Introductory
Mathematical Analysis

Introductory Mathematical Analysis:

For Students of Business and Economics

Second Edition

Ernest F. Haeussler, Jr.
Richard S. Paul

Department of Mathematics
The Pennsylvania State University

RESTON PUBLISHING COMPANY, INC., RESTON, VIRGINIA
A Prentice-Hall Company

Library of Congress Cataloging in Publication Data

Haeussler, Ernest F
  Introductory mathematical analysis for students
of business and economics.

  Includes index.
  1. Mathematical analysis. 2. Economics, Mathe-
matical. I. Paul, Richard S., joint author.
II. Title.
QA300.H33   1976   515   75-43820
ISBN 0-87909-359-5

© 1976 by
Reston Publishing Company, Inc.
A Prentice-Hall Company
Reston, Virginia 22090

10

Printed in the United States of America

Contents

Preface

This text is designed to provide a mathematical foundation, including calculus and matrix algebra, for students enrolled in business and economics curricula. It considers topics that these students may encounter in later courses in their major fields of study.

The material is presented in both a readable and comprehensible manner. Concepts are thoroughly and carefully explained at an appropriate level and are motivated wherever possible. The text is slow-paced at first so that confidence is gained by the student. Where appropriate, diagrams are included to convey and reinforce ideas. Errors that are frequently made by students are explicitly pointed out under the format "PITFALL." Since students have various mathematical backgrounds, we have included a basic algebra refresher, Chapter 0, for the convenience of those students who would benefit from such a review.

With the exception of Chapter 0, each chapter has a review section that contains a listing of important terms and symbols together with page numbers that indicate where these terms and symbols first appear. Also in each of these sections is a programmed review and numerous review problems.

In order to make the material meaningful and relevant to the student, we have included many topics in this text that show how mathematical concepts are applied to describe business and economic phenomena. Among these applications are supply and demand, equilibrium, break-even point, marginal revenue, marginal cost, marginal propensity to consume, marginal propensity to save, marginal revenue product, maximization of profit under monopoly, elasticity, consumer's surplus, producers' surplus, and budget equations. However, the text is virtually self-contained in the sense that it *assumes no prior exposure to the concepts on which the applications are based*.

In this second edition we have inserted additional examples and problems where we felt they were needed. There are now more than 685 examples, which are explained in step-by-step detail, and more than 3,470 problems that relate to the examples and material in the text.

Answers to odd-numbered problems appear at the end of the book. For many of the differentiation problems in Chapter 7, the answers appear in both unsimplified and simplified forms. This allows the student to readily check his procedures and work. Available from the publisher is an extensive instructor's manual that contains answers to all problems and detailed solutions to a great many of them, including all applied problems. Included also are problems suitable for examination purposes.

Several changes appear in this second edition. Various sections were rewritten for greater clarity and understanding by the student. Chapter 0 is presented in a less formal way and contains more examples and problems. Less emphasis is placed on sets. Some chapters have been broken up to make the material more manageable and to provide more flexibility for the instructor in designing a course. The approach to functions is now via a rule of correspondence. Continuity is presented more informally. The chain rule is presented in a clearer fashion with increased emphasis on its use. The approach to definite integration now allows the student to see the connection between definite and indefinite integration earlier than before. Also, the rigor of evaluating definite integrals by Riemann sums has been toned down. More steps have been included in the examples of integration by substitution. There is more discussion and examples on exponential growth. The following additional topics are discussed in this edition: combinations of functions; multiple integration; adjoint and finding inverses with the adjoint; input-output analysis; and a new chapter on linear programming including the simplex method and the dual.

We wish to express our appreciation to those people who contributed to this edition by offering their opinions and suggestions for improvement. They include F. Miles and C. L. Chang of California State College at Dominguez Hills; Dean B. Priest of Harding College; Therese Butzen and students of Harper College; B. Watson of Huron College; Peter Evanovich and John K. Hampson of Lafayette College; Stanley T. Uyemura of Leeward Community College; Ira Marshak of Loyola University of Chicago; B. A. Banatmy, Kenneth E. Carlson, and David W. Hansen of Monterey Peninsula College; Larry Hayman of Mt. San Antonio College; S. Hinthorne of Palomar College; John D. Baildon, R. Barshinger, Stephen Currier, Anabeth Dollins, Nicholas S. Ford, Robert P. Hostetler, Joe Lambert, Stephen L. Littell, James Mettler, Yoon Yong Oh, Norman B. Patterson, C. O. Pope, Richard F. Reynolds, Henry R. Riley, Jacqueline Wells, and James VanDeventer of Pennsylvania State University; Sid Huff of Queens University; Philip T. Church and Gary Hensler of Syracuse University; Robert W. Brown of University of Alaska; Thomas W. McCullough of University of California at Berkeley; Dean Lebestky and John O. Tellefson of University of Kansas; S. K. Berberian, Larry E. Knop, and David P. Wright of University of Texas at Austin; Joe W. Fitzpatrick and J. R. Provencio of University of Texas at El Paso; R. G. Biggs, M. Hey, and C. Brandt Miller of University of Western Ontario; and Ron Morgan, W. H. Seybold, and Ruth S. Stanley of West Chester State College.

In addition, we again wish to acknowledge and thank those who contributed to the first edition: Frank Kocher of the Department of Mathematics, Lawrence L. Biacchi of the Department of Economics, and Nicholas Skimbo of the Department of Accounting and Quantitative Business Analysis of the Pennsylvania State University; George W. Schultz of the Department of Mathematics of St. Petersburg Junior College; and Martin Brutosky, one of our former students.

Ernest F. Haeussler, Jr.
Richard S. Paul

Algebra Refresher

0-1 PURPOSE

This chapter is designed to give you a brief review of some terms and methods of manipulative mathematics. No doubt you have been exposed to much of this material before. However, because these topics are important in handling the mathematics that comes later, perhaps an immediate second exposure to them would be beneficial. Devote whatever time is necessary to those sections in which you need review.

0-2 SETS AND REAL NUMBERS

In simplest terms, a *set* is a collection of objects. For example, we can speak of the set of even numbers between 5 and 11, namely 6, 8, and 10. An object in a set is called a *member* or *element* of the set.

One way to specify a set is by listing its members inside braces. For example, the set above is

$$\{6, 8, 10\}.$$

Certain sets of numbers have special names. The numbers 1, 2, 3, etc. form the set of **positive integers** (or **natural numbers**):

$$\begin{array}{l} set\ of \\ positive \\ integers \end{array} = \{1, 2, 3, \ldots\}.$$

The three dots mean that the listing of elements is unending, although we know what the elements are.

The positive integers together with 0 and the **negative integers** -1, -2, -3, ... form the set of **integers:**

$$\begin{array}{l} set\ of \\ integers \end{array} = \{\ldots, -3, -2, -1, 0, 1, 2, 3, \ldots\}.$$

The set of **rational numbers** consists of numbers, such as $\frac{1}{2}$ and $\frac{5}{3}$, which can be written as a ratio (or quotient) of two integers. That is, a rational number is one that can be written as p/q, where p and q are integers and $q \neq 0$. The symbol "$\neq$" is read "is not equal to." **We never divide by zero.** Other rational numbers are $\frac{19}{20}$, $\frac{-2}{7}$, and $\frac{-6}{-2}$. The integer 2 is rational since $2 = \frac{2}{1}$. In fact, every integer is rational. Note that $\frac{2}{4}$, $\frac{1}{2}$, $\frac{3}{6}$, $\frac{-4}{-8}$, and .5 all represent the same rational number.

Geometrically, numbers can be represented by points on a straight line. To do this, we first choose a point on the line to represent zero. This point is called the *origin*. Then a unit of distance is chosen and is successively marked off both to the right and to the left of the origin. With each point on the line we associate a directed distance, or *signed number,* which depends on the position of the point with respect to the origin. Positions to the right of the origin are considered positive (+), and positions to the left are negative (−). Thus, with the point one unit to the right of the origin there corresponds the signed number +1 (or 1), positive one; with the point two and one-half units to the left of the origin there corresponds the signed number $-2\frac{1}{2}$, negative two and one-half (Fig. 0-1).

All of the rational numbers, and hence the integers, can be represented by points on the line. However, it can be shown that there are points whose

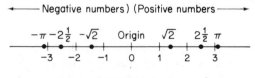

Fig. 0-1

directed distances from zero *cannot* be represented by rational numbers. Numbers that represent directed distances of this type are said to be **irrational**—that is, not rational. For example, $\sqrt{2}$ and π are known to be irrational.

Together, the rational numbers and irrational numbers form the set of **real numbers.** In Fig. 0-1 some points and their associated real numbers are identified. To each point on the line there corresponds a unique real number, and to each real number there corresponds a unique point on the line. For this reason we say that there is a *one-to-one correspondence* between points on the line and real numbers. For obvious reasons we call this line the **real number line.**

EXERCISE 0-2

In problems 1-12, classify the statement as either true or false.

1. -7 is an integer.

2. $\frac{1}{6}$ is rational.

3. -3 is a natural number.

4. 0 is not rational.

5. 5 is rational.

6. $\frac{7}{0}$ is a real number.

7. $\frac{4}{2}$ is not a positive integer.

8. π is a real number.

9. $\frac{0}{6}$ is rational.

10. 0 is a natural number.

11. -3 is to the right of -4 on the real number line.

12. Every integer is positive or negative.

0-3 SOME PROPERTIES OF REAL NUMBERS

In this section we shall give a few properties of the real numbers.

I. The Transitive Property.
   Let a, b, and c be real numbers.

$$\text{If} \quad a = b \quad \text{and} \quad b = c, \quad \text{then} \quad a = c.$$

Thus, two quantities that are both equal to a third quantity are equal to each other. For example, if $x = y$ and $y = 7$, then $x = 7$.

II. The Commutative Properties.
   If a and b are real numbers, then

$$a + b = b + a \quad \text{and} \quad ab = ba.$$

This means that we can add or multiply two real numbers in any order. For example, $3 + 4 = 4 + 3$ and $7(-4) = (-4)(7)$.

III. **The Associative Properties.**

   If a, b, and c are real numbers, then

$$a + (b + c) = (a + b) + c \quad and \quad a(bc) = (ab)c.$$

This means that in addition or multiplication, numbers can be grouped in any order.

For example, $2 + (3 + 4) = (2 + 3) + 4$, $6(\frac{1}{3} \cdot 5) = (6 \cdot \frac{1}{3}) \cdot 5$, and $2x + (x + y) = (2x + x) + y$.

IV. **The Inverse Properties.**

   a. *For each real number a, there is a unique real number denoted $-a$ such that*

$$a + (-a) = 0.$$

   The number $-a$ is called the **additive inverse,** *or* **negative,** *of a.*

For example, since $6 + (-6) = 0$, the additive inverse of 6 is -6. The additive inverse of a number is not necessarily a negative number. For example, the additive inverse of -6 is 6, since $(-6) + (6) = 0$. That is, the negative of -6 is 6.

   b. *For each real number a, except 0, there is a unique real number a^{-1} such that*

$$a \cdot a^{-1} = 1.$$

   The number a^{-1} is called the **multiplicative inverse** *of a.*

Thus all numbers except 0 have a multiplicative inverse. You may recall that a^{-1} can be written $\dfrac{1}{a}$ and is called the *reciprocal* of a. For example, the multiplicative inverse of 3 is $\frac{1}{3}$, since $3(\frac{1}{3}) = 1$. Thus $\frac{1}{3}$ is the reciprocal of 3. The reciprocal of $\frac{1}{3}$ is 3, since $(\frac{1}{3})(3) = 1$. We emphasize that **the reciprocal of 0 is not defined.**

V. **The Distributive Properties.**

   If a, b, and c are real numbers, then

$$a(b + c) = ab + ac \quad and \quad (b + c)a = ba + ca.$$

For example,

$$2(3 + 4) = 2(3) + 2(4) = 6 + 8 = 14,$$
$$(2 + 3)(4) = 2(4) + 3(4) = 8 + 12 = 20,$$
$$x(z + 4) = x(z) + x(4) = xz + 4x.$$

The distributive property can be extended to the form $a(b + c + d) = ab + ac + ad$. In fact, it can be extended to sums involving any other number of terms.

It is by the additive inverse property that we formally define *subtraction:*

$a - b$ means $a + (-b)$, where $-b$ is the additive inverse of b. Thus $6 - 8$ means $6 + (-8)$. Subtraction is therefore defined in terms of addition.

In a similar way we define *division* in terms of multiplication. If $b \neq 0$, then $a \div b$, or $\dfrac{a}{b}$, is defined by

$$\frac{a}{b} = a(b^{-1}).$$

Since $b^{-1} = \dfrac{1}{b}$,

$$\frac{a}{b} = a(b^{-1}) = a\left(\frac{1}{b}\right).$$

Thus $\frac{3}{5}$ means 3 times $\frac{1}{5}$ where $\frac{1}{5}$ is the multiplicative inverse of 5. Sometimes we refer to $a \div b$ or $\dfrac{a}{b}$ as the *ratio* of a to b.

The following examples show some manipulations involving the above properties.

EXAMPLE 1

a. $x(y - 3z + 2w) = (y - 3z + 2w)\,x$, by the commutative property of multiplication.

b. By the associative property of multiplication, $3(4 \cdot 5) = (3 \cdot 4)5$. Thus, the result of multiplying 3 by the product of 4 and 5 is the same as the result of multiplying the product of 3 and 4 by 5. In either case the result is 60.

c. By the definition of subtraction, $2 - \sqrt{2} = 2 + (-\sqrt{2})$. However, by the commutative property, $2 + (-\sqrt{2}) = -\sqrt{2} + 2$. Thus, by the transitive property, $2 - \sqrt{2} = -\sqrt{2} + 2$. More concisely we can write

$$2 - \sqrt{2} = 2 + (-\sqrt{2}) = -\sqrt{2} + 2.$$

d. $\quad\quad (8 + x) - y = (8 + x) + (-y) \quad\quad$ (definition of subtraction)

$$= 8 + [x + (-y)] \quad\quad \text{(associative property)}$$

$$= 8 + (x - y) \quad\quad \text{(definition of subtraction).}$$

Hence, by the transitive property,

$$(8 + x) - y = 8 + (x - y).$$

e. By the definition of division,

$$\frac{ab}{c} = (ab) \cdot \frac{1}{c} \quad \text{for} \quad c \neq 0.$$

But by the associative property,

$$(ab) \cdot \frac{1}{c} = a \left(b \cdot \frac{1}{c} \right).$$

However, by the definition of division $b \cdot \dfrac{1}{c} = \dfrac{b}{c}$. Thus

$$\frac{ab}{c} = a \left(\frac{b}{c} \right).$$

EXAMPLE 2

a. *Show* $3(4x + 2y + 8) = 12x + 6y + 24.$

By the distributive property,

$$3(4x + 2y + 8) = 3(4x) + 3(2y) + 3 \cdot 8.$$

But by the associative property of multiplication,

$$3(4x) = (3 \cdot 4)x = 12x \text{ and similarly } 3(2y) = 6y.$$

Thus $3(4x + 2y + 8) = 12x + 6y + 24.$

b. *Show* $x(y - z) = xy - xz.$

By the definition of subtraction and the distributive property,

$$
\begin{aligned}
x(y - z) &= x[y + (-z)] \\
&= xy + x(-z).
\end{aligned}
$$

Recalling that $-z = (-1)z$, we can then say $x(-z) = x[(-1)z]$. But $x[(-1)z] = (-1)(xz)$. Why? Hence,

$$
\begin{aligned}
x(y - z) &= xy + x(-z) \\
&= xy + (-1)xz.
\end{aligned}
$$

Referring again to the definition of subtraction, we have $x(y - z) = xy - xz.$

c. *Show that if* $c \neq 0$, *then* $\dfrac{a + b}{c} = \dfrac{a}{c} + \dfrac{b}{c}.$

By the definition of division and the distributive property,

$$\frac{a + b}{c} = (a + b)\frac{1}{c} = a \cdot \frac{1}{c} + b \cdot \frac{1}{c}.$$

But

$$a \cdot \frac{1}{c} + b \cdot \frac{1}{c} = \frac{a}{c} + \frac{b}{c}.$$

Hence,

$$\frac{a+b}{c} = \frac{a}{c} + \frac{b}{c}.$$

This important result does *not* mean that $\dfrac{a}{b+c} = \dfrac{a}{b} + \dfrac{a}{c}$, a very common error.

Finding the product of several numbers can be done only by considering products of numbers taken two at a time. For example, to find the product of x, y, and z we could first multiply x by y and then multiply that product by z, or alternatively we could multiply x by the product of y and z. The associative property of multiplication says that both results are identical, regardless of how the numbers are grouped. Thus it is not ambiguous to write xyz. This concept can be extended to more than three numbers and applies equally well to addition.

One final comment before we end this section. Not only should you be aware of the manipulative aspects of the properties of the real numbers, but you should also be aware of and familiar with the terminology involved.

EXERCISE 0-3

In problems 1–10, classify the statements as either true or false.

1. Every real number has a reciprocal.

2. The reciprocal of $\frac{2}{5}$ is $\frac{5}{2}$.

3. The additive inverse of 5 is $\frac{1}{5}$.

4. $2(3 \cdot 4) = (2 \cdot 3)(2 \cdot 4)$

5. $-x + y = y - x$

6. $(x + 2)(4) = 4x + 8$

7. $\dfrac{x+2}{2} = \dfrac{x}{2} + 1$

8. $3\left(\dfrac{x}{4}\right) = \dfrac{3x}{4}$

9. $x + (y + 5) = (x + y) + (x + 5)$

10. $8(9x) = 72x$

In problems 11–20, tell which properties of the real numbers are being used.

11. $2(x + y) = 2x + 2y$

12. $(x + 5) + y = y + (x + 5)$

13. $2(3y) = (2 \cdot 3)y$

14. $\frac{6}{7} = 6 \cdot \frac{1}{7}$

15. $2(x - y) = (x - y)(2)$

16. $x + (x + y) = (x + x) + y$

17. $8 - y = 8 + (-y)$

18. $5(4 + 7) = 5(7 + 4)$

19. $(7 + x)y = 7y + xy$

20. $(-1)[-3 + 4] = (-1)(-3) + (-1)(4)$

In problems 21–26, show that the statements are true by using properties of the real numbers.

21. $5a(x + 3) = 5ax + 15a$

22. $(2 - x) + y = 2 + (y - x)$

list.

23. $(x - y)(2) = 2x - 2y$

dist.

25. $x[(2y + 1) + 3] = 2xy + 4x$

associative

24. $2[27 + (x + y)] = 2[(y + 27) + x]$

26. $(x + 1)(y + 1) = xy + x + y + 1$ *dist.*

27. Show $a(b + c + d) = ab + ac + ad$. Hint: $b + c + d = (b + c) + d$.

dist.

0-4 OPERATIONS WITH SIGNED NUMBERS

Listed below are important properties of signed numbers which you should study thoroughly. Being able to manipulate signed numbers is essential to your success in mathematics. A numerical example follows each property. All denominators are different from zero and a knowledge of addition and subtraction of signed numbers is assumed.

Property	*Example*
1. $a - b = a + (-b)$	$2 - 7 = 2 + (-7) = -5$
2. $a - (-b) = a + b$	$2 - (-7) = 2 + 7 = 9$
3. $-a = (-1)(a)$	$-7 = (-1)(7)$
4. $a(b + c) = ab + ac$	$6(7 + 2) = 6 \cdot 7 + 6 \cdot 2 = 54$
5. $a(b - c) = ab - ac$	$6(7 - 2) = 6 \cdot 7 - 6 \cdot 2 = 30$
6. $-(a + b) = -a - b$	$-(7 + 2) = -7 - 2 = -9$
7. $-(a - b) = -a + b$	$-(2 - 7) = -2 + 7 = 5$
8. $-(-a) = a$	$-(-2) = 2$
9. $a(0) = (-a)(0) = 0$	$2(0) = (-2)(0) = 0$
10. $(-a)(b) = -(ab) = a(-b)$	$(-2)(7) = -(2 \cdot 7) = 2(-7)$
11. $(-a)(-b) = ab$	$(-2)(-7) = 2 \cdot 7 = 14$
12. $\dfrac{a}{1} = a$	$\dfrac{7}{1} = 7, \quad \dfrac{-2}{1} = -2$
13. $\dfrac{a}{b} = a\left(\dfrac{1}{b}\right)$	$\dfrac{2}{7} = 2\left(\dfrac{1}{7}\right)$
14. $\dfrac{1}{-a} = -\dfrac{1}{a} = \dfrac{-1}{a}$	$\dfrac{1}{-4} = -\dfrac{1}{4} = \dfrac{-1}{4}$
15. $\dfrac{a}{-b} = -\dfrac{a}{b} = \dfrac{-a}{b}$	$\dfrac{2}{-7} = -\dfrac{2}{7} = \dfrac{-2}{7}$

16. $\dfrac{-a}{-b} = \dfrac{a}{b}$ $\dfrac{-2}{-7} = \dfrac{2}{7}$

17. $\dfrac{0}{a} = 0$ when $a \neq 0$ $\dfrac{0}{7} = 0$

18. $\dfrac{a}{a} = 1$ when $a \neq 0$ $\dfrac{2}{2} = 1, \quad \dfrac{-5}{-5} = 1$

19. $a\left(\dfrac{b}{a}\right) = b$ $2\left(\dfrac{7}{2}\right) = 7$

20. $\dfrac{1}{a} \cdot \dfrac{1}{b} = \dfrac{1}{ab}$ $\dfrac{1}{2} \cdot \dfrac{1}{7} = \dfrac{1}{2 \cdot 7} = \dfrac{1}{14}$

21. $\dfrac{ab}{c} = \left(\dfrac{a}{c}\right)b = a\left(\dfrac{b}{c}\right)$ $\dfrac{2 \cdot 7}{3} = \dfrac{2}{3} \cdot 7 = 2 \cdot \dfrac{7}{3}$

22. $\dfrac{a}{bc} = \left(\dfrac{a}{b}\right)\left(\dfrac{1}{c}\right) = \left(\dfrac{1}{b}\right)\left(\dfrac{a}{c}\right)$ $\dfrac{2}{3 \cdot 7} = \dfrac{2}{3} \cdot \dfrac{1}{7} = \dfrac{1}{3} \cdot \dfrac{2}{7}$

23. $\dfrac{a}{b} = \left(\dfrac{a}{b}\right)\left(\dfrac{c}{c}\right) = \dfrac{ac}{bc}$ when $c \neq 0$ $\dfrac{2}{7} = \left(\dfrac{2}{7}\right)\left(\dfrac{5}{5}\right) = \dfrac{2 \cdot 5}{7 \cdot 5}$

24. $\dfrac{a}{b(-c)} = \dfrac{a}{(-b)(c)} = \dfrac{-a}{bc}$ $\dfrac{2}{3(-5)} = \dfrac{2}{(-3)(5)} = \dfrac{-2}{3(5)}$

$= \dfrac{-a}{(-b)(-c)} = -\dfrac{a}{bc}$ $= \dfrac{-2}{(-3)(-5)} = -\dfrac{2}{15}$

25. $\dfrac{a}{c} + \dfrac{b}{c} = \dfrac{a+b}{c}$ $\dfrac{2}{9} + \dfrac{3}{9} = \dfrac{2+3}{9} = \dfrac{5}{9}$

26. $\dfrac{a}{c} - \dfrac{b}{c} = \dfrac{a-b}{c}$ $\dfrac{2}{9} - \dfrac{3}{9} = \dfrac{2-3}{9} = \dfrac{-1}{9}$

27. $\dfrac{a}{b} + \dfrac{c}{d} = \dfrac{ad+bc}{bd}$ $\dfrac{4}{5} + \dfrac{2}{3} = \dfrac{4 \cdot 3 + 5 \cdot 2}{5 \cdot 3} = \dfrac{22}{15}$

28. $\dfrac{a}{b} - \dfrac{c}{d} = \dfrac{ad-bc}{bd}$ $\dfrac{4}{5} - \dfrac{2}{3} = \dfrac{4 \cdot 3 - 5 \cdot 2}{5 \cdot 3} = \dfrac{2}{15}$

29. $\dfrac{a}{b} \cdot \dfrac{c}{d} = \dfrac{ac}{bd}$ $\dfrac{2}{3} \cdot \dfrac{4}{5} = \dfrac{2 \cdot 4}{3 \cdot 5} = \dfrac{8}{15}$

30. $\dfrac{\dfrac{a}{b}}{c} = a \div \dfrac{b}{c} = \dfrac{ac}{b}$ $\dfrac{\dfrac{2}{3}}{5} = 2 \div \dfrac{3}{5} = \dfrac{2 \cdot 5}{3} = \dfrac{10}{3}$

31. $\dfrac{\dfrac{a}{b}}{c} = \dfrac{a}{b} \div c = \dfrac{a}{bc}$

$\dfrac{\dfrac{2}{3}}{5} = \dfrac{2}{3} \div 5 = \dfrac{2}{3 \cdot 5} = \dfrac{2}{15}$

32. $\dfrac{\dfrac{a}{b}}{\dfrac{c}{d}} = \dfrac{a}{b} \div \dfrac{c}{d} = \dfrac{a}{b} \cdot \dfrac{d}{c} = \dfrac{ad}{bc}$

$\dfrac{\dfrac{2}{3}}{\dfrac{7}{5}} = \dfrac{2}{3} \div \dfrac{7}{5} = \dfrac{2}{3} \cdot \dfrac{5}{7} = \dfrac{10}{21}$

Property 23 is essentially the **fundamental principle of fractions.** It says that *multiplying or dividing both the numerator and denominator of a fraction by the same number, except 0, results in a fraction which is equivalent to the original fraction.* Thus,

$$\frac{7}{\dfrac{1}{8}} = \frac{7 \cdot 8}{\dfrac{1}{8} \cdot 8} = \frac{56}{1} = 56.$$

Properties 27 and 23 say that

$$\frac{2}{5} + \frac{4}{15} = \frac{2 \cdot 15 + 5 \cdot 4}{5 \cdot 15} = \frac{50}{75} = \frac{2 \cdot 25}{3 \cdot 25} = \frac{2}{3}.$$

We can do this problem another way. For the fractions $\frac{2}{5}$ and $\frac{4}{15}$, a common denominator is $5 \cdot 15$; however, 15 is the *least common denominator* (L.C.D.), and we can write

$$\frac{2}{5} + \frac{4}{15} = \frac{2 \cdot 3}{5 \cdot 3} + \frac{4}{15} = \frac{6}{15} + \frac{4}{15} = \frac{10}{15} = \frac{2}{3}.$$

Similarly,

$$\frac{3}{8} - \frac{5}{12} = \frac{3 \cdot 3}{8 \cdot 3} - \frac{5 \cdot 2}{12 \cdot 2}$$

$$= \frac{9}{24} - \frac{10}{24} = \frac{9 - 10}{24} = -\frac{1}{24}.$$

EXERCISE 0-4

Find each of the following if possible.

1. $-2 + (-4)$

2. $-6 + 2$

3. $6 + (-4)$

4. $7 - 2$

5. $7 - (-4)$

6. $-7 - (-4)$

7. $-8 - (-6)$

8. $(-2)(9)$

9. $7(-9)$

10. $(-2)(-12)$

11. $(-1)6$

12. $-(-9)$

13. $-(-6 + x)$

14. $-7(x)$

15. $-12(x - y)$

16. $-[-6 + (-y)]$

17. $-2 \div 6$

18. $-2 \div (-4)$

19. $4 \div (-2)$

20. $2(-6 + 2)$

21. $3[-2(3) + 6(2)]$

22. $(-2)(-4)(-1)$

23. $(-5)(-5)$

24. $x(0)$

25. $3(x - 4)$

26. $4(5 + x)$

27. $-(x - 2)$

28. $0(-x)$

29. $8(\frac{1}{11})$

30. $\frac{7}{1}$

31. $\dfrac{-5x}{7y}$

32. $\dfrac{3}{-2x}$

33. $\dfrac{2}{3} \cdot \dfrac{1}{x}$

34. $\dfrac{x}{y}(2z)$

35. $(2x)\left(\dfrac{3}{2x}\right)$

36. $\dfrac{-15x}{-3y}$

37. $\dfrac{7}{y} \cdot \dfrac{1}{x}$

38. $\dfrac{2}{x} \cdot \dfrac{5}{y}$

39. $\dfrac{1}{2} + \dfrac{1}{3}$

40. $\dfrac{5}{12} + \dfrac{3}{4}$

41. $\dfrac{3}{10} - \dfrac{7}{15}$

42. $\dfrac{2}{3} + \dfrac{7}{3}$

43. $\dfrac{x}{9} - \dfrac{y}{9}$

44. $\dfrac{3}{2} - \dfrac{1}{4} + \dfrac{1}{6}$

45. $\dfrac{2}{3} - \dfrac{5}{8}$

46. $\dfrac{6}{\dfrac{x}{y}}$

47. $\dfrac{\frac{x}{6}}{y}$ 48. $\dfrac{\frac{-7}{2}}{\frac{5}{8}}$

49. $\dfrac{7}{0}$ 50. $\dfrac{0}{7}$

51. $\dfrac{0}{0}$ 52. $0 \cdot 0$

0-5   EXPONENTS AND RADICALS

The expression

$$x \cdot x \cdot x$$

is abbreviated x^3. In general, for n a positive integer, x^n is the product of n x's. The letter n in x^n is called the *exponent* and x is called the *base*. More specifically, if n is a positive integer we define:

1. $x^n = \underbrace{x \cdot x \cdot x \cdot \ldots \cdot x}_{n\,\text{factors}}.$

2. $x^{-n} = \dfrac{1}{x^n} = \underbrace{\dfrac{1}{x \cdot x \cdot x \cdot \ldots \cdot x}}_{n\,\text{factors}}.$

3. $x^0 = 1$ if $x \neq 0$. 0^0 is not defined.

EXAMPLE 3

a. $3^{-5} = \dfrac{1}{3^5} = \dfrac{1}{3 \cdot 3 \cdot 3 \cdot 3 \cdot 3} = \dfrac{1}{243}.$

b. $\dfrac{1}{3^{-5}} = \dfrac{1}{\frac{1}{3^5}} = 1 \cdot \dfrac{3^5}{1} = 3^5.$

c. $2^0 = 1, \pi^0 = 1, (-5)^0 = 1.$

The generalization of Example 3(b) is

$$\dfrac{1}{x^{-n}} = x^n.$$

If $r^n = x$ where n is a positive integer, then r is an nth *root* of x. For example, $3^2 = 9$ and so 3 is a second root (usually called a *square root*) of 9. Since $(-3)^2 = 9$, -3 is also a square root of 9. Similarly, -2 is a *cube root* of -8 since $(-2)^3 = -8$.

The **principal nth root** of x is that nth root of x which is positivé if x is positive, and is negative if x is negative and n is odd. We denote it by $\sqrt[n]{x}$. Thus,

$$\sqrt[n]{x} \text{ is } \begin{cases} \text{positive if } x \text{ is positive,} \\ \text{negative if } x \text{ is negative and } n \text{ is odd.} \end{cases}$$

For example, $\sqrt[2]{9} = 3$, $\sqrt[3]{-8} = -2$, and $\sqrt[3]{\frac{1}{27}} = \frac{1}{3}$. For completeness we define $\sqrt[n]{0} = 0$.

The symbol $\sqrt[n]{x}$ is called a **radical**. We say that n is the *index*, x is the *radicand*, and $\sqrt{}$ is the *radical sign*. With principal square roots we usually drop the index and write $\sqrt{x}$ instead of $\sqrt[2]{x}$. Thus $\sqrt{9} = 3$.

PITFALL. *Although 2 and -2 are square roots of 4, the principal square root of 4 is 2, not -2. Hence $\sqrt{4} = 2$.*

If x is positive, the expression $x^{p/q}$ where p and q are integers and q is positive is defined to be $\sqrt[q]{x^p}$. Thus,

$$x^{3/4} = \sqrt[4]{x^3}; \qquad 8^{2/3} = \sqrt[3]{8^2} = \sqrt[3]{64} = 4;$$

$$4^{-\frac{1}{2}} = 4^{-\frac{1}{2}} = \sqrt[2]{4^{-1}} = \sqrt{\frac{1}{4}} = \frac{1}{2}.$$

We now state some basic laws of exponents and radicals.†

Law	Example
1. $x^m \cdot x^n = x^{m+n}$	$2^3 \cdot 2^5 = 2^8 = 256;\quad x^2 \cdot x^3 = x^5$
2. $x^0 = 1$ if $x \neq 0$	$2^0 = 1$
3. $x^{-n} = \dfrac{1}{x^n}$	$2^{-3} = \dfrac{1}{2^3} = \dfrac{1}{8}$
4. $\dfrac{1}{x^{-n}} = x^n$	$\dfrac{1}{2^{-3}} = 2^3 = 8;\quad \dfrac{1}{x^{-5}} = x^5$
5. $\dfrac{x^m}{x^n} = x^{m-n} = \dfrac{1}{x^{n-m}}$	$\dfrac{2^{12}}{2^8} = 2^4 = 16;\quad \dfrac{x^8}{x^{12}} = \dfrac{1}{x^4}$
6. $\dfrac{x^m}{x^m} = 1$ if $x \neq 0$	$\dfrac{2^4}{2^4} = 1$

† Although some laws involve restrictions, they are not vital to our discussion.

7. $(x^m)^n = x^{mn}$ $(2^3)^5 = 2^{15}; \quad (x^2)^3 = x^6$

8. $(xy)^n = x^n y^n$ $(2 \cdot 4)^3 = 2^3 \cdot 4^3 = 8 \cdot 64$

9. $\left(\dfrac{x}{y}\right)^n = \dfrac{x^n}{y^n}$ $\left(\dfrac{2}{3}\right)^3 = \dfrac{2^3}{3^3}; \quad \left(\dfrac{1}{3}\right)^5 = \dfrac{1^5}{3^5} = \dfrac{1}{3^5} = 3^{-5}$

10. $\left(\dfrac{x}{y}\right)^{-n} = \left(\dfrac{y}{x}\right)^n$ $\left(\dfrac{3}{4}\right)^{-2} = \left(\dfrac{4}{3}\right)^2 = \dfrac{4^2}{3^2} = \dfrac{16}{9}$

11. $x^{1/n} = \sqrt[n]{x}$ $3^{1/5} = \sqrt[5]{3}$

12. $x^{-1/n} = \dfrac{1}{x^{1/n}} = \dfrac{1}{\sqrt[n]{x}}$ $4^{-1/2} = \dfrac{1}{4^{1/2}} = \dfrac{1}{\sqrt{4}} = \dfrac{1}{2}$

13. $\sqrt[n]{x}\,\sqrt[n]{y} = \sqrt[n]{xy}$ $\sqrt[3]{9}\,\sqrt[3]{2} = \sqrt[3]{18}$

14. $\dfrac{\sqrt[n]{x}}{\sqrt[n]{y}} = \sqrt[n]{\dfrac{x}{y}}$ $\dfrac{\sqrt[3]{90}}{\sqrt[3]{10}} = \sqrt[3]{\dfrac{90}{10}} = \sqrt[3]{9}$

15. $\sqrt[m]{\sqrt[n]{x}} = \sqrt[mn]{x}$ $\sqrt[3]{\sqrt[4]{2}} = \sqrt[12]{2}$

16. $x^{m/n} = \sqrt[n]{x^m} = (\sqrt[n]{x})^m$ $8^{2/3} = \sqrt[3]{8^2} = (\sqrt[3]{8})^2 = 2^2 = 4$

17. $(\sqrt[n]{x})^m = x$ $(\sqrt[8]{7})^8 = 7$

EXAMPLE 4

a. By Law 1,

$$x^6 x^8 = x^{6+8} = x^{14},$$
$$a^3 b^2 a^5 b = a^3 a^5 b^2 b = a^8 b^3,$$
$$x^{11} x^{-5} = x^{11-5} = x^6,$$
$$z^{2/5} z^{3/5} = z^1 = z,$$
$$x x^{1/2} = x^1 x^{1/2} = x^{3/2}.$$

b. By Law 16,

$$\left(\frac{1}{4}\right)^{3/2} = \left(\sqrt{\frac{1}{4}}\right)^3 = \left(\frac{1}{2}\right)^3 = \frac{1}{8}.$$

c. $\left(-\dfrac{8}{27}\right)^{4/3} = \left(\sqrt[3]{\dfrac{-8}{27}}\right)^4 = \left(\dfrac{\sqrt[3]{-8}}{\sqrt[3]{27}}\right)^4$ (Laws 16 and 14)

$$= \left(\frac{-2}{3}\right)^4$$

$$= \frac{(-2)^4}{3^4} = \frac{16}{81}. \qquad\qquad \text{(Law 9)}$$

d. $(8a^3)^{2/3} = 8^{2/3}(a^3)^{2/3}$ (Law 8)

$\quad\quad\quad\quad = (\sqrt[3]{8})^2 a^2$ (Laws 16 and 7)

$\quad\quad\quad\quad = (2)^2 a^2 = 4a^2.$

Rationalizing the denominator of a fraction is a procedure in which a fraction having a radical in its denominator is expressed as an equivalent fraction without a radical in its denominator. We use the fundamental principle of fractions.

EXAMPLE 5

Rationalize the denominators.

a. $\dfrac{2}{\sqrt{5}} = \dfrac{2}{5^{1/2}} = \dfrac{2}{5^{1/2}} \cdot \dfrac{5^{1/2}}{5^{1/2}} = \dfrac{2 \cdot 5^{1/2}}{5^1} = \dfrac{2\sqrt{5}}{5}.$

b. $\dfrac{2}{\sqrt[6]{3x^5}} = \dfrac{2}{\sqrt[6]{3} \cdot \sqrt[6]{x^5}} = \dfrac{2}{3^{1/6} x^{5/6}} = \dfrac{2}{3^{1/6} x^{5/6}} \cdot \dfrac{3^{5/6} x^{1/6}}{3^{5/6} x^{1/6}} = \dfrac{2(3^5 x)^{1/6}}{3x} = \dfrac{2\sqrt[6]{3^5 x}}{3x}.$

The following examples illustrate various applications of the laws of exponents and radicals.

EXAMPLE 6

a.   *Eliminate negative exponents in* $\dfrac{x^{-2} y^3}{z^{-2}}.$

$$\dfrac{x^{-2} y^3}{z^{-2}} = \dfrac{y^3 z^2}{x^2}.$$

Thus we can bring a factor of the numerator down to the denominator by changing the sign of the exponent, and vice versa.

b.   *Simplify* $\sqrt[4]{48}.$

$$\sqrt[4]{48} = \sqrt[4]{16 \cdot 3} = \sqrt[4]{16}\,\sqrt[4]{3} = 2\sqrt[4]{3}.$$

c.   *Simplify* $\dfrac{x^2 y^7}{x^3 y^5}.$

$$\dfrac{x^2 y^7}{x^3 y^5} = \dfrac{y^{7-5}}{x^{3-2}} = \dfrac{y^2}{x}.$$

d.   *Eliminate negative exponents in* $x^{-1} + y^{-1}$ *and simplify.*

$$x^{-1} + y^{-1} = \dfrac{1}{x} + \dfrac{1}{y} = \dfrac{y + x}{xy}. \quad \left(\text{Note: } x^{-1} + y^{-1} \neq \dfrac{1}{x + y}.\right)$$

e. *Use exponents to rewrite* $\sqrt{2 + 5x}$.

$$\sqrt{2 + 5x} = (2 + 5x)^{1/2}.$$

f. *Rationalize the denominator of* $\dfrac{\sqrt[5]{2}}{\sqrt[3]{6}}$ *and simplify.*

$$\frac{\sqrt[5]{2}}{\sqrt[3]{6}} = \frac{2^{1/5}}{6^{1/3}} \cdot \frac{6^{2/3}}{6^{2/3}} = \frac{2^{3/15} 6^{10/15}}{6} = \frac{(2^3 6^{10})^{1/15}}{6} = \frac{\sqrt[15]{2^3 6^{10}}}{6}.$$

g. *Simplify* $x^{3/2} - x^{1/2}$ *by using the distributive property.*

$$x^{3/2} - x^{1/2} = x^{1/2}(x - 1).$$

h. *Simplify* $\dfrac{\sqrt{20}}{\sqrt{5}}$.

$$\frac{\sqrt{20}}{\sqrt{5}} = \sqrt{\frac{20}{5}} = \sqrt{4} = 2.$$

i. *Simplify* $(x^5 y^8)^5$.

$$(x^5 y^8)^5 = x^{25} y^{40}.$$

j. *Simplify* $(x^{5/9} y^{4/3})^{18}$.

$$(x^{5/9} y^{4/3})^{18} = (x^{5/9})^{18} (y^{4/3})^{18} = x^{10} y^{24}.$$

k. *Simplify* $\left(\dfrac{x^{1/5} y^{6/5}}{z^{2/5}}\right)^5$.

$$\left(\frac{x^{1/5} y^{6/5}}{z^{2/5}}\right)^5 = \frac{(x^{1/5} y^{6/5})^5}{(z^{2/5})^5} = \frac{xy^6}{z^2}.$$

l. *Simplify* $\sqrt{\dfrac{2}{7}}$.

$$\sqrt{\frac{2}{7}} = \sqrt{\frac{2}{7} \cdot \frac{7}{7}} = \sqrt{\frac{14}{7^2}} = \frac{\sqrt{14}}{\sqrt{7^2}} = \frac{\sqrt{14}}{7}.$$

m. *Simplify* $\sqrt[3]{x^6 y^4}$.

$$\sqrt[3]{x^6 y^4} = \sqrt[3]{(x^2)^3 y^3 y} = \sqrt[3]{(x^2)^3} \cdot \sqrt[3]{y^3} \cdot \sqrt[3]{y}$$

$$= x^2 y \sqrt[3]{y}.$$

n. *Eliminate negative exponents in* $7x^{-2} + (7x)^{-2}$.

$$7x^{-2} + (7x)^{-2} = \frac{7}{x^2} + \frac{1}{(7x)^2} = \frac{7}{x^2} + \frac{1}{49x^2}.$$

o. *Eliminate negative exponents in* $(x^{-1} - y^{-1})^{-2}$.

$$(x^{-1} - y^{-1})^{-2} = \left(\frac{1}{x} - \frac{1}{y}\right)^{-2}$$

$$= \left(\frac{y - x}{xy}\right)^{-2} = \left(\frac{xy}{y - x}\right)^2$$

$$= \frac{x^2 y^2}{(y - x)^2}.$$

p. *Apply the distributive law to* $x^{2/5}(y^{1/2} + 2z^{6/5})$.

$$x^{2/5}(y^{1/2} + 2z^{6/5}) = x^{2/5} y^{1/2} + 2x^{2/5} z^{6/5}.$$

q. *Simplify* $\sqrt{250} - \sqrt{50} + 15\sqrt{2}$.

$$\sqrt{250} - \sqrt{50} + 15\sqrt{2} = \sqrt{25 \cdot 10} - \sqrt{25 \cdot 2} + 15\sqrt{2}$$

$$= 5\sqrt{10} - 5\sqrt{2} + 15\sqrt{2}$$

$$= 5\sqrt{10} + 10\sqrt{2}.$$

r. *Simplify* $\dfrac{x^3}{y^2} \div \dfrac{x^6}{y^5}$.

$$\frac{x^3}{y^2} \div \frac{x^6}{y^5} = \frac{x^3}{y^2} \cdot \frac{y^5}{x^6} = \frac{y^3}{x^3}.$$

s.

$$\sqrt{x^2} = \begin{cases} x \text{ if } x \text{ is positive} \\ -x \text{ if } x \text{ is negative} \\ 0 \text{ if } x = 0. \end{cases}$$

Thus, $\sqrt{2^2} = 2$ and $\sqrt{(-3)^2} = -(-3) = 3$.

EXERCISE 0-5

Evaluate the following expressions.

1. $\sqrt{25}$

2. $\sqrt[3]{64}$

3. $\sqrt[5]{-32}$

4. $\sqrt{.04}$

5. $\sqrt[4]{\frac{1}{16}}$

6. $\sqrt[3]{-\frac{8}{27}}$

7. $(100)^{1/2}$ **8.** $(64)^{1/3}$

9. $4^{3/2}$ **10.** $(25)^{-3/2}$

11. $(32)^{-2/5}$ **12.** $(.09)^{-1/2}$

13. $\left(\dfrac{1}{16}\right)^{5/4}$ **14.** $\left(-\dfrac{27}{64}\right)^{2/3}$

Simplify the following expressions.

15. $\sqrt{32}$ **16.** $\sqrt[3]{24}$

17. $\sqrt[3]{2x^3}$ **18.** $\sqrt{4x}$

19. $\sqrt{16x^4}$ $= \quad 4x^2$ **20.** $\sqrt[4]{x/16}$

21. $(9z^4)^{1/2}$ $= \quad 3z^2$ **22.** $(16y^8)^{3/4}$

23. $\left(\dfrac{27t^3}{8}\right)^{2/3}$ $= \quad \dfrac{3t}{2} \quad \dfrac{9t^2}{4}$ **24.** $\left(\dfrac{1000}{a^9}\right)^{-2/3}$

Write the following expressions in terms of positive exponents only. Avoid all radicals in the final form. For example, $y^{-1}\sqrt{x} = \dfrac{x^{1/2}}{y}$.

25. $\dfrac{x^3 y^{-2}}{z^2}$ $\dfrac{x^3}{z^2 y^2}$ **26.** $\sqrt[5]{x^2 y^3 z^{-10}}$

27. $2x^{-1} x^{-3}$ **28.** $x + y^{-1}$

29. $(3t)^{-2}$ $\frac{1}{3}\ \frac{2}{3}$ $7\ \ s$ **30.** $(3 - z)^{-4}$

31. $\sqrt[3]{7s^2}$ **32.** $(x^{-2} y^2)^{-2}$

33. $\sqrt{x} - \sqrt{y}$ $x^{1/2} - y^{1/2}$ **34.** $\dfrac{x^{-2} y^{-6} z^2}{xy^{-1}}$

35. $x^2 \sqrt[4]{xy^{-2} z^3}$ $x^2\ x^{1/4}(y\cdot 4)\ z^{3/4} 2^{3/4}$ $y^{1/2}$ **36.** $(\sqrt[5]{xy^{-3}})x^{-1} y^{-2}$

Write the following exponential forms in equivalent forms involving radicals.

37. $(8x - y)^{4/5}$ N   **38.** $(ab^2 c^3)^{3/4}$

39. $x^{-4/5}$ **40.** $2x^{1/2} - (2y)^{1/2}$

41. $2x^{-2/5} - (2x)^{-2/5}$ **42.** $[(x^{-4})^{1/5}]^{1/6}$

Simplify the following. Express all answers in terms of positive exponents. Rationalize the denominator where necessary to avoid fractional exponents in the denominator.

43. $2x^2 y^{-3} x^4$ **44.** $\dfrac{2}{x^{3/2} y^{1/3}}$

45. $\sqrt{\sqrt[3]{t^4}}$ **46.** $\{[(2x^2)^3]^{-4}\}^{-1}$

47. $\dfrac{2^0}{(2^{-2}x^{1/2}y^{-2})^3}$

48. $\dfrac{\sqrt{s^5}}{\sqrt[3]{s^2}}$

49. $\sqrt[3]{x^2yz^3}\ \sqrt[3]{xy^2}$

50. $(\sqrt[5]{2})^{10}$

51. $3^2(27)^{-4/3}$

52. $(\sqrt[5]{x^2y})^{2/5}$

53. $(2x^{-1}y^2)^2$

54. $\dfrac{3}{\sqrt[3]{y}\ \sqrt[4]{x}}$

55. $\sqrt{x}\ \sqrt{x^2y^3}\ \sqrt{xy^2}$

56. $\sqrt{75k^4}$

57. $\dfrac{(x^2y^{-1}z)^{-2}}{(xy^2)^{-4}}$

58. $\sqrt{6(6)}$

59. $\dfrac{(x^2)^3}{x^4} \div \left[\dfrac{x^3}{(x^3)^2}\right]^{-2}$

60. $\sqrt{(-6)(-6)}$

61. $-\dfrac{8s^{-2}}{2s^3}$

62. $(x^{-1}y^{-2}\sqrt{z})^4$

63. $(2x^2y \div 3y^3z^{-2})^2$

64. $\dfrac{1}{\left(\dfrac{\sqrt{2}\,x^{-2}}{\sqrt{16}\,x^3}\right)^2}$

65. Given that $\sqrt{2}$ is approximately 1.4142, find $\dfrac{1}{\sqrt{2}}$ by long division. Then compute $\dfrac{\sqrt{2}}{2}$ by long division. At what conclusion do you arrive about the use of rationalizing the denominator in the approximation of certain expressions?

0-6   OPERATIONS WITH ALGEBRAIC EXPRESSIONS

If numbers, represented by symbols, are combined by the operations of addition, subtraction, multiplication, division, or extraction of roots, then the resulting expression is called an *algebraic expression.*

EXAMPLE 7

a. $\sqrt[3]{\dfrac{3x^3 - 5x - 2}{10 - x}}$ is an algebraic expression in the variable x.

b. $10 - 3\sqrt{y} + \dfrac{5}{7 + y^2}$ is an algebraic expression in the variable y.

c. $\dfrac{(x + y)^3 - xy}{y} + 2$ is an algebraic expression in the variables x and y.

The algebraic expression $5ax^3 - 2bx + 3$ consists of three *terms:* $+5ax^3$, $-2bx$, and $+3$. Some of the *factors* of the first term $5ax^3$ are 5, a, x, x^2, x^3, $5ax$, and ax^2. Also, $5a$ is the *coefficient* of x^3 and 5 is the *numerical coefficient* of ax^3. The symbols a and b are called *constants*. They represent fixed numbers throughout a discussion.

Algebraic expressions with exactly one term are called *monomials*. Those having exactly two terms are *binomials*, and those with exactly three terms are *trinomials*. Algebraic expressions with more than one term are classified as *multinomials*. Thus the multinomial $2x - 5$ is a binomial and the multinomial $3\sqrt{y} + 2y - 4y^2$ is a trinomial.

A *polynomial in x* is an algebraic expression of the form

$$a_0 x^n + a_1 x^{n-1} + \ldots + a_{n-1} x + a_n \dagger$$

where n is a positive integer and a_0, a_1, ..., a_n are real numbers with $a_0 \neq 0$. We call n the *degree* of the polynomial. Hence $4x^3 - 5x^2 + x - 2$ is a polynomial in x of degree 3, and $y^5 - 2$ is a polynomial in y of degree 5. A nonzero constant is treated as a polynomial of degree zero; thus 5 is a polynomial of degree zero.

EXAMPLE 8

Simplify $(3x^2 y - 2x + 1) + (4x^2 y + 6x - 3)$.

We shall first remove the parentheses. Next, using the commutative property of addition, we gather all similar terms together. *Similar terms* are those terms which differ only by their numerical coefficients. In our case, $3x^2 y$ and $4x^2 y$ are similar, as are the pairs $-2x$ and $6x$, and 1 and -3. Thus,

$$(3x^2 y - 2x + 1) + (4x^2 y + 6x - 3)$$

$$= 3x^2 y - 2x + 1 + 4x^2 y + 6x - 3$$

$$= 3x^2 y + 4x^2 y - 2x + 6x + 1 - 3.$$

By the distributive property,

$$3x^2 y + 4x^2 y = (3 + 4)x^2 y = 7x^2 y$$

and

$$-2x + 6x = (-2 + 6)x = 4x.$$

Hence,

$$(3x^2 y - 2x + 1) + (4x^2 y + 6x - 3) = 7x^2 y + 4x - 2.$$

---

†The three dots indicate the terms which are understood to be included in the sum.

EXAMPLE 9

Simplify $(3x^2 y - 2x + 1) - (4x^2 y + 6x - 3)$.

Here we apply the definition of subtraction and the distributive property:

$$(3x^2 y - 2x + 1) - (4x^2 y + 6x - 3)$$
$$= (3x^2 y - 2x + 1) + (-1)(4x^2 y + 6x - 3)$$
$$= (3x^2 y - 2x + 1) + (-4x^2 y - 6x + 3)$$
$$= 3x^2 y - 2x + 1 - 4x^2 y - 6x + 3$$
$$= 3x^2 y - 4x^2 y - 2x - 6x + 1 + 3$$
$$= (3 - 4)x^2 y + (-2 - 6)x + 1 + 3$$
$$= -x^2 y - 8x + 4.$$

EXAMPLE 10

Simplify $3\{2x[2x + 3] + 5[4x^2 - (3 - 4x)]\}$.

We shall first remove the innermost grouping symbols (parentheses) by using the distributive property. Then we repeat the process until all grouping symbols are removed—combining similar terms whenever possible.

$$3\{2x[2x + 3] + 5[4x^2 - (3 - 4x)]\}$$
$$= 3\{2x[2x + 3] + 5[4x^2 - 3 + 4x]\}$$
$$= 3\{4x^2 + 6x + 20x^2 - 15 + 20x\}$$
$$= 3\{24x^2 + 26x - 15\}$$
$$= 72x^2 + 78x - 45.$$

The distributive property is the key tool in multiplying expressions. For example, to multiply $ax + c$ by $bx + d$ we can consider $ax + c$ as a single number and then use the distributive property.

$$(ax + c)(bx + d) = (ax + c)bx + (ax + c)d.$$

Using the distributive property again, we have

$$(ax + c)bx + (ax + c)d = abx^2 + cbx + adx + cd$$
$$= abx^2 + (ad + cb)x + cd.$$

Thus, $(ax + c)(bx + d) = abx^2 + (ad + cb)x + cd$. In particular, if $a = 2$, $b = 1$, $c = 3$, and $d = -2$, then

$$(2x + 3)(x - 2) = 2(1)x^2 + [2(-2) + 3(1)]x + 3(-2)$$
$$= 2x^2 - x - 6.$$

Below is a list of special products. Each one may be obtained from the distributive property. Verify those products which are unfamiliar to you.

SPECIAL PRODUCTS

(I) $x(y + z) = xy + xz$ (Distributive property).

(II) $(x + a)(x + b) = x^2 + (a + b)x + ab$.

(III) $(ax + c)(bx + d) = abx^2 + (ad + cb)x + cd$.

(IV) $(x + a)^2 = x^2 + 2ax + a^2$ (Square of a binomial).

(V) $(x - a)^2 = x^2 - 2ax + a^2$ (Square of a binomial).

(VI) $(x - a)(x + a) = x^2 - a^2$ (Product of sum and difference).

EXAMPLE 11

a. By II, $(x + 2)(x - 5) = [x + 2][x + (-5)]$

$$= x^2 + (2 - 5)x + 2(-5)$$

$$= x^2 - 3x - 10.$$

b. By III, $(3z + 5)(7z + 4) = 3 \cdot 7z^2 + (3 \cdot 4 + 5 \cdot 7)z + 5 \cdot 4$

$$= 21z^2 + 47z + 20.$$

c. By V, $(x - 4)^2 = x^2 - 2(4)x + 4^2$

$$= x^2 - 8x + 16.$$

d. By VI, $(\sqrt{y^2 + 1} - 3)(\sqrt{y^2 + 1} + 3) = [(y^2 + 1)^{1/2} - 3][(y^2 + 1)^{1/2} + 3]$

$$= [(y^2 + 1)^{1/2}]^2 - 3^2$$

$$= (y^2 + 1) - 9$$

$$= y^2 - 8.$$

EXAMPLE 12

Multiply $(2t - 3)(5t^2 + 3t - 1)$.

We treat $2t - 3$ as a single number and apply the distributive property.

$$(2t - 3)(5t^2 + 3t - 1) = (2t - 3)5t^2 + (2t - 3)3t - (2t - 3)1$$

$$= 10t^3 - 15t^2 + 6t^2 - 9t - 2t + 3$$

$$= 10t^3 - 9t^2 - 11t + 3.$$

In Example 2(c) we showed that $\dfrac{a + b}{c} = \dfrac{a}{c} + \dfrac{b}{c}$. Similarly, $\dfrac{a - b}{c} = \dfrac{a}{c} - \dfrac{b}{c}$. Using these results, we can divide a multinomial by a monomial.

EXAMPLE 13

a. $\dfrac{x^3 + 3x}{x} = \dfrac{x^3}{x} + \dfrac{3x}{x} = x^2 + 3.$

b. $\dfrac{4z^3 - 8z^2 + 3z - 6}{2z} = \dfrac{4z^3}{2z} - \dfrac{8z^2}{2z} + \dfrac{3z}{2z} - \dfrac{6}{2z}$

$= 2z^2 - 4z + \dfrac{3}{2} - \dfrac{3}{z}.$

To divide a polynomial by a polynomial we use so-called "long division."

EXAMPLE 14

Divide $2x^3 - 14x - 5$ *by* $x - 3$.

Here $2x^3 - 14x - 5$ is the *dividend* and $x - 3$ is the *divisor*. To avoid errors it is best to write the dividend as $2x^3 + 0x^2 - 14x - 5$. Note that the powers of x are in decreasing order.

$$
\begin{array}{r}
2x^2 \ + \ 6x \ + \ 4 \leftarrow \text{Quotient} \\
x - 3 \overline{)2x^3 + 0x^2 - 14x - \ 5} \\
\underline{2x^3 - 6x^2} \quad\quad\quad\quad \\
6x^2 - 14x \quad\quad \\
\underline{6x^2 - 18x} \quad\quad \\
4x - \ 5 \\
\underline{4x - 12} \\
7 \leftarrow \text{Remainder}
\end{array}
$$

Here we divided x into $2x^3$ and got $2x^2$. Then we multiplied $2x^2$ by $x - 3$ getting $2x^3 - 6x^2$. After subtracting $2x^3 - 6x^2$ from $2x^3 + 0x^2$, we obtained $6x^2$ and then "brought down" the term $-14x$. This process is continued until we arrive at 7, the *remainder*. We always stop when the remainder is a polynomial whose degree is less than the degree of the divisor. Our answer may be written as

$$2x^2 + 6x + 4 + \dfrac{7}{x - 3}.$$

A way of checking a division is to verify that

(Quotient)(Divisor) + Remainder = Dividend.

By using this equation you should verify the result of the example.

EXERCISE 0-6

Simplify the following expressions.

1. $(8x - 4y + 2) + (3x + 2y - 5)$

2. $(6x^2 - 10xy + 2) + (2z - xy + 4)$

3. $(8t^2 - 6s^2) + (4s^2 - 2t^2 + 6)$

4. $(\sqrt{x} + 2\sqrt{x}) + (\sqrt{x} + 3\sqrt{x})$

5. $(\sqrt{x} + \sqrt{2y}) + (\sqrt{x} + \sqrt{3z})$

6. $(3x + 2y - 5) - (8x - 4y + 2)$

7. $(6x^2 - 10xy + \sqrt{2}) - (2z - xy + 4)$

8. $(\sqrt{x} + 2\sqrt{x}) - (\sqrt{x} + 3\sqrt{x})$

9. $(\sqrt{x} + \sqrt{2y}) - (\sqrt{x} + \sqrt{3z})$

10. $4(2z - w) - 3(w - 2z)$

11. $3(3x + 2y - 5) - 2(8x - 4y + 2)$

12. $(2s + t) - 3(s - 6) + 4(1 - t)$

13. $3(x^2 + y^2) - x(y + 2x) + 2y(x + 3y)$

14. $2 - [3 + 4(s - 3)]$

15. $2\{3[3(x^2 + 2) - 2(x^2 - 5)]\}$

16. $4\{3(t + 5) - t[1 - (t + 1)]\}$

17. $-3\{4x(x + 2) - 2[x^2 - (3 - x)]\}$

18. $-\{-2[2a + 3b - 1] + 4[a - 2b] - a[2(b - 3)]\}$

19. $(x + 3)(x - 2)$

20. $(z - 7)(z - 3)$

21. $(2x + 3)(5x + 2)$

22. $(y - 4)(2y + 3)$

23. $(x - 5)^2$

24. $(\sqrt{x} - 1)(2\sqrt{x} + 5)$

25. $(\sqrt{2y} + 3)^2$

26. $(y - 3)(y + 3)$

27. $(2s - 1)(2s + 1)$

28. $(z^2 - 3w)(z^2 + 3w)$

29. $(x^2 - 3)(x + 4)$

30. $(x + 1)(x^2 + x + 3)$

31. $(x^2 - 1)(2x^2 + 2x - 3)$

32. $(2x - 1)(3x^3 + 7x^2 - 5)$

33. $x\{3(x - 1)(x - 2) + 2[x(x + 7)]\}$

34. $[(2z + 1)(2z - 1)](4z^2 + 1)$

35. $(x + y + 2)(3x + 2y - 4)$

36. $(x^2 + x + 1)^2$

37. $\dfrac{z^2 - 4z}{z}$

38. $\dfrac{2x^3 - 7x + 4}{x}$

39. $\dfrac{6x^5 + 4x^3 - 1}{2x^2}$

40. $\dfrac{(3x - 4) - (x + 8)}{4x}$

41. $(x^2 + 3x - 1) \div (x + 3)$

42. $(x^2 - 5x + 4) \div (x - 4)$

43. $(3x^3 - 2x^2 + x - 3) \div (x + 2)$

44. $(x^4 + 2x^2 + 1) \div (x - 1)$

45. $t^2 \div (t - 8)$

46. $(4x^2 + 6x + 1) \div (2x - 1)$

47. $(3x^2 - 4x + 3) \div (3x + 2)$

48. $(z^3 + z^2 + z) \div (z^2 - z + 1)$

0-7 FACTORING

You should read this section with pencil and paper in hand so that you can reproduce the manipulations for yourself.

If two or more expressions are multiplied together, the expressions are called *factors* of the product. Thus if $c = ab$, then a and b are both factors of the product c. For example, in $3ax$ some factors are 3, a, x, and $3a$. The process by which an expression is written as a product of its factors is called *factoring*.

Listed below are the special products discussed in Section 0-6. The right side of each identity is written as a product of factors of the left side.

(I) $xy + xz = x(y + z)$ (Common factor).

(II) $x^2 + (a + b)x + ab = (x + a)(x + b)$.

(III) $abx^2 + (ad + cb)x + cd = (ax + c)(bx + d)$.

(IV) $x^2 + 2ax + a^2 = (x + a)^2$ (Perfect-square trinomial).

(V) $x^2 - 2ax + a^2 = (x - a)^2$ (Perfect-square trinomial).

(VI) $x^2 - a^2 = (x - a)(x + a)$ (Difference of two squares).

When factoring a polynomial we usually choose factors which themselves are polynomials. Thus, $x^2 - 4 = (x - 2)(x + 2)$. We do not write $x - 4 = (\sqrt{x} - 2)(\sqrt{x} + 2)$.

Always factor completely. For example,

$$2x^2 - 8 = 2(x^2 - 4) = 2(x - 2)(x + 2).$$

EXAMPLE 15

a. *Completely factor* $3k^2 x^2 + 9k^3 x$.

Since $3k^2 x^2 = (3k^2 x)(x)$ and $9k^3 x = (3k^2 x)(3k)$, each term of the original expression contains the common factor $3k^2 x$. Thus by the distributive property $3k^2 x^2 + 9k^3 x = 3k^2 x(x + 3k)$. Note that although $3k^2 x^2 + 9k^3 x = 3(k^2 x^2 + 3k^3 x)$, we do not say that the expression is completely factored, since $k^2 x^2 + 3k^3 x$ can yet be factored.

b. *Completely factor* $8a^5 x^2 y^3 - 6a^2 b^3 yz - 2a^4 b^4 xy^2 z^2$.

$$8a^5 x^2 y^3 - 6a^2 b^3 yz - 2a^4 b^4 xy^2 z^2$$

$$= 2a^2 y(4a^3 x^2 y^2 - 3b^3 z - a^2 b^4 xyz^2).$$

c. *Completely factor* $3x^2 - 12$.

By the distributive property, $3x^2 - 12 = 3(x^2 - 4)$. But by Rule VI, $x^2 - 4 = (x - 2) \cdot (x + 2)$. Thus, $3x^2 - 12 = 3(x - 2)(x + 2)$ and the expression is completely factored.

EXAMPLE 16

a. *Completely factor* $x^2 - x - 6$.

If this trinomial factors into the form $x^2 - x - 6 = (x + a)(x + b)$, which is a product of two binomials, then all we must do is determine a and b. Since $(x + a)(x + b) = x^2 + (a + b)x + ab$, then

$$x^2 + (-1)x + (-6) = x^2 + (a + b)x + ab.$$

By equating corresponding coefficients, we want

$$a + b = -1 \text{ and } ab = -6.$$

The sum of a and b must be -1 and their product must be -6. If $a = -3$ and $b = 2$, then both conditions are met and hence

$$x^2 - x - 6 = (x - 3)(x + 2).$$

b. *Completely factor $x^2 - 7x + 12$.*

$$x^2 - 7x + 12 = (x - 3)(x - 4).$$

EXAMPLE 17

Listed below are expressions that are completely factored. The numbers in parentheses refer to the rules used.

a. $x^2 + 8x + 16 = (x + 4)^2$.   (IV)

b. $9x^2 + 9x + 2 = (3x + 1)(3x + 2)$.   (III)

c. $6y^3 + 3y^2 - 18y = 3y(2y^2 + y - 6)$ (I)

                    $= 3y(2y - 3)(y + 2)$.   (III)

d. $x^2 - 6x + 9 = (x - 3)^2$.   (V)

e. $z^{1/4} + z^{5/4} = z^{1/4}(1 + z)$.   (I)

f. $x^4 - 1 = (x^2 - 1)(x^2 + 1)$ (VI)

             $= (x - 1)(x + 1)(x^2 + 1)$.   (VI)

g. $x^{2/3} - 5x^{1/3} + 4 = (x^{1/3} - 1)(x^{1/3} - 4)$.   (II)

h. $ax^2 - ay^2 + bx^2 - by^2 = (ax^2 - ay^2) + (bx^2 - by^2)$

                       $= a(x^2 - y^2) + b(x^2 - y^2)$ (I)

                       $= (a + b)(x^2 - y^2)$ (I)

                       $= (a + b)(x - y)(x + y)$.   (VI)

Note in Example 17(f) that $x^2 - 1$ is factorable but $x^2 + 1$ is not. In 17(h) we factored by making use of grouping.

EXERCISE 0-7

Completely factor the expressions.

1. $6x + 4$

2. $6y^2 - 4y$

3. $10xy + 5xz$

4. $3x^2 y - 9x^3 y^3$

5. $8a^3 bc - 12ab^3 cd + 4b^4 c^2 d^2$

6. $6z^2 t^3 + 3zst^4 - 12z^2 t^3$

7. $x^2 - 25$ 8. $x^2 + 3x - 4$

9. $p^2 + 4p + 3$ 10. $s^2 - 6s + 8$

11. $16x^2 - 9$ 12. $x^2 + 5x - 24$

13. $z^2 + 6z + 8$ 14. $4t^2 - 9s^2$

15. $x^2 + 6x + 9$ 16. $y^2 - 15y + 50$

17. $2x^2 + 12x + 16$ 18. $2x^2 + 7x - 15$

19. $3x^2 - 3$ 20. $4y^2 - 8y + 3$

21. $6y^2 + 13y + 2$ 22. $4x^2 - x - 3$

23. $12s^3 + 10s^2 - 8s$ 24. $9z^2 + 24z + 16$

25. $x^{2/3}y - 4x^{8/3}y^3$ 26. $9x^{4/7} - 1$

27. $2x^3 + 2x^2 - 12x$ 28. $x^2y^2 - 4xy + 4$

29. $(4x + 2)^2$ 30. $3s^2(3s - 9s^2)^2$

31. $x^3y^2 - 10x^2y + 25x$ 32. $(3x^2 + x) + (6x + 2)$

33. $(x^3 - 4x) + (8 - 2x^2)$ 34. $(x^2 - 1) + (x^2 - x - 2)$

35. $(y^{10} + 8y^6 + 16y^2) - (y^8 + 8y^4 + 16)$ 36. $x^3y - xy + z^2x^2 - z^2$

0-8   FRACTIONS

By using the fundamental principle of fractions (Sec. 0-4), we are able to simplify fractions. That principle allows us to multiply or divide both numerator and denominator of a fraction by the same nonzero quantity. The resulting fraction will be equivalent to the original one. The fractions that we shall consider are assumed to have nonzero denominators.

EXAMPLE 18

a. *Simplify* $\dfrac{x^2 - x - 6}{x^2 - 7x + 12}$.

First, completely factor the numerator and denominator:

$$\frac{x^2 - x - 6}{x^2 - 7x + 12} = \frac{(x - 3)(x + 2)}{(x - 3)(x - 4)}.$$

Since both numerator and denominator have the common factor $x - 3$, we multiply each of them by the multiplicative inverse of $x - 3$, namely $\dfrac{1}{x - 3}$, and simplify.

$$\frac{(x-3)(x+2)}{(x-3)(x-4)} = \frac{\dfrac{1}{x-3}(x-3)(x+2)}{\dfrac{1}{x-3}(x-3)(x-4)}$$

$$= \frac{1(x+2)}{1(x-4)} = \frac{x+2}{x-4}.$$

Usually we just write

$$\frac{x^2 - x - 6}{x^2 - 7x + 12} = \frac{\overset{1}{\cancel{(x-3)}}(x+2)}{\underset{1}{\cancel{(x-3)}}(x-4)} = \frac{x+2}{x-4}$$

or

$$\frac{x^2 - x - 6}{x^2 - 7x + 12} = \frac{(x-3)(x+2)}{(x-3)(x-4)} = \frac{x+2}{x-4}.$$

The process we have used here is commonly referred to as "cancellation."

b. *Simplify* $\dfrac{2x^2 + 6x - 8}{8 - 4x - 4x^2}$.

$$\frac{2x^2 + 6x - 8}{8 - 4x - 4x^2} = \frac{2(x-1)(x+4)}{4(1-x)(2+x)}$$

$$= \frac{2(x-1)(x+4)}{2(2)[(-1)(x-1)](2+x)}$$

$$= \frac{x+4}{-2(x+2)}$$

$$= -\frac{x+4}{2(x+2)}.$$

c. *Rationalize the denominator of* $\dfrac{x}{\sqrt{2} - 6}$.

$$\frac{x}{\sqrt{2} - 6} = \frac{x}{\sqrt{2} - 6} \cdot \frac{\sqrt{2} + 6}{\sqrt{2} + 6}$$

$$= \frac{x(\sqrt{2} + 6)}{2 - 36}$$

$$= -\frac{x(\sqrt{2} + 6)}{34}.$$

In Example 2(c) it was shown that $\dfrac{a}{c} + \dfrac{b}{c} = \dfrac{a+b}{c}$. That is, if we add two fractions having a common denominator, then the result is a fraction whose denominator is the common denominator. The numerator is the sum of the numerators of the original fractions. Similarly, $\dfrac{a}{c} - \dfrac{b}{c} = \dfrac{a-b}{c}$.

EXAMPLE 19

a.
$$\dfrac{p^2 - 5}{p - 2} + \dfrac{3p + 2}{p - 2} = \dfrac{(p^2 - 5) + (3p + 2)}{p - 2}$$
$$= \dfrac{p^2 + 3p - 3}{p - 2}.$$

b.
$$\dfrac{x^2 - 5x + 4}{x^2 + 2x - 3} - \dfrac{x^2 + 2x}{x^2 + 5x + 6} = \dfrac{(x - 1)(x - 4)}{(x - 1)(x + 3)} - \dfrac{x(x + 2)}{(x + 2)(x + 3)}$$
$$= \dfrac{x - 4}{x + 3} - \dfrac{x}{x + 3} = \dfrac{(x - 4) - x}{x + 3}$$
$$= -\dfrac{4}{x + 3}.$$

c.
$$\dfrac{x^2 + x - 5}{x - 7} - \dfrac{x^2 - 2}{x - 7} + \dfrac{-4x + 8}{x^2 - 9x + 14} = \dfrac{x^2 + x - 5}{x - 7} - \dfrac{x^2 - 2}{x - 7} + \dfrac{-4(x - 2)}{(x - 2)(x - 7)}$$
$$= \dfrac{(x^2 + x - 5) - (x^2 - 2) + (-4)}{x - 7}$$
$$= \dfrac{x - 7}{x - 7}$$
$$= 1.$$

d.
$$\dfrac{4}{q - 1} + 3 = \dfrac{4}{q - 1} + \dfrac{3(q - 1)}{q - 1}$$
$$= \dfrac{4 + 3(q - 1)}{q - 1} = \dfrac{3q + 1}{q - 1}.$$

Suppose that you want to add (or subtract) two fractions with different denominators. Transform the fractions by the fundamental principle of fractions into equivalent fractions that have the same denominator. Then proceed with the addition (or subtraction) by the method described above.

For example, to find

$$\frac{2}{x^3(x-3)} + \frac{3}{x(x-3)^2},$$

we can convert the first fraction into the equivalent fraction

$$\frac{2(x-3)}{x^3(x-3)^2},$$

and we can convert the second fraction into

$$\frac{3x^2}{x^3(x-3)^2}.$$

These fractions have the same denominator. Hence,

$$\frac{2}{x^3(x-3)} + \frac{3}{x(x-3)^2} = \frac{2(x-3)}{x^3(x-3)^2} + \frac{3x^2}{x^3(x-3)^2}$$

$$= \frac{3x^2 + 2x - 6}{x^3(x-3)^2}.$$

We could have converted the original fractions into equivalent fractions with any common denominator. However, we chose to convert them into fractions with the denominator $x^3(x-3)^2$. This is the **least common denominator (L.C.D.)** of the fractions $2/[x^3(x-3)]$ and $3/[x(x-3)^2]$.

In general, to find the L.C.D. of two or more fractions, first factor each denominator completely. *The L.C.D. is the product of each of the distinct factors appearing in the denominators, each raised to the highest power to which it occurs in any one denominator.*

EXAMPLE 20

Subtract: $\dfrac{t}{3t+2} - \dfrac{4}{t-1}.$

Here the denominators are already factored. The L.C.D. is $(3t+2)(t-1)$.

$$\frac{t}{3t+2} - \frac{4}{t-1} = \frac{t(t-1)}{(3t+2)(t-1)} - \frac{4(3t+2)}{(3t+2)(t-1)}$$

$$= \frac{t(t-1) - 4(3t+2)}{(3t+2)(t-1)}$$

$$= \frac{t^2 - t - 12t - 8}{(3t+2)(t-1)}$$

$$= \frac{t^2 - 13t - 8}{(3t+2)(t-1)}.$$

EXAMPLE 21

$$\frac{2}{x^2 - 2x + 1} - \frac{3}{x^2 + x - 2} + \frac{1}{x^2 + 2x + 1}$$

$$= \frac{2}{(x-1)^2} - \frac{3}{(x-1)(x+2)} + \frac{1}{(x+1)^2} \qquad [\text{L.C.D.} = (x-1)^2(x+2)(x+1)^2]$$

$$= \frac{2(x+2)(x+1)^2}{(x-1)^2(x+2)(x+1)^2} - \frac{3(x-1)(x+1)^2}{(x-1)^2(x+2)(x+1)^2} + \frac{(x-1)^2(x+2)}{(x+1)^2(x-1)^2(x+2)}$$

$$= \frac{2(x+2)(x+1)^2 - 3(x-1)(x+1)^2 + (x-1)^2(x+2)}{(x-1)^2(x+2)(x+1)^2}$$

$$= \frac{5x^2 + 10x + 9}{(x-1)^2(x+2)(x+1)^2}.$$

If we wish to multiply $\dfrac{a}{b}$ by $\dfrac{c}{d}$, then

$$\frac{a}{b} \cdot \frac{c}{d} = \frac{ac}{bd}.$$

To divide $\dfrac{a}{b}$ by $\dfrac{c}{d}$, where $c \neq 0$, we have

$$\frac{a}{b} \div \frac{c}{d} = \frac{\dfrac{a}{b}}{\dfrac{c}{d}} = \frac{a}{b} \cdot \frac{d}{c}.$$

EXAMPLE 22

a. $\dfrac{x}{x+2} \cdot \dfrac{x+3}{x-5} = \dfrac{x(x+3)}{(x+2)(x-5)}.$

b. $\dfrac{x^2 - 4x + 4}{x^2 + 2x - 3} \cdot \dfrac{6x^2 - 6}{x^2 + 2x - 8} = \dfrac{[(x-2)^2][6(x-1)(x+1)]}{[(x+3)(x-1)][(x+4)(x-2)]}$

$$= \frac{6(x-2)(x+1)}{(x+3)(x+4)}.$$

c. $\dfrac{x}{x+2} \div \dfrac{x+3}{x-5} = \dfrac{x}{x+2} \cdot \dfrac{x-5}{x+3} = \dfrac{x(x-5)}{(x+2)(x+3)}.$

d. $\dfrac{\dfrac{\dfrac{x^2 - 4x + 4}{x^2 + 2x - 3}}{\dfrac{6x^2 - 6}{x^2 + 2x - 8}}}{} = \dfrac{x^2 - 4x + 4}{x^2 + 2x - 3} \cdot \dfrac{x^2 + 2x - 8}{6x^2 - 6}$

$$= \dfrac{[(x-2)^2][(x+4)(x-2)]}{[(x+3)(x-1)][6(x-1)(x+1)]}$$

$$= \dfrac{(x-2)^3(x+4)}{6(x+3)(x-1)^2(x+1)}.$$

e. $\dfrac{\dfrac{x-5}{x-3}}{2x} = \dfrac{\dfrac{x-5}{x-3}}{\dfrac{2x}{1}} = \dfrac{x-5}{x-3} \cdot \dfrac{1}{2x} = \dfrac{x-5}{2x(x-3)}.$

f. $\dfrac{x + 7 + \dfrac{x-1}{x-2}}{2 - \dfrac{\dfrac{3}{x-2}}{x}} = \dfrac{\dfrac{(x+7)(x-2)}{x-2} + \dfrac{x-1}{x-2}}{2 - \left[\left(\dfrac{3}{x-2}\right)\left(\dfrac{1}{x}\right)\right]}$

$$= \dfrac{\dfrac{x^2 + 6x - 15}{x-2}}{2 - \dfrac{3}{x(x-2)}} = \dfrac{\dfrac{x^2 + 6x - 15}{x-2}}{\dfrac{2x(x-2) - 3}{x(x-2)}}$$

$$= \dfrac{(x^2 + 6x - 15)\, x(x-2)}{(x-2)[2x(x-2) - 3]}$$

$$= \dfrac{x(x^2 + 6x - 15)}{2x^2 - 4x - 3}.$$

EXERCISE 0-8

In problems 1-24, perform the operations and simplify as much as possible.

1. $\dfrac{x^2}{x+3} + \dfrac{5x+6}{x+3}$

2. $\dfrac{2}{x+2} + \dfrac{x}{x+2}$

3. $\dfrac{1}{t} + \dfrac{2}{3t}$

4. $\dfrac{4}{x^2} - \dfrac{1}{x}$

5. $1 - \dfrac{p^2}{p^2 - 1}$

6. $\dfrac{4}{s+4} + s$

7. $\dfrac{4}{2x-1} + \dfrac{x}{x+3}$

8. $\dfrac{x+1}{x-1} - \dfrac{x-1}{x+1}$

9. $\dfrac{1}{x^2-x-2} + \dfrac{1}{x^2-1}$

10. $\dfrac{y}{3y^2-5y-2} - \dfrac{2}{3y^2-7y+2}$

11. $\dfrac{4}{x-1} - 3 + \dfrac{-3x^2}{5-4x-x^2}$

12. $\dfrac{2x-3}{2x^2+11x-6} - \dfrac{3x+1}{3x^2+16x-12} + \dfrac{1}{3x-2}$

13. $\dfrac{y^2}{y-3} \cdot \dfrac{-1}{y+2}$

14. $\dfrac{z^2-4}{z^2+2z} \cdot \dfrac{z^2}{z-2}$

15. $\dfrac{2x-3}{x-2} \cdot \dfrac{2-x}{2x+3}$

16. $\dfrac{x^2-y^2}{x+y} \cdot \dfrac{x^2+2xy+y^2}{y-x}$

17. $\dfrac{2x-2}{x^2-2x-8} \div \dfrac{x^2-1}{x^2+5x+4}$

18. $\dfrac{x^2+2x}{3x^2-18x+24} \div \dfrac{x^2-x-6}{x^2-4x+4}$

19. $\dfrac{\dfrac{4x^2-9}{x^2+3x-4}}{\dfrac{2x-3}{1-x^2}}$

20. $\dfrac{\dfrac{6x^2y+7xy-3y}{xy-x+5y-5}}{\dfrac{x^3y+4x^2y}{xy-x+4y-4}}$

21. $\dfrac{1+\dfrac{1}{x}}{3}$

22. $\dfrac{\dfrac{x+3}{x}}{x-\dfrac{9}{x}}$

23. $\dfrac{3-\dfrac{1}{2x}}{x+\dfrac{x}{x+2}}$

24. $\dfrac{\dfrac{x-1}{x^2+5x+6} - \dfrac{1}{x+2}}{3+\dfrac{x-7}{3}}$

In problems 25–28, simplify and express your answer in a form which is free of radicals in the denominator.

25. $\dfrac{1}{x+\sqrt{5}}$

26. $\dfrac{x-3}{\sqrt{x}-1} + \dfrac{4}{\sqrt{x}-1}$

27. $\dfrac{5}{1+\sqrt{3}} - \dfrac{4}{2-\sqrt{2}}$

28. $\dfrac{4}{\sqrt{x}+2} \cdot \dfrac{x^2}{3}$

Chapter 1

Equations

Even a beginning student of economics or business is faced with solving elementary equations. In this chapter we shall develop techniques to accomplish this task. These methods will be applied in the next chapter to some practical situations.

1-1 EQUATIONS—LINEAR EQUATIONS

DEFINITION.   *An **equation** is a statement that two expressions are equal.*

The two expressions that make up an equation are called its **sides** or **members**. They are separated by the **equality sign** "=."

EXAMPLE 1

The following are equations.

(a) $x + 2 = 3$
(b) $x^2 + 3x + 2 = 0$

(c) $\dfrac{y}{y-5} = 7$

(d) $x + a = 4b$

(e) $w + z = 7$

(f) $I = Prt$

In Example 1 each equation contains at least one variable. A **variable** is a symbol that can be replaced by any one of a set of different numbers. The most popular symbols for variables are letters from the latter part of the alphabet, such as x, y, z, w, and s. Hence equations (a) and (c) are in the variables x and y, respectively. Equation (e) is in the variables w and z.

We never allow a variable to have a value for which any expression in the equation is undefined. Thus in $y/(y-5) = 7$, y cannot equal 5, since this would result in division by 0.

To *solve* an equation means to find all values of its variables for which the equation is true. These values are called *solutions* of the equation and are said to *satisfy* the equation. When only one variable is involved, a solution is also called a **root**. The set of all solutions is called the **solution set** of the equation. Sometimes a letter representing an unknown quantity in an equation is simply called an *unknown*. Let us illustrate these terms.

EXAMPLE 2

a. In the equation $x + 2 = 3$, the variable x is the unknown. The only value of x which satisfies the equation is 1. Hence 1 is a root and the solution set is $\{1\}$.

b. $w + z = 7$ is an equation in two unknowns. One solution is $w = 4$ and $z = 3$. However, there are infinitely many solutions. Can you think of another?

c. A root of $x^2 + 3x + 2 = 0$ is -2 because $(-2)^2 + 3(-2) + 2 = 0$.

In the equation $x + 2 = 3$, the numbers 2 and 3 are called *constants*. They are fixed numbers. Equations in which some of the constants are represented by letters are called **literal equations**. For example, in the literal equation $x + a = 4b$ we consider a and b to be constants. Formulas, such as $I = Prt$, which express a relationship between certain quantities may be regarded as literal equations. If we want to express a particular letter in a formula in terms of the others, this letter is considered the unknown.

EXAMPLE 3

The formula $I = Prt$ has the variables I, P, r, and t. If r is to be expressed in terms of I, P, and t, then r is the unknown.

In solving an equation we want any operation on it to result in another equation having exactly the same roots as the given equation. When this occurs the equations are said to be **equivalent**. Three operations which guarantee equivalence are:

(1) *Adding (subtracting) the same polynomial to (from) both sides of an equation where the polynomial is in the same variable as that occurring in the equation;*

(2) *Multiplying (dividing) both sides of an equation by the same constant, except zero;*

(3) *Replacing either side of an equation by an equal expression.*

We repeat: Applying operations 1–3 guarantees that the resulting equation is equivalent to the given one.

Sometimes in solving an equation we have to apply operations other than 1–3. These operations may not necessarily result in equivalent equations. They include:

(4) *Multiplying both sides of an equation by an expression involving the variable;*

(5) *Dividing both sides of an equation by an expression involving the variable;*

(6) *Raising both sides of an equation to equal powers.*

For example, by inspection the only root of $x - 1 = 0$ is 1. Multiplying each side by x gives $x^2 - x = 0$, which is satisfied if x is 0 or 1 (you should check this by substitution). But 0 *does not* satisfy the *original* equation. Thus the equations are not equivalent.

Continuing, you may check that $(x - 4)(x - 3) = 0$ is satisfied when x is 3 or 4. Dividing both sides by $(x - 4)$ gives $x - 3 = 0$, whose only root is 3. Again, we do not have equivalence since, in this case, a root has been "lost." Note that when x is 4, division by $x - 4$ is actually division by 0, an invalid operation.

Finally, squaring each side of the equation $x = 2$ gives $x^2 = 4$, which is true if $x = 2$ or -2. But -2 is not a root of the given equation.

From our discussion it is clear that when operations 4–6 are performed, we must be careful about drawing conclusions concerning the roots of a given equation. Operations 4 and 6 *can* produce an equation with more roots. Thus you should check whether or not each "solution" obtained by these operations satisfies the *original* equation. Operation 5 *can* produce an equation with fewer roots. In this case, any "lost" roots may never be determined. Thus, avoid operation 5 whenever possible.

The principles presented so far will now be demonstrated in the solution of a *linear equation*.

DEFINITION. *A **linear equation** in the variable x is one which can be written in the form*

$$ax + b = 0 \tag{1}$$

where a and b are constants and a ≠ 0.

Equation (1) is also called a *first-degree equation* or an *equation of degree one,* since the highest power of the variable that occurs is one.

To solve a linear equation we perform operations on it until the roots are obvious, as the following examples show.

EXAMPLE 4

Solve the following equations.

a. $5x - 6 = 3x.$

$$5x - 6 = 3x$$

$$5x - 6 + (-3x) = 3x + (-3x) \qquad \text{(adding } -3x \text{ to both sides)}$$

$$2x - 6 = 0 \qquad \text{(simplifying)}$$

$$2x - 6 + 6 = 0 + 6 \qquad \text{(adding 6 to both sides)}$$

$$2x = 6 \qquad \text{(simplifying)}$$

$$\frac{2x}{2} = \frac{6}{2} \qquad \text{(dividing both sides by 2)}$$

$$x = 3.$$

Clearly 3 is the only root of the last equation. Since each equation is equivalent to the one before it, we conclude that 3 must be the only root of $5x - 6 = 3x.$ That is, the solution set is {3}. We can describe the first step in the solution as moving a term from one side of an equation to the other while changing its sign; this is commonly called *transposing.* Note that since the original equation can be put in the form $2x + (-6) = 0,$ it is a linear equation.

b. $2(p + 4) = 7p + 2.$

$$2(p + 4) = 7p + 2$$

$$2p + 8 = 7p + 2 \qquad \text{(distributive property)}$$

$$2p = 7p - 6 \qquad \text{(subtracting 8 from both sides)}$$

$$-5p = -6 \qquad \text{(subtracting } 7p \text{ from both sides)}$$

$$p = \frac{-6}{-5} \qquad \text{(dividing both sides by } -5\text{)}$$

$$p = \frac{6}{5}.$$

c. $y(7y + 5) - y^2 = 4y(y + 4) + 2y^2 + 1$.

$$y(7y + 5) - y^2 = 4y(y + 4) + 2y^2 + 1$$
$$7y^2 + 5y - y^2 = 4y^2 + 16y + 2y^2 + 1$$
$$6y^2 + 5y = 6y^2 + 16y + 1$$
$$-1 = 11y$$
$$-\frac{1}{11} = y \quad \text{or} \quad y = -\frac{1}{11}.$$

d. $\dfrac{7x + 3}{2} - \dfrac{9x - 8}{4} = 6$.

We first clear the equation of fractions by multiplying *both* sides by the least common denominator (L.C.D.), which is 4.

$$4\left(\frac{7x + 3}{2} - \frac{9x - 8}{4}\right) = 4(6)$$
$$2(7x + 3) - 1(9x - 8) = 24$$
$$14x + 6 - 9x + 8 = 24$$
$$5x + 14 = 24$$
$$5x = 10$$
$$x = 2.$$

Each equation in Example 4 has one and only one root. This is typical of every linear equation in one variable.

Now let us look at some literal equations.

EXAMPLE 5

a. *The equation $I = Prt$ is the formula for the simple interest I on a principal of P dollars at the annual interest rate of r for a period of t years. Express r in terms of I, P, and t.*

$$I = Prt$$
$$\frac{I}{Pt} = \frac{Prt}{Pt}$$
$$\frac{I}{Pt} = r \quad \text{or} \quad r = \frac{I}{Pt}.$$

b. *If $S = P + Prt$, solve for P.*

$$S = P + Prt$$

$$S = P(1 + rt)$$

$$\frac{S}{1 + rt} = P.$$

c. *Solve $(a + c)x + x^2 = (x + a)^2$ for x.*

$$(a + c)x + x^2 = (x + a)^2$$

$$ax + cx + x^2 = x^2 + 2ax + a^2$$

$$cx - ax = a^2$$

$$x(c - a) = a^2$$

$$x = \frac{a^2}{c - a}.$$

Actually we assumed $c - a \neq 0$ to avoid division by 0.

EXERCISE 1-1

In problems 1-6, determine by substitution which of the given numbers, if any, satisfy the given equation.

1. $x^2 - 2x = 0$;   0, 2

2. $20 - 9x = -x^2$;   5, 4

3. $y + 2(y - 3) = 4$; $\frac{10}{3}$, 1

4. $2x + x^2 - 8 = 0$;   2, -4

5. $x(7 + x) - 2(x + 1) - 3x = -2$; -3

6. $(x + 1)^2(x + 2)(x - 3) = 0$; $-1, -2, 3$

In problems 7-16, determine what operations were applied to the first equation to obtain the second. State whether or not the operations **guarantee** that the equations are equivalent. Do not solve.

7. $x - 5 = 4x + 10$; $x = 4x + 15$

8. $8x - 4 = 16$; $x - \frac{1}{2} = 2$

9. $x = 4$; $x^2 = 16$

10. $\frac{1}{2}x^2 + 3 = x - 9$; $x^2 + 6 = 2x - 18$

11. $x^2 - 2x = 0$; $x - 2 = 0$

12. $\dfrac{2}{x - 2} + x = x^2$; $2 + x(x - 2) = x^2(x - 2)$

13. $\dfrac{x^2 - 1}{x - 1} = 3; \quad x^2 - 1 = 3(x - 1)$

14. $x(x + 5)(x + 9) = x(x + 1); \quad (x + 5)(x + 9) = x + 1$

15. $\dfrac{x(x + 1)}{x - 5} = x(x + 9); \quad x + 1 = (x + 9)(x - 5)$

16. $2x^2 - 9 = x; \quad x^2 - \frac{1}{2}x = \frac{9}{2}$

In problems 17–44, solve the equations.

17. $6x = 45$

18. $.2x = 5$

19. $3y = 0$

20. $3 - 2x = 4$

21. $5x - 3 = 9$

22. $\sqrt{2}\,x + 3 = 8$

23. $7x + 7 = 2(x + 1)$

24. $6z + 5z - 3 = 41$

25. $2(p - 1) - 3(p - 4) = 4p$

26. $t = 2 - 2[2t - 3(1 - t)]$

27. $\dfrac{x}{5} = 2x - 6$

28. $\dfrac{5y}{7} - \dfrac{6}{7} = 2 - 4y$

29. $5 + \dfrac{4x}{9} = \dfrac{x}{2}$

30. $\dfrac{x}{3} - 4 = \dfrac{x}{5}$

31. $q = \dfrac{3}{2}q - 4$

32. $\dfrac{x}{2} + \dfrac{x}{3} = 7$

33. $3x + \dfrac{x}{5} - 5 = \dfrac{1}{5} + 5x$

34. $y - \dfrac{y}{2} + \dfrac{y}{3} - \dfrac{y}{4} = \dfrac{y}{5}$

35. $w + \dfrac{w}{2} - \dfrac{w}{3} + \dfrac{w}{4} = 5$

36. $\dfrac{p}{3} + \dfrac{3}{4}p = \dfrac{9}{2}(p - 1)$

37. $\dfrac{2y - 3}{4} = \dfrac{6y + 7}{3}$

38. $\dfrac{7 + 2(x + 1)}{3} = \dfrac{8x}{5}$

39. $\dfrac{x + 2}{3} - \dfrac{2 - x}{6} = x - 2$

40. $\dfrac{x}{5} + \dfrac{2(x - 4)}{10} = 7$

41. $\frac{9}{5}(3 - x) = \frac{3}{4}(x - 3)$

42. $\dfrac{2y - 7}{3} + \dfrac{8y - 9}{14} = \dfrac{3y - 5}{21}$

43. $\frac{3}{2}(4x - 3) = 2[x - (4x - 3)]$

44. $(3x - 1)^2 - (5x - 3)^2 = -(4x - 2)^2$

In problems 45–52, express the indicated symbol in terms of the remaining symbols.

45. $I = Prt; \; P$

46. $ax + b = 0; \; x$

47. $p = 6x - 1; x$ **48.** $p = -3x + 6; x$

49. $S = P(1 + rt); r$ **50.** $S = \dfrac{R\left[(1 + i)^n - 1\right]}{i}; R$

51. $S = \dfrac{n}{2}(a_1 + a_n); a_1$ **52.** $r = \dfrac{2mI}{B(n + 1)}; m$

1-2   EQUATIONS LEADING TO LINEAR EQUATIONS

Some equations that are not linear can lead to linear equations, as the following examples show.

EXAMPLE 6

Solve the following equations.

a. $\dfrac{5}{x - 4} = \dfrac{6}{x - 3}.$

To solve this *fractional equation* we first clear it of fractions. Multiplying both sides by the L.C.D., $(x - 4)(x - 3)$, we have

$$(x - 4)(x - 3)\left(\frac{5}{x - 4}\right) = (x - 4)(x - 3)\left(\frac{6}{x - 3}\right)$$

$$5(x - 3) = 6(x - 4)$$

$$5x - 15 = 6x - 24$$

$$9 = x.$$

In the first step we multiplied each side by an expression involving the variable x. As we mentioned in Sec. 1-1, this means that we must check whether or not 9 satisfies the *original* equation. If 9 is substituted for x in that equation, the left side is

$$\frac{5}{9 - 4} = \frac{5}{5} = 1$$

and the right side is

$$\frac{6}{9 - 3} = \frac{6}{6} = 1.$$

Since both sides are equal, 6 is a root.

b. $\dfrac{3x + 4}{x + 2} - \dfrac{3x - 5}{x - 4} = \dfrac{12}{x^2 - 2x - 8}.$

Notice that $x^2 - 2x - 8 = (x + 2)(x - 4)$. Thus the L.C.D. of the fractions is clearly $(x + 2)(x - 4)$. Multiplying both sides by the L.C.D., we have

$$(x - 4)(3x + 4) - (x + 2)(3x - 5) = 12$$

$$3x^2 - 8x - 16 - (3x^2 + x - 10) = 12$$

$$3x^2 - 8x - 16 - 3x^2 - x + 10 = 12$$

$$-9x - 6 = 12$$

$$-9x = 18$$

$$x = -2.$$

However, the *original* equation is not defined for $x = -2$ (division by zero), and so there are no roots. The solution set is a set having no elements in it, { }. This is called the **empty set** or **null set,** which we denote by $\emptyset$.

c. $\sqrt{x^2 + 33} = x + 3$ is a *radical equation.* One way to solve it is to raise both sides to the same power so as to eliminate the radical.

$$\sqrt{x^2 + 33} = x + 3$$

$$x^2 + 33 = (x + 3)^2 \qquad \text{(squaring both sides)}$$

$$x^2 + 33 = x^2 + 6x + 9$$

$$24 = 6x$$

$$4 = x.$$

You should check by substitution that 4 is indeed a root.

d. $\sqrt{y - 3} - \sqrt{y} = -3$.

When an equation contains two terms involving radical expressions, you should first write the equation so that one radical is on each side, if possible.

$$\sqrt{y - 3} = \sqrt{y} - 3$$

$$y - 3 = y - 6\sqrt{y} + 9 \qquad \text{(squaring both sides)}$$

$$6\sqrt{y} = 12$$

$$\sqrt{y} = 2$$

$$y = 4. \qquad \text{(squaring both sides)}$$

Substituting 4 into the left side of the *original* equation gives $\sqrt{1} - \sqrt{4}$, which is -1. Since this does not equal the right side, -3, the solution set is $\emptyset$.

EXERCISE 1-2

Solve the equations in problems 1–32.

1. $\dfrac{4}{x} = 16$

2. $\dfrac{4}{x-1} = 2$

3. $\dfrac{4}{8-x} = \dfrac{3}{4}$

4. $\dfrac{x+3}{x} = \dfrac{2}{5}$

5. $\dfrac{x}{3x-4} = 3$

6. $\dfrac{4q}{7-q} = 1$

7. $\dfrac{1}{p-1} = \dfrac{2}{p-2}$

8. $\dfrac{2x-3}{4x-5} = 6$

9. $\dfrac{1}{x} + \dfrac{1}{5} = \dfrac{4}{5}$

10. $\dfrac{4}{t-3} = \dfrac{3}{t-4}$

11. $\dfrac{3x-2}{2x+3} = \dfrac{3x-1}{2x+1}$

12. $\dfrac{x+2}{x-1} + \dfrac{x+1}{2-x} = 0$

13. $\dfrac{y-6}{y} - \dfrac{6}{y} = \dfrac{y+6}{y-6}$

14. $\dfrac{y-3}{y+3} = \dfrac{y-3}{y+2}$

15. $\dfrac{-4}{x-1} = \dfrac{7}{2-x} + \dfrac{3}{x+1}$

16. $\dfrac{1}{x-3} - \dfrac{3}{x-2} = \dfrac{4}{1-2x}$

17. $\dfrac{9}{x-3} = \dfrac{3x}{x-3}$

18. $\dfrac{x}{x+3} - \dfrac{x}{x-3} = \dfrac{3x-4}{x^2-9}$

19. $\sqrt{x-5} = 2$

20. $\sqrt{z-2} = 3$

21. $\sqrt{5x-6} - 16 = 0$

22. $6 - \sqrt{2x+5} = 0$

23. $\sqrt{\dfrac{x}{2} + 1} = \dfrac{2}{3}$

24. $(x+6)^{1/2} = 7$

25. $\sqrt{4x-6} = \sqrt{x}$

26. $\sqrt{7-2x} = \sqrt{x-1}$

27. $(x-3)^{3/2} = 8$

28. $\sqrt{y^2-9} = 9 - y$

29. $\sqrt{y} + \sqrt{y+2} = 3$

30. $\sqrt{x} - \sqrt{x+1} = 1$

31. $\sqrt{z^2+2z} = 3 + z$

32. $\sqrt{\dfrac{1}{w}} - \sqrt{\dfrac{2}{5w-2}} = 0$

In problems 33–35 express the indicated letter in terms of the remaining letters.

33. $r = \dfrac{d}{1 - dt}$; d

34. $\dfrac{x - a}{b - x} = \dfrac{x - b}{a - x}$; x

35. $r = \dfrac{2mI}{B(n + 1)}$; n

1-3 QUADRATIC EQUATIONS

To learn how to solve more complicated problems, we turn to methods of solving quadratic equations.

DEFINITION. *A **quadratic equation** in the variable x is an equation which can be written in the form*

$$ax^2 + bx + c = 0$$

where a, b, and c are constants and a $\neq$ 0.

A quadratic equation is also called a *second-degree equation* or an *equation of degree two* since the highest power of the variable that occurs is the second. While a linear equation has only one root, some quadratic equations have two roots.

A useful method of solving quadratic equations is based on factoring $ax^2 + bx + c$, as the following example shows.

EXAMPLE 7

a. *Solve the quadratic equation $x^2 + x - 12 = 0$.*

The left side factors easily:

$$(x - 3)(x + 4) = 0.$$

Think of this as two quantities, $(x - 3)$ and $(x + 4)$, whose product is zero. But whenever a product of two or more quantities is zero, at least one of the quantities *must* be zero. This means either $x - 3 = 0$ or $x + 4 = 0$. Solving these gives $x = 3$ and $x = -4$. The roots are 3 and -4 and the solution set is $\{3, -4\}$.

b. *Solve $6w^2 = 5w$.*

We *do not* divide both sides by w (a variable). Instead, write the equation as

$$6w^2 - 5w = 0.$$

Factoring, we obtain

$$w(6w - 5) = 0.$$

Setting each factor equal to 0, we have

$$w = 0 \quad \text{and} \quad 6w - 5 = 0.$$

Thus

$$w = 0 \quad \text{and} \quad w = \tfrac{5}{6}.$$

Check these by substitution.

c. *Solve* $4x - 4x^3 = 0$.

Although the equation is not quadratic, the method of factoring applies.

$$4x - 4x^3 = 0$$
$$4x(1 - x^2) = 0$$
$$4x(1 - x)(1 + x) = 0.$$

Setting each factor equal to 0, we get

$$x = 0, 1, -1,$$

which we can write as $x = 0, \pm 1$.

EXAMPLE 8

a. *Solve* $(3x - 4)(x + 1) = -2$.

PITFALL.   *You should approach a problem like this with caution. If the product of two quantities is equal to* -2, *it is not true that at least one of the quantities must be* -2. *Why?*

We first multiply the factors in the left side:

$$3x^2 - x - 4 = -2.$$

Adding 2 to both sides gives

$$3x^2 - x - 2 = 0.$$

Factoring, we have

$$(3x + 2)(x - 1) = 0.$$

Thus

$$x = -\frac{2}{3}, 1.$$

b. *Solve*
$$\frac{y + 1}{y + 3} + \frac{y + 5}{y - 2} = \frac{7(2y + 1)}{y^2 + y - 6}. \tag{1}$$

Multiplying both sides by the L.C.D., $(y + 3)(y - 2)$, we get

$$(y + 1)(y - 2) + (y + 5)(y + 3) = 7(2y + 1). \tag{2}$$

Since Eq. (1) was multiplied by a quantity which involved the variable y, remember (from Sec. 1-1) that Eq. (2) is not necessarily equivalent to Eq. (1). After simplifying Eq. (2) we have

$$2y^2 - 7y + 6 = 0$$

$$(2y - 3)(y - 2) = 0.$$

Thus, $\frac{3}{2}$ and 2 are *possible* roots of the given equation. But 2 cannot be a root of Eq. (1), since this involves division by 0. However, you should check that $\frac{3}{2}$ does indeed satisfy the original equation.

EXAMPLE 9

Solve $x^2 = 3$.

This equation is equivalent to

$$x^2 - 3 = 0.$$

Factoring, we obtain

$$(x - \sqrt{3})(x + \sqrt{3}) = 0.$$

Thus $x - \sqrt{3} = 0$ or $x + \sqrt{3} = 0$. The roots are $\pm\sqrt{3}$. More generally,

$$\text{if } u^2 = k, \quad \text{then } u = \pm\sqrt{k}.$$

Solving quadratic equations by factoring can be quite difficult, as is evident by trying that method on $.7x^2 - \sqrt{2}x - 8\sqrt{5} = 0$. However, there is a formula for solving every quadratic equation.

The roots of the quadratic equation $ax^2 + bx + c = 0$ are given by the **quadratic formula** †

$$\boxed{x = \frac{-b \pm \sqrt{b^2 - 4ac}}{2a}.}$$

EXAMPLE 10

a. *Solve $4x^2 - 17x + 15 = 0$ by the quadratic formula.*

Here $a = 4$, $b = -17$, and $c = 15$.

$$x = \frac{-b \pm \sqrt{b^2 - 4ac}}{2a} = \frac{-(-17) \pm \sqrt{(-17)^2 - 4(4)(15)}}{2(4)}$$

$$= \frac{17 \pm \sqrt{49}}{8} = \frac{17 \pm 7}{8}.$$

---

† A derivation of the quadratic formula appears in a supplement in the next section.

The roots are $\dfrac{17 + 7}{8} = \dfrac{24}{8} = 3$ and $\dfrac{17 - 7}{8} = \dfrac{10}{8} = \dfrac{5}{4}$.

b. *Solve* $2 + 6\sqrt{2}\,y + 9y^2 = 0$ *by the quadratic formula.*

Look at the arrangement of the terms. Here $a = 9$, $b = 6\sqrt{2}$, and $c = 2$.

$$y = \frac{-b \pm \sqrt{b^2 - 4ac}}{2a} = \frac{-6\sqrt{2} \pm \sqrt{0}}{2(9)}.$$

Thus, $y = \dfrac{-6\sqrt{2} + 0}{18} = -\dfrac{\sqrt{2}}{3}$ or $y = \dfrac{-6\sqrt{2} - 0}{18} = -\dfrac{\sqrt{2}}{3}$. The only root is

$-\dfrac{\sqrt{2}}{3}$.

c. *Solve* $z^2 + z + 1 = 0$ *by the quadratic formula.*

Here $a = 1$, $b = 1$, and $c = 1$. The roots are

$$\frac{-b \pm \sqrt{b^2 - 4ac}}{2a} = \frac{-1 \pm \sqrt{-3}}{2}.$$

Since $\sqrt{-3}$ is not a real number, there are no real roots.†

PITFALL. *Be certain that you use the quadratic formula correctly. Do not write*
$$x = -b \pm \frac{\sqrt{b^2 - 4ac}}{2a}.$$

From Example 10 we see that a quadratic equation may have no real roots, exactly one real root, or two different real roots.

EXERCISE 1-3

In problems 1–26, solve by factoring.

1. $x^2 + 3x + 2 = 0$ **2.** $t^2 - 4t + 4 = 0$

3. $y^2 - 7y + 12 = 0$ **4.** $x^2 + x - 12 = 0$

5. $x^2 - 2x - 3 = 0$ **6.** $x^2 - 16 = 0$

7. $x^2 - 12x = -36$ **8.** $3w^2 - 12w + 12 = 0$

9. $x^2 - 4 = 0$ **10.** $2x^2 + 4x = 0$

11. $z^2 - 8z = 0$ **12.** $x^2 + 9x = -14$

13. $4x^2 + 1 = 4x$ **14.** $2z^2 + 7z = 4$

---

† $\dfrac{-1 \pm \sqrt{-3}}{2}$ can be expressed as $\dfrac{-1 \pm i\sqrt{3}}{2}$, where $i(= \sqrt{-1})$ is called the imaginary unit.

15. $y(2y + 3) = 5$

16. $8 + 2x - 3x^2 = 0$

17. $-x^2 + 3x + 10 = 0$

18. $\frac{1}{7} y^2 = \frac{3}{7} y$

19. $2p^2 = 3p$

20. $-r^2 - r + 12 = 0$

21. $6x^3 + 5x^2 - 4x = 0$

22. $x^3 - 4x^2 - 5x = 0$

23. $x^3 - 64x = 0$

24. $(x + 1)^2 - 5x + 1 = 0$

25. $(x + 3)(x^2 - x - 2) = 0$

26. $3(x^2 + 2x - 8)(x - 5) = 0$

In problems 27–40, find all real roots by using the quadratic formula.

27. $x^2 + 2x - 15 = 0$

28. $x^2 - 2x - 24 = 0$

29. $4x^2 - 12x + 9 = 0$

30. $p^2 + 2p = 0$

31. $p^2 - 5p + 3 = 0$

32. $2 - 2x + x^2 = 0$

33. $4 - 2n + n^2 = 0$

34. $2x^2 + x = 5$

35. $6x^2 + 7x - 5 = 0$

36. $w^2 - 2\sqrt{2}\,w + 2 = 0$

37. $2x^2 - 3x = 20$

38. $.01x^2 + .2x - .6 = 0$

39. $2x^2 + 4x = 5$

40. $-2x^2 - 6x + 5 = 0$

In problems 41–62, solve by any method.

41. $x^2 = \dfrac{x + 5}{6}$

42. $\dfrac{x}{3} = \dfrac{6}{x} - 1$

43. $\dfrac{3}{x - 4} + \dfrac{x - 3}{x} = 2$

44. $\dfrac{2}{x - 1} - \dfrac{6}{2x + 1} = 5$

45. $\dfrac{6x + 7}{2x + 1} - \dfrac{6x + 1}{2x} = 1$

46. $\dfrac{6(w + 1)}{2 - w} + \dfrac{w}{w - 1} = 3$

47. $\dfrac{2}{r - 2} - \dfrac{r + 1}{r + 4} = 0$

48. $\dfrac{2x - 3}{2x + 5} + \dfrac{2x}{3x + 1} = 1$

49. $\dfrac{y + 1}{y + 3} + \dfrac{y + 5}{y - 2} = \dfrac{14y + 7}{y^2 + y - 6}$

50. $\dfrac{3}{t + 1} + \dfrac{4}{t} = \dfrac{12}{t + 2}$

51. $\dfrac{2}{x^2 - 1} - \dfrac{1}{x(x - 1)} = \dfrac{2}{x^2}$

52. $5 - \dfrac{3(x + 3)}{x^2 + 3x} = \dfrac{1 - x}{x}$

53. $\sqrt{x + 2} = x - 4$

54. $3\sqrt{x + 4} = x - 6$

55. $q + 2 = 2\sqrt{4q - 7}$

56. $x + \sqrt{x} - 2 = 0$

57. $\sqrt{x + 7} - \sqrt{2x} - 1 = 0$

58. $\sqrt{x} - \sqrt{2x - 8} - 2 = 0$

59. $\sqrt{x} - \sqrt{2x + 1} + 1 = 0$

60. $\sqrt{y - 2} + 2 = \sqrt{2y + 3}$

61. $\sqrt{x+5} + 1 = 2\sqrt{x}$ **62.** $\sqrt{\sqrt{x}+2} = \sqrt{2x-4}$

63. On page 353 of Samuelson's *Economics*† it is stated that one root of the equation

$$\overline{M} = \frac{Q(Q+10)}{44}$$

is $-5 + \sqrt{25 + 44\overline{M}}$. Verify this by using the quadratic formula to solve for Q in terms of $\overline{M}$.

1-4 SUPPLEMENT

The following is a derivation of the quadratic formula.

Suppose $ax^2 + bx + c = 0$ is a quadratic equation. Since $a \neq 0$, we can divide both sides by a:

$$x^2 + \frac{b}{a}x + \frac{c}{a} = 0$$

$$x^2 + \frac{b}{a}x = -\frac{c}{a}.$$

If we add $\left(\dfrac{b}{2a}\right)^2$ to both sides,

$$x^2 + \frac{b}{a}x + \left(\frac{b}{2a}\right)^2 = \left(\frac{b}{2a}\right)^2 - \frac{c}{a},$$

then the left side factors into $\left(x + \dfrac{b}{2a}\right)^2$ and the right side simplifies into $\dfrac{b^2 - 4ac}{4a^2}$. Thus,

$$\left(x + \frac{b}{2a}\right)^2 = \frac{b^2 - 4ac}{4a^2}.$$

This equation is of the form $u^2 = k$ where $u = x + \dfrac{b}{2a}$ and $k = \dfrac{b^2 - 4ac}{4a^2}$.

Therefore, by Example 9, we have

$$x + \frac{b}{2a} = \pm\sqrt{\frac{b^2 - 4ac}{4a^2}} = \pm\frac{\sqrt{b^2 - 4ac}}{2a}.$$

Solving for x, we obtain

---

†From Paul A. Samuelson, *Economics*, 9th ed, (New York: McGraw Hill, Inc., 1973).

$$x = -\frac{b}{2a} \pm \frac{\sqrt{b^2 - 4ac}}{2a} = \frac{-b \pm \sqrt{b^2 - 4ac}}{2a}.$$

It can be verified that the two values $\dfrac{-b + \sqrt{b^2 - 4ac}}{2a}$ and $\dfrac{-b - \sqrt{b^2 - 4ac}}{2a}$

do indeed satisfy $ax^2 + bx + c = 0$. Summarizing, we say that the roots of the quadratic equation $ax^2 + bx + c = 0$ are given by the **quadratic formula**

$$x = \frac{-b \pm \sqrt{b^2 - 4ac}}{2a}.$$

1-5 REVIEW

Important Terms and Symbols in Chapter 1

equation *(p. 34)*   side of equation *(p. 34)*

equivalent equations *(p. 36)*   solution set *(p. 35)*

root of equation *(p. 35)*   empty set *(p. 42)*

linear equation *(p. 37)*   quadratic equation *(p. 44)*

∅ *(p. 42)*   variable *(p. 35)*

quadratic formula *(p. 46)*   literal equation *(p. 35)*

Review Section

1. In the equation $x^3 + 7x^2 + 5 = x + 7$, we call $x^3 + 7x^2 + 5$ the __(a)__ side and $x + 7$ the __(b)__ side.

  Ans. (a) left,   (b) right

2. The number -3 (is)(is not) a root of $-x^2 + 2x = 15$.

  Ans. is not

3. The equation $2x + 5 = 7$ is of the __(a)__ degree and its only root is __(b)__ .

  Ans. (a) first,   (b) 1

4. The equation $x + 2 = 3$ (is)(is not) (a) equivalent to $x + 4 = 5$. The equation $x + 2 = 3$ (is)(is not) (b) equivalent to $2x + 4 = 3$.

  Ans. (a) is,   (b) is not

5. The roots of $x^2 - 4 = 0$ are _____.

> *Ans.* ±2

6. The roots of $x^2(x - 2)(2x + 1)$ are _____.

> *Ans.* $0, 2, -\dfrac{1}{2}$

7. If $I = Prt$, then $t =$ _____.

> *Ans.* $\dfrac{I}{Pr}$

8. True or false: Every quadratic equation has two different roots. _____

> *Ans.* false

9. A quadratic equation is of the __(a)__ degree and can be written in the form __(b)__ .

> *Ans.* (a) second,   (b) $ax^2 + bx + c = 0, \ a \neq 0$

10. The roots of $x^2 + 50x = 0$ are _____.

> *Ans.* $0, -50$

11. The number of roots of a linear equation is _____.

> *Ans.* one

Review Problems

Solve the following equations.

1. $4 - 3x = 2 + 5x$

2. $\frac{5}{7}x - \frac{2}{3}x = \frac{3}{21}x$

3. $3[2 - 4(1 + x)] = 5 - 3(3 - x)$

4. $3(x + 4)^2 + 6x = 3x^2 + 7$

5. $2 - w = 3 + w$

6. $x = 2x$

7. $x = 2x - (7 + x)$

8. $3x - 8 = 4(x - 2)$

9. $2(4 - \frac{3}{5}p) = 5$

10. $\frac{5}{7}x - \frac{2}{3}x = \frac{3}{21}$

11. $\dfrac{2x}{x - 3} - \dfrac{x + 1}{x + 2} = 1$

12. $\dfrac{t + 3t + 4}{7 - t} = 14$

13. $3x^2 + 2x - 5 = 0$

14. $x^2 - 2x - 2 = 0$

15. $5q^2 = 7q$

16. $2x^2 - x = 0$

17. $x^2 - 10x + 25 = 0$

18. $r^2 + 10r - 25 = 0$

19. $3x^2 - 5 = 0$

20. $x(x - 9) = 0$

21. $(8t - 5)(2t + 6) = 0$

22. $2(x^2 - 1) + 2x = x^2 - 6x + 1$

23. $-3x^2 + 5x - 1 = 0$

24. $y^2 = 6$

25. $\dfrac{6w + 7}{2w + 1} - \dfrac{6w + 1}{2w} = 1$

26. $\dfrac{3}{x + 1} + \dfrac{4}{x} - \dfrac{12}{x + 2} = 0$

27. $\dfrac{2}{x^2 - 9} - \dfrac{3x}{x + 3} = \dfrac{1}{x - 3}$

28. $\dfrac{3}{x^2 - 4} + \dfrac{2}{x^2 + 4x + 4} - \dfrac{4}{x + 2} = 0$

29. $x + 2 = 2\sqrt{4x - 7}$

30. $\sqrt{3z} - \sqrt{5z + 1} + 1 = 0$

Chapter **2**

Applications of Equations and Inequalities

2-1 APPLICATIONS OF EQUATIONS

To solve verbal problems you must express in mathematical symbols the relationships stated in the problems. There is no prescribed method for the solution of these problems. Skill can only come with practice. The following examples illustrate basic techniques and concepts. Examine each of them carefully before going to the exercises.

EXAMPLE 1

The Anderson Company produces Product A for which their cost (including labor and material) is $6 per unit. Fixed charges (that is, charges incurred in a given time period, regardless of output) for the business are $80,000. Each unit has a selling price of $10. Determine the number of units which must be sold for the company to earn a profit of $60,000.

Here we shall use the fact that

$$\text{Profit} = \text{Total Revenue} - \text{Total Cost.}$$

If the number of units which must be sold is denoted by n, then their cost (in dollars) is $6n$. The total cost for the business is therefore $6n + 80,000$. The total revenue from the sale of n units will be $10n$. Since

$$\text{Profit} = \text{Total Revenue} - \text{Total Cost,}$$
$$60,000 = 10n - (6n + 80,000)$$
$$60,000 = 10n - 6n - 80,000$$
$$140,000 = 4n$$
$$35,000 = n.$$

Thus 35,000 units must be sold to earn a profit of $60,000.

EXAMPLE 2

A manufacturer of women's sportswear is planning to sell his new line of slacks sets to various retail outlets. The cost to the retailer will be $16 per set. As a convenience to the retailer, the manufacturer will attach a price tag to each set. What should the tag price be to allow the retailer to reduce this price by 20 percent during a sale and still make a profit of 15 percent on his cost?

Let p be the selling price per set in dollars. During the sale the retailer receives $p - .2p$. This must equal his cost, 16, plus his profit, $(.15)(16)$. Hence,

$$\text{Sale Price} = \text{Cost} + \text{Profit}$$
$$p - .2p = 16 + (.15)(16)$$
$$.8p = 18.40$$
$$p = 23.$$

The manufacturer should mark the price tag at $23.

EXAMPLE 3

A total of $10,000 was invested in two business ventures, A and B. At the end of the first year, A and B yielded returns on the original investment of 6 percent and $5\frac{3}{4}$ percent, respectively. How was the original amount allocated if the total amount earned was $588.75?

Suppose that x is the amount invested at 6 percent. Then $10,000 - x$ is the amount invested at $5\frac{3}{4}$ percent. The interest earned was $(.06)(x)$ and $(.0575)(10,000 - x)$ which totals 588.75. Hence,

$$(.06)x + (.0575)(10,000 - x) = 588.75$$

$$.06x + 575 - .0575x = 588.75$$

$$.0025x = 13.75$$

$$x = 5500.$$

Thus, $5500 was invested at 6 percent and $10,000 - $5500 = $4500 was invested at $5\frac{3}{4}$ percent.

EXAMPLE 4

The board of directors of the Fuddy Duddy Corporation agrees to redeem some of its callable preferred stock in two years. At that time $1,102,500 will be required. Suppose they presently set aside $1,000,000. At what annual rate of interest, compounded annually, will this money have to be invested in order that its future value be sufficient to redeem the shares?

Let r be the required annual rate of interest. At the end of the first year, the accumulated amount will be $1,000,000 plus the interest, 1,000,000r, for a total of

$$1,000,000 + 1,000,000r = 1,000,000(1 + r).$$

At the end of the second year, the accumulated amount will be $1,000,000(1 + r)$ plus the interest on this amount, which is $[1,000,000(1 + r)]r$. Thus the total at the end of the second year will be $1,000,000(1 + r) + 1,000,000(1 + r)r$. This must equal $1,102,500:

$$1,000,000(1 + r) + 1,000,000(1 + r)r = 1,102,500. \tag{1}$$

Since $1,000,000(1 + r)$ is common to each term on the left side,

$$1,000,000(1 + r)[1 + r] = 1,102,500$$

$$1,000,000(1 + r)^2 = 1,102,500$$

$$(1 + r)^2 = \frac{1,102,500}{1,000,000} = \frac{11,025}{10,000} = \frac{441}{400}$$

$$1 + r = \pm\frac{21}{20}$$

$$r = -1 \pm\frac{21}{20}.$$

Thus, $r = -1 + (21/20) = .05$ or $r = -1 - (21/20) = -2.05$. Although .05 and -2.05 are roots of Eq. (1), we reject -2.05, since we want r to be nonnegative. Hence $r = .05 =$ 5 percent is the desired rate.

At times there may be more than one way to set up a verbal problem. Example 5 will illustrate.

EXAMPLE 5

A real estate firm owns the Shantytown Garden Apartments, which consists of 70 apartments. At $125 per month each apartment can be rented. However, for each $5 per month increase there will be two vacancies with no possibility of filling them. The firm wants to receive $8,990 per month from rents. What rent should be charged for each apartment?

Method I.   Suppose r is the rent to be charged per apartment. The increase over the $125 level is then $r - 125$. Thus the number of $5 increases is $\dfrac{r - 125}{5}$. Since each $5 increase results in two vacancies, the total number of vacancies will be $2\left(\dfrac{r - 125}{5}\right)$. Hence the total number of apartments rented will be $70 - 2\left(\dfrac{r - 125}{5}\right)$. Since

$$\text{total rent} = (\text{rent per apartment})(\text{number of apartments rented}),$$

we have

$$8990 = r\left[70 - \frac{2(r - 125)}{5}\right]$$

$$8990 = r\left[\frac{350 - 2(r - 125)}{5}\right]$$

$$8990 = r\left[\frac{350 - 2r + 250}{5}\right]$$

$$44{,}950 = r[600 - 2r]$$

$$2r^2 - 600r + 44{,}950 = 0$$

$$r^2 - 300r + 22{,}475 = 0.$$

By the quadratic formula,

$$r = \frac{300 \pm \sqrt{(300)^2 - 4(1)(22{,}475)}}{2(1)}$$

$$= \frac{300 \pm \sqrt{100}}{2} = \frac{300 \pm 10}{2}.$$

Thus the rent for each apartment should be $155 or $145.

Method II.   Suppose n is the number of $5 increases. Then the increase in rent per apartment will be $5n$ and there will be $2n$ vacancies. Since

$$\text{total rent} = (\text{rent per apartment})(\text{number of apartments rented}),$$

$$8990 = (125 + 5n)(70 - 2n)$$

$$8990 = 8750 + 100n - 10n^2$$

$$10n^2 - 100n + 240 = 0$$

$$n^2 - 10n + 24 = 0$$

$$(n - 6)(n - 4) = 0.$$

Thus, $n = 6$ or $n = 4$. The rent charged should be $125 + 5(6) = \$155$ or $125 + 5(4) = \$145$.

EXERCISE 2-1

1. The Geometric Products Company produces Product Z at a unit cost of $2.15. If fixed costs are $93,500 and each unit sells for $3, how many must be sold for the company to have a profit of $51,000?

2. The Clark Company management would like to know the total sales units that are required for the company to earn a profit of $100,000. The following data are available: unit selling price of $20; unit cost of $15; total fixed cost of $600,000. From these data, determine the required sales units.

3. A man has $8000 which he wishes to invest in two enterprises so that his total income per year will be $425. One enterprise pays $5\frac{1}{2}$ percent annually and the other 5 percent annually. How much must he invest in each?

4. A man invests $20,000, with a part at an interest rate of 6 percent annually and the remainder at 7 percent annually. The total interest at the end of one year is equivalent to an annual $6\frac{3}{4}$ percent rate. How much was invested at each rate?

5. The cost of an article to a retailer is $3.40. If he wishes to make a profit of 20 percent on the selling price, at what price should it be sold?

6. In two years a company will require $1,123,600 in order to retire some bonds. If the company now invests $1,000,000 for this purpose, what annual rate of interest, compounded annually, must it receive on this amount in order to retire the bonds?

7. In two years the Dimwit Power Company will begin an expansion program. It has decided to invest $2,000,000 now so that in two years the total value of the investment will be $2,163,200, the amount required for the expansion. What is the annual rate of interest, compounded annually, that the company must receive to achieve its purpose?

8. A company finds that if it produces and sells x units of a product, its total sales revenue in dollars is $100\sqrt{x}$. If the expense of producing one unit is $2 and the expense of maintaining the plant is fixed at $1200, find the values of x for which:

Total sales revenue = Total production expense + Fixed expense

(that is, profit is zero).

9. Suppose that consumers will purchase x units of a product when the price is $\dfrac{80 - x}{4}$ dollars each. How many units must be sold in order that sales revenue be $400?

10. How long would it take to double an investment at simple interest with a rate of 5 percent per year? (*Hint:* See Example 5(a) of Chapter 1 and express 5 percent as .05.)

11. The inventor of a new toy offers the Kiddy Toy Company exclusive rights to manufacture and sell his new product for a lump-sum payment of $25,000. After estimating that future sales possibilities beyond one year are nonexistent, the company management is reviewing the following alternate proposal: to make a lump-sum payment of $2000 plus a royalty of $0.50 for each unit sold. What must be the sales the first year to make this alternative as economically attractive to the inventor as his original request? (*Hint:* Determine when his incomes under both proposals are the same.)

12. A company parking lot is 120 ft long and 80 ft wide. Due to an increase in personnel, it is decided to double the area of the lot by adding strips of equal width to one end and one side. Find the width of one such strip.

13. You are the chief financial advisor to the Howard Muse Corp. The corporation owns an office complex consisting of 50 suites. At $400 per month each suite can be rented. However, for each $20 per month increase there will be two vacancies with no possibility of filling them. Mr. Muse phones and informs you that he wants to receive a total of $20,240 per month from rents in the complex. He asks you to determine the rent that should be charged for each suite. What is your reply?

14. Six months ago an investment company had a $3,000,000 portfolio consisting of blue chip and glamour stocks. Since then, the value of the blue chip investment increased by $1/10$, while the value of the glamour stocks decreased by $1/10$. The current value of the portfolio is $3,140,000. What is the *current* value of the blue chip investment?

15. The monthly revenue R of a certain company is given by $R = 800p - 7p^2$, where p is the price in dollars of the commodity they produce. At what price will the revenue be $10,000 if the price is greater than $50?

16. The *price-earning ratio* (P/E ratio) of a company is the ratio of the price of one share of its common stock outstanding to the earnings per share. If the P/E ratio increases by 10 percent and the earnings per share increase by 20 percent, determine the percentage increase in the price per share of the common stock.

17. Suppose that at a price of p dollars each, a manufacturer will supply to the market $2p - 8$ units of a product and consumers will demand to buy $300 - 2p$ units. At the value of p for which supply equals demand, the market is said to be in equilibrium. Find this value of p.

18. Repeat Problem 17 for the following conditions: at a price of p dollars each, the supply is $3p^2 - 4p$ and the demand is $24 - p^2$.

19. A *compensating balance* refers to that practice wherein a bank requires a borrower to maintain on deposit a certain portion of a loan during the term of the loan. For example, if a firm makes a $100,000 loan which requires a compensating balance of 20 percent, it would have to leave $20,000 on deposit and would have the use of $80,000.

   To meet the expenses of retooling, the Victor Manufacturing Company finds it must borrow additional funds of $95,000. The Third National Bank, with whom they have had no prior association, requires a compensating balance of 15 percent. To the nearest thousand dollars what must be the amount of the loan to obtain the needed funds?

20. The Dingle-Dangle Machine Co. has an incentive plan for its salesmen. For each Dingle-Dangle machine that a salesman sells he receives a commission of $20. His commission for *every* machine sold will increase by $0.02 for each machine sold over 600. For example, if a salesman sells 602 machines his commission on each of the machines is $20.04. How many machines must a salesman sell in order to earn $15,400?

21. A land investment company purchased a parcel of land for $7200. After having sold all but 20 acres at a profit of $30 per acre, the entire cost of the parcel had been regained. How many acres were sold?

22. The *margin of profit* of a company is the net profit divided by the total revenue. The Ipsy-Wipsy Co. makes the famous Ipsy-Wipsy pot. The company's margin of profit increased by .02 from last year. In that year the company sold its pots at $3.00 each and had a net profit of $4500. This year it increased the price of its pots by $0.50 each, sold 2000 more pots, and had a net profit of $7140. The company never has had a margin of profit greater than .15. How many pots were sold last year and how many were sold this year?

23. The Dinky-Winky Co. manufactures the ever-popular dinkys and winkys. The cost of producing each dinky is $2 more than that of a winky. The costs of production of dinkys and winkys are $1500 and $1000, respectively, and 25 more dinkys are produced than winkys. How many of each are produced?

2-2   LINEAR INEQUALITIES

Suppose a and b are two points on the real number line. Then either a and b coincide, or a lies to the left of b, or a lies to the right of b (Fig. 2-1).

Fig. 2-1

   If a and b coincide, then $a = b$. If a lies to the left of b, we say a is less than b and write $a < b$, the *inequality symbol* $<$ being read "is less than." On the other hand, if a lies to the right of b, we say a is greater than b, written $a > b$. To write $a < b$ is equivalent to writing $b > a$.

   Another inequality symbol $\leq$ is read "is less than or equal to" and is defined: $a \leq b$ if and only if $a < b$ or $a = b$. Similarly, the symbol $\geq$ is defined: $a \geq b$ if and only if $a > b$ or $a = b$. In this case we say "*a is greater than or equal to b.*"

We shall use the words *real numbers* and *points* interchangeably, since there is a one-to-one correspondence between real numbers and points on a line. Thus, we can speak of the points -5, -2, 0, 7, and 9 and write $7 < 9$, $-2 > -5$, $7 \leq 7$, and $7 \geq 0$ (Fig. 2-2). Clearly if $a > 0$, then a is positive, and if $a < 0$, then a is negative.

Fig. 2-2

Suppose that $a < b$ and x is between a and b (Fig. 2-3). Then not only is $a < x$, but $x < b$. We indicate this by writing $a < x < b$. For example, $0 < 7 < 9$ (see Fig. 2-2).

Fig. 2-3

In defining an inequality below we shall use the greater than relation ($>$), but the others ($<$, $\geq$, $\leq$) would also apply.

DEFINITION.   *An **inequality** is a statement that one number is greater than another number.*

Of course we represent inequalities by means of inequality symbols. If two inequalities have their inequality symbols pointing in the same direction, then the inequalities are said to have the *same sense.* If not, they are said to be *opposite in sense* or one is said to have the *reverse sense* of the other. Hence, $a < b$ and $c < d$ have the same sense, but $a < b$ has the reverse sense of $c > d$.

To solve an inequality, such as $2(x - 3) < 4$, means to find all values of the variable for which the inequality is true. This involves the application of certain rules which we now state.

(1) *If the same number is added to or subtracted from both sides of an inequality, the resulting inequality has the same sense as the original inequality.*

Symbolically, if $a < b$, then $a + c < b + c$ and $a - c < b - c$.

For example, $7 < 10$ and $7 + 3 < 10 + 3$.

(2) *If both sides of an inequality are multiplied or divided by the same **positive** number, the resulting inequality has the same sense as the original inequality.*

Symbolically, if $a < b$ and $c > 0$, then $ac < bc$ and $\dfrac{a}{c} < \dfrac{b}{c}$.

For example, since $3 < 7$ and $2 > 0$, then $3(2) < 7(2)$. Also, $\frac{3}{2} < \frac{7}{2}$.

(3) *If both sides of an inequality are multiplied or divided by the same **negative** number, then the resulting inequality has the reverse sense of the original inequality.*

Symbolically, if $a < b$ and $c < 0$, then $ac > bc$ and $\dfrac{a}{c} > \dfrac{b}{c}$.

For example, $4 < 7$ but $4(-2) > 7(-2)$. Also $\frac{4}{-2} > \frac{7}{-2}$.

(4) *Any member of an inequality can be replaced by an expression equal to it.*

Symbolically, if $a < b$ and $a = c$, then $c < b$.

For example, if $x < 2$ and $x = y + 4$, then $y + 4 < 2$.

(5) *If no side of an inequality is zero and both sides are of the same sign, then their respective reciprocals† are unequal in the reverse sense.*

For example, $2 < 4$ but $\frac{1}{2} > \frac{1}{4}$.

(6) *If both sides of an inequality are positive and we raise each side to the same positive power, then the resulting inequality has the same sense as the original inequality.*

Thus if $a > b > 0$ and $n > 0$, then

$$a^n > b^n$$

and $\sqrt[n]{a} > \sqrt[n]{b}$.

For example, $9 > 4$ and $9^2 > 4^2$ and $\sqrt{9} > \sqrt{4}$.

The result of applying rules 1-4 to an inequality is called an *equivalent inequality*. It is an inequality whose solution is exactly the same as that of the original inequality.

DEFINITION.   *A **linear inequality** in the variable x is an inequality which is equivalent to*

$$ax + b < 0$$

where a and b are constants and a ≠ 0.

We shall now give some examples of solving linear inequalities. The property used is indicated to the right. In each step the given inequality will be replaced by an equivalent one until the solution is evident.

---

†The *reciprocal* of a nonzero number a is defined to be $\dfrac{1}{a}$.

EXAMPLE 6

a. *Solve* $2(x - 3) < 4$.

$$2(x - 3) < 4$$

$$2x - 6 < 4 \qquad \text{(Distributive property)}$$

$$2x - 6 + 6 < 4 + 6 \qquad (1)$$

$$2x < 10$$

$$\frac{2x}{2} < \frac{10}{2} \qquad (2)$$

$$x < 5.$$

All of the inequalities are equivalent. Thus the original inequality is true for *all* real numbers x such that $x < 5$. We shall consider $x < 5$ as our solution. Geometrically, we may represent this by the bold line segment in Fig. 2-4. The parenthesis indicates that 5 *is not included* in the solution.

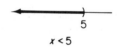

$$x < 5$$

Fig. 2-4

b. *Solve* $3 - 2x \le 6$.

$$3 - 2x \le 6$$

$$-2x \le 3 \qquad (1)$$

$$x \ge -\frac{3}{2}. \qquad (3)$$

The solution is $x \ge -3/2$. Geometrically this is represented in Fig. 2-5. The square bracket indicates that $-3/2$ *is included* in the solution.

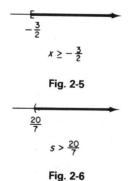

$$-\frac{3}{2}$$

$$x \ge -\frac{3}{2}$$

Fig. 2-5

$$\frac{20}{7}$$

$$s > \frac{20}{7}$$

Fig. 2-6

c. *Solve* $\dfrac{3}{2}(s - 2) + 1 > -2(s - 4).$

$$\frac{3}{2}(s - 2) + 1 > -2(s - 4)$$

$$3(s - 2) + 2 > -4(s - 4) \qquad (2)$$

$$3s - 4 > -4s + 16$$

$$7s > 20 \qquad (1)$$

$$s > \frac{20}{7}. \qquad (2)$$

See Fig. 2-6.

EXAMPLE 7

a. *Solve* $2(x - 4) - 3 > 2x - 1.$

$$2(x - 4) - 3 > 2x - 1$$

$$2x - 8 - 3 > 2x - 1$$

$$-11 > -1. \qquad (1)$$

Since $-11 > -1$ is never true, the solution set is $\emptyset$.

b. *Solve* $2(x - 4) - 3 < 2x - 1.$

Proceeding in the same manner as in (a), we obtain $-11 < -1$. This inequality is true for all real numbers x. We write our solution as $-\infty < x < \infty$. See Fig. 2-7. The symbols $-\infty$ and ∞ are not numbers, but are merely a convenience for indicating that the solution is all real numbers.

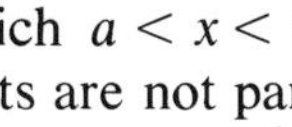

$$-\infty < x < \infty$$

Fig. 2-7

Frequently we shall use the term *interval* to describe certain sets of numbers. For example, the set of all numbers x for which $a \le x \le b$ is called a **closed interval** because it includes the *endpoints* a and b. We denote it by $[a, b]$. The set of all x for which $a < x < b$ is called an **open interval** and is denoted by (a, b). The endpoints are not part of this set. See Fig. 2-8.

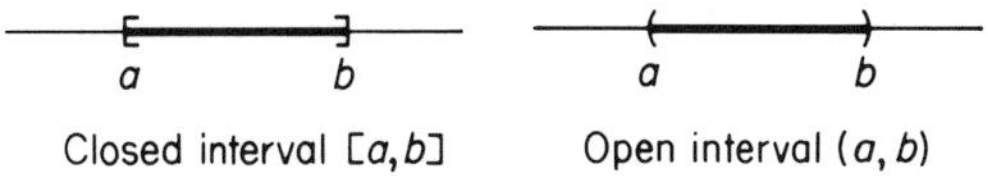

Closed interval $[a, b]$ Open interval (a, b)

Fig. 2-8

Extending these concepts, we have the intervals shown in Fig. 2-9, where the symbols ∞ and $-\infty$ are not numbers but merely a convenience for indicating that an interval extends indefinitely in some direction.

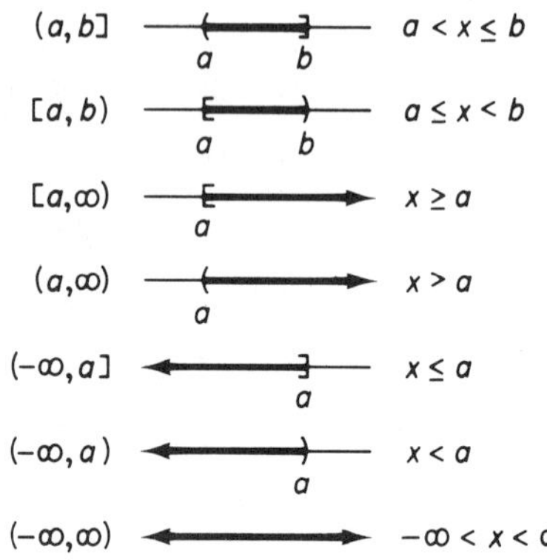

Fig. 2-9

EXERCISE 2-2

In problems 1-32, solve the inequalities and indicate your answers geometrically on the real number line.

1. $4x > 8$

2. $8x < -2$

3. $3x - 4 \le 2$

4. $5x \ge 0$

5. $3 < 2y + 3$

6. $2y + 1 > 0$

7. $-4x \ge 2$

8. $6 \le 5 - 3y$

9. $3 - 5s > 5$

10. $4s - 1 < -5$

11. $2x - 3 \le 4 + 7x$

12. $-3 \ge 8(2 - x)$

13. $3(2 - 3x) > 4(1 - 4x)$

14. $8(x + 1) + 1 < 3(2x) + 1$

15. $2(3x - 2) > 3(2x - 1)$

16. $3 - 2(x - 1) \le 2(4 + x)$

17. $x + 2 < \sqrt{3} - x$

18. $\sqrt{2}\,(x + 2) > \sqrt{8}\,(3 - x)$

19. $\dfrac{9y + 1}{4} \le 2y - 1$

20. $\dfrac{4y - 3}{2} \ge \dfrac{1}{3}$

21. $4x - 1 \ge 4(x - 2) + 7$

22. $0x \le 0$

23. $\dfrac{1 - t}{2} < \dfrac{3t - 7}{3}$

24. $\dfrac{3(2t - 2)}{2} > \dfrac{6t - 3}{5} + \dfrac{t}{10}$

25. $2x + 3 \ge \frac{1}{2}x - 4$

26. $4x - \frac{1}{2} \le \frac{3}{2}x$

27. $\frac{2}{3}r < \frac{5}{6}r$

28. $\frac{7}{4}t > -\frac{2}{3}t$

29. $.1(.03x + 4) \geq .02x + .434$

30. $9 - .1x \leq (2 - .01x)/(.2)$

31. $\dfrac{y}{2} + \dfrac{y}{3} > y + \dfrac{y}{5}$

32. $\dfrac{5y - 1}{-3} < \dfrac{7(y + 1)}{-2}$

33. Each month last year, National Doo-Dad Company had earnings that were greater than \$37,000 but less than \$53,000. If S represents the total earnings for the year, what can be said about S using inequalities?

34. Using inequalities, symbolize the statement: The number of man-hours x to produce a commodity is not less than $2\frac{1}{2}$ nor more than 4.

2-3 QUADRATIC INEQUALITIES

An inequality which can be written in the form $ax^2 + bx + c < 0$ where $a \neq 0$ is called a **quadratic inequality** in the variable x. Quadratic inequalities also occur when the symbol "$<$" is replaced by "$\leq$", "$>$", or "$\geq$."

For example, $x^2 + 4 > 0$ is a quadratic inequality. Its solution consists of all real numbers, since the square of any real number when added to 4 is always positive. The inequality $x^2 < 0$ has no solution, since the square of every real number is never negative.

EXAMPLE 8

Solve $x^2 + 3x - 4 > 0$.

Since $x^2 + 3x - 4 = (x + 4)(x - 1)$, then

$$(x + 4)(x - 1) > 0.$$

Here we have a product of two factors that is positive. Thus either both factors must be positive *or* both must be negative. We shall consider these two cases individually.

Case 1.   Suppose $x + 4 > 0$ *and* $x - 1 > 0$.
Then $x > -4$ *and* $x > 1$. On the real number line x must lie not only to the right of -4, but it must also simultaneously lie to the right of 1. Since both conditions are met when $x > 1$, the solution for this case is $x > 1$. See Fig. 2-10.

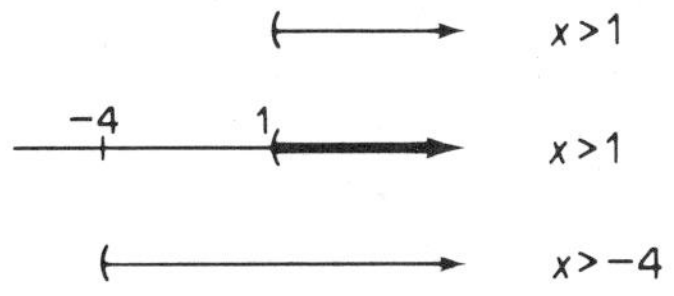

Fig. 2-10

Case 2.   Suppose $x + 4 < 0$ *and* $x - 1 < 0$.
           Then $x < -4$ *and* $x < 1$. Thus x must lie not only to the left of 1, but it
           also must simultaneously lie to the left of -4. Since both conditions are
           met when $x < -4$, the solution in this case is $x < -4$, as is indicated in
           Fig. 2-11.

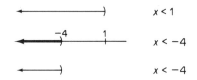

Fig. 2-11

Since the original inequality is true when and only when $x > 1$ *or* $x < -4$, its solution
can be written as $x < -4$, $x > 1$. See Fig. 2-12.

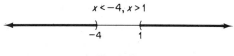

Fig. 2-12

EXAMPLE 9

Solve $x^2 - 1 \le 0$.

Factoring yields

$$(x - 1)(x + 1) \le 0.$$

The product $(x - 1)(x + 1)$ can be less than or equal to zero only when one factor
is less than or equal to zero and the other factor is greater than or equal to zero.
There are two cases to consider.

Case 1.   Suppose $x - 1 \le 0$ *and* $x + 1 \ge 0$.
           Then $x \le 1$ *and* $x \ge -1$. All numbers x between and including -1 and 1
           meet both conditions (Fig. 2-13). For this case we write our solution as
           $-1 \le x \le 1$.

Case 2.   Suppose $x - 1 \ge 0$ *and* $x + 1 \le 0$.
           Then $x \ge 1$ *and* $x \le -1$. But no value of x simultaneously satisfies both
           conditions (Fig. 2-14).
The solution of $x^2 - 1 \le 0$ is thus $-1 \le x \le 1$ (see Fig. 2-15).

Factoring the left side of $ax^2 + bx + c < 0$ may at times be difficult.
However, you may verify that

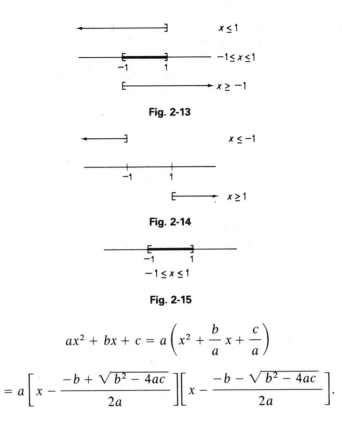

Fig. 2-13

Fig. 2-14

Fig. 2-15

$$ax^2 + bx + c = a\left(x^2 + \frac{b}{a}x + \frac{c}{a}\right)$$

$$= a\left[x - \frac{-b + \sqrt{b^2 - 4ac}}{2a}\right]\left[x - \frac{-b - \sqrt{b^2 - 4ac}}{2a}\right].$$

Thus we have a formula for factoring $ax^2 + bx + c$. For example,

$$x^2 + 2x - 1 = 1\left[x - \frac{-2 + \sqrt{2^2 - 4(1)(-1)}}{2(1)}\right]\left[x - \frac{-2 - \sqrt{2^2 - 4(1)(-1)}}{2(1)}\right]$$

$$= \left[x - \frac{-2 + \sqrt{8}}{2}\right]\left[x - \frac{-2 - \sqrt{8}}{2}\right]$$

$$= \left[x - \frac{-2 + 2\sqrt{2}}{2}\right]\left[x - \frac{-2 - 2\sqrt{2}}{2}\right]$$

$$= [x - (-1 + \sqrt{2})][x - (-1 - \sqrt{2})].$$

Although the inequality $x(x - 1)(x + 4) < 0$ is not quadratic, it can be solved by the technique used in Examples 8 and 9. Since we have three quantities the product of which is negative, four cases must be considered as shown in the table below. It gives the situations in which exactly one factor is negative and the situation in which all three are negative. For example, in Case 2 we see that $x(x - 1)(x + 4) < 0$ when $x > 0$, $x - 1 < 0$, and $x + 4 > 0$. This means that $x > 0$ *and* $x < 1$ *and* $x > -4$ simultaneously. Thus the solution in this case is $0 < x < 1$. The complete solution is left as an exercise for you.

$$x(x - 1)(x + 4) < 0$$

CASE	x	$x - 1$	$x + 4$
1	>0	>0	<0
2	>0	<0	>0
3	<0	>0	>0
4	<0	<0	<0

The following example concerns an inequality involving a variable in the denominator. Although this inequality is not quadratic, the method involved is fundamental.

EXAMPLE 10

Solve $\dfrac{p - 2}{p + 4} > 2.$

Subtracting 2 from both sides and simplifying, we have

$$\frac{p - 2}{p + 4} - 2 > 0$$

$$\frac{p - 2 - 2(p + 4)}{p + 4} > 0$$

$$\frac{-p - 10}{p + 4} > 0.$$

Since a quotient is positive if and only if the numerator and denominator are *both* positive or *both* negative, there are two cases to consider.

Case 1.   If $-p - 10 > 0$ *and* $p + 4 > 0$, then $p < -10$ *and* $p > -4$. But no number can simultaneously satisfy these inequalities.

Case 2.   If $-p - 10 < 0$ *and* $p + 4 < 0$, then $p > -10$ *and* $p < -4$. Thus we must have $-10 < p < -4$.

The solution of the original inequality is $-10 < p < -4$ (Fig. 2-16).

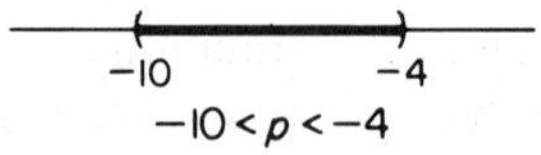

Fig. 2-16

EXERCISE 2-3

Solve each inequality and indicate the solution on the real number line.

1. $x^2 - 9 < 0$

2. $9x^2 - 4 < 0$

3. $x^2 - 3 > 0$

4. $x^2 - 5 \geq 0$

5. $(x - 1)(x + 7) > 0$

6. $(2x - 1)(3x + 4) > 0$

7. $x^2 - x - 6 < 0$

8. $x^2 - 2x - 3 < 0$

9. $x^2 + 4x - 5 > 3x + 15$

10. $x^2 + 9x + 9 > 2 - x^2$

11. $s^2 - 5s < 0$

12. $2t^2 - 5t - 12 < 0$

13. $x^2 + 5x \leq -6$

14. $x^2 - 12 \geq x$

15. $4(t^2 + t) - 1 < 2$

16. $3s^2 < 11s - 10$

17. $3x^2 + 2 \geq 1$

18. $2x^2 + 5 \leq x^2 - 2$

19. $x^2 + 3x + 1 \leq 0$

20. $x^2 - 4x + 1 \geq 0$

21. $y^2 + 2y + 1 < 0$

22. $x^2 + 4x + 4 \geq 0$

23. $\dfrac{5}{x - 3} > 0$

24. $-\dfrac{4}{4 - x} > 0$

25. $-\dfrac{x}{4 - x} \leq 0$

26. $\dfrac{x + 3}{x + 5} \leq 0$

27. $\dfrac{2t}{t + 1} < 3$

28. $\dfrac{s - 1}{2s - 1} < -1$

29. $\dfrac{4x + 5}{x + 3} > 2$

30. $\dfrac{5x - 3}{2x + 3} > 1$

31. $x(x - 1)(x + 4) < 0$

32. $x^2 (x + 5) \geq 0$

2-4   APPLICATIONS OF INEQUALITIES

Solving verbal problems may sometimes involve inequalities, as the following examples illustrate.

EXAMPLE 11

The Hotsy-Totsy Company manufactures thermostats. The combined cost for labor and material is $4 per thermostat. Fixed costs (costs incurred in a given time period, regardless of output) are $60,000. If the selling price of a thermostat is $7, how many must be sold for the company to earn a profit?

Let n be the number of thermostats that must be sold. Then their cost is $4n$. The total cost for the company is therefore $4n + 60{,}000$. The total revenue from the sale of n thermostats will be $7n$. But

$$\text{Profit} = \text{Total Revenue} - \text{Total Cost}$$

and we want Profit > 0. Thus,

$$\text{Total Revenue} - \text{Total Cost} > 0$$

$$7n - (4n + 60{,}000) > 0$$

$$3n > 60{,}000$$

$$n > 20{,}000.$$

Therefore, at least 20,001 thermostats must be sold for the company to earn a profit.

EXAMPLE 12

Gene Fierro is president of the Fierro Construction Company. He is interested in comparing costs involved in purchasing or renting a piece of machinery needed for excavation. If he were to purchase it, his fixed annual cost would be $2000 and daily operation and maintenance costs would be $40 for each day it is used. In "Digger," a local trade journal, he finds that he can rent the same machinery for $300 per month (on a yearly basis). If the machinery were rented, the daily cost (gas, oil, driver) would be $30 for each day it is used. Neglecting any other considerations, determine the least number of days he would have to use the machinery each year to justify renting the equipment rather than purchasing it.

Let d be the number of days the machinery is used. By renting the machine, the total yearly cost consists of rental fees which are $(12)(300)$ and daily charges of $30d$. By purchasing the machine, the cost per year is $2000 + 40d$. We want

$$\text{Cost}_{\text{Rent}} < \text{Cost}_{\text{Purchase}}$$

$$12(300) + 30d < 2000 + 40d$$

$$1600 < 10d$$

$$160 < d.$$

Thus he must use the machine at least 161 days to justify renting it.

EXAMPLE 13

The *current ratio* of a business is the ratio of its current assets (such as cash, merchandise inventory, and accounts receivable) to its current liabilities (such as short-term loans and taxes payable).

After consulting with the comptroller, the president of the Ace Sports Equipment Company decides to make a short-term loan to build up its inventory. The company has current assets of $350,000 and current liabilities of $80,000. How much can they borrow if they *want their current ratio to be no less than 2.5? (Note: The funds they receive are considered as current assets and the loan as a current liability.)*

Let x denote the amount which the company can borrow. Then their current assets will be $350,000 + x$, and their current liabilities will be $80,000 + x$. Thus

$$\text{Current Ratio} = \frac{\text{Current Assets}}{\text{Current Liabilities}} = \frac{350,000 + x}{80,000 + x}.$$

For our problem, we want

$$\frac{350,000 + x}{80,000 + x} \geq 2.5.$$

Simplifying, we have

$$350,000 + x \geq 2.5(80,000 + x)$$

$$150,000 \geq 1.5x$$

$$100,000 \geq x.$$

Hence they may borrow as much as $100,000 and yet maintain a current ratio of no less than 2.5. Note that when the original inequality was cleared of fractions, the sense of the resulting inequality did not change, since we could assume that $80,000 + x$ was a positive quantity.

EXAMPLE 14

Imperial Educational Services (I.E.S.) is considering offering a workshop in resource allocation to key personnel at Acme Corporation. If successful, it will be extended to other companies. To make the idea economically feasible, I.E.S. feels that at least thirty persons must attend at a cost of $50 to each participant. Moreover, I.E.S. will agree to reduce the charge for everybody by $1.25 for each person over the thirty who attends. As financial adviser to I.E.S., you are asked to limit the size of the group so that the total revenue received by I.E.S. will never be less than that received for thirty persons.

Let n be the number of persons *over* the thirty who attend. Then each of $30 + n$ persons will pay $50 - 1.25n$ dollars each. The total revenue from the $30 + n$ persons will be $(30 + n)(50 - 1.25n)$. But the revenue from 30 persons is $(30)(50)$. We want

$$(30 + n)(50 - 1.25n) \geq 30(50)$$

$$30(50) - 37.5n + 50n - 1.25n^2 \geq 30(50)$$

$$12.5n - 1.25n^2 \geq 0$$

$$1.25(n)(10 - n) \geq 0.$$

Since $n \geq 0$, we must have $10 - n \geq 0$. Thus $10 \geq n$ and the group must be limited to forty persons.

EXAMPLE 15

Scandal Publishing Company finds that the cost of publishing each copy of a certain magazine is $0.11. The revenue from dealers is $0.10 per copy. The advertising revenue is 12 percent of the revenue received from dealers for all copies sold beyond 10,000. What is the least number of copies which must be sold so as to have a profit for the company?

Let x be the number of copies *beyond* 10,000 which must be sold. The revenue from dealers is $(10,000 + x)(.10)$ and the revenue from advertising is $(.12)[(.10)(x)]$. The total cost of publication is $(10,000 + x)(.11)$. Since Profit = Total Revenue − Total Cost, we want

$$\text{Total Revenue} - \text{Total Cost} > 0$$

$$(10,000 + x)(.10) + (.12)(.10)(x) - (10,000 + x)(.11) > 0$$

$$.002x - 100 > 0$$

$$.002x > 100$$

$$x > 50,000.$$

Thus the total number of copies sold must be greater than $x + 10,000 = 60,000$. That is, at least 60,001 copies must be sold to guarantee a profit.

EXERCISE 2-4

1. The Davis Company manufactures a product that has a unit selling price of $20 and a unit cost of $15. If total fixed costs are $600,000, determine the least number of units that must be sold for the company to have a profit.

2. To produce one unit of a new product, a company determines that the cost for material is $2.50 and the cost of labor is $4. The constant overhead, regardless of sales volume, is $5000. If the cost to a wholesaler is $7.40 per unit, determine the least number of units that must be sold by the company to realize a profit.

3. For business purposes Mr. Michael Joseph wants to determine the difference between the costs of owning and renting an automobile. He can rent a compact for $122 per month (on an annual basis). Under this plan, his cost per mile (gas and oil) is $0.03. If he were to purchase the car, his fixed annual expense would be $800 and other costs would amount to $0.09 per mile. What is the least number of miles he would have to drive per year to make renting less expensive than purchasing? (Give your answer to the nearest mile.)

4. A shirt manufacturer produces N shirts at a total labor cost (in dollars) of $1.2N$ and a total material cost of $.3N$. The constant overhead for the plant is $6000. If each shirt sells for $3, how many must be sold by the company to realize a profit?

5. Imperial Educational Services (I.E.S.) is offering a workshop in data processing to key personnel at Zeta Corporation. The price per person is $50 and Zeta Corporation guarantees that at least fifty persons will attend. Suppose I.E.S. offers to reduce

the charge for *everybody* by $0.50 for each person over the fifty who attends. How should I.E.S. limit the size of the group so that the total revenue they receive will never be less than that received for fifty persons?

6. The cost of publication of each copy of Rinky Tink Magazine is $6\frac{1}{2}$ cents. It is sold to dealers for 6 cents each, and the amount received for advertising is 10 percent of the amount received for all magazines issued beyond 10,000. Find the least number of magazines that can be issued without loss. (Assume that all issues will be sold.)

7. The Ding-a-ling Company produces alarm clocks. During the regular work week the labor cost for producing one clock is $2.00. However, if a clock is produced in overtime, the labor cost is $3.00. Management has decided to spend no more than a total of $25,000 per week for labor. The company must produce 11,000 clocks this week. What is the minimum number of clocks that must be produced during the regular work week?

8. A company invests a total of $30,000 of surplus funds at two annual rates of interest: 5 percent and $6\frac{3}{4}$ percent. It wishes an annual yield of no less than $6\frac{1}{2}$ percent. What is the least amount of money that it must invest at the $6\frac{3}{4}$ percent rate?

9. The current ratio of Precision Machine Products is 3.8. If their current assets are $570,000, what are their current liabilities? To raise additional funds, what is the maximum amount they can borrow on a short-term basis if they want their current ratio to be no less than 2.6? (See Example 13 for an explanation of current ratio.)

10. In order to begin an expansion program in two years, a company will require $108,160. If the company now invests $100,000 for this purpose, what is the minimum annual rate of interest, compounded annually, that it must receive?

11. A container manufacturer wishes to make an open box by cutting a 4-in. square from each corner of a square sheet of aluminum and then turning up the sides. The box is to contain at least 324 cu in. Find the dimensions of the smallest sheet of aluminum that can be used.

12. A lumber company owns a forest which is of rectangular shape, 1 mi × 2 mi. The company wants to cut a uniform strip of trees along the outer edges of the forest. At most how wide can the strip be if the company wants at least $\frac{3}{4}$ sq mi of forest to remain?

13. A manufacturer presently has 2500 units of his product in stock. The product is now selling at $4 per unit. Next month the unit price will increase by $0.50. The manufacturer wants the total revenue received from the sale of the 2500 units to be no less than $10,750. What is the maximum number of units that can be sold this month?

14. Suppose that consumers will purchase x units of a product at a price of $\dfrac{100}{x} + 1$ dollars per unit. What is the minimum number of units that must be sold in order that sales revenue be greater than $5000?

15. Suppose that consumers will purchase x units of a product when the price of each unit is $20 - .1x$ dollars. How many units must be sold in order that sales revenue will be greater than \$750?

2-5 ABSOLUTE VALUE†

Sometimes it is useful to consider the distance on the real number line that a number x is from 0. We call this distance the **absolute value** of x and denote it by $|x|$. For example, $|5| = 5$ and $|-5| = 5$ because both 5 and -5 are five units from 0 (see Fig. 2-17). Similarly, $|0| = |0|$.

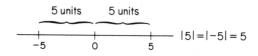

Fig. 2-17

If x is positive, clearly $|x| = x$. Since we can write $|-5| = 5 = -(-5)$, it should not be difficult to convince yourself that if x is any negative number, then $|x|$ is the positive number $-x$. Thus, aside from its geometrical interpretation, absolute value can be defined as follows:

DEFINITION. *The absolute value of a real number x, written $|x|$, is*

$$|x| = \begin{cases} x, & \text{if } x > 0 \\ 0, & \text{if } x = 0 \\ -x, & \text{if } x < 0. \end{cases}$$

Applying the definition, we have $|3| = 3$; $|-8| = -(-8) = 8$; $|\frac{1}{2}| = \frac{1}{2}$; $-|2| = -2$; and $-|-2| = -2$. Notice that $|x|$ is always positive or zero; that is, $|x| \geq 0$.

PITFALL. $\sqrt{x^2}$ is not necessarily x, but $\sqrt{x^2} = |x|$. For example, $\sqrt{(-2)^2} = |-2| = 2$, not -2.

EXAMPLE 16

a. *Solve* $|x - 3| = 2$.

This equation states that $x - 3$ is a number two units from 0. Thus, either

$$x - 3 = 2 \quad or \quad x - 3 = -2.$$

Solving these gives $x = 5$ and $x = 1$.

b. *Solve* $|7 - 3x| = 5$.

---

†This section may be omitted without loss of continuity if Chapter 13 is not covered.

The equation is true if $7 - 3x = 5$ *or* if $7 - 3x = -5$. Solving these gives $x = \frac{2}{3}$ and $x = 4$.

c. *Solve* $|x - 4| = -3$.

The absolute value of a number is never negative. Thus the solution set is $\emptyset$.

The numbers 5 and 9 are 4 units apart. Also

$$|9 - 5| = |4| = 4,$$
$$|5 - 9| = |-4| = 4.$$

In general, we may interpret $|a - b| = |b - a|$ as the distance between a and b.

For example, the equation $|x - 3| = 2$ states that the distance between x and 3 is 2 units. Thus x can be 1 or 5, as shown in Example 16(a) and Fig. 2-18.

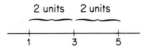

Fig. 2-18

Let us turn now to inequalities. If $|x| < 3$, then x is less than 3 units from 0. Thus x must lie between -3 and 3. Equivalently, $-3 < x < 3$ [Fig. 2-19(a)]. On the other hand, if $|x| > 3$, then x must be greater than 3 units from 0. Thus there are two cases: either $x > 3$ or $x < -3$ [Fig. 2-19(b)]. Extending these ideas, we say that if $|x| \leq 3$, then $-3 \leq x \leq 3$, and if $|x| \geq 3$, then $x \geq 3$ or $x \leq -3$.

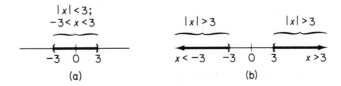

Fig. 2-19

EXAMPLE 17

a. *Solve* $|x - 2| < 4$.

The number $x - 2$ must be less than 4 units from 0. From our discussion above this means $-4 < x - 2 < 4$. We may set up the procedure for solving this inequality as follows:

$$-4 < x - 2 < 4$$

$$-4 + 2 < x < 4 + 2 \qquad \text{(adding 2 to each member)}$$

$$-2 < x < 6.$$

b. *Solve* $|3 - 2x| \leq 5$.

$$-5 \leq 3 - 2x \leq 5$$

$$-5 - 3 \leq -2x \leq 5 - 3 \quad \text{(subtracting 3 from each member)}$$

$$-8 \leq -2x \leq 2$$

$$4 \geq x \geq -1 \qquad \text{(dividing each member by } -2\text{)}$$

$$-1 \leq x \leq 4. \qquad \text{(rewriting)}$$

Note that the sense of the original inequality was reversed when we divided by a negative number.

EXAMPLE 18

a. *Solve* $|x + 5| \geq 7$.

The number $x + 5$ must be at least 7 units from 0: either $x + 5 \leq -7$ *or* $x + 5 \geq 7$. Thus, either $x \leq -12$ *or* $x \geq 2$.

b. *Solve* $|3x - 4| > 1$.

Either $3x - 4 < -1$ or $3x - 4 > 1$. Equivalently, either $x < 1$ or $x > \frac{5}{3}$.

EXAMPLE 19

Using absolute value notation, express the fact that

a. *x is less than* 3 *units from* 5.

$$|x - 5| < 3.$$

b. *x differs from* 6 *by at least* 7.

$$|x - 6| \geq 7.$$

c. *x* < 3 *and x* > −3 *simultaneously.*

$$|x| < 3.$$

d. *x is strictly within* 1 *unit of* −2.

$$|x - (-2)| = |x + 2| < 1.$$

e. *x is strictly within* σ *(sigma) units of* μ *(mu).*

$$|x - \mu| < \sigma.$$

Three basic properties of absolute value are:

(1) $|ab| = |a| \cdot |b|$.

$$(2) \quad \left| \frac{a}{b} \right| = \frac{|a|}{|b|}. \qquad (b \neq 0)$$

$$(3) \quad |a - b| = |b - a|.$$

EXAMPLE 20

a. $|(-7) \cdot 3| = |-7| \cdot |3| = 21; \quad |(-7)(-3)| = |-7| \cdot |-3| = 21.$

b. $|7 - x| = |(-1)(x - 7)| = |-1| \cdot |x - 7| = |x - 7|.$

c. $|4 - 2| = |2 - 4| = 2.$

d. $\left| \dfrac{-7}{3} \right| = \dfrac{|-7|}{|3|} = \dfrac{7}{3}; \quad \left| \dfrac{-7}{-3} \right| = \dfrac{|-7|}{|-3|} = \dfrac{7}{3}.$

e. $\left| \dfrac{x - 3}{-5} \right| = \dfrac{|x - 3|}{|-5|} = \dfrac{|x - 3|}{5}.$

EXERCISE 2-5

In problems 1-10, write an equivalent form without the absolute value symbol.

1. $|-13|$

2. $|2^{-1}|$

3. $|8 - 2|$

4. $|(-4 - 6)/2|$

5. $|3 (-\frac{5}{3})|$

6. $|2 - 7| - |7 - 2|$

7. $|x| < 3$

8. $|x| < 10$

9. $|2 - \sqrt{5}|$

10. $|\sqrt{5} - 2|$

11. Using the absolute value symbol, express the fact that

a. x is strictly within 3 units of 7.

b. x differs from 2 by less than 3.

c. x is no more than 5 units from 7.

d. the distance between 7 and x is 4.

e. $x + 4$ is strictly within 2 units of 0.

f. x is strictly between -3 and 3.

g. $x < -6$ or $x > 6$.

h. $x - 6 > 4$ or $x - 6 < -4$.

i. the number x of hours that a machine will operate efficiently differs from 105 by less than 3.

j. the average monthly income x (in dollars) of a family differs from 600 by less than 100.

12. Use absolute value notation to indicate that x and μ differ by no more than σ.

13. Use absolute value notation to indicate that the prices, p and q, of two products may differ by no more than 2 (dollars).

14. Find all values of x such that $|x - \mu| \le 2\sigma$.

In problems 15-36, solve the given equation or inequality.

15. $|x| = 7$ **16.** $|-x| = 2$

17. $\left|\dfrac{x}{3}\right| = 2$ **18.** $\left|\dfrac{4}{x}\right| = 8$

19. $|x - 5| = 8$ **20.** $|4 + 3x| = 2$

21. $|5x - 2| = 0$ **22.** $|7x + 3| = x$

23. $|7 - 4x| = 5$ **24.** $|1 - 2x| = 1$

25. $|x| < 4$ **26.** $|-x| < 3$

27. $\left|\dfrac{x}{4}\right| > 2$ **28.** $\left|\dfrac{3}{x}\right| > \dfrac{1}{2}$

29. $|x + 7| < 2$ **30.** $|5x - 1| < -6$

31. $\left|x - \tfrac{1}{2}\right| > \tfrac{1}{2}$ **32.** $|1 - 3x| > 2$

33. $|5 - 2x| \le 1$ **34.** $|4x - 1| \ge 0$

35. $\left|\dfrac{3x - 8}{2}\right| \ge 4$ **36.** $\left|\dfrac{x - 8}{4}\right| \le 2$

37. In statistical analysis, the Chebychev inequality asserts that if x is a random variable, μ its mean, and σ its standard deviation, then

$$\text{(Probability that } |x - \mu| > h\sigma) \le \frac{1}{h^2}.$$

Find those values of x such that $|x - \mu| > h\sigma$.

38. In the manufacture of widgets, the average dimension of a part is .01 cm. Using the absolute value symbol, express the fact that an individual measurement x of a part does not differ from the average by more than .005 cm.

2-6   REVIEW

Important Terms and Symbols in Chapter 2

inequality *(p. 60)* $a < b$, $a \le b$ *(p. 59, 60)*

linear inequality *(p. 61)* $a > b$, $a \ge b$ *(p. 59, 60)* quadratic inequality *(p. 65)* $a < x < b$ *(p. 60)*

absolute value, $|x|$ *(p. 74)* $-\infty < x < \infty$ *(p. 63)*

Review Section

1. True or false: If $x > -3$, then $-x > 3$.__(a)__

If $x > 4$, then $2x > 8$.__(b)__

Ans. (a) false,   (b) true

2. True or false: If $x < 1$, then $x^2 < 1$.__(a)__

If $2 < x < 3$, then $x > 2$ and $x < 3$.__(b)__

Ans. (a) false,   (b) true

3. $2x + 5 < 0$ is a linear inequality while $3x^2 - 4x + 1 < 0$ is a _____ inequality.

Ans. quadratic

4. If $x > -5$ *and* $x > -2$, then $x >$ _____.

Ans. -2

5. The solution of $(x - 2)^2 \geq 0$ is _____.

Ans. $-\infty < x < \infty$

6. The solution set of $(3x - 1)^2 < -1$ is _____.

Ans. Ø

7. The solution of $2x - 6 < 0$ is _____.

Ans. $x < 3$

8. The solution of $x^2 > 4$ is _____.

Ans. $x < -2$ or $x > 2$

9. The solution of $\dfrac{3}{x - 1} > 0$ is _____.

Ans. $x > 1$

†10. If $x = 0$, then $|x| =$ __(a)__ . Otherwise, $|x|$ is always (positive) (negative) (b) .

Ans. (a) 0,   (b) positive

---

† Refers to Section 5 of this chapter.

†**11.** The solution of $|x - 2| = 0$ is _____.

> *Ans.* 2

†**12.** If $-x > 0$, then $|x| =$ _____.

> *Ans.* $-x$

†**13.** In absolute value notation, the fact that $2x$ is strictly within 5 units of 6 would be written _____.

> *Ans.* $|2x - 6| < 5$

†**14.** The solution of $|x - 4| \leq 2$ is _____.

> *Ans.* $2 \leq x \leq 6$

Review Problems

Solve each of the following.

1. $3x - 8 \geq 4(x - 2)$

2. $2x - (7 + x) \leq x$

3. $3p(1 - p) > 3(2 + p) - 3p^2$

4. $2(4 - \frac{3}{5}q) < 5$

5. $\dfrac{x + 1}{3} - \dfrac{1}{2} \leq 2$

6. $\dfrac{5}{x} < 2$

7. $4s^2 + 12s + 9 \geq 0$

8. $t^2 - t - 2 > 0$

9. $6x^2 + x \leq 2$

10. $x^2 + 6 < 5x$

11. $\dfrac{x + 2}{x - 1} \leq 0$

12. $x(x - 1)(x + 1) \geq 0$

†**13.** $|3 - 2x| = 7$

†**14.** $\left| \dfrac{5x - 8}{13} \right| = 0$

†**15.** $|4t - 1| < 1$

†**16.** $1 \geq |x^2|$

†**17.** $|3 - 2x| \geq 4$

18. A profit of 40 percent on the selling price of a product is equivalent to what percent profit on the cost?

19. On a certain day, there were 1132 issues traded on the New York Stock Exchange. There were 48 more issues showing an increase than showing a decline and no issues remained the same. How many issues suffered a decline?

20. In Transylvania the sales tax is 6 percent. If a total of $3017.29 in purchases, including tax, is made in the course of a year, how much of it is tax?

---

† Refers to Section 5 of this chapter.

21. A company will manufacture a total of 10,000 units of its product at plants A and B. Available data is shown in the table below.

	Plant A	Plant B
Unit cost for labor and material	$5	$5.50
Fixed costs	$30,000	$35,000

Between the two plants the company has decided to allot no more than $117,000 for total costs. What is the minimum number of units that must be produced at plant A?

Chapter **3**

Functions & Graphs

3-1 FUNCTIONS

In 1694 Gottfried Wilhelm Leibniz, one of the developers of calculus, introduced the word *function* into the mathematical vocabulary. The concept of a "function" is no doubt one of the most basic in all of mathematics.

To introduce it, let us consider the equation

$$y = x + 2.$$

Replacing x by various numbers, we get corresponding values of y. For example,

if $x = 0$, then $y = 0 + 2 = 2$;

if $x = 1$, then $y = 1 + 2 = 3$.

Notice that for each value of x that "goes into" the equation, only *one* value of y "comes out."

Think of y as defining an operation: adding 2 to x. This operation assigns to each *input number x* exactly one *output number y.*

$$x \longrightarrow y \quad (= x + 2)$$

input output
number number

We call this operation a *function* in the following sense:

DEFINITION. *A function is an operation that assigns to each input number exactly one output number. The set of all input numbers that can be used in the operation is called the domain of the function. The set of all output numbers is called the range.*

For the function defined by $y = x + 2$, the input x can be any real number. Thus the domain of this function is all real numbers. To the input number 0 is assigned the output number 2:

$$x \to y \, (= x + 2)$$
$$0 \to 2 \, (= 0 + 2).$$

Thus 2 is in the range.

A variable that represents input numbers for a function is called an **independent variable.** One representing output numbers is a **dependent variable** because its value *depends* on the chosen value of the independent variable. We say that the dependent variable is a *function of* the independent variable. Thus in the equation $y = x + 2$ the independent variable is x, the dependent variable is y, and y is a function of x.

EXAMPLE 1

Let $y^2 = x.$

a. Suppose x is an input number, say $x = 9$. Then $y^2 = 9$ and so $y = \pm 3$. Thus with the input number 9 there are assigned *two* output numbers, +3 and −3. Hence y is **not** a function of x.

b. Now, suppose y is an input number.

$$y \to x \, (= y^2)$$

It determines exactly one output number, x. For example, if $y = 3$, then $x = y^2 = 3^2 = 9$. Thus x is a function of y. The domain is all real numbers, the independent variable is y, and the dependent variable is x.

EXAMPLE 2

Suppose $p = \dfrac{100}{x}$ is the demand equation for a manufacturer's product (p is the price per unit when x units are demanded). With each input number x there is assigned exactly one output number p.

$$x \rightarrow \frac{100}{x} = p$$

For example,

$$20 \rightarrow \frac{100}{20} = 5.$$

Thus price p is a function of quantity demanded x. Here x is the independent variable and p is the dependent variable. Since x cannot equal 0 (division by 0) and since x cannot be negative (x represents quantity), the domain is all values of x such that $x > 0$.

Usually we use letters such as f, g, h, F, G, etc. to denote functions. Suppose we let f represent the function defined by $y = x + 2$. Then we use the notation

$$f(x), \text{ which is read "} f \text{ of } x,"$$

to denote the output number corresponding to the input number x.

input
↓
$f(x)$
output

Thus $f(x) = y$. But since $y = x + 2$ we may write

$$f(x) = x + 2. \qquad (1)$$

To find $f(3)$, the output corresponding to the input 3, replace x in Eq. (1) by 3:

$$f(3) = 3 + 2 = 5.$$

Similarly,

$$f(8) = 8 + 2 = 10,$$
$$f(-4) = -4 + 2 = -2,$$
$$f(0) = 0 + 2 = 2.$$

Sometimes output numbers, such as $f(3)$, $f(8)$, etc., are called *functional values*. They are in the range of f.

PITFALL. *$f(x)$ is **not** the product of f and x.*

Quite often, functions are defined by functional notation. For example, $g(x) = x^3 + x^2$ defines the function g which assigns to an input number x the output number $x^3 + x^2$.

$$g: x \rightarrow x^3 + x^2$$

Some functional values are

$$g(0) = 0^3 + 0^2 = 0,$$
$$g(2) = 2^3 + 2^2 = 12,$$
$$g(-1) = (-1)^3 + (-1)^2 = -1 + 1 = 0,$$
$$g(t) = t^3 + t^2,$$
$$g(x + 1) = (x + 1)^3 + (x + 1)^2.$$

Note that $g(x + 1)$ was found by replacing each x in $x^3 + x^2$ by $(x + 1)$. That is, g sums the cube and the square of an input number.

Since the equation $g(x) = x^3 + x^2$ defines a function, we shall take the liberty of referring to $g(x)$ as a function itself. Similarly, we speak of the function $y = x + 2$.

EXAMPLE 3

a. The function $f(x) = 2x + 3$ is called a **linear function.** It has the form $f(x) = ax + b$ where a and b are real numbers and $a \neq 0$. Its domain is all real numbers.

$$f(0) = 2(0) + 3 = 3,$$
$$f(t + 7) = 2(t + 7) + 3 = 2t + 17.$$

b. The equation $y = 2$ defines a **constant function,** say g, one of the form $g(x) = c$, where c is a fixed real number. The domain of g is all real numbers and the range is just 2.

$$g(.10) = 2; \qquad g(-420) = 2; \qquad g(0) = 2.$$

c. $y = h(x) = -3x^2 + x - 5$ is a **quadratic function,** one of the form $h(x) = ax^2 + bx + c$, where a, b, and c are real numbers and $a \neq 0$. The domain of h is all real numbers, and y is a function of x.

$$h(2) = -3(2)^2 + 2 - 5 = -15,$$

$$h\left(\frac{1}{t}\right) = -3\left(\frac{1}{t}\right)^2 + \left(\frac{1}{t}\right) - 5,$$

$$h(x + t) - h(x) = -3(x + t)^2 + (x + t) - 5 - (-3x^2 + x - 5)$$

$$= -6xt - 3t^2 + t.$$

d. If $f(x) = 5 - 3x$, then

$$\frac{f(x + h) - f(x)}{h} = \frac{[5 - 3(x + h)] - (5 - 3x)}{h} = \frac{-3h}{h} = -3.$$

EXAMPLE 4

a. $f(t) = \dfrac{2t}{t^2 - 1}.$

Here the input number is t. The domain of f is all real numbers except ± 1 (to avoid division by 0).

$$f\left(\frac{1}{2}\right) = \frac{2(\frac{1}{2})}{(\frac{1}{2})^2 - 1} = -\frac{4}{3}; \quad f(-t) = \frac{2(-t)}{(-t)^2 - 1} = -\frac{2t}{t^2 - 1}.$$

b. $g(x) = \sqrt{x}.$

We want input numbers to give rise only to real output numbers. For $\sqrt{x}$ to be a real number, x cannot be negative. Thus the domain of g is all $x \geq 0$.

$$g(0) = \sqrt{0} = 0; \qquad g(4) = \sqrt{4} = 2;$$

$$\frac{g(x + h) - g(x)}{h} = \frac{\sqrt{x + h} - \sqrt{x}}{h}.$$

c. $h(q) = \sqrt{q - 3}.$

Here we must have $q - 3 \geq 0$. Thus the domain of h is all $q \geq 3$.

$$h(3) = \sqrt{3 - 3} = 0; \qquad h(5) = \sqrt{5 - 3} = \sqrt{2};$$

$$h(q^2) = \sqrt{q^2 - 3}.$$

d. The function

$$F(s) = \begin{cases} 1, & \text{if } s > 0 \\ 0, & \text{if } s = 0 \\ -1, & \text{if } s < 0 \end{cases}$$

has three parts. It is interpreted as follows:

$$\text{if } s \text{ is positive, } F(s) = 1,$$

$$\text{if } s \text{ is zero, } F(s) = 0,$$

$$\text{if } s \text{ is negative, } F(s) = -1.$$

The domain of F is all real numbers, while the range consists of $1, 0, -1$.

$$F(0) = 0; \qquad F(78.36) = 1; \qquad F(-13) = -1.$$

The symbol $|x|$ is read "**absolute value of x**" and is defined:

$$|x| = \begin{cases} x, \text{ if } x > 0 \\ 0, \text{ if } x = 0 \\ -x, \text{ if } x < 0. \end{cases}$$

For example, since $2 > 0$, $|2| = 2$. Since $-4 < 0$, $|-4| = -(-4) = 4$. Of course, $|0| = 0$. Notice that $|x| \geq 0$ for all x.

EXAMPLE 5

$f(x) = |x|$ is called the *absolute value function*. Its domain is all real numbers.

$$f(16) = |16| = 16,$$

$$f(-\tfrac{4}{3}) = |-\tfrac{4}{3}| = -(-\tfrac{4}{3}) = \tfrac{4}{3},$$

$$f(0) = |0| = 0,$$

$$f(2x + 3) = |2x + 3|,$$

$$f(x^2 + 1) = |x^2 + 1| = x^2 + 1 \text{ since } x^2 + 1 > 0.$$

For some equations containing two variables, either variable may be a function of the other. For example, if $y = 2x$, then y is a function of x and x is the independent variable. Letting f denote this function, we have $y = f(x) = 2x$. However, since $x = y/2$, then x is a function of y where y is the independent variable. If g denotes this function, then $x = g(y) = y/2$.

We have seen that a function is essentially a *rule of correspondence* which assigns to each input number in the domain, exactly one output number in the range. The correspondence given by $f(x) = x^2$ is shown by the arrows in Fig. 3-1.

EXAMPLE 6

The table in Fig. 3-2 is a *supply schedule*. It gives a correspondence between the price p of a certain product and the quantity q that producers will supply per week at that price.

If p is the independent variable, then q is a function of p, say $q = f(p)$, and

$$f(500) = 11, \qquad f(600) = 14, \qquad f(700) = 17, \quad \text{and} \quad f(800) = 20.$$

If q is the independent variable, then p is a function of q, say $p = g(q)$, and

$$g(11) = 500, \qquad g(14) = 600, \qquad g(17) = 700, \quad \text{and} \quad g(20) = 800.$$

We speak of f and g as *supply functions*.

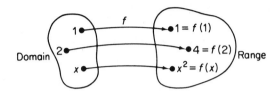

Fig. 3-1

Supply schedule

p	q
Price per unit in dollars	Quantity supplied per week
500	11
600	14
700	17
800	20

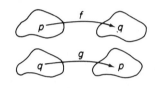

Fig. 3-2

EXERCISE 3-1

For each function in problems 1-26, determine the independent variable and domain. Also, find the indicated functional values.

1. $f(x) = 4x$; $f(0)$, $f(3)$, $f(-\frac{1}{4})$, $f(t)$

2. $F(x) = x + 8$; $F(4)$, $F(-\frac{1}{2})$, $F(12)$, $F(-3)$, $F(x_1)$

3. $g(x) = 1 - 2x$; $g(0)$, $g(-u)$, $g(7)$, $g(-2x)$, $g(x + h)$

4. $h(x) = -\frac{9}{2}$; $h(0)$, $h[(13)^2]$, $h(t)$, $h(x + 1)$

5. $G(t) = 1.02$; $G(5)$, $G(-107.3)$, $G(x^2)$, $G(2 + x)$

6. $F(s) = 2(4 - s)$; $F(0)$, $F\left(\dfrac{1}{s}\right)$, $F(1 + \frac{1}{3})$, $F\left(\dfrac{s}{2}\right)$

7. $h = q(p) = \dfrac{3(4p + 1)}{2}$; $q(1)$, $q\left(\dfrac{p}{2}\right)$, $q\left(\dfrac{1}{p}\right)$

8. $g(x) = 3x^2$; $g(-4)$, $g(-3u)$, $g(x^3)$, $g(2/x)$

9. $f(p) = p^2 + 2p + 1$; $f(0)$, $f(2)$, $f(x_1)$, $f(w)$, $f(p + h)$

10. $x = H(y) = 2y^2 - 3y + 1$; $H(1)$, $H(-\frac{1}{2})$, $H(z)$, $H(z + 1)$

11. $y = G(t) = (t + 4)^2$; $G(0)$, $G(2)$, $G(2 + h)$, $\dfrac{G(2 + h) - G(2)}{h}$

12. $F(x) = |x - 3|$; $F(10)$, $F(3)$, $F(-3)$, $F(4t + 2)$

13. $f(q) = |2q - 7|$; $f(6)$, $f(2)$, $f(7/2)$, $f(x^2 + 5)$

14. $s = h(t) = \sqrt{6t}$; $h(0)$, $h(6)$, $h(\frac{2}{3})$, $h(6t)$

15. $H(x) = \sqrt{4 + x}$; $H(0)$, $H(-4)$, $H(-3)$, $H(x + 1) - H(x)$

16. $y = F(t) = \dfrac{t}{t - 3}$; $F(0)$, $F(4)$, $F(-1)$, $F(t + 2)$

17. $g(s) = \dfrac{4}{s^2 - 9}$; $g(1)$, $g(-1)$, $g(-2w)$, $g(s - 1)$, $g(s) - 1$

18. $h(z) = \left(\dfrac{z + 1}{z - 1}\right)^2$; $h(0)$, $h(1)$, $h(-\frac{1}{2})$, $h(z - 1)$

19. $f(x) = \begin{cases} 4, \text{ if } x \geq 0 \\ 3, \text{ if } x < 0 \end{cases}$; $f(3)$, $f(-4)$, $f(\frac{17}{3})$, $f(-7.3)$

20. $H(x) = \begin{cases} 1, \text{ if } x > 1 \\ x + 1, \text{ if } -1 \leq x \leq 1; \\ 1, \text{ if } x < -1 \end{cases}$ $H(7)$, $H(-7)$, $H(.5)$, $H(-\frac{1}{2})$

21. $h(r) = \begin{cases} 3r - 1 \text{ if } r > 2 \\ r^2 - 4r + 7 \text{ if } r < -2 \end{cases}$; $h(3)$, $h(-3)$, $h(5)$, $h(-5)$

22. $y = g(x) = \dfrac{1}{x - 2} + \dfrac{1}{x + 3}$; $g(-2)$, $g(3)$, $g(0)$

23. $f(z) = \dfrac{z}{z^2 - 7z + 12}$; $f(1)$, $f(2)$, $f(-2)$, $f(z + h)$

24. $g(x) = \dfrac{1}{x - \dfrac{3}{x + 2}}$; $g(0)$, $g(-1)$, $g(2)$, $g(-\frac{3}{2})$

25. $y = f(x) = \dfrac{1}{\sqrt{x}}$; $f(1)$, $f(\sqrt{16})$

26. $F(t) = \dfrac{2}{3(2t^2 - 3t - 5)}$; $F(1)$, $F(-2)$, $F(t + 1)$, $F(2t)$

27. If $z = 4x^2$, can z be considered a function of x? Can x be considered a function of z?

28. If $2p = 3q - 2$, can p be considered a function of q? Can q be considered a function of p?

In problems 29-32, find $\dfrac{f(x + h) - f(x)}{h}$ if

29. $f(x) = 3x - 4$

30. $f(x) = \dfrac{x}{2}$

31. $f(x) = x^2 + 2x$

32. $f(x) = 2x^2 - 3x - 5$

33. If a $30,000 machine depreciates 2 percent of its original value each year, find a function f which expresses its value V after t years have elapsed.

34. A business with original capital of $10,000 has income and expenses each week of $2000 and $1600, respectively. If all profits are retained in the business, express as a function of t, the value V of the business at the end of t weeks.

35. If x units of a certain product are sold (x is a nonnegative integer), the profit P is given by the equation $P = 1.25x$. Is P a function of x? What is the dependent variable; the independent variable? If no more than 7000 units can be produced, what is the domain of this function?

36. If a principal of P dollars is invested at a simple annual interest rate of r for t years, express the total accumulated amount of the principal and interest as a function of t. Is your result a linear function of t?

37. In manufacturing a component for a machine, the initial cost of a die is $850 and all other additional costs are $3 per unit produced. Express the total cost C as a function of the number x of units produced.

38. Suppose that when x units of a product can be sold, the price per unit is $f(x)$. What would be the total revenue TR obtained?

39. The following table, called a *demand schedule*, establishes a correspondence between the price p of a product and the quantity q that consumers will demand (that is, purchase) at that price. (a) If $p = f(q)$, list the numbers in the domain of f. Find $f(2900)$ and $f(3000)$. (b) If $q = g(p)$, list the numbers in the domain of g. Find $g(10)$ and $g(17)$.

p	*q*
PRICE PER UNIT IN DOLLARS	QUANTITY DEMANDED PER WEEK
10	3000
12	2900
17	2300
20	2000

3-2   COMBINATIONS OF FUNCTIONS

If f and g are functions, we can combine them to create new functions. For example, suppose

$$f(x) = x^2 \quad \text{and} \quad g(x) = x + 1.$$

Adding $f(x)$ and $g(x)$ in the obvious way gives

$$f(x) + g(x) = x^2 + (x + 1).$$

This sum defines a new function—let us call it H:

$$H: x \to f(x) + g(x) = x^2 + (x + 1).$$

Thus,

$$H(x) = f(x) + g(x) = x^2 + x + 1.\dagger$$

Similarly, we can create other functions:

$$f(x) - g(x) = x^2 - (x + 1),$$
$$f(x) \cdot g(x) = x^2(x + 1),$$
$$\frac{f(x)}{g(x)} = \frac{x^2}{x + 1}, \quad \text{if } g(x) \neq 0.$$

EXAMPLE 7

Let $f(x) = 3x - 1$ and $g(x) = x^2 + 3x + 3$.

a. $f(x) + g(x) = (3x - 1) + (x^2 + 3x + 3)$
$\qquad = x^2 + 6x + 2 = H(x)$

Thus, $f(2) + g(2) = H(2) = 2^2 + 6(2) + 2 = 18$.

b. $f(x) - g(x) = (3x - 1) - (x^2 + 3x + 3)$
$\qquad = -4 - x^2$.

c. $f(x) \cdot g(x) = (3x - 1)(x^2 + 3x + 3)$
$\qquad = 3x^3 + 8x^2 + 6x - 3$.

d. $\dfrac{f(x)}{g(x)} = \dfrac{3x - 1}{x^2 + 3x + 3}$.

EXAMPLE 8

Let $f(x) = \sqrt{x}$, $g(x) = 6x + 1$, and $H(x) = f(x) + g(x)$.

a. $H(4x) = f(4x) + g(4x)$
$\qquad = \sqrt{4x} + 6(4x) + 1 = 2\sqrt{x} + 24x + 1$.

b. $H(x + h) = f(x + h) + g(x + h) = \sqrt{x + h} + 6(x + h) + 1$.

It may be possible to combine functions in yet another way. In Fig. 3-3 we see that x is in the domain of g. Applying g to x, we get $g(x)$, which

---

$\dagger$We assume that x is in the domains of both f and g.

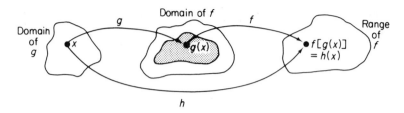

Fig. 3-3

is in the range of g (the shaded region). But suppose *the range of g is in the domain of f.* By applying f to $g(x)$ we get $f[g(x)]$, which is in the range of f. The procedure of applying g and then f defines a so-called "composite" function h. This function assigns to the input number x the output number $f[g(x)]$. Thus $h(x) = f[g(x)]$.

DEFINITION.   *If f and g are functions, then the* **composition of f with g** *is the function h defined by*

$$h(x) = f[g(x)].$$

EXAMPLE 9

> Let $f(x) = \sqrt{x}$ *and* $g(x) = x + 1$. *Find*
>
> a. $f[g(x)]$.
>
> f takes the square root of an input number. But the input number is $g(x)$ or $x + 1$. Thus f takes the square root of it.
>
> $$f[g(x)] = f[x + 1] = \sqrt{x + 1}.$$
>
> Note that the domain of this composite function is all $x \geq -1$.
>
> b. $g[f(x)]$.
>
> g adds 1 to an input number. But the input number is $f(x)$ or $\sqrt{x}$. Thus g adds 1 to $\sqrt{x}$.
>
> $$g[f(x)] = g[\sqrt{x}] = \sqrt{x} + 1.$$
>
> Here the domain is all $x \geq 0$.

From Example 9 we see that $f[g(x)] \neq g[f(x)]$.

PITFALL.   *Do not confuse $f[g(x)]$ with the product $f(x) \cdot g(x)$, for if $f(x) = \sqrt{x}$ and $g(x) = x + 1$, then*

$$f[g(x)] = \sqrt{x + 1}$$

but

$$f(x) \cdot g(x) = \sqrt{x}\,(x + 1).$$

EXAMPLE 10

If $F(p) = p^2 + 4p - 3$ and $G(p) = 2p + 1$, then

a. $F[G(p)] = F[2p + 1] = (2p + 1)^2 + 4(2p + 1) - 3$
$$= 4p^2 + 12p + 2.$$

b. $G[F(p)] = 2(p^2 + 4p - 3) + 1 = 2p^2 + 8p - 5.$

EXAMPLE 11

If $f(x) = 5x^2 - 2$ and $g(x) = \sqrt{10 - x^2}$, find $f[g(-1)]$ and $g[f(2)]$.

a. $f[g(-1)] = f[\sqrt{10 - (-1)^2}] = f[3] = 5(3)^2 - 2 = 43.$

b. $g[f(2)] = g[5(2)^2 - 2] = g[18] = \sqrt{10 - (18)^2}$, which is not a real number. Thus you must be careful with composition.

EXAMPLE 12

If $f(s) = \dfrac{1}{s - 1}$ and $g(t) = t^2 + t + 1$, find $f[g(t)]$ and $g[f(s)]$.

a. $f[g(t)] = f[t^2 + t + 1]$

$$= \frac{1}{(t^2 + t + 1) - 1} = \frac{1}{t^2 + t} = \frac{1}{t(t + 1)}.$$

The domain of this composition is all real numbers except 0 and -1.

b. $g[f(s)] = g\left[\dfrac{1}{s - 1}\right] = \left(\dfrac{1}{s - 1}\right)^2 + \dfrac{1}{s - 1} + 1$

$$= \frac{1 + (s - 1) + (s - 1)^2}{(s - 1)^2}$$

$$= \frac{s^2 - s + 1}{(s - 1)^2}.$$

Here the domain is all real numbers except 1.

EXAMPLE 13

The function $y = (x^2 + 2x + 3)^3$ can be considered a composition. If we let

$$f(x) = x^3 \quad \text{and} \quad g(x) = x^2 + 2x + 3,$$

then

$$f[g(x)] = f[x^2 + 2x + 3] = (x^2 + 2x + 3)^3.$$

Thus,

$$y = f[g(x)].$$

EXERCISE 3-2

In problems 1-6, find

a. $f(x) + g(x)$ b. $f(x) - g(x)$ c. $f(x) \cdot g(x)$

d. $\dfrac{f(x)}{g(x)}$ e. $f[g(x)]$ f. $g[f(x)]$.

1. $f(x) = x + 5$, $g(x) = x + 4$ 2. $f(x) = 3$, $g(x) = -1$

3. $f(x) = 3x + 4$, $g(x) = x^2 - 1$ 4. $f(x) = x^2$, $g(x) = x^3 + 1$

5. $f(x) = x^2 + 3x - 4$, $g(x) = 2x^2 - 7$

6. $f(x) = 1/x$, $g(x) = 4x + 5$

Problems 7-9 refer to the functions

$H(x) = f(x) + g(x)$, $F(x) = f(x) - g(x)$,

$G(x) = f(x) \cdot g(x)$, $Q(x) = \dfrac{f(x)}{g(x)}$.

7. If $f(x) = 6x - 5$ and $g(x) = 4x + 1$, find

a. $H(3)$ b. $H(2x)$ c. $F(-1)$ d. $F(-w)$

e. $G(\frac{1}{2})$ f. $G(x + 1)$ g. $Q(0)$ h. $Q(t^2)$

8. If $f(x) = 4x$ and $g(x) = x^2 + 6x - 1$, find

a. $H(1)$ b. $H(2x + 1)$ c. $F(-3)$ d. $F(x/2)$

e. $G(-.5)$ f. $G(1/x)$ g. $Q(0)$ h. $Q(-z^2)$

9. If $f(x) = 2x^2 + 3$ and $g(x) = 1 - 3x$, find

a. $H(-2)$ b. $H(x + h)$ c. $F(-2)$ d. $F(x + h)$

e. $G(0)$ f. $G(\sqrt{x})$ g. $Q(1)$ h. $Q(2p/3)$

10. If $f(x) = 4x$ and $g(x) = x^2 + 6x - 1$, find $f[g(1)]$ and $g[f(1)]$.

11. If $f(x) = 2x^2 + 3$ and $g(x) = 1 - 3x$, find $f[g(2)]$ and $g[f(2)]$.

12. If $f(p) = \dfrac{4}{p}$ and $g(p) = \dfrac{p - 2}{3}$, find $f[g(p)]$ and $g[f(p)]$.

13. If $F(t) = t^2 + 3t + 1$ and $G(t) = \dfrac{2}{t - 1}$, find $F[G(t)]$ and $G[F(t)]$.

14. If $F(s) = \sqrt{s}$ and $G(t) = 3t^2 + 4t + 2$, find $F[G(t)]$ and $G[F(s)]$.

15. If $f(w) = \dfrac{1}{w^2 + 1}$ and $g(v) = \sqrt{v + 2}$, find $f[g(v)]$ and $g[f(w)]$.

16. If $f(x) = x^2 + 3$, find $f[f(x)]$.

17. Let $f(x) = 3x + 8$ and $g(x) = 2$. (a) Find $f[g(x)]$ and give the domain and range of this composition. (b) Find $g[f(x)]$ and give the domain and range of this composition.

In problems 18–23, find functions f and g such that $h(x) = f[g(x)]$.

18. $h(x) = (x^2 + 2)^2$

19. $h(x) = \sqrt{x - 2}$

20. $h(x) = \sqrt[5]{\dfrac{x + 1}{3}}$

21. $h(x) = \left(\dfrac{4x - 5}{x^2 + 1}\right)^{2/3}$

22. $h(x) = (x^2 - 1)^2 + 2(x^2 - 1)$

23. $h(x) = (3x^3 - 2x)^3 - (3x^3 - 2x)^2 + 7$

3-3   GRAPHS IN RECTANGULAR COORDINATES

A **rectangular** (or **Cartesian**) **coordinate system** lets us specify and locate points in a plane. It also provides a geometric way to represent equations in two variables as well as functions.

In a plane two real number lines, called *coordinate axes*, are constructed perpendicular to each other so that their origins coincide as in Fig. 3-4. Their point of intersection is called the *origin* of the coordinate system. Right now we shall call the horizontal line the *x-axis* and the vertical line the *y-axis*.

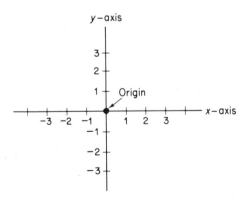

Fig. 3-4

The plane on which the coordinate axes are placed is called a *rectangular coordinate plane* or, more simply, an *xy-plane*. The unit distance on the axes need not necessarily be the same.

Every point in the xy-plane can be labeled to indicate its position. To label point P in Fig. 3-5(a) we draw perpendiculars from P to the x-axis and y-axis. They meet these axes at 4 and 2, respectively.

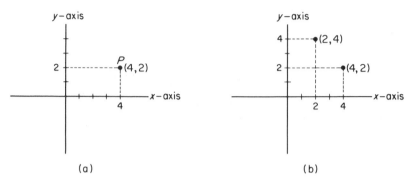

Fig. 3-5

Thus P determines two numbers, 4 and 2. We say that the **rectangular coordinates** of P are given by the **ordered pair** (4, 2). The word "ordered" is important. In Fig. 3-5(b) the point corresponding to (4, 2) is not the same as that for (2, 4):

$$(4, 2) \neq (2, 4).$$

In general, if P is any point, then its rectangular coordinates will be given by an ordered pair of the form (x, y). See Fig. 3-6. We call x the *abscissa* or *x-coordinate* of P, and y the *ordinate* or *y-coordinate*.

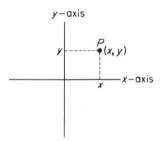

Fig. 3-6

Thus with each point in the coordinate plane we can associate exactly one ordered pair (x, y) of real numbers. Also it should be clear that with each ordered pair (x, y) of real numbers we can associate exactly one point in the plane. Since there is a *one-to-one correspondence* between the points in the plane and all ordered pairs of real numbers, we shall refer to a point P with abscissa x and ordinate y simply as the point (x, y), or as $P(x, y)$. Moreover, we shall use the words "point" and "ordered pair" interchangeably.

In Fig. 3-7 the coordinates of various points are indicated. For example, the point $(1, -4)$ is located one unit to the right of the y-axis and four units below the x-axis. The origin is $(0, 0)$. The x-coordinate of every point on the

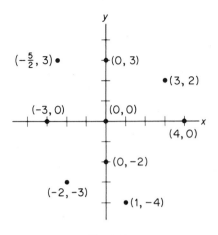

Fig. 3-7

y-axis is 0, and the y-coordinate of every point on the x-axis is 0.

The coordinate axes divide the plane into four regions called *quadrants* (Fig. 3-8). For example, quadrant I consists of all points (x_1, y_1) such that $x_1 > 0$ and $y_1 > 0$. The points on the axes do not lie in any quadrant.

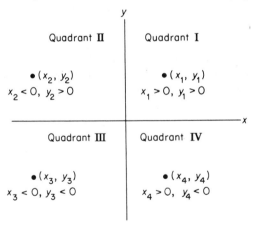

Fig. 3-8

Using a rectangular coordinate system, we can geometrically represent equations in two variables.

For example, let us look at

$$y = x^2 + 2x - 3.$$

A solution of this equation is a value of x and a value of y that make the equation true.

If $x = 1$, then $y = 1^2 + 2(1) - 3 = 0$.

Thus $x = 1$, $y = 0$ is a solution. Similarly,

$$\text{if } x = -2, \text{ then } y = (-2)^2 + 2(-2) - 3 = -3$$

and so $x = -2$, $y = -3$ is also a solution. By choosing other values for x we can get more solutions [see table in Fig. 3-9(a)]. It should be clear that there are infinitely many solutions.

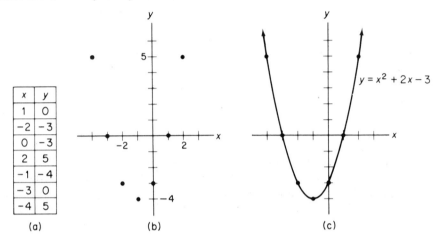

x	y
1	0
-2	-3
0	-3
2	5
-1	-4
-3	0
-4	5

(a)   (b)   (c)

Fig. 3-9

Each solution gives rise to a point (x, y). For example, to $x = 1$ and $y = 0$ corresponds $(1, 0)$. The **graph** of $y = x^2 + 2x - 3$ is the geometric representation of all its solutions. In Fig. 3-9(b) we have plotted the points corresponding to the solutions in the table.

But the equation has infinitely many solutions. So it seems impossible to determine its graph precisely. However, we are concerned only with the graph's general shape. For this reason we locate only enough points so that its general behavior is clear. Then we join these points by a smooth curve wherever conditions permit. See Fig. 3-9(c). Of course, the more points we plot, the better is our graph. Note that the graph extends indefinitely upward.

EXAMPLE 14

a. *Graph $y = 2x + 3$.*

See Fig. 3-10 on page 99.

b. *Graph $s = \dfrac{100}{t}$.*

Using t for the horizontal axis and s for the vertical, we get Fig. 3-11 (page 99).

c. *Graph $x = 3$.*

We can think of this as an equation in two variables if we write it as $x = 3 + 0y$. Here y can be any value, but x must be 3. See Fig. 3-12.

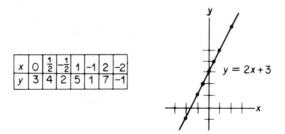

x	0	$\frac{1}{2}$	$-\frac{1}{2}$	1	-1	2	-2
y	3	4	2	5	1	7	-1

$y = 2x + 3$

Fig. 3-10

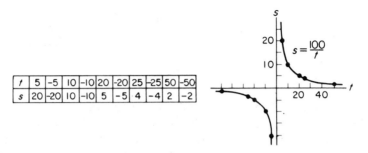

t	5	-5	10	-10	20	-20	25	-25	50	-50
s	20	-20	10	-10	5	-5	4	-4	2	-2

$s = \dfrac{100}{t}$

Fig. 3-11

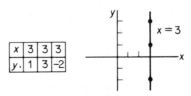

x	3	3	3
y	1	3	-2

$x = 3$

Fig. 3-12

We can also represent functions in a coordinate plane. If f is a function and x is the independent variable, then the graph of f is all points $(x, f(x))$, where x is in the domain of f.

EXAMPLE 15

a. *Graph* $f(x) = \sqrt{x}$.

The domain of f is all $x \geq 0$. See Fig. 3-13 on page 100.

b. *Graph* $p = G(q) = |q|$ *(absolute value function).*

It is customary to *use the independent variable to label the horizontal axis.* See Fig. 3-14 (page 100).

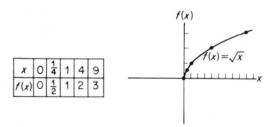

Fig. 3-13

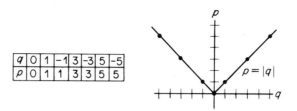

Fig. 3-14

In Fig. 3-15 is the graph of the function $y = f(x)$. Corresponding to the input number x on the horizontal axis is the output number $f(x)$ on the vertical axis. In particular $f(4) = 3$. Since there is an output number for any value of x, the domain of f is all real numbers. Notice that the y-coordinates of all points on the graph are nonnegative. In fact, for any $y \geq 0$ there is an x such that $y = f(x)$. Thus the range of f is all $y \geq 0$.

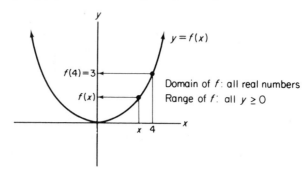

Fig. 3-15

EXAMPLE 16

The domain of F in Fig. 3-16 (page 101) is all $t \geq 0$. To the right of 4 we assume that the graph repeats itself indefinitely. Thus, the range is $-1 \leq s \leq 1$. Some functional values are

$$F(0) = 0, \qquad F(1) = 1, \qquad F(2) = 0, \qquad F(3) = -1.$$

In the leftmost diagram in Fig. 3-17 is the graph of some equation in

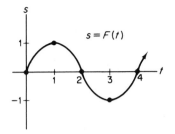

Fig. 3-16

x and y. Notice that with the given x there are associated *two* values of y—namely y_1 and y_2. Thus the equation *does not* define y as a function of x.

In general, if a vertical line L can be drawn which meets the graph of an equation in at least two points, then the equation does *not* define a function of x. When no such vertical line can be drawn, the graph is that of a function of x. Thus the graphs in Fig. 3-17 do not represent functions of x, but those in Fig. 3-18 do.

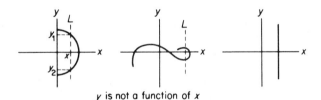

y is not a function of *x*

Fig. 3-17

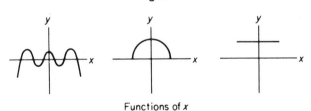

Functions of *x*

Fig. 3-18

EXAMPLE 17

Graph $x = 2y^2$.

Here it is easier to choose values of y and then find the corresponding values of x. The equation does *not* define a function of x. See Fig. 3-19 on page 102.

EXERCISE 3-3

In problems 1 and 2, locate and label each of the points and give the quadrant, if possible, in which each point lies.

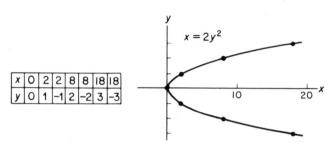

x	0	2	2	8	8	18	18
y	0	1	-1	2	-2	3	-3

Fig. 3-19

1. $(2, 7)$, $(8, -3)$, $(-\frac{1}{2}, -2)$, $(0, 0)$

2. $(-4, 5)$, $(3, 0)$, $(1, 1)$, $(0, -6)$

In problems 3-16, sketch the graph of each equation. Based on your graph, is y a function of x and if so, what is the domain and range?

3. $y = x$

4. $y = x + 1$

5. $y = 3x - 5$

6. $y = 3 - 2x$

7. $y = x^2$

8. $y = \dfrac{3}{x}$

9. $x = 0$

10. $y = x^2 - 9$

11. $y = x^3$

12. $x = -4$

13. $x = -3y^2$

14. $x^2 = y^2$

15. $2x + y - 2 = 0$

16. $x + y = 1$

In problems 17-28, sketch the graph of each function and give its domain and range.

17. $y = g(x) = 2$

18. $v = H(u) = |u - 3|$

19. $f(t) = -t^3$

20. $G(s) = -8$

21. $s = F(r) = \sqrt{r - 5}$

22. $y = f(x) = x^2 + 2x - 8$

23. $f(x) = |2x - 1|$

24. $p = h(q) = q(2 - q)$

25. $y = h(x) = x^2 - 4x + 1$

26. $F(r) = -\dfrac{1}{r}$

27. $F(t) = \dfrac{16}{t^2}$

28. $y = f(x) = \dfrac{x + 1}{x}$

29. Graph $s = 4 - t^2$ and label the horizontal axis with t.

30. Graph $c = \begin{cases} p \text{ if } 0 \le p < 2 \\ 2 \text{ if } p \ge 2 \end{cases}$ and label the horizontal axis with p.

31. Graph $y = x^2 - 4x - 5$ and then solve the equation $x^2 - 4x - 5 = 0$. What can you say about the solution of $x^2 - 4x - 5 = 0$ and the points where the graph of $y = x^2 - 4x - 5$ intersects the x-axis?

32. The dividends paid per share (in cents) by a corporation during the last ten years are as follows:

year	1	2	3	4	5	6	7	8	9	10
dividend	5	5	5	6	$11\frac{1}{2}$	15	20	22	$27\frac{1}{4}$	30

These data give rise to ordered pairs (1, 5), (2, 5), etc. Plot these points and connect them by a smooth curve.

33. The following table indicates the quantities of Brand X that consumers will demand to buy each week at alternative prices per unit. Plot each quantity-price pair by choosing the vertical axis for the possible prices.

price/unit	20	10	5	4
quantity/week	5	10	20	25

Connect the points with a smooth curve. In this way we approximate points in between the given data. The result is called a *demand curve*. From the graph, determine the relationship between the price of Brand X and the amount that will be consumed. (That is, as price decreases, what happens to the quantity demanded?)

34. Given the following supply schedule (see Example 6), plot each quantity-price pair by choosing the horizontal axis for the possible quantities.

Price per unit in dollars	Quantity supplied per week
10	30
20	100
30	150
40	190
50	210

Approximate the points in between the data by connecting the data points with a smooth curve. Thus you get a *supply curve*. From the graph determine the relationship between price and supply. (That is, as price increases, what happens to the quantity supplied?)

3-4   REVIEW

Important Terms and Symbols in Chapter 3

function *(p. 83)* $f(x)/g(x)$ *(p. 91)*

domain *(p. 83)*   composition of functions *(p. 92)*

range *(p. 83)* $f[g(x)]$ *(p. 92)*

independent variable *(p. 83)*   rectangular coordinate system
                                              (p. 95)

dependent variable *(p. 83)*   origin *(p. 95)*

$f(x)$ *(p. 84)*   ordered pair *(p. 96)*

constant function *(p. 85)* (x, y) *(p. 96)*

linear function *(p. 85)*   coordinates of a point *(p. 96)*

quadratic function *(p. 85)* x-coordinate, y-coordinate
                                              (p. 96)

absolute value, $|x|$ *(p. 87)*   abscissa, ordinate *(p. 96)*

$f(x) + g(x)$ *(p. 91)*   quadrant *(p. 97)*

$f(x) - g(x)$ *(p. 91)*   graph of equation *(p. 98)*

$f(x) \cdot g(x)$ *(p. 91)*   graph of function *(p. 99)*

Review Section

1. If f is a function, the set of all input numbers is called the __(a)__ of f. The set of all output numbers is the __(b)__ of f.

> *Ans.* (a) domain;   (b) range

2. If $f(x) = -x^2 - 1$, then $f(-1) = $ __(a)__ . If $g(x) = 3$, then $g(1) = $ __(b)__ . If $h(x) = |6x - 15|$, then $h(2) = $ __(c)__ .

> *Ans.* (a) -2;   (b) 3;   (c) 3

3. If $h(u) = 2u$, then $h(t + 1) = 2($_____$)$.

> *Ans.* $t + 1$

4. If $f(x) = x$, then the domain of f is _____.

> *Ans.* all real numbers

5. True or false:

a. 12 is in the domain of $f(x) = 5x + 3$. _____

b. 6 is in the domain of $g(x) = \sqrt{25 - x^2}$. _____

c. 0 is in the domain of $h(z) = \dfrac{z}{z^2 - 9}$. _____

d. -3 is in the domain of $F(t) = \dfrac{t}{t^2 - 9}$. _____

> *Ans.* (a) true;   (b) false;   (c) true;   (d) false

6. If $g(x) = 5$, then g is called a __(a)__ function and all functional values are equal to __(b)__ .

> *Ans.* (a) constant;   (b) 5

7. The domain of the function

$$f(x) = \frac{3(x - 1)(x + 6)}{(x - 4)(x + 2)}$$

consists of all real numbers except __(a)__ and __(b)__ .

> *Ans.* (a) 4;   (b) -2

8. A variable representing input numbers of a function is called a(n) (dependent) (independent) variable.

> *Ans.* independent

9. If $h(x) = f(x) + g(x)$ where $f(x) = x + 2$ and $g(x) = 5x$, then $h(1) =$ _____.

> *Ans.* 8

10. If $f(x) = x^2$ and $g(x) = x + 1$, then $g[f(x)] =$ __(a)__ and $f[g(x)] =$ __(b)__ .

> *Ans.* (a) $x^2 + 1$;   (b) $(x + 1)^2$

11. The origin of a rectangular coordinate system has coordinates _____.

> *Ans.* (0, 0)

12. The abscissa of the point (1, 2) is __(a)__ and the ordinate is __(b)__ .

> *Ans.* (a) 1;   (b) 2

13. A point on the horizontal axis has its (a)(abscissa)(ordinate) equal to 0. A point on the vertical axis has its (b)(abscissa)(ordinate) equal to 0.

> *Ans.* (a) ordinate;   (b) abscissa

14. The coordinate axes divide a rectangular coordinate plane into four regions called

_____.

> *Ans.* quadrants

15. The point $(3, -7)$ lies in Quadrant ___(a)___ while the point $(-3, 7)$ lies in Quadrant ___(b)___ .

> *Ans.* (a) IV;   (b) II

16. Which of the graphs in Fig. 3-20 represent functions of x? _____ .

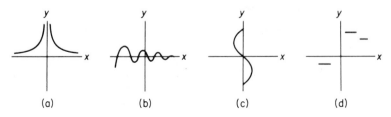

(a)   (b)   (c)   (d)

Fig. 3-20

> *Ans.* (a), (b), (d)

17. The domain of the function whose graph is in Fig. 3-21 is ___(a)___ and its range is ___(b)___ .

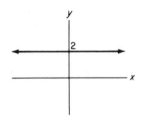

Fig. 3-21

> *Ans.* (a) all real numbers;   (b) 2

Review Problems

In problems 1-4, find the given functional values and the domain of the function.

1. $f(x) = 3x^2 - 4x + 7$; $f(0)$, $f(-3)$, $f(5)$, $f(x^2)$

2. $g(t) = \dfrac{t - 3}{t + 4}$; $g(3)$, $g(-1)$, $g(2)$, $g(2 + h) - g(2)$

3. $H(u) = 6u^2$; $H(\tfrac{1}{2})$, $H(-\sqrt{3})$, $H(\sqrt[4]{u})$, $H(u + h) - H(u)$

4. $f(x) = \sqrt{2x - 1}$; $f(\tfrac{1}{2})$, $f(5)$, $f(x + 3)$, $f(s/2)$

In problems 5-6, find (a) $f(x) + g(x)$, (b) $f(x) - g(x)$, (c) $f(x) \cdot g(x)$, (d) $f(x)/g(x)$, (e) $f[g(x)]$, (f) $g[f(x)]$.

5. $f(x) = 4 - 3x;$ $g(x) = 2x - 8$

6. $f(x) = x^2 + 7x - 3;$ $g(x) = 2x + 1$

7. If $f(s) = s^2 + 5s - 3$ and $g(r) = \sqrt{r + 13}$, find $f[g(10)]$ and $g[f(-2)]$.

8. If $F(x) = \dfrac{1}{2x}$ and $G(x) = \dfrac{3x + 1}{2}$, find $F[G(4x)]$ and $G[F(x^2)]$.

In problems 9–10, graph the equations. If y is a function of x, determine the domain and range.

9. $y = 9 - x^2$ **10.** $y = 3x - 7$

In problems 11–14, graph each function and give its domain and range.

11. $y = f(x) = \begin{cases} 1 - x, \text{ if } x \le 0 \\ \quad 1, \text{ if } x > 0 \end{cases}$ **12.** $y = f(x) = |x| + 1$

13. $g(t) = \dfrac{2}{t - 4}$ **14.** $g(t) = \sqrt{4t}$

15. The predicted annual sales S (in dollars) of a new product is given by $S = 150{,}000 + 3000t$, where t is the time in years from 1975. Such an equation is called a *trend equation*. Find the predicted annual sales for 1980. Is S a function of t?

Chapter 4

Straight Lines and Systems of Equations

4-1 STRAIGHT LINES

Many relationships in economics can be represented conveniently by using straight lines. One feature of a straight line is its "steepness." For example, in Fig. 4-1 line L_1 rises faster as it goes from left to right than line L_2. In this sense it is steeper.

To measure the steepness of a line we introduce the notion of *slope*. Look at line L in Fig. 4-2. As x increases from 2 to 4, notice that y increases from 1 to 5. The average rate of change of y with respect to x is the ratio

$$\frac{\text{change in } y}{\text{change in } x} = \frac{5 - 1}{4 - 2} = \frac{4}{2} = 2.$$

In fact, it turns out that no matter which two points on L are chosen to compute this ratio, the result is always 2. We say that 2 is the *slope* of L. This means that for each 1-unit increase in x, there is a 2-unit *increase* in y. Thus the line must *rise* from left to right.

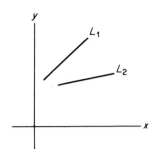

Fig. 4-1

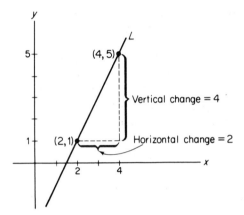

Fig. 4-2

DEFINITION.   *Suppose that (x_1, y_1) and (x_2, y_2) are two different points on a line. The* **slope** *m of the line is the number*

$$m = \frac{y_2 - y_1}{x_2 - x_1} \left(= \frac{\text{vertical change}}{\text{horizontal change}} \right).$$

PITFALL.   *In the slope formula, always align the subscripts correctly.* **Do not** *write* $m = \dfrac{y_2 - y_1}{x_1 - x_2}.$

EXAMPLE 1

Suppose that the line in Fig. 4-3 shows the relationship between the price p of a widget (in dollars) and the quantity q of widgets (in thousands) that consumers will buy at that price. Find and interpret the slope.

In the slope formula we replace the y's by p's, and the x's by q's. Either point may be chosen as (q_1, p_1). Letting $(2, 4) = (q_1, p_1)$ and $(6, 1) = (q_2, p_2)$, then we have

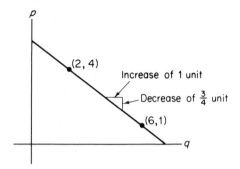

Fig. 4-3

$$m = \frac{p_2 - p_1}{q_2 - q_1} = \frac{1 - 4}{6 - 2} = \frac{-3}{4} = -\frac{3}{4}.$$

The slope is negative, $-\frac{3}{4}$. This means that for each increase in quantity of 1 (thousand widgets), there corresponds a **decrease** in price of $\frac{3}{4}$ (dollars per widget). Due to this decrease the line **falls** from left to right.

EXAMPLE 2

The slope of the *horizontal* line through (2, 2) and (3, 2) is (see Fig. 4-4)

$$m = \frac{y_2 - y_1}{x_2 - x_1} = \frac{2 - 2}{3 - 2} = \frac{0}{1} = 0.$$

But the slope of the *vertical* line through (2, 2) and (2, 3) is (see Fig. 4-4)

$$m = \frac{3 - 2}{2 - 2} = \frac{1}{0}, \text{ which is not defined}.$$

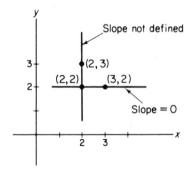

Fig. 4-4

In fact,

> The slope of every horizontal line is 0. The slope of every vertical line is not defined.

In summary,

> Zero slope: horizontal line
> No slope: vertical line
> Positive slope: line rises from left to right
> Negative slope: line falls from left to right

Lines with different slopes are shown in Fig. 4-5. Notice that *the closer the slope is to* 0, *the more horizontal is the line.* It should also be mentioned that **two lines are parallel if and only if they are both vertical or both have the same slope.**

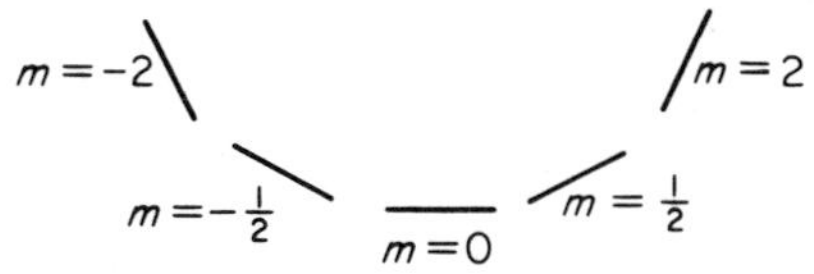

Fig. 4-5

Suppose that line L has slope m and passes through (x_1, y_1). If (x, y) is *any* other point on L (see Fig. 4-6), we want to find a relationship between x and y. By the slope formula,

$$\frac{y - y_1}{x - x_1} = m$$

$$y - y_1 = m(x - x_1). \tag{1}$$

That is, every point on L satisfies Eq. (1). It is also true that any point satisfying Eq. (1) must lie on L. Thus we say that

> $$y - y_1 = m(x - x_1)$$
> is the point-slope form of an equation of the line through (x_1, y_1) and having slope m.

EXAMPLE 3

Determine and sketch an equation of the line that has slope 2 *and passes through* $(1, -3)$.

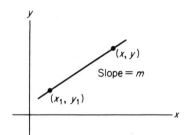

Fig. 4-6

Here $m = 2$ and $(x_1, y_1) = (1, -3)$. Using a point-slope form,

$$y - (-3) = 2(x - 1)$$

$$y + 3 = 2x - 2$$

or

$$y = 2x - 5.$$

To sketch the line only two points need be plotted since two points determine a straight line. See Fig. 4-7.

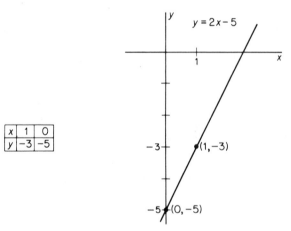

Fig. 4-7

An equation of the line passing through two points can be found easily. First determine the line's slope and then use a point-slope form with either point as (x_1, y_1).

EXAMPLE 4

Determine an equation of the line passing through $(4, -2)$ and $(-3, 8)$.

$$m = \frac{8 - (-2)}{-3 - 4} = -\frac{10}{7}.$$

Choosing $(4, -2)$ as (x_1, y_1), we have

$$y - (-2) = -\frac{10}{7}(x - 4)$$

$$y + 2 = -\frac{10}{7}(x - 4).$$

Choosing $(-3, 8)$ as (x_1, y_1) would give an equivalent result.

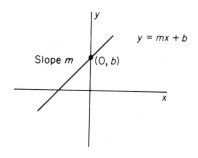

Fig. 4-8

A point $(0, b)$ where a graph intersects the y-axis is called a **y-intercept** (Fig. 4-8). If the slope and y-intercept of a line L are known, an equation for L is (using a point-slope form)

$$y - b = m(x - 0).$$

Solving for y, we have

$$\boxed{y = mx + b}$$

which is the **slope-intercept form** of an equation of the line with slope m and y-intercept $(0, b)$.

EXAMPLE 5

a. An equation of the line with slope 3 and y-intercept $(0, -4)$ is (see Fig. 4-9 on page 114)

$$y = mx + b$$

$$y = 3x + (-4)$$

$$y = 3x - 4.$$

b. *Find the slope-intercept form of an equation of the line passing through* $(4, -2)$ *and* $(-3, 8)$.

From Example 4, a point-slope form is

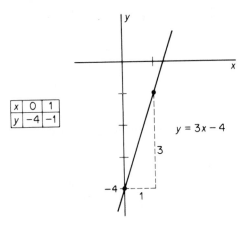

x	0	1
y	-4	-1

$y = 3x - 4$

Fig. 4-9

$$y + 2 = -\frac{10}{7}(x - 4).$$

Solving for y gives the slope-intercept form:

$$y = -\frac{10}{7}x + \frac{26}{7} \qquad \text{(form: } y = mx + b\text{)}.$$

From this we note that the y-intercept is $(0, \frac{26}{7})$.

c. The line $y = \frac{3}{2}x - 6$ has the form $y = mx + b$, where $m = \frac{3}{2}$ and $b = -6$. Thus the line has slope $\frac{3}{2}$ and y-intercept $(0, -6)$.

If a vertical line L passes through (a, b) (see Fig. 4-10), then any other point (x, y) lies on L if and only if $x = a$. Hence an equation of L is $x = a$. Similarly, an equation of the horizontal line passing through (a, b) is $y = b$ (see Fig. 4-11).

Fig. 4-10

Fig. 4-11

EXAMPLE 6

An equation of the vertical line through $(-2, 3)$ is $x = -2$ (see Fig. 4-12). An equation of the horizontal line through $(-2, 3)$ is $y = 3$ (see Fig. 4-13).

Fig. 4-12   Fig. 4-13

On the basis of our discussions we can show that every straight line is the graph of an equation of the form $Ax + By + C = 0$, where A and B are not both zero. We call this a **general linear equation** (or *an equation of the first degree*) **in the variables x and y,** and x and y are said to be **linearly related.** For example, a general linear equation for the line $y = 7x - 2$ is $(-7)x + (1)y + (2) = 0$. Conversely, the graph of a general linear equation is a straight line. Thus, since $3x + 4y + 5 = 0$ is equivalent to $y = (-\frac{3}{4})x + (-\frac{5}{4})$, its graph is a straight line with slope $-\frac{3}{4}$ and y-intercept $(0, -\frac{5}{4})$.

EXAMPLE 7

Sketch the graph of $2x - 3y + 6 = 0$.

Since this is a general linear equation, its graph is a straight line. Thus we need only determine two points on the graph. If $x = 0$, then $y = 2$. If $y = 0$, then $x = -3$. We now draw the line passing through $(0, 2)$ and $(-3, 0)$ (see Fig. 4-14). The point $(-3, 0)$ is called an **x-intercept** of the graph.

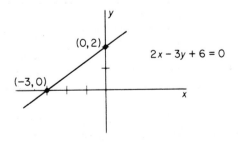

Fig. 4-14

EXAMPLE 8

Suppose a manufacturer has 100 lbs of material from which he can produce two products, *A* and *B*, which require 4 lbs and 2 lbs of material per unit, respectively. If *x* and *y* denote the number of units produced of *A* and *B*, respectively, then all levels of production are given by the combinations of *x* and *y* satisfying the linear equation

$$4x + 2y = 100 \quad \text{where} \quad x, y \geq 0.$$

Solving for *y* we get the slope-intercept form

$$y = -2x + 50,$$

and hence the slope is -2. The slope reflects the rate of change of the level of production of *B* with respect to the level of production of *A*. For example, if one more unit of *A* is to be produced, it will require 4 more lbs of material resulting in $\frac{4}{2} = 2$ *fewer* units of *B*. Thus as *x* increases by one unit, the corresponding value of *y* decreases two units. To sketch the graph of $y = -2x + 50$, we can use the *y*-intercept $(0, 50)$ and the fact that when $x = 10$, then $y = 30$ (see Fig. 4-15).

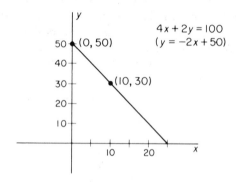

Fig. 4-15

The following table gives the various forms of equations of straight lines.

FORMS OF EQUATIONS OF STRAIGHT LINES	
Point-slope form	$y - y_1 = m(x - x_1)$
Slope-intercept form	$y = mx + b$
General linear form	$Ax + By + C = 0$
Vertical line	$x = a$
Horizontal line	$y = b$

Before we conclude, one point is worthy of mention. The equation $f(x) = mx + b$ defines a *linear function* of *x*. If $y = f(x)$, then $y = mx + b$ and thus *the graph of a linear function is a straight line.* We say that the slope of the linear function is m and the y-intercept is $(0, b)$. Thus the linear function $f(x) = 3x + 5$ has slope 3 and y-intercept $(0, 5)$.

EXERCISE 4-1

In problems 1–8, find the slope of the straight line which passes through the given points.

1. $(5, 2), (7, 5)$ **2.** $(-3, 4), (0, 1)$

3. $(-2, 3), (3, -1)$ **4.** $(2, -4), (3, -4)$

5. $(-2, 4), (-2, 8)$ **6.** $(0, -6), (3, 0)$

7. $(5, -2), (4, -2)$ **8.** $(1, -6), (1, 0)$

In problems 9–22, determine a general linear equation of the straight line that has the indicated properties and sketch each line.

9. Passes through $(1, 2)$ and has slope 6.

10. Passes through origin and has slope -5.

11. Passes through $(-2, 5)$ and has slope $-\frac{1}{4}$.

12. Passes through $(\frac{1}{2}, 6)$ and has slope $\frac{1}{3}$.

13. Passes through $(1, 4)$ and $(8, 7)$.

14. Passes through $(7, 1)$ and $(7, -5)$.

15. Passes through $(3, -1)$ and $(-2, -9)$.

16. Passes through $(0, 0)$ and $(2, 3)$.

17. Passes through $(-2, 5)$ and $(3, 5)$.

18. Passes through $(4, 3)$ and $(2, 0)$.

19. Passes through $(2, -8)$ and is vertical.

20. Passes through $(7, 4)$ and is horizontal.

21. Passes through $(-1, 3)$ and is parallel to the line $y = 4x - 5$.

22. Passes through $(2, 1)$ and is parallel to the line $y = 3 + 2x$.

In problems 23–36, find, if possible, the slope and y-intercept of the straight line determined by the equation and sketch the graph.

23. $y = 2x - 1$ **24.** $x - 1 = 5$

25. $3x - 8y = 8$ **26.** $(x - 1) + (y - 2) = 0$

27. $x + 2y - 3 = 0$ **28.** $x + 4 = 7$

29. $x = -5$ **30.** $x - 1 = 5y + 3$

31. $y = 3x$ **32.** $y - 7 = 3(x - 4)$

33. $y = 1$

34. $2y - 3 = 0$

35. $\dfrac{x}{5} - 8y = 4$

36. $y + 7 = 0$

In problems 37–46, determine a general linear form and the slope-intercept form of the given equation.

37. $x = -2y + 4$

38. $3x + 2y = 6$

39. $4x + 9y - 5 = 0$

40. $2(x - 3) - 4(y + 2) = 8$

41. $\dfrac{3}{4}x = \dfrac{7}{3}y + \dfrac{1}{4}$

42. $\dfrac{y}{-2} + \dfrac{x}{3} = 1$

43. $\dfrac{x}{2} - \dfrac{y}{3} = -4$

44. $y = \dfrac{1}{300}x + 8$

45. $3x + 4y - 7 = 2x + 3y - 6$

46. $3x - 4y = 13$

In problems 47–50, determine the slope and y-intercept of the given linear function and sketch the graph.

47. $f(x) = x + 1$

48. $f(x) = x$

49. $f(x) = -3x + 5$

50. $f(x) = 2x - 3$

51. Suppose x and p are related linearly such that $p = 12$ when $x = 40$, and $p = 18$ when $x = 25$. Find an equation that satisfies these conditions. Find p when $x = 30$.

52. Suppose the cost expenditure needed to produce 10 units of a product is $40 and the cost of 20 units is $70. If a linear relationship exists between cost y and output x, describe this in terms of a linear equation.

53. In production analysis, an *isocost line* is a line whose points represent all combinations of two factors of production which can be purchased for the same amount. Suppose a farmer has allocated $20,000 for the purchase of x tons of fertilizer (costing $200 per ton) and y acres of land (costing $2000 per acre). Find an equation of the isocost line which describes the various combinations which can be purchased for $20,000. Observe that neither x nor y can be negative.

54. Suppose the value of a piece of machinery decreases each year by 10 percent of its original value. If the original value is $8000, find an equation that expresses the value v of the machinery after t years of purchase where $0 \le t \le 10$. Sketch the equation, choosing t as the horizontal axis and v as the vertical axis. What is the slope of the resulting line? This method of considering the value of equipment is called *straight-line depreciation*.

4-2   SYSTEMS OF LINEAR EQUATIONS

A company pays its salesmen on a basis of a certain percentage of the first $100,000 in sales, plus a certain percentage of any sales beyond $100,000. If a salesman earned $17,000 on sales of $300,000 and another earned $12,500 on sales of $225,000, what are the two rates?

Suppose we let x be the rate on the first $100,000 in sales and y be the rate on sales beyond $100,000. The salesman who had $300,000 in sales will receive $100,000x$ (which is his pay for the first $100,000) and $200,000y$ (for the remaining sales). Thus,

$$100,000x + 200,000y = 17,000.$$

Similarly, for the other salesman

$$100,000x + 125,000y = 12,500.$$

The problem is to find values of x and y for which *both* linear equations above are true. Let us consider this situation on a more general level. We shall return to our particular problem shortly.

The set of linear equations

$$\begin{cases} a_1 x + b_1 y = c_1 & (1) \\ a_2 x + b_2 y = c_2 & (2) \end{cases}$$

is called a **system** of two linear equations in the variables (or unknowns) x and y. Its solution consists of values of x and y which satisfy *both* equations *simultaneously*.

Geometrically, Eqs. (1) and (2) represent straight lines, say L_1 and L_2. Since the coordinates of any point on a line satisfy the equation of that line, the coordinates of any point of intersection of L_1 and L_2 will satisfy both equations. Hence a point of intersection will give a solution of the system. If L_1 and L_2 are sketched on the same plane, there are three possibilities as to their relative orientations:

(1) L_1 and L_2 may be parallel and have no points in common (see Fig. 4-16 on page 120). Thus there is no solution.

(2) L_1 and L_2 may intersect at exactly one point, (x_0, y_0) [see Fig. 4-17]. Thus the system has the solution $x = x_0$ and $y = y_0$.

(3) L_1 and L_2 may coincide (see Fig. 4-18). Thus the coordinates of any point on L_1 is a solution of the system and so there are infinitely many solutions. In this case the given equations must be equivalent.

Our main concern now is algebraic methods of solving a system of linear

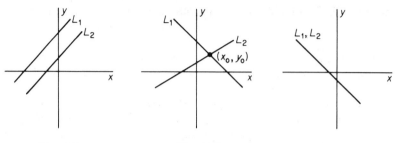

Fig. 4-16   Fig. 4-17   Fig. 4-18

equations. Essentially we successively replace the system by other systems which have the same solution (that is, by *equivalent systems*), but whose equations have a progressively more desirable form for determining the solution. More precisely, we seek an equivalent system containing an equation in which one of the variables does not appear (that is, has been eliminated). We shall illustrate this procedure.

In the problem originally posed,

$$\begin{cases} 100{,}000x + 200{,}000y = 17{,}000 & (3) \\ 100{,}000x + 125{,}000y = 12{,}500, & (4) \end{cases}$$

the left and right sides of Eq. (4) are equal. Thus each side can be subtracted from the corresponding side of Eq. (3):

$$100{,}000x + 200{,}000y - (100{,}000x + 125{,}000y) = 17{,}000 - 12{,}500$$

$$75{,}000\,y = 4500$$

$$y = .06.$$

Replacing Eq. (3) with the last equation, we get the equivalent system:

$$\begin{cases} y = .06 & (5) \\ 100{,}000x + 125{,}000y = 12{,}500. & (6) \end{cases}$$

Note that x does not appear in Eq. (5). Replacing y in Eq. (6) by .06, we get

$$100{,}000x + 125{,}000(.06) = 12{,}500$$

$$100{,}000x = 5000$$

$$x = .05.$$

Thus, the original system is equivalent to

$$\begin{cases} y = .06 \\ x = .05 \end{cases}$$

and must have the same solution, namely $x = .05$ and $y = .06$. To check our answer, substitute these values into the *original* equations.

To solve

$$\begin{cases} 3x - 4y = 13 & (7) \\ 2x + 3y = 3 & (8) \end{cases}$$

we can multiply Eq. (7) by 2 [that is, multiply both sides of Eq. (7) by 2] and multiply Eq. (8) by -3. This gives an equivalent system in which the coefficients of x in each equation differ only in sign:

$$\begin{cases} 6x - 8y = 26 & (9) \\ -6x - 9y = -9. & (10) \end{cases}$$

Adding corresponding sides of Eq. (10) to Eq. (9), we can replace Eq. (9) with $-17y = 17$ or, more simply, $y = -1$:

$$\begin{cases} y = -1 & (11) \\ -6x - 9y = -9. & (12) \end{cases}$$

Replacing y in Eq. (12) by -1 means that Eq. (12) is equivalent to $-6x - 9(-1) = -9$ or $x = 3$:

$$\begin{cases} y = -1 \\ x = 3. \end{cases}$$

The solution is $x = 3$ and $y = -1$, which should be checked by substituting these values into both Eqs. (7) and (8). Our procedure is referred to as *elimination by addition*. Although we chose to eliminate x first, we could have done the same for y by a similar procedure. Figure 4-19 shows a geometrical representation of the system.

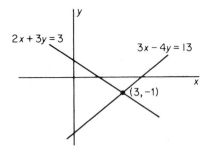

$2x + 3y = 3$

$3x - 4y = 13$

$(3, -1)$

Fig. 4-19

To solve the same system

$$\begin{cases} 3x - 4y = 13 & (13) \\ 2x + 3y = 3 & (14) \end{cases}$$

by an alternate approach, we first choose an equation, for example Eq. (13), and solve it for one unknown in terms of the other, say x in terms of y. Hence Eq. (13) is equivalent to

$$x = \frac{4}{3}y + \frac{13}{3}$$

and we obtain

$$\begin{cases} x = \dfrac{4}{3}y + \dfrac{13}{3} & \qquad (15) \\[2mm] 2x + 3y = 3. & \qquad (16) \end{cases}$$

By *substitution*, Eq. (16) is equivalent to

$$2\left(\frac{4}{3}y + \frac{13}{3}\right) + 3y = 3$$

which when solved gives

$$y = -1.$$

Replacing y in Eq. (15) by -1 gives $x = 3$, and the original system is equivalent to

$$\begin{cases} x = 3 \\ y = -1. \end{cases}$$

Our procedure in this case is called *elimination by substitution*.

EXAMPLE 9

   a. *Solve the system*

$$\begin{cases} x + 2y - 8 = 0 \\ 2x + 4y + 4 = 0. \end{cases}$$

In the equivalent system

$$\begin{cases} x = -2y + 8 & \qquad (17) \\ 2x + 4y + 4 = 0 & \qquad (18) \end{cases}$$

we replace x in Eq. (18) by $-2y + 8$, obtaining

$$2(-2y + 8) + 4y + 4 = 0.$$

This simplifies to $20 = 0$.

$$\begin{cases} x = -2y + 8 & \qquad (19) \\ 20 = 0. & \qquad (20) \end{cases}$$

Since Eq. (20) is never true, there is no solution to the original system. Observe that the original equations can be written in slope-intercept form as

$$\begin{cases} y = -\dfrac{1}{2}x + 4 \\ \\ y = -\dfrac{1}{2}x - 1. \end{cases}$$

These equations represent straight lines having slopes of $-\frac{1}{2}$ but different y-intercepts, $(0, 4)$ and $(0, -1)$. That is they determine different parallel lines (see Fig. 4-20).

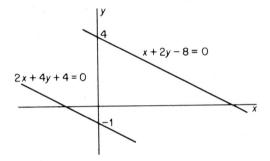

Fig. 4-20

b. *Solve*

$$\begin{cases} x + 5y = 2 & (21) \\ \\ \dfrac{1}{2}x + \dfrac{5}{2}y = 1. & (22) \end{cases}$$

Multiplying Eq. (22) by -2, we have

$$\begin{cases} x + 5y = 2 & (23) \\ -x - 5y = -2. & (24) \end{cases}$$

Adding Eq. (23) to Eq. (24) gives

$$\begin{cases} x + 5y = 2 & (25) \\ 0 = 0. & (26) \end{cases}$$

Any solution of Eq. (25) is a solution of the system, because Eq. (26) is always true. Looking at it another way, by writing Eqs. (21) and (22) in their slope-intercept forms, we get the equivalent system

$$\begin{cases} y = -\dfrac{1}{5}x + \dfrac{2}{5} \\[2ex] y = -\dfrac{1}{5}x + \dfrac{2}{5} \end{cases}$$

in which both equations represent the same line. Hence the lines coincide (Fig. 4-21), and Eqs. (21) and (22) are equivalent. The coordinates of any point on the line $y = -\frac{1}{5}x + \frac{2}{5}$ are a solution, and so there are infinitely many solutions. For example, $x = 0$ and $y = \frac{2}{5}$ is a solution.

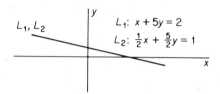

L_1, L_2

$L_1: x + 5y = 2$

$L_2: \frac{1}{2}x + \frac{5}{2}y = 1$

Fig. 4-21

EXAMPLE 10

a. *Solve*

$$\begin{cases} 2x + y + z = 3 & (27) \\ -x + 2y + 2z = 1 & (28) \\ x - y - 3z = -6. & (29) \end{cases}$$

This system consists of three linear equations in three variables. We follow the same basic procedure as before. From Eq. (29), $x = y + 3z - 6$. Substituting for x in Eqs. (27) and (28) and simplifying, we obtain

$$\begin{cases} 3y + 7z = 15 & (30) \\ y - z = -5 & (31) \\ x = y + 3z - 6. & (32) \end{cases}$$

Note that x does not appear in Eqs. (30) and (31). Since any solution of the original system must satisfy Eqs. (30) and (31), we shall consider their solution first:

$$\begin{cases} 3y + 7z = 15 & (30) \\ y - z = -5. & (31) \end{cases}$$

From Eq. (31), $y = z - 5$. This means we can replace Eq. (30) by $3(z - 5) + 7z = 15$ or $z = 3$. Since z is 3, we can replace Eq. (31) with $y = -2$. Hence the above system is equivalent to

$$\begin{cases} z = 3 \\ y = -2. \end{cases}$$

The original system becomes

$$\begin{cases} x = y + 3z - 6 \\ z = 3 \\ y = -2 \end{cases}$$

from which $x = 1$. The solution is $x = 1$, $y = -2$, and $z = 3$, which you may verify.

b. *Solve*

$$\begin{cases} 2x + y + z = -2 & (33) \\ x - 2y = \dfrac{13}{2} & (34) \\ 3x + 2y - 2z = -\dfrac{9}{2}. & (35) \end{cases}$$

Since Eq. (34) can be written $x - 2y + 0z = \frac{13}{2}$, we can view Eqs. (33) to (35) as a system of three linear equations in the variables x, y, and z. From Eq. (34), $x = 2y + \frac{13}{2}$. By substituting for x in Eqs. (33) and (35) and simplifying, we obtain

$$\begin{cases} 5y + z = -15 & (36) \\ x = 2y + \dfrac{13}{2} & (37) \\ 4y - z = -12. & (38) \end{cases}$$

Solving the system formed by Eqs. (36) and (38),

$$\begin{cases} 5y + z = -15 \\ 4y - z = -12, \end{cases}$$

we find that $y = -3$ and $z = 0$. Substituting these values in Eq. (37) gives $x = \frac{1}{2}$. Hence the solution of the original system is $x = \frac{1}{2}$, $y = -3$, and $z = 0$.

EXAMPLE 11

A chemical manufacturer wishes to fill a request for 500 gallons of a 25 percent acid solution (25 percent by volume is acid). If solutions of 30 and 18 percent are available in stock, how many gallons of each must he mix to fill the order?

Let x and y, respectively, be the number of gallons of the 30 and 18 percent solutions which should be mixed. Then

$$x + y = 500. \qquad (39)$$

In 500 gallons of a 25 percent solution, there will be $.25(500) = 125$ gallons of acid.

This acid comes from two sources: $.30x$ gallons of acid come from the 30 percent solution and $.18y$ gallons of acid come from the 18 percent solution. Hence

$$.30x + .18y = 125. \tag{40}$$

Equations (39) and (40) form a system of two linear equations in two unknowns. Solving Eq. (39) for x and substituting in Eq. (40) gives

$$.30(500 - y) + .18y = 125. \tag{41}$$

Solving Eq. (41) for y, we find $y = 208\frac{1}{3}$ gallons and thus $x = 500 - 208\frac{1}{3} = 291\frac{2}{3}$ gallons.

EXERCISE 4-2

In problems 1–16, solve the systems algebraically.

1. $\begin{cases} 3x + y = 7 \\ 2x + 2y = -2 \end{cases}$

2. $\begin{cases} 2x - y = -11 \\ y + 5x = -7 \end{cases}$

3. $\begin{cases} 3x - 4y = 13 \\ 2x + 3y = 3 \end{cases}$

4. $\begin{cases} 2x - y = 1 \\ -x + 2y = 7 \end{cases}$

5. $\begin{cases} 5v + 2w = 36 \\ 8v - 3w = -54 \end{cases}$

6. $\begin{cases} p + q = 3 \\ 3p + 2q = 19 \end{cases}$

7. $\begin{cases} 4x - 3y - 2 = 3x - 7y \\ x + 5y - 2 = y + 4 \end{cases}$

8. $\begin{cases} 5x + 7y + 2 = 9y - 4x + 6 \\ \frac{21}{2}x - \frac{4}{3}y - \frac{11}{4} = \frac{3}{2}x + \frac{2}{3}y + \frac{5}{4} \end{cases}$

9. $\begin{cases} \frac{2}{3}x + \frac{1}{2}y = 2 \\ \frac{3}{8}x + \frac{5}{6}y = -\frac{11}{2} \end{cases}$

10. $\begin{cases} \frac{1}{2}z - \frac{1}{4}w = \frac{1}{6} \\ z + \frac{1}{2}w = \frac{2}{3} \end{cases}$

11. $\begin{cases} 4p + 12q = 6 \\ 2p + 6q = 3 \end{cases}$

12. $\begin{cases} 5x - 3y = 2 \\ -10x + 6y = 4 \end{cases}$

13. $\begin{cases} 2x + y + 6z = 3 \\ x - y + 4z = 1 \\ 3x + 2y - 2z = 2 \end{cases}$

14. $\begin{cases} x + y + z = -1 \\ 3x + y + z = 1 \\ 4x - 2y + 2z = 0 \end{cases}$

15. $\begin{cases} 5x - 7y + 4z = 2 \\ 3x + 2y - 2z = 3 \\ 2x - y + 3z = 4 \end{cases}$

16. $\begin{cases} 3x - 2y + z = 0 \\ -2x + y - 2z = 5 \\ \frac{3}{2}x + \frac{4}{5}y + 4z = 10 \end{cases}$

17. A chemical manufacturer wishes to obtain 700 gallons of a 24 percent acid solution by mixing a 20 percent solution with a 30 percent solution. How many gallons of each solution should he use?

18. A company has taxable income of $312,000. The federal tax is 25 percent of that portion which is left after the state tax has been paid. The state tax is 10 percent

of that portion which is left after the federal tax has been paid. Find the federal and state taxes.

19. National Wigwam Co., manufacturer of prefabricated houses, produces two models, Early American and Little Big Horn. From past experience management has determined that 20 percent more of the Early American models can be sold than the Little Big Horn models. A profit of $250 is made on each Early American sold, while one of $350 is made on each Little Big Horn. If, in the forthcoming year, management desires a total profit of $130,000, how many units of each model must be sold?

20. Snoopy Surveys was awarded a contract to perform a product rating survey for Moldy Crackers. A total of 250 people were interviewed. Snoopy Surveys reported that 62.5 percent more people liked Moldy Crackers than disliked them. However, the report did not indicate that 16 percent of those interviewed had no comment. How many of those surveyed liked Moldy Crackers? How many disliked them? How many had no comment?

21. United Dum Dum Co. has plants in the cities of Exton and Whyton. Each plant is devoted to the manufacturing of electric forks. At the Exton plant, fixed costs are $7000 per month, and the cost of producing each fork is $7.50. At the Whyton plant, fixed costs are $8800 per month, and each fork costs $6.00 to produce. Next month, United Dum Dum must manufacture 1500 forks. Find the production order for each plant if the total cost for each plant is to be the same.

22. A coffee wholesaler blends together three types of coffee that sell for 65, 70, 75 cents per lb so as to obtain 100 lb of coffee worth 71 cents per lb. If he uses the same amount of the two higher priced coffees, how much of each type must be used in the blend?

23. Company A pays its salesmen on a basis of a certain percentage of the first $100,000 in sales plus a certain percentage of any amount over $100,000 in sales. If a salesman earned $8500 on sales of $175,000 and another salesman earned $14,800 on sales of $280,000, find the two rates.

24. A businessman made two investments and the percentage return per year on each was the same. Of the total amount invested, $\frac{3}{10}$ of it plus $600 was invested in one venture and at the end of one year he received a return of $384 from that venture. If the total return after one year was $1120, find the total amount invested.

25. A total of $35,000 is invested at three interest rates: 4, 5, and 6 percent. The interest for the first year was $1780, which was not reinvested. The second year the amount originally invested at 6 percent earned 7 percent instead, and the other rates remained the same. The total interest the second year was $1910. How much was invested at each rate?

4-3   SOME APPLICATIONS OF SYSTEMS OF EQUATIONS

For each price level of a product there is a corresponding quantity of the product that consumers will demand (that is, purchase) during some time period. Usually, the higher the price, the smaller the quantity demanded; as the price falls, the quantity demanded increases.

On the other hand, in response to various prices, there is a corresponding quantity of output of a product that producers are willing to place on the market during some time period. Usually, the higher the price, the larger the quantity that producers are willing to supply to the consumer; as the price falls, so will the quantity supplied.

The quantities of a product that will be demanded or supplied per unit of time at all possible alternative prices can be indicated geometrically on a coordinate plane by a *demand* or *supply curve*, as in Figs. 4-22 and 4-23. In keeping with the practice of most economists, quantity per unit of time is measured along the horizontal axis, the x-axis, while the vertical axis, the p-axis, measures price per unit. Some economists also use q or Q as the quantity variable, rather than x. Although straight lines are not necessarily typical of these curves, their use is convenient for illustrative purposes.

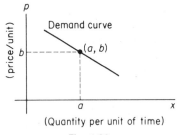

Fig. 4-22

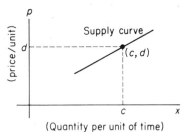

Fig. 4-23

Throughout our discussion we shall assume that price per unit is given in dollars and that the time period is one week. The point (a, b) in Fig. 4-22 indicates that at a price of b dollars per unit, consumers will demand a units per week. Similarly, in Fig. 4-23 the point (c, d) indicates that at a price of d dollars each, producers will supply c units per week. Since negative prices or quantities are not meaningful, the coordinates of (a, b) and (c, d) must be nonnegative.

In most cases a demand curve falls from left to right (that is, has a negative slope). This reflects the relationship that consumers will buy more of a product as its price goes down. A supply curve usually rises from left to right (that is, has a positive slope). This indicates that a producer will supply more of a product at higher prices.

An equation that relates price per unit and quantity demanded (supplied) is called a *demand equation* (*supply equation*). Suppose that the linear demand equation for Product Z is

$$p = -\frac{1}{180}x + 12 \qquad\qquad (1)$$

and its linear supply equation is

$$p = \frac{1}{300}x + 8, \qquad\qquad (2)$$

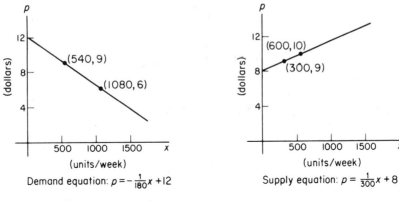

Fig. 4-24   Fig. 4-25

where x, $p \geq 0$. The demand and supply curves defined by Eqs. (1) and (2), respectively, are given in Figs. 4-24 and 4-25. In analyzing Fig. 4-24, we see that consumers will purchase 540 units/week when the price is $9 per unit; 1080 units when the price is $6; etc. Figure 4-25 shows that when the price is $9 per unit, producers will place 300 units per week on the market; at $10 they will supply 600 units; etc.

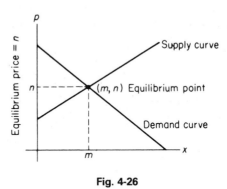

Fig. 4-26

When both the demand and supply curves of a product are represented on the same coordinate plane, the point (m, n) at which the curves intersect is called the *point of equilibrium* (see Fig. 4-26). The price n, called the *equilibrium price,* is the price at which consumers will purchase the same quantity of a product that producers wish to sell at that price. In short, n is the price at which stability in the producer-consumer relationship occurs. The quantity m is called the *equilibrium quantity.*

To determine precisely the equilibrium point, we solve the system formed by the supply and demand equations. Let us do this for our previous data, namely the system

$$\begin{cases} p = -\dfrac{1}{180}x + 12 & \text{(demand equation)} \\[2em] p = \dfrac{1}{300}x + 8. & \text{(supply equation)} \end{cases}$$

By substituting $\dfrac{1}{300}x + 8$ for p in the demand equation we get

$$\frac{1}{300}x + 8 = -\frac{1}{180}x + 12$$

$$\left(\frac{1}{300} + \frac{1}{180}\right)x = 4$$

$$x = 450. \qquad \text{(equilibrium quantity)}$$

Thus,

$$p = \frac{1}{300}(450) + 8$$

$$= 9.50 \qquad \text{(equilibrium price)}$$

and the equilibrium point is (450, 9.50). Therefore, at the price of \$9.50 per unit, manufacturers will produce exactly the quantity (450) of units per week that consumers will purchase at that price (see Fig. 4-27).

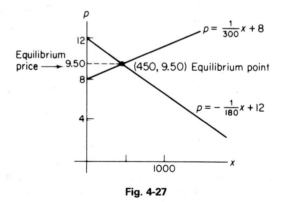

Fig. 4-27

EXAMPLE 12

Let $p = \frac{8}{100}x + 50$ be the supply equation for a certain manufacturer. Suppose the demand per week for his product is 100 units when the price is \$58 per unit, and 200 units per week at \$51 each.

a. *Determine the demand equation, assuming that it is linear.*

b. *If a tax of $1.50 per unit is to be imposed on the manufacturer, how will the original equilibrium price be affected if the demand remains the same?*

c. *Determine the total revenue obtained by the manufacturer at the equilibrium point both before and after the tax.*

a. Since the demand equation is linear, the demand curve must be a straight line. From the given data we conclude that the points (100, 58) and (200, 51) lie on this line. Thus,

$$m = \frac{51 - 58}{200 - 100} = -\frac{7}{100}$$

$$p - p_1 = m(x - x_1)$$

$$p - 58 = -\frac{7}{100}(x - 100).$$

Hence, the demand equation is

$$p = -\frac{7}{100}x + 65.$$

b. Before the tax, the equilibrium price is obtained by solving the system

$$\begin{cases} p = \frac{8}{100}x + 50 \\ \\ p = -\frac{7}{100}x + 65. \end{cases}$$

By substitution,

$$-\frac{7}{100}x + 65 = \frac{8}{100}x + 50$$

$$15 = \frac{15}{100}x$$

$$100 = x$$

and

$$p = \frac{8}{100}(100) + 50 = 58.$$

Thus, $58 is the original equilibrium price. Before the tax the manufacturer supplies x units at a price of $p = \frac{8}{100}x + 50$ per unit. After the tax he will sell the same

x units for an additional \$1.50 per unit. The price per unit will then be $(\frac{8}{100}x + 50) + 1.50$ and the new supply equation will be $p = \frac{8}{100}x + 51.50$. Solving the system

$$\begin{cases} p = \dfrac{8}{100}x + 51.50 \\[4mm] p = -\dfrac{7}{100}x + 65 \end{cases}$$

will give the new equilibrium price.

$$\frac{8}{100}x + 51.50 = -\frac{7}{100}x + 65$$

$$\frac{15}{100}x = 13.50$$

$$x = 90$$

$$p = \frac{8}{100}(90) + 51.50 = 58.70.$$

The tax of \$1.50 per unit increases the equilibrium price by \$0.70 (Fig. 4-28). Note that there is also a decrease in the equilibrium quantity from $x = 100$ to $x = 90$ due to the change in the equilibrium price. (In the exercises, you are asked to find

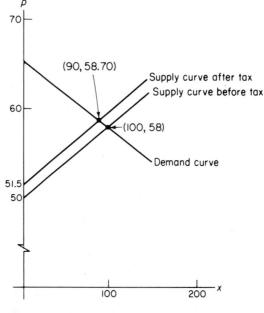

Fig. 4-28

the effect of a subsidy given to the manufacturer which will reduce the price of the product.)

c. If x units of a product are sold at a price of p dollars each, then the total revenue, which we shall denote by y_{TR}, is given by

$$y_{TR} = px.$$

Before the tax the revenue at (100, 58) is (in dollars)

$$y_{TR} = (58)(100) = 5800.$$

After the tax it is

$$y_{TR} = (58.70)(90) = 5283,$$

which is a decrease.

EXAMPLE 13

Find the equilibrium point if the supply and demand equations of a product are $p = \dfrac{x}{40} + 10$

and $p = \dfrac{8000}{x}$, *respectively.*

Although the demand equation is not linear, the method of solution is the same as if both equations were linear. Solving

$$\begin{cases} p = \dfrac{x}{40} + 10 \\ p = \dfrac{8000}{x} \end{cases}$$

by substitution gives

$$\frac{8000}{x} = \frac{x}{40} + 10$$

$$320{,}000 = x^2 + 400x$$

$$x^2 + 400x - 320{,}000 = 0$$

$$(x + 800)(x - 400) = 0$$

$$x = -800 \quad \text{or} \quad x = 400.$$

We disregard $x = -800$ since x represents quantity. Choosing $x = 400$, then we have $p = (8{,}000/400) = 20$ and the required point is (400, 20) (see Fig. 4-29).

Suppose a manufacturer produces and sells product A at \$8.00 per unit. Then the total revenue y_{TR} he receives (in dollars) from selling x units is

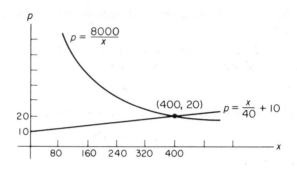

Fig. 4-29

$$y_{TR} = 8x. \qquad \text{(total revenue)}$$

The difference between the total revenue received for x units and the total cost of producing x units is the manufacturer's profit (or loss).

$$\text{Profit (or Loss)} = \text{Total Revenue} - \text{Total Cost.}$$

Total cost, y_{TC}, is the sum of total variable costs y_{VC} and total fixed costs y_{FC}.

$$y_{TC} = y_{VC} + y_{FC}.$$

Fixed costs are those costs that under normal conditions do not depend on the level of production; that is, over some period of time they remain constant at all levels of output (examples are rent, officers' salaries and normal maintenance). *Variable costs* are those costs that vary with the level of production (such as cost of materials, labor, maintenance due to wear and tear, etc.). For x units of product A, suppose

$$y_{FC} = 5000 \qquad \text{(fixed cost)}$$

and

$$y_{VC} = \frac{22}{9}x. \qquad \text{(variable cost)}$$

Then

$$y_{TC} = \frac{22}{9}x + 5000. \qquad \text{(total cost)}$$

The graphs of fixed cost, total cost, and total revenue appear in Fig. 4-30. The horizontal axis represents level of production x, and the vertical axis represents the total dollar value, be it revenue or costs. The *break-even point* is the point at which Total Revenue = Total Cost ($TR = TC$). It occurs when the levels of production and sales result in neither a profit nor a loss to the manufacturer. In the diagram, called a *break-even chart*, it is the point

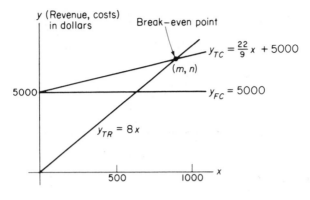

Fig. 4-30

(m, n) at which the graphs of $y_{TR} = 8x$ and $y_{TC} = \frac{22}{9}x + 5000$ intersect. We call m the *break-even quantity* and n the *break-even revenue*. When variable costs and revenue are linearly related to output, as in our case, any production level greater than m units will produce a profit, while any level less than m units will produce a loss. Thus, at an output of m units the profit is zero. In the following example we shall examine our data in more detail.

EXAMPLE 14

A manufacturer sells his product at $8 per unit, selling all that he produces. His fixed cost is $5000 and the cost per unit is $\frac{22}{9}$ (dollars). *Find*

a. *the total output and revenue at the break-even point.*

b. *the profit when 1800 units are produced.*

c. *the loss when 450 units are produced.*

d. *the sales volume in order to obtain a profit of* $10,000.

a. At an output level of x units, the variable cost is $y_{VC} = \frac{22}{9}x$ and the total revenue is $y_{TR} = 8x$. Hence

$$y_{TR} = 8x$$

$$y_{TC} = y_{VC} + y_{FC} = \frac{22}{9}x + 5000.$$

At the break-even point, Total Revenue = Total Cost. Thus we solve the system formed by the above equations. Since

$$y_{TR} = y_{TC},$$

we have

$$8x = \frac{22}{9}x + 5000$$

$$\frac{50}{9}x = 5000$$

$$x = 900.$$

Thus, the desired output is 900 units resulting in a total revenue (in dollars) of

$$y_{TR} = 8(900) = 7200.$$

b. Since Profit = Total Revenue − Total Cost, when $x = 1800$ we have

$$y_{TR} - y_{TC} = 8(1800) - \left[\frac{22}{9}(1800) + 5000 \right]$$

$$= 5000.$$

The profit when 1800 units are produced and sold is $5000.

c. When $x = 450$,

$$y_{TR} - y_{TC} = 8(450) - \left[\frac{22}{9}(450) + 5000 \right]$$

$$= -2500.$$

A loss of $2500 occurs when the level of production is 450 units.

d. In order to obtain a profit of $10,000, the total revenue must cover the total cost plus the desired profit.

$$\text{Total Revenue} = \text{Total Cost} + \text{Profit}$$

$$8x = \left(\frac{22}{9}x + 5000 \right) + 10,000$$

$$\frac{50}{9}x = 15,000$$

$$x = 2700.$$

Thus 2700 units must be produced.

EXAMPLE 15

Determine the break-even quantity of XYZ Manufacturing Co. given the following data: total fixed cost, $1200; total unit cost, $2; total revenue for selling x units, $y_{TR} = 100\sqrt{x}$.

Although the revenue equation is not linear, we shall proceed using previous techniques. For x units of output,

$$y_{TR} = 100\sqrt{x}$$

$$y_{TC} = 2x + 1200.$$

Equating total revenue to total cost gives

$$100\sqrt{x} = 2x + 1200$$

or

$$50\sqrt{x} = x + 600.$$

Squaring both sides, we have

$$2500x = x^2 + 1200x + (600)^2$$

$$0 = x^2 - 1300x + 360,000.$$

By the quadratic formula

$$x = \frac{1300 \pm \sqrt{250,000}}{2}$$

$$x = 400 \quad \text{or} \quad x = 900.$$

Although both $x = 400$ and $x = 900$ are break-even quantities, observe in Fig. 4-31 that there will always be a loss when $x > 900$.

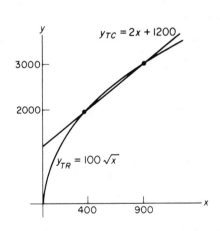

Fig. 4-31

EXERCISE 4-3

1. Suppose a manufacturer of shoes will place on the market 50 (thousand pairs) when the price is 35 (dollars/pair) and 35 when the price is 30. Find the supply equation, assuming that it is linear.

2. Suppose consumers will demand 20 (thousand) pairs of shoes when the price is 35 (dollars/pair) and 25 pairs when the price is 30. Find the demand equation, assuming that it is linear.

In problems 3–6, the first equation is a supply equation and the second is a demand equation for a product. If p represents price per unit in dollars and x represents the number of units per unit of time, find the equilibrium point. In problems 3 and 4 sketch the system.

3. $p = \frac{3}{100}x + 2$

   $p = -\frac{7}{100}x + 12$

4. $p = \frac{1}{2000}x + 3$

   $p = -\frac{1}{2500}x + \frac{42}{5}$

5. $35x - 2p + 250 = 0$

   $65x + p - 537.5 = 0$

6. $246p - 3.25x - 2460 = 0$

   $410p + 3x - 14{,}452.5 = 0$

In problems 7–10, y_{TR} represents total revenue in dollars and y_{TC} represents total cost in dollars for a manufacturer. If x represents both the number of units produced and the number of units sold, find the break-even quantity. Sketch a break-even chart in problems 7 and 8.

7. $y_{TR} = 3x$

   $y_{TC} = 2x + 4500$

8. $y_{TR} = 14x$

   $y_{TC} = \frac{40}{3}x + 1200$

9. $y_{TR} = .05x$

   $y_{TC} = .85x + 600$

10. $y_{TR} = .25x$

    $y_{TC} = .16x + 360$

11. The supply and demand equations for a certain product are $3x - 200p + 1800 = 0$ and $3x + 100p - 1800 = 0$, respectively, where p represents the price per unit in dollars, and x represents the number of units per time period.

    a. Find the equilibrium price algebraically, and derive it graphically.

    b. Find the equilibrium price when a tax of 27 cents per unit is imposed on the supplier.

12. A manufacturer of a product sells all that he produces. His total revenue is given by $y_{TR} = 7x$ and his total cost is given by $y_{TC} = 6x + 800$, where x represents the number of units produced and sold.

    a. Find the level of production at the break-even point and draw the break-even chart.

    b. Find the level of production at the break-even point if the total cost increases by 5 percent.

13. A manufacturer sells his product at $8.35 per unit, selling all he produces. His fixed cost is $2116 and his variable cost is $7.20 per unit. At what level of production will he have a profit of $4600? At what level of production will he have a loss of $1150? At what level of production will he break even?

14. The market equilibrium point for a product occurs when 13,500 units are produced at a price of $4.50 per unit. The producer will supply no units at $1 and the consumers will demand no units at $20. Find the supply and demand equations if they are both linear.

15. The Lambda Co., a manufacturer of electric widgets, will break even at a sales volume of $200,000. Fixed costs are $40,000 and each unit of output sells for $5. Determine the average variable cost per unit.

16. The Footsie Sandal Co. manufactures sandals for which the material cost is $0.80/pair and the labor cost is $0.90/pair. Additional variable costs amount to $0.30/pair. Fixed costs are $70,000. If each pair sells for $2.50, how many pairs must be sold for the company to break even?

17. Find the break-even point for Company Z, which sells all it produces, if the cost of one unit is $2. Fixed costs are $1050 and $y_{TR} = 50\sqrt{x}$, where x is the number of units of output.

18. A company has determined that the demand equation for its product is $p = \dfrac{1000}{x}$, where p is the price per unit for x units in some time period. Determine the quantity demanded when the price/unit is: (a) $4; (b) $2; and (c) $0.50. For each of these prices, determine the total revenue that the company will receive. What will be the revenue regardless of the price? (*Hint:* Find the revenue when the price is p dollars.)

19. By using the data in Example 12, determine how the original equilibrium price will be affected if the company is given a government subsidy of $1.50 per unit.

20. The Monroe Forging Company sells a corrugated steel product to the Standard Manufacturing Company and is in competition on such sales with other suppliers of the Standard Manufacturing Co. The vice president of sales of Monroe Forging Co. believes that by reducing the price of the product, a 40 percent increase in the volume of units sold to the Standard Manufacturing Co. could be secured. As the manager, Cost and Analysis Department, you have been asked to analyze the proposal of the vice president and submit your recommendations as to whether it is financially beneficial to the Monroe Forging Co.

You are specifically requested to determine the following.

(1) Net profit or loss based on the pricing proposal.
(2) Unit sales volume under the proposed price that is required to make the same $40,000 profit now earned at the current price and unit sales volume.

The following data are available for use in your analysis.

	CURRENT OPERATIONS	PROPOSAL OF VICE PRESIDENT OF SALES
Unit Price	$2.50	$2.00
Unit Sales Volume	200,000 units	280,000 units
Variable Cost-total	$350,000	
-per unit	$1.75	$1.75
Fixed Cost	$110,000	$110,000
Profit	$40,000	???

21. Suppose products A and B have demand and supply equations that are related to each other. If q_A and q_B are quantities of A and B, and p_A and p_B are their prices, the demand equations are

$$q_A = 8 - p_A + p_B$$

$$q_B = 26 + p_A - p_B$$

and the supply equations are

$$q_A = -2 + 5p_A - p_B$$

$$q_B = -4 - p_A + 3p_B.$$

Eliminate q_A and q_B to get the equilibrium prices.

4-4   REVIEW

Important Terms and Symbols in Chapter 4

y-intercept *(p. 113)*

slope of a straight line *(p. 109)*

point-slope form *(p. 112)*

slope-intercept form *(p.113)*

general linear form *(p. 115)*

linearly related *(p. 115)*

linear function *(p. 116)*

system of linear equations
        (p. 119)

equivalent systems *(p. 120)*

elimination by addition *(p. 121)*

elimination by substitution *(p. 122)*

supply curve, supply equation *(p. 128)*

demand curve, demand equation
        (p. 128)

point of equilibrium *(p. 129)*

equilibrium price *(p. 129)*

total cost *(p. 134)*

fixed cost, variable cost *(p. 134)*

break-even point *(p. 134)*

Review Section

1. A linear equation in x and y is one which can be written in the general form _____ .

> *Ans.* $Ax + By + C = 0$; A, B not both zero

2. The line in Fig. 4–32 on page 141 has a (positive)(negative) slope.

> *Ans.*   negative

3. The slope of a horizontal line is equal to __(a)__ and the slope of a vertical line is __(b)__ .

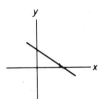

Fig. 4-32

Ans. (a) zero;   (b) not defined

4. Two methods by which a system of two linear equations in two variables can be solved are elimination by __(a)__ and elimination by __(b)__ .

Ans. (a) addition; (b) substitution

5. The graph of $x = 7$ is a line parallel to the _____ axis.

Ans. y

6. If the points (7, 6) and (3, 4) lie on the graph of a straight line, then the line has a slope equal to _____ .

Ans. $\frac{1}{2}$

7. The y-intercepts of the lines $y = x$ and $y = 2x$ are __(a)__ and __(b)__ respectively.

Ans. (a) (0, 0);   (b) (0, 0)

8. If a system of two linear equations is represented geometrically by two parallel lines, what can be said about the solution of the system? _____

Ans. no solution or infinitely many solutions

9. The point-slope form of an equation of the line through (1, −2), having slope 4, is _____ .

Ans. $y + 2 = 4(x - 1)$

10. The slope of the straight line $y = 4x - 3$ is _____ .

Ans. 4

11. An equation of the vertical line passing through (2, −3) is _____ .

Ans. $x = 2$

12. The graphs of a demand equation usually (a)(rises)(falls) from left to right, while the graph of a supply equation usually (b)(rises)(falls) from left to right.

Ans. (a) falls;   (b) rises

13. In the graph of a supply or demand equation, price per unit is usually measured along the (horizontal) (vertical) axis.

> *Ans.* vertical

14. The point at which supply and demand curves intersect is called the __(a)__ . The price at which the quantity supplied is equal to the quantity demanded is called the __(b)__ price.

> *Ans.* (a) point of equilibrium;   (b) equilibrium

15. Total cost is the sum of __(a)__ cost and __(b)__ cost. The point at which total revenue equals total cost is called the __(c)__ point.

> *Ans.* (a) variable;   (b) fixed;   (c) break-even

16. To solve the system

$$\begin{cases} 3x - 4y = 10 \\ 8x + 5y = -40 \end{cases}$$

by the method of elimination of y, first multiply the top equation by 5, the bottom equation by __(a)__ , and then __(b)__ the resulting equations.

> *Ans.* (a) 4;   (b) add

17. The slope of the line $2y = 3x + 2$ is _____ .

> *Ans.* $\frac{3}{2}$

18. A straight line whose slope is 0 has an equation of the form (a) $(x = c)(y = c)$ and is (b) (parallel) (perpendicular) to the y-axis.

> *Ans.* (a) $y = c$;   (b) perpendicular

Review Problems

1. The slope of the line through (2, 5) and (3, k) is 4. Find k.

2. The slope of the line through (2, 3) and (k, 3) is 0. Find k.

In problems 3–7, determine the slope-intercept form and a general linear form of an equation of the straight line that has the indicated properties.

3. Passes through (3, −2) and (−7, 8).

4. Passes through (−1, −1) and is parallel to the line $9x - 3y + 14 = 0$.

5. Passes through (10, 4) and has slope $\frac{1}{2}$.

6. Passes through (3, 5) and is vertical.

7. Passes through $(-2, 4)$ and is horizontal.

8. Determine whether the point $(0, -7)$ lies on the line passing through $(1, -3)$ and $(4, 9)$.

In problems 9-12, write each line in the slope-intercept form and sketch. What is the slope of the line?

9. $3x - 2y = 4$

10. $x = -3y + 4$

11. $4 - 3y = 0$

12. $y = 2x$

In problems 13-20, solve the given system.

13. $\begin{cases} 2x - y = 6 \\ 3x + 2y = 5 \end{cases}$

14. $\begin{cases} 8x - 4y = 7 \\ y = 2x - 4 \end{cases}$

15. $\begin{cases} 4x + 5y = 3 \\ 3x + 4y = 2 \end{cases}$

16. $\begin{cases} 3x + 6y = 9 \\ 4x + 8y = 12 \end{cases}$

17. $\begin{cases} \frac{1}{4}x - \frac{3}{2}y = -4 \\ \frac{3}{4}x + \frac{1}{2}y = 8 \end{cases}$

18. $\begin{cases} \frac{1}{3}x - \frac{1}{4}y = \frac{1}{12} \\ \frac{4}{3}x + 3y = \frac{5}{3} \end{cases}$

19. $\begin{cases} 3x - 2y + z = -2 \\ 2x + y + z = 1 \\ x + 3y - z = 3 \end{cases}$

20. $\begin{cases} x + \dfrac{2y + x}{6} = 14 \\ y + \dfrac{3x + y}{4} = 20 \end{cases}$

21. If the supply and demand equations of a certain commodity are $125p - x - 250 = 0$ and $100p + x - 1100 = 0$, respectively, find the equilibrium price.

22. The difference in price of two items before a five-percent sales tax is imposed is \$4. The difference in price after the sales tax is imposed is \$4.20. Find the price of each item before the sales tax.

23. A manufacturer of a certain product sells all that he produces. Determine his break-even point if he sells his product at \$16 per unit, his fixed cost is \$10,000, and his variable cost is given by $y_{VC} = 8x$, where x is the number of units produced (y_{VC} expressed in dollars).

Chapter **5**

Exponential and Logarithmic Functions

5-1 EXPONENTIAL AND LOGARITHMIC FUNCTIONS

There is a function which has an important role not only in mathematics but in business and economics as well. It involves a constant raised to a variable power.

DEFINITION. *The function f defined by*

$$y = f(x) = b^x$$

*where $b > 0$, $b \neq 1$, and the exponent x is any real number, is called an **exponential function.***

The restriction $b \neq 1$ merely excludes from our consideration the rather trivial constant function $f(x) = 1^x = 1$. Since the exponent can be any real number, the question comes up as to how we define something like $b^{\sqrt{2}}$. Stated simply, we use an approximation method. First, $b^{\sqrt{2}}$ is approximately $b^{1.4} = b^{7/5} = \sqrt[5]{b^7}$, which *is* defined. Better approximations are $b^{1.41} = \sqrt[100]{b^{141}}$ and $b^{1.414}$, etc. In this way a meaning of $b^{\sqrt{2}}$ becomes clear.

In Fig. 5-1 are the graphs of $y = 2^x$, $y = 3^x$, and $y = (\frac{1}{2})^x = 2^{-x}$. Notice that

(1) the *domain* of an exponential function is all real numbers, and

(2) the *range* is all positive numbers.

Also, $b^0 = 1$ for every base b, as shown by the point of intersection (0, 1) of the graphs.

We also see in Fig. 5-1 that $y = b^x$ has two basic shapes, depending on whether $b > 1$ or $0 < b < 1$. If $b > 1$, then as x increases y also increases. But y can also take on values very close to 0. Now suppose $0 < b < 1$ as in $y = (\frac{1}{2})^x$. Then as x increases y *decreases*, taking on values close to zero.

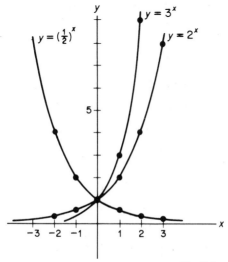

x	2^x	3^x	$(\frac{1}{2})^x$
-2	$\frac{1}{4}$	$\frac{1}{9}$	4
-1	$\frac{1}{2}$	$\frac{1}{3}$	2
0	1	1	1
1	2	3	$\frac{1}{2}$
2	4	9	$\frac{1}{4}$
3	8	27	$\frac{1}{8}$

Fig. 5-1

One of the most **useful** numbers that is used as a base in $y = b^x$ is a certain irrational number denoted by the letter e in honor of the mathematician Euler.

$$e \text{ is approximately } 2.71828 \ldots .$$

See Fig. 5-2 on page 146 for the graph of $y = e^x$.

Although e seems to be a strange number to use as a base, it arises quite naturally in the calculus (as you will see in later chapters). It also occurs in economic analysis and problems involving natural growth (or decay), such as compound interest and population studies. A table of values of e^x and e^{-x} is in Appendix B.

EXAMPLE 1

The predicted population P of a city is given by

$$P = 100,000e^{.05t},$$

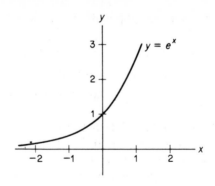

Fig. 5-2

where *t is the number of years after 1976. Predict the population at 1996.*

Here $t = 20$.

$$P = 100,000e^{.05(20)} = 100,000e.$$

Since $e \approx 2.71828$ ($\approx$ means "is approximately"),

$$P \approx 271,828.$$

Many economic forecasts are based on population studies.

EXAMPLE 2

A mail order firm finds that the percentage P (expressed as a decimal) of small towns having exactly x persons responding to a magazine advertisement is given approximately by the formula

$$P = \frac{e^{-.5}\,(.5)^{x}}{1 \cdot 2 \cdot 3 \cdots x}.$$

From what percentage of small towns can the firm expect exactly two people to respond?

If we let $P = g(x)$, then we want to find $g(2)$.

$$g(2) = \frac{e^{-.5}\,(.5)^{2}}{1 \cdot 2}.$$

From the table in Appendix B, $e^{-.5} = .6065$ and so

$$g(2) = \frac{(.6065)(.25)}{2} \approx .0758.$$

Thus, the firm can expect such a response from approximately 7.58 percent. The basis for the above formula is a function used in probability theory called the *Poisson probability function.*

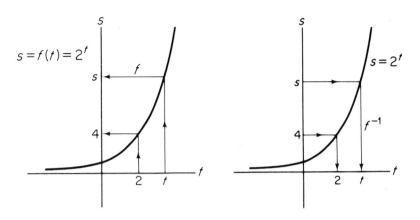

Fig. 5-3   **Fig. 5-4**

In Fig. 5-3 is the graph of $s = f(t) = 2^t$. The function f sends an input number t into a *positive* output number s.

$$f: t \rightarrow s \quad \text{where} \quad s = 2^t.$$

For example, f sends 2 into 4.

$$f: 2 \rightarrow 4.$$

Moreover, from the arrows in Fig. 5-4 it is clear that with each positive number s we can associate exactly one value of t. Notice with $s = 4$ we associate $t = 2$. Thus if we think here of s as an input and t as an output, then we have a function that sends s's into t's. Let us denote this function by the symbol f^{-1}, read "f inverse."†

$$f^{-1}: s \rightarrow t \quad \text{where} \quad s = 2^t.$$

Thus $f^{-1}(s) = t$.

The relationship between f and f^{-1} is shown in Fig. 5-5. The function f^{-1} *reverses* the action of f, and conversely. For example,

$$f \text{ sends 2 into 4, and } f^{-1} \text{ sends 4 into 2.}$$

In terms of composition,

$$f^{-1}[f(2)] = f^{-1}[4] = 2.$$

More generally,

$$f^{-1}[f(t)] = t.$$

This is what is really meant by saying f^{-1} reverses the action of f. We also have $f[f^{-1}(4)] = f[2] = 4$. Generalizing this, we have

---

† f^{-1} is a symbol for a new function. It does not mean $\dfrac{1}{f}$.

$$f[f^{-1}(s)] = s.$$

Notice that the domain of f^{-1} is the range of f, and the range of f^{-1} is the domain of f.

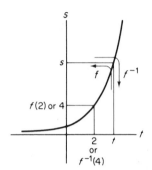

Fig. 5-5

We give a special name to f^{-1}: the **logarithmic function base 2.** Usually we write f^{-1} as $\log_2$, read "log base 2." Thus $\log_2$ is just a symbol for a special function.

In summary,

$$\text{if} \quad s = f(t) = 2^t \quad \text{then} \quad f^{-1}(s) = \log_2(s) = t. \qquad (1)$$

The domain of $\log_2$ is all positive numbers and the range is all reals.

Generalizing to other bases and replacing s by x and t by y in (1) gives the following definition.

DEFINITION. *The **logarithmic function base b,** denoted $\log_b$, is defined by*

$$y = \log_b x \quad \text{if and only if} \quad b^y = x.$$

The domain of $\log_b$ is all positive numbers and its range is all real numbers.

Since the logarithmic function reverses the action of the exponential function, we sometimes call the logarithmic function the *inverse* of the exponential function.

Remember: To say that the log (or logarithm) base b of x is y means that b raised to the y power is x.

$$\boxed{\log_b x = y \quad \text{means} \quad b^y = x.}$$

For example, $\log_2 8 = 3$ because $2^3 = 8$. We say $\log_2 8 = 3$ is the *logarithmic form* of the exponential form $2^3 = 8$.

EXAMPLE 3

    a. Since $25 = 5^2$, then $\log_5 25 = 2$.

    b. Since $10^0 = 1$, then $\log_{10} 1 = 0$.

    c. If $6y = e^{2r}$, then $\log_e 6y = 2r$ and so $r = [\log_e (6y)]/2$.

    d. $\log_{10} 100 = 2$ means $10^2 = 100$.

    e. $\log_{64} 8 = \frac{1}{2}$ means $64^{1/2} = 8$.

    f. $\log_2 \frac{1}{16} = -4$ means $2^{-4} = \frac{1}{16}$.

EXAMPLE 4

    Graph the function $y = \log_2 x$.

    To plot points we shall use the equivalent form $2^y = x$. If $y = 0$, then $x = 1$, giving the point $(1, 0)$. Other points are shown in Fig. 5-6. Note that the domain is all positive numbers and the range is all real numbers.

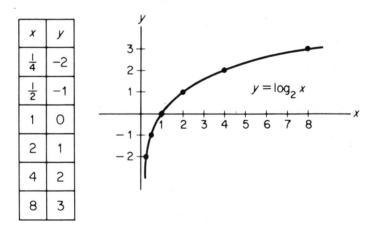

x	y
$\frac{1}{4}$	-2
$\frac{1}{2}$	-1
1	0
2	1
4	2
8	3

Fig. 5-6

    The graph of $y = \log_e x$ is shown in Fig. 5-7. Notice the similarity to Fig. 5-6.

    Logarithms to the base 10, called **common logarithms,** were frequently used for computational purposes before the pocket-calculator age. The subscript 10 is generally omitted from the notation. Thus

$$\log x \quad \text{means} \quad \log_{10} x.$$

    Important in the calculus are logarithms to the base e, called **natural** (or Naperian) **logarithms.** We use the notation "ln" for such logarithms. Thus

$$\ln x \quad \text{means} \quad \log_e x.$$

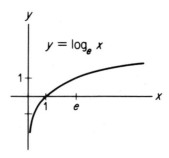

Fig. 5-7

EXAMPLE 5

Find

a. log 1000.

Here the base is 10. Let log 1000 = y. Converting to exponential form, we have

$$10^y = 1000.$$

Clearly y must be 3. Thus log 1000 = 3.

b. ln 1.

Here the base is *e*. Let ln 1 = y. Converting to exponential form, we have

$$e^y = 1.$$

Clearly y must be 0. Thus ln 1 = 0.

c. log .1.

$$\log .1 = y$$

$$10^y = .1 = \tfrac{1}{10} = 10^{-1}.$$

Thus y = −1 and log .1 = −1.

d. ln *e*.

$$\ln e = y$$

$$e^y = e.$$

Thus y = 1 and ln *e* = 1.

EXAMPLE 6

Solve each equation for x.

a. $\log_3 x = 4$.

$$\log_3 x = 4,$$

or equivalently

$$3^4 = x$$

$$81 = x.$$

b. $x + 1 = \log_4 16$.

$$x + 1 = \log_4 16$$

$$4^{x+1} = 16.$$

Thus, from inspection the exponent $x + 1$ must be 2 and so $x = 1$.

c. $\log_x 49 = 2$.

$$\log_x 49 = 2$$

$$x^2 = 49$$

$$x = 7.$$

We reject $x = -7$, since a negative number cannot be a base of a logarithmic function.

EXERCISE 5-1

In problems 1-6, graph each function.

1. $y = f(x) = 4^x$ **2.** $y = f(x) = (\frac{1}{3})^x$

3. $y = f(x) = 4^{-x}$ **4.** $y = f(x) = 3^{x/2}$

5. $y = f(x) = \log_3 x$ **6.** $y = f(x) = \log_2 x$

In problems 7-18 express each logarithmic form exponentially and each exponential form logarithmically.

7. $16^{1/2} = 4$ **8.** $2 = \log_{12} 144$

9. $10^4 = 10,000$ **10.** $\log_{1/2} 4 = -2$

11. $\log_2 64 = 6$ **12.** $8^{2/3} = 4$

13. $\log_2 x = 14$ **14.** $10^{.48302} = 3.041$

15. $e^{.33647} = 1.4$ **16.** $e^2 = 7.3891$

17. $\ln 3 = 1.0986$ **18.** $\log 5 = .6990$

In problems 19-42, find x.

19. $\log_2 x = 4$ **20.** $\log_3 x = 2$

21. $\log_5 x = 3$ **22.** $\log_4 x = 0$

23. $\log x = -1$ **24.** $\ln x = 1$

25. $\ln x = 2$ **26.** $\log_x 100 = 2$

27. $\log_x 8 = 3$

28. $\log_x 3 = \frac{1}{2}$

29. $\log_x \frac{1}{6} = -1$

30. $\log_x y = 1$

31. $\log_4 16 = x$

32. $\log_3 1 = x$

33. $\log 10{,}000 = x$

34. $\log_2 \frac{1}{16} = x$

35. $\log_{25} 5 = x$

36. $\log_9 9 = x$

37. $\log_3 x = -4$

38. $\log_x (2x - 3) = 1$

39. $\log_x (6 - x) = 2$

40. $\log_8 64 = x - 1$

41. $2 + \log_2 4 = 3x - 1$

42. $\log_3 (x + 2) = -2$

43. The probability P that a telephone operator will receive exactly x calls during a certain time interval is

$$P = \frac{e^{-3} 3^x}{1 \cdot 2 \cdot 3 \cdot \ldots \cdot x}.$$

Find the probability that exactly two calls will be received.

44. Repeat Problem 43 for the case of exactly one call being received.

Problems 45 and 46 make use of the following definition: Interest is said to be *compounded continuously* if the amount A of a principal P after n years at an annual rate of r (expressed as a decimal) is given by $A = Pe^{rn}$.

45. Find the amount that $1000 will become after eight years with interest compounded continuously at an annual rate of 5 percent.

46. Find the amount at the end of one year for $100 at 5 percent, compounded continuously.

47. The formula $A = Pe^{-rn}$ gives the amount at the end of n years of a principal P which depreciates at a rate of r (expressed as a decimal) per year compounded continuously. What is the value at the end of ten years of $50,000 of machinery which depreciates at a rate of 8 percent, compounded continuously?

48. The demand equation for a certain product is $x = 80 - 2^p$. Sketch its graph.

49. P. P. Piddle is president of United Dum Dum Co., a manufacturer of electric forks. In *Prong*, a trade journal, he finds an article that says for most electric fork manufacturers the daily output y of electric forks on the tth day of a production run is given by $y = 500(1 - e^{-.2t})$. Such an equation is called a *learning equation* and indicates that as time progresses, output per day will increase. This may be due to the gain of the workers' proficiency at their jobs. If Mr. Piddle's company is typical of the industry, determine to the nearest complete unit the output on the (a) first day, and (b) tenth day after the start of a production run. After how many days will a daily production run of 400 forks be reached? Assume $\ln 0.2 = -1.6$.

50. An important function used in economic and business decisions is the *normal distribution density function*, which in standard form is

$$y = f(x) = \frac{1}{\sqrt{2\pi}} \, e^{-x^2/2}.$$

Evaluate $f(0)$, $f(-1)$, and $f(1)$, using $\dfrac{1}{\sqrt{2\pi}} = .399$.

51. The demand equation for a new toy is $q = 10,000(.9512)^p$. It is desired to evaluate q when $p = 10$. To convert the equation into a more desirable computational form, use Appendix B to show that $q = 10,000e^{-.05p}$. Then evaluate. *Hint:* Find a number x such that $.9512 = e^{-x}$.

5-2   PROPERTIES OF LOGARITHMS

Some basic properties of logarithms deserve mention.

PROPERTY 1. $\log_b (mn) = \log_b m + \log_b n$.

      Proof.   Let $x = \log_b m$ and $y = \log_b n$. Then $b^x = m$ and $b^y = n$. Thus

$$mn = b^x b^y = b^{x+y}.$$

Since $mn = b^{x+y}$, then $\log_b (mn) = x + y$. Thus

$$\log_b (mn) = \log_b m + \log_b n.$$

We shall not prove the next two properties, since their proofs are similar to that of Property 1.

PROPERTY 2. $\log_b \dfrac{m}{n} = \log_b m - \log_b n$.

PROPERTY 3. $\log_b m^n = n \log_b m$.

In some of the examples and exercises that follow, the following table of common logarithms will be used. Most entries are approximate. Notice that $\log 4 = .6021$, which means $10^{.6021} = 4$.

x	2	3	4	5	6
log x	.3010	.4771	.6021	.6990	.7782

x	7	8	9	10	e
log x	.8451	.9031	.9542	1.0000	.43429

EXAMPLE 7

a. *Find* log 56.

$$\log 56 = \log (8 \cdot 7) = \log 8 + \log 7 = .9031 + .8451 = 1.7482.$$

b. *Find* log $\frac{9}{2}$.

$$\log \tfrac{9}{2} = \log 9 - \log 2 = .9542 - .3010 = .6532.$$

c. *Find* log 64.

$$\log 64 = \log 8^2 = 2 \log 8 = 2(.9031) = 1.8062.$$

d. *Find* log $\sqrt{5}$.

$$\log \sqrt{5} = \log 5^{1/2} = \tfrac{1}{2} \log 5 = \tfrac{1}{2}(.6990) = .3495.$$

e. *Find* log $\frac{15}{7}$.

$$\log \frac{15}{7} = \log \frac{3 \cdot 5}{7} = \log (3 \cdot 5) - \log 7$$

$$= \log 3 + \log 5 - \log 7$$

$$= .4771 + .6990 - .8451 = .3310.$$

EXAMPLE 8

a. *Simplify* $\log_3 \dfrac{1}{x^2}$.

$$\log_3 \frac{1}{x^2} = \log_3 x^{-2} = -2 \log_3 x.$$

b. *Express* $3 \log_2 10 + \log_2 15$ *as a single logarithm.*

$$3 \log_2 10 + \log_2 15 = \log_2 10^3 + \log_2 15 = \log_2 [(10)^3 (15)]$$

$$= \log_2 15{,}000.$$

c. *Write* $\ln \sqrt[3]{\dfrac{x^5 (x - 2)^8}{x - 3}}$ *in terms of* $\ln x$, $\ln (x - 2)$, *and* $\ln (x - 3)$.

$$\ln \sqrt[3]{\frac{x^5(x-2)^8}{x-3}} = \ln \left[\frac{x^5(x-2)^8}{x-3}\right]^{1/3} = \frac{1}{3} \ln \frac{x^5(x-2)^8}{x-3}$$

$$= \frac{1}{3} \{\ln [x^5(x-2)^8] - \ln (x-3)\}$$

$$= \frac{1}{3} [\ln x^5 + \ln (x-2)^8 - \ln (x-3)]$$

$$= \frac{1}{3} [5 \ln x + 8 \ln (x-2) - \ln (x-3)].$$

Since $b^0 = 1$ and $b^1 = b$ we have the following properties.

PROPERTY 4. $\log_b 1 = 0.$

PROPERTY 5. $\log_b b = 1.$

EXAMPLE 9

    a. *Find* $\ln e$.

$$\ln e = \log_e e = 1.$$

    b. *Find* $\log 10^c$.

$$\log 10^c = c \log 10 = c \log_{10} 10 = c \cdot 1 = c.$$

    c. *Find* $\log \frac{200}{21}$.

$$\log \frac{200}{21} = \log 200 - \log 21 = \log (2 \cdot 100) - \log (7 \cdot 3)$$

$$= \log 2 + \log 100 - (\log 7 + \log 3)$$

$$= .3010 + 2 - (.8451 + .4771) \text{ [since } \log 100 = \log 10^2 = 2 \log 10 = 2]$$

$$= .9788.$$

    d. *Find* $\log_7 \sqrt[9]{7^8}$.

$$\log_7 \sqrt[9]{7^8} = \log_7 (7^8)^{1/9} = \log_7 7^{8/9} = \tfrac{8}{9} \log_7 7 = \tfrac{8}{9}.$$

    e. *Find* $\log_3 (\frac{27}{81})$.

$$\log_3 \left(\frac{27}{81}\right) = \log_3 \left(\frac{3^3}{3^4}\right) = \log_3 (3^{-1}) = (-1) \log_3 3 = -1.$$

    f. *Find* $\ln e + \log \frac{1}{10}$.

$$\ln e + \log \tfrac{1}{10} = \ln e + \log 10^{-1} = \log_e e + (-1) \log_{10} 10$$

$$= 1 + (-1)(1) = 0.$$

Notice in Fig. 5-8 that if x_1 and x_2 are different, then their logarithms are different. This means that if $\log_2 m = \log_2 n$, then $m = n$. Generalizing to base b, we have the following property:

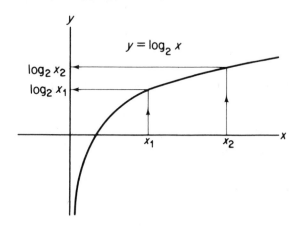

Fig. 5-8

PROPERTY 6.   If $\log_b m = \log_b n$, then $m = n$.

There is a similar property for exponentials.

PROPERTY 7.   If $b^m = b^n$, then $m = n$.

EXAMPLE 10

a. *Solve* $\log_b x + \log_b (2x) = \log_b 100$ *for x.*

$$\log_b x + \log_b (2x) = \log_b 100$$
$$\log_b [(x)(2x)] = \log_b 100.$$
$$\log_b (2x^2) = \log_b 100.$$

By Property 6,

$$2x^2 = 100$$
$$x^2 = 50$$
$$x = 5\sqrt{2}.$$

(Why do we ignore $x = -5\sqrt{2}$?)

b. *Find x if* $(25)^{x+2} = 5^{3x-4}$.

Since $25 = 5^2$, we can express both sides of the equation as powers of 5.

$$(25)^{x+2} = 5^{3x-4}$$

$$(5^2)^{x+2} = 5^{3x-4}$$

$$5^{2x+4} = 5^{3x-4}$$

$$2x + 4 = 3x - 4 \qquad \text{(Property 7)}$$

$$x = 8.$$

PROPERTY 8. $b^{\log_b x} = x$, and in particular $10^{\log x} = x$ and $e^{\ln x} = x$.

Proof.   Let $t = b^{\log_b x}$. Writing this in logarithmic form, we have $\log_b t = \log_b x$. By Property 6, $t = x$ and so $x = b^{\log_b x}$.

EXAMPLE 11

a. *Find* $2^{\log_2 6}$.

$$2^{\log_2 6} = 6.$$

b. *Simplify* $10^{\log x^2}$.

$$10^{\log x^2} = x^2.$$

c. *Evaluate* $e^{(\ln 3 + 2 \ln 4)}$.

$$e^{(\ln 3 + 2 \ln 4)} = e^{(\ln 3 + \ln 4^2)} = e^{\ln(3 \cdot 4^2)} = 3 \cdot 4^2 = 48.$$

EXAMPLE 12

Find $\log_5 2$.

Let $x = \log_5 2$. Then $5^x = 2$, and by taking common logs of both sides we get

$$\log 5^x = \log 2$$

$$x \log 5 = \log 2$$

$$x = \frac{\log 2}{\log 5} = \frac{.3010}{.6990} = .4306.$$

Generalizing the method used in Example 12, we have

$$\log_b N = \frac{\log N}{\log b}$$

and

$$\log_b N = \frac{\log_a N}{\log_a b}.$$

With these formulas we can convert logarithms from one base to another. In particular, in the last formula if $b = e$ and $a = 10$, then

$$\ln N = \frac{\log N}{\log e} = \frac{\log N}{.43429}$$

$$= 2.30259 \log N.$$

EXAMPLE 13

Find $\ln 6$.

$$\ln 6 = 2.30259 \log 6 = 2.30259 \,(.7782) \approx 1.7919.$$

Thus, $e^{1.7919} \approx 6$.

EXAMPLE 14

A demand equation for a product is defined by $p = 12^{1-.1x}$. *Express x in terms of p.*

$$p = 12^{1-.1x}$$

Taking common logs of both sides gives

$$\log p = \log (12^{1-.1x})$$

$$\log p = (1 - .1x) \log 12$$

$$\frac{\log p}{\log 12} = 1 - .1x$$

$$.1x = 1 - \frac{\log p}{\log 12}$$

$$x = 10 \left(1 - \frac{\log p}{\log 3 + \log 4} \right)$$

$$x = 10 \left(1 - \frac{\log p}{1.0792} \right).$$

EXERCISE 5-2

In problems 1–18, find the given values.

1. $\log 35$ **2.** $\log 12$

3. $\log \frac{9}{4}$ **4.** $\log \frac{7}{10}$

5. $\log 25$ **6.** $\log .0001$

7. $\log 2000$ **8.** $\log 900$

9. $\log_3 \sqrt[3]{3}$ **10.** $\log_5 (5\sqrt{5})^5$

11. $\ln 7$ **12.** $\log_7 4$

13. $\log_2 3$ **14.** $\ln e$

15. $\log_7 7^{48}$ **16.** $\log_2 4$

17. $\log 10 + \ln e^3$ **18.** $\log 10^e$

In problems 19–24, express each of the given forms as a single logarithm.

19. $\log_2 (2x) - \log_2 (x + 1)$ **20.** $2 \log x - \frac{1}{2} \log (x - 2)$

21. $9 \log 7 + 5 \log 23$ **22.** $3 (\log x + \log y - 2 \log z)$

23. $2 + 10 \log 1.05$ **24.** $\frac{1}{2} (\log 215 + 8 \log 6 - 3 \log 121)$

In problems 25–36, find x.

25. $e^{2x} \cdot e^{5x} = e^{14}$ **26.** $(e^{5x+1})^2 = e$

27. $(16)^{3x} = 2$ **28.** $(27)^{2x+1} = \frac{1}{3}$

29. $e^{\ln (2x)} = 5$ **30.** $4^{\log_4 x + \log_4 2} = 3$

31. $10^{\log x^2} = 4$ **32.** $e^{3 \ln x} = 8$

33. $\log (2x + 1) = \log (x + 6)$ **34.** $\log x - \log (x - 1) = .6021$

35. $\log (x + 2)^2 = 2$, where $x > 0$ **36.** $\ln x = \ln (3x + 1) + 1$

In problems 37–42, write each expression in terms of $\log x$, $\log (x + 2)$, and $\log (x - 3)$.

37. $\log [x(x + 2)(x - 3)]$ **38.** $\log \dfrac{x^2(x + 2)}{x - 3}$

39. $\log \dfrac{(\sqrt{x})^3}{(x + 2)(x - 3)^2}$ **40.** $\log [(x - 3)(x + 2)^2 \sqrt{x(x + 2)}]$

41. $\log \sqrt{\dfrac{x^2(x - 3)^3}{x + 2}}$ **42.** $\log \dfrac{1}{x(x - 3)^2 (x + 2)^3}$

43. The demand equation for a certain product is $x = 80 - 2^p$. Solve for p and express your answer in terms of common logarithms as in Example 14. Evaluate p to two decimal places when $x = 60$.

44. In statistics, the sample regression equation $y = ab^x$ is reduced to a linear form by taking logarithms of both sides. Find $\log y$.

45. The vice president of a company believes that for his company's product, the number of units x sold per year after t years from the date he assumed his position is given by $x = 1000(.5)^{.8^t}$. Such an equation is called a *Gompertz equation* and describes natural growth in many areas of study. Solve this equation for t in the same manner as in Example 14.

46. A manufacturer has determined that his supply equation is $p = \log [10 + (x/2)]$, where x is the number of units he will supply at a price p per unit. At what price will he supply (a) 1980 units; (b) 11,980 units?

47. The cost c for a firm producing x units of a product is given by the cost equation $c = (2x \ln x) + 20$. Evaluate the cost when $x = 6$. (Give your answer to two decimal places.)

5-3 REVIEW

Important Terms and Symbols in Chapter 5

exponential function *(p. 144)*   log x *(p. 149)*

e *(p. 145)*   natural logarithm *(p. 149)*

logarithmic function *(p. 148)*   ln x *(p. 149)*

common logarithm *(p. 149)*

Review Section

1. The domain of the exponential function $f(x) = b^x$ is __(a)__ and its range is __(b)__ .

> *Ans.* (a) all real numbers;   (b) all positive numbers

2. The domain of the logarithmic function $g(x) = \log_b x$ is __(a)__ and its range is __(b)__ .

> *Ans.* (a) all positive numbers;   (b) all real numbers

3. The graph in Fig. 5-9 is typical of a(n) (exponential)(logarithmic) function.

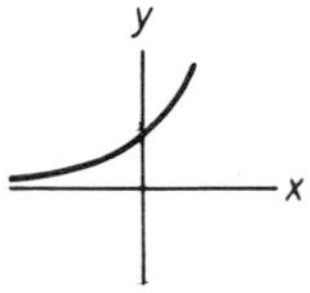

Fig. 5-9

> *Ans.* exponential

4. $10^{\log 4} =$ _____ .

> *Ans.* 4

5. If $\log_2 (x + 1) = \log_2 4$, then $x =$ _____ .

> *Ans.* 3

6. The expression $e^{2(\ln x)}$ is equal to the square of what quantity? _____.

> *Ans.* x

7. If $\log x = 1.2222$, then $\log \sqrt{x} =$ _____.

> *Ans.* .6111

8. $e^{\ln x} =$ _____.

> *Ans.* x

9. $\log 10^{5x} =$ _____.

> *Ans.* $5x$

10. $\ln \dfrac{x^2 y^3}{z^4} = $ ___(a)___ $\ln x + $ ___(b)___ $\ln y - $ ___(c)___ $\ln z.$

> *Ans.* (a) 2;   (b) 3;   (c) 4

11. The graphs of $y = e^{x+2}$ and $y = e^2 e^x$ (are)(are not) identical.

> *Ans.* are

Review Problems

1. Convert $3^4 = 81$ to logarithmic form.

2. Convert $\log_5 \frac{1}{5} = -1$ to exponential form.

In problems 3–10, find x.

3. $\log_5 125 = x$

4. $\log_x \frac{1}{8} = -3$

5. $\log x = -2$

6. $\ln \dfrac{1}{e} = x$

7. $\log_x (2x + 3) = 2$

8. $\log (4x + 1) = \log (x + 2)$

9. $e^{\ln (x+4)} = 7$

10. $\log x + \log 2 = 1$

11. Find the value of $\log_3 4$.

12. Find the value of $\log 2500$.

13. If $\log 3 = x$ and $\log 4 = y$, express $\log (16\sqrt{3})$ in terms of x and y.

14. Express

$$\log \frac{x^2 \sqrt{x + 1}}{\sqrt[3]{x^2 + 2}}$$

in terms of $\log x$, $\log (x + 1)$, and $\log (x^2 + 2)$.

15. Simplify $e^{\ln x} + \ln e^x + \ln 1$.

16. Simplify $\log 10^2 + \log 1000 - 5$.

17. If $\ln y = x^2 + 2$, find y.

18. Sketch the graphs of $y = 3^x$ and $y = \log_3 x$.

19. Due to ineffective advertising, the Kleer-Kut Razor Company finds its annual revenues have been cut sharply. Moreover, the annual revenue R at the end of t years of business satisfies the equation $R = 200,000e^{-.2t}$. Find the annual revenue at the end of 2 years; at the end of 3 years.

Chapter 6

Limits and Continuity

6-1 LIMITS

Our study of the calculus will begin in the next chapter. However, since the notion of a *limit* lies at the foundation of the calculus, we must not only develop some understanding of that concept, but also insight. We shall first attempt to cultivate a "feeling" for the concept of a limit by some examples.

Suppose we consider the function

$$f(x) = \frac{2x^2 - 5x + 2}{x - 2}.$$

Note that $f(x)$ is defined for all values of x except $x = 2$, for at that point the denominator is zero. Hence 2 is not in the domain of f. Let us examine the behavior of $f(x)$ for values of x "near" 2. Some values of $f(x)$ for x less than 2 and then greater than 2 are given in Table 6-1; in each case x takes on values closer and closer to 2.

TABLE 6-1

$x < 2$	$x > 2$
$f(1.7) = 2.4$	$f(2.3) = 3.6$
$f(1.8) = 2.6$	$f(2.2) = 3.4$
$f(1.9) = 2.8$	$f(2.1) = 3.2$
$f(1.99) = 2.98$	$f(2.01) = 3.02$
$f(1.999) = 2.998$	$f(2.001) = 3.002$

After inspection of both situations, it is apparent that as x takes on values closer and closer to 2, regardless of whether x approaches 2 *from the left* $(x < 2)$ or *from the right* $(x > 2)$, the corresponding values of $f(x)$ become closer and closer to 3. To express this, we say that 3 is the **limit** of f as x approaches 2. Symbolically we write

$$\lim_{x \to 2} \frac{2x^2 - 5x + 2}{x - 2} = 3.$$

Actually we can make the number $f(x)$ as close to 3 as we wish by taking x sufficiently close to 2.

We can reach the same conclusion by viewing f another way. Since $2x^2 - 5x + 2 = (2x - 1)(x - 2)$, then

$$f(x) = \frac{(2x - 1)(x - 2)}{(x - 2)}.$$

For $x \neq 2$, we can find another form for $f(x)$ by dividing both numerator and denominator by the common factor $(x - 2)$; thus

$$f(x) = 2x - 1, \quad x \neq 2.$$

By considering this simplified form we see that if x is sufficiently close to 2, the number $2x - 1$ will be as close to 3 as we please. Figure 6-1 illustrates this. Note that the point $(2, 3)$ is not part of the graph since 2 is not in the domain of f.

As another example, suppose we find the limit of $f(x) = x^2$ as x approaches -1. In Fig. 6-2 we see that as x approaches -1 both from the left and right, the corresponding functional values, x^2, approach 1. Thus,

$$\lim_{x \to -1} x^2 = 1.$$

Be aware that in determining this limit we are *not* at all concerned with what happens to the function when x *equals* -1.

Our results can be generalized to any function f. To say

$$\lim_{x \to a} f(x) = L$$

(read: "the limit of $f(x)$, as x approaches a, is L") means that $f(x)$ will be as close to the number L as we please for all x sufficiently close to the number a. Again, we are not concerned with what happens to $f(x)$ when $x = a$, but only with what happens to it when x is *close to a*. Indeed, in our first example the function $f(x) = (2x^2 - 5x + 2)/(x - 2)$ was not even defined for $x = a = 2$. We emphasize that a limit is independent of the way in which $x \to a$. The limit must be the same whether x approaches a from the left or from the right (for $x < a$ or $x > a$, respectively).

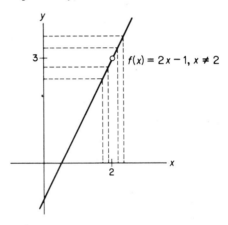

Fig. 6-1

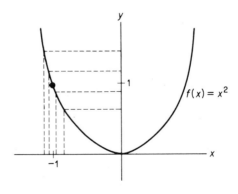

Fig. 6-2

We shall now state some properties of limits which should seem reasonable to you.

I.   If $f(x) = c$ is a constant function, then $\lim_{x \to a} c = c$.

II. $\lim_{x \to a} x^n = a^n$, for any positive integer n.

EXAMPLE 1

a. $\lim\limits_{x \to 2} 7 = 7; \quad \lim\limits_{x \to -5} 7 = 7.$

b. $\lim\limits_{x \to 6} x^2 = 6^2 = 36.$

c. $\lim\limits_{t \to -2} t^4 = (-2)^4 = 16.$

If $\lim\limits_{x \to a} f(x) = L_1$ and $\lim\limits_{x \to a} g(x) = L_2$ where L_1 and L_2 are real numbers, then

III. $\lim\limits_{x \to a} [f(x) \pm g(x)] = \lim\limits_{x \to a} f(x) \pm \lim\limits_{x \to a} g(x) = L_1 \pm L_2.$

       This property can be extended to the limit of a finite number of sums and differences.

IV. $\lim\limits_{x \to a} [f(x) \cdot g(x)] = \lim\limits_{x \to a} f(x) \cdot \lim\limits_{x \to a} g(x) = L_1 \cdot L_2.$

V. $\lim\limits_{x \to a} [cf(x)] = c \cdot \lim\limits_{x \to a} f(x) = cL_1,$ where c is a constant.

EXAMPLE 2

a. $\begin{aligned}\lim\limits_{x \to 2} (x^2 + x) &= \lim\limits_{x \to 2} x^2 + \lim\limits_{x \to 2} x \\ &= 2^2 + 2 = 6.\end{aligned}$

b. $\begin{aligned}\lim\limits_{x \to 3} (x^3 - x) &= \lim\limits_{x \to 3} x^3 - \lim\limits_{x \to 3} x \\ &= 3^3 - 3 = 24.\end{aligned}$

c. $\begin{aligned}\lim\limits_{x \to -1} (x^3 - x + 1) &= \lim\limits_{x \to -1} x^3 - \lim\limits_{x \to -1} x + \lim\limits_{x \to -1} 1 \\ &= (-1)^3 - (-1) + 1 \\ &= 1.\end{aligned}$

d. $\begin{aligned}\lim\limits_{x \to 2} [(x + 1)(x - 3)] &= \lim\limits_{x \to 2} (x + 1) \cdot \lim\limits_{x \to 2} (x - 3) \\ &= [\lim\limits_{x \to 2} x + \lim\limits_{x \to 2} 1] \cdot [\lim\limits_{x \to 2} x - \lim\limits_{x \to 2} 3] \\ &= [2 + 1] \cdot [2 - 3] \\ &= -3.\end{aligned}$

e. $\begin{aligned}\lim\limits_{x \to -2} 3x^3 &= 3 \lim\limits_{x \to -2} x^3 \\ &= 3(-2)^3 = -24.\end{aligned}$

EXAMPLE 3

Let $f(x) = c_0 x^n + c_1 x^{n-1} + \ldots + c_{n-1} x + c_n$ define a polynomial function f. Then

$$\lim_{x \to a} f(x) = \lim_{x \to a} (c_0 x^n + c_1 x^{n-1} + \ldots + c_{n-1} x + c_n)$$

$$= c_0 \cdot \lim_{x \to a} x^n + c_1 \cdot \lim_{x \to a} x^{n-1} + \ldots + c_{n-1} \cdot \lim_{x \to a} x + \lim_{x \to a} c_n$$

$$= c_0 a^n + c_1 a^{n-1} + \ldots + c_{n-1} a + c_n = f(a).$$

Thus, **if f is a polynomial function, then**

$$\lim_{x \to a} f(x) = f(a).$$

This result allows us to find many limits by just substituting a for x. For example,

$$\lim_{x \to -3} (x^3 + 4x^2 - 7) = (-3)^3 + 4(-3)^2 - 7 = 2,$$

$$\lim_{h \to 3} [2(h - 1)] = 2 \cdot \lim_{h \to 3} (h - 1) = 2(3 - 1) = 4.$$

If $\lim_{x \to a} f(x) = L_1$ and $\lim_{x \to a} g(x) = L_2$ where L_1 and L_2 are real numbers, then

VI. $\displaystyle \lim_{x \to a} \frac{f(x)}{g(x)} = \frac{\lim_{x \to a} f(x)}{\lim_{x \to a} g(x)} = \frac{L_1}{L_2}$ **providing $L_2 \neq 0$.**

VII. $\displaystyle \lim_{x \to a} \sqrt[n]{f(x)} = \sqrt[n]{\lim_{x \to a} f(x)} = \sqrt[n]{L_1}$ **if $\sqrt[n]{L_1}$ is defined.**

EXAMPLE 4

a. $\displaystyle \lim_{x \to 1} \frac{2x^2 + x - 3}{x^3 + 4} = \frac{\lim_{x \to 1} (2x^2 + x - 3)}{\lim_{x \to 1} (x^3 + 4)} = \frac{0}{5} = 0.$

b. $\displaystyle \lim_{t \to 4} \sqrt{t^2 + 1} = \sqrt{\lim_{t \to 4} (t^2 + 1)} = \sqrt{17}.$

c. $\displaystyle \lim_{x \to 2} \frac{x^2 + 1}{4x - 1} = \frac{\lim_{x \to 2} (x^2 + 1)}{\lim_{x \to 2} (4x - 1)} = \frac{5}{7}.$

d. $\displaystyle \lim_{x \to 3} \sqrt[3]{x^2 + 7} = \sqrt[3]{\lim_{x \to 3} (x^2 + 7)} = \sqrt[3]{16} = 2\sqrt[3]{2}.$

EXAMPLE 5

a. *Find* $\displaystyle \lim_{h \to 0} \frac{(2 + h)^2 - 4}{h}.$

As $h \to 0$, both numerator and denominator approach zero. Thus we cannot use property VI. However, since what happens when h equals zero is of no concern, we can assume $h \neq 0$. But for $h \neq 0$ we can simplify:

$$\frac{(2 + h)^2 - 4}{h} = \frac{4 + 4h + h^2 - 4}{h} = \frac{4h + h^2}{h} = \frac{h(4 + h)}{h} = 4 + h.$$

Thus,

$$\lim_{h \to 0} \frac{(2 + h)^2 - 4}{h} = \lim_{h \to 0} (4 + h) = 4.$$

b. *Find* $\lim\limits_{x \to -1} \dfrac{x^2 - 1}{x + 1}$.

Since both numerator and denominator approach 0 as $x \to -1$, we try to express $(x^2 - 1)/(x + 1)$ in a different form.

$$\lim_{x \to -1} \frac{x^2 - 1}{x + 1} = \lim_{x \to -1} \frac{(x - 1)(x + 1)}{x + 1} = \lim_{x \to -1} (x - 1) = -2.$$

EXERCISE 6-1

In problems 1–36, find the limits.

1. $\lim\limits_{x \to 3} 14$

2. $\lim\limits_{x \to 0} 4x$

3. $\lim\limits_{x \to 6} (x - 17)$

4. $\lim\limits_{s \to 1} 2$

5. $\lim\limits_{t \to -2} (t^2 + 1)$

6. $\lim\limits_{t \to 1/2} (3t - 5)$

7. $\lim\limits_{x \to 0.3} (3 - 2x^2)$

8. $\lim\limits_{x \to -3} (x^3 - 4)$

9. $\lim\limits_{h \to 6} (h^2 - 5h - 6)$

10. $\lim\limits_{x \to -2} (x^2 - 2x + 1)$

11. $\lim\limits_{x \to -1} (x^3 - 3x^2 - 2x + 1)$

12. $\lim\limits_{r \to 9} \dfrac{4r - 3}{11}$

13. $\lim\limits_{t \to -3} \dfrac{t - 2}{t + 5}$

14. $\lim\limits_{x \to -6} \dfrac{x^2 + 6}{x - 6}$

15. $\lim\limits_{h \to 0} \dfrac{h}{h^2 - 7h + 1}$

16. $\lim\limits_{h \to 0} \dfrac{h^2 - 2h - 4}{h^3 - 1}$

17. $\lim\limits_{p \to 4} \sqrt{p^2 + p + 5}$

18. $\lim\limits_{y \to 9} \sqrt{y + 3}$

19. $\lim\limits_{x \to -2} \sqrt{\dfrac{4x - 1}{x + 1}}$

20. $\lim\limits_{x \to -1} \sqrt[3]{x^2}$

21. $\displaystyle\lim_{x \to 2} \frac{(x + 3)\sqrt{x^2 - 1}}{(x - 4)(x + 1)}$

22. $\displaystyle\lim_{t \to 3} \sqrt{\frac{2t + 3}{3t - 5}}$

23. $\displaystyle\lim_{t \to 1} \frac{t^2}{\sqrt[3]{(t^2 - 2)^2}}$

24. $\displaystyle\lim_{t \to 2} \frac{(t + 3)(t + 7)}{(t - 1)(t + 4)}$

25. $\displaystyle\lim_{x \to -1} \frac{x^2 + 2x + 1}{x + 1}$

26. $\displaystyle\lim_{t \to 1} \frac{t^2 - 1}{t - 1}$

27. $\displaystyle\lim_{x \to 0} \frac{(x + 2)^2 - 4}{x}$

28. $\displaystyle\lim_{x \to -4} \frac{x^2 + 2x - 8}{x^2 + 5x + 4}$

29. $\displaystyle\lim_{x \to e} \frac{2x^2 - 2xe}{x - e}$

30. $\displaystyle\lim_{x \to 0} \frac{x^2 - 2x}{x}$

31. $\displaystyle\lim_{h \to 0} \frac{(2 + h)^2 - 2^2}{h}$

32. $\displaystyle\lim_{x \to 2} \frac{x^2 - 2x}{x - 2}$

33. $\displaystyle\lim_{x \to 2} \frac{3x^2 - x - 10}{x^2 + 5x - 14}$

34. $\displaystyle\lim_{x \to a} \frac{x^4 - a^4}{x^2 - a^2}$

35. $\displaystyle\lim_{x \to 0} \frac{x}{2x - \dfrac{7}{x}}$

36. $\displaystyle\lim_{x \to 3} \frac{x - 3}{\dfrac{1}{x - 3}}$

37. Find $\displaystyle\lim_{h \to 0} \frac{(x + h)^2 - x^2}{h}$ by treating x as a constant.

38. Find $\displaystyle\lim_{h \to 0} \frac{2(x + h)^2 + 5(x + h) - 2x^2 - 5x}{h}$ by treating x as a constant.

39. If $f(x) = x + 5$, show that $\displaystyle\lim_{h \to 0} \frac{f(x + h) - f(x)}{h} = 1$. (See problem 37.)

40. If $f(x) = x^2$, show that $\displaystyle\lim_{h \to 0} \frac{f(x + h) - f(x)}{h} = 2x$. (See problem 37.)

6-2   LIMITS, CONTINUED

Let us now consider

$$\lim_{x \to 0} \frac{|x|}{x}.$$

If $x > 0$, then $|x| = x$ and so $|x|/x = x/x = 1$. If $x < 0$, then $|x| = -x$ and so $|x|/x = (-x)/x = -1$. If $x = 0$, then $|x|/x$ is not defined. Using this information, we easily sketch the graph of $f(x) = |x|/x$ in Fig. 6-3. We see that as x approaches 0 *from the right*, $f(x)$ approaches 1. We write this as

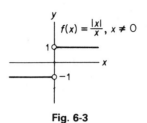

Fig. 6-3

$$\lim_{x \to 0^+} \frac{|x|}{x} = 1.$$

On the other hand, as x approaches 0 *from the left*, $f(x)$ approaches -1 and we write

$$\lim_{x \to 0^-} \frac{|x|}{x} = -1.$$

Limits like these are called *one-sided limits*. From the last section we know that the limit of a function as $x \to a$ is independent of the way x approaches a. Thus the limit will exist if and only if both one-sided limits exist and are equal. We therefore conclude that

$$\lim_{x \to 0} \frac{|x|}{x} \text{ does not exist.}$$

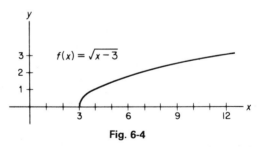

Fig. 6-4

As another example, consider $f(x) = \sqrt{x - 3}$ as x approaches 3 (see Fig. 6-4). Since f is defined only when $x \geq 3$, we speak of the limit as x approaches 3 from the right. From the diagram we conclude that

$$\lim_{x \to 3^+} \sqrt{x - 3} = 0.$$

Now let us look at $y = f(x) = 1/x^2$ near $x = 0$. Figure 6-5 shows a table of values of $f(x)$ for x near 0, together with the graph of the function. Observe that as $x \to 0$, both from the left and from the right, $f(x)$ increases without bound. Hence no limit exists at 0. We say that as $x \to 0$, $f(x)$ becomes positively infinite and symbolically we write

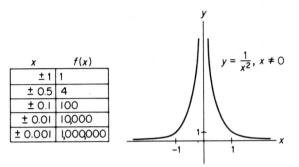

x	f(x)
± 1	1
± 0.5	4
± 0.1	100
± 0.01	10,000
± 0.001	1,000,000

Fig. 6-5

$$\lim_{x \to 0} \frac{1}{x^2} = \infty.$$

PITFALL.   *Keep in mind that the use of the limit notation in this situation does not mean that the limit exists. On the contrary, the symbolism here (∞) is a way of saying specifically that there is no limit.*

Now let us look at the graph of $y = f(x) = \dfrac{1}{x}$ for $x \neq 0$ (see Fig. 6-6).

As x approaches 0 from the right, $\dfrac{1}{x}$ becomes positively infinite; as x approaches 0 from the left, $\dfrac{1}{x}$ becomes negatively infinite. Symbolically we write

$$\lim_{x \to 0^+} \frac{1}{x} = \infty \quad \text{and} \quad \lim_{x \to 0^-} \frac{1}{x} = -\infty.$$

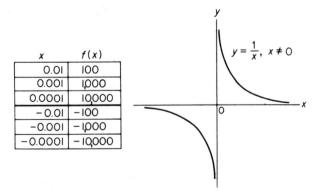

x	f(x)
0.01	100
0.001	1,000
0.0001	10,000
− 0.01	−100
−0.001	−1,000
−0.0001	−10,000

Fig. 6-6

Now let us examine this function as x becomes infinite in both a positive and negative sense. From Table 6-2 we can see that as x increases without bound through positive values, the values of $f(x)$ approach 0. Likewise, as x decreases without bound through negative values, the values of $f(x)$ also approach 0.

TABLE 6-2

x	$f(x)$
1,000	.001
10,000	.0001
100,000	.00001
1,000,000	.000001

x	$f(x)$
−1,000	−.001
−10,000	−.0001
−100,000	−.00001
−1,000,000	−.000001

Symbolically we write

$$\lim_{x \to \infty} \frac{1}{x} = 0 \quad \text{and} \quad \lim_{x \to -\infty} \frac{1}{x} = 0.$$

Let us now turn to the limit of a quotient of two polynomials where the variable becomes infinite.

For example, consider

$$\lim_{x \to \infty} \frac{8x^2 + 2x + 3}{2x^3 + 3x - 1}.$$

It is clear that as $x \to \infty$, both numerator and denominator become infinite. However, the form of the quotient can be changed so that we can draw a conclusion as to whether or not a limit exists. Since $x \to \infty$, we are concerned only with those values of x which are very large. Thus we can assume $x \neq 0$. A frequently used "gimmick" in a case like this is to divide both the numerator and denominator by the largest power of x which occurs in either the numerator or demoninator. In our example it is x^3. Thus

$$\lim_{x \to \infty} \frac{8x^2 + 2x + 3}{2x^3 + 3x - 1} = \lim_{x \to \infty} \frac{\dfrac{8x^2 + 2x + 3}{x^3}}{\dfrac{2x^3 + 3x - 1}{x^3}}$$

$$= \lim_{x \to \infty} \frac{\dfrac{8}{x} + \dfrac{2}{x^2} + \dfrac{3}{x^3}}{2 + \dfrac{3}{x^2} - \dfrac{1}{x^3}}$$

$$= \frac{8 \cdot \lim\limits_{x \to \infty} \dfrac{1}{x} + 2 \cdot \lim\limits_{x \to \infty} \dfrac{1}{x^2} + 3 \cdot \lim\limits_{x \to \infty} \dfrac{1}{x^3}}{\lim\limits_{x \to \infty} 2 + 3 \cdot \lim\limits_{x \to \infty} \dfrac{1}{x^2} - \lim\limits_{x \to \infty} \dfrac{1}{x^3}}.$$

As $x \to \infty$, $\dfrac{1}{x^2} = \dfrac{1}{x} \cdot \dfrac{1}{x}$ approaches $0 \cdot 0 = 0$. In fact,

$$\lim_{x \to \infty} \frac{1}{x^p} = 0 \qquad \text{for } p > 0.$$

Thus,

$$\lim_{x \to \infty} \frac{8x^2 + 2x + 3}{2x^3 + 3x - 1} = \frac{8(0) + 2(0) + 3(0)}{2 + 3(0) - 0} = \frac{0}{2} = 0.$$

EXAMPLE 6

a. $\lim\limits_{x \to \infty} \dfrac{2x + 5}{3x + 2} = \lim\limits_{x \to \infty} \dfrac{\dfrac{2x + 5}{x}}{\dfrac{3x + 2}{x}} = \lim\limits_{x \to \infty} \dfrac{2 + \dfrac{5}{x}}{3 + \dfrac{2}{x}} = \dfrac{2 + 0}{3 + 0} = \dfrac{2}{3}.$

b. *Find* $\lim\limits_{x \to 0} \dfrac{10x^2}{x}$.

As $x \to 0$, both numerator and denominator approach 0. The result is $0/0$, which is not defined. Since $x \neq 0$ for $x \to 0$,

$$\lim_{x \to 0} \frac{10x^2}{x} = \lim_{x \to 0} 10x = 0.$$

c. *Find* $\lim\limits_{x \to -\infty} \dfrac{10x^2}{x}$.

Dividing both numerator and denominator by x, we have

$$\lim_{x \to -\infty} 10x.$$

As $x \to -\infty$, the factor 10 remains the same and the factor x becomes negatively infinite. This results in the product's becoming negatively infinite. Thus,

$$\lim_{x \to -\infty} \frac{10x^2}{x} = \lim_{x \to -\infty} 10x = -\infty$$

and no limit exists.

d. $\lim\limits_{t \to 2} \dfrac{t - 2}{t^2 - 4} = \lim\limits_{t \to 2} \dfrac{t - 2}{(t - 2)(t + 2)} = \lim\limits_{t \to 2} \dfrac{1}{t + 2} = \dfrac{1}{4}.$

e. $\lim\limits_{x \to 2} \dfrac{x + 2}{x^2 - 4} = \lim\limits_{x \to 2} \dfrac{1}{x - 2}$ does not exist because $\lim\limits_{x \to 2^+} \dfrac{1}{x - 2} = \infty$ and $\lim\limits_{x \to 2^-} \dfrac{1}{x - 2} = -\infty.$

We conclude this section with a note concerning a most important limit, namely

$$\lim_{x \to 0} (1 + x)^{1/x}.$$

TABLE 6-3

x	$(1 + x)^{1/x}$	x	$(1 + x)^{1/x}$
.5	2.2500	−.5	4.0000
.1	2.5937	−.1	2.8680
.01	2.7048	−.01	2.7320
.001	2.7169	−.001	2.7195

Table 6-3 shows some typical values of $(1 + x)^{1/x}$ for values of x near 0. It can be shown that the limit does indeed exist. It is approximately 2.7183 and is denoted by the letter e. This, you recall, is the base of the system of natural logarithms. The limit

$$\lim_{x \to 0} (1 + x)^{1/x} = e$$

can actually be considered the definition of e, and it will be met again in our study of calculus.

EXERCISE 6-2

In each of problems 1–44, find the limit (if it exists).

1. $\lim\limits_{x \to \infty} 3$

2. $\lim\limits_{x \to -\infty} 5x$

3. $\lim\limits_{x \to 3^+} (x - 2)$

4. $\lim\limits_{x \to -1^-} (1 - x^2)$

5. $\lim\limits_{x \to 0^-} \dfrac{6x}{x^4}$

6. $\lim\limits_{x \to 0} \dfrac{5}{x - 1}$

7. $\lim\limits_{x \to -\infty} x^2$

8. $\lim\limits_{t \to \infty} (t - 1)^3$

9. $\lim\limits_{h \to 0^+} \sqrt{h}$

10. $\lim\limits_{h \to 5^-} \sqrt{5 - h}$

11. $\lim\limits_{x \to 5} \dfrac{3}{x - 5}$

12. $\lim\limits_{x \to 1/2} \dfrac{1}{2x - 1}$

13. $\lim\limits_{x\to1^+} (4\sqrt{x-1})$

14. $\lim\limits_{x\to2^+} (x\sqrt{x^2-4})$

15. $\lim\limits_{x\to\infty} \dfrac{x+2}{x+3}$

16. $\lim\limits_{x\to\infty} \dfrac{2x-4}{3-2x}$

17. $\lim\limits_{x\to-\infty} \dfrac{x^2-1}{x^3+4x-3}$

18. $\lim\limits_{r\to\infty} \dfrac{r^3}{r^2-1}$

19. $\lim\limits_{t\to\infty} \dfrac{5t^2+2t+1}{4t+7}$

20. $\lim\limits_{x\to-\infty} \dfrac{2x}{3x^6-x+4}$

21. $\lim\limits_{x\to\infty} \dfrac{3-4x-2x^3}{5x^3-8x+1}$

22. $\lim\limits_{x\to\infty} \dfrac{7-2x-x^4}{9-3x^4+2x^2}$

23. $\lim\limits_{x\to3^-} \dfrac{x+3}{x^2-9}$

24. $\lim\limits_{x\to-2^+} \dfrac{2x}{4-x^2}$

25. $\lim\limits_{w\to\infty} \dfrac{2w^2-3w+4}{5w^2+7w-1}$

26. $\lim\limits_{x\to\infty} \dfrac{4-3x^3}{x^3-1}$

27. $\lim\limits_{x\to-5} \dfrac{2x^2+9x-5}{x^2+5x}$

28. $\lim\limits_{t\to2} \dfrac{t^2+2t-8}{2t^2-5t+2}$

29. $\lim\limits_{x\to1} \dfrac{x^2-3x+1}{x^2+1}$

30. $\lim\limits_{x\to-1} \dfrac{3x^3-x^2}{2x+1}$

31. $\lim\limits_{x\to1^+} \left[1+\dfrac{1}{x-1}\right]$

32. $\lim\limits_{x\to0} f(x)$ where

$$f(x) = \begin{cases} x \text{ if } x<0 \\ -x \text{ if } x>0 \end{cases}$$

33. $\lim\limits_{x\to0^+} \dfrac{2}{x+x^2}$

34. $\lim\limits_{x\to-\infty} \dfrac{x^3+2x^2+1}{x^3-4}$

35. $\lim\limits_{x\to\infty} \dfrac{1}{x+\dfrac{1}{x}}$

36. $\lim\limits_{x\to\infty} \left(x+\dfrac{1}{x}\right)$

37. $\lim\limits_{x\to1} x(x-1)^{-1}$

38. $\lim\limits_{x\to0^-} 2^{1/2}$

39. $\lim\limits_{x\to0^+} \left(-\dfrac{3}{x}\right)$

40. $\lim\limits_{x\to0} \left(-\dfrac{3}{x}\right)$

41. $\lim\limits_{x\to0} |x|$

42. $\lim\limits_{x\to0} \left|\dfrac{1}{x}\right|$

43. $\lim\limits_{x\to-\infty} \dfrac{x+1}{x}$

44. $\lim\limits_{x\to\infty} \dfrac{x^3}{\sqrt{1+x^6}}$

45. If c is the total cost in dollars to produce x units of a product, then the average cost per unit $\bar{c}$ for an output of x units is given by $\bar{c} = c/x$. Thus, if the total cost equation is $c = 5000 + 6x$, then $\bar{c} = (5000/x) + 6$. For example, for an output of 5 units the total cost would be \$5030, and the average cost per unit at this level of production would be \$1006. By finding $\lim\limits_{x \to \infty} \bar{c}$, show that the average cost approaches a level of stability if the producer continually increases output. What is the limiting value of the average cost? Sketch the graph of the average cost function.

46. Repeat Problem 45 given that fixed cost is \$12,000 and the variable cost is given by the function $c_v = 7x$.

In problems 47–50, find $\lim\limits_{h \to 0} \dfrac{f(x + h) - f(x)}{h}$ by treating x as a constant.

47. $f(x) = 2x + 3$ **48.** $f(x) = 4 - x$

49. $f(x) = x^2 + x + 1$ **50.** $f(x) = x^2 - 3$

6-3   CONTINUITY

Let us consider the functions

$$f(x) = x \quad \text{and} \quad g(x) = \begin{cases} x \text{ if } x \neq 1 \\ 2 \text{ if } x = 1. \end{cases}$$

Their graphs appear in Fig. 6-7 and Fig. 6-8, respectively. The significant difference between the graphs is that there is a "break" in the graph of g when $x = 1$, while there is *no* "break" at all in the graph of f. Stated another way, if we were to trace both graphs with a pencil, we would have to lift the pencil on the graph of g when $x = 1$, but we would not have to lift it on the graph of f. These situations can be expressed by limits. As x approaches 1,

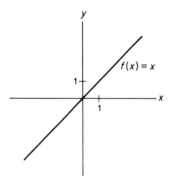

Fig. 6-7

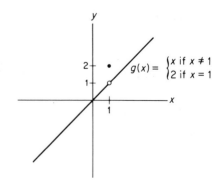

Fig. 6-8

$$\lim_{x \to 1} f(x) = 1 = f(1)$$

while

$$\lim_{x \to 1} g(x) = 1 \neq g(1) = 2.$$

The limit of f as $x \to 1$ is the same as $f(1)$, but the limit of g as $x \to 1$ is *not* the same as $g(1)$. For these reasons we say f is *continuous* at $x = 1$ and g is *discontinuous* at $x = 1$.

DEFINITION. *A function f is **continuous** at $x = a$ if and only if the following three conditions are met:*

    (1) $f(x)$ *is defined at $x = a$.*

    (2) $\lim_{x \to a} f(x)$ *exists.*

    (3) $\lim_{x \to a} f(x) = f(a)$.

DEFINITION. *A function is **discontinuous** at $x = a$ if and only if it is not continuous at $x = a$.*

Continuous functions have many useful properties that discontinuous functions do not have. These properties are not only important from a mathematical point of view, but also from the point of view of economics. We shall say more about this in Sec. 6-5.

EXAMPLE 7

   a. *Show that $f(x) = 5$ is continuous at $x = 7$.*

     We must verify that three conditions are met. First, f is indeed defined at $x = 7$. Second,

$$\lim_{x \to 7} f(x) = \lim_{x \to 7} 5 = 5.$$

     Thus f has a limit as $x \to 7$. Third,

$$\lim_{x \to 7} f(x) = 5 = f(7).$$

     Therefore $f(x) = 5$ is continuous at $x = 7$.

   b. *Show that $g(x) = x^2 - 3$ is continuous at $x = -4$.*

     The function g is defined at $x = -4$; $g(-4) = 13$. Also,

$$\lim_{x \to -4} g(x) = \lim_{x \to -4} (x^2 - 3) = 13 = g(-4).$$

     Therefore, $g(x) = x^2 - 3$ is continuous at $x = -4$.

   c. *Show that $f(x) = \dfrac{7}{x^2}$ is continuous at $x = -2$.*

$$f(-2) = \tfrac{7}{4}$$

$$\lim_{x \to -2} \frac{7}{x^2} = \frac{7}{4}.$$

Since the limit as $x \to -2$ equals $f(-2)$, the function is continuous at $x = -2$.

d. *Show that* $g(s) = \sqrt{s - 3}$ *is continuous at* $s = 12$.

$$g(12) = \sqrt{9} = 3$$

$$\lim_{s \to 12} \sqrt{s - 3} = \sqrt{9} = 3.$$

Hence g is continuous at $s = 12$.

We say that a function is *continuous on an interval* if it is continuous at each point there. Thus, over an interval a continuous function has a graph that is connected. For example, $f(x) = x^2$ is continuous on $[2, 5]$. In fact, in Example 3 we showed that $\lim_{x \to a} f(x) = f(a)$ for *any* polynomial function f. Thus, **a polynomial function is continuous at every point** and hence on every interval. We say that polynomial functions are continuous everywhere, or, more simply, that they are continuous.

EXAMPLE 8

The functions $f(x) = 7$ and $g(x) = x^3 - 9x + 3$ are polynomial functions. Therefore, they are continuous. In particular, they are continuous at $x = 3$.

If a function is not defined at a, it is automatically discontinuous there. If it *is* defined at a, then it is discontinuous at a if

(1) it has no limit as $x \to a$,

or

(2) as $x \to a$ it has a limit that is different from $f(a)$.

In Fig. 6-9 we can find points of discontinuity by inspection.

EXAMPLE 9

a. Let $f(x) = \dfrac{1}{x}$ (Fig. 6-10). Since f is not defined at $x = 0$, it is discontinuous there.

Moreover, $\lim_{x \to 0^+} f(x) = \infty$ and $\lim_{x \to 0^-} f(x) = -\infty$. A function is said to have an **infinite discontinuity** at $x = a$ when at least one of the one-sided limits is either ∞ or $-\infty$ as $x \to a$. Hence f has an *infinite discontinuity* at $x = 0$.

b. Let $f(x) = \begin{cases} 1 \text{ if } x > 0 \\ 0 \text{ if } x = 0 \\ -1 \text{ if } x < 0 \end{cases}$ (see Fig. 6-11). Since $\lim_{x \to 0} f(x)$ does not exist, f is discontinuous

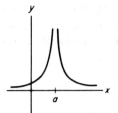
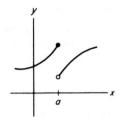
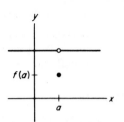

Not defined at a Defined at a Defined at a
                             but no limit as   and limit as
                             $x \to a$ $x \to a$, but limit
                                                      is not $f(a)$

Discontinuities at a

Fig. 6-9

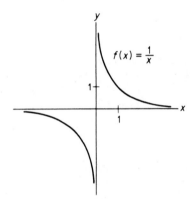

$f(x) = \dfrac{1}{x}$

Fig. 6-10

$f(x) = \begin{cases} 1 \text{ if } x > 0 \\ 0 \text{ if } x = 0 \\ -1 \text{ if } x < 0 \end{cases}$

Fig. 6-11

at $x = 0$. However, note that $\lim_{x \to 0^+} f(x) = 1$ and $\lim_{x \to 0^-} f(x) = -1$; that is, both of the one-sided limits exist but are not equal. In this case f is said to have a *jump discontinuity* at $x = 0$. More precisely, a function f has a **jump discontinuity** at $x = a$ if and only if both $\lim_{x \to a^+} f(x)$ and $\lim_{x \to a^-} f(x)$ exist but are *not* equal.

EXAMPLE 10

Find any points of discontinuity for each of the following.

a. $f(x) = \dfrac{x^4 - 3x^3 + 2x - 1}{x^2 - 4}$

The denominator is zero when $x = \pm 2$. Hence f is not defined at ± 2 and is therefore discontinuous at these points. Otherwise the function is "well-behaved." In fact, **any quotient of polynomials is discontinuous at points where the denominator is 0, and is continuous elsewhere.**

b. $g(x) = \begin{cases} x + 6, & \text{if } x \ge 3 \\ x^2, & \text{if } x < 3 \end{cases}$

The only possible trouble may occur when $x = 3$. We know $g(3) = 3 + 6 = 9$. As $x \to 3^+$, then $g(x) \to 3 + 6 = 9$. As $x \to 3^-$, then $g(x) \to 3^2 = 9$. Thus the function is continuous at $x = 3$ as well as at all other x. We can reach the same conclusion by inspecting the graph of g (Fig. 6–12).

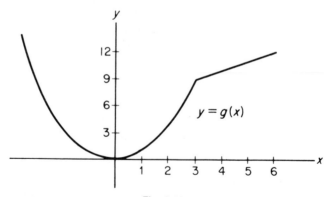

Fig. 6-12

c. $f(x) = \begin{cases} x + 2, & \text{if } x > 2 \\ x^2, & \text{if } x < 2 \end{cases}$

Since f is not defined at $x = 2$, it is discontinuous there. It is continuous for all other x.

EXAMPLE 11

In Table 6-4 data are listed relative to redemption values of a fifty dollar savings bond for the first six successive periods after the date of issue. These data are displayed

TABLE 6-4

NUMBER OF YEARS AFTER ISSUE DATE		REDEMPTION VALUE
(greater than)	— (not more than)	
0	— $\frac{1}{2}$	$37.50
$\frac{1}{2}$	— 1	38.10
1	— $1\frac{1}{2}$	39.02
$1\frac{1}{2}$	— 2	39.90
2	— $2\frac{1}{2}$	40.80
$2\frac{1}{2}$	— 3	41.76

by the graph of the function $y = f(x)$ where y is the redemption value x years after the date of issue (Fig. 6-13). Obviously f has jump discontinuities when $x = \frac{1}{2}, 1, \frac{3}{2}, 2,$ and $\frac{5}{2}$ and is constant for values of x between successive discontinuities. Such a function is called a *step function* because of the appearance of its graph.

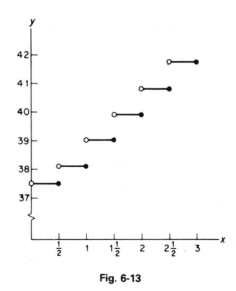

Fig. 6-13

There is another way to express continuity besides that given in the definition. If we take the statement

$$\lim_{x \to a} f(x) = f(a)$$

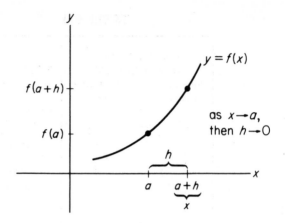

Fig. 6-14

and replace x by $a + h$, then as $x \to a$ we have $h \to 0$ (Fig. 6-14). Thus the statement

$$\lim_{h \to 0} f(a + h) = f(a)$$

defines continuity at a.

EXERCISE 6-3

In problems 1-10, use the definition of continuity to show that the given function is continuous at the indicated point.

1. $f(x) = x^3 - 5x,\ x = 2$

2. $f(x) = \dfrac{x - 3}{9x},\ x = -3$

3. $f(x) = \dfrac{1}{x},\ x = 1$

4. $f(x) = x^2 - 3x + 4,\ x = 0$

5. $g(x) = \sqrt{2 - 3x},\ x = 0$

6. $f(x) = \frac{1}{8},\ x = 2$

7. $h(x) = \dfrac{x - 4}{x + 4},\ x = 4$

8. $f(x) = \sqrt[3]{x},\ x = -1$

9. $f(x) = \begin{cases} x^2, & \text{if } x \geq 0 \\ x, & \text{if } x < 0 \end{cases},\ x = 0$

10. $g(x) = \begin{cases} \dfrac{2}{x}, & \text{if } x \geq 2 \\ 1, & \text{if } x < 2 \end{cases},\ x = 0$

In problems 11-16, determine whether the function is continuous at the given points.

11. $f(x) = \dfrac{x + 4}{x - 2};\ -2, 0$

12. $f(x) = \dfrac{x^2 - 4x + 4}{6};\ 2, -2$

13. $g(x) = \dfrac{x-3}{x^2-9}; 3, -3$

14. $h(x) = \dfrac{3}{x^2+4}; 2, -2$

15. $F(x) = \begin{cases} x+2, & \text{if } x \geq 2 \\ x^2, & \text{if } x < 2 \end{cases}; 2, 0$

16. $f(x) = \begin{cases} \dfrac{1}{x}, & \text{if } x \neq 0 \\ 0, & \text{if } x = 0 \end{cases}; 0, -1$

In problems 17–20, show that the functions are continuous everywhere.

17. $f(x) = 2x^2 - 3$

18. $f(x) = \dfrac{x+2}{5}$

19. $f(x) = \dfrac{x-1}{x^2+4}$

20. $f(x) = x(1-x)$

In problems 21–38, find all points of discontinuity.

21. $f(x) = 3x^2 - 3$

22. $h(x) = x - 2$

23. $f(x) = \dfrac{3}{x-4}$

24. $f(x) = \dfrac{x^2+3x-4}{x+4}$

25. $g(x) = |x|$

26. $f(x) = \begin{cases} 5, & \text{if } x \geq 3 \\ 2x-1, & \text{if } x < 3 \end{cases}$

27. $f(x) = \dfrac{x^2+6x+9}{x^2+2x-15}$

28. $g(x) = \dfrac{x-3}{x^2+x}$

29. $h(x) = \dfrac{x-7}{x^3-x}$

30. $f(x) = \dfrac{|x|}{x}$

31. $p(x) = \dfrac{x}{x^2+1}$

32. $f(x) = \dfrac{3}{4x - \dfrac{1}{x}}$

33. $f(x) = \begin{cases} x^2, & \text{if } x > 2 \\ x-1, & \text{if } x < 2 \end{cases}$

34. $f(x) = \begin{cases} \dfrac{1}{x}, & \text{if } x \neq 3 \\ 5, & \text{if } x = 3 \end{cases}$

35. $f(x) = \begin{cases} \dfrac{1}{x-3}, & \text{if } x > 4 \\ x, & \text{if } x < 4 \end{cases}$

36. $f(x) = \begin{cases} 10x-3, & \text{if } x \geq 1 \\ \dfrac{1}{x+1}, & \text{if } x < 1 \end{cases}$

37. $f(x) = \begin{cases} \dfrac{-3}{x-2}, & \text{if } x > 0 \\ 4-x, & \text{if } x \leq 0 \end{cases}$

38. $f(x) = \dfrac{5x+2}{3} - \dfrac{7}{x}$

39. Suppose the long distance rate for a telephone call from Hazleton, Pa. to Washington, D.C. is \$0.85 for the first three minutes and \$0.25 for each additional minute or fraction thereof. If $y = f(t)$ is a function which indicates the total charge y for a call of t minutes' duration, sketch the graph of f for $0 < t \le 6$.

40. The *greatest integer function,* $f(x) = [x]$, is defined as the greatest integer less than or equal to x, where x is any real number. For example, $[3] = 3$, $[1.999] = 1$, $[\frac{1}{4}] = 0$, and $[-4.5] = -5$. Sketch the graph of this function for $-4 \le x \le 4$.

41. Sketch the graph of

$$y = f(x) = \begin{cases} -100x + 600, & \text{if } 0 \le x \le 5 \\ -100x + 1100, & \text{if } 5 < x \le 10 \\ -100x + 1600, & \text{if } 10 < x \le 15. \end{cases}$$

A function such as this might describe the inventory y of a company at time x.

42. Sketch the "post-office function"

$$c = f(x) = \begin{cases} 10, & \text{if } 0 < x \le 1 \\ 20, & \text{if } 1 < x \le 2 \\ 30, & \text{if } 2 < x \le 3 \\ & \text{etc.} \end{cases}$$

for $0 < x \le 6$. Here c could be the cost of sending a parcel of weight x (ounces). Where do discontinuities occur?

6-4   CONTINUITY APPLIED TO INEQUALITIES

In Chapter 2 a method for solving the inequality $x^2 + 3x - 4 > 0$ was developed. We wrote it as $(x + 4) \cdot (x - 1) > 0$. Then two cases were analyzed: one where both factors were positive and the other where both factors were negative.

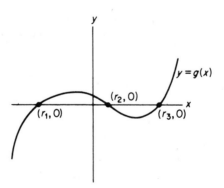

Fig. 6-15

In this section we shall show how our intuitive knowledge of continuity can be applied to solve this and other inequalities. But first we must take a moment to provide a framework on which to build our technique.

In particular, we wish to draw your attention to the relationship between the x-intercepts of the graph of a function g (that is, the points where the graph meets the x-axis) and the roots of the equation $g(x) = 0$. If the graph of g has an x-intercept $(r, 0)$, then $g(r) = 0$ and so r is a root of the equation $g(x) = 0$. Hence, from the graph of $y = g(x)$ in Fig. 6-15, we conclude that r_1, r_2, and r_3 are roots of $g(x) = 0$. On the other hand, if r is any real root of the equation $g(x) = 0$, then $g(r) = 0$ and hence $(r, 0)$ lies on the graph of g. This means that all real roots of the equation $g(x) = 0$ can be represented by the points where the graph of g meets the x-axis.

Returning to the inequality $x^2 + 3x - 4 > 0$, we shall let $f(x) = x^2 + 3x - 4$. Since f is a polynomial function, it is continuous everywhere. The roots of $f(x) = 0$ are -4 and 1; hence the graph of f has x-intercepts $(-4, 0)$ and $(1, 0)$ [see Fig. 6-16]. The roots, or to be more precise the intercepts, determine three intervals on the real line:

$$(-\infty, -4), (-4, 1), \text{ and } (1, \infty).$$

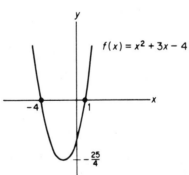

$$f(x) = x^2 + 3x - 4$$

Fig. 6-16

Consider the interval $(-\infty, -4)$. Since f is continuous on this interval, we claim that either $f(x) > 0$ or $f(x) < 0$ throughout the interval. Suppose $f(x)$ did indeed change sign there. Then by the continuity of f there would be a point where the graph would intersect the x-axis, for example at $(x_0, 0)$ (refer to Fig. 6-17); but then x_0 would be a root of the equation $f(x) = 0$. This cannot

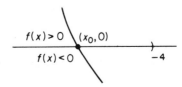

$$f(x) > 0 \quad (x_0, 0)$$
$$f(x) < 0 \qquad -4$$

Fig. 6-17

occur since there is no root of $x^2 + 3x - 4 = 0$ which is less than -4. Hence $f(x)$ must be strictly positive or strictly negative on $(-\infty, -4)$ as well as on the other intervals.

To determine the sign of $f(x)$ on any interval, it is sufficient to determine its sign at any point in the interval. For instance, -5 is in $(-\infty, -4)$ and $f(-5) = 6 > 0$. Thus $f(x) > 0$ on $(-\infty, -4)$. Since 0 is in $(-4, 1)$ and $f(0) = -4 < 0$, then $f(x) < 0$ on $(-4, 1)$. Similarly, 3 is in $(1, \infty)$ and $f(3) = 14 > 0$; thus, $f(x) > 0$ on $(1, \infty)$ [see Fig. 6-18]. Therefore, $x^2 + 3x - 4 > 0$ for $x < -4$ and for $x > 1$.

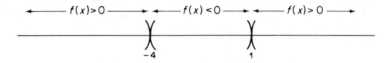

$$\text{—— } f(x) > 0 \text{ ——} \quad \text{—— } f(x) < 0 \text{ ——} \quad \text{—— } f(x) > 0 \text{ ——}$$

Fig. 6-18

EXAMPLE 12

Solve $x(x - 1)(x + 4) \leq 0$.

If $f(x) = x(x - 1)(x + 4)$, then f is continuous everywhere. The roots of $f(x) = 0$ are 0, 1, and -4 which are shown in Fig. 6-19.

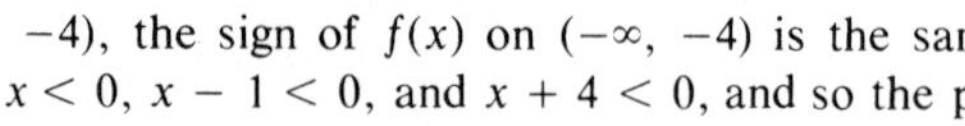

Fig. 6-19

These roots determine four intervals:

$$(-\infty, -4), (-4, 0), (0, 1), \text{ and } (1, \infty).$$

Since -5 is in $(-\infty, -4)$, the sign of $f(x)$ on $(-\infty, -4)$ is the same as that of $f(-5)$. When $x = -5$, then $x < 0$, $x - 1 < 0$, and $x + 4 < 0$, and so the product $x(x - 1)(x + 4) < 0$. That is, $f(-5) < 0$ and therefore $f(x) < 0$ on $(-\infty, -4)$. Note that it is not necessary that we actually evaluate $f(-5)$. Knowing the sign of each factor is enough. We summarize this argument by using the following notations:

$$f(-5) = (-)(-)(-) = (-) \text{ and so } f(x) < 0 \text{ on } (-\infty, -4).$$

For the other intervals we find

$$f(-2) = (-)(-)(+) = (+) \text{ and so } f(x) > 0 \text{ on } (-4, 0),$$

$$f(\tfrac{1}{2}) = (+)(-)(+) = (-) \text{ and so } f(x) < 0 \text{ on } (0, 1),$$

and

$$f(2) = (+)(+)(+) = (+) \text{ and so } f(x) > 0 \text{ on } (1, \infty).$$

Thus $x(x - 1)(x + 4) \leq 0$ for $x \leq -4$ and $0 \leq x \leq 1$. Note that -4, 0, and 1 are included in the solution. Why?

EXAMPLE 13

Solve $\dfrac{x^2 - 6x + 5}{x} \le 0.$

Let $f(x) = \dfrac{x^2 - 6x + 5}{x} = \dfrac{(x - 1)(x - 5)}{x}$. For the case of a quotient, we solve the inequality by considering the intervals determined by the roots of $f(x) = 0$, namely 1 and 5, and the points where f is discontinuous. The function is discontinuous at $x = 0$ and continuous otherwise. In Fig. 6-20 we have placed a circle at 0 to indicate that

Fig. 6-20

f is not defined there. We thus consider the intervals

$$(-\infty, 0), (0, 1), (1, 5), \text{ and } (5, \infty).$$

Determining the sign of $f(x)$ at a point in each interval, we find

$$\text{since } f(-1) = \frac{(-)(-)}{(-)} = (-), \text{ then } f(x) < 0 \text{ on } (-\infty, 0),$$

$$\text{since } f\left(\frac{1}{2}\right) = \frac{(-)(-)}{(+)} = (+), \text{ then } f(x) > 0 \text{ on } (0, 1),$$

$$\text{since } f(2) = \frac{(+)(-)}{(+)} = (-), \text{ then } f(x) < 0 \text{ on } (1, 5),$$

and

$$\text{since } f(6) = \frac{(+)(+)}{(+)} = (+), \text{ then } f(x) > 0 \text{ on } (5, \infty).$$

Therefore, $f(x) \le 0$ for $x < 0$ and $1 \le x \le 5$ (see Fig. 6-21 on page 188).

EXERCISE 6-4

By the technique discussed in this section, solve the following inequalities.

1. $x^2 - 3x - 4 > 0$
2. $x^2 - 8x + 15 > 0$
3. $x^2 - 5x + 6 \le 0$
4. $14 - 5x - x^2 \le 0$
5. $2x^2 + 11x + 14 < 0$
6. $x^2 - 4 < 0$
7. $x^2(x^2 - 1) < 0$
8. $2x^2 - x - 2 \le 0$
9. $(x + 2)(x - 3)(x + 6) \le 0$
10. $(x - 5)(x - 2)(x + 3) \ge 0$
11. $-x(x - 5)(x + 4) > 0$
12. $(x + 2)^2(x^2 - 1) < 0$

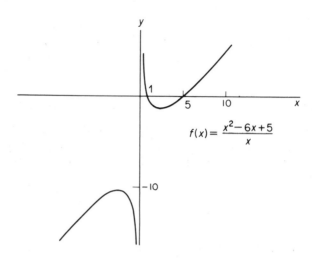

$$f(x) = \frac{x^2 - 6x + 5}{x}$$

Fig. 6-21

13. $x^2 + 2x \geq 2$

14. $x^3 - 4x^2 + 4x > 0$

15. $\dfrac{x}{x^2 - 1} < 0$

16. $\dfrac{x^2 - 1}{x} < 0$

17. $\dfrac{x^2 - x - 6}{x^2 + 4x - 5} \geq 0$

18. $\dfrac{x^2 + 2x - 8}{x^2 + 3x + 2} \geq 0$

19. $\dfrac{3}{x^2 + 6x + 8} \leq 0$

20. $\dfrac{2x + 1}{x^2} \leq 0$

6-5 WHY CONTINUOUS FUNCTIONS?

Quite often it is desirable to describe a given situation by a continuous function. For example, the demand schedule in Table 6-5 indicates the number of units of a particular product that consumers will demand per week at various prices. This information can be depicted graphically as in Fig. 6-22 by plotting each quantity-price pair as a point. Clearly this graph does not represent a continuous function. Furthermore, it gives us no information as to the price at which, say, 35 units would be demanded. However, if we were to connect the points in Fig. 6-22 by a smooth curve (see Fig. 6-23), we get a demand curve. We could conjecture from it that at $2.50 per unit, 35 units would be demanded.

Frequently, it is possible and advantageous to describe a graph, as in Fig. 6-23, by means of an explicit equation which defines a continuous function f. Such a function not only gives us a demand equation, $p = f(x)$, which allows us to anticipate corresponding prices and quantities demanded, but it also permits a convenient mathematical analysis of the nature and basic properties of demand. Of course some discretion must be used in working with equations such as

TABLE 6-5
DEMAND SCHEDULE

Price/unit (dollars)	Quantity per week
p	x
20	0
10	5
5	15
4	20
2	45
1	95

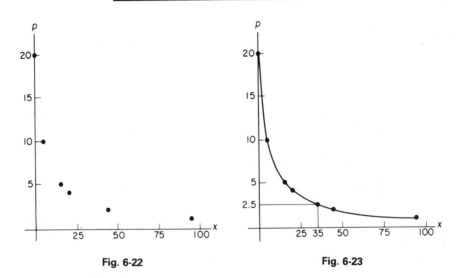

Fig. 6-22   **Fig. 6-23**

$p = f(x)$. Mathematically, f may be defined when $x = \sqrt{37}$, but from a practical standpoint a demand of $\sqrt{37}$ units would be meaningless to our particular situation.

In general, it will be our desire to view practical situations in terms of continuous functions whenever possible so that we may be better able to analyze their nature.

6-6   REVIEW

Important Terms and Symbols in Chapter 6

$\lim_{x \to a} f(x) = L$ *(p. 165)*   one-sided limits *(p. 170)*

$\lim_{x \to a} f(x) = \infty$ *(p. 171)*   continuity *(p. 177)*

$$\lim_{x \to \infty} f(x) = L \ (p. \ 172)$$ discontinuous *(p. 177)*

$$\lim_{x \to -\infty} f(x) = L \ (p. \ 172)$$ infinite discontinuity *(p. 178)*

$$\lim_{x \to a^+} f(x) \ (p. \ 170)$$ continuous everywhere *(p. 178)*

$$\lim_{x \to a^-} f(x) \ (p. \ 170)$$ step function *(p. 181)*

Review Section

1. $\lim_{x \to a} x =$ _____ .

Ans. *a*

2. True or false: In general, $\lim_{x \to a} f(x) = f(a)$. _____

Ans. false

3. True or false: For a function to have a limit at a point, the function must be defined at that point. _____

Ans. false

4. If $\lim_{x \to a} f(x) = \infty$, then $\lim_{x \to a} \dfrac{1}{f(x)} =$ _____ .

Ans. 0

5. If $\lim_{x \to a} f(x) = 10$, then $\lim_{x \to a} [6 \, f(x)] =$ _____ .

Ans. 60

6. $\lim_{x \to \infty} \dfrac{1}{x} = $ __(a)__ , $\lim_{x \to \infty} \dfrac{1}{x^2} = $ __(b)__ , and $\lim_{x \to \infty} \dfrac{\dfrac{1}{x}}{\dfrac{1}{x^2}} = $ __(c)__ .

Ans. (a) 0,   (b) 0,   (c) ∞

7. $\lim_{h \to 0} (x + h) =$ _____ .

Ans. *x*

8. To solve $x(x - 2) > 0$ we consider how many intervals on the real number line?

_____

Ans. 3

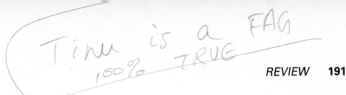

9. If $\lim\limits_{x \to a^+} f(x) = L_1$ and $\lim\limits_{x \to a^-} f(x) = L_2$ and $L_1 \neq L_2$, then f (is) (is not) continuous at $x = a$. _____

  Ans. is not

10. The function $f(x) = (4 - 2x)/(2 + x)$ is discontinuous at $x = $ _____.

  Ans. -2

11. The function $f(x) = 3/(x - 4)$ has a(n) _____ discontinuity at $x = 4$.

  Ans. infinite

12. If f is continuous at $x = a$, then $\lim\limits_{x \to a} f(x) = $ _____.

  Ans. $f(a)$

Review Problems

In problems 1–20, find the limits if they exist.

1. $\lim\limits_{x \to -1} (2x^2 + 6x - 1)$

2. $\lim\limits_{x \to 0} \dfrac{2x^2 - 3x + 1}{2x^2 - 2}$

3. $\lim\limits_{x \to 3} \dfrac{x^2 - 9}{x^2 - 3x}$

4. $\lim\limits_{x \to -2} \dfrac{x + 1}{x^2 - 2}$

5. $\lim\limits_{h \to 0} (x + h)$

6. $\lim\limits_{x \to 2} \dfrac{x^2 - 4}{x^2 - 3x + 2}$

7. $\lim\limits_{x \to \infty} \dfrac{2}{x + 1}$

8. $\lim\limits_{x \to \infty} \dfrac{x^2 + 1}{x^2}$

9. $\lim\limits_{x \to \infty} \dfrac{3x - 2}{5x + 3}$

10. $\lim\limits_{x \to -\infty} \dfrac{1}{x^4}$

11. $\lim\limits_{t \to 3} \dfrac{2t - 3}{t - 3}$

12. $\lim\limits_{x \to -\infty} \dfrac{x^6}{x^5}$

13. $\lim\limits_{x \to -\infty} \dfrac{x + 3}{1 - x}$

14. $\lim\limits_{x \to 4} \sqrt{4}$

15. $\lim\limits_{y \to 5^+} \sqrt{y - 5}$

16. $\lim\limits_{x \to 1} f(x)$ if $f(x) = \begin{cases} x^2, & \text{if } 0 \le x < 1 \\ x, & \text{if } x > 1 \end{cases}$

17. $\lim\limits_{x \to \infty} \dfrac{x^2 - 1}{(3x + 2)^2}$

18. $\lim\limits_{x \to 1} \dfrac{x^2 + x - 2}{x - 1}$

19. $\lim\limits_{x \to 0} |x|$

20. $\lim\limits_{x \to 1} \dfrac{|x - 1|}{x - 1}$

21. Using the definition of continuity, show that $f(x) = x + 5$ is continuous at $x = 7$.

22. Using the definition of continuity, show that $f(x) = (x - 3)/(x^2 + 4)$ is continuous at $x = 3$.

23. State whether $f(x) = x/4$ is continuous everywhere. Give a reason for your answer.

24. State whether $f(x) = x^2 - 2$ is continuous everywhere. Give a reason for your answer.

In problems 25–28, determine the points of discontinuity for each function.

25. $f(x) = \dfrac{x^2}{x + 3}$

26. $f(x) = \dfrac{0}{x^3}$

27. $f(x) = \begin{cases} x + 4, \text{ if } x > -2 \\ 3x - 1, \text{ if } x \le -2 \end{cases}$

28. $f(x) = \begin{cases} \dfrac{x}{x + 1}, \text{ if } x > 1 \\ \dfrac{3}{x + 4}, \text{ if } x < 1 \end{cases}$

In problems 29–32, solve the given inequalities.

29. $x^2 + 4x - 12 > 0$

30. $2x^2 - 6x + 4 \le 0$

31. $\dfrac{x^2 + 3x}{x^2 + 2x - 8} \ge 0$

32. $\dfrac{x(x + 5)(x + 8)}{3} < 0$

Chapter 7

Differential Calculus

This chapter begins our study of differential calculus. The objective will be not only to understand what the so-called "derivative" of a function is and means, but also to learn the techniques of finding the derivatives of functions by applying certain rules properly. Chapter 8 will cover additional interpretations of the derivative.

7-1 THE DERIVATIVE

One of the main problems that calculus deals with is finding the slope of the *tangent line* at a point on a curve. In geometry you probably thought of a tangent line, or *tangent*, to a circle as a line which meets the circle at exactly one point (Fig. 7-1). But this idea of a tangent is not too good for other kinds of curves.

For example, in Fig. 7-2(a) the lines L_1 and L_2 intersect the curve at exactly one point. Intuitively we would not think of L_2 as the tangent at this

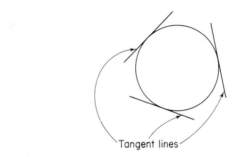

Fig. 7-1

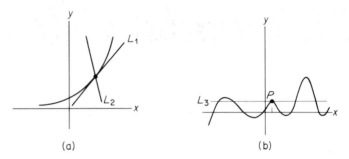

(a)   (b)

Fig. 7-2

point, but it seems natural that L_1 is. Also, in Fig. 7-2(b) we would consider L_3 to be the tangent at point P even though it intersects the curve at other points. From these examples, it seems clear that we must drop the idea that a tangent intersects a curve at only one point. To develop a suitable definition of tangent line, we use a limit concept.

Look at the graph of the function $y = f(x)$ in Fig. 7-3. Here $P(x_1, y_1)$ and $Q(x_2, y_2)$ are two different points on the curve. The line passing through them is called a *secant line*. From the slope formula, the slope of the secant line PQ is

$$m_{PQ} = \frac{y_2 - y_1}{x_2 - x_1}.$$

If Q moves along the curve and approaches P, the secant line has a limiting position as shown in Fig. 7-4. This limiting position is the same if Q approaches P from the left. In Fig. 7-4, as Q approaches P from the right, the positions of the secant lines are PQ', PQ'', etc. As Q approaches P from the left, they are PQ_1, PQ_2, etc. *In both cases, the same limiting position is obtained.* This common limiting position of secant lines is called the **tangent line** to the curve at P. This definition is in agreement with our intuition and avoids the failings previously discussed.

Not every curve has a tangent at each of its points. For example, the

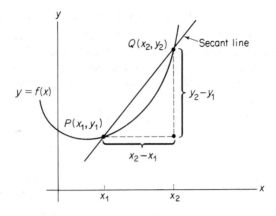

Fig. 7-3

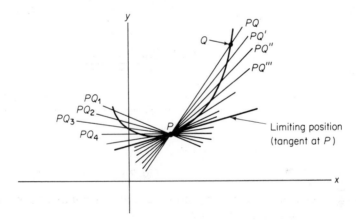

Fig. 7-4

curve $y = |x|$ does not have a tangent at $(0, 0)$. In Fig. 7-5 a secant line from the right must always be the line $y = x$, and from the left it is the line $y = -x$. Since there is no common limiting position, there is no tangent.

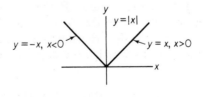

Fig. 7-5

Now that we have a suitable definition of a tangent to a curve at a point, we can define the *slope* of a curve at a point.

DEFINITION.   *The slope of a curve at a point P is the slope of the tangent line at P.*

Since the tangent is a limiting position of secant lines, the slope is the limiting value of the slopes of the secant lines PQ as Q approaches P. We shall now find an expression for the slope of the curve $y = f(x)$ at the point $(x_1, f(x_1))$. In Fig. 7-6, the slope of the secant line PQ is

$$m_{PQ} = \frac{f(x_2) - f(x_1)}{x_2 - x_1}.$$

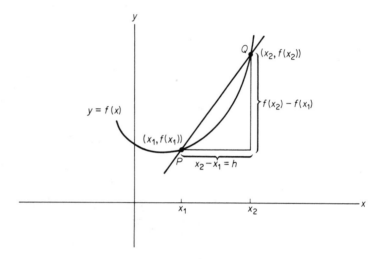

Fig. 7-6

Since x_2 can be obtained by adding a nonzero number to x_1, we can say that $x_2 = x_1 + h$ where $h \neq 0$. Thus,

$$m_{PQ} = \frac{f(x_1 + h) - f(x_1)}{(x_1 + h) - x_1}$$

$$= \frac{f(x_1 + h) - f(x_1)}{h}.$$

As Q moves along the curve towards P, then $x_2 \to x_1$. This means h is getting closer and closer to zero. Note that $h \neq 0$, for if $h = 0$ then $x_2 = x_1$ and no secant line would exist. Finally, the limiting value of the slopes of the secant lines at the point $(x_1, f(x_1))$—which is the slope of the tangent line at $(x_1, f(x_1))$—is the limit:

$$\lim_{h \to 0} \frac{f(x_1 + h) - f(x_1)}{h}. \tag{1}$$

Note that the limit in (1) may exist, aside from any geometrical interpretation at all.

EXAMPLE 1

The slope of the curve $y = f(x) = x^2$ at the point $(1,1)$ is

$$\lim_{h \to 0} \frac{f(1 + h) - f(1)}{h} = \lim_{h \to 0} \frac{(1 + h)^2 - (1)^2}{h}$$

$$= \lim_{h \to 0} \frac{1 + 2h + h^2 - 1}{h} = \lim_{h \to 0} \frac{2h + h^2}{h}$$

$$= \lim_{h \to 0} \frac{h(2 + h)}{h}$$

$$= \lim_{h \to 0} (2 + h) = 2.$$

Thus the tangent line to $y = x^2$ at $(1,1)$ has a slope of 2 (Fig. 7-7).

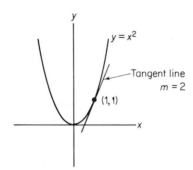

Fig. 7-7

Since x_1 in (1) can be any number, we may replace it by x to make the result more general. We thus have the following definition:

DEFINITION.   *If $y = f(x)$ defines a function f, the limit*

$$\lim_{h \to 0} \frac{f(x + h) - f(x)}{h},$$

*if it exists, is called the **derivative** of f with respect to x and is denoted $f'(x)$, which is read "f prime of x." The process of finding the derivative is called **differentiation.***

Other ways of denoting the derivative of $y = f(x)$ are

$\dfrac{dy}{dx}$ (pronounced "dee y, dee x"), f' (f prime),

$\dfrac{df}{dx}$ (dee f, dee x), $D_x y$ (dee x of y),

$$\frac{d}{dx} [f(x)] \text{ (dee } f(x), \text{ dee } x), \qquad\qquad D_x f \text{ (dee } x \text{ of } f),$$

$$y' \text{ (y prime)}, \qquad\qquad D_x [f(x)] \text{ (dee } x \text{ of } f(x)).$$

PITFALL. $\dfrac{dy}{dx}$ *is not a fraction, but is a symbol for a derivative. We have not yet attached any meaning to symbols such as dy and dx considered independently.*

EXAMPLE 2

If $f(x) = x^2$, find the derivative of f.

$$f'(x) = \lim_{h \to 0} \frac{f(x + h) - f(x)}{h}$$

$$= \lim_{h \to 0} \frac{(x + h)^2 - x^2}{h} = \lim_{h \to 0} \frac{x^2 + 2xh + h^2 - x^2}{h}$$

$$= \lim_{h \to 0} \frac{2xh + h^2}{h} = \lim_{h \to 0} \frac{h(2x + h)}{h} = \lim_{h \to 0} (2x + h) = 2x.$$

Note that as $h \to 0$, we treat x as a constant. Also note that $f'(x) = 2x$ is a function of x. In all cases, **the derivative of a function is also a function.**

If the derivative of f can be evaluated at $x = x_1$, the resulting number is called the derivative of f at x_1, denoted $f'(x_1)$, and the function is said to be *differentiable* at that point. This means that

$$\boxed{f'(x_1) \text{ is the slope of the tangent to } y = f(x) \text{ at } (x_1, f(x_1)).}$$

In addition to the notation $f'(x_1)$ we can also write

$$\left.\frac{dy}{dx}\right|_{x=x_1}, \left.\frac{df}{dx}\right|_{x=x_1}, \text{ and } y'(x_1).$$

EXAMPLE 3

If $f(x) = 2x^2 + 2x + 3$, find $f'(1)$.

$$f'(x) = \lim_{h \to 0} \frac{f(x + h) - f(x)}{h}$$

$$= \lim_{h \to 0} \frac{[2(x + h)^2 + 2(x + h) + 3] - (2x^2 + 2x + 3)}{h}$$

$$= \lim_{h \to 0} \frac{2x^2 + 4xh + 2h^2 + 2x + 2h + 3 - 2x^2 - 2x - 3}{h}$$

$$= \lim_{h \to 0} \frac{4xh + 2h^2 + 2h}{h} = \lim_{h \to 0} (4x + 2h + 2)$$

$$= 4x + 2.$$

$$f'(1) = 4(1) + 2 = 6.$$

EXAMPLE 4

a. *Find the slope of the curve $y = x^2$ at the point $(3, 9)$. Also find an equation of the tangent line at $(3, 9)$.*

From Example 2, $y' = 2x$. Thus, $y'(3) = 2(3) = 6$. That is, the tangent line to the curve $y = x^2$ at $(3, 9)$ has a slope of 6. A point-slope form of the tangent line is $y - 9 = 6(x - 3)$ (see Fig. 7-8).

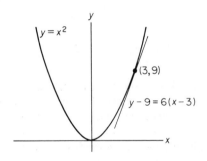

Fig. 7-8

PITFALL.   It is not correct to say that since the derivative of $y = x^2$ is $2x$, the tangent at $(3, 9)$ is $y - 9 = 2x(x - 3)$. The derivative must be **evaluated** at the point of tangency to determine the slope of the tangent line.

b. *Find the slope of the curve $y = 2x + 3$ at the point where $x = 6$.*

Letting $y = f(x) = 2x + 3$, we have

$$y' = \lim_{h \to 0} \frac{f(x + h) - f(x)}{h}$$

$$= \lim_{h \to 0} \frac{[2(x + h) + 3] - (2x + 3)}{h}$$

$$= \lim_{h \to 0} \frac{2h}{h} = \lim_{h \to 0} 2 = 2.$$

Since $y' = 2$, the slope when $x = 6$, or at any point, is 2. Note that the curve is a straight line and thus has a constant slope at each point.

EXAMPLE 5

Find $D_x(\sqrt{x})$.

If $f(x) = \sqrt{x}$, then

$$D_x(\sqrt{x}) = \lim_{h \to 0} \frac{f(x+h) - f(x)}{h} = \lim_{h \to 0} \frac{\sqrt{x+h} - \sqrt{x}}{h}.$$

As $h \to 0$, both the numerator and denominator approach zero. This can be avoided by rationalizing the numerator.

$$\frac{\sqrt{x+h} - \sqrt{x}}{h} = \frac{\sqrt{x+h} - \sqrt{x}}{h} \cdot \frac{\sqrt{x+h} + \sqrt{x}}{\sqrt{x+h} + \sqrt{x}} = \frac{(x+h) - x}{h(\sqrt{x+h} + \sqrt{x})}$$

$$= \frac{1}{\sqrt{x+h} + \sqrt{x}}.$$

Thus,

$$D_x(\sqrt{x}) = \lim_{h \to 0} \frac{1}{\sqrt{x+h} + \sqrt{x}} = \frac{1}{\sqrt{x} + \sqrt{x}} = \frac{1}{2\sqrt{x}}.$$

Note that the original function, $\sqrt{x}$, is defined for $x \geq 0$. But the derivative, $1/(2\sqrt{x})$, is defined only when $x > 0$. A sketch of $y = \sqrt{x}$ indicates that when $x = 0$, the tangent is a vertical line and hence does not have a slope (see Fig. 7-9).

If a variable, say q, is a function of some variable, say p, then we would speak of the derivative of q with respect to p and could write dq/dp.

EXAMPLE 6

If $q = f(p) = \dfrac{1}{2p}$, find dq/dp.

$$\frac{dq}{dp} = \lim_{h \to 0} \frac{f(p+h) - f(p)}{h}$$

$$= \lim_{h \to 0} \frac{\dfrac{1}{2(p+h)} - \dfrac{1}{2p}}{h} = \lim_{h \to 0} \frac{p - (p+h)}{h[2p(p+h)]}$$

$$= \lim_{h \to 0} \frac{-h}{h[2p(p+h)]} = \lim_{h \to 0} \frac{-1}{2p(p+h)} = -\frac{1}{2p^2}.$$

Note that when $p = 0$, neither the function nor its derivative exists.

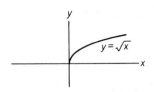

Fig. 7-9

EXERCISE 7-1

In problems 1–16, use the definition of the derivative to find

1. $f'(x)$ if $f(x) = 3$

2. $f'(x)$ if $f(x) = 7.01$

3. $\dfrac{df}{dx}$ if $f(x) = x$

4. $\dfrac{df}{dx}$ if $f(x) = 4x - 1$

5. $\dfrac{dy}{dx}$ if $y = 2x + 4$

6. $\dfrac{dy}{dx}$ if $y = -3x$

7. $\dfrac{d}{dx}(3 - 2x)$

8. $\dfrac{d}{dx}\left(4 - \dfrac{x}{2}\right)$

9. $D_x y$ if $y = \dfrac{1}{x}$

10. $D_x y$ if $y = x^2 + 5$

11. $D_x(x^2 + 4x - 8)$

12. $D_x(x^2 - x - 3)$

13. $\dfrac{dq}{dp}$ if $q = 2p^2 + 5p - 1$

14. $\dfrac{dC}{dq}$ if $C = 7 + 2q - 3q^2$

15. $f'(x)$ if $f(x) = \sqrt{x + 2}$

16. $g'(x)$ if $g(x) = \dfrac{2}{x - 3}$

17. Find the slope of the curve $y = x^2 + 4$ at the point $(-2, 8)$.

18. Find the slope of the curve $y = 2 - 3x^2$ at the point $(1, -1)$.

19. Find the slope of the curve $y = 4x^2 - 5$ when $x = 0$.

In problems 20–25, find an equation of the tangent line to the curve at the given point.

20. $y = x + 4$; $(3, 7)$

21. $y = -2x^2$; $(1, -2)$

22. $y = 2x^2 - 5$; $(-2, 3)$

23. $y = \dfrac{3}{x}$; $(3, 1)$

24. $y = \dfrac{5}{1 - 3x}$; $(2, -1)$

25. $y = 3x^2 + 3x - 4$; $(-1, -4)$

7-2   RULES FOR DIFFERENTIATION

You will probably agree that differentiating a function by direct use of the definition of a derivative can be tedious. Fortunately there are rules that give us completely mechanical and efficient procedures for differentiation. They also avoid direct use of limits. In each of the following cases we assume that the derivatives of the given functions exist.

RULE 1.   *If $f(x) = c$ where c is a constant, then $f'(x) = 0$.*
That is, the derivative of a constant function is zero.

Proof.   If $f(x) = c$, applying the definition of the derivative gives

$$f'(x) = \lim_{h \to 0} \frac{f(x + h) - f(x)}{h} = \lim_{h \to 0} \frac{c - c}{h}$$

$$= \lim_{h \to 0} \frac{0}{h} = \lim_{h \to 0} 0 = 0.$$

Therefore,

$$\boxed{\text{If } f(x) = c, \text{ then } f'(x) = 0.}$$

The graph of $f(x) = c$ is a horizontal line. Thus Rule 1 says that the slope of a horizontal line is zero everywhere—a previously known fact.

EXAMPLE 7

a.   If $f(x) = 3$, then $f'(x) = 0$.

b.   If $g(x) = \sqrt{15}$, then $g'(x) = 0$. For example, the derivative of g when $x = 4$ is $g'(4) = 0$.

c.   If $s(t) = (1{,}938{,}623)^{807.4}$, then $ds/dt = 0$ since s is a constant function.

The next rule requires that we expand a binomial. Recall that

$$(x + h)^2 = x^2 + 2xh + h^2.$$

By direct multiplication we can show

$$(x + h)^3 = x^3 + 3x^2 h + 3xh^2 + h^3.$$

In both expansions, notice in reading from left to right that the exponents of x decrease while those of h increase. This is true for the general case $(x + h)^n$, for n a positive integer. That is,

$$(x + h)^n = x^n + nx^{n-1} h + (\ \ )x^{n-2} h^2 + \dots + (\ \ )xh^{n-1} + h^n$$

where the missing numbers inside the parentheses are constants. This formula will get us through the next rule.

RULE 2.   *If $f(x) = x^n$ where n is any real number, then $f'(x) = nx^{n-1}$.*

Proof.   We shall prove this rule for the case that n is a positive integer. If $f(x) = x^n$, applying the definition of the derivative gives

$$f'(x) = \lim_{h \to 0} \frac{f(x + h) - f(x)}{h} = \lim_{h \to 0} \frac{(x + h)^n - x^n}{h}.$$

By our discussion above,

$$(x + h)^n = x^n + nx^{n-1} h + (\ \ ) x^{n-2} h^2 + \ldots + h^n.$$

Thus,

$$f'(x) = \lim_{h \to 0} \frac{x^n + nx^{n-1} h + (\ \ ) x^{n-2} h^2 + \ldots + h^n - x^n}{h}$$

$$= \lim_{h \to 0} \left[nx^{n-1} + (\ \ ) x^{n-2} h + \ldots + h^{n-1} \right].$$

Each term after the first has h as a factor and must approach 0 as $h \to 0$. Hence,

$$f'(x) = nx^{n-1}.$$

Therefore,

$$\boxed{\text{If } f(x) = x^n, \text{ then } f'(x) = nx^{n-1}.}$$

EXAMPLE 8

a. If $f(x) = x^2$, then by Rule 2,

$$f'(x) = 2x^{2-1} = 2x.$$

b. If $g(w) = w^{9/4}$, then by Rule 2,

$$g'(w) = \frac{9}{4} w^{(9/4)-1}$$

$$= \frac{9}{4} w^{5/4}.$$

c. If $F(x) = x = x^1$, then

$$\frac{dF}{dx} = \frac{d}{dx}(x) = 1 \cdot x^{1-1} = 1 \cdot x^0 = 1.$$

d. If $y = x\sqrt{x} = x^{3/2}$, then

$$D_x y = \frac{3}{2} x^{(3/2)-1} = \frac{3}{2} x^{1/2} = \frac{3}{2}\sqrt{x}.$$

e. Let $h(x) = \dfrac{1}{x^{3/2}}$. To apply Rule 2 we *must* write $h(x)$ as $h(x) = x^{-3/2}$.

$$D_x\left(\frac{1}{x^{3/2}}\right) = D_x(x^{-3/2}) = -\frac{3}{2} x^{(-3/2)-1} = -\frac{3}{2} x^{-5/2}.$$

PITFALL. $D_x\left(\dfrac{1}{x^{3/2}}\right) \neq \dfrac{1}{\dfrac{3}{2} x^{1/2}}.$

RULE 3.   *If $g(x) = cf(x)$, then $g'(x) = cf'(x)$.*
This says that the derivative of a constant times a function is the constant times the derivative of the function.

Proof.   If $g(x) = cf(x)$, applying the definition of the derivative of g gives

$$g'(x) = \lim_{h \to 0} \frac{g(x+h) - g(x)}{h} = \lim_{h \to 0} \frac{cf(x+h) - cf(x)}{h}$$

$$= \lim_{h \to 0}\left[c \cdot \frac{f(x+h) - f(x)}{h}\right] = c \cdot \lim_{h \to 0} \frac{f(x+h) - f(x)}{h}.$$

But $\displaystyle\lim_{h \to 0} \frac{f(x+h) - f(x)}{h} = f'(x)$ and thus $g'(x) = cf'(x)$.

Therefore,

$$\boxed{\text{If } g(x) = cf(x), \text{ then } g'(x) = cf'(x).}$$

EXAMPLE 9

Find the derivative of each of the following functions.

a. $g(x) = 5x^3$.

If we let $f(x) = x^3$, then $g(x) = 5 f(x)$.

$$
\begin{aligned}
g'(x) &= 5 f'(x) && \text{(Rule 3)}\\
&= 5 D_x(x^3) = 5(3x^{3-1}) && \text{(Rule 2)}\\
&= 15x^2.
\end{aligned}
$$

b. $g(p) = \frac{13}{2} p$.

If we let $f(p) = p$, then $g(p) = \frac{13}{2} f(p)$ and

$$g'(p) = \frac{13}{2} f'(p) \qquad \text{(Rule 3)}$$

$$= \frac{13}{2} D_p(p)$$

$$= \frac{13}{2}(1 \cdot p^{1-1}) = \frac{13}{2}. \qquad \text{(Rule 2)}$$

c. $y = \dfrac{.702}{x^2 \sqrt{x}} = .702x^{-5/2}$.

Note that y can be considered a constant times a function.

$$D_x y = .702 \, D_x(x^{-5/2}) \qquad \text{(Rule 3)}$$

$$= .702 \left(-\tfrac{5}{2} x^{-7/2}\right) \qquad \text{(Rule 2)}$$

$$= -1.755x^{-7/2}.$$

RULE 4.   *If $F(x) = f(x) + g(x)$, then $F'(x) = f'(x) + g'(x)$.*
This says that the derivative of a sum of two functions is the sum of the derivatives
of the functions.

Proof.   If $F(x) = f(x) + g(x)$, applying the definition of the derivative of F
gives

$$F'(x) = \lim_{h \to 0} \frac{F(x + h) - F(x)}{h}$$

$$= \lim_{h \to 0} \frac{[f(x + h) + g(x + h)] - [f(x) + g(x)]}{h}$$

$$= \lim_{h \to 0} \frac{[f(x + h) - f(x)] + [g(x + h) - g(x)]}{h} \qquad \text{(regrouping)}$$

$$= \lim_{h \to 0} \left[\frac{f(x + h) - f(x)}{h} + \frac{g(x + h) - g(x)}{h} \right].$$

Since the limit of a sum is the sum of the limits,

$$F'(x) = \lim_{h \to 0} \frac{f(x + h) - f(x)}{h} + \lim_{h \to 0} \frac{g(x + h) - g(x)}{h}.$$

But these two limits are $f'(x)$ and $g'(x)$. Thus,

$$F'(x) = f'(x) + g'(x).$$

Therefore,

$$\boxed{\begin{array}{l} \text{If } F(x) = f(x) + g(x), \text{ then} \\ \quad F'(x) = f'(x) + g'(x). \end{array}}$$

Rule 4 can be extended to the derivative of the sum of any finite number of functions. For example, if we have $F(x) = f(x) + g(x) + h(x) + k(x)$, then $F'(x) = f'(x) + g'(x) + h'(x) + k'(x)$.

The proof of the following is similar to that of Rule 4.

RULE 5. *If $F(x) = f(x) - g(x)$, then $F'(x) = f'(x) - g'(x)$.*

Verbally, the derivative of a difference of two functions is the difference of the derivatives of the functions.

$$\boxed{\begin{array}{l} \text{If } F(x) = f(x) - g(x), \text{ then} \\ \quad F'(x) = f'(x) - g'(x). \end{array}}$$

EXAMPLE 10

Differentiate each of the following functions.

a. $F(x) = 3x^5 + \sqrt{x}$.

Let $f(x) = 3x^5$ and $g(x) = \sqrt{x} = x^{1/2}$. Then $F(x) = f(x) + g(x)$, a sum of two functions.

$$\begin{aligned} F'(x) &= f'(x) + g'(x) & \text{(Rule 4)} \\ &= D_x(3x^5) + D_x(x^{1/2}) \\ &= 3\,D_x(x^5) + D_x(x^{1/2}) & \text{(Rule 3)} \\ &= 3(5x^4) + \frac{1}{2}x^{-1/2} & \text{(Rule 2)} \\ &= 15x^4 + \frac{1}{2\sqrt{x}}. \end{aligned}$$

b. $f(x) = x^5 - \sqrt[3]{x^2}$.

Since f is the difference of two functions,

$$f'(x) = D_x(x^5) - D_x(\sqrt[3]{x^2}) \qquad \text{(Rule 5)}$$

$$= D_x(x^5) - D_x(x^{2/3})$$

$$= 5x^4 - \frac{2}{3}x^{-1/3} \qquad \text{(Rule 2)}$$

$$= 5x^4 - \frac{2}{3\sqrt[3]{x}}.$$

c. $f(z) = \dfrac{z^4}{4} - \dfrac{5}{z^{1/3}}.$

Note that we can write $f(z) = \dfrac{1}{4}z^4 - 5z^{-1/3}.$

$$\frac{df}{dz} = \frac{d}{dz}\left(\frac{1}{4}z^4 - 5z^{-1/3}\right)$$

$$= D_z\left(\frac{1}{4}z^4\right) - D_z(5z^{-1/3}) \qquad \text{(Rule 5)}$$

$$= \frac{1}{4}D_z(z^4) - 5D_z(z^{-1/3}) \qquad \text{(Rule 3)}$$

$$= \frac{1}{4}(4z^3) - 5\left(-\frac{1}{3}z^{-4/3}\right) \qquad \text{(Rule 2)}$$

$$= z^3 + \frac{5}{3}z^{-4/3}.$$

d. $y = 6x^3 - 2x^2 + 7x - 8.$

$$D_x y = D_x(6x^3) - D_x(2x^2) + D_x(7x) - D_x(8)$$

$$= 6D_x(x^3) - 2D_x(x^2) + 7D_x(x) - D_x(8)$$

$$= 6(3x^2) - 2(2x) + 7(1) - 0$$

$$= 18x^2 - 4x + 7.$$

EXAMPLE 11

a. *Find the derivative of $f(x) = 2x(x^2 - 5x + 2)$ when $x = 2$.*

By the distributive property,

$$f(x) = 2x^3 - 10x^2 + 4x.$$

Thus,

$$f'(x) = 2(3x^2) - 10(2x) + 4(1)$$
$$= 6x^2 - 20x + 4$$

and

$$f'(2) = 6(2)^2 - 20(2) + 4 = -12.$$

b. *Find an equation of the tangent line to the curve* $y = \dfrac{3x^2 - 2}{x}$ *when* $x = 1.$

Since $y = \dfrac{3x^2}{x} - \dfrac{2}{x} = 3x - 2x^{-1},$

$$\frac{dy}{dx} = 3(1) - 2[(-1)x^{-2}]$$

$$= 3 + \frac{2}{x^2}.$$

The slope of the tangent line to the curve when $x = 1$ is

$$\frac{dy}{dx}\bigg|_{x=1} = 3 + \frac{2}{1^2} = 5.$$

When $x = 1$, then $y = [3(1)^2 - 2]/1 = 1$. Hence the point $(1, 1)$ lies on the tangent line. Therefore an equation of the tangent line is

$$y - 1 = 5(x - 1)$$
$$y = 5x - 4.$$

EXERCISE 7-2

In problems 1–56, differentiate the functions.

1. $f(x) = 7$

2. $f(x) = (\frac{933}{465})^{2/3}$

3. $f(x) = x$

4. $f(x) = .7x$

5. $f(x) = .3x^{6.907}$

6. $f(x) = \sqrt{2}\, x^{83/4}$

7. $f(x) = 4x^{-14/5}$

8. $v(x) = x^e$

9. $f(x) = 3x - 2$

10. $f(w) = 5w - 7 \ln{(\frac{4}{5})}$

11. $f(p) = \frac{13}{5}p + \frac{7}{3}$

12. $q(x) = \dfrac{5x + 2}{8}$

13. $g(x) = 3x^2 - 5x - e^3$

14. $f(q) = 7q^2 - 5q + 3$

15. $f(t) = -13t^2 + 14t + 2$

16. $p(x) = 97x^2 - 383x + 205$

17. $f(x) = 14x^3 - 6x^2 + 7x - 8$

18. $f(r) = -8r^3 + 6$

19. $f(q) = -3q^3 + \frac{9}{2}q^2 + 9q + 9$

20. $f(x) = 100x^{-3} - 50x^{-1/2} + 10x - 1$

21. $f(x) = x^8 - 7x^6 + 3x^2 + 9$

22. $f(u) = 3u^{12} - 8u^8 + 3u^{-3} + 2u^2 - 9$

23. $f(x) = 2x^{501} - 125x^{100} + 4x^{27} + 3\sqrt[5]{x}$

24. $f(x) = 17 + 8x^{1/7} - 10x^{12} - 3x^{-15}$

25. $f(x) = 2(13 - x^4)$

26. $f(s) = 5(s^4 - 3)$

27. $g(x) = \dfrac{13 - x^4}{3}$

28. $f(x) = \dfrac{5(x^4 - 3)}{2}$

29. $f(x) = x^{-4} - 9x^{1/3} + 5x^{-2/5}$

30. $f(z) = 3z^{1/4} - 12^2 - 8z^{-3/4}$

31. $h(x) = -2(27x - 14x^5)$

32. $f(x) = \dfrac{-(1 + x - x^2 + x^3 + x^4 - x^5)}{2}$

33. $f(x) = -2x^2 + \dfrac{3}{2}x + \dfrac{x^4}{4} + 2$

34. $p(x) = \dfrac{x^7}{7} + \dfrac{x}{2}$

35. $f(x) = \dfrac{1}{x}$

36. $f(x) = \dfrac{7}{x}$

37. $f(s) = \dfrac{1}{4s^5}$

38. $g(w) = \dfrac{2}{3w^3}$

39. $f(u) = 4\sqrt{u}$

40. $f(x) = \dfrac{4}{\sqrt{x}}$

41. $q(x) = \dfrac{1}{\sqrt[5]{x}}$

42. $f(x) = \dfrac{3}{\sqrt[4]{x^3}}$

43. $f(x) = x(3x^2 - 7x + 7)$

44. $f(x) = x^3(3x^6 - 5x^2 + 4)$

45. $g(t) = \dfrac{t^2}{2} - \dfrac{2}{t^2}$

46. $f(x) = x\sqrt{x}$

47. $f(x) = \sqrt{x}(4\sqrt{x^3} - x)$

48. $f(x) = \sqrt{x}(5 - 6x + 3\sqrt[4]{x})$

49. $v(x) = x^{-2/3}(x + 5)$

50. $f(x) = x^{3/5}(x^2 + 7x + 1)$

51. $f(q) = \dfrac{4q^3 + 7q - 4}{q}$

52. $f(w) = \dfrac{w - 5}{w^5}$

53. $f(x) = (x + 1)(x + 3)$

54. $f(x) = x^2(x - 2)(x + 4)$

55. $w(x) = \dfrac{x^2 + x^3}{x^2}$

56. $f(x) = \dfrac{7x^3 + x}{2\sqrt{x}}$

For each curve in problems 57–60, find the slope at the indicated points.

57. $y = 3x^2 + 4x - 8$; $(0, -8), (2, 12), (-3, 7)$

58. $y = 5 - 6x - 2x^3$; $(0, 5), (\frac{3}{2}, -\frac{43}{4}), (-3, 77)$

59. $y = 4$;   when $x = -4, x = 7, x = 22$

60. $y = 2x - 3\sqrt{x}$;   when $x = 1, x = 16, x = 25$

In problems 61 and 62, find an equation of the tangent line to the curve at the indicated point.

61. $y = 4x^2 + 5x + 2$; $(1, 11)$ **62.** $y = (1 - x^2)/5$; $(4, -3)$

63. Find an equation of the tangent line to the curve $y = 3 + x - 5x^2 + x^4$ when $x = 0$.

64. Repeat Problem 63 for the curve $y = \dfrac{\sqrt{x}\,(2 - x^2)}{x}$ when $x = 4$.

7-3   THE DERIVATIVE AS A RATE OF CHANGE

Suppose that a manufacturer's total cost c (in dollars) of producing and marketing x lb of a product is given by the cost function

$$c = f(x) = .3x^2 + 1.2x + 3.$$

For example, the cost of 2 lb is $f(2) = 6.6$. If there is a 2 lb change in output from $x = 2$ to $x = 2 + 2 = 4$, then there is a change in cost from $c = f(2) = 6.6$ to $c = f(4) = 12.6$. The average cost per lb of producing these two additional pounds is

$$\frac{\text{change in total cost } c}{\text{change in output } x} = \frac{f(4) - f(2)}{2} = \frac{12.6 - 6.6}{2} = \$3 \text{ per lb.}$$

If the changes in c and x are denoted by the symbols Δc (delta c) and Δx (delta x) respectively, then the above ratio $\Delta c/\Delta x$ is called the *average rate of change of c with respect to x* from $x = 2$ to $x = 2 + \Delta x = 4$. Recall from Sec. 2-2 that the set of x such that $2 \le x \le 4$ is called a closed interval and is denoted $[2, 4]$. Thus

$$\frac{\Delta c}{\Delta x} = 3 \quad \text{on } [2, 4].$$

In passing, observe in Fig. 7-10 that $\Delta c/\Delta x$ is merely the slope of the secant line through the points $(2, 6.6)$ and $(4, 12.6)$ on the total cost curve.

If the change in output is 1 (that is, $\Delta x = 1$), then on the *smaller* interval from $x = 2$ to $x = 2 + \Delta x = 3$ we have

$$\frac{\Delta c}{\Delta x} = \frac{f(3) - f(2)}{\Delta x} = \frac{9.3 - 6.6}{1} = 2.7.$$

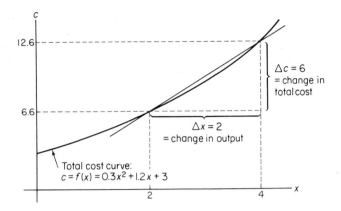

Fig. 7-10

Thus on $[2, 3]$ the average cost of producing one more pound beyond 2 lb is \$2.70. Similarly, for changes in output of .1 and .01 the following results are obtained:

CHANGE IN OUTPUT Δx	INTERVAL $[2, 2 + \Delta x]$	AVERAGE COST PER LB OF ADDITIONAL OUTPUT $\Delta c / \Delta x$
.1	$[2, 2.1]$	$[f(2.1) - f(2)]/\Delta x$ $= (6.843 - 6.6)/.1 = 2.43$
.01	$[2, 2.01]$	$[f(2.01) - f(2)]/\Delta x$ $= (6.62403 - 6.6)/.01 = 2.403$

Observe that as the additional output decreases (that is, $\Delta x \to 0$), the average cost per lb of the additional output appears to get closer to 2.4. This must indeed be the case, as will be shown soon. But first, let us analyze the situation on a more general level.

The **average rate of change of cost** $c = f(x)$ **with respect to output** x over the interval $[x, x + \Delta x]$ is

$$\frac{\Delta c}{\Delta x} = \frac{f(x + \Delta x) - f(x)}{\Delta x}.$$

As the length of the interval from x to $x + \Delta x$ decreases, then $\Delta x \to 0$. The limit of the average rate of change as $\Delta x \to 0$ is called the **marginal cost** or the **instantaneous rate of change of c with respect to x:**

$$\lim_{\Delta x \to 0} \frac{\Delta c}{\Delta x} = \lim_{\Delta x \to 0} \frac{f(x + \Delta x) - f(x)}{\Delta x}.$$

This is merely a restatement of the definition of the derivative of c with respect to x, where Δx plays the role of h. Thus, *speaking of the derivative of f at a point is the same as speaking of the instantaneous rate of change of f at the point.* Since our discussion applies equally well to *any* function $y = f(x)$, we have:

$$\left.\begin{array}{l} \text{instantaneous rate} \\ \text{of change of } y = f(x) \\ \text{with respect to } x \end{array}\right\} = \lim_{\Delta x \to 0} \frac{\Delta y}{\Delta x}$$

$$= \lim_{\Delta x \to 0} \frac{f(x + \Delta x) - f(x)}{\Delta x} \tag{1}$$

$$= \lim_{h \to 0} \frac{f(x + h) - f(x)}{h} \tag{2}$$

$$= \frac{dy}{dx}.$$

It follows that the instantaneous rate of change of $y = f(x)$ at a point is the slope of the tangent line to the graph of $y = f(x)$ at that point. We can use either form (1) or (2) to find a derivative. In some instances we use the delta notation when cumbersome notation would otherwise result. In using (1), we speak of using the "delta process."

Summing up, if $c = f(x)$ is a total cost function, then the marginal cost is defined to be the instantaneous rate of change of total cost c with respect to output x.

$$\textbf{marginal cost} = \frac{dc}{dx}.$$

Now let us find the marginal cost for our original cost function $c = f(x) = .3x^2 + 1.2x + 3$. We shall use the delta process for practice.

$$\frac{dc}{dx} = \lim_{\Delta x \to 0} \frac{f(x + \Delta x) - f(x)}{\Delta x}$$

$$= \lim_{\Delta x \to 0} \frac{.3(x + \Delta x)^2 + 1.2(x + \Delta x) + 3 - (.3x^2 + 1.2x + 3)}{\Delta x}$$

$$= \lim_{\Delta x \to 0} \frac{.6x\Delta x + .3(\Delta x)^2 + 1.2\Delta x}{\Delta x} = \lim_{\Delta x \to 0} (.6x + .3\Delta x + 1.2)$$

$$= .6x + 1.2. \qquad \text{(marginal cost function)}$$

To find marginal cost when 2 lb are produced, we evaluate dc/dx when $x = 2$:

$$\frac{dc}{dx}\bigg|_{x=2} = .6(2) + 1.2 = \$2.40 \text{ per lb.}$$

We saw that the actual cost of producing one more lb beyond 2 lb was $\frac{f(3) - f(2)}{1} = 2.70$. Also, the marginal cost is 2.40. The reason these numbers are close to each other is because the slope of the tangent of the cost curve at $x = 2$ is a good approximation to the slope of the secant line through $(2, f(2))$ and $(3, f(3))$. See Fig. 7-11. For this reason *we interpret marginal cost as the approximate change in cost resulting from one additional unit of output.*

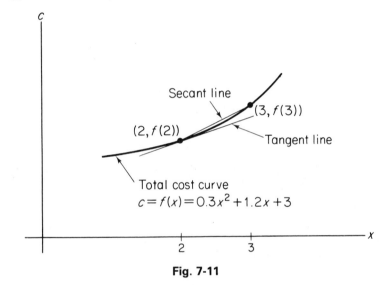

Fig. 7-11

Before we proceed to more applications, here is another example of the delta process.

EXAMPLE 12

Use the delta process to find the instantaneous rate of change of $y = x^3$ *with respect to x. Evaluate when* $x = 2$.

Letting $y = f(x) = x^3$, then we have

$$\lim_{\Delta x \to 0} \frac{\Delta y}{\Delta x} = \lim_{\Delta x \to 0} \frac{(x + \Delta x)^3 - x^3}{\Delta x}$$

$$= \lim_{\Delta x \to 0} \frac{x^3 + 3x^2 \, \Delta x + 3x(\Delta x)^2 + (\Delta x)^3 - x^3}{\Delta x}$$

$$= \lim_{\Delta x \to 0} \left[3x^2 + 3x(\Delta x) + (\Delta x)^2\right] = 3x^2.$$

Thus the rate at which x^3 changes with respect to x is $3x^2$. When $x = 2$, x^3 is changing $3(2)^2 = 12$ times as fast as x.

EXAMPLE 13

Let $p = 100 - q^2$ be the demand function for a manufacturer's product. Find the instantaneous rate of change of price p per unit with respect to quantity q. How fast is the price changing with respect to q when $q = 5$?

$$\lim_{\Delta q \to 0} \frac{\Delta p}{\Delta q} = \frac{dp}{dq} = \frac{d}{dq}(100 - q^2) = -2q.$$

Thus,

$$\frac{dp}{dq}\bigg|_{q=5} = -2(5) = -10.$$

This means that when 5 units are demanded, an *increase* of one extra unit demanded will *decrease* the price per unit by approximately $10. .

EXAMPLE 14

If c is the total cost for producing x units of a product, then the average cost per unit, $\bar{c}$, for producing x units is

$$\bar{c} = \frac{c}{x}. \qquad (3)$$

Multiplying both sides of Eq. (3) by x, we have

$$c = x\bar{c}.$$

Thus total cost is the product of the number of units produced and the average cost per unit. For example, suppose

$$\bar{c} = .0001x^2 - .02x + 4 + \frac{5000}{x}$$

is the average cost equation for a certain manufacturer. Then his total cost equation is

$$c = .0001x^3 - .02x^2 + 4x + 5000.$$

Differentiating c we have his marginal cost function:

$$\frac{dc}{dx} = .0001(3x^2) - .02(2x) + 4(1) + 0$$

$$= .0003x^2 - .04x + 4.$$

The marginal cost when 50 units are produced is

$$\frac{dc}{dx}\bigg|_{x=50} = .0003(50)^2 - .04(50) + 4$$

$$= 2.75.$$

Suppose $r = f(x)$ is the total revenue function of a manufacturer. The equation $r = f(x)$ states that the total dollar value received for selling x units of his product is r. The **marginal revenue** is defined as the instantaneous rate of change of the total dollar value received with respect to the total number of units sold. Hence, marginal revenue is just the derivative of r with respect to x.

$$\textbf{marginal revenue} = \frac{dr}{dx}.$$

Marginal revenue indicates the rate at which revenue changes with respect to units sold. We interpret it as the approximate change in revenue that results from selling one additional unit of output.

EXAMPLE 15

Suppose a manufacturer sells his product at $5 per unit. If he sells x units, his total revenue is given by

$$r = 5x.$$

Thus the marginal revenue function is

$$\frac{dr}{dx} = \frac{d}{dx}(5x) = 5.$$

The marginal revenue when $x = 10$ is

$$\frac{dr}{dx}\bigg|_{x=10} = 5.$$

EXERCISE 7-3

In problems 1–6, find the instantaneous rate of change of y with respect to x by the Δ-process.

1. $y = x + 4$ **2.** $y = 4 - 2x$

3. $y = 3x + 1$ **4.** $y = 2 - x^2$

5. $y = x^2 - 8$ **6.** $y = x^2 + 3x - 4$

Use the rules for differentiation in problems 7–27.

In problems 7–10, cost functions are given where c is the cost of producing x units of a product. In each case find the marginal cost function. What is the marginal cost when $x = 3$?

7. $c = 500 + 10x$ **8.** $c = 5000 + 6x$

9. $c = .3x^2 + 2x + 850$ **10.** $c = .1x^2 + 3x + 2$

11. For the cost function $c = .2x^2 + 1.2x + 4$, how fast does c change with respect to x when $x = 5$?

12. For the cost function $c = .4x^2 + 4x + 5$, find the instantaneous rate of change of c with respect to x when $x = 2$. Also, what is $\Delta c / \Delta x$ over the interval $[2, 3]$?

In problems 13-20, c represents total cost and $\bar{c}$ represents average cost. Both are functions of the number x of units produced. Find the marginal cost function and the marginal cost for the indicated values of x.

13. $c = x^2 + 50x + 1000;$ $x = 15, x = 16, x = 17$

14. $c = 1.35x + 200;$ $x = 10, x = 100, x = 1000$

15. $c = .000034x^3 - .017x^2 + 5x + 10,000;$ $x = 10, x = 50, x = 100$

16. $c = .03x^3 - .6x^2 + 4.5x + 7700;$ $x = 10, x = 20, x = 100$

17. $\bar{c} = .01x + 5 + \dfrac{500}{x};$ $x = 50, x = 100$

18. $\bar{c} = 2 + \dfrac{1000}{x};$ $x = 25, x = 235$

19. $\bar{c} = .00002x^2 - .01x + 6 + \dfrac{20,000}{x};$ $x = 100, x = 500$

20. $\bar{c} = .001x^2 - .3x + 40 + \dfrac{7000}{x};$ $x = 10, x = 20$

In problems 21-24, r represents total revenue and is a function of the number x of units sold. Find the marginal revenue function and the marginal revenue for the indicated values of x.

21. $r = .7x;$ $x = 8, x = 100, x = 200$

22. $r = x(15 - \frac{1}{30}x);$ $x = 5, x = 15, x = 150$

23. $r = 250x + 45x^2 - x^3;$ $x = 5, x = 10, x = 25$

24. $r = 2x(30 - .1x);$ $x = 10, x = 20$

25. Suppose that for a certain manufacturer, the revenue r obtained from the sale of x units of his product is given by $r = 30x - .2x^2$. Find the instantaneous rate of change of r with respect to x.

26. Repeat Problem 25 for the revenue function $r = 20x - .1x^2$. How fast does r change with respect to x when $x = 4$?

27. Using the straight-line method of depreciation, the value v of a certain machine after t years have elapsed is given by $v = 50,000 - 5000t$ where $0 \le t \le 10$. How fast is v changing with respect to t when $t = 2$? $t = 3$? at any time t?

7-4 DIFFERENTIABILITY AND CONTINUITY

In the next section we shall make use of an important relationship between differentiability and continuity.

> If f is differentiable at $x = a$,
> then f is continuous at $x = a$.

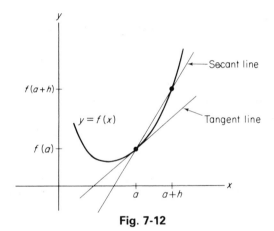

Fig. 7-12

Intuitively we can see why this is true in Fig. 7-12. If the derivative exists at $x = a$, then as $h \to 0$ the limiting position of the secant line is the tangent line. For this position to be approached, the curve must be smooth and connected at a. This means $f(a + h)$ approaches $f(a)$:

$$\lim_{h \to 0} f(a + h) = f(a),$$

which is another way of saying that $f(x)$ is continuous at $x = a$.

If a function is not continuous at a point, then it can not have a derivative there. For example, the function in Fig. 7-13 is discontinuous at $x = a$. The curve has no tangent at that point, and so the function is not differentiable there.

EXAMPLE 16

a. Let $f(x) = x^2$. Since $f'(x) = 2x$ is defined for all values of x, we are assured that $f(x) = x^2$ is continuous for all values of x.

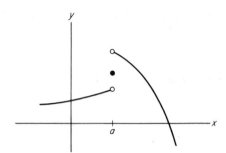

Fig. 7-13

b. The function $f(p) = \dfrac{1}{2p}$ is not continuous at $p = 0$ because $f(0) = \frac{1}{0}$ is not defined.

Thus the derivative does not exist at $p = 0$. In fact, $f'(p) = -\dfrac{1}{2p^2}$ which is undefined at $p = 0$.

The converse of the statement that differentiability implies continuity is *false*. In Example 17 you will see a function that is continuous at a point but not differentiable there.

EXAMPLE 17

The function $y = f(x) = |x|$ is continuous at $x = 0$. See Fig. 7-14. But as we mentioned in Sec. 7-1, there is no tangent line at $x = 0$. Thus the derivative does not exist there. This shows that continuity does *not* imply differentiability.

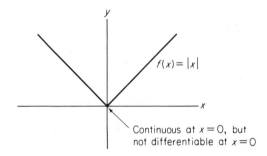

Fig. 7-14

7-5   PRODUCT AND QUOTIENT RULES

In this section we shall introduce two more rules for differentiation: the *product rule* and the *quotient rule*.

RULE 6.   (*Product Rule.*) Let $F(x) = f(x) \cdot g(x)$. If $f'(x)$ and $g'(x)$ exist, then

$$F'(x) = f(x) \cdot g'(x) + g(x) \cdot f'(x).$$

Proof.   By the definition of the derivative of F, we have

$$F'(x) = \lim_{h \to 0} \frac{F(x+h) - F(x)}{h}$$

$$= \lim_{h \to 0} \frac{f(x+h) \cdot g(x+h) - f(x) \cdot g(x)}{h}.$$

Now we use a "trick." Adding and subtracting $f(x+h) \cdot g(x)$, we have

$$F'(x) = \lim_{h \to 0} \frac{f(x+h) \cdot g(x+h) - f(x) \cdot g(x) + [f(x+h) \cdot g(x) - f(x+h) \cdot g(x)]}{h}$$

Regrouping gives

$$F'(x) = \lim_{h \to 0} \frac{[f(x+h) \cdot g(x+h) - f(x+h) \cdot g(x)] + [f(x+h) \cdot g(x) - f(x) \cdot g(x)]}{h}$$

$$= \lim_{h \to 0} \frac{f(x+h)[g(x+h) - g(x)] + g(x)[f(x+h) - f(x)]}{h}$$

$$= \lim_{h \to 0} \frac{f(x+h)[g(x+h) - g(x)]}{h} + \lim_{h \to 0} \frac{g(x)[f(x+h) - f(x)]}{h}$$

$$= \lim_{h \to 0} f(x+h) \cdot \lim_{h \to 0} \frac{g(x+h) - g(x)}{h} + \lim_{h \to 0} g(x) \cdot \lim_{h \to 0} \frac{f(x+h) - f(x)}{h}.$$

Since we assumed that f and g are differentiable, we can say that

$$\lim_{h \to 0} \frac{f(x+h) - f(x)}{h} = f'(x)$$

and

$$\lim_{h \to 0} \frac{g(x+h) - g(x)}{h} = g'(x).$$

Moreover, the differentiability of f implies that f is continuous, and from Sec. 7-4,

$$\lim_{h \to 0} f(x+h) = f(x).$$

Thus,

$$F'(x) = f(x) \cdot g'(x) + g(x) \cdot f'(x).$$

(See how important continuity is!) Therefore, we have the *product rule:*

$$\boxed{\begin{aligned} &\text{If } F(x) = f(x) \cdot g(x), \text{ then} \\ &F'(x) = f(x) \cdot g'(x) + g(x) \cdot f'(x). \end{aligned}}$$

PITFALL.   *The derivative of a product of two functions is **not** the product of the derivatives.*

EXAMPLE 18

a. *If $F(x) = (x^2 + 3x)(4x + 5)$, find $F'(x)$.*

Here F can be considered a product of two functions: $f(x) = x^2 + 3x$ and $g(x) = 4x + 5$. By Rule 6, the product rule,

$$\begin{aligned} F'(x) &= f(x) \cdot g'(x) + g(x) \cdot f'(x) \\ &= (x^2 + 3x) D_x(4x + 5) + (4x + 5) D_x(x^2 + 3x) \\ &= (x^2 + 3x)(4) + (4x + 5)(2x + 3) \\ &= 12x^2 + 34x + 15. \end{aligned}$$

$F'(x)$ can also be obtained by first multiplying $x^2 + 3x$ by $4x + 5$, obtaining $F(x) = 4x^3 + 17x^2 + 15x$, and then differentiating this form of F. This gives

$$\begin{aligned} F'(x) &= 4(3x^2) + 17(2x) + 15(1) \\ &= 12x^2 + 34x + 15 \end{aligned}$$

b. *Find the slope of the graph of $F(x) = (7x^3 - 5x + 2)(2x^4 + x + 7)$ when $x = 1$.*

Let $f(x) = 7x^3 - 5x + 2$ and $g(x) = 2x^4 + x + 7$. Then $F(x) = f(x) \cdot g(x)$, a product of two functions. By the product rule,

$$\begin{aligned} F'(x) &= (7x^3 - 5x + 2) D_x(2x^4 + x + 7) + (2x^4 + x + 7) D_x(7x^3 - 5x + 2) \\ &= (7x^3 - 5x + 2)(8x^3 + 1) + (2x^4 + x + 7)(21x^2 - 5). \end{aligned}$$

Evaluating $F'(x)$ at $x = 1$ gives the slope of the graph at that point:

$$F'(1) = 4(9) + 10(16) = 196.$$

Note: we do not have to simplify $F'(x)$ before evaluating it.

c. *If $y = (x^{2/3} + 3)(x^{-1/3} + 5x)$, find $D_x y$.*

$$\begin{aligned} D_x y &= (x^{2/3} + 3) D_x(x^{-1/3} + 5x) + (x^{-1/3} + 5x) D_x(x^{2/3} + 3) \\ &= (x^{2/3} + 3)\left(-\frac{1}{3}x^{-4/3} + 5\right) + (x^{-1/3} + 5x)\left(\frac{2}{3}x^{-1/3}\right) \\ &= \frac{25}{3}x^{2/3} + \frac{1}{3}x^{-2/3} - x^{-4/3} + 15. \end{aligned}$$

d. *If $y = (x + 2)(x + 3)(x + 4)$, find y'.*

Since y can be written as

$$y = [(x + 2)(x + 3)](x + 4),$$

by the product rule we have

$$y' = [(x + 2)(x + 3)] D_x(x + 4) + (x + 4) D_x[(x + 2)(x + 3)]$$
$$= [(x + 2)(x + 3)] (1) + (x + 4) D_x[(x + 2)(x + 3)].$$

Applying the product rule again, we have

$$y' = [(x + 2)(x + 3)] (1) + (x + 4)[(x + 2) D_x(x + 3) + (x + 3) D_x(x + 2)]$$
$$= [(x + 2)(x + 3)] (1) + (x + 4)[(x + 2) (1) + (x + 3)(1)].$$

After simplifying,

$$y' = 3x^2 + 18x + 26.$$

RULE 7. **(Quotient Rule.)** *Let* $F(x) = \dfrac{f(x)}{g(x)}$ *such that* $g(x) \neq 0$. *If* $f'(x)$ *and* $g'(x)$ *exist, then*

$$F'(x) = \frac{g(x) \cdot f'(x) - f(x) \cdot g'(x)}{[g(x)]^2}.$$

Proof. Since $F(x) = \dfrac{f(x)}{g(x)}$,

$$F(x) \cdot g(x) = f(x).$$

By the product rule,

$$F(x)g'(x) + g(x)F'(x) = f'(x).$$

Solving for $F'(x)$, we have

$$F'(x) = \frac{f'(x) - F(x)g'(x)}{g(x)}.$$

But $F(x) = f(x)/g(x)$. Thus

$$F'(x) = \frac{f'(x) - \dfrac{f(x)g'(x)}{g(x)}}{g(x)}$$

$$= \frac{g(x)f'(x) - f(x)g'(x)}{[g(x)]^2}.$$

Therefore †, we have the *quotient rule:*

_____

†You may have observed that this proof assumes the existence of $F'(x)$. However, the quotient rule can be proven without this assumption.

> If $F(x) = f(x)/g(x)$, then
>
> $$F'(x) = \frac{g(x) \cdot f'(x) - f(x) \cdot g'(x)}{[g(x)]^2}.$$

PITFALL.   *The derivative of a quotient of two functions is **not** the quotient of the derivatives of the functions.*

EXAMPLE 19

a. If $F(x) = \dfrac{4x^2 - 2x + 3}{2x - 1}$, *find* $F'(x)$.

Let $f(x) = 4x^2 - 2x + 3$ and $g(x) = 2x - 1$. Then $F(x) = f(x)/g(x)$ and by Rule 7, the quotient rule,

$$F'(x) = \frac{g(x) \cdot f'(x) - f(x) \cdot g'(x)}{[g(x)]^2}$$

$$= \frac{(2x - 1) D_x(4x^2 - 2x + 3) - (4x^2 - 2x + 3) D_x(2x - 1)}{(2x - 1)^2}$$

$$= \frac{(2x - 1)(8x - 2) - (4x^2 - 2x + 3)(2)}{(2x - 1)^2}$$

$$= \frac{8x^2 - 8x - 4}{(2x - 1)^2} = \frac{4(2x^2 - 2x - 1)}{(2x - 1)^2}.$$

b. If $y = \dfrac{1}{x^2}$, *find* y'.

Here y can be considered a quotient and by the quotient rule,

$$y' = \frac{(x^2) D_x(1) - (1) D_x(x^2)}{(x^2)^2}$$

$$= \frac{x^2(0) - 1(2x)}{x^4}$$

$$= \frac{-2x}{x^4} = -\frac{2}{x^3}.$$

A simpler and more direct method of differentiating y is by writing $y = x^{-2}$ and using Rule 2: $y' = -2x^{-3} = -2/x^3$.

PITFALL.   *Remember that* $D_x(1/x^2) \neq 1/(2x)$.

c. *Find an equation of the tangent line to the curve* $y = \dfrac{(x + 1)(x^2 + 2x + 5)}{1 - x}$ *at* $(0,5)$.

By the quotient rule,

$$y' = \frac{(1 - x)\, D_x[(x + 1)(x^2 + 2x + 5)] - [(x + 1)(x^2 + 2x + 5)]\, D_x(1 - x)}{(1 - x)^2}.$$

Using the product rule to find $D_x[(x + 1)(x^2 + 2x + 5)]$ we have

$$y' = \frac{(1 - x)\,[(x + 1)(2x + 2) + (x^2 + 2x + 5)(1)] - [(x + 1)(x^2 + 2x + 5)]\,(-1)}{(1 - x)^2}.$$

The slope of the curve at $(0, 5)$ is $y'(0) = 12$. An equation of the tangent line is

$$y - 5 = 12(x - 0)$$

$$y = 12x + 5.$$

A function that plays an important role in economic analysis is the *consumption function*. The consumption function $C = f(I)$ expresses a relationship between the total national income I and the total national consumption C. Usually, both I and C are expressed in billions of dollars. The *marginal propensity to consume* is defined as the instantaneous rate of change of consumption with respect to income. It is merely the derivative of C with respect to I.

$$\textbf{marginal propensity to consume} = \frac{dC}{dI}.$$

The marginal propensity to consume indicates how fast consumption changes with respect to income.

If we assume that the difference between income I and consumption C is savings S, then

$$S = I - C.$$

Differentiating both sides with respect to I gives

$$\frac{dS}{dI} = \frac{d}{dI}(I) - \frac{dC}{dI} = 1 - \frac{dC}{dI}.$$

We define dS/dI as the *marginal propensity to save*. Consequently, the marginal propensity to save indicates how fast savings change with respect to income.

EXAMPLE 20

If the consumption function is given by

$$C = \frac{12\sqrt{I} + .6\sqrt{I^3} + I}{\sqrt{I} + 1} = \frac{12I^{1/2} + .6I^{3/2} + I}{I^{1/2} + 1},$$

determine the marginal propensity to consume and the marginal propensity to save when I = 100.

$$\frac{dC}{dI} = \frac{(I^{1/2} + 1)\, D_I(12I^{1/2} + .6I^{3/2} + I) - (12I^{1/2} + .6I^{3/2} + I)\, D_I(I^{1/2} + 1)}{(I^{1/2} + 1)^2}$$

$$= \frac{(I^{1/2} + 1)(6I^{-1/2} + .9I^{1/2} + 1) - (12I^{1/2} + .6I^{3/2} + I)(.5I^{-1/2})}{(I^{1/2} + 1)^2}.$$

When I = 100, the marginal propensity to consume is

$$\frac{dC}{dI}\bigg|_{I=100} = \frac{75.6}{121} = .625.$$

The marginal propensity to save when I = 100 is 1 − .625 = .375. This means that if a current income of $100 billion increases by $1 billion, then the nation will consume approximately 62.5% (625/1000) and save 37.5% (375/1000) of that increase.

EXAMPLE 21

If the demand equation for a manufacturer's product is $p = 1000/(x + 5)$, *find his marginal revenue function.*
The revenue r he receives for selling x units is

$$r = px.$$

Thus his revenue function is

$$r = \left(\frac{1000}{x + 5}\right) x$$

or

$$r = \frac{1000x}{x + 5}.$$

To find his marginal revenue function, all we must determine is dr/dx.

$$\frac{dr}{dx} = \frac{(x + 5)\, D_x(1000x) - (1000x)\, D_x(x + 5)}{(x + 5)^2}$$

$$= \frac{(x + 5)1000 - (1000x)(1)}{(x + 5)^2} = \frac{5000}{(x + 5)^2}.$$

EXERCISE 7-5

In problems 1–50, differentiate the functions.

1. $f(x) = (3x - 1)(7x + 2)$

2. $f(x) = (4x + 1)(6x + 3)$

3. $Q(x) = (5 - 2x)(x^2 + 1)$

4. $s(t) = (8 - 7t)(t^2 - 2)$

5. $f(r) = (3r^2 - 4)(r^2 - 5r + 1)$

6. $C(I) = (2I^2 - 3)(3I^2 - 4I + 1)$

7. $y = (x^2 + 3x - 2)(2x^2 - x - 3)$

8. $y = (2 - 3x + 4x^2)(1 + 2x - 3x^2)$

9. $f(w) = (8w^2 + 2w - 3)(5w^3 + 2)$

10. $f(x) = (3x - x^2)(3 - x - x^2)$

11. $g(x) = 3(x^3 - 2x^2 + 5x - 4)(x^4 - 2x^3 + 7x + 1)$

12. $y = -\frac{3}{2}(2x^4 - 3x + 1)(3x^3 - 6x^2 + 2x - 4)$

13. $y = (x^2 - 1)(3x^3 - 6x + 5) - (x + 4)(4x^2 + 2x + 1)$

14. $h(x) = 4(x^5 - 3)(2x^3 + 4) + 3(8x^2 - 5)(3x + 2)$

15. $f(p) = \frac{3}{2}(\sqrt{p} - 4)(4p - 5)$

16. $g(x) = (\sqrt{x} - 3x + 1)(\sqrt[4]{x} - 2\sqrt{x})$

17. $y = (2x^{.45} - 3)(x^{1.3} - 7x)$

18. $y = (x - 1)(x - 2)(x - 3)$

19. $y = (2x - 1)(3x + 4)(x + 7)$

20. $y = \dfrac{x}{x - 3}$

21. $y = 7 \cdot \frac{2}{3}$

22. $y = \dfrac{3x - 5}{2x + 1}$

23. $f(x) = \dfrac{x}{x - 1}$

24. $f(x) = \dfrac{-2x}{1 - x}$

25. $y = \dfrac{x - 1}{x + 2}$

26. $h(w) = \dfrac{3w^2 + 5w - 1}{w - 3}$

27. $h(z) = \dfrac{5 - 2z}{z^2 - 4}$

28. $y = \dfrac{x^2 - 4x + 2}{x^2 + x + 1}$

29. $y = \dfrac{8x^2 - 2x + 1}{x^2 - 5x}$

30. $f(x) = \dfrac{x^3 - x^2 + 1}{x^2 + 1}$

31. $y = \dfrac{x^2 - 4x + 3}{2x^2 - 3x + 2}$

32. $F(z) = \dfrac{z^4 + 4}{3z}$

33. $g(x) = \dfrac{1}{x^{100} + 1}$

34. $y = \dfrac{3}{7x^3}$

35. $u(v) = \dfrac{v^5 - 8}{v}$

36. $y = \dfrac{x - 5}{2\sqrt{x}}$

37. $y = \dfrac{3x^2 - x - 1}{\sqrt[3]{x}}$

38. $y = \dfrac{x^{.3} - 2}{2x^{2.1} + 1}$

39. $y = 7 - \dfrac{4}{x - 8} + \dfrac{2x}{3x + 1}$

40. $q(x) = 13x^2 + \dfrac{x - 1}{2x + 3} - \dfrac{4}{x}$

41. $H(s) = \dfrac{(s + 2)(s - 4)}{s - 5}$

42. $y = \dfrac{(2x - 1)(3x + 2)}{4 - 5x}$

43. $y = \dfrac{x - 5}{(x + 2)(x - 4)}$

44. $y = \dfrac{4 - 5x}{(2x - 1)(3x + 2)}$

45. $s(t) = \dfrac{t^2 + 3t}{(t^2 - 1)(t^3 + 7)}$

46. $y = \dfrac{(2x - 3)(x^2 - 4x + 1)}{3x^3 + 1}$

47. $y = \dfrac{(x - 1)(x - 2)}{(x - 3)(x - 4)}$

48. $f(s) = \dfrac{17}{s(5s^2 - 10s + 4)}$

49. $y = 3x - \dfrac{\dfrac{2}{x} - \dfrac{3}{x - 1}}{x - 2}$

50. $y = 7 - 10x^2 + \dfrac{1 - \dfrac{7}{x^2 + 3}}{x + 2}$

✓ **51.** Find the slope of the curve $y = (4x^2 + 2x - 5)(x^3 + 7x + 4)$ at $(-1, 12)$.

In problems 52–56, find an equation of the tangent line to the curve at the given point.

52. $y = 6/(x - 1);$ $(3, 3)$

53. $y = (2x + 3)[2(x^4 - 5x^2 + 4)];$ $(0, 24)$

54. $y = \dfrac{4x + 5}{x^2};$ $(-1, 1)$

55. $y = \dfrac{x + 1}{x^2(x - 4)};$ $(2, -\tfrac{3}{8})$

56. $y = 3x - \dfrac{5}{x + 2} + \dfrac{2x^2}{3x - 6};$ $(3, 14)$

In problems 57-61, each equation represents a consumption function. Find the marginal propensity to consume and the marginal propensity to save for the given value of I.

57. $C = 2 + 2\sqrt{I};$ $I = 9$

58. $C = 6 + \dfrac{3I}{4} - \dfrac{\sqrt{I}}{3};$ $I = 25$

59. $C = \dfrac{16\sqrt{I} + .8\sqrt{I^3} - .2I}{\sqrt{I} + 4};$ $I = 36$

60. $C = \dfrac{20\sqrt{I} + .5\sqrt{I^3} - .4I}{\sqrt{I} + 5}$; $I = 100$

61. $C = \dfrac{5(2\sqrt{I^3} + 3)}{I + 10}$; $I = 100$

In problems 62–65, each equation represents a demand function for a certain product where p denotes price per unit for x units. Find the marginal revenue function in each case.

62. $p = 25 - .02x$ **63.** $p = 500/x$

64. $p = \dfrac{108}{x + 2} - 3$ **65.** $p = \dfrac{x + 750}{x + 50}$

66. If the total cost function for a manufacturer is given by

$$c = \frac{5x^2}{x + 3} + 5000,$$

find the marginal cost function.

7-6   THE CHAIN RULE AND POWER RULE

Our next rule, the chain rule, is probably one of the most important rules for finding derivatives.

To begin, suppose

$$y = f(u) = 2u^2 - 3u - 2 \qquad (1)$$

and

$$u = g(x) = x^2 + x. \qquad (2)$$

Here y is a function of u and u is a function of x. If we substitute $x^2 + x$ for u in Eq. (1), we can consider y to be a function of x.

$$y = 2(x^2 + x)^2 - 3(x^2 + x) - 2.$$

By expanding we can find dy/dx in the usual way.

$$y = 2x^4 + 4x^3 + 2x^2 - 3x^2 - 3x - 2$$
$$= 2x^4 + 4x^3 - x^2 - 3x - 2.$$

$$\frac{dy}{dx} = 8x^3 + 12x^2 - 2x - 3.$$

From this example you can easily see that finding dy/dx by first performing a substitution could be quite cumbersome, especially if $2u^2$ in Eq. (1) were $2u^{200}$. The chain rule allows us to find dy/dx with some ease.

RULE 8. (*Chain Rule.*) *If* $y = f(u)$ *is a differentiable function of u and u is a differentiable function of x, then y is a differentiable function of x and*

$$\frac{dy}{dx} = \frac{dy}{du} \cdot \frac{du}{dx}.$$

Let us see why the chain rule is reasonable. Suppose $y = 8u + 5$ and $u = 2x - 3$. Let x change by one unit. How does u change? Answer: $\dfrac{du}{dx} = 2$. But for *each* one-unit change in u there is a change in y of $dy/du = 8$. Therefore, what is the change in y if x changes by one unit, that is, what is $\dfrac{dy}{dx}$? Answer: $8 \cdot 2$, which is $\dfrac{dy}{du} \cdot \dfrac{du}{dx}$. Thus $\dfrac{dy}{dx} = \dfrac{dy}{du} \cdot \dfrac{du}{dx}$.

EXAMPLE 22

a. *If* $y = 2u^2 - 3u - 2$ *and* $u = x^2 + x$, *find* dy/dx.

By Rule 8, the chain rule,

$$\frac{dy}{dx} = \frac{dy}{du} \cdot \frac{du}{dx} = \frac{d}{du}(2u^2 - 3u - 2) \cdot \frac{d}{dx}(x^2 + x)$$

$$= (4u - 3)(2x + 1).$$

We can write our answer exclusively in terms of x by replacing u by $x^2 + x$.

$$\frac{dy}{dx} = [4(x^2 + x) - 3](2x + 1)$$

$$= (4x^2 + 4x - 3)(2x + 1)$$

$$= 8x^3 + 12x^2 - 2x - 3 \quad \text{(as we saw before)}.$$

b. *If* $y = \sqrt{u}$ *and* $u = 7 - x^3$, *find* dy/dx.

By the chain rule,

$$\frac{dy}{dx} = \frac{dy}{du} \cdot \frac{du}{dx}$$

$$= \frac{d}{du}(\sqrt{u}) \cdot \frac{d}{dx}(7 - x^3)$$

$$= \frac{1}{2\sqrt{u}} \cdot (-3x^2)$$

$$= -\frac{3x^2}{2\sqrt{u}} = -\frac{3x^2}{2\sqrt{7 - x^3}}.$$

c. *If* $y = u^{10}$ *and* $u = 8 - t^2 + t^5$, *find* dy/dt.

By the chain rule,

$$\frac{dy}{dt} = \frac{dy}{du} \cdot \frac{du}{dt} = \frac{d}{du}(u^{10}) \cdot \frac{d}{dt}(8 - t^2 + t^5)$$

$$= (10u^9)(-2t + 5t^4)$$

$$= 10(8 - t^2 + t^5)^9(-2t + 5t^4).$$

d. *If* $y = 4u^3 + 10u^2 - 3u - 7$ *and* $u = 4/(3x - 5)$, *find* dy/dx *when* $x = 1$.

By the chain rule,

$$\frac{dy}{dx} = \frac{dy}{du} \cdot \frac{du}{dx} = \frac{d}{du}(4u^3 + 10u^2 - 3u - 7) \cdot \frac{d}{dx}\left(\frac{4}{3x - 5}\right)$$

$$= (12u^2 + 20u - 3) \cdot \frac{(3x - 5)\,D_x(4) - 4D_x(3x - 5)}{(3x - 5)^2}$$

$$= (12u^2 + 20u - 3) \cdot \frac{-12}{(3x - 5)^2}.$$

When $x = 1$, then $u = \dfrac{4}{3(1) - 5} = -2$ and thus

$$\left.\frac{dy}{dx}\right|_{x=1} = [12(-2)^2 + 20(-2) - 3] \cdot \frac{-12}{[3(1) - 5]^2}$$

$$= -15.$$

Suppose we wanted to find dy/dx where $y = (x^3 - x^2 + 6)^{100}$. Notice that the right side is like u^{100} where $x^3 - x^2 + 6$ plays the role of u. This suggests a substitution. Let $x^3 - x^2 + 6$ be u. Then

$$y = u^{100} \quad \text{where } u = x^3 - x^2 + 6.$$

By the chain rule,

$$\frac{dy}{dx} = \frac{dy}{du} \cdot \frac{du}{dx}$$

$$= (100u^{99})(3x^2 - 2x)$$

$$= 100(x^3 - x^2 + 6)^{99}(3x^2 - 2x).$$

EXAMPLE 23

a. *If* $y = \sqrt[5]{8x^2 - 7x}$, *find* y'.

Let $u = 8x^2 - 7x$. Then $y = \sqrt[5]{u}$.

$$\frac{dy}{dx} = \frac{dy}{du} \cdot \frac{du}{dx}$$

$$= (\tfrac{1}{5}u^{-4/5})(16x - 7)$$

$$= \frac{(16x - 7)(8x^2 - 7x)^{-4/5}}{5}.$$

b. *If* $y = \left(\dfrac{x}{x + 1}\right)^4$, *find* y'.

Let $u = \dfrac{x}{x + 1}$. Then $y = u^4$ and

$$\frac{dy}{dx} = \frac{dy}{du} \cdot \frac{du}{dx}$$

$$= \frac{d}{du}(u^4) \cdot \frac{d}{dx}\left(\frac{x}{x + 1}\right)$$

$$= 4u^3 \cdot \frac{(x + 1)(1) - x(1)}{(x + 1)^2}$$

$$= 4\left(\frac{x}{x + 1}\right)^3 \left[\frac{1}{(x + 1)^2}\right] = \frac{4x^3}{(x + 1)^5}.$$

c. *If* $y = \dfrac{1}{(x^2 - 2)^4}$, *find* y'.

Let $u = x^2 - 4$. Then $y = \dfrac{1}{u^4} = u^{-4}$. Thus

$$\frac{dy}{dx} = \frac{dy}{du} \cdot \frac{du}{dx} = (-4u^{-5})(2x)$$

$$= -\frac{8x}{u^5} = -\frac{8x}{(x^2 - 2)^5}.$$

The following rule generalizes Example 23 and is known as the *power rule.*

RULE 9.   (*Power Rule.*) *If* $y = u^n$, *where* n *is any real number and* u *is a differentiable function of* x, *then*

$$\frac{dy}{dx} = nu^{n-1}\frac{du}{dx}.$$

Proof. By the chain rule,

$$\frac{dy}{dx} = \frac{dy}{du} \cdot \frac{du}{dx}.$$

But by Rule 2, $\quad \dfrac{dy}{du} = \dfrac{d}{du}(u^n) = nu^{n-1}$ and so

$$\frac{dy}{dx} = nu^{n-1}\frac{du}{dx}.$$

Therefore, we have the *power rule:*

> If $y = u^n$ where u is a
> function of x, then
> $$\frac{dy}{dx} = nu^{n-1}\frac{du}{dx}.$$

EXAMPLE 24

a. *If* $y = (x^3 - 1)^7$, *find* y'.

Since y is a power of a function of x, the power rule applies. Letting $u = x^3 - 1$ and $n = 7$, we have

$$y' = nu^{n-1}\frac{du}{dx}$$

$$= 7(x^3 - 1)^{7-1}\frac{d}{dx}(x^3 - 1)$$

$$= 7(x^3 - 1)^6(3x^2) = 21x^2(x^3 - 1)^6.$$

b. *If* $y = \sqrt{4x^2 + 3x - 1}$, *find* dy/dx *when* $x = -2$.

Since $y = (4x^2 + 3x - 1)^{1/2}$, we use the power rule with $u = 4x^2 + 3x - 1$ and $n = \frac{1}{2}$.

$$\frac{dy}{dx} = \frac{1}{2}(4x^2 + 3x - 1)^{(1/2)-1}\frac{d}{dx}(4x^2 + 3x - 1)$$

$$= \frac{8x + 3}{2\sqrt{4x^2 + 3x - 1}}.$$

$$\frac{dy}{dx}\bigg|_{x=-2} = -\frac{13}{6}.$$

c. If $z = \left(\dfrac{2s + 5}{s^2 + 1}\right)^4$, find $\dfrac{dz}{ds}$.

Since z is a power of a function, we use the power rule.

$$\frac{dz}{ds} = 4\left(\frac{2s + 5}{s^2 + 1}\right)^{4-1} \frac{d}{ds}\left(\frac{2s + 5}{s^2 + 1}\right).$$

By the quotient rule,

$$\frac{dz}{ds} = 4\left(\frac{2s + 5}{s^2 + 1}\right)^3 \frac{(s^2 + 1)(2) - (2s + 5)(2s)}{(s^2 + 1)^2}.$$

Simplifying, we have

$$\frac{dz}{ds} = 4 \cdot \frac{(2s + 5)^3}{(s^2 + 1)^3} \cdot \frac{(-2s^2 - 10s + 2)}{(s^2 + 1)^2}$$

$$= \frac{-8(s^2 + 5s - 1)(2s + 5)^3}{(s^2 + 1)^5}.$$

d. If $y = (x^2 - 4)^5(3x + 5)^4$, find y'.

Since y is a product, we first apply the product rule.

$$y' = (x^2 - 4)^5 D_x[(3x + 5)^4] + (3x + 5)^4 D_x[(x^2 - 4)^5].$$

Now we can use the power rule.

$$y' = (x^2 - 4)^5 [4(3x + 5)^3(3)] + (3x + 5)^4 [5(x^2 - 4)^4(2x)].$$

Simplifying, we have

$$y' = 12(x^2 - 4)^5(3x + 5)^3 + 10x(3x + 5)^4(x^2 - 4)^4$$

$$= 2(x^2 - 4)^4(3x + 5)^3 [6(x^2 - 4) + 5x(3x + 5)]$$

$$= 2(x^2 - 4)^4(3x + 5)^3(21x^2 + 25x - 24).$$

Usually, the power rule should be used to differentiate $y = [f(x)]^n$. Although a function such as $y = (x^2 + 2)^2$ may be written $y = x^4 + 4x^2 + 4$ and differentiated easily, this method is impractical for a function such as $y = (x^2 + 2)^{1000}$. Since $y = (x^2 + 2)^{1000}$ is of the form $y = [f(x)]^n$, we have

$$y' = 1000(x^2 + 2)^{999}(2x).$$

Let us now use our knowledge of calculus to develop analytically a concept relevant to economic studies. Suppose a manufacturer hires m employees who produce a total of x units per day. We can think of x as a function of m. If r is the total revenue the manufacturer receives for selling the x units produced by the m employees, then r can be considered a function of m. Thus we can look at dr/dm, the instantaneous rate of change of revenue with respect to the number of employees. We know that total revenue is given by

$$r = px,$$

where p is the price per unit. Here p is a function of x and is determined by the manufacturer's demand equation. By the product rule,

$$\frac{dr}{dm} = p\frac{d}{dm}(x) + x\frac{d}{dm}(p) = p\frac{dx}{dm} + x\frac{dp}{dm}.$$

But by the chain rule,

$$\frac{dp}{dm} = \frac{dp}{dx} \cdot \frac{dx}{dm}.$$

Therefore,

$$\frac{dr}{dm} = p\frac{dx}{dm} + x\frac{dp}{dx} \cdot \frac{dx}{dm}$$

or

$$\frac{dr}{dm} = \frac{dx}{dm}\left(p + x\frac{dp}{dx}\right). \tag{3}$$

The derivative dr/dm is called the **marginal revenue product.** It is approximately the change in revenue that results when a manufacturer hires an extra employee.

EXAMPLE 25

A manufacturer determines that m employees will produce a total of x units per day where $x = 10m^2/\sqrt{m^2 + 19}$. If his demand equation is $p = 900/(x + 9)$, determine the marginal revenue product when $m = 9$.

First we find dx/dm and dp/dx. Using the quotient and power rules, we obtain

$$\frac{dx}{dm} = \frac{(m^2 + 19)^{1/2}D_m(10m^2) - (10m^2)D_m[(m^2 + 19)^{1/2}]}{[(m^2 + 19)^{1/2}]^2}$$

$$= \frac{(m^2 + 19)^{1/2}(20m) - 10m^2[(1/2)(m^2 + 19)^{-1/2}(2m)]}{m^2 + 19}$$

$$= \frac{10m(m^2 + 38)}{(m^2 + 19)^{3/2}}.$$

Since $p = 900(x + 9)^{-1}$, then by the power rule,

$$\frac{dp}{dx} = 900[(-1)(x + 9)^{-2}(1)] = -\frac{900}{(x + 9)^2}.$$

Substituting into Eq. (3), we have the marginal revenue product:

$$\frac{dr}{dm} = \frac{10m(m^2 + 38)}{(m^2 + 19)^{3/2}} \left[p + x \left(-\frac{900}{[x + 9]^2} \right) \right].$$

When $m = 9$, then $x = 81$ and $p = 10$. Thus

$$\frac{dr}{dm} \bigg|_{m=9} = 10.71.$$

EXERCISE 7-6

In problems 1–8, use the chain rule.

1. If $y = u^2 - 2u$ and $u = x^2 - x$, find dy/dx.

2. If $y = 2u^3 - 8u$ and $u = 7x - x^3$, find dy/dx.

3. If $y = \dfrac{1}{w^2}$ and $w = 2 - x$, find dy/dx.

4. If $y = \sqrt[3]{z}$ and $z = x^6 - x^2 + 1$, find dy/dx.

5. If $w = u^2$ and $u = \dfrac{t + 1}{t - 1}$, find dw/dt.

6. If $z = u^2 + \sqrt{u} + 9$ and $u = 2s^2 - 1$, find dz/ds.

7. If $y = 3w^2 - 8w + 4$ and $w = 3x^2 + 1$, find dy/dx when $x = 0$.

8. If $y = 3u^3 - u^2 + 7u - 2$ and $u = 3x - 2$, find dy/dx when $x = 1$.

In problems 9–46, find y'.

9. $y = (7x + 4)^8$

10. $y = (4 - 3x)^{25}$

11. $y = (3 - 2p^2)^{14}$

12. $y = (x^2 - 8x)^{40}$

13. $y = \dfrac{(4x^3 - 8x + 2)^{10}}{3}$

14. $y = \dfrac{(7 - q^2 + q)^{12}}{9}$

15. $y = (4r^2 - 10r + 3)^{-15}$

16. $y = (t^2 - 5)^{-4}$

17. $y = \dfrac{7}{(x^3 - x^2 + 2)^7}$

18. $y = \dfrac{6}{(2 - x^2 + x)^4}$

19. $y = 15(4z^3 - z^2 + 2)^{1/5}$

20. $y = 2(8x - 2)^{2/3}$

21. $y = \sqrt{2x^2 - x + 3}$

22. $y = \sqrt[3]{8s^2 - 1}$

23. $y = \sqrt[5]{(x^2 + 1)^3}$

24. $y = \dfrac{1}{(3x^2 - x)^{2/3}}$

25. $y = (x^5 + 7x^3 - 8x + 4)^{-6.5}$

26. $y = (4x^3 - 6x^2 + 7)^{3.8}$

27. $y = \left(\dfrac{x-7}{x+4}\right)^{10}$

28. $y = \left(\dfrac{2w}{w+2}\right)^4$

29. $y = 2\left(\dfrac{q^3 - 2q + 4}{5q^2 + 1}\right)^5$

30. $y = 3\left(\dfrac{x^2 + 2x - 2}{x^3 + x}\right)^8$

31. $y = \sqrt{\dfrac{x-2}{x+3}}$

32. $y = \sqrt[3]{\dfrac{8x^2 - 3}{x^2 + 2}}$

33. $y = (x^2 + 2x - 1)^3(5x + 7)$

34. $y = (8x^3 - 1)^3(2x^2 + 1)^2$

35. $y = [(4x + 3)(6x^2 + x + 8)]^8$

36. $y = \dfrac{2t - 5}{(t^2 + 4)^3}$

37. $y = \dfrac{(2w + 3)^3}{w^2 + 4}$

38. $y = \sqrt{(x - 1)(x + 2)^3}$

39. $y = 6(5x^2 + 2)\sqrt{x^4 + 5}$

40. $y = \sqrt[3]{\dfrac{8x - 7}{5x^2 + 6}}$

41. $y = 8t + \dfrac{t - 1}{t + 4} - \left(\dfrac{8t - 7}{4}\right)^2$

42. $y = 4[(3p - 8)(3p^2 - 2p + 1)^3]^4$

43. $y = [(4 - 3x^2)^2(2 - 3x)^3]^2$

44. $y = 6 + 3x - 4x(7x + 1)^2$

45. $y = \dfrac{(8x - 1)^5}{(3x - 1)^3}$

46. $y = \dfrac{(4x^2 - 2)(8x - 1)}{(3x - 1)^2}$

47. If $y = (5u + 6)^3$ and $u = (x^2 + 1)^4$, find dy/dx when $x = 0$.

48. If $z = 2y^2 - 4y + 5$, $y = 6x - 5$, and $x = 2t$, find dz/dt when $t = 1$.

49. Find the slope of the curve $y = (x^2 - 7x - 8)^3$ at the point $(8, 0)$.

50. Find the slope of the curve $y = \sqrt{x + 1}$ at the point $(8, 3)$.

In problems 51–54, find an equation of the tangent line to the curve at the given point.

51. $y = \sqrt[3]{(x^2 - 8)^2}$; $(3, 1)$

52. $y = (2x + 3)^2$; $(-2, 1)$

53. $y = \dfrac{\sqrt{7x + 2}}{x + 1}$; $(1, \tfrac{3}{2})$

54. $y = \dfrac{-3}{(3x^2 + 1)^3}$; $(0, -3)$

In problems 55–58, x is the total number of units produced per day by m employees of a manufacturer, and p is the price per unit at which the x units are sold. In each case find the marginal revenue product for the given value of m.

55. $x = 2m$, $p = -.5x + 20$; $m = 5$

56. $x = (200m - m^2)/20$, $p = -.1x + 70$; $m = 40$

57. $x = 10m^2/\sqrt{m^2 + 9}$, $p = 525/(x + 3)$; $m = 4$

58. $x = 100m/\sqrt{m^2 + 19}$, $p = 4500/(x + 10)$; $m = 9$

59. If $p = c/x$, where c is a constant, is the demand equation of a manufacturer, and $x = f(m)$ defines a function that gives the total number of units produced per day by m employees, show that the marginal revenue product is always zero.

60. If $p = 100 - \sqrt{x^2 + 20}$ is a demand equation, find the instantaneous rate of change of p with respect to x.

61. Suppose the cost c of producing x units of a product is given by $c = 4000 + 10x + .1x^2$. If the price per unit p is given by the equation $x = 800 - 2.5p$, find the rate of change of cost with respect to price per unit when $p = 80$.

62. Suppose that for a certain group of 20,000 births, the number l_x of people surviving to age x years is

$$l_x = 2000\sqrt{100 - x}, \quad 0 \le x \le 100.$$

Find the instantaneous rate of change of l_x with respect to x. Evaluate your answer for $x = 36$.

In problems 63-64, each equation represents a consumption function. Find the marginal propensity to consume and the marginal propensity to save for the given value of I.

63. $C = \dfrac{20\sqrt{I} + .5\sqrt{I^3} - .4I}{\sqrt{I + 100}}; \quad I = 100$

64. $C = \dfrac{5(2I + \sqrt{I + 9})}{\sqrt{I + 9}}; \quad I = 135$

65. If the total cost function for a manufacturer is given by

$$c = \frac{5x^2}{\sqrt{x^2 + 3}} + 5000,$$

find the marginal cost function.

7-7 DERIVATIVES OF THE LOGARITHMIC AND EXPONENTIAL FUNCTIONS

In this section we shall study differentiation formulas for the logarithmic function $y = \log_b u$ and the exponential function $y = a^u$. We shall first find the derivative of the logarithmic function. Using this result and the fact that the exponential function can be written logarithmically, we shall then determine the derivative of $y = a^u$.

We shall begin with the derivative of $\ln x$. Let

$$y = f(x) = \ln x$$

where x is positive.

$$\frac{d}{dx}(\ln x) = \lim_{h \to 0} \frac{\ln (x + h) - \ln x}{h}$$

$$= \lim_{h \to 0} \frac{\ln\left(\dfrac{x+h}{x}\right)}{h} \qquad \left(\text{since } \ln r - \ln s = \ln \frac{r}{s}\right)$$

$$= \lim_{h \to 0} \left[\frac{1}{h} \ln\left(\frac{x+h}{x}\right)\right] = \lim_{h \to 0} \left[\frac{1}{h} \ln\left(1 + \frac{h}{x}\right)\right]$$

$$= \lim_{h \to 0} \left[\frac{1}{x} \cdot \frac{x}{h} \ln\left(1 + \frac{h}{x}\right)\right] \qquad \left(\text{introducing the factor } \frac{x}{x}\right)$$

$$= \lim_{h \to 0} \left[\frac{1}{x} \ln\left(1 + \frac{h}{x}\right)^{x/h}\right] \qquad (\text{since } n \ln r = \ln r^n)$$

$$= \frac{1}{x} \cdot \lim_{h \to 0} \left[\ln\left(1 + \frac{h}{x}\right)^{x/h}\right].$$

Since the logarithmic function is continuous where it is defined, it can be shown that we can write

$$\frac{d}{dx}(\ln x) = \frac{1}{x} \ln\left[\lim_{h \to 0}\left(1 + \frac{h}{x}\right)^{x/h}\right].$$

To evaluate $\lim\limits_{h \to 0}\left(1 + \dfrac{h}{x}\right)^{x/h}$, we first note that as $h \to 0$, then $\dfrac{h}{x} \to 0$. Then by replacing $\dfrac{h}{x}$ by k, the limit has the form

$$\lim_{k \to 0}(1 + k)^{1/k}.$$

As mentioned in Sec. 6-2, this limit is e, the base of natural logarithms. Thus,

$$\frac{d}{dx}(\ln x) = \frac{1}{x} \ln e = \frac{1}{x}.$$

Hence,

$$\boxed{\frac{d}{dx}(\ln x) = \frac{1}{x}.} \qquad (1)$$

EXAMPLE 26

If $y = x \ln x$, then by the product rule and Eq. (1)

$$y' = x\left(\frac{1}{x}\right) + (\ln x)(1) = 1 + \ln x.$$

We now extend Eq. (1) to cover a broader class of functions. Let

$$y = \ln u \text{ where } u = f(x). \quad (u \text{ positive and differentiable})$$

By the chain rule,

$$\frac{d}{dx}(\ln u) = \frac{dy}{du} \cdot \frac{du}{dx}$$

$$= \frac{d}{du}(\ln u) \cdot \frac{du}{dx}$$

$$= \frac{1}{u} \cdot \frac{du}{dx}.$$

Thus

$$\boxed{\frac{d}{dx}(\ln u) = \frac{1}{u} \cdot \frac{du}{dx}.} \qquad (2)$$

EXAMPLE 27

Differentiate each of the following.

a. $y = \ln(x^2 + 1)$.

This function has the form $\ln u$ with $u = x^2 + 1$. Using Eq. (2) we have

$$\frac{dy}{dx} = \frac{1}{x^2 + 1}\frac{d}{dx}(x^2 + 1) = \frac{1}{x^2 + 1}(2x) = \frac{2x}{x^2 + 1}.$$

b. $y = x^2 \ln(4x + 2)$.

Using the product rule and then Eq. (2) with $u = 4x + 2$, we obtain

$$D_x y = x^2 D_x[\ln(4x + 2)] + [\ln(4x + 2)] D_x(x^2)$$

$$= x^2\left(\frac{1}{4x + 2}\right)(4) + [\ln(4x + 2)](2x)$$

$$= \frac{4x^2}{4x + 2} + 2x \ln(4x + 2).$$

c. $y = \ln(\ln x)$.

This has the form $y = \ln u$ where $u = \ln x$. Using Eqs. (2) and (1) we obtain

$$y' = \frac{1}{\ln x}\frac{d}{dx}(\ln x) = \frac{1}{\ln x}\left(\frac{1}{x}\right) = \frac{1}{x \ln x}.$$

d. $y = \ln (2x + 5)^3$.

By using properties of logarithms, the function can be simplified before the differentiation.

$$y = \ln (2x + 5)^3 = 3 \ln (2x + 5).$$

$$\frac{dy}{dx} = 3\left(\frac{1}{2x + 5}\right)(2) = \frac{6}{2x + 5}.$$

If the simplification were not performed first,

$$\frac{dy}{dx} = \frac{1}{(2x + 5)^3} D_x[(2x + 5)^3]$$

$$= \frac{1}{(2x + 5)^3}(3)(2x + 5)^2(2) = \frac{6}{2x + 5}.$$

e. $f(p) = \ln [(p + 1)^2(p + 2)^3(p + 3)^4]$.

$$f(p) = 2 \ln (p + 1) + 3 \ln (p + 2) + 4 \ln (p + 3).$$

$$f'(p) = 2\left(\frac{1}{p + 1}\right)(1) + 3\left(\frac{1}{p + 2}\right)(1) + 4\left(\frac{1}{p + 3}\right)(1)$$

$$= \frac{2}{p + 1} + \frac{3}{p + 2} + \frac{4}{p + 3}.$$

f. $f(w) = \ln \sqrt{\dfrac{1 + w^2}{w^2 - 1}}$.

$$f(w) = \frac{1}{2} [\ln (1 + w^2) - \ln (w^2 - 1)].$$

$$f'(w) = \frac{1}{2}\left[\frac{1}{1 + w^2}(2w) - \frac{1}{w^2 - 1}(2w)\right]$$

$$= \frac{w}{1 + w^2} - \frac{w}{w^2 - 1} = -\frac{2w}{w^4 - 1}.$$

g. $f(x) = \ln^3 [(2x + 1)^4] = [\ln (2x + 1)^4]^3 = [4 \ln (2x + 1)]^3$.

By the power rule,

$$f'(x) = 3[4 \ln (2x + 1)]^2 D_x[4 \ln (2x + 1)]$$

$$= 3[4 \ln (2x + 1)]^2 \left[4\left(\frac{1}{2x + 1}\right)(2)\right]$$

$$= \frac{24}{2x + 1} [\ln (2x + 1)^4]^2$$

$$= \frac{24}{2x + 1} \ln^2 [(2x + 1)^4].$$

We can generalize Eq. (2) to any base b. Since $\ln u = \dfrac{\log_b u}{\log_b e}$ (from Sec. 5-2), we have

$$\frac{d}{dx} (\log_b u) = \frac{d}{dx} [(\log_b e) \ln u]$$

$$= (\log_b e) \frac{d}{dx} (\ln u)$$

$$= (\log_b e) \left(\frac{1}{u} \frac{du}{dx} \right).$$

Thus,

$$\boxed{\frac{d}{dx} (\log_b u) = \frac{1}{u} (\log_b e) \frac{du}{dx}.} \qquad\qquad (3)$$

Since the use of natural logarithms gives a value of 1 to the factor $\log_b e$ in Eq. (3), natural logarithms are used extensively in calculus.

EXAMPLE 28

Find y' if $y = \log (2x + 1)$.

We use Eq. (3) with $u = 2x + 1$ and $b = 10$.

$$\frac{dy}{dx} = \frac{1}{2x + 1} (\log e) D_x(2x + 1) = \frac{1}{2x + 1} (\log e)(2) = \frac{2 \log e}{2x + 1}.$$

We now turn to the exponential function $y = e^u$ where u is a differentiable function of x. Since $y = e^u$, then

$$u = \ln y. \qquad\qquad (4)$$

Now we take derivatives with respect to x of both sides of Eq. (4).

$$\frac{d}{dx}(u) = \frac{d}{dx}(\ln y).$$

Using Eq. (2) where y is a function of u, we obtain

$$\frac{du}{dx} = \frac{1}{y} \frac{dy}{dx}.$$

Solving for dy/dx, we have

$$\frac{dy}{dx} = y \frac{du}{dx} = e^u \frac{du}{dx}.$$

Thus

$$\frac{d}{dx}(e^u) = e^u \frac{du}{dx}. \tag{5}$$

In particular, if $u = x$, then $du/dx = 1$ and

$$\frac{d}{dx}(e^x) = e^x. \tag{6}$$

PITFALL.   *Notice that we do **not** use the power rule to find $D_x(e^x)$. $D_x(e^x) \neq xe^{x-1}$.*

EXAMPLE 29

a. *Find* $\dfrac{d}{dx}(e^{x^3+3x})$.

The function has the form e^u with $u = x^3 + 3x$. Using Eq. (5), we obtain

$$\frac{d}{dx}(e^{x^3+3x}) = e^{x^3+3x} D_x(x^3 + 3x) = e^{x^3+3x}(3x^2 + 3)$$

$$= 3(x^2 + 1) e^{x^3+3x}.$$

b. *If* $y = \dfrac{x}{e^x}$, *find* y'.

We first use the quotient rule and then Eq. (6).

$$\frac{dy}{dx} = \frac{e^x D_x(x) - xD_x(e^x)}{(e^x)^2} = \frac{e^x(1) - x(e^x)}{(e^x)^2} = \frac{e^x(1 - x)}{e^{2x}} = \frac{1 - x}{e^x}.$$

c. *If* $f(w) = w^4 e^{2w}$, *find* $f'(w)$.

We first use the product rule and then Eq. (5), where $u = 2w$.

$$f'(w) = w^4 D_w(e^{2w}) + e^{2w} D_w(w^4)$$

$$= w^4(e^{2w})(2) + e^{2w}(4w^3) = 2e^{2w} w^3 (w + 2).$$

d. *Find* $D_x[e^{x+1} \ln (x^2 + 1)]$.

By the product rule,

$$D_x[e^{x+1} \ln(x^2 + 1)] = e^{x+1} D_x[\ln(x^2 + 1)] + [\ln(x^2 + 1)] D_x(e^{x+1})$$

$$= e^{x+1}\left(\frac{1}{x^2 + 1}\right)(2x) + [\ln(x^2 + 1)] e^{x+1}(1)$$

$$= e^{x+1}\left[\frac{2x}{x^2 + 1} + \ln(x^2 + 1)\right].$$

e. *If $y = e^2 + e^x + \ln 3$, find y'.*

Since e^2 and $\ln 3$ are constants,

$$y' = 0 + e^x + 0 = e^x.$$

We can generalize Eq. (5) by considering the derivative of a^u where $a > 0$, $a \neq 1$. Since $a = e^{\ln a}$ (Sec. 5-2, Property 8),

$$D_x(a^u) = D_x[(e^{\ln a})^u] = D_x(e^{u \ln a})$$

$$= e^{u \ln a} D_x(u \ln a)$$

$$= e^{u \ln a}\left(\frac{du}{dx}\right) \ln a \qquad (\text{In } a \text{ is constant})$$

$$= a^u(\ln a)\frac{du}{dx}.$$

Thus,

$$\boxed{\frac{d}{dx}(a^u) = a^u(\ln a)\frac{du}{dx}.} \qquad (7)$$

EXAMPLE 30

a. *Find dy/dx if $y = 4^{2x^3 + 5x}$.*

Using Eq. (7) with $a = 4$ and $u = 2x^3 + 5x$, we obtain

$$\frac{dy}{dx} = 4^{2x^3 + 5x}(\ln 4)\frac{d}{dx}(2x^3 + 5x)$$

$$= 4^{2x^3 + 5x}(\ln 4)(6x^2 + 5) = (\ln 4)(6x^2 + 5)4^{2x^3 + 5x}.$$

b. *If $y = x^{100} + 100^x$, find $D_x y$.*

Note that this function involves a variable to a constant power and a constant raised to a variable power. Do not confuse the two!

$$D_x y = 100x^{99} + 100^x(\ln 100) D_x(x) = 100x^{99} + 100^x \ln 100.$$

EXAMPLE 31

*An important function used in economic and business decisions is the **normal distribution density function***

$$y = f(x) = \frac{1}{\sigma\sqrt{2\pi}}\, e^{-(1/2)[(x-\mu)/\sigma]^2}$$

where σ (sigma) and μ (mu) are constants. Its graph, called the normal curve, is bell-shaped. Determine the instantaneous rate of change of y with respect to x when $x = \mu$.

$$\frac{dy}{dx} = \frac{1}{\sigma\sqrt{2\pi}}\, [e^{-(1/2)[(x-\mu)/\sigma]^2}]\left[-\frac{1}{2}(2)\left(\frac{x-\mu}{\sigma}\right)\left(\frac{1}{\sigma}\right)\right].$$

Evaluating dy/dx when $x = \mu$, we obtain

$$\left.\frac{dy}{dx}\right|_{x=\mu} = 0.$$

EXERCISE 7-7

In problems 1–60, differentiate the functions.

1. $y = \ln(3x - 4)$

2. $y = \ln(5x - 6)$

3. $y = \ln x^2$

4. $y = \ln(ax^2 + b)$

5. $y = \ln(1 - x^2)$

6. $y = \ln(-x^2 + 6x)$

7. $f(p) = \ln(2p^3 + 3p)$

8. $f(r) = \ln(2r^4 - 3r^2 + 2r + 1)$

9. $y = \ln^4(ax)$

10. $y = \ln^2(2x + 3)$

11. $y = \ln(x^2 + 4x + 5)$

12. $y = \ln x^{100}$

13. $f(t) = t \ln t$

14. $y = x^2 \ln x$

15. $y = \log_3(2x - 1)$

16. $f(w) = \log(w^2 + w)$

17. $y = (x^2 + 1)\ln(2x + 1)$

18. $y = (ax + b)\ln(ax)$

19. $y = \ln[(x^2 + 2)^2(x^3 + x - 1)]$

20. $y = \ln[(5x + 2)^4(8x - 3)^6]$

21. $f(l) = \ln\left(\dfrac{1 + l}{1 - l}\right)$

22. $y = \ln\left(\dfrac{2x + 3}{3x - 4}\right)$

23. $y = \ln\sqrt{1 + x^2}$

24. $f(s) = \ln\left(\dfrac{s^2}{1 + s^2}\right)$

25. $y = \ln \sqrt[4]{\dfrac{1 + x^2}{1 - x^2}}$

26. $y = \ln \sqrt{\dfrac{x^4 - 1}{x^4 + 1}}$

27. $f(z) = \dfrac{\ln z}{z}$

28. $y = \dfrac{x^2 - 1}{\ln x}$

29. $y = x \ln \sqrt{x - 1}$

30. $y = \ln (x^2 \sqrt{3x - 2})$

31. $y = \sqrt{4 + \ln x}$

32. $y = \ln (x + \sqrt{1 + x^2})$

33. $y = e^{x^2 + 1}$

34. $y = e^{2x^2 + 5}$

35. $y = e^{3 - 5x}$

36. $f(q) = e^{-q^3 + 6q - 1}$

37. $f(r) = e^{3r^2 + 4r + 4}$

38. $y = e^{9x^2 + 5x^3 - 6}$

39. $y = xe^x$

40. $y = x^2 e^{-x}$

41. $y = x^2 e^{-x^2}$

42. $y = xe^{2x}$

43. $y = \dfrac{e^x + e^{-x}}{2}$

44. $y = \dfrac{e^x - e^{-x}}{2}$

45. $y = 4^{3x^2}$

46. $y = 4^{3x + 1}$

47. $f(w) = \dfrac{e^{2w}}{w^2}$

48. $y = 2^x x^2$

49. $y = e^{1 + \sqrt{x}}$

50. $y = e^{x - \sqrt{x}}$

51. $y = \dfrac{e^x - 1}{e^x + 1}$

52. $f(z) = e^{1/z}$

53. $y = e^{e^x}$

54. $y = e^{2x}(x + 1)$

55. $y = e^{\ln x}$

56. $y = e^{\ln(x^2 + 1)}$

57. $y = e^{x \ln x}$

58. $y = e^{-x} \ln x$

59. $y = (\log 2)^x$

60. $y = \ln e^{4x + 1}$

61. Find an equation of the tangent line to the graph of $y = e^x$ when $x = 2$.

62. Find the slope of the tangent line to the graph of $y = 2e^{-4x^2}$ when $x = 0$.

63. Find the marginal revenue for a product if its demand function is $p = 25/\ln (x + 2)$.

64. A total cost function is given by $c = 25 \ln(x + 1) + 12$. Find the marginal cost when $x = 6$.

For each of the demand equations in problems 65 and 66, find the function that gives the instantaneous rate of change of price p with respect to quantity x. What is the instantaneous rate of change for the indicated value of x?

65. $p = 15e^{-.001x}$; $x = 500$

66. $p = 8e^{-3x/800}$; $x = 400$

67. The population P of a city t years from now is given by $P = 20,000e^{.03t}$. Show that $dP/dt = kP$ where k is a constant. This means that the rate of change of population at any time is proportional to the population at that time.

In problems 68 and 69, $\bar{c}$ is the average cost of producing x units of a product. Find the marginal cost function and the marginal cost for the given values of x.

68. $\bar{c} = (7000e^{x/700})/x;$ $x = 350, x = 700$

69. $\bar{c} = \dfrac{850}{x} + 4000\dfrac{e^{(2x+6)/800}}{x};$ $x = 97, x = 197$

70. For a firm the daily output y on the t-th day of a production run is given by $y = 500(1 - e^{-.2t})$. Find the instantaneous rate of change of output y with respect to t on the tenth day.

71. For the normal distribution density function

$$f(x) = \frac{1}{\sqrt{2\pi}}e^{-x^2/2},$$

find $f'(0)$.

72. After t years, the value V of a principal of A dollars which is invested at a nominal rate of r percent (expressed as a decimal) per year and compounded continuously is given by $V = Ae^{rt}$. Show that $(dV/dt)/V = r$.

7-8 IMPLICIT DIFFERENTIATION

To introduce implicit differentiation, we shall find the slope of a tangent line to a circle. Let us take the circle of radius 2 whose center is at the origin (Fig. 7-15). Its equation is

$$x^2 + y^2 = 4$$

$$x^2 + y^2 - 4 = 0. \tag{1}$$

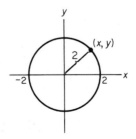

Fig. 7-15

To find the slope at $(\sqrt{2}, \sqrt{2})$ we need to find dy/dx at this point. Until now we have always had y given explicitly in terms of x before determining y'; that is, in the form $y = f(x)$. In Eq. (1) this is not so. We say that Eq. (1) has the form $F(x, y) = 0$ where $F(x, y)$ denotes a function of two variables. The obvious thing to do is to solve Eq. (1) for y in terms of x:

$$x^2 + y^2 - 4 = 0$$

$$y^2 = 4 - x^2$$

$$y = \pm\sqrt{4 - x^2}. \qquad (2)$$

A problem now occurs—Eq. (2) may give two values of y for a value of x. It does not define y explicitly as a function of x. We can, however, "consider" Eq. (1) as implicitly defining y as the two different functions of x

$$y = +\sqrt{4 - x^2} \quad \text{and} \quad y = -\sqrt{4 - x^2}$$

whose graphs are given in Fig. 7-16. Since $(\sqrt{2}, \sqrt{2})$ lies on the graph of $y = \sqrt{4 - x^2}$, we should differentiate that function:

$$y = \sqrt{4 - x^2}$$

$$\frac{dy}{dx} = \frac{1}{2}(4 - x^2)^{-1/2}(-2x)$$

$$= -\frac{x}{\sqrt{4 - x^2}}.$$

$$\frac{dy}{dx}\bigg|_{x=\sqrt{2}} = -\frac{\sqrt{2}}{\sqrt{4 - 2}} = -1.$$

Thus the slope of the circle $x^2 + y^2 - 4 = 0$ at the point $(\sqrt{2}, \sqrt{2})$ is -1.

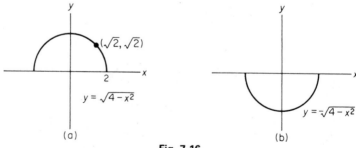

(a) (b)

Fig. 7-16

Let us summarize the difficulties we had. First, y was not originally given explicitly in terms of x. Second, after we tried to find such a relation, we ended up with more than one function of x. In fact, depending on the equation given, it may be very complicated or even impossible to find an explicit expression for y. For example, it would be difficult to solve $ye^x + \ln(x + y) + e^y = 0$ for y. We shall now consider a method which avoids such difficulties.

An equation of the form $F(x, y) = 0$, such as we had originally, is said to express y *implicitly* as a function of x. The word "implicitly" is used since y is not given *explicitly* as a function of x. However, it is assumed or *implied* that the equation defines y as at least one differentiable function of x. Thus we assume that the equation $x^2 + y^2 - 4 = 0$ defines at least one function of x, say $y = f(x)$. Hence, to find dy/dx we treat y as a function of x and differentiate both sides of the equation with respect to x.

$$\frac{d}{dx}(x^2 + y^2 - 4) = \frac{d}{dx}(0)$$

$$\frac{d}{dx}(x^2) + \frac{d}{dx}(y^2) - \frac{d}{dx}(4) = \frac{d}{dx}(0).$$

Since y is assumed to be a function of x, the y^2 has the form u^n. It follows from the power rule that $\frac{d}{dx}(y^2) = 2y\frac{dy}{dx} = 2yy'$. Hence the above equation becomes

$$2x + 2yy' = 0.$$

Solving for y', we obtain

$$y' = -\frac{x}{y}. \tag{3}$$

Thus

$$y'|_{(\sqrt{2}, \sqrt{2})} = -\frac{\sqrt{2}}{\sqrt{2}} = -1 \text{ as before.}$$

This method of finding dy/dx is called **implicit differentiation**. We note that Eq. (3) is not defined when $y = 0$. Geometrically this is clear, since the tangent line to the circle at either $(2, 0)$ or $(-2, 0)$ is vertical and the slope is not defined.

EXAMPLE 32

For each of the following, find y' by implicit differentiation.

a. $x^2 + 5xy - 3y^3 - 5 = 0$.

We assume that y is a function of x and differentiate both sides with respect to x.

$$D_x(x^2) + 5D_x(xy) - 3D_x(y^3) - D_x(5) = D_x(0)$$

$$[2x] + 5[xD_x(y) + yD_x(x)] - 3[3y^2 D_x(y)] - 0 = 0$$

$$[2x] + 5[xy' + y] - 3[3y^2 y'] = 0$$

$$y'(5x - 9y^2) = -2x - 5y$$

$$y' = \frac{2x + 5y}{9y^2 - 5x}.$$

b. $e^{xy} = x + y.$

Differentiating both sides with respect to x and treating y as a function of x, we obtain

$$D_x(e^{xy}) = D_x(x) + D_x(y)$$

$$e^{xy} D_x(xy) = 1 + D_x(y)$$

$$e^{xy}(xD_x y + yD_x x) = 1 + D_x(y)$$

$$e^{xy}(xy' + y) = 1 + y'$$

$$y'(xe^{xy} - 1) = 1 - ye^{xy}$$

$$y' = \frac{1 - ye^{xy}}{xe^{xy} - 1}.$$

c. $\sqrt{x} + \sqrt{y} = 4.$

Since $x^{1/2} + y^{1/2} = 4$, then $D_x(x^{1/2}) + D_x(y^{1/2}) = D_x(4)$:

$$\frac{1}{2x^{1/2}} + \frac{1}{2y^{1/2}}(y') = 0$$

$$y' = -\frac{y^{1/2}}{x^{1/2}} = -\frac{\sqrt{y}}{\sqrt{x}}.$$

Using the original equation we can express y' in terms of x:

$$y' = -\frac{4 - \sqrt{x}}{\sqrt{x}}.$$

d. $x^3 = (y - x^2)^2.$

$$D_x(x^3) = D_x[(y - x^2)^2]$$

$$3x^2 = 2(y - x^2)(y' - 2x)$$

$$3x^2 = 2(yy' - 2xy - x^2 y' + 2x^3)$$

$$3x^2 + 4xy - 4x^3 = 2y'(y - x^2)$$

$$y' = \frac{3x^2 + 4xy - 4x^3}{2(y - x^2)}.$$

If we want to find the slope of the curve $x^3 = (y - x^2)^2$ at the point $(1, 2)$, we have

$$y'\big|_{(1,2)} = \frac{3(1)^2 + 4(1)(2) - 4(1)^3}{2[2 - (1)^2]} = \frac{7}{2}.$$

EXAMPLE 33

If $x + p = \ln x + \ln p$, find dx/dp, the instantaneous rate of change of x with respect to p.

$$D_p(x) + D_p(p) = D_p(\ln x) + D_p(\ln p)$$

$$D_p(x) + 1 = \frac{1}{x} D_p(x) + \frac{1}{p}$$

$$\frac{dx}{dp} + 1 = \frac{1}{x} \frac{dx}{dp} + \frac{1}{p}$$

$$\frac{dx}{dp} = \left(\frac{1}{p} - 1\right) \frac{x}{x - 1}.$$

EXERCISE 7-8

In problems 1–20 find dy/dx by implicit differentiation.

1. $x^2 + 4y^2 = 4$ 2. $3x^2 + 6y^2 = 1$

3. $xy = 4$ 4. $x + xy - 2 = 0$

5. $xy - y - 4x = 5$ 6. $x^2 + y^2 = 2xy + 3$

7. $x^3 + y^3 - 12xy = 0$ 8. $2x^2 - 3y^2 = 4$

9. $x^{3/4} + y^{3/4} = 7$ 10. $y^3 = 4x$

11. $3y^4 - 5x = 0$ 12. $x^{1/5} + y^{1/5} = 4$

13. $\sqrt{x} + \sqrt{y} = 3$ 14. $2x^3 + 3xy + y^3 = 0$

15. $x = \sqrt{y} + \sqrt[3]{y}$ 16. $y^2 + y = \ln x$

17. $y \ln x = xe^y$ 18. $\ln (xy) + x = 4$

19. $xe^y + y = 4$ 20. $ax^2 - by^2 = c$

21. If $x + xy + y^2 = 7$, find y' at $(1, 2)$.

22. Find the slope of the graph of $4x^2 + 9y^2 = 1$ at the point $(0, \frac{1}{3})$; at the point (x_0, y_0).

For the demand equations in problems 23–25, find the instantaneous rate of change of x with respect to p.

23. $p = 100 - x^2$ **24.** $p = 20/(x^2 + 5)$

25. $p = 20/(x + 5)^2$

7-9   LOGARITHMIC DIFFERENTIATION

Logarithmic differentiation is a technique which can at times be used to simplify differentiation. It is useful in differentiating a function involving many factors or a function whose equation is of the form $y = u^v$, where both u and v are differentiable functions of x. The procedure involves taking the natural logarithm of each side of the given equation. After simplifying by using properties of logarithms, we differentiate both sides with respect to x. The following examples will illustrate the logarithmic differentiation process.

EXAMPLE 34

Find y' for each of the following:

a. $y = x^x$.

This has the form $y = u^v$, where u and v are functions of x. Taking the natural logarithm of each side, we obtain

$$y = x^x$$

$$\ln y = \ln x^x.$$

Using properties of logarithms, we have

$$\ln y = x \ln x.$$

Differentiating both sides with respect to x, we have

$$\left(\frac{1}{y}\right) y' = x\left(\frac{1}{x}\right) + (\ln x)(1)$$

$$\frac{y'}{y} = 1 + \ln x.$$

Solving for y', we obtain

$$y' = y(1 + \ln x).$$

Since $y = x^x$,

$$y' = x^x(1 + \ln x).$$

b. $y = \sqrt[4]{\dfrac{(x - 1)(x^2 + 2)^2}{(x + 3)(x - 4)^3}}.$

Taking the natural logarithm of both sides, we obtain

$$\ln y = \ln \sqrt[4]{\dfrac{(x - 1)(x^2 + 2)^2}{(x + 3)(x - 4)^3}} = \dfrac{1}{4} \ln \dfrac{(x - 1)(x^2 + 2)^2}{(x + 3)(x - 4)^3}$$

$$\ln y = \dfrac{1}{4} [\ln (x - 1) + 2 \ln (x^2 + 2) - \ln (x + 3) - 3 \ln (x - 4)].$$

Differentiating both sides with respect to x, we have

$$\left(\dfrac{1}{y}\right) y' = \dfrac{1}{4} \left[\dfrac{1}{x - 1} + (2) \cdot \dfrac{1}{x^2 + 2} (2x) - \dfrac{1}{x + 3} - (3) \cdot \dfrac{1}{x - 4} \right].$$

Solving for y' yields

$$y' = \dfrac{y}{4} \left[\dfrac{1}{x - 1} + \dfrac{4x}{x^2 + 2} - \dfrac{1}{x + 3} - \dfrac{3}{x - 4} \right]$$

where y is given in the original equation.

c. $y = x^{e^{-x^2}}.$

$$\ln y = \ln x^{e^{-x^2}} = e^{-x^2} \ln x$$

$$\left(\dfrac{1}{y}\right) y' = e^{-x^2} \left(\dfrac{1}{x}\right) + (\ln x)[(e^{-x^2})(-2x)]$$

$$\dfrac{y'}{y} = \dfrac{e^{-x^2}}{x} - 2xe^{-x^2} \ln x = e^{-x^2}\left(\dfrac{1}{x} - 2x \ln x\right)$$

$$y' = ye^{-x^2}\left(\dfrac{1}{x} - 2x \ln x\right) = x^{e^{-x^2}} e^{-x^2}\left(\dfrac{1}{x} - 2x \ln x\right).$$

PITFALL. *When using properties of logarithms, you must at all times be able to justify your steps. Thus, if* $y = \ln (x + y)$, *then* $\ln y \neq \ln (x + y)$. *Similarly, if* $y = x^x + x^5$, $\ln y \neq \ln x^x + \ln x^5$.

Be sure to use the right technique for differentiating each of the following forms:

$$y = \begin{cases} [f(x)]^n & \text{(a)} \\ a^{f(x)} & \text{(b)} \\ [f(x)]^{g(x)}. & \text{(c)} \end{cases}$$

For type (a), use the power rule; for type (b), use the differentiation formula for exponential functions; for type (c), use logarithmic differentiation. It would be sheer nonsense to write $D_x(x^x) = x \cdot x^{x-1}$. Be sure that all steps in a calculation are justified by the basic concepts that have been developed.

EXERCISE 7-9

In problems 1–21, find y' by the method of logarithmic differentiation.

1. $y = (x + 1)^2(x - 1)(x^2 + 3)$

2. $y = (3x + 4)(8x - 1)^2(3x^2 + 1)^4$

3. $y = (3x^3 - 1)^2(2x + 5)^3$

4. $y = (3x + 1)\sqrt{8x - 1}$

5. $y = \sqrt{x + 1}\ \sqrt{x^2 - 2}\ \sqrt{x + 4}$

6. $y = (x + 2)\sqrt{x^2 + 9}\ \sqrt[3]{2x + 1}$

7. $y = \dfrac{(2x^2 + 2)^2}{(x + 1)^2(3x + 2)}$

8. $y = \sqrt{\dfrac{(x - 1)(x + 1)}{3x - 4}}$

9. $y = \dfrac{(8x + 3)^{1/2}(x^2 + 2)^{1/3}}{(1 + 2x)^{1/4}}$

10. $y = \dfrac{x(1 + x^2)^2}{\sqrt{2 + x^2}}$

11. $y = \dfrac{\sqrt{1 - x^2}}{1 - 2x}$

12. $y = \sqrt{\dfrac{x^2 + 5}{x + 9}}$

13. $y = x^{1/x}$

14. $y = x^{\sqrt{x}}$

15. $y = x^{\ln x}$

16. $y = \left(\dfrac{2}{x}\right)^x$

17. $y = x^{x^2}$

18. $y = x^{e^x}$

19. $y = e^x x^{3x}$

20. $y = (\ln x)^{e^x}$

21. $x^y = y^x$

22. Without using logarithmic differentiation, find the derivative of $y = x^x$. *Hint:* First show $y = x^x = e^{x \ln x}$.

7-10 HIGHER-ORDER DERIVATIVES

Since the derivative of a function is itself a function, it too may be differentiated. When this is done, the result (being a function itself) may also be differentiated. Continuing in this manner, we obtain *higher-order derivatives*.

If $y = f(x)$, then $f'(x)$ is called the **first derivative** of f with respect to x. The derivative of $f'(x)$, denoted $f''(x)$, is called the **second derivative** of f with respect to x, etc. Some of the various ways in which higher-order derivatives may be denoted are given next.

MAGIC shell—chocolate

first derivative	y',	$f'(x)$,	$\dfrac{dy}{dx}$,	$\dfrac{d}{dx}[f(x)]$,	$D_x y$
second derivative	y'',	$f''(x)$,	$\dfrac{d^2 y}{dx^2}$,	$\dfrac{d^2}{dx^2}[f(x)]$,	$D_x^2 y$
third derivative	y''',	$f'''(x)$,	$\dfrac{d^3 y}{dx^3}$,	$\dfrac{d^3}{dx^3}[f(x)]$,	$D_x^3 y$
fourth derivative	$y^{(4)}$,	$f^{(4)}(x)$,	$\dfrac{d^4 y}{dx^4}$,	$\dfrac{d^4}{dx^4}[f(x)]$,	$D_x^4 y$

PITFALL.   *The symbol $D_x^2 y$ represents the second derivative of y. It is not the same as $[D_x y]^2$, the square of the first derivative of y.*

$$D_x^2 y \neq [D_x y]^2.$$

EXAMPLE 35

a. *If $y = 2x^4 + 6x^3 - 12x^2 + 6x - 2$, find y'''.*

Differentiating y, we obtain

$$y' = 8x^3 + 18x^2 - 24x + 6.$$

Differentiating y', we obtain

$$y'' = 24x^2 + 36x - 24.$$

Differentiating y'', we obtain

$$y''' = 48x + 36.$$

b. *If $f(x) = 7$, find $f''(x)$.*

$$f'(x) = 0.$$

$$f''(x) = 0.$$

c. *If $y = e^{x^2}$, find $\dfrac{d^2 y}{dx^2}$.*

$$\frac{dy}{dx} = e^{x^2}(2x) = 2xe^{x^2}.$$

$$\frac{d^2 y}{dx^2} = 2[x(e^{x^2})(2x) + e^{x^2}(1)]$$

$$= 2e^{x^2}(2x^2 + 1).$$

d. If $y = \dfrac{x^2}{x+4}$, find $\dfrac{d^2 y}{dx^2}$ and evaluate it when $x = 4$.

$$\frac{dy}{dx} = \frac{(x+4)(2x) - (x^2)(1)}{(x+4)^2} = \frac{x^2 + 8x}{(x+4)^2}.$$

$$\frac{d^2 y}{dx^2} = \frac{(x+4)^2(2x+8) - (x^2 + 8x)(2)(x+4)}{(x+4)^4}$$

$$= \frac{32}{(x+4)^3}.$$

$$\frac{d^2 y}{dx^2}\bigg|_{x=4} = \frac{1}{16}.$$

e. If $f(x) = x \ln x$, *find the instantaneous rate of change of* $f''(x)$.

To find the rate of change of any function, we must find its derivative. Thus we want $D_x[f''(x)]$ which is $f'''(x)$.

$$f'(x) = x\left(\frac{1}{x}\right) + (\ln x)(1) = 1 + \ln x.$$

$$f''(x) = 0 + \frac{1}{x} = \frac{1}{x}.$$

$$f'''(x) = -\frac{1}{x^2}.$$

We shall now find higher-order derivatives by means of implicit differentiation. Keep in mind that we shall assume y to be a function of x.

EXAMPLE 36

a. *Find* y'' *if* $x^2 + 4y^2 = 4$.

$$x^2 + 4y^2 = 4.$$

Differentiating both sides with respect to x, we obtain

$$2x + 8yy' = 0$$

$$y' = \frac{-x}{4y}$$

$$y'' = \frac{4y D_x(-x) - (-x) D_x(4y)}{(4y)^2}$$

$$= \frac{4y(-1) - (-x)(4y')}{16y^2}$$

$$= \frac{-4y + 4xy'}{16y^2}.$$

Since $y' = \dfrac{-x}{4y}$,

$$y'' = \frac{-4y + 4x\left(\dfrac{-x}{4y}\right)}{16y^2} = \frac{-4y^2 - x^2}{16y^3}$$

$$= -\frac{4y^2 + x^2}{16y^3}.$$

Since $x^2 + 4y^2 = 4$,

$$y'' = -\frac{4}{16y^3} = -\frac{1}{4y^3}.$$

b. *Find y'' if $y^2 = e^{x+y}$.*

$$y^2 = e^{x+y}$$

$$2yy' = e^{x+y}(1 + y').$$

Solving for y', we obtain

$$y' = \frac{e^{x+y}}{2y - e^{x+y}}.$$

Since $y^2 = e^{x+y}$,

$$y' = \frac{y^2}{2y - y^2} = \frac{y}{2 - y}.$$

$$y'' = \frac{(2 - y)(y') - y(-y')}{(2 - y)^2}$$

$$= \frac{2y'}{(2 - y)^2}.$$

Since $y' = \dfrac{y}{2 - y}$,

$$y'' = \frac{2y}{(2 - y)^3}.$$

EXERCISE 7-10

In problems 1–20, find the indicated derivatives.

1. $y = 4x^3 - 12x^2 + 6x + 2$, y'''

2. $y = 2x^4 - 6x^2 + 7x - 2$, y'''

3. $y = 7 - x$, $\dfrac{d^2y}{dx^2}$

4. $y = -x - x^2$, $\dfrac{d^2y}{dx^2}$

5. $y = x^3 + e^x$, $y^{(4)}$

6. $f(q) = \ln q$, $f'''(q)$

7. $f(x) = x^2 \ln x$, $D_x^2[f(x)]$

8. $y = \dfrac{1}{x}$, y'''

9. $f(p) = \dfrac{1}{6p^3}$, $f'''(p)$

10. $f(x) = \sqrt{x}$, $D_x^2[f(x)]$

11. $f(r) = \sqrt{1 - r}$, $f''(r)$

12. $y = e^{-4x^2}$, y''

13. $y = \dfrac{1}{5x - 6}$, $\dfrac{d^2y}{dx^2}$

14. $y = (2x + 1)^4$, y''

15. $y = \dfrac{x + 1}{x - 1}$, y''

16. $y = 2x^{1/2} + (2x)^{1/2}$, y''

17. $y = \ln[x(x + 1)]$, y''

18. $y = \ln \dfrac{(2x - 3)(4x - 5)}{x + 3}$, y''

19. $f(z) = z^2 e^z$, $f''(z)$

20. $y = \dfrac{x}{e^x}$, $\dfrac{d^2y}{dx^2}$

In problems 21–30, find y''.

21. $x^2 + 4y^2 - 16 = 0$

22. $x^2 - y^2 = 16$

23. $y^2 = 4x$

24. $4x^2 + 3y^2 = 4$

25. $\sqrt{x} + 4\sqrt{y} = 4$

26. $y^2 - 6xy = 4$

27. $xy + y - x = 4$

28. $xy + y^2 = 1$

29. $y^2 = e^{x+y}$

30. $e^x - e^y = x^2 + y^2$

7-11 DIFFERENTIATION FORMULAS

For your convenience, we list below the important differentiation formulas of this chapter. We emphasize that you should not only be totally familiar with these formulas and the mechanics involved in applying them, but you should also know both the definition and the interpretations of a derivative.

$$\frac{d}{dx}(c) = 0 \text{ where } c \text{ is any constant}$$

$$\frac{d}{dx}(x^n) = nx^{n-1} \text{ where } n \text{ is any real number}$$

$$\frac{d}{dx}[cf(x)] = c\frac{df}{dx}$$

$$\frac{d}{dx}[f(x) + g(x)] = \frac{df}{dx} + \frac{dg}{dx}$$

$$\frac{d}{dx}[f(x) - g(x)] = \frac{df}{dx} - \frac{dg}{dx}$$

$$\frac{d}{dx}[f(x) \cdot g(x)] = f(x)\frac{dg}{dx} + g(x)\frac{df}{dx}$$

$$\frac{d}{dx}\left[\frac{f(x)}{g(x)}\right] = \frac{g(x)\dfrac{df}{dx} - f(x)\dfrac{dg}{dx}}{[g(x)]^2}$$

$$\frac{dy}{dx} = \frac{dy}{du} \cdot \frac{du}{dx} \text{ where } y \text{ is a function of } u \text{ and } u \text{ is a function of } x$$

$$\frac{d}{dx}(u^n) = nu^{n-1}\frac{du}{dx}$$

$$\frac{d}{dx}(\log_b u) = \frac{1}{u}(\log_b e)\frac{du}{dx}$$

$$\frac{d}{dx}(\ln u) = \frac{1}{u}\frac{du}{dx}$$

$$\frac{d}{dx}(a^u) = a^u(\ln a)\frac{du}{dx}$$

$$\frac{d}{dx}(e^u) = e^u\frac{du}{dx}$$

7-12 REVIEW

Important Terms and Symbols in Chapter 7

derivative *(p. 197)*

y', $f'(x)$, $D_x y$ *(p. 197)*

$\lim\limits_{h \to 0} \dfrac{f(x+h) - f(x)}{h}$ *(p. 197)*

$\dfrac{dy}{dx}, \dfrac{d^3 y}{dx^3}, \dfrac{d^4}{dx^4} [f(x)], D_x^2 y$ *(p. 253)*

tangent line *(p. 194)*

product rule *(p. 219)*

slope of a curve *(p. 195)*

quotient rule *(p. 221)*

Δc, Δx *(p. 210)*

chain rule *(p. 228)*

Δ-process *(p. 212)*

power rule *(p. 230)*

higher-order derivatives *(p. 252)*

marginal cost *(p. 211)*

implicit differentiation *(p. 247)*

marginal revenue *(p. 215)*

slope of a tangent line *(p. 196)*

instantaneous rate of change *(p. 212)*

average cost *(p. 214)*

marginal propensity to consume *(p. 223)*

marginal revenue product *(p. 233)*

marginal propensity to save *(p. 223)*

logarithmic differentiation *(p. 250)*

consumption function *(p. 223)*

Review Section

1. In terms of a limit, the definition of the derivative of $f(x)$ with respect to x is _____.

Ans. $\lim\limits_{h \to 0} \dfrac{f(x+h) - f(x)}{h}$

2. Geometrically, the derivative $f'(x)$ evaluated at $x = a$ is the _____ of the tangent line to the graph of $y = f(x)$ at $x = a$.

Ans. slope

3. If $f'(x) = 2x^3 + 7$, then $f'''(x) =$ _____.

Ans. $12x$

4. The slope of the tangent line to $y = x^2$ at $(1, 1)$ is _____.

Ans. 2

5. If $y = e^{8x^2+3}$, then $y' = \underline{\hspace{1cm}}$.

> *Ans.* $16xe^{8x^2+3}$

6. If $y = \ln(8x^2 + 3)$, then $dy/dx = \underline{\hspace{1cm}}$.

> *Ans.* $16x/(8x^2 + 3)$

7. Does the derivative of $y = |x|$ exist at $x = 0?$ $\underline{\hspace{1cm}}$

> *Ans.*   No

8. True or false: If a function is continuous at a point, then it is differentiable there. $\underline{\text{(a)}}$. If a function is differentiable at a point, then it is continuous there. $\underline{\text{(b)}}$.

> *Ans.*   (a) false;   (b) true

9. If $y = e^x$, then $d^4y/dx^4 = \underline{\hspace{1cm}}$.

> *Ans.* e^x

10. The slope of the curve $y = x + e^x$ at $x = 0$ is $\underline{\hspace{1cm}}$.

> *Ans.*   2

11. If $y = 7$, then $D_x^3\, y = \underline{\hspace{1cm}}$.

> *Ans.*   0

12. If u is a function of x, then the power rule asserts that $D_x(u^n) = \underline{\hspace{1cm}}$.

> *Ans.* $nu^{n-1}\dfrac{du}{dx}$

13. If $f'(x) = 7$, then $D_x(8f(x)) = \underline{\hspace{1cm}}$.

> *Ans.*   56

14. If $y = f(x)$, then dy/dx denotes an (average)(instantaneous) rate of change of y with respect to x.

> *Ans.*   instantaneous

15. True or false: $\dfrac{\Delta y}{\Delta x} = \dfrac{dy}{dx}$. $\underline{\hspace{1cm}}$

> *Ans.*   false

16. The derivative of a function (is)(is not) a function.

> *Ans.*   is

17. True or false: If $y = f(x) \cdot g(x)$, then $y' = f'(x) \cdot g'(x)$. ___(a)___ . If $y = f(x)/g(x)$, then $y' = f'(x)/g'(x)$. ___(b)___ .

> *Ans.* (a) false;   (b) false

18. If $f(x) = 7x + 1$, then $f'(1) =$ _____.

> *Ans.* 7

19. If the marginal propensity to consume is .6, then the marginal propensity to save is _____.

> *Ans.* .4

20. True or false: $D_x(x^2 + 7)^3 = 3(x^2 + 7)^2$. _____

> *Ans.* false

21. The instantaneous rate of change of total revenue with respect to the number of units sold is called ___(a)___ and the instantaneous rate of change of total cost with respect to the number of units produced is called ___(b)___ .

> *Ans.* (a) marginal revenue;   (b) marginal cost

Review Problems

In problems 1–46, differentiate.

○   **1.** $y = 6^3$

$28x^3 - 18x^2 + 10x$ **3.** $y = 7x^4 - 6x^3 + 5x^2 + 1$

$2e^x + 2e + 2xe^{x^2}$ **5.** $y = 2e^x + e^2 + e^{x^2}$

7. $f(r) = \ln(r^2 + 5r)$

9. $y = (x^2 + 6x)(x^3 - 6x^2 + 4)$

11. $f(x) = (2x^2 + 4x)^{100}$

13. $y = (8 + 2x)(x^2 + 1)^4$

15. $y = e^x(x^2 + 2)$

17. $f(z) = \dfrac{z^2 - 1}{z^2 + 1}$

19. $y = \dfrac{\ln x}{e^x}$

21. $y = e^{x^2 + 4x + 5}$

2. $y = x$

4. $y = \sqrt{x + 3}$

6. $y = \dfrac{1}{x^3}$

8. $y = e^{\ln x}$

10. $y = (x^2 + 1)^{100}(x - 6)$

12. $y = 2^{7x^2}$

14. $f(t) = \log_6 \sqrt{t^2 + 1}$

16. $f(w) = we^w + w^2$

18. $y = \dfrac{x - 5}{(x + 2)^2}$

20. $y = \dfrac{e^x + e^{-x}}{x^2}$

22. $y = (2x)^{3/5} + e$

23. $2xy + y^2 = 6$

24. $y = (x - 6)^4(x + 4)^3(6 - x)^2$

25. $y = \sqrt{(x - 6)(x + 5)(9 - x)}$

26. $4x^2 - 9y^2 = 4$

27. $f(q) = \ln\left[(q + 1)^2(q + 2)^3\right]$

28. $y = x^{x^3}$

29. $y = \dfrac{1}{\sqrt{1 - x}}$

30. $y = \sqrt{\dfrac{(x - 2)(x + 3)}{\sqrt{x - 1}}}$

31. $y = \log_2 (8x + 5)^2$

32. $y + xy + y^2 = 1$

33. $y = (x + 1)^{x+1}$

34. $y = (x + 2)^{\ln x}$

35. $y = \dfrac{x^2 + 6}{\sqrt{x^2 + 5}}$

36. $y = \dfrac{(x + 3)^5}{x}$

37. $y = 2x^{-3/8} + (2x)^{-3/8}$

38. $f(t) = e^{\sqrt{t}}$

39. $f(l) = \ln (1 + l + l^2 + l^3)$

40. $y = \sqrt{\dfrac{x}{2}} + \sqrt{\dfrac{2}{x}}$

41. $y = (x^3 + 6x^2 + 9)^{3/5}$

42. $y = (e + e^2)^0$

43. $f(u) = \ln (u^2 \sqrt{1 - u})$

44. $y = \dfrac{1 + e^x}{1 - e^x}$

45. $y = \dfrac{(x^2 + 2)^{3/2}(x^2 + 9)^{4/9}}{(x^3 + 6x)^{4/11}}$

46. $y = \dfrac{\ln x}{\sqrt{x}}$

In problems 47–54, find the indicated derivative at the given point. It is not necessary to simplify the derivative before substituting the coordinates.

47. $y = x^4 - 2x^3 + 6x$, y''', $(1, 5)$

48. $y = x^2 e^x$, y''', $(1, e)$

49. $y = \dfrac{x}{\sqrt{x - 1}}$, y'', $\left(5, \dfrac{5}{2}\right)$

50. $y = \dfrac{2}{1 - x}$, y'', $\left(-2, \dfrac{2}{3}\right)$

51. $x + xy + y = 5$, y'', $(2, 1)$

52. $xy + y^2 = 2$, y'', $(1, 1)$

53. $y = \dfrac{4x}{x^2 + 4}$, y'', $(2, 1)$

54. $y = (x + 1)^3(x - 1)$, y'', $(-1, 0)$

In problems 55–60, find an equation of the tangent line to the curve at the point corresponding to the given value of x.

55. $y = x^2 - 6x + 4$, $x = 1$

56. $y = -2x^3 + 6x + 1$, $x = 2$

57. $y = e^x$, $x = \ln 2$

58. $y = \dfrac{x}{1 - x}$, $x = 3$

59. $x^2 - y^2 = 9$, $x = 7$, $y > 0$

60. $xy = 6$, $x = 1$

61. If $r = x(20 - .1x)$ is a total revenue function, find the marginal revenue function.

62. If $c = .0001x^3 - .02x^2 + 3x + 6000$ is a total cost function, find the marginal cost when $x = 100$.

63. If $C = 7 + .6I - .25\sqrt{I}$ is a consumption function, find the marginal propensity to consume and the marginal propensity to save when $I = 16$.

64. If $p = (x + 14)/(x + 4)$ is a demand equation, find the instantaneous rate of change of price p with respect to quantity x.

65. If $p = -.5x + 450$ is a demand equation, find the marginal revenue function.

66. If $\bar{c} = (500/x)\, e^{x/300}$ is an average cost function, find the marginal cost function.

67. A manufacturer has determined that m employees will produce a total of x units per day where $x = m(50 - m)$. If his demand function is given by $p = -.01x + 9$, find the marginal revenue product when $m = 10$.

Chapter 8

Applications of Differential Calculus

8-1 INTERCEPTS, SYMMETRY, AND ASYMPTOTES

Examining the graphical behavior of equations is a basic part of business and economic analysis. In this section we shall examine equations to determine whether their graphs have certain features. Specifically, we shall consider *intercepts*, *symmetry*, and *asymptotes*.

A point where a graph intersects the x-axis is called an *x-intercept* of the graph and has the form $(x, 0)$. A *y-intercept* is a point $(0, y)$ where the graph intersects the y-axis.

EXAMPLE 1

Find the x- and y-intercepts of the graphs of the following equations.

a. $x^2 + y^2 = 25$.

If $(x, 0)$ is an x-intercept, its coordinates must satisfy $x^2 + y^2 = 25$. Setting $y = 0$

and solving for x will give the abscissas of the x-intercepts.

$$x^2 + 0^2 = 25.$$

$$x = \pm 5.$$

The x-intercepts are thus $(5, 0)$ and $(-5, 0)$. Similarly, to determine the ordinates of the y-intercepts we set $x = 0$ in $x^2 + y^2 = 25$ and solve for y.

$$0^2 + y^2 = 25.$$

$$y = \pm 5.$$

Thus the y-intercepts are $(0, 5)$ and $(0, -5)$. See Fig. 8-1.

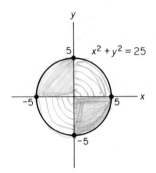

Fig. 8-1

b. $y = 1/x$.

Since x cannot be 0, the graph has no y-intercept. If $y = 0$, then $0 = 1/x$ and this equation has no solution. Thus no x-intercepts exist (see Fig. 8-2).

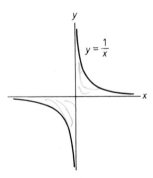

Fig. 8-2

At times it may be quite difficult or even impossible to find intercepts. For example, it would be difficult to find the x-intercepts of the graph of $y - \sqrt{2}\, x^5 - 3ex^4 + \pi x^3 - 4x^2 - 7 = 0$, although the y-intercept is easily found to be $(0, 7)$. In cases such as this, we settle for those intercepts that we can find conveniently.

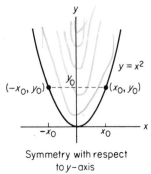

Symmetry with respect
to y-axis

Fig. 8-3

Consider the graph of $y = x^2$ in Fig. 8-3. The portion for which $x \leq 0$ is the reflection (or mirror image) through the y-axis of that portion for which $x \geq 0$. The converse is also true. More precisely, if (x_0, y_0) is any point on the graph of $y = x^2$, then the point $(-x_0, y_0)$ must also lie on the graph. We say that this graph is *symmetric with respect to the y-axis.*

DEFINITION.   *A graph is **symmetric with respect to the y-axis** if and only if* $(-x_0, y_0)$ *lies on the graph when* (x_0, y_0) *does.*

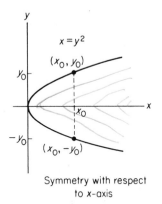

Symmetry with respect
to x-axis

Fig. 8-4

The graph of $x = y^2$ appears in Fig. 8-4. Here the portion for which $y \leq 0$ is the reflection through the x-axis of that portion for which $y \geq 0$, and the converse also holds. If (x_0, y_0) lies on the graph, then $(x_0, -y_0)$ also lies on it. We say that this graph is *symmetric with respect to the x-axis.*

DEFINITION.   *A graph is **symmetric with respect to the x-axis** if and only if* $(x_0, -y_0)$ *lies on the graph when* (x_0, y_0) *does.*

A third type of symmetry, *symmetry with respect to the origin*, is illustrated by the graph of $y = x^3$ (Fig. 8-5). Whenever (x_0, y_0) lies on the graph, then $(-x_0, -y_0)$ also lies on it. Note that the line segment joining (x_0, y_0) and $(-x_0, -y_0)$ is bisected by the origin.

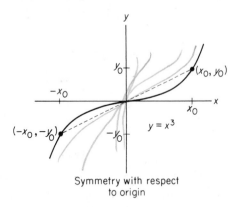

Symmetry with respect
to origin

Fig. 8-5

DEFINITION.   *A graph is **symmetric with respect to the origin** if and only if $(-x_0, -y_0)$ lies on the graph when (x_0, y_0) does.*

PITFALL.   *In Fig. 8-5, (x_0, y_0) is in Quadrant I. In general, however, (x_0, y_0) may be in any quadrant.*

EXAMPLE 2

Find the intercepts of the graph of $f(x) = 1 - x^4$ and determine whether or not the graph is symmetric with respect to the x-axis, the y-axis, or the origin. Sketch the graph.

Intercepts.   Let $y = 1 - x^4$. Testing for x-intercepts, we set $y = 0$. Then

$$1 - x^4 = 0$$

$$(1 - x^2)(1 + x^2) = 0$$

$$(1 - x)(1 + x)(1 + x^2) = 0$$

$$x = 1 \text{ or } x = -1.$$

The x-intercepts are thus $(1, 0)$ and $(-1, 0)$. Testing for y-intercepts, we set $x = 0$. Then $y = 1$ and so $(0, 1)$ is the only y-intercept.

Symmetry.   Suppose (x_0, y_0) is *any* point on the graph of $y = 1 - x^4$. Then

$$y_0 = 1 - x_0^4.$$

To test for x-axis symmetry, we determine whether the coordinates of $(x_0, -y_0)$ satisfy $y = 1 - x^4$:

$$(-y_0) \overset{?}{=} 1 - (x_0)^4$$

$$-y_0 \overset{?}{=} 1 - x_0^4.$$

But as stated above, $y_0 = 1 - x_0^4$ and so $-y_0 \neq 1 - x_0^4$. Thus the graph is *not* symmetric with respect to the x-axis.

To test for y-axis symmetry, we determine whether the coordinates of $(-x_0, y_0)$ satisfy $y = 1 - x^4$:

$$y_0 \overset{?}{=} 1 - (-x_0)^4$$

$$y_0 \overset{?}{=} 1 - x_0^4.$$

But we know $y_0 = 1 - x_0^4$. Thus the graph *is* symmetric with respect to the y-axis. To test for symmetry with respect to the origin, we determine whether the coordinates of $(-x_0, -y_0)$ satisfy $y = 1 - x^4$:

$$(-y_0) \overset{?}{=} 1 - (-x_0)^4$$

$$-y_0 \overset{?}{=} 1 - x_0^4.$$

As stated above, $-y_0 \neq 1 - x_0^4$ and so the graph is *not* symmetric with respect to the origin.

Discussion.   If the intercepts and some points (x, y) where $x > 0$ are plotted, we can sketch the entire graph by using the property of symmetry with respect to the y-axis (Fig. 8-6).

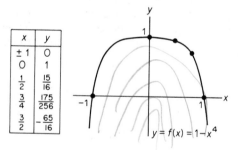

x	y
± 1	0
0	1
$\frac{1}{2}$	$\frac{15}{16}$
$\frac{3}{4}$	$\frac{175}{256}$
$\frac{3}{2}$	$-\frac{65}{16}$

$$y = f(x) = 1 - x^4$$

Fig. 8-6

In testing for symmetry in Example 2, (x_0, y_0) can be any point. Thus, for convenience we shall drop the subscripts in the future. This means that we will have symmetry with respect to the x-axis if the equation that results when y is replaced by $-y$ is equivalent to the original equation. For y-axis symmetry or symmetry with respect to the origin, we replace x by $-x$, or both x by $-x$ and y by $-y$, respectively.

EXAMPLE 3

Test the graph of $4x^2 + 9y^2 = 36$ for intercepts and symmetry. Sketch the graph.

Intercepts.   If $y = 0$, then $x = \pm 3$. Thus the x-intercepts are $(3, 0)$ and $(-3, 0)$. If $x = 0$, then $y = \pm 2$ and the y-intercepts are $(0, 2)$ and $(0, -2)$.

Symmetry. Testing for x-axis symmetry, we replace y by $-y$:

$$4x^2 + 9(-y)^2 \stackrel{?}{=} 36$$

$$4x^2 + 9y^2 \stackrel{?}{=} 36.$$

Since we get the original equation, the graph is symmetric with respect to the x-axis. Testing for y-axis symmetry, we replace x by $-x$:

$$4(-x)^2 + 9y^2 \stackrel{?}{=} 36$$

$$4x^2 + 9y^2 \stackrel{?}{=} 36.$$

Again we have the original equation, and so the graph is also symmetric with respect to the y-axis.

Testing for symmetry with respect to the origin, we replace x by $-x$ and y by $-y$:

$$4(-x)^2 + 9(-y)^2 \stackrel{?}{=} 36$$

$$4x^2 + 9y^2 \stackrel{?}{=} 36.$$

Since this is the original equation, the graph is also symmetric with respect to the origin.

Discussion. In Fig. 8-7 the intercepts and some points in the first quadrant are plotted and connected by a smooth curve. By symmetry with respect to the x-axis, the points in the fourth quadrant are obtained. Then by symmetry with respect to the y-axis the complete graph is found. There are other ways of graphing the equation by use of symmetry. For example, after plotting the intercepts and some points in the first quadrant, then by symmetry with respect to the origin we can obtain the points in the third quadrant. By symmetry with respect to the x-axis (or y-axis) we can then obtain the entire graph.

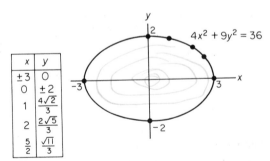

x	y
± 3	0
0	± 2
1	$\frac{4\sqrt{2}}{3}$
2	$\frac{2\sqrt{5}}{3}$
$\frac{5}{2}$	$\frac{\sqrt{11}}{3}$

Fig. 8-7

We saw in Example 3 that the graph of $4x^2 + 9y^2 = 36$ is symmetric with respect to the x-axis, the y-axis, and the origin. **For any graph, if any two of the three types of symmetry that we have discussed exist, then the third type must also exist.**

In Example 1(b) we showed that the graph of the function $y = 1/x$ has no intercepts. Although this graph is symmetric with respect to the origin (as you may verify), it has other distinguishing features (see Fig. 8-8). As x approaches

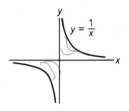

Fig. 8-8

zero from the right, $1/x$ becomes positively infinite; as x approaches zero from the left, $1/x$ becomes negatively infinite. In terms of limits, we may express these observations by writing

$$\lim_{x\to 0^+} \frac{1}{x} = \infty \quad \text{and} \quad \lim_{x\to 0^-} \frac{1}{x} = -\infty.$$

We say that the line $x = 0$ (the y-axis) is a *vertical asymptote* of the graph of $y = 1/x$. This means it is a vertical line near which the graph "blows up" (that is, the graph increases or decreases, so to speak, without bound).

On the other hand, as x approaches ∞, as well as $-\infty$, $1/x$ approaches 0. Symbolically

$$\lim_{x\to \infty} \frac{1}{x} = 0 \quad \text{and} \quad \lim_{x\to -\infty} \frac{1}{x} = 0.$$

We say that the line $y = 0$ (the x-axis) is a *horizontal asymptote* of the graph of $y = 1/x$. That is, it is a line near which the graph "settles down" as $x \to \infty$ or $x \to -\infty$.

DEFINITION. *The line $x = a$ is a **vertical asymptote** of the graph of the function f if and only if*

$$\lim_{x\to a^+} f(x) = \infty \ (\text{or } -\infty)$$

or

$$\lim_{x\to a^-} f(x) = \infty \ (\text{or } -\infty).$$

*The line $y = b$ is a **horizontal asymptote** of the graph of f if and only if*

$$\lim_{x\to \infty} f(x) = b \quad \text{or} \quad \lim_{x\to -\infty} f(x) = b.$$

Note that if $x = a$ is a vertical asymptote, the function cannot be continuous at a—in fact, it will have an infinite discontinuity at a.

EXAMPLE 4

Determine the horizontal and vertical asymptotes for the graphs of the following functions.

a. $y = \dfrac{1}{x - 2} + 3.$

Testing for horizontal asymptotes, we obtain

$$\lim_{x \to \infty} \left[\frac{1}{x - 2} + 3 \right] = \lim_{x \to \infty} \frac{1}{x - 2} + \lim_{x \to \infty} 3.$$

As x increases without bound, so does $x - 2$ and so $1/(x - 2)$ approaches zero. Thus

$$\lim_{x \to \infty} \left[\frac{1}{x - 2} + 3 \right] = 3$$

and the line $y = 3$ is a horizontal asymptote. Also,

$$\lim_{x \to -\infty} \left[\frac{1}{x - 2} + 3 \right] = \lim_{x \to -\infty} \frac{1}{x - 2} + \lim_{x \to -\infty} 3$$

$$= 0 + 3 = 3.$$

Hence the graph will settle down near the line $y = 3$ both as $x \to \infty$ and $x \to -\infty$.

To determine vertical asymptotes, we must find where $\dfrac{1}{x - 2} + 3$ blows up. Note that the denominator of $1/(x - 2)$ is 0 when $x = 2$. If x is slightly larger than 2, then $x - 2$ is both close to 0 and positive. Thus $1/(x - 2)$ is very large and consequently,

$$\lim_{x \to 2^+} \left[\frac{1}{x - 2} + 3 \right] = \infty.$$

Hence, the line $x = 2$ is a vertical asymptote. If x is slightly less than 2, then $x - 2$ is very close to 0 but negative. Thus $1/(x - 2)$ is "very negative" and so

$$\lim_{x \to 2^-} \left[\frac{1}{x - 2} + 3 \right] = -\infty.$$

We conclude that the function increases without bound as $x \to 2^+$ and decreases without bound as $x \to 2^-$. The graph appears in Fig. 8-9. The dotted lines indicate the asymptotes and are not part of the graph. **Usually a good place to look for vertical asymptotes of $y = f(x)$ are at those values of x for which a denominator of $f(x)$ is 0.**

b. $y = e^x - 1.$

Testing for horizontal asymptotes, we let $x \to \infty$. Then e^x increases without bound and so

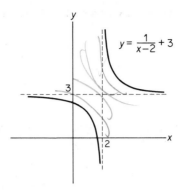

Fig. 8-9

$$\lim_{x \to \infty} (e^x - 1) = \infty.$$

Thus the graph does not settle down as $x \to \infty$. However, as $x \to -\infty$, then $e^x \to 0$ and so

$$\lim_{x \to -\infty} (e^x - 1) = \lim_{x \to -\infty} e^x - \lim_{x \to -\infty} 1$$

$$= 0 - 1 = -1.$$

Therefore $y = -1$ is a horizontal asymptote. The graph has no vertical asymptotes, since $e^x - 1$ neither increases nor decreases without bound around any fixed value of x (see Fig. 8-10).

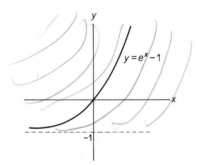

Fig. 8-10

EXAMPLE 5

Sketch the graph of $y = \dfrac{x^2}{x^2 - 1}$ *with the aid of intercepts, symmetry, and asymptotes.*

Intercepts.   If $x = 0$, then $y = 0$; if $y = 0$, then $x = 0$. Therefore the x-intercept, as well as the y-intercept, is $(0, 0)$.

Symmetry.   Testing for x-axis symmetry, we replace y by $-y$:

$$(-y) \overset{?}{=} \frac{x^2}{x^2 - 1}$$

$$-y \overset{?}{=} \frac{x^2}{x^2 - 1}.$$

We conclude that the graph is *not* symmetric with respect to the x-axis. Testing for y-axis symmetry, we replace x by $-x$:

$$y \overset{?}{=} \frac{(-x)^2}{(-x)^2 - 1}$$

$$y \overset{?}{=} \frac{x^2}{x^2 - 1}.$$

The graph *is* symmetric with respect to the y-axis. *Symmetry with respect to exactly one axis implies that the graph cannot be symmetric with respect to the origin.*

Asymptotes.
Horizontal:

$$\lim_{x \to \infty} \frac{x^2}{x^2 - 1} = \lim_{x \to \infty} \frac{1}{1 - \dfrac{1}{x^2}}$$ (dividing both numerator and denominator by x^2)

$$= \frac{1}{1 - 0} = 1.$$

Therefore as $x \to \infty$, the graph approaches the line $y = 1$, a horizontal asymptote. By symmetry, as $x \to -\infty$, the graph again approaches the line $y = 1$.

Vertical:
Since

$$\frac{x^2}{x^2 - 1} = \frac{x^2}{(x - 1)(x + 1)},$$

it is easy to see from the denominator that the graph will blow up when x is close to 1 or -1. In fact,

$$\lim_{x \to 1^-} \frac{x^2}{(x - 1)(x + 1)} = -\infty \quad \text{and} \quad \lim_{x \to 1^+} \frac{x^2}{(x - 1)(x + 1)} = \infty.$$

By symmetry,

$$\lim_{x \to -1^+} \frac{x^2}{(x - 1)(x + 1)} = -\infty \quad \text{and} \quad \lim_{x \to -1^-} \frac{x^2}{(x - 1)(x + 1)} = \infty.$$

Thus the lines $x = 1$ and $x = -1$ are vertical asymptotes.

Discussion.   By plotting the intercept and other points on the graph when $x > 0$, and by using the properties of symmetry and asymptotes, it is relatively easy to sketch the graph (see Fig. 8-11).

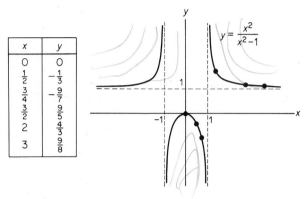

x	y
0	0
$\frac{1}{2}$	$-\frac{1}{3}$
$\frac{3}{4}$	$-\frac{9}{7}$
$\frac{3}{2}$	$\frac{9}{5}$
2	$\frac{4}{3}$
3	$\frac{9}{8}$

$$y = \frac{x^2}{x^2 - 1}$$

Fig. 8-11

EXERCISE 8-1

Find the x- and y-intercepts of the graphs of each of the equations in problems 1–20. Also determine whether or not the graphs are symmetric with respect to the x-axis, the y-axis, or the origin. Do not sketch.

1. $y = 5x$ **2.** $y = 7$

3. $x = -2$ **4.** $y = x^2 - 4$

5. $x - 4y - y^2 + 21 = 0$ **6.** $y = |2x| - 2$

7. $|x| - |y| = 0$ **8.** $y = x^3 - x$

9. $y = x^3 - 4x$ **10.** $y = \sqrt{x^2 - 4}$

11. $x = -y^{-4}$ **12.** $y = e^{x^2}$

13. $e^{x^2 + y^2} - 5 = 0$ **14.** $x^2 - y^2 = 1$

15. $4x^2 - 9y^2 = 36$ **16.** $x^2 + y^2 = 16$

17. $16x^2 + y^2 = 16$ **18.** $x^3 - xy = 0$

19. $y = x^3/(x^2 + 5)$ **20.** $x^2 + xy + y^2 = 0$

Determine the horizontal and vertical asymptotes of the graphs of the functions in problems 21–30. Do not sketch.

21. $y = \dfrac{4}{x}$ **22.** $y = -\dfrac{4}{x^2}$

23. $y = \dfrac{4}{x - 6} + 4$

24. $y = \dfrac{2x + 1}{2x - 1}$

25. $f(x) = \dfrac{x - 1}{2x + 3}$

26. $f(x) = \dfrac{x^2}{5}$

27. $f(x) = \sqrt[3]{x^2}$

28. $f(x) = e^{x^3}$

29. $y = 2e^{x+2} + 4$

30. $y = \dfrac{x^2(x^2 - 9)}{x^2}$

For each of the functions in problems 31–40, determine the same properties as instructed in problems 1–20, the same as instructed in problems 21–30, and sketch the graphs.

31. $y = \dfrac{3}{x - 1}$

32. $y = \dfrac{x}{4 - x}$

33. $f(x) = \dfrac{8}{x^3}$

34. $f(x) = \dfrac{1}{x^4}$

35. $f(x) = \dfrac{x^2}{x^2 - 4}$

36. $f(x) = \dfrac{1}{x^2 - 1}$

37. $y = 3 - e^{2x}$

38. $y = e^{-x} - 1$

39. $y = \dfrac{x^2(x^2 - 9)}{x^2}$

40. $y = \dfrac{x^3 - x}{x}$

41. In discussing the time pattern of purchasing, Mantell and Sing† use the curve

$$y = \frac{x}{a + bx}$$

as a mathematical model. They claim that $y = 1/b$ is an asymptote. Verify this.

42. Sketch the graphs of $y = 6 - 3e^{-x}$ and $y = 6 + 3e^{-x}$. Show that they are both asymptotic to the same line. What is the equation of this line?

43. For a new product, Instant Eggroll, the yearly number of thousand packages sold, y, after t years from its introduction is given by

$$y = f(t) = 150 - 76e^{-t}.$$

Show that $y = 150$ is a horizontal asymptote of the graph. This shows that after the product is established with consumers, the market tends to be constant.

---

† L. H. Mantell and F. P. Sing, *Economics for Business Decisions* (New York: McGraw-Hill Book Co., 1972), p. 107.

8-2 THE FIRST DERIVATIVE AND RELATIVE MAXIMA AND MINIMA

In curve sketching, plotting points at random usually is not good enough to properly determine a curve's shape. For example, the points $(-1, 0)$, $(0, -1)$, and $(1, 0)$ satisfy the equation $y = (x + 1)^3 (x - 1)$. You might hastily conclude that its graph should appear as in Fig. 8-12(a) when in fact the actual shape is given in Fig. 8-12(b). In this section, as well as in the following one, we shall explore the role that differentiation plays in analyzing an equation so that we may determine the true shape and behavior of its graph.

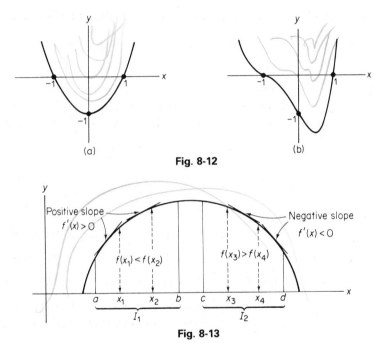

(a)   (b)

Fig. 8-12

Fig. 8-13

Suppose Fig. 8-13 gives the graph of a function f whose equation is $y = f(x)$. As x increases (goes from left to right) on the interval I_1 determined by a and b, the corresponding values of y increase and the curve is rising. Symbolically, if x_1 and x_2 are any two points in I_1 such that $x_2 > x_1$, then $f(x_2) > f(x_1)$ and f is said to be an *increasing function* on I_1. Moreover, for this portion of the curve, any tangent line will have a positive slope, and thus the derivative $f'(x)$ must be positive for all x in I_1. On the other hand, as x increases on the interval I_2 determined by c and d, the curve is falling. Here $x_4 > x_3$ implies $f(x_4) < f(x_3)$ and f is said to be a *decreasing function* on I_2. In this case any tangent line has a negative slope, and thus $f'(x) < 0$ for all x in I_2.

DEFINITION.   *A function f is an **increasing** [**decreasing**] **function** on the interval I if and only if for any two points x_1, x_2 in I such that $x_2 > x_1$, then $f(x_2) > f(x_1)$ $[f(x_2) < f(x_1)]$.*

RULE 1.   *If $f'(x) > 0$ on an interval I, then f is an increasing function on I. If $f'(x) < 0$ on I, then f is a decreasing function on I.*

A function f is said to be increasing at a *point* x_0 if there is an interval around x_0 on which f is increasing. Thus in Fig. 8-13, f is increasing at x_1 and is decreasing at x_3.

To illustrate these notions we shall use Rule 1 to find when $y = 18x - \dfrac{2x^3}{3}$ is increasing or decreasing. Letting $y = f(x)$, we have

$$f'(x) = 18 - 2x^2 = 2(3 + x)(3. - x).$$

Using the technique of Sec. 6-4, we can find the sign of $f'(x)$ by considering the intervals determined by the roots of $2(3 + x)(3 - x) = 0$, namely 3 and -3 (see Fig. 8-14). In each interval the sign of $f'(x)$ is determined by the

Fig. 8-14

signs of its factors:

if $x < -3$, then $f'(x) = 2(-)(+) = (-)$ and f is decreasing;

if $-3 < x < 3$, then $f'(x) = 2(+)(+) = (+)$ and f is increasing;

if $x > 3$, then $f'(x) = 2(+)(-) = (-)$ and f is decreasing (see Fig. 8-15).

Thus f is decreasing on $(-\infty, -3)$ and $(3, \infty)$, and is increasing on $(-3, 3)$ as seen in Fig. 8-16. These results could be sharpened. Actually f is decreasing

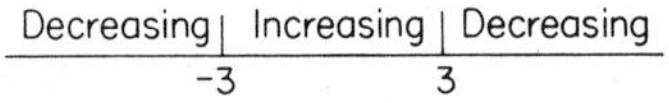

Decreasing | Increasing | Decreasing
                 -3   3

Fig. 8-15

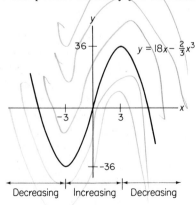

Fig. 8-16

on $(-\infty, -3]$ and $[3, \infty)$, and increasing on $[-3, 3]$. However, for our purposes, open intervals are quite sufficient. *It will be our practice to determine open intervals on which a function is increasing or decreasing.*

Look now at the graph of $y = f(x)$ in Fig. 8-17. Three observations can be made.

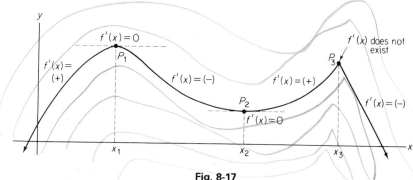

Fig. 8-17

First, there is something special about the points P_1, P_2, and P_3. Notice that P_1 is *higher* than any other "nearby" points on the curve—likewise for P_3. The point P_2 is *lower* than any other "nearby" points on the curve. Since P_1, P_2, and P_3 may not necessarily be the highest or lowest points on the *entire* curve, we simply say that f has a *relative maximum* when $x = x_1$ and when $x = x_3$, and a *relative minimum* when $x = x_2$. Actually, there is an *absolute maximum* (highest point) when $x = x_1$, but there is no *absolute minimum* (lowest point), since the curve is assumed to extend downward indefinitely. We define these new terms as follows:

DEFINITION. *A function f has an **absolute maximum** [**minimum**] when $x = x_0$ if $f(x_0) \geq f(x)$ $[f(x_0) \leq f(x)]$ for all x in the domain of f.*

DEFINITION. *A function f has a **relative maximum** [**minimum**] when $x = x_0$ if there is an interval around x_0 on which f has an absolute maximum [minimum] when $x = x_0$.*

Our second observation is that at a relative maximum or minimum, the derivative $f'(x)$ may not be defined (as at $x = x_3$). But whenever it is defined, it is 0 (as at $x = x_1$ and $x = x_2$), and hence the tangent line is horizontal as shown in Fig. 8-17. We may state:

RULE 2. *If f has a relative maximum or minimum when $x = x_0$, then $f'(x_0) = 0$ or $f'(x_0)$ is not defined.*

Third, each relative maximum or minimum occurs at a point at which the sign of $f'(x)$ is changing, regardless of whether or not the derivative is defined at the point. For the relative maximum when $x = x_1$, $f'(x)$ goes from $(+)$ for $x < x_1$ to $(-)$ for $x > x_1$, *as long as x is near x_1*. At the relative minimum when $x = x_2$, $f'(x)$ goes from $(-)$ to $(+)$, and at the relative maximum when $x = x_3$, it again goes from $(+)$ to $(-)$. Thus, around relative maxima, f is increasing and then decreasing, and the reverse holds for relative minima.

RULE 3.   *If x_0 is in the domain of f and $f'(x)$ changes from positive to negative as x increases through x_0, then f has a relative maximum when $x = x_0$. If $f'(x)$ changes from negative to positive as x increases through x_0, then f has a relative minimum when $x = x_0$.*

From Rules 1, 2, and 3, it should be evident that relative maxima or minima may occur at values of x for which $f'(x) = 0$ or is not defined, for it is there that $f'(x)$ may change sign. These values of x, called *critical values*, determine intervals (on the real number line) over which the sign of $f'(x)$ should be examined.

DEFINITION.   *If $f'(x_0) = 0$ or $f'(x_0)$ is not defined, x_0 is called a **critical value** of f. If x_0 is a critical value and is in the domain of f, then $(x_0, f(x_0))$ is called a **critical point**.*

PITFALL.   *Not every critical value corresponds to a relative maximum or minimum.*
For example, if $y = f(x) = x^3$, then $f'(x) = 3x^2$. Since $f'(0) = 0, 0$ is a critical value. But if $x < 0$, then $3x^2 > 0$. If $x > 0$, then $3x^2 > 0$. Since $f'(x)$ does not change sign, no relative maximum or minimum exists. Indeed, since $f'(x) \geq 0$ for all x, the graph of f never falls and f is said to be *nondecreasing* (see Fig. 8-18). On the other hand, if $y = f(x) = 1/x^2$, then $y' = -2/x^3$. Since y' is not defined when $x = 0, 0$ is a critical value. If $x < 0$, then $y' > 0$. If $x > 0$, then $y' < 0$. Although a change in sign of y' occurs around $x = 0$, no relative maximum exists there, since 0 is not in the domain of f. Nevertheless, this critical value is important in determining the intervals over which f is increasing or decreasing. Our results are that f is increasing on $(-\infty, 0)$ and decreasing on $(0, \infty)$ (See Fig. 8-19).

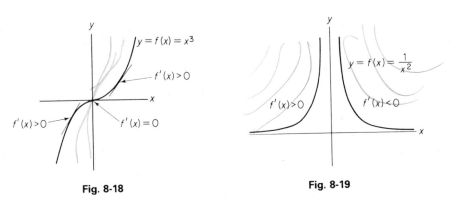

Fig. 8-18   Fig. 8-19

Summarizing the results of this section, we have the *first-derivative test* for relative maxima or minima of $y = f(x)$:

First-Derivative Test.

1. **Find $f'(x)$.**

2. **Determine critical values.**

3. **On the intervals suggested by the critical values, determine whether f is increasing ($f'(x) > 0$) or decreasing ($f'(x) < 0$).**

4. **For each critical value x_0 in the domain of f, determine whether $f'(x)$ changes sign as x increases through x_0. There is a relative maximum when $x = x_0$ if $f'(x)$ changes from $(+)$ to $(-)$ and a relative minimum if $f'(x)$ changes from $(-)$ to $(+)$. If $f'(x)$ does not change sign, there is no relative maximum or minimum when $x = x_0$.**

EXAMPLE 6

If $y = f(x) = x + \dfrac{4}{x + 1}$, use the first-derivative test to determine intervals on which f is increasing or decreasing and locate all relative maxima and minima.

1. $f'(x) = 1 - \dfrac{4}{(x + 1)^2} = \dfrac{(x + 1)^2 - 4}{(x + 1)^2} = \dfrac{(x + 3)(x - 1)}{(x + 1)^2}.$

2. Setting $f'(x) = 0$ gives the critical values $x = -3, 1$. Since $f'(-1)$ does not exist, $x = -1$ is also a critical value.

3. There are four intervals to consider (Fig. 8-20):

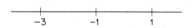

$$-3 \qquad -1 \qquad 1$$

Fig. 8-20

if $x < -3$, then $f'(x) = \dfrac{(-)(-)}{(+)} = (+)$ and f is increasing;

if $-3 < x < -1$, then $f'(x) = \dfrac{(+)(-)}{(+)} = (-)$ and f is decreasing;

if $-1 < x < 1$, then $f'(x) = \dfrac{(+)(-)}{(+)} = (-)$ and f is decreasing;

if $x > 1$, then $f'(x) = \dfrac{(+)(+)}{(+)} = (+)$ and f is increasing (Fig. 8-21).

Thus f is increasing on $(-\infty, -3)$ and $(1, \infty)$ and is decreasing on $(-3, -1)$ and $(-1, 1)$.

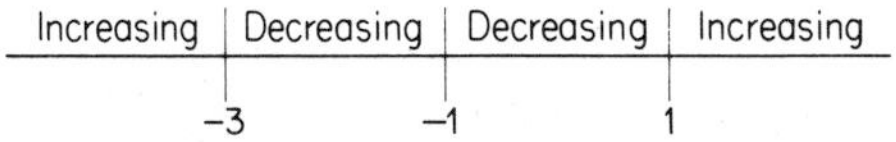

Increasing	Decreasing	Decreasing	Increasing
-3		-1	1

Fig. 8-21

4. When $x = -3$, there is a relative maximum since $f'(x)$ changes from $(+)$ to $(-)$. When $x = 1$, there is a relative minimum since $f'(x)$ changes from $(-)$ to $(+)$. We ignore $x = -1$ since -1 is not in the domain of f (Fig. 8-22).

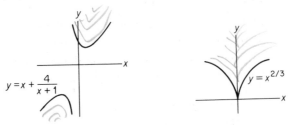

$y = x + \dfrac{4}{x+1}$

$y = x^{2/3}$

Fig. 8-22   **Fig. 8-23**

EXAMPLE 7

Test $y = f(x) = x^{2/3}$ for relative maxima or minima.

We have $f'(x) = 2/(3\sqrt[3]{x})$. When $x = 0$, then $f'(x)$ is not defined and thus $x = 0$ is a critical value. If $x < 0$, then $f'(x) < 0$. If $x > 0$, then $f'(x) > 0$. Since 0 is also in the domain of f, there is a relative (as well as an absolute) minimum when $x = 0$ (Fig. 8-23).

EXAMPLE 8

Sketch the graph of $y = f(x) = 2x^2 - x^4$.

Intercepts.   If $x = 0$, then $y = 0$. If $y = 0$, then $0 = 2x^2 - x^4 = x^2(\sqrt{2} + x)(\sqrt{2} - x)$ and thus $x = 0, \pm\sqrt{2}$. The intercepts are $(0, 0)$ $(\sqrt{2}, 0)$, and $(-\sqrt{2}, 0)$.

Symmetry.   Testing for y-axis symmetry, we have

$$y \overset{?}{=} 2(-x)^2 - (-x)^4$$

$$y \overset{?}{=} 2x^2 - x^4.$$

Since this is the original equation, there is y-axis symmetry. There is no x-axis symmetry and hence no symmetry with respect to the origin.

Asymptotes.   No horizontal or vertical asymptotes exist.

First-Derivative Test.

1. $y' = 4x - 4x^3 = 4x(1 + x)(1 - x)$.

2. Setting $y' = 0$ gives the critical values $x = 0, \pm 1$. The critical points are $(-1, 1)$, $(0, 0)$, and $(1, 1)$.

3. There are four intervals to consider in Fig. 8-24:

    if $x < -1$, then $y' = 4(-)(-)(+) = (+)$ and f is increasing;

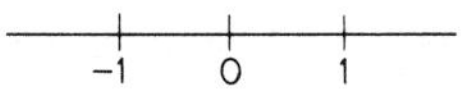

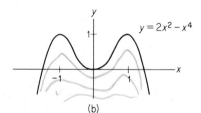

Fig. 8-24

if $-1 < x < 0$, then $y' = 4(-)(+)(+) = (-)$ and f is decreasing;

if $0 < x < 1$, then $y' = 4(+)(+)(+) = (+)$ and f is increasing;

if $x > 1$, then $y' = 4(+)(+)(-) = (-)$ and f is decreasing (Fig. 8-25).

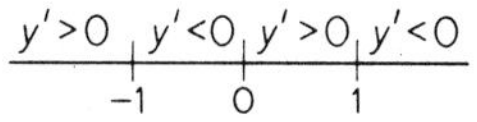

$$y'>0 \quad y'<0 \quad y'>0 \quad y'<0$$
$$\begin{array}{ccc} & & \\ -1 & 0 & 1 \end{array}$$

Fig. 8-25

4. Relative maxima occur at $(-1, 1)$ and $(1, 1)$; a relative minimum occurs at $(0, 0)$.

Discussion.   In Fig. 8-26(a) we have plotted the intercepts and the horizontal tangents at the relative maximum and minimum points. We know the curve rises from the left, has a relative maximum, then falls, has a relative minimum, then rises to a relative maximum, and falls thereafter. A sketch is shown in Fig. 8-26(b).

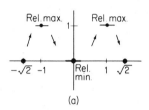

(a)

$$y = 2x^2 - x^4$$

(b)

Fig. 8-26

   In Example 8 relative maxima, as well as absolute maxima, occur at $x = \pm 1$ [see Fig. 8-26(b)]. Although there is a relative minimum, there is no absolute minimum.

   If the domain of a function is a closed interval, to determine absolute maxima or minima we must not only examine the function for relative maxima and minima, but we must also take into consideration the values of $f(x)$ at the endpoints. Although endpoints are not considered to be relative maxima or minima, they may yield *absolute* maxima or minima. Example 9 will illustrate.

EXAMPLE 9

Find all maxima and minima (relative and absolute) for $y = f(x) = x^2 - 4x + 5$ on $[1, 4]$.

1. $f'(x) = 2x - 4 = 2(x - 2)$.

2. Setting $f'(x) = 0$ gives the critical value $x = 2$ which is in the domain of f.

3. The intervals to consider are when $x < 2$ and when $x > 2$.

4. If $x < 2$, then $f'(x) < 0$ and f is decreasing; if $x > 2$, then $f'(x) > 0$ and f is increasing. Thus, there is a relative minimum when $x = 2$. It occurs on the graph at the point $(2, 1)$ [see Fig. 8-27].

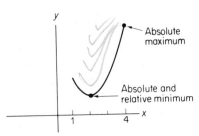

Fig. 8-27

5. Since f is decreasing for $x < 2$, then an absolute maximum may *possibly* occur at the left-hand endpoint of the domain of f, that is, when $x = 1$. Similarly, since f is increasing for $x > 2$, an absolute maximum may *possibly* occur at the right-hand endpoint, that is, when $x = 4$. Testing the endpoints, we have $f(1) = 2$ and $f(4) = 5$. Noting that $f(4) > f(1)$, we conclude that an absolute maximum occurs when $x = 4$. When $x = 2$ there is an absolute, as well as a relative, minimum.

EXERCISE 8-2

In problems 1–32 determine when the function is increasing or decreasing and locate all relative maxima and minima. Do not sketch.

1. $y = x^2 + 2$

2. $y = x^2 + 4x + 3$

3. $y = x - x^2 + 2$

4. $y = 4x - x^2$

5. $y = x^2 - 6x - 7$

6. $y = 2x^2 - 5x - 12$

7. $y = 3x - x^3$

8. $y = x^3 - 9x^2 + 24x - 19$

9. $y = 2x^3 - 9x^2 + 12x$

10. $y = x^3 - 3x^2 + 3x - 3$

11. $y = -\dfrac{x^3}{3} - 2x^2 + 5x - 2$

12. $y = 4x^3 - 3x^4$

13. $y = x^4 - 2x^2$

14. $y = -2 + 12x - x^3$

15. $y = x^3 - 6x^2 + 9x$

16. $y = x^3 - 6x^2 + 12x - 6$

17. $y = 3x^5 - 5x^3$

18. $y = 5x - x^5$

19. $y = -x^5 - 5x^4 + 200$

20. $y = 3x^4 - 4x^3 + 1$

21. $y = \dfrac{1}{x - 1}$

22. $y = \dfrac{3}{x}$

23 $y = \dfrac{10}{\sqrt{x}}$ **24.** $y = \dfrac{x}{x + 1}$

25. $y = \dfrac{x^2}{1 - x}$ **26.** $y = x + \dfrac{4}{x}$

27. $y = e^{-2x}$ **28.** $y = x \ln x$

29. $y = x^2 - 2 \ln x$ **30.** $y = xe^x$

31. $y = e^x + e^{-x}$ **32.** $y = e^{-x^2}$

33–37. Sketch the graphs of the equations given in problems 5–9.
In problems 38–42, find when absolute maxima and minima occur for the given function on the given interval.

38. $f(x) = x^2 - 2x + 3,\ [-1, 2]$

39. $f(x) = -2x^2 - 6x + 5,\ [-2, 3]$

40. $f(x) = \frac{1}{3} x^3 - x^2 - 3x + 1,\ [0, 2]$

41. $f(x) = \frac{1}{4} x^4 - \frac{3}{2} x^2,\ [0, 1]$

42. $f(x) = 4x^3 + 3x^2 - 18x + 3,\ [\frac{1}{2}, 3]$

43. If $c_f = 25{,}000$ is a fixed cost function, show that the average fixed cost function $\bar{c}_f = c_f/x$ is a decreasing function for $x > 0$. Thus, as output x increases, each unit's portion of fixed cost declines.

44. If $c = 4x - x^2 + 2x^3$ is a cost function, when is marginal cost increasing?

45. Given the demand function $p = 400 - 2x$, find when marginal revenue is increasing.

46. For the cost function $c = \sqrt{x}$, show that marginal and average costs are always decreasing for $x > 0$.

47. For a manufacturer's product, the demand function is $x = 10{,}000e^{-.02p}$. Find the value of p for which maximum revenue is obtained.

48. If $c = .01x^2 + 5x + 100$ is a cost equation, find the average cost equation. At what level of production x is there a minimum average cost? Show algebraically that the graph of the marginal cost function intersects the graph of the average cost function at this point.

8-3 THE SECOND DERIVATIVE AND CONCAVITY

We have seen how the first derivative is used to determine when a function is increasing or decreasing and to locate relative maxima and minima. However, for us to know with assurance the actual shape of a curve, we must have additional information. For example, consider the curve $y = f(x) = x^2$. Since

$f'(x) = 2x$ and $f'(0) = 0$, then $x = 0$ is a critical value. If $x < 0$, then $f'(x) < 0$ and f is decreasing; if $x > 0$, then $f'(x) > 0$ and f is increasing. Thus there is a relative minimum when $x = 0$. Figures 8-28(a) and (b) both satisfy the

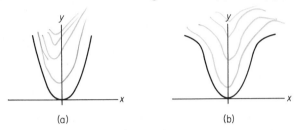

(a)   (b)

Fig. 8-28

preceding conditions. But which one truly describes the curve? This question will easily be settled by using the second derivative and the notion of *concavity*.

In Fig. 8-29, note that in each case the curve $y = f(x)$ "bends" (or opens) upward. Moreover, for each curve, if tangent lines are drawn their slopes increase in value as x increases. In (a) the slopes go from small positive values to larger values; in (b) they are negative and approaching zero (thus increasing); in (c) they pass from negative values to positive values. Since $f'(x)$ gives the slope at a point, f' is an increasing function here. In each case we say that the curve (or function f) is *concave up*. By a similar analysis, in Fig. 8-30 it can be seen in each case that as x increases, the slopes of the tangent lines are decreasing and the curves are bending downward. Thus f' is a decreasing function here, and we say f is *concave down*.

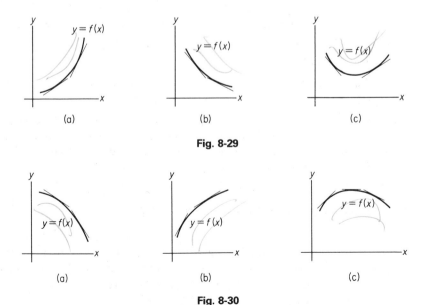

(a)   (b)   (c)

Fig. 8-29

(a)   (b)   (c)

Fig. 8-30

DEFINITION.   *A function f is said to be **concave up** [**concave down**] on an interval I if f'
is an increasing [decreasing] function on I.*

PITFALL.   *Concavity relates to whether f', not f, is increasing or decreasing. Thus in Fig.
8-29(b), note that f is concave up and decreasing, but in Fig. 8-30(a) note that f is
concave down and decreasing.*

Since f' is increasing when its derivative $D_x[f'(x)] = f''(x)$ is positive
and f' is decreasing when $f''(x)$ is negative, we can state the following rule:

RULE 4.   *A function f is concave up on an interval I if f'' (x) > 0 on I. It is concave down
on I if f''(x) < 0 on I.*

A function f is also said to be concave up at a *point* x_0 if there exists
an interval around x_0 on which f is concave up. In fact, for the functions
that we shall consider, if $f''(x_0) > 0$, then f is concave up at x_0.† Similarly,
f is concave down at x_0 if $f''(x_0) < 0$.

EXAMPLE 10

a. *Test $y = f(x) = (x - 1)^3 + 1$ for concavity.*

Since $y' = 3(x - 1)^2$, then $y'' = 6(x - 1)$. Thus f is concave up when $6(x - 1) > 0$;
that is, when $x > 1$. Similarly, f is concave down when $x < 1$ (Fig. 8-31). [For example,
since $f''(2) > 0$, f is concave up at $x = 2$.]

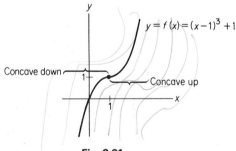

Fig. 8-31

b. *Test $y = x^2$ for concavity.*

Since $y' = 2x$, then $y'' = 2 > 0$. Thus the graph of $y = x^2$ must always be concave
up, as in Fig. 8-28(a). The graph of $y = x^2$ cannot appear as in Fig. 8-28(b), for
in that situation there are intervals on which the curve is concave down.

A point on a graph, such as (1, 1) in Fig. 8-31, where concavity changes
from downward to upward, or vice versa, is called a **point of inflection.** For
this to occur, the sign of $f''(x)$ must go from (−) to (+) or from (+) to (−).

---

†This is guaranteed for functions f such that f'' is continuous.

Possible inflection points are points where $f''(x) = 0$ or is not defined. In fact, such points determine intervals that should be examined when testing for concavity. We use the same method as that for determining when a function is increasing or decreasing.

EXAMPLE 11

Test $y = 6x^4 - 8x^3 + 1$ *for concavity and points of inflection.*

$$y' = 24x^3 - 24x^2$$

$$y'' = 72x^2 - 48x = 24x(3x - 2) = 72x\left(x - \tfrac{2}{3}\right).$$

Setting $y'' = 0$ gives $x = 0, \tfrac{2}{3}$ as *possible* points of inflection. There are three intervals to consider (Fig. 8-32):

Fig. 8-32

if $x < 0$, then $y'' = 72(-)(-) = (+)$ and the curve is concave up;

if $0 < x < \tfrac{2}{3}$, then $y'' = 72(+)(-) = (-)$ and the curve is concave down;

if $x > \tfrac{2}{3}$, then $y'' = 72(+)(+) = (+)$ and the curve is concave up (Fig. 8-33).

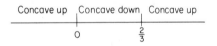

Fig. 8-33

Since concavity changes when $x = 0$ and $x = \tfrac{2}{3}$, inflection points occur for these values of x (Fig. 8-34). Summarizing, the curve is concave up on $(-\infty, 0)$ and $(\tfrac{2}{3}, \infty)$ and is concave down on $(0, \tfrac{2}{3})$. Inflection points occur when $x = 0$ or $x = \tfrac{2}{3}$.

PITFALL. *If* $f''(x_0) = 0$, *this does not prove that f has an inflection point when* $x = x_0$. *For if* $f(x) = x^4$, *then* $f''(x) = 12x^2$ *and* $f''(0) = 0$. *But* $x < 0$ *implies* $f''(x) > 0$, *and* $x > 0$ *implies* $f''(x) > 0$. *Thus, concavity does not change and there are no inflection points* (*Fig. 8-35*).

EXAMPLE 12

Sketch the graph of $y = 2x^3 - 9x^2 + 12x$.

Intercepts.   When $x = 0$, then $y = 0$. Setting $y = 0$ gives $0 = x(2x^2 - 9x + 12)$ which has $x = 0$ as the only real root. Thus the only intercept is $(0, 0)$.

Symmetry.   None.

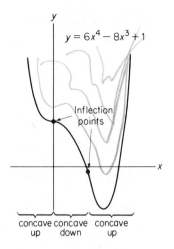

Fig. 8-34

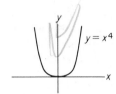

Fig. 8-35

Asymptotes.   None.

Letting $y = f(x)$, we have

$$f'(x) = 6x^2 - 18x + 12 = 6(x - 1)(x - 2)$$

$$f''(x) = 12x - 18 = 12\left(x - \tfrac{3}{2}\right).$$

Maxima and Minima.   From $f'(x)$ the critical values are $x = 1, 2$ (Fig. 8-36).

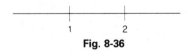

Fig. 8-36

If $x < 1$, then $f'(x) = 6(-)(-) = (+)$ and f is increasing;
if $1 < x < 2$, then $f'(x) = 6(+)(-) = (-)$ and f is decreasing;
if $x > 2$, then $f'(x) = 6(+)(+) = (+)$ and f is increasing [Fig. 8-37].
There is a relative maximum when $x = 1$ and a relative minimum when $x = 2$.

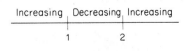

Fig. 8-37

Concavity. Setting $f''(x) = 0$ gives a possible inflection point at $x = \frac{3}{2}$. When $x < \frac{3}{2}$, then $f''(x) < 0$ and f is concave down. When $x > \frac{3}{2}$, then $f''(x) > 0$ and f is concave up. See Fig. 8-38.

Concave   Concave
down   up

$\dfrac{3}{2}$

Fig. 8-38

Since concavity changes, there is a point of inflection when $x = \frac{3}{2}$.

Discussion. We now find the coordinates of the important points on the graph (and

x	0	1	$\frac{3}{2}$	2
y	0	5	$\frac{9}{2}$	4

any other points if there is doubt as to the behavior of the curve). As x increases, the function is first concave down and increases to a relative maximum at $(1, 5)$; it then decreases to $(\frac{3}{2}, \frac{9}{2})$; it then becomes concave up but continues to decrease until it reaches a relative minimum at $(2, 4)$; thereafter it increases and is still concave up (Fig. 8-39).

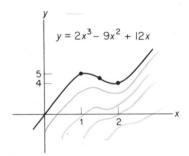

$$y = 2x^3 - 9x^2 + 12x$$

Fig. 8-39

EXAMPLE 13

Sketch the graph of $y = \dfrac{4x}{x^2 + 1}$.

Intercepts. When $x = 0$, then $y = 0$; when $y = 0$, then $x = 0$. Thus, $(0, 0)$ is the only intercept.

Symmetry. There is symmetry only with respect to the origin: replacing x by $-x$ and y by $-y$ gives

$$-y = \frac{4(-x)}{(-x)^2 + 1}$$

which is equivalent to

$$y' = \frac{4x}{x^2 + 1}.$$

Asymptotes. Testing for horizontal asymptotes, we have

$$\lim_{x \to \infty} \frac{4x}{x^2 + 1} = \lim_{x \to \infty} \frac{\dfrac{4}{x}}{1 + \dfrac{1}{x^2}} = \frac{0}{1} = 0.$$

$$\lim_{x \to -\infty} \frac{4x}{x^2 + 1} = 0.$$

The x-axis ($y = 0$) is a horizontal asymptote. There are no vertical asymptotes because the denominator is never 0.

Letting $y = f(x)$, we have

$$f'(x) = \frac{(x^2 + 1)(4) - 4x(2x)}{(x^2 + 1)^2} = \frac{4 - 4x^2}{(x^2 + 1)^2} = \frac{4(1 + x)(1 - x)}{(x^2 + 1)^2}$$

$$f''(x) = \frac{(x^2 + 1)^2 (-8x) - (4 - 4x^2)(2)(x^2 + 1)(2x)}{(x^2 + 1)^4}$$

$$= \frac{8x(x^2 + 1)(x^2 - 3)}{(x^2 + 1)^4} = \frac{8x(x + \sqrt{3})(x - \sqrt{3})}{(x^2 + 1)^3}.$$

Maxima and Minima. From $f'(x)$, the critical values are $x = \pm 1$.

If $x < -1$, then $f'(x) = \dfrac{4(-)(+)}{(+)} = (-)$ and f is decreasing;

if $-1 < x < 1$, then $f'(x) = \dfrac{4(+)(+)}{(+)} = (+)$ and f is increasing;

if $x > 1$, then $f'(x) = \dfrac{4(+)(-)}{(+)} = (-)$ and f is decreasing [Fig. 8-40].

There is a relative minimum when $x = -1$ and a relative maximum when $x = 1$.

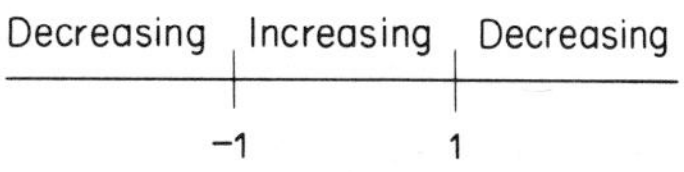

Decreasing   Increasing   Decreasing

-1 1

Fig. 8-40

Concavity. Setting $f''(x) = 0$, we see that the possible points of inflection are when $x = \pm\sqrt{3}, 0$.

If $x < -\sqrt{3}$, $f''(x) = \dfrac{8(-)(-)(-)}{(+)} = (-)$ and f is concave down;

if $-\sqrt{3} < x < 0$, $f''(x) = \dfrac{8(-)(+)(-)}{(+)} = (+)$ and f is concave up;

if $0 < x < \sqrt{3}$, $f''(x) = \dfrac{8(+)(+)(-)}{(+)} = (-)$ and f is concave down;

if $x > \sqrt{3}$, $f''(x) = \dfrac{8(+)(+)(+)}{(+)} = (+)$ and f is concave up (Fig. 8-41).

Inflection points occur when $x = 0, \pm\sqrt{3}$.

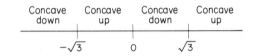

Fig. 8-41

Discussion. After considering all of the above information, the graph of $y = 4x/(x^2 + 1)$ is given in Fig. 8-42 together with a table of coordinates of important points.

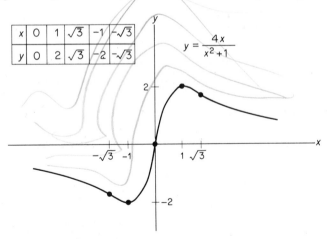

x	0	1	$\sqrt{3}$	-1	$-\sqrt{3}$
y	0	2	$\sqrt{3}$	-2	$-\sqrt{3}$

$$y = \frac{4x}{x^2+1}$$

Fig. 8-42

EXAMPLE 14

Sketch the graph of $y = \dfrac{1}{4 - x^2}$.

Intercepts. $(0, \frac{1}{4})$.

Symmetry.   Symmetrical to the y-axis.

Asymptotes.   As $x \to \infty$, $y \to 0$; as $x \to -\infty$, then $y \to 0$. Thus $y = 0$ (the x-axis) is a horizontal asymptote. Since $1/(4 - x^2)$ blows up near $x = \pm 2$, the vertical asymptotes are the lines $x = 2$ and $x = -2$.

Maxima and Minima.   Since $y = (4 - x^2)^{-1}$,

$$y' = -1(4 - x^2)^{-2}(-2x) = \frac{2x}{(4 - x^2)^2}.$$

The critical values are $x = 0, \pm 2$. If $x < -2$, then $y' < 0$; if $-2 < x < 0$, then $y' < 0$; if $0 < x < 2$, then $y' > 0$; if $x > 2$, then $y' > 0$. The function is decreasing on $(-\infty, -2)$ and $(-2, 0)$ and increasing on $(0, 2)$ and $(2, \infty)$. There is a relative minimum when $x = 0$ (Fig. 8-43).

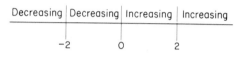

Fig. 8-43

Concavity.

$$y'' = \frac{(4 - x^2)^2 (2) - (2x) 2 (4 - x^2)(-2x)}{(4 - x^2)^4} = \frac{2(4 - x^2)(4 + 3x^2)}{(4 - x^2)^4} = \frac{8 + 6x^2}{(4 - x^2)^3}.$$

Setting $y'' = 0$ we get no real roots, but y'' is undefined when $x = \pm 2$. If $x < -2$, then $y'' < 0$; if $-2 < x < 2$, then $y'' > 0$; if $x > 2$, then $y'' < 0$. The graph is concave up on $(-2, 2)$ and concave down on $(-\infty, -2)$ and $(2, \infty)$ (Fig. 8-44). Although concavity changes around $x = \pm 2$, these values of x do not give points of inflection since y *itself* is not defined at $x = \pm 2$.

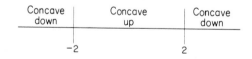

Fig. 8-44

Discussion.   Plotting the points in the table, some arbitrarily chosen, and using the above information, we get the graph in Fig. 8-45. Due to symmetry our table has only $x > 0$.

EXERCISE 8-3

In problems 1-10, determine concavity and points of inflection. Do not sketch.

1. $y = -2x^2 + 4x$

2. $y = 3x^2 - 6x + 5$

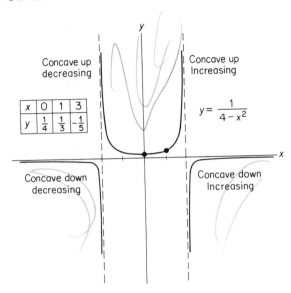

Fig. 8-45

3. $y = 4x^3 + 12x^2 - 12x$

4. $y = x^3 - 6x^2 + 9x + 1$

5. $y = x^4 - 6x^2 + 5x - 6$

6. $y = -\dfrac{x^4}{4} + \dfrac{9x^2}{2} + 2x$

7. $y = e^x$

8. $y = e^x - e^{-x}$

9. $y = xe^x$

10. $y = xe^{-x}$

In problems 11-40 sketch each curve. Determine: intervals on which the function is increasing, decreasing, concave up, concave down; relative maxima and minima; inflection points; symmetry; horizontal and vertical asymptotes; those intercepts which can be obtained conveniently.

11. $y = x^2 + 4x + 3$

12. $y = x^2 + 2$

13. $y = 4x - x^2$

14. $y = x - x^2 + 2$

15. $y = 2x^2 - 5x - 12$

16. $y = x^2 - 6x - 7$

17. $y = x^3 - 9x^2 + 24x - 19$

18. $y = 3x - x^3$

19. $y = \dfrac{x^3}{3} - 3x$

20. $y = x^3 - 6x^2 + 9x$

21. $y = x^3 - 3x^2 + 3x - 3$

22. $y = 2x^3 - 9x^2 + 12x$

23. $y = 4x^2 - x^4$

24. $y = -\dfrac{x^3}{3} - 2x^2 + 5x - 2$

25. $y = 4x^3 - 3x^4$

26. $y = x^4 - 2x^2$

27. $y = -2 + 12x - x^3$

28. $y = (3 + 2x)^3$

29. $y = x^3 - 6x^2 + 12x - 6$

30. $y = 3x^5 - 5x^3$

31. $y = 5x - x^5$

32. $y = \dfrac{x^5}{100} - \dfrac{x^4}{20}$

33. $y = 3x^4 - 4x^3 + 1$

34. $y = x(1 - x)^3$

35. $y = \dfrac{3}{x}$

36. $y = \dfrac{1}{x - 1}$

37. $y = \dfrac{x}{x + 1}$

38. $y = \dfrac{10}{\sqrt{x}}$

39. $y = x^2 + \dfrac{1}{x^2}$

40. $y = \dfrac{x^2}{1 - x}$

41. Show that the graph of the demand equation $p = 100/(x + 2)$ is decreasing and concave up for $x > 0$.

42. For the cost function $c = 3x^2 + 5x + 6$, show that the graph of the average cost function $\bar{c}$ is always concave up for $x > 0$.

8-4 THE SECOND-DERIVATIVE TEST

Concavity gives us another way of determining whether certain critical points are relative maxima or minima. Observe in Fig. 8-46 that when $x = x_0$ we have $f'(x) = 0$. This suggests a relative maximum or minimum. However, we see also that the curve is bending upward there (that is, $f''(x_0) > 0$). This leads us to conclude that there is a relative minimum when $x = x_0$. On the other hand, $f'(x_1) = 0$ but the curve is bending downward where $x = x_1$ (that is, $f''(x_1) < 0$). From this we conclude that a relative maximum exists there. This technique of examining the second derivative at points for which $f'(x) = 0$ is called the *second-derivative test* for relative maxima and minima of $y = f(x)$.

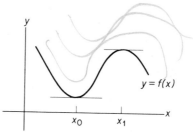

Fig. 8-46

Second-Derivative Test.

Suppose $f'(x_0) = 0$ and x_0 is in the domain of f. Then
if $f''(x_0) < 0$, there is a relative maximum when $x = x_0$;
if $f''(x_0) > 0$, there is a relative minimum when $x = x_0$;
if $f''(x_0) = 0$, the test fails (use the first-derivative test).

PITFALL. *In the case where* $f'(x_0) = f''(x_0) = 0$, *some students conclude that there is no relative maximum or minimum at* x_0. *This inference is erroneous as Example 15(c) will show.*

EXAMPLE 15

Using the second-derivative test, examine the following for relative maxima and minima.

a. $y = 18x - \frac{2}{3}x^3$.

$$y' = 18 - 2x^2 = 2(3 + x)(3 - x)$$

$$y'' = -4x.$$

Setting $y' = 0$ gives the critical values $x = \pm 3$. If $x = 3$, then $y'' < 0$ and thus there is a relative maximum when $x = 3$. If $x = -3$, then $y'' > 0$ and thus there is a relative minimum when $x = -3$ (Fig. 8-16).

b. $y = 6x^4 - 8x^3 + 1$.

$$y' = 24x^3 - 24x^2 = 24x^2(x - 1)$$

$$y'' = 72x^2 - 48x.$$

Setting $y' = 0$ gives the critical values $x = 0, 1$. Since $y'' > 0$ if $x = 1$, there is a relative minimum when $x = 1$. For $x = 0$, then $y'' = 0$ and the second-derivative test fails. Turning to the first-derivative test, if $x < 0$, then $y' < 0$; if $0 < x < 1$, then $y' < 0$. Thus no relative maximum or minimum exists at $x = 0$ (Fig. 8-34).

c. $y = x^4$.

$$y' = 4x^3$$

$$y'' = 12x^2.$$

Setting $y' = 0$ gives the critical value $x = 0$. But if $x = 0$, then $y'' = 0$ and the second-derivative test fails. Since $y' < 0$ for $x < 0$ and $y' > 0$ for $x > 0$, there is a relative minimum when $x = 0$ (Fig. 8-35).

EXERCISE 8-4

In problems 1-10, test for relative maxima and minima by using the second-derivative test.

1. $y = x^2 - 5x + 6$

2. $y = -2x^2 + 6x + 12$

3. $y = -4x^2 + 2x - 8$

4. $y = 3x^2 - 5x + 6$

5. $y = x^3 - 27x + 1$

6. $y = x^3 - 12x + 1$

7. $y = -x^3 + 3x^2 + 1$

8. $y = x^4 - 2x^2 + 4$

9. $y = 2x^4 + 2$

10. $y = -x^7$

8-5 APPLIED MAXIMA AND MINIMA

By using techniques of the previous sections, we can examine situations in business and economics which require determining the value of a variable which will maximize or minimize a function. For example, we might want to maximize profit or minimize cost. The crucial part is setting up the function to be investigated. Then by Rule 2 we set its derivative equal to 0 and test the resulting critical values. For this the first-derivative test or second-derivative test may be used, although it is often obvious from the nature of the problem whether or not the value represents an appropriate answer. We should not overlook those critical values which are in the domain of the function and for which the first derivative is not defined. For the problems that we will consider, our interest is in *absolute* maxima and minima. In some cases they may occur at endpoints, and we should not forget this fact.

Read each of the examples carefully so that you may gain insight into setting up the function to be analyzed.

EXAMPLE 16

A manufacturer determines that his total cost function is $c = \dfrac{x^2}{4} + 3x + 400$ where x is the number of units produced. At what level of output will average cost per unit be a minimum?

The quantity to be minimized is average cost $\bar{c}$. It is given by

$$\bar{c} = \frac{c}{x} = \frac{\dfrac{x^2}{4} + 3x + 400}{x} = \frac{x}{4} + 3 + \frac{400}{x}.$$

Setting $D_x\bar{c} = 0$, we have

$$D_x\bar{c} = \frac{1}{4} - \frac{400}{x^2} = 0.$$

Solving for x, we have

$$x^2 - 1600 = 0$$

$$(x - 40)(x + 40) = 0$$

$$x = 40 \quad \text{(since we assume } x > 0\text{)}.$$

Now,

$$D_x^2 \bar{c} = \frac{800}{x^3}$$

which is positive for $x > 0$. Thus the cost curve is always concave up for $x > 0$ and so we indeed have an absolute minimum when $x = 40$.

Calculus can be applied to inventory decisions as the following example shows.

EXAMPLE 17

A manufacturer annually produces and sells 10,000 units of a product. Sales are uniformly distributed throughout the year. He wishes to determine the number of units to be manufactured in each production run in order to minimize annual set-up costs and carrying costs. This is referred to as the **economic lot size** *or* **economic order quantity.** *The production cost of each unit is $20 and carrying costs (insurance, interest, storage, etc.) are estimated to be 10 percent of the value of the average inventory. Set-up costs per production run are $40. Find the economic lot size.*

Let q be the number of units in a production run. Since sales are distributed at a uniform rate, we shall assume that inventory varies uniformly from q to 0 between production runs. Thus we take the average inventory to be $q/2$ units. The production costs are $20 per unit, and so the value of the average inventory is $20(q/2)$. Carrying costs are 10 percent of this value:

$$.10(20)\left(\frac{q}{2}\right).$$

The number of production runs per year is $10,000/q$. Thus the total set-up costs are

$$40\left(\frac{10,000}{q}\right).$$

Hence the total annual carrying costs and set-up costs C are

$$C = .10(20)\left(\frac{q}{2}\right) + 40\left(\frac{10,000}{q}\right)$$

$$= q + \frac{400,000}{q}.$$

$$\frac{dC}{dq} = 1 - \frac{400,000}{q^2} = \frac{q^2 - 400,000}{q^2}.$$

Setting $dC/dq = 0$, we get

$$q^2 = 400,000.$$

We choose

$$q = \sqrt{400,000} = 200\sqrt{10} \approx 632.4.$$

If $0 < q < \sqrt{400,000}$, then $dC/dq < 0$. If $q > \sqrt{400,000}$, then $dC/dq > 0$. Thus there is an *absolute* minimum at $q = 632.4$. The number of production runs is $10,000/632.4 \approx 15.8$. For practical purposes, there would be 16 lots, each having an economic lot size of 625 units.

EXAMPLE 18

The demand equation for a manufacturer's product is $p = (80 - x)/4$ where x is the number of units and p is price/unit. At what value of x will there be maximum revenue?

Let r be total revenue. Then revenue $=$ (price) (quantity). Thus,

$$r = px = \frac{80 - x}{4} \cdot x = \frac{80x - x^2}{4}.$$

Setting $dr/dx = 0$:

$$\frac{dr}{dx} = \frac{80 - 2x}{4} = 0$$

$$x = 40.$$

Since $d^2r/dx^2 = -\frac{1}{2}$, the revenue curve is always concave down and maximum revenue is achieved at $x = 40$. This revenue would be $40(80 - 40)/4 = 400$.

EXAMPLE 19

The Fuzzy TV Cable Co. currently has 2000 subscribers who are paying a monthly rate of \$5. A survey reveals that there will be 50 more subscribers for each \$.10 decrease in the rate. At what rate will maximum revenue be obtained and how many subscribers will there be at this rate?

Let x be the rate. Then the total decrease in the rate is $5 - x$ and the number of \$.10 decreases is $\dfrac{5 - x}{.10}$. For *each* of these decreases there will be 50 more subscribers.

Thus the total of *new* subscribers is $50\left(\dfrac{5 - x}{.10}\right)$ and the total of all subscribers is

$$2000 + 50\left(\frac{5 - x}{.10}\right). \tag{1}$$

The revenue r is given by $r =$ (rate) (number of subscribers):

$$r = x\left[2000 + 50\left(\frac{5 - x}{.10}\right)\right]$$

$$= 4500x - 500x^2.$$

Setting $r' = 0$, we have

$$r' = 4500 - 1000x = 0$$

$$x = 4.50.$$

Since $r'' = -1000 < 0$, r is indeed a maximum when $x = 4.50$. Substituting $x = 4.50$ in (1) gives 2250 subscribers.

EXAMPLE 20

The cost per hour (in dollars) of operating an automobile is given by

$$C = .03s - .0003s^2 + .02, \quad 0 \le s \le 60$$

where s is the speed in miles per hour. At what speed is the cost per hour a minimum?

Setting $dC/ds = 0$, we have

$$\frac{dC}{ds} = .03 - .0006s = 0$$

$$s = 50.$$

Since $d^2C/ds^2 = -.0006$, a *maximum* occurs when $s = 50$. Thus a minimum can occur only at an endpoint of the domain. If $s = 0$, then $C = .02$ and if $s = 60$, then $C = .74$. Thus the minimum cost of $.02 per hour occurs for $s = 0$ and might be due to depreciation, insurance, registration fees, etc.

Suppose $p = f(x)$ is the demand function for a firm where p is price per unit and x is the number of units produced and sold. Then the total revenue $r = xp = xf(x)$ is a function of x. Let the total cost c of producing x units be given by the cost function $c = g(x)$. Thus, the total profit P, which is given by $P =$ total revenue $-$ total cost, is also a function of x:

$$P = r - c = xf(x) - g(x).$$

Let us consider the most profitable output for the firm. Ignoring special cases, we know that profit is maximized when $dP/dx = 0$ and $d^2P/dx^2 < 0$.

$$\frac{dP}{dx} = \frac{d}{dx}(r - c) = \frac{dr}{dx} - \frac{dc}{dx} = 0.$$

Thus

$$\frac{dr}{dx} = \frac{dc}{dx}.$$

That is, at the level of maximum profit the slope of the tangent to the total revenue curve must equal the slope of the tangent to the total cost curve (Fig. 8-47). But dr/dx is marginal revenue MR, and dc/dx is marginal cost MC.

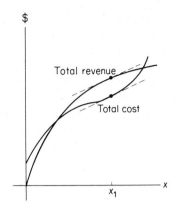

Fig. 8-47

Thus, under typical conditions, *to maximize profits it is necessary that*

$$MR = MC.$$

For this to indeed correspond to a maximum, it is necessary that $d^2 P/dx^2 < 0$.

$$\frac{d^2 P}{dx^2} = \frac{d^2 r}{dx^2} - \frac{d^2 c}{dx^2} < 0, \quad \text{or} \quad \frac{d^2 r}{dx^2} < \frac{d^2 c}{dx^2}.$$

That is, when $MR = MC$, the slope of the marginal revenue curve must be less than the slope of the marginal cost curve in order to insure maximum profit.

The condition that $d^2 P/dx^2 < 0$ when $dP/dx = 0$ can be viewed another way. Equivalently, to have $MR = MC$ correspond to a maximum it is necessary that dP/dx go from $(+)$ to $(-)$; that is, from $dr/dx - dc/dx > 0$ to $dr/dx - dc/dx < 0$. Hence, as output increases, we must have $MR > MC$ and then $MR < MC$. This means that at the point x_1 of maximum profit, *the marginal cost curve must cut the marginal revenue curve from below* (Fig. 8-48). For

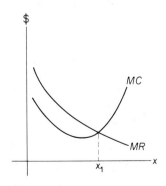

Fig. 8-48

production up to x_1, the revenue from additional output would be greater than the cost of such output and total profit would increase. For output beyond x_1, $MC > MR$ and each unit of output would add more to total costs than to total revenue. Hence, total profits would decline.

In the next example we use the word *monopolist*. Under a situation of monopoly, there is only one seller of a product for which there are no similar substitutes, and he, the monopolist, controls the market. By considering the demand equation for his product, he may set the price (or volume of output) so that maximum profit will be obtained.

EXAMPLE 21

Suppose for a monopolist the demand equation for his product is $p = 400 - 2x$ and his average cost function is $\bar{c} = .2x + 4 + (400/x)$, where x is the number of units, and both p and $\bar{c}$ are expressed in dollars. Determine:

a. *The level of output at which profit is maximized*

b. *The price at which this occurs and*

c. *The maximum profit.*

d. *If, as a regulatory device, the government imposes a tax of $22 per unit on the monopolist, what is the new price for profit maximization?*

Since revenue $r = px = 400x - 2x^2$ and total cost $c = x\bar{c} = .2x^2 + 4x + 400$, profit P is

$$P = r - c = 400x - 2x^2 - (.2x^2 + 4x + 400)$$

$$P = 396x - 2.2x^2 - 400. \tag{2}$$

a. Setting $dP/dx = 0$, we have

$$\frac{dP}{dx} = 396 - 4.4x = 0$$

$$x = 90.$$

Since $d^2P/dx^2 = -4.4 < 0$, $x = 90$ gives a maximum.

b. $p = 400 - 2(90) = 220$.

c. Substituting $x = 90$ in (2) gives $P = 17,420$.

d. The tax of 22/unit is a variable cost. His new cost function is $c_1 = .2x^2 + 4x + 400 + 22x$ and the profit P_1 is given by

$$P_1 = 400x - 2x^2 - (.2x^2 + 4x + 400 + 22x)$$

$$P_1 = 374x - 2.2x^2 - 400.$$

Setting $dP_1/dx = 0$ gives

$$\frac{dP_1}{dx} = 374 - 4.4x = 0$$

$$x = 85.$$

Thus to maximize profit, the monopolist restricts output to 85 units at a higher price of $p_1 = 400 - 170 = 230$. Since this is only $10 more than before, only part of the tax has been shifted to the consumer and the monopolist must bear the cost of the balance. His new profit is $15,495, which is lower than the former profit.

EXERCISE 8-5

In each of the following, p is price per unit and x is output per unit of time.

1. A manufacturer finds that the total cost c of producing his product is given by the cost function $c = .05x^2 + 5x + 500$. At what level of output will average cost per unit be at a minimum?

2. For a monopolist's product, the revenue function is given by $r = 240x + 57x^2 - x^3$. Determine the output for maximum revenue.

3. A monopolist estimates the demand equation for his product to be $p = 72 - .04x$. If his cost function is $c = 500 + 30x$, at what level of output will his profit be maximized? At what price does this occur and what is the profit?

4. The demand equation for a monopolist's product is $p = -5x + 30$. At what price will revenue be maximized?

5. For XYZ Manufacturing Co., total fixed costs are $1200, material and labor costs combined are $2 per unit, and the demand equation is $p = 100/\sqrt{x}$. What level of output will maximize profit? Show that this occurs when marginal revenue is equal to marginal cost. What is the price at profit maximization?

6. For a monopolist, the demand function is $p = 50/\sqrt{x}$ and his average cost function is $\bar{c} = .50 + (1000/x)$. Find the profit-maximizing price and output. At this level, show marginal revenue is equal to marginal cost.

7. A monopolist determines that his cost function is $c = 100 + .2x$, but is not sure whether the demand equation should be $p = 3 - 2x$ or $p = 5 - 4x$. He decides to set a price within the limits determined by both conditions. Within what price range should he set the price?

8. For a monopolist, the cost per unit of producing a product is $3 and the demand equation is $p = 10/\sqrt{x}$. What price will give the greatest profit?

9. A manufacturer finds that for the first 500 units of his product that are produced and sold, the profit is $50/unit. The profit on each of the units beyond 500 is decreased by $.10 times the number of additional units produced. For example, the total profit when 502 units are produced and sold is 500(50) + 2(49.80). What level of output will maximize his profit?

10. A real estate firm owns the Shantytown Apartments which consist of 70 garden-type apartments. At $125 per month each apartment can be rented. However, for each

$5 per month increase, there will be two vacancies with no possibility of filling them. What rent per apartment will maximize monthly revenue?

11. Imperial Educational Services (I.E.S.) is considering offering a workshop in resource allocation to key personnel at Acme Corp. To make the offering economically feasible, I.E.S. feels that at least thirty persons must attend at a cost of $50 each. Moreover, I.E.S. will agree to reduce the charge for *everybody* by $1.25 for each person over the thirty who attends. How many people should be in the group for I.E.S. to maximize revenue? Assume that the maximum allowable number in the group is forty.

12. For a monopolist, the demand equation is $p = 42 - 4x$ and the average cost function is $\bar{c} = 2 + (80/x)$. Find the profit-maximizing price.

13. The demand equation for a monopolist is $p = 600 - 2x$ and his total cost function is $c = .2x^2 + 28x + 200$. Find the profit-maximizing output and price, and determine the corresponding profits. If the government were to impose a tax of $22 per unit on the manufacturer, what would be the new profit-maximizing output and price? What is his profit now?

14. Use the *original* data in Problem 13 and assume the government imposes a license fee of $100 on the manufacturer. This is a lump-sum amount without regard to output. Show that marginal revenue and marginal cost do not change and, hence, the profit maximizing price and output remain the same. Show, however, that he will have less profit.

15. A manufacturer has to produce annually 1000 units of a product that is sold at a uniform rate during the year. The production cost of each unit is $10 and carrying costs (insurance, interest, storage, etc.) are estimated to be 12.8 percent of the value of average inventory. Set-up costs per production run are $40. Find the economic lot size.

16. A TV cable company has 1000 subscribers who are paying $5 per month. It can get 100 more subscribers for each $.10 decrease in the monthly fee. What rate will yield maximum revenue and what will this revenue be?

17. For a manufacturer, the cost of making a part is $3/unit for labor and $1/unit for materials; overhead is fixed at $2000/week. If more than 5000 units are made each week, he must pay for labor $4.50/unit for those units in excess of 5000. At what level of production will average cost per unit be at a minimum?

18. For a monopolist, the cost function is $c = .004x^3 + 20x + 5000$ and the demand function is $p = 450 - 4x$. Find the profit-maximizing output. At this level, show that marginal cost = marginal revenue.

19. The cost of operating a truck on a throughway (excluding the salary of the driver) is $.11 + \dfrac{s}{600}$ dollars per mile, where s is the (steady) speed of the truck in miles per hour. The truck driver's salary is $6 per hour. At what speed should the truck driver operate the truck to make a 700-mile trip most economical?

20. A company produces daily x tons of chemical $A (x \leq 4)$ and y tons of chemical

B where $y = (24 - 6x)/(5 - x)$. The profit on chemical *A* is $2000 per ton and on *B* it is $1000 per ton. How much of chemical *A* should be produced per day to maximize profit? Answer the same question if the profit on *A* is *P* per ton and that on *B* is $P/2$ per ton.

21. The Kiddie Toy Company plans to lease an electric motor to be used 90,000 horsepower-hours per year in manufacturing. One horsepower-hour is the work done in one hour by a one-horsepower motor. The annual cost to lease a suitable motor is $150 plus $.60 per horsepower. The cost per horsepower-hour of operating the motor is $.006/N$ where *N* is the horsepower. What size motor should be leased in order to minimize cost?

22. To erect an office building, fixed costs are $250,000 and include land, architect's fee, basement, foundation, etc. If *x* floors are to be constructed, the cost (excluding fixed costs) is $c = (x/2)[100,000 + 5000(x - 1)]$. The revenue/month is $5000/floor. Find the number of floors that will yield a maximum rate of return on investment (rate of return = total revenue/total cost).

8-6   DIFFERENTIALS

We shall now give a reason for the frequent use of the symbol dy/dx in denoting the derivative of *y* with respect to *x*. To do this we introduce the notion of the *differential* of a function.

DEFINITION.   *If $y = f(x)$ is a differentiable function of x, then the **differential of** y, denoted dy or $d[f(x)]$, is*

$$dy = f'(x) \cdot h$$

where h is any real number. Note that dy is a function of two variables, x and h.

EXAMPLE 22

Find the differentials of the following functions.

a. $y = x^3 - 2x^2 + 3x - 4$.

$$dy = D_x(x^3 - 2x^2 + 3x - 4) \cdot h$$

$$dy = (3x^2 - 4x + 3)h.$$

For example, if $x = 1$ and $h = .04$, then

$$dy = [3(1)^2 - 4(1) + 3](.04) = .08.$$

b. $f(x) = \ln(x^2 + 5)$.

$$d[f(x)] = d[\ln(x^2 + 5)] = D_x[\ln(x^2 + 5)] \cdot h$$

$$= \frac{2x}{x^2 + 5}h = \frac{2xh}{x^2 + 5}.$$

If $f(x) = x$, then $d[f(x)] = d[x] = D_x[x]h = 1h = h$. Hence the differential of x is h. From now on we shall use the symbol dx for $d[x] = h$. For example,

$$d(\sqrt{x^2 + 5}) = \frac{x}{\sqrt{x^2 + 5}} dx.$$

Summarizing, if $y = f(x)$ defines a differentiable function of x, we have

$$dy = f'(x)dx.$$

If $dx \neq 0$, we can divide both sides by dx:

$$\frac{dy}{dx} = f'(x).$$

That is, the derivative of f with respect to x, $f'(x)$, is nothing more than the quotient of two differentials, dy divided by dx. It is for this reason that in Chapter 7 we introduced the symbol dy/dx to denote the derivative.

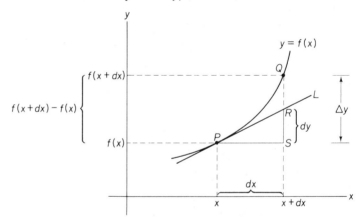

Fig. 8-49

The differential can be interpreted geometrically. In Fig. 8-49 $P(x, f(x))$ is a point on the graph of a function $y = f(x)$. Suppose x changes by dx, where dx is a real number, and $Q(x + dx, f(x + dx))$ is the corresponding point on the curve. Through P and Q we construct horizontal and vertical lines, respectively, which intersect at S. If a line L tangent to the curve is constructed at P, it will intersect $\overline{QS}$ at R, forming the right triangle PRS. The slope of L is $f'(x)$ or, equivalently, it is $\overline{SR}/\overline{PS}$:

$$f'(x) = \frac{\overline{SR}}{\overline{PS}}.$$

Since $dy = f'(x) dx$, and $dx = \overline{PS}$,

$$dy = f'(x)\,dx$$

$$= \frac{\overline{SR}}{\overline{PS}} \cdot \overline{PS}$$

$$= \overline{SR}.$$

Thus, if dx is a change in x at P, dy is the corresponding vertical change in the *tangent line* at P. Note that for the same dx, the vertical change in the *curve* is $\Delta y = \overline{SQ} = f(x + dx) - f(x)$. However, it is apparent from Fig. 8-49 that

when dx is *small*, dy is an approximation to Δy.

Observe that the graph of f near P is approximated by the tangent line at P.

EXAMPLE 23

Suppose the total profit P (in dollars) of producing x units of a product is

$$P = P(x) = \frac{x^3}{1000} - \frac{1}{4}x^2 + 30x.$$

Use differentials to find the approximate change in profit if the level of production changes from $x = 200$ to $x = 205$.

We want ΔP when x goes from 200 to 205. We approximate ΔP by dP where $x = 200$ and $dx = 5$.

$$\Delta P \approx dP = P'\,dx = \left(\frac{3x^2}{1000} - \frac{x}{2} + 30 \right) dx$$

$$= \left[\frac{3(200)^2}{1000} - \frac{200}{2} + 30 \right] 5$$

$$= 250.$$

The actual change is $P(205) - P(200) = 258.875$.

We said that if $y = f(x)$, then $\Delta y \approx dy$ if dx is small. Thus

$$\Delta y = f(x + dx) - f(x) \approx dy$$

or

$$\boxed{f(x + dx) \approx f(x) + dy.} \qquad\qquad (1)$$

For example, suppose we approximate ln (1.06). If we let $y = f(x) = \ln x$, then we want to approximate $f(1.06)$. By (1) and the fact that $d(\ln x) = (1/x)dx$,

$$f(x + dx) \approx f(x) + dy$$

$$\ln(x + dx) \approx \ln x + \frac{1}{x}dx.$$

Note that $1.06 = 1 + .06$. Since .06 is small and we know the exact value of $\ln 1 = 0$, we shall let $x = 1$ and $dx = .06$:

$$\ln(1.06) = \ln(1 + .06) \approx \ln(1) + \frac{1}{1}(.06) = .06.$$

The actual value of $\ln(1.06)$ to five decimal places is .05827.

EXAMPLE 24

The demand function for a product is given by $p = f(x) = 20 - \sqrt{x}$ where p is the price per unit in dollars for x units. By means of differentials, approximate the price when 99 units are demanded.

We want $f(99)$. By (1),

$$f(x + dx) \approx f(x) + dp$$

where

$$dp = -\frac{1}{2\sqrt{x}}dx.$$

We choose $x = 100$ since $f(100) = 20 - \sqrt{100} = 10$ is easy to compute and 100 is near 99. Choosing $dx = -1$, we have

$$f(99) = f[100 + (-1)] \approx f(100) - \frac{1}{2\sqrt{100}}(-1)$$

$$f(99) \approx 10 + .05 = 10.05.$$

Thus the price per unit when 99 units are demanded is approximately $10.05.

The equation $y = x^3 + 4x + 5$ defines x implicitly as a function of y. Thus we can look at the derivative of x with respect to y, dx/dy. Since dx/dy can be considered a quotient of differentials,

$$\boxed{\frac{dx}{dy} = \frac{1}{\dfrac{dy}{dx}}, \quad dy \neq 0, \quad dx \neq 0.}$$

But dy/dx is the derivative of y with respect to x and equals $3x^2 + 4$. Thus

$$\frac{dx}{dy} = \frac{1}{3x^2 + 4}.$$

This is the *reciprocal* of dy/dx.

EXAMPLE 25

Find dp/dx if $x = \sqrt{2500 - p^2}$.

Since $x = (2500 - p^2)^{1/2}$,

$$\frac{dx}{dp} = \frac{1}{2}(2500 - p^2)^{-1/2}(-2p) = -\frac{p}{\sqrt{2500 - p^2}}.$$

Hence,

$$\frac{dp}{dx} = \frac{1}{\dfrac{dx}{dp}} = -\frac{\sqrt{2500 - p^2}}{p}.$$

EXERCISE 8-6

In problems 1–10, find the differentials of the functions in terms of x and dx.

1. $y = 3x - 4$
2. $y = 2$
3. $f(x) = \sqrt{x^4 + 2}$
4. $f(x) = (4x^2 - 5x + 2)^3$
5. $g(x) = (2x + 1)/(x^2 + 3)$
6. $g(x) = (x + 4)(x^2 - 5)^4$
7. $p = \ln (x^2 + 7)$
8. $p = e^{x^3 + 5}$
9. $y = (4x + 3)e^{2x^2 + 3}$
10. $y = \ln \sqrt{x^4 + 1}$

In problems 11–14, evaluate $d[f(x)]$ for the indicated values of x and dx.

11. $f(x) = 4 - 7x;\ x = 3,\ dx = .02$

12. $f(x) = 4x^2 - 3x + 10;\ x = -1,\ dx = .25$

13. $f(x) = \sqrt{25 - x^2};\ x = 4,\ dx = -.1$

14. $f(x) = e^{x^2};\ x = 0,\ dx = -.01$

15. Suppose the profit P (in dollars) of producing x units of a product is

$$P = 396x - 2.2x^2 - 400.$$

Using differentials, find the approximate change in profit if the level of production changes from $x = 80$ to $x = 81$. Find the actual change.

16. Given the revenue function

$$r = 250x + 45x^2 - x^3,$$

use differentials to find the approximate change in revenue if the number of units increases from $x = 40$ to $x = 41$. Find the actual change.

In problems 17-22, approximate each expression by using differentials.

17. $\sqrt{101}$ **18.** $\sqrt{2497}$ **19.** $\ln .97$

20. $\ln 1.01$ **21.** $\sqrt[4]{17}$ **22.** $e^{.01.}$

In problems 23-28, find dx/dy or dp/dx.

23. $y = 2x - 1$ **24.** $y = 5x^2 + 3x + 2$

25. $x = (p^2 + 5)^3$ **26.** $x = \sqrt{p + 5}$

27. $x = \dfrac{1}{p}$ **28.** $x = e^{5-p}$

In problems 29 and 30, find the instantaneous rate of change of x with respect to p for the indicated value of x.

29. $p = \dfrac{500}{x + 2}$; $x = 18$ **30.** $p = 50 - \sqrt{x}$; $x = 100$

31. The demand equation for a monopolist is $p = \dfrac{10}{\sqrt{x}}$. Using differentials, approximate the price when 24 units are demanded.

32. Answer the same question in Problem 31 if 101 units are demanded.

8-7 ELASTICITY

Elasticity of demand is a means by which economists measure how a change in price of a product will affect quantity demanded. That is, it refers to consumer response to price changes. Loosely speaking, elasticity of demand is the ratio of the resulting percentage change in quantity demanded to a given percentage change in price:

$$\frac{\text{percentage change in quantity}}{\text{percentage change in price}}.$$

For example, if for a price increase of 5 percent, quantity demanded were to decrease by 2 percent, we would *loosely say* that elasticity of demand is $-.02/.05 = -\frac{2}{5}$.

Suppose $p = f(x)$ is the demand function for a product. Consumers will demand x units at a price of $f(x)$ per unit and $x + h$ units at a price of $f(x + h)$ per unit (Fig. 8-50). The *percentage* change in quantity demanded from

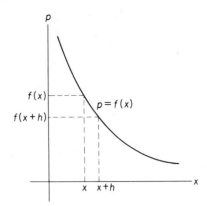

Fig. 8-50

x to $x + h$ is $\dfrac{(x + h) - x}{x} = \dfrac{h}{x}$. The percentage change in price per unit from

$f(x)$ to $f(x + h)$ is $\dfrac{f(x + h) - f(x)}{f(x)}$. The ratio of these percentage changes
is

$$\frac{\dfrac{h}{x}}{\dfrac{f(x + h) - f(x)}{f(x)}} = \frac{h}{x} \cdot \frac{f(x)}{f(x + h) - f(x)}$$

$$= \frac{f(x)}{x} \cdot \frac{h}{f(x + h) - f(x)}$$

$$= \frac{\dfrac{f(x)}{x}}{\dfrac{f(x + h) - f(x)}{h}}. \qquad (1)$$

If f is differentiable, then as $h \to 0$ we have $[f(x + h) - f(x)]/h \to dp/dx$
and thus (1) approaches

$$\frac{\dfrac{f(x)}{x}}{\dfrac{dp}{dx}} = \frac{\dfrac{p}{x}}{\dfrac{dp}{dx}}.$$

DEFINITION. *If $p = f(x)$ is a differentiable demand function, the* **point elasticity of demand,** *denoted by the Greek letter η (eta), at (x, p) is*

$$\eta = \frac{\dfrac{p}{x}}{\dfrac{dp}{dx}}.$$

Let us determine the point elasticity of demand for the function $p = 1200 - x^2$.

$$\eta = \frac{\dfrac{p}{x}}{\dfrac{dp}{dx}} = \frac{\dfrac{1200 - x^2}{x}}{-2x} = -\left[\frac{600}{x^2} - \frac{1}{2}\right]. \qquad (2)$$

For example, when $x = 10$, $\eta = -[(600/10^2) - \frac{1}{2}] = -5\frac{1}{2}$. Thus, if price were increased by 1 percent when $x = 10$, the quantity demanded would decrease by approximately $5\frac{1}{2}$ percent. Increasing price by $\frac{1}{2}$ percent results in a decrease of approximately 2.75 percent in demand.

Note that when elasticity is evaluated, no units are attached to it—it is nothing more than a real number. For normal behavior of demand, as price increases (decreases), quantity decreases (increases). Thus, dp/dx will always be negative or 0 and consequently η will always be negative or 0. Some economists disregard the minus sign; in the above example they would consider the elasticity to be $5\frac{1}{2}$. We shall not adopt this practice.

There are three categories of elasticity:

(1) When $|\eta| > 1$, demand is *elastic.*
(2) When $|\eta| = 1$, demand has *unit elasticity.*
(3) When $|\eta| < 1$, demand is *inelastic.*

In Eq. (2), since $|\eta| = 5\frac{1}{2}$ when $x = 10$, demand is elastic. When $x = 20$, $|\eta| = |-[(600/20^2) - \frac{1}{2}]| = 1$ and so demand has unit elasticity. When $x = 25$, $|\eta| = |-\frac{23}{50}|$ and demand is inelastic.

Loosely speaking, for a given percentage change in price, there will be a greater percentage change in quantity demanded if demand is elastic, a smaller percentage change if demand is inelastic, and an equal percentage change if demand has unit elasticity.

For example, suppose that there is a price increase of 5 percent. If this results in a decrease in demand of 10 percent, then demand is elastic. Here the price change caused a proportionately larger change in demand. On the other hand, if the demand decreases 2 percent, then demand is inelastic. Here the price change caused a proportionately smaller change in demand. Finally, if the price increase causes the same proportionate change in demand, then demand has unit elasticity.

EXAMPLE 26

Determine the point elasticity of the following demand equations for $x > 0$.

a. $p = \dfrac{k}{x}$ where $k > 0$.

$$\eta = \frac{\dfrac{p}{x}}{\dfrac{dp}{dx}} = \frac{\dfrac{k}{x^2}}{\dfrac{-k}{x^2}} = -1.$$

Thus the demand has unit elasticity for all $x > 0$. The graph of $p = k/x$ is called an *equilateral hyperbola* and is often found in economics texts in discussions of elasticity. See Example 14(b), Chapter 3 for a graph of such a curve.

b. $x = p^2 - 40p + 400$.

  This equation defines p implicitly as a function of x. From Sec. 8-6,

$$\frac{dp}{dx} = \frac{1}{\dfrac{dx}{dp}}.$$

Therefore, $dp/dx = 1/(2p - 40)$ and

$$\eta = \frac{\dfrac{p}{x}}{\dfrac{dp}{dx}} = \frac{\dfrac{p}{x}}{\dfrac{1}{2p - 40}} = \frac{p(2p - 40)}{x}.$$

For example, if $p = 15$, then $x = 25$; hence $\eta = [15(-10)]/25 = -6$ and demand is elastic.

Point elasticity of a *linear* demand equation is quite interesting. Suppose the equation has the form

$$p = mx + b \quad \text{where} \quad m < 0 \text{ and } b > 0.$$

See Fig. 8-51. We shall assume $x > 0$; thus $p < b$. The point elasticity of demand is

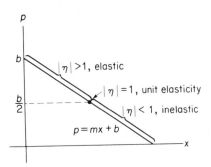

Fig. 8-51

$$\eta = \dfrac{\dfrac{p}{x}}{\dfrac{dp}{dx}} = \dfrac{\dfrac{p}{x}}{m} = \dfrac{p}{mx} = \dfrac{p}{p-b}.$$

By considering $d\eta/dp$, we shall show that η is a decreasing function of p.

$$\frac{d\eta}{dp} = \frac{(p-b)-p}{(p-b)^2} = -\frac{b}{(p-b)^2}.$$

Since $b > 0$, then $d\eta/dp < 0$ and thus η is a decreasing function of p—as p increases, η must decrease. However p ranges between 0 and b, and at the midpoint of this range, $b/2$,

$$\eta = \frac{\dfrac{b}{2}}{\dfrac{b}{2}-b} = -1.$$

Therefore, if $p < b/2$, then $\eta > -1$; if $p > b/2$, then $\eta < -1$. Stating this another way, when $p < b/2$, $|\eta| < 1$ and demand is inelastic; when $p = b/2$, $|\eta| = 1$ and demand has unit elasticity; when $p > b/2$, $|\eta| > 1$ and demand is elastic. This shows that the slope of a demand curve is not a measure of elasticity. The slope of the above line is m everywhere, but elasticity varies with the point on the line.

It is possible to relate how elasticity of demand affects changes in revenue (marginal revenue). If $p = f(x)$ is a manufacturer's demand function, his total revenue is

$$r = px.$$

To find marginal revenue dr/dx we differentiate r, using the product rule.

$$\frac{dr}{dx} = p + x\frac{dp}{dx}. \tag{3}$$

Factoring the right side of Eq. (3), we have

$$\frac{dr}{dx} = p\left(1 + \frac{x}{p}\frac{dp}{dx}\right).$$

But

$$\frac{x}{p}\frac{dp}{dx} = \frac{\dfrac{dp}{dx}}{\dfrac{p}{x}} = \frac{1}{\eta}.$$

Thus,

$$\frac{dr}{dx} = p\left(1 + \frac{1}{\eta}\right). \tag{4}$$

If demand is elastic, then $\eta < -1$ and $1 + \dfrac{1}{\eta} > 0$. If demand is inelastic, then $\eta > -1$ and $1 + \dfrac{1}{\eta} < 0$. Let us assume that $p > 0$. From Eq. (4) we can conclude that $dr/dx > 0$ on intervals for which demand is elastic; hence, total revenue r is increasing there. On the other hand, marginal revenue is negative on intervals for which demand is inelastic; hence, total revenue is decreasing there.

Thus we conclude from the above argument that as more units are sold, a manufacturer's total revenue increases if demand is elastic, but decreases if demand is inelastic. That is, if demand is elastic, a lower price will increase revenue. If inelastic, a lower price will decrease revenue. For unit elasticity, a lower price leaves total revenue unchanged.

EXERCISE 8-7

In problems 1-14, find the point elasticity of the demand equations for the indicated values of x or p and determine whether demand is elastic, inelastic, or has unit elasticity.

1. $p = 40 - 2x$; $x = 5$

2. $p = 12 - .03x$; $x = 300$

3. $x = 600 - 100p$; $p = 3$

4. $x = 100 - p$; $p = 50$

5. $p = \dfrac{1000}{x}$; $x = 288$

6. $p = \dfrac{1000}{x^2}$; $x = 156$

7. $p = \dfrac{500}{x + 2}$; $x = 100$

8. $p = \dfrac{800}{2x + 1}$; $x = 25$

9. $x = \sqrt{2500 - p}$; $p = 900$

10. $x = \sqrt{2500 - p^2}$; $p = 20$

11. $x = \dfrac{(p - 100)^2}{2}$; $p = 20$

12. $x = p^2 - 60p + 898$; $p = 10$

13. $p = 150 - e^{x/100}$; $x = 100$

14. $p = 100e^{-x/200}$; $x = 200$

15. For the linear demand equation $p = 13 - .05x$, verify that demand is elastic when $p = 10$, is inelastic when $p = 3$, and demand has unit elasticity when $p = 6.50$.

16. For what value (or values) of x do the following demand equations have unit elasticity?

   a. $p = 26 - .10x$

   b. $p = 1200 - x^2$

17. The demand equation for a product is

$$x = 500 - 40p + p^2$$

where p is the price per unit (in dollars) and x is the quantity of units demanded (in thousands). Find the point elasticity of demand when $p = 15$. If this price of 15 is increased by $\frac{1}{2}$ percent, what is the approximate change in demand?

18. The demand equation of a product is

$$x = \sqrt{2500 - p^2}.$$

Find the point elasticity of demand when $p = 30$. If the price of 30 decreases 2/3 percent, what is the approximate change in demand?

19. For the demand equation $p = 500 - 2x$, verify that demand is elastic and total revenue is increasing for $0 < x < 125$. Verify that demand is inelastic and total revenue is decreasing for $125 < x < 250$.

20. Verify that $\dfrac{dr}{dx} = p\left(1 + \dfrac{1}{\eta}\right)$ if $p = 40 - 2x$.

21. Repeat Problem 20 for $p = \dfrac{1000}{x^2}$.

22. Let $p = mx + b$ be a linear demand equation where $m \neq 0$ and $b > 0$.

   a. Show that $\lim\limits_{p \to b^-} \eta = -\infty$.

   b. Show that $\eta = 0$ when $p = 0$.

23. For the demand equation $p = 1000 - x^2$, if $5 \leq x \leq 30$, for what value of x is $|\eta|$ a maximum? For what value is it a minimum?

24. Repeat Problem 23 for $p = 200/(x + 5)$ and $5 \leq x \leq 95$.

8-8 REVIEW

Important Terms and Symbols in Chapter 8

x-axis symmetry *(p. 265)*   critical value *(p. 278)*

y-axis symmetry *(p. 265)*   first-derivative test *(p. 279)*

symmetry about origin *(p. 266)*   second-derivative test *(p. 294)*

horizontal asymptote *(p. 269)*   differential *(p. 303)*

vertical asymptote *(p. 269)*   *dy, dx (p. 304)*

relative maximum *(p. 277)*   point elasticity of demand
                                          (p. 310)

relative minimum *(p. 277)*   η *(p. 310)*

inflection point *(p. 285)*   elastic *(p. 310)*

increasing function *(p. 275)*   inelastic *(p. 310)*

decreasing function *(p. 275)*   unit elasticity *(p. 310)*

Review Section

1. The graph of $y = x^2 + 1$ has no (a)(x)(y)-intercept but has one (b)(x)(y)-intercept.

    Ans. (a) x;   (b) y

2. The y-intercept of the graph of $y = 8x^3 - 7x + 4$ is _____ .

    Ans. (0, 4)

3. The graph of $y = x^4 - x^2 + 3$ is symmetric with respect to the __(a)__ -axis but not the __(b)__ -axis.

    Ans. (a) y;   (b) x

4. If a graph is symmetric with respect to both the x-axis and y-axis, then it (is)(is not) symmetric with respect to the origin.

    Ans. is

5. In the graph of $y = 6/(x + 2) + 3$ the line $x =$ __(a)__ is a vertical asymptote and the line $y =$ __(b)__ is a horizontal asymptote.

    Ans. (a) -2;   (b) 3

6. The graph of $y = e^x$ has a (a)(horizontal)(vertical) but no (b)(horizontal)(vertical) asymptote.

    Ans. (a) horizontal;   (b) vertical

7. Suppose f is a function defined on an interval I. If $f'(x) < 0$ on I, then f is (a)(increasing)(decreasing) on I and the graph of f is (b)(rising)(falling). If $f'(x) > 0$ on I, then f is (c)(increasing)(decreasing) on I. If $f'(x_1) = 0$ or is not defined, then $x = x_1$ is called a __(d)__ value. At such a point, f may have a relative __(e)__ or __(f)__ or neither.

Ans. (a) decreasing; (b) falling; (c) increasing;
(d) critical; (e) maximum; (f) minimum

8. If $f''(x) > 0$ on I, then f is concave (up)(down) on I.

Ans. up

9. If $f''(x_1) = 0$ or is not defined, then there may be a point of __(a)__ when $x = x_1$. If $f'(x_1) = 0$ and $f''(x_1) > 0$, then f has a relative __(b)__ when $x = x_1$.

Ans. (a) inflection; (b) minimum

10. If $f(x_1) \geq f(x)$ for all x in the domain of f, then when $x = x_1$ there occurs a(n) _____ maximum.

Ans. absolute

11. Under typical conditions, profit is maximized at the level of output for which marginal revenue = _____ .

Ans. marginal cost

12. If f has a relative maximum when $x = x_1$, then as x increases through x_1, $f'(x)$ changes from (a)(+)(−) to (b)(+)(−). At a relative minimum, $f'(x)$ changes from (c)(+)(−) to (d)(+)(−).

Ans. (a) +; (b) −; (c) −; (d) +

13. True or false: If $f'(x_1) = 0$, then f has a relative maximum or minimum when $x = x_1$, __(a)__ . If $f''(x_2) = 0$, then f has a point of inflection when $x = x_2$, __(b)__ .

Ans. (a) false; (b) false

14. In the graph of $y = f(x)$ in Fig. 8-52, an absolute maximum occurs at point(s) __(a)__ , an absolute minimum at __(b)__ , a relative maximum at __(c)__ , a relative minimum at __(d)__ , and inflection point(s) at __(e)__ .

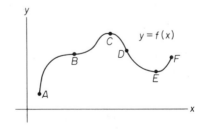

Fig. 8-52

Ans. (a) C; (b) A; (c) C; (d) E; (e) B, D

15. The differential of $y = x^2 + 3$ is _____ .

Ans. $2x\,dx$

16. If $\dfrac{dy}{dx} = \dfrac{2}{3}$, then $\dfrac{dx}{dy} = $ _____ .

Ans. $\frac{3}{2}$

17. The differential of $y = x$ when $x = 6$ and $dx = .001$ is _____ .

Ans. $.001$

18. If the elasticity of a demand function at a point is -1.301, then the demand is said to be (elastic) (inelastic) there.

Ans. elastic

Review Problems

In problems 1-8 sketch the graphs of the functions. Indicate intervals on which the function is increasing, decreasing, concave up, concave down; indicate relative maximum points, relative minimum points, points of inflection, horizontal asymptotes, vertical asymptotes, symmetry, and intercepts, if they can be obtained conveniently.

1. $y = x^2 - 2x - 24$

2. $y = x^3 - 27x$

3. $y = x^3 - 12x + 20$

4. $y = x^4 - 4x^3 - 20x^2 + 150$

5. $f(x) = \dfrac{e^x + e^{-x}}{2}$

6. $f(x) = 1 + \ln (x^2)$

7. $f(x) = \dfrac{100(x + 5)}{x^2}$

8. $f(x) = \dfrac{1}{x^2 - 5}$

9. The demand function for a monopolist's product is $p = 400 - 2x$; p is given in dollars. If the average cost per unit for producing x units is $\bar{c} = x + 160 + (2000/x)$, find the maximum profit that the monopolist can achieve.

10. A manufacturer determines that m employees on a certain production line will produce x units per month where $x = 80m^2 - .1m^4$. To obtain maximum monthly production, how many employees should be assigned to the production line?

11. The demand function for a monopolist's product is $p = \sqrt{600 - x}$. If he wants to produce at least 100 units but not more than 300 units, how many units should he produce to maximize total revenue?

In problems 12 and 13, determine the differentials of the functions in terms of x and dx.

12. $f(x) = x^2 \ln (x + 5)$

13. $f(x) = (x^2 + 5)/(x - 7)$

Approximate the expressions in problems 14 and 15 by use of differentials.

14. $\sqrt{25.5}$ **15.** $e^{-.01}$

For the demand equations in problems 16–18, determine whether demand is elastic, inelastic, or has unit elasticity for the indicated value of x.

16. $p = 18 - .02x$; $x = 600$ **17.** $p = \dfrac{500}{x}$; $x = 200$

18. $p = 900 - x^2$; $x = 10$

Chapter 9

Integral Calculus

Chapters 7 and 8 were concerned with differential calculus. We differentiated a function and obtained another function called its derivative. The study of *integral calculus* is concerned with the opposite process. We are given the derivative of a function and must find the original function. Just as the derivative geometrically gives the slope of a tangent line to a curve, the so-called integral is sometimes associated geometrically with area. Moreover, you will see that it too involves a limiting process.

9-1 THE INDEFINITE INTEGRAL

If F is a function such that

$$\frac{dF}{dx} = f(x), \tag{1}$$

then F is said to be an *antiderivative* of f. Thus an antiderivative of f is nothing more than a function F which when differentiated gives f. Since dF/dx can be considered a quotient of differentials, multiplying both sides of Eq. (1) by dx gives

$$dF = f(x)\,dx.$$

Thus on the differential level, a useful interpretation of an antiderivative of f is that it is a function whose differential is $f(x)\,dx$.

DEFINITION. *An antiderivative of a function f is a function F such that*

$$\frac{dF}{dx} = f(x),$$

or equivalently

$$dF = f(x)\, dx.$$

For example, since

$$d\left(\frac{x^3}{3}\right) = x^2\, dx,$$

$x^3/3$ is an antiderivative of x^2. Is this the *only* antiderivative of x^2? The answer is "no"! Since

$$d\left(\frac{x^3}{3} + 1\right) = x^2\, dx,$$

$$d\left(\frac{x^3}{3} - 5\right) = x^2\, dx,$$

and

$$d\left(\frac{x^3}{3} + 3895.6\right) = x^2\, dx,$$

then $(x^3/3) + 1$, $(x^3/3) - 5$, and $(x^3/3) + 3895.6$ are also antiderivatives of x^2. In fact, it can be shown that any antiderivative of x^2 must have the form $(x^3/3) + C$ where C is a constant. Thus any two antiderivatives of x^2 differ only by a constant. The symbol we shall use for any antiderivative of x^2 is $\int x^2\, dx$, which is read "the *indefinite integral* of x^2 with respect to x." Since all antiderivatives of x^2 have the form $\dfrac{x^3}{3} + C$, we write

$$\int x^2\, dx = \frac{x^3}{3} + C.$$

The symbol $\int$ is called the *integral sign*, x^2 is the *integrand*, and C is the *constant of integration*.

More generally, the **indefinite integral** of $f(x)$ is written $\int f(x)\, dx$ and means *any* antiderivative of $f(x)$. Thus if $F(x)$ is an antiderivative of $f(x)$, then

$$\int f(x)\, dx = F(x) + C.$$

To integrate f, that is, to find $\int f(x)\, dx$, we just determine an antiderivative of f and then tack on the constant of integration. Thus

$$\int f(x) \, dx = F(x) + C \quad \text{if and only if}$$

$$dF = f(x) \, dx \quad \text{or} \quad \frac{dF}{dx} = f(x).$$

EXAMPLE 1

Find $\int 5 \, dx$.

First we must find (perhaps better words are "guess at") a function whose differential is $5 \, dx$ (or equivalently, a function whose derivative is 5). Since $d(5x) = 5 \, dx$, $5x$ is an antiderivative of 5. Thus

$$\int 5 \, dx = 5x + C.$$

PITFALL. *It is incorrect to write* $\int 5 \, dx = 5x$. *Do not forget the constant of integration.*

Using differentiation formulas from Chapter 7, we have compiled a list of basic integration formulas in Table 9-1. These formulas are easily verified. For example, formula (2) is true since the differential of $x^{n+1}/(n+1)$ is $x^n \, dx$ for $n \neq -1$. To verify formula (4) we must show that k times an antiderivative of f is an antiderivative of kf. To demonstrate this, let F be an antiderivative

Table 9-1

BASIC INTEGRATION FORMULAS
1. $\int k \, dx = kx + C,$ k a constant
2. $\int x^n \, dx = \dfrac{x^{n+1}}{n+1} + C,$ $n \neq -1$
3. $\int e^x \, dx = e^x + C$
4. $\int kf(x) \, dx = k \int f(x) \, dx,$ k a constant
5. $\int [f(x) \pm g(x)] \, dx = \int f(x) \, dx \pm \int g(x) \, dx$

of f. Then $dF = f(x)\, dx$ and $d(kF) = kf(x)\, dx$. Thus kF is an antiderivative of kf and the validity of formula (4) is established. You should verify the other formulas. Formula (5) can be extended to any finite number of sums and/or differences.

EXAMPLE 2

Find the following indefinite integrals.

a. $\displaystyle\int 1\, dx.$

By formula (1) with $k = 1$,

$$\int 1\, dx = 1x + C = x + C.$$

Usually we write $\displaystyle\int 1\, dx$ as $\displaystyle\int dx$. Thus,

$$\int dx = x + C.$$

b. $\displaystyle\int x^5\, dx.$

By formula (2) with $n = 5$,

$$\int x^5\, dx = \frac{x^{5+1}}{5+1} + C = \frac{x^6}{6} + C.$$

c. $\displaystyle\int 7x\, dx.$

By formula (4) with $k = 7$ and $f(x) = x$,

$$\int 7x\, dx = 7\int x\, dx.$$

But $\displaystyle\int x\, dx = \int x^1\, dx$ and by formula (2) with $n = 1$,

$$\int x^1\, dx = \frac{x^{1+1}}{1+1} + C_1 = \frac{x^2}{2} + C_1$$

where C_1 is the constant of integration. Therefore,

$$\int 7x\, dx = 7\int x\, dx = 7\left[\frac{x^2}{2} + C_1\right] = \frac{7}{2}x^2 + 7C_1.$$

Letting $C = 7C_1$, we have

$$\int 7x \, dx = \frac{7}{2} x^2 + C.$$

It is not necessary to write all intermediate steps when integrating. More concisely we have

$$\int 7x \, dx = 7 \int x \, dx = (7)\frac{x^2}{2} + C = \frac{7}{2} x^2 + C.$$

d. $\int -\frac{3}{5} e^x \, dx.$

$$\int -\frac{3}{5} e^x \, dx = -\frac{3}{5} \int e^x \, dx \qquad\qquad \text{(formula 4)}$$

$$= -\frac{3}{5} e^x + C. \qquad\qquad \text{(formula 3)}$$

EXAMPLE 3

Find the following indefinite integrals.

a. $\int \frac{1}{\sqrt{t}} \, dt.$

Here t is the *variable of integration*. We rewrite the integrand so that one of the basic forms can be used.

$$\int \frac{1}{\sqrt{t}} \, dt = \int t^{-1/2} \, dt.$$

By formula (2) with $n = -\frac{1}{2}$,

$$\int \frac{1}{\sqrt{t}} \, dt = \int t^{-1/2} \, dt = \frac{t^{(-1/2)+1}}{-\frac{1}{2} + 1} + C = \frac{t^{1/2}}{\frac{1}{2}} + C = 2\sqrt{t} + C.$$

b. $\int \frac{1}{6x^3} \, dx.$

$$\int \frac{1}{6x^3} \, dx = \frac{1}{6} \int x^{-3} \, dx$$

$$= \left(\frac{1}{6}\right) \frac{x^{-3+1}}{-3 + 1} + C$$

$$= -\frac{1}{12x^2} + C.$$

c. $\int (x^2 + 2x - 4)\, dx.$

By formula (5),

$$\int (x^2 + 2x - 4)\, dx = \int x^2\, dx + \int 2x\, dx - \int 4\, dx.$$

Now

$$\int x^2\, dx = \frac{x^{2+1}}{2+1} + C_1 = \frac{x^3}{3} + C_1,$$

$$\int 2x\, dx = 2 \int x\, dx = (2)\frac{x^{1+1}}{1+1} + C_2 = x^2 + C_2,$$

and

$$\int 4\, dx = 4x + C_3.$$

Thus,

$$\int (x^2 + 2x - 4)\, dx = \frac{x^3}{3} + x^2 - 4x + C_1 + C_2 - C_3.$$

Letting $C = C_1 + C_2 - C_3$, we have

$$\int (x^2 + 2x - 4)\, dx = \frac{x^3}{3} + x^2 - 4x + C.$$

Omitting intermediate steps, we simply write

$$\int (x^2 + 2x - 4)\, dx = \int x^2\, dx + 2 \int x\, dx - \int 4\, dx$$

$$= \frac{x^3}{3} + (2)\frac{x^2}{2} - 4x + C$$

$$= \frac{x^3}{3} + x^2 - 4x + C.$$

d. $\int (2\sqrt[5]{x^4} - 7x^3 + 10e^x - 1)\, dx.$

$$\int (2\sqrt[5]{x^4} - 7x^3 + 10e^x - 1)\, dx$$

$$= 2 \int x^{4/5}\, dx - 7 \int x^3\, dx + 10 \int e^x\, dx - \int 1\, dx$$

$$= (2)\frac{x^{9/5}}{\frac{9}{5}} - (7)\frac{x^4}{4} + 10e^x - x + C$$

$$= \frac{10}{9}x^{9/5} - \frac{7}{4}x^4 + 10e^x - x + C.$$

PITFALL. *Only a constant factor can "jump" in front of an integral sign. It is correct to write* $\int 7x\,dx = 7\int x\,dx = (7/2)x^2 + C$, *but it is **incorrect** to write* $\int 7x\,dx = 7x \int dx = (7x)(x + C) = 7x^2 + 7Cx.$

EXAMPLE 4

Find the following indefinite integrals.

a. $\displaystyle\int y^2\left(y + \frac{2}{3}\right) dy.$

By multiplying the integrand, we obtain

$$\int y^2\left(y + \frac{2}{3}\right) dy = \int\left(y^3 + \frac{2}{3}y^2\right) dy$$

$$= \int y^3\,dy + \frac{2}{3}\int y^2\,dy$$

$$= \frac{y^4}{4} + \left(\frac{2}{3}\right)\frac{y^3}{3} + C$$

$$= \frac{y^4}{4} + \frac{2y^3}{9} + C.$$

b. $\displaystyle\int \frac{(3x + \sqrt{x})(\sqrt[3]{x} - 2)}{6}\,dx.$

By factoring out $\frac{1}{6}$ and multiplying the binomials we get

$$\int \frac{(3x + x^{1/2})(x^{1/3} - 2)}{6}\,dx$$

$$= \frac{1}{6}\int (3x^{4/3} + x^{5/6} - 6x - 2x^{1/2})\,dx$$

$$= \frac{3}{6}\int x^{4/3}\,dx + \frac{1}{6}\int x^{5/6}\,dx - \frac{6}{6}\int x\,dx - \frac{2}{6}\int x^{1/2}\,dx$$

$$= \left(\frac{1}{2}\right)\frac{x^{7/3}}{\frac{7}{3}} + \frac{1}{6}\frac{x^{11/6}}{\frac{11}{6}} - (1)\frac{x^2}{2} - \frac{1}{3}\frac{x^{3/2}}{\frac{3}{2}} + C$$

$$= \frac{3x^{7/3}}{14} + \frac{x^{11/6}}{11} - \frac{x^2}{2} - \frac{2x^{3/2}}{9} + C.$$

EXAMPLE 5

a. *If* $dy/dx = 2x - 4$, *and* $y = 2$ *when* $x = 1$, *find* y.

Since $dy/dx = 2x - 4$, y is an antiderivative of $2x - 4$. Thus

$$y = \int (2x - 4)\, dx = 2\int x\, dx - \int 4\, dx$$

$$= (2)\frac{x^2}{2} - 4x + C = x^2 - 4x + C.$$

Thus *any* function y of the form

$$y = x^2 - 4x + C \qquad (2)$$

satisfies $dy/dx = 2x - 4$. To determine the *specific* one for which $y = 2$ when $x = 1$, we must find the right C. Substituting $y = 2$ and $x = 1$ into Eq. (2), we obtain

$$2 = (1)^2 - 4(1) + C.$$

Therefore $C = 5$ and

$$y = x^2 - 4x + 5.$$

b. *Given that* $y'' = x^2 - 6$, $y'(0) = 2$, *and* $y(1) = -1$, *find* y.

Since $y'' = \dfrac{d}{dx}(y') = x^2 - 6$, y' is an antiderivative of $x^2 - 6$. Thus

$$y' = \int (x^2 - 6)\, dx = \frac{x^3}{3} - 6x + C_1. \qquad (3)$$

Since $y'(0) = 2$ means $y' = 2$ when $x = 0$, from Eq. (3) we have

$$2 = \frac{0^3}{2} - 6(0) + C_1.$$

Hence $C_1 = 2$ and

$$y' = \frac{x^3}{3} - 6x + 2.$$

By integration we can find y:

$$y = \int \left(\frac{x^3}{3} - 6x + 2 \right) dx$$

$$= \left(\frac{1}{3} \right) \frac{x^4}{4} - (6) \frac{x^2}{2} + 2x + C_2.$$

$$y = \frac{x^4}{12} - 3x^2 + 2x + C_2. \tag{4}$$

Since $y = -1$ when $x = 1$, then from Eq. (4)

$$-1 = \frac{1^4}{12} - 3(1)^2 + 2(1) + C_2.$$

Therefore $C_2 = -\frac{1}{12}$ and

$$y = \frac{x^4}{12} - 3x^2 + 2x - \frac{1}{12}.$$

EXAMPLE 6

a. *Mr. Yohito Ling, president of Ding-a-Ling Alarm Clock Co., has determined that the marginal revenue function for his U.S. subsidiary is*

$$dr/dx = 2000 - 20x - 3x^2.$$

Determine the demand function for Ding-a-Ling alarm clocks in the U.S.

Since dr/dx is the derivative of total revenue r,

$$r = \int (2000 - 20x - 3x^2) \, dx$$

$$= 2000x - (20) \frac{x^2}{2} - (3) \frac{x^3}{3} + C$$

$$r = 2000x - 10x^2 - x^3 + C. \tag{5}$$

When no units are sold, total revenue is 0; that is, $r = 0$ when $x = 0$. From Eq. (5),

$$0 = 2000(0) - 10(0)^2 - 0^3 + C.$$

Hence $C = 0$ and

$$r = 2000x - 10x^2 - x^3.$$

But $r = px$ where p is the price per unit. Solving for p gives the demand function.

$$p = \frac{r}{x} = \frac{2000x - 10x^2 - x^3}{x}$$

$$p = 2000 - 10x - x^2.$$

b. *J. P. Jellybelly, president of Jellybelly Jelly Bean Corp., asked his vice president of production to determine the total cost of producing 10,000 pounds of Jellybelly jelly beans in one week. In his files the vice president found that the marginal cost function dc / dx is*

$$\frac{dc}{dx} = \frac{1}{1,000,000} \left[\frac{1}{500} x^2 - 25x \right] + .2$$

where x is pounds of jelly beans per week, and fixed costs per week are $400. What reply should the vice president give to Mr. Jellybelly?

Since dc / dx is the derivative of total cost c,

$$c = \int \left\{ \frac{1}{1,000,000} \left[\frac{1}{500} x^2 - 25x \right] + .2 \right\} dx$$

$$= \frac{1}{1,000,000} \int \left[\frac{1}{500} x^2 - 25x \right] dx + \int .2 \, dx$$

$$c = \frac{1}{1,000,000} \left[\frac{x^3}{1500} - \frac{25 x^2}{2} \right] + .2x + C.$$

When $x = 0$, then $c = 400$ and so $C = 400$. Thus

$$c = \frac{1}{1,000,000} \left[\frac{x^3}{1500} - \frac{25 x^2}{2} \right] + .2x + 400. \qquad (6)$$

From Eq. (6), when $x = 10,000$ then $c = 1816\frac{2}{3}$. The vice president should reply that the total cost for producing 10,000 pounds of jelly beans in one week is $1,816.67.

EXERCISE 9-1

In problems 1-62, find the indefinite integrals.

1. $\int 5 \, dx$

2. $\int \frac{1}{2} \, dx$

3. $\int x^8 \, dx$

4. $\int 2x^{25} \, dx$

5. $\int t^{13/2} \, dt$

6. $\int \frac{1}{2} x^{5/3} \, dx$

7. $\int x^{-7} \, dx$

8. $\int \frac{z^{-3}}{3} \, dz$

9. $\int \frac{1}{x^{10}} \, dx$

10. $\int \frac{7}{x^4} \, dx$

11. $\displaystyle\int \frac{1}{y^{11/5}}\, dy$

12. $\displaystyle\int \frac{7}{2x^{9/4}}\, dx$

13. $\displaystyle\int \sqrt[5]{x^6}\, dx$

14. $\displaystyle\int -\tfrac{3}{2}\sqrt{x}\, dx$

15. $\displaystyle\int \frac{1}{\sqrt[8]{x^7}}\, dx$

16. $\displaystyle\int \frac{3}{4\sqrt[8]{x}}\, dx$

17. $\displaystyle\int (7 + e)\, dx$

18. $\displaystyle\int (5 - 6)\, dx$

19. $\displaystyle\int x^{\sqrt{2}}\, dx$

20. $\displaystyle\int x^{1.2}\, dx$

21. $\displaystyle\int 3x^7\, dx$

22. $\displaystyle\int 5x^4\, dx$

23. $\displaystyle\int (8 + x)\, dx$

24. $\displaystyle\int (r^3 + 2r)\, dr$

25. $\displaystyle\int (y^5 + 5y)\, dy$

26. $\displaystyle\int (7 - 3w - 2w^2)\, dw$

27. $\displaystyle\int (3t^2 - 4t - 5)\, dt$

28. $\displaystyle\int (1 + u + u^2 + u^3)\, du$

29. $\displaystyle\int \left(\frac{x}{7} - \frac{3}{4}x^4\right) dx$

30. $\displaystyle\int \left(\frac{2x^2}{7} - \frac{8}{3}x^4\right) dx$

31. $\displaystyle\int 3e^x\, dx$

32. $\displaystyle\int \left(\frac{e^x}{3} + 2x\right) dx$

33. $\displaystyle\int (6 - \tfrac{5}{4}z^2 + 2e^z)\, dz$

34. $\displaystyle\int \tfrac{1}{12}\left(\tfrac{1}{3}x^5\right) dx$

35. $\displaystyle\int \left(\frac{e^u}{4} + 1\right) du$

36. $\displaystyle\int \left(3y^3 - 2y^2 + \frac{e^y}{6}\right) dy$

37. $\displaystyle\int (x^{-2} - 5x^{-3} + 2x^{-4})\, dx$

38. $\displaystyle\int (-3x^{-2} - 2x^{-3})\, dx$

39. $\displaystyle\int (x^{8.3} - 9x^6 + 3x^{-4} + x^{-3})\, dx$

40. $\displaystyle\int (.3y^4 - 8y^{-3} + 2)\, dy$

41. $\displaystyle\int \left(\frac{x^3}{3} - \frac{3}{x^3}\right) dx$

42. $\displaystyle\int \left(\frac{1}{2x^3} - \frac{1}{x^4}\right) dx$

43. $\displaystyle\int \left(\frac{3w^2}{2} - \frac{2}{3w^2}\right) dw$

44. $\displaystyle\int \frac{2}{e^{-s}}\, ds$

45. $\int (\sqrt[3]{x} - \sqrt[4]{x} + \sqrt[5]{x}) \, dx$

46. $\int \left(\dfrac{\sqrt[4]{x}}{2} - \dfrac{2}{3} \sqrt[3]{x} \right) dx$

47. $\int (2\sqrt{x} - 3\sqrt[4]{x}) \, dx$

48. $\int 0 \, dx$

49. $\int 2x^{-6/5} \, dx$

50. $\int (x^{-4/5} + 2) \, dx$

51. $\int \left(-\dfrac{\sqrt[3]{x^2}}{5} - \dfrac{7}{2\sqrt{x}} + 6x \right) dx$

52. $\int \left(\sqrt[3]{x} - \dfrac{1}{\sqrt[3]{x}} \right) dx$

53. $\int (x^2 + 5)(x - 3) \, dx$

54. $\int x^4 (x^3 + 3x^2 + 7) \, dx$

55. $\int \sqrt{x} \, (x + 3) \, dx$

56. $\int (z + 2)^2 \, dz$

57. $\int (2u + 1)^2 \, du$

58. $\int \left(\dfrac{1}{\sqrt[3]{x}} + 1 \right)^2 dx$

59. $\int v^{-2} (2v^4 + 3v^2 - 2v^{-3}) \, dv$

60. $\int [6e^u - u^3 (\sqrt{u} + 1)] \, du$

61. $\int \dfrac{e^6 + e^x}{2} \, dx$

62. $\int \dfrac{\sqrt{x} \, (x^5 - \sqrt[3]{x} + 2)}{3} \, dx$

In problems 63–68, find y subject to the given conditions.

63. $dy/dx = 0$; $y(2) = 3$

64. $dy/dx = 3x - 4$; $y(-1) = \frac{13}{2}$

65. $y'' = x + 1$; $y'(0) = 0$, $y(0) = 5$

66. $y'' = 2e^x$; $y'(2) = 0$, $y(0) = 3$

67. $y''' = 2x$; $y''(-1) = 3$, $y'(3) = 10$, $y(0) = 2$

68. $y''' = e^x + 1$; $y''(0) = 1$, $y'(0) = 2$, $y(0) = 3$

In problems 69–72, dc/dx is a marginal cost function and fixed costs are indicated in braces. For problems 69 and 70 find the total cost function. For problems 71 and 72, find the total cost for the indicated value of x.

69. $dc/dx = 1.35$; $\{200\}$

70. $dc/dx = 2x + 50$; $\{1000\}$

71. $dc/dx = .09x^2 - 1.2x + 4.5$; $\{7700\}$; $x = 10$

72. $dc/dx = .000102x^2 - .034x + 5$; $\{10,000\}$; $x = 100$

73. Yankee Doodle Dummy Co., a manufacturer of manikins, has determined that their marginal cost function is $dc/dx = .003x^2 - .4x + 40$, where x is the number of manikins produced. If their marginal cost when 50 manikins are produced is $27.50 and fixed costs are $5000, what is the *average* cost of producing 100 manikins?

In problems 74–76, dr/dx is a marginal revenue function. Find the demand function.

74. $dr/dx = .7$ **75.** $dr/dx = 15 - \frac{1}{15}x$

76. $dr/dx = 275 - x - .3x^2$

77. Blinko Co. is the sole producer of artificial lightning bugs. Management has determined that the company's marginal revenue function is $dr/dx = 100 - 3x^2$. Determine the point elasticity of demand for artificial lightning bugs when $x = 5$. *Hint:* First find the demand function.

9-2 INTEGRATION BY SUBSTITUTION

In Sec. 9-1 we saw that

$$\int x^n \, dx = \frac{x^{n+1}}{n+1} + C \quad \text{if } n \neq -1.$$

If u is substituted for x, then $du = dx$ and

$$\boxed{\int u^n \, du = \frac{u^{n+1}}{n+1} + C \quad \text{if } n \neq -1.} \qquad (1)$$

Similarly,

$$\boxed{\int e^u \, du = e^u + C.} \qquad (2)$$

Sometimes for a complicated integral involving x (say), we may substitute a simple one involving u. It involves replacing a function of x by the variable u. Example 7 will illustrate.

EXAMPLE 7

Find the following indefinite integrals.

a. $\int (x + 1)^{20} \, dx.$

Let us set $u = x + 1$; then $du = dx$. Thus $\int (x + 1)^{20} \, dx$ has the form $\int u^{20} \, du$. By Eq. (1),

$$\int (x + 1)^{20} \, dx = \int u^{20} \, du$$

$$= \frac{u^{21}}{21} + C$$

$$= \frac{(x + 1)^{21}}{21} + C.$$

It will be our custom to give our answer in terms of the variable of the original integral.

b. $\int 2xe^{x^2} \, dx.$

Let $u = x^2$. Then $du = 2x \, dx$ and

$$\int 2xe^{x^2} \, dx = \int e^{x^2} (2x \, dx)$$

$$= \int e^u \, du$$

$$= e^u + C \qquad\qquad\qquad [\text{by Eq. (2)}]$$

$$= e^{x^2} + C.$$

c. $\int x\sqrt{x^2 + 5} \, dx.$

We can write this integral as

$$\int x(x^2 + 5)^{1/2} \, dx.$$

If $u = x^2 + 5$, then $du = 2x \, dx$. The integral would have the form $\int u^{1/2} \, du$ if the integrand contained a factor of 2. Although this is not the case, we can remedy the situation by expressing the integrand in a suitable equivalent form.

$$\int x(x^2 + 5)^{1/2} \, dx = \int \frac{2}{2} x(x^2 + 5)^{1/2} \, dx.$$

Since the integrand now has $1/2$ as a *constant* factor, we have

$$\int \frac{2}{2} x(x^2 + 5)^{1/2} \, dx = \frac{1}{2} \int (x^2 + 5)^{1/2} (2x \, dx)$$

$$= \frac{1}{2} \int u^{1/2} \, du$$

$$= \frac{1}{2} \left[\frac{u^{3/2}}{\frac{3}{2}} \right] + C.$$

Going back to x, we have

$$\int x\sqrt{x^2+5}\ dx = \frac{(x^2+5)^{3/2}}{3} + C.$$

In summary, to integrate $x\sqrt{x^2+5}$ the integrand was multiplied by 2 and this step was compensated for by inserting the factor $\frac{1}{2}$ before the integral sign.

d. $\int \sqrt[3]{6y}\ dy.$

If we set $u = 6y$, then $du = 6\ dy$. Thus we insert a factor of 6 and adjust for it with a factor of $\frac{1}{6}$.

$$\int \sqrt[3]{6y}\ dy = \int (6y)^{1/3}\ dy = \frac{1}{6}\int (6y)^{1/3}\ (6\ dy)$$

$$= \frac{1}{6}\int u^{1/3}\ du$$

$$= \left(\frac{1}{6}\right)\frac{u^{4/3}}{\frac{4}{3}} + C = \frac{(6y)^{4/3}}{8} + C.$$

e. $\int (x^2+1)\ e^{x^3+3x}\ dx.$

If $u = x^3 + 3x$, then $du = (3x^2+3)\ dx = 3(x^2+1)\ dx$. If the integrand contained a factor of 3, the integral would have the form $\int e^u\ du$. Thus we write

$$\int (x^2+1)\ e^{x^3+3x}\ dx = \tfrac{1}{3}\int 3(x^2+1)\ e^{x^3+3x}\ dx$$

$$= \tfrac{1}{3}\int e^{x^3+3x}\ [3(x^2+1)\ dx]$$

$$= \tfrac{1}{3}\int e^u\ du = \tfrac{1}{3}e^u + C$$

$$= \tfrac{1}{3}e^{x^3+3x} + C.$$

PITFALL. *Equation (1) should not be used indiscriminately. For example, it does not apply to the integration of* e^{2x}:

$$\int e^{2x}\ dx \neq \frac{e^{2x+1}}{2x+1} + C.$$

Equation (2) must be used with u = 2x and du = 2 dx.

$$\int e^{2x}\, dx = \tfrac{1}{2} \int e^{2x}\,(2\,dx)$$

$$= \tfrac{1}{2} \int e^u\, du = \tfrac{1}{2} e^u + C$$

$$= \tfrac{1}{2} e^{2x} + C.$$

For $\int \dfrac{1}{u}\, du = \int u^{-1}\, du$, Eq. (1) cannot be used since it assumes $n \neq -1$. To determine this integral we turn to logarithms. Recall from Chapter 5 that the logarithm of a number is defined if and only if that number is positive. Suppose $u > 0$. Then

$$d\,(\ln u) = \frac{d}{du}\,(\ln u)\, du$$

$$= \frac{1}{u}\, du.$$

Thus,

$$\int \frac{1}{u}\, du = \ln(u) + C, \quad \text{if } u > 0.$$

On the other hand, suppose $u < 0$. Then $-u > 0$ and

$$d\,[\ln(-u)] = \frac{d}{du}\,[\ln(-u)]\, du$$

$$= \frac{-1}{-u}\, du = \frac{1}{u}\, du.$$

Thus,

$$\int \frac{1}{u}\, du = \ln(-u) + C, \quad \text{if } u < 0.$$

Combining these cases, we have

$$\boxed{\int \frac{1}{u}\, du = \ln|u| + C, \quad \text{if } u \neq 0.} \tag{3}$$

EXAMPLE 8

Find the following indefinite integrals.

a. $\int \dfrac{7}{x}\, dx.$

$$\int \frac{7}{x}\, dx = 7 \int \frac{1}{x}\, dx.$$

By Eq. (3) with $u = x$ and $du = dx$,

$$\int \frac{7}{x}\, dx = 7 \ln |x| + C.$$

Using properties of logarithms, we can express the answer another way:

$$\int \frac{7}{x}\, dx = \ln |x^7| + C.$$

b. $\int \dfrac{2x}{x^2 + 5}\, dx.$

Let $u = x^2 + 5$. Then $du = 2x\, dx$. Thus

$$\int \frac{2x}{x^2 + 5}\, dx = \int \frac{1}{x^2 + 5}\, (2x\, dx)$$

$$= \int \frac{1}{u}\, du$$

$$= \ln |u| + C \qquad\qquad \text{[by Eq. (3)]}$$

$$= \ln |x^2 + 5| + C.$$

Since $x^2 + 5 > 0$ for all x, we can omit the vertical bars and write

$$\int \frac{2x}{x^2 + 5}\, dx = \ln (x^2 + 5) + C.$$

c. $\int \dfrac{2x^3 + 3x}{x^4 + 3x^2 + 7}\, dx.$

If $u = x^4 + 3x^2 + 7$, then $du = (4x^3 + 6x)\, dx$ which is 2 times the given numerator. Thus we insert a factor of 2 and adjust for it with a factor of $\frac{1}{2}$.

$$\int \frac{2x^3 + 3x}{x^4 + 3x^2 + 7}\, dx = \frac{1}{2} \int \frac{2(2x^3 + 3x)}{x^4 + 3x^2 + 7}\, dx$$

$$= \frac{1}{2} \int \frac{1}{x^4 + 3x^2 + 7}\, [(4x^3 + 6x)\, dx]$$

$$= \frac{1}{2} \int \frac{1}{u} \, du$$

$$= \frac{1}{2} \ln |u| + C$$

$$= \frac{1}{2} \ln |x^4 + 3x^2 + 7| + C$$

$$= \ln \sqrt{x^4 + 3x^2 + 7} + C.$$

d. $\int \left[\dfrac{1}{(1-w)^2} + \dfrac{1}{w-1} \right] dw.$

$$\int \left[\frac{1}{(1-w)^2} + \frac{1}{w-1} \right] dw = \int (1-w)^{-2} \, dw + \int \frac{1}{w-1} \, dw$$

$$= -1 \int (1-w)^{-2} \, (-dw) + \int \frac{1}{w-1} \, dw.$$

The integrands have the forms $u^{-2} \, du$ and $\dfrac{1}{v} \, dv$, respectively. Thus by formulas (1) and (3) we have

$$\int \left[\frac{1}{(1-w)^2} + \frac{1}{w-1} \right] dw = -\frac{(1-w)^{-1}}{-1} + \ln |w-1| + C$$

$$= \frac{1}{1-w} + \ln |w-1| + C.$$

It should be clear from the examples that an *appropriate* substitution may transform an integral into a familar form. We say appropriate in the sense that in Example 8(c) you would *not* be able to proceed very far if, for instance, you let $u = 2x^3 + 3x$. At times you may find it necessary to try many different substitutions before recognizing a familiar form. **Skill at integration comes only after many hours of practice and conscientious study.**

For your convenience we list in Table 9-2 the basic integration formulas so far discussed. We assume that u is a function of x.

EXERCISE 9-2

In problems 1–76, find the indefinite integrals.

1. $\displaystyle\int (x+4)^8 \, dx$

2. $\displaystyle\int 2(x+3)^3 \, dx$

3. $\displaystyle\int 2x(x^2+16)^3 \, dx$

4. $\displaystyle\int (3x^2+14x)(x^3+7x^2+1) \, dx$

Table 9-2

BASIC INTEGRATION FORMULAS

1. $\int k\,du = ku + C,\qquad k$ a constant

2. $\int u^n\,du = \dfrac{u^{n+1}}{n+1} + C,\qquad n \neq -1$

3. $\int e^u\,du = e^u + C$

4. $\int \dfrac{1}{u}\,du = \ln|u| + C,\qquad u \neq 0$

5. $\int k\,f(x)\,dx = k\int f(x)\,dx$

6. $\int [f(x) \pm g(x)]\,dx = \int f(x)\,dx \pm \int g(x)\,dx$

5. $\displaystyle\int (3y^2 + 6y)(y^3 + 3y^2 + 1)^{2/3}\,dy$

6. $\displaystyle\int (-12z^2 - 12z + 1)(-4z^3 - 6z^2 + z)^{18}\,dz$

7. $\displaystyle\int \frac{3}{(3x-1)^3}\,dx$

8. $\displaystyle\int \frac{4x}{(2x^2-7)^{10}}\,dx$

9. $\displaystyle\int 3e^{3x}\,dx$

10. $\displaystyle\int 2e^{2t+5}\,dt$

11. $\displaystyle\int (2t+1)\,e^{t^2+t}\,dt$

12. $\displaystyle\int -3w^2\,e^{-w^3}\,dw$

13. $\displaystyle\int \frac{1}{x+5}\,dx$

14. $\displaystyle\int \frac{2x+1}{x+x^2}\,dx$

15. $\displaystyle\int \frac{3x^2 + 4x^3}{x^3 + x^4}\,dx$

16. $\displaystyle\int \frac{3x^2 - 2x}{1 - x^2 + x^3}\,dx$

17. $\displaystyle\int \sqrt{x+10}\,dx$

18. $\displaystyle\int \frac{1}{\sqrt{x-2}}\,dx$

19. $\displaystyle\int (7x-6)^4\,dx$

20. $\displaystyle\int x^2(3x^3 + 7)^3\,dx$

21. $\int x(x^2 + 3)^{12} \, dx$

22. $\int x \sqrt{1 + 2x^2} \, dx$

23. $\int x^4 (27 + x^5)^{1/3} \, dx$

24. $\int x^3 \, e^{4x^4} \, dx$

25. $\int xe^{5x^2} \, dx$

26. $\int (3 - 2x)^{10} \, dx$

27. $\int 6e^{-2x} \, dx$

28. $\int x^4 \, e^{-6x^5} \, dx$

29. $\int \dfrac{6z}{(z^2 - 6)^5} \, dz$

30. $\int \dfrac{1}{(8y - 3)^3} \, dy$

31. $\int \dfrac{4}{x} \, dx$

32. $\int \dfrac{3}{1 + 2y} \, dy$

33. $\int \dfrac{s^2}{s^3 + 5} \, ds$

34. $\int \dfrac{2x^2}{3 - 4x^3} \, dx$

35. $\int \dfrac{7}{5 - 3x} \, dx$

36. $\int \dfrac{7t}{5t^2 - 6} \, dt$

37. $\int \sqrt{5x} \, dx$

38. $\int \dfrac{1}{(4x)^7} \, dx$

39. $\int \dfrac{x}{\sqrt{x^2 - 4}} \, dx$

40. $\int \dfrac{7}{3 - 2x} \, dx$

41. $\int 2y^3 \, e^{y^4 + 1} \, dy$

42. $\int \sqrt{4x - 3} \, dx$

43. $\int v^2 \, e^{-2v^3 + 1} \, dv$

44. $\int \dfrac{x^2}{\sqrt[3]{2x^3 + 9}} \, dx$

45. $\int (e^{-5x} + 2e^x) \, dx$

46. $\int 4 \sqrt[3]{y + 1} \, dy$

47. $\int (x + 1)(3 - 3x^2 - 6x)^3 \, dx$

48. $\int 2ye^{3y^2} \, dy$

49. $\int \dfrac{x^2 + 2}{x^3 + 6x} \, dx$

50. $\int (e^x - e^{-x} + e^{2x}) \, dx$

51. $\int \dfrac{16s - 4}{3 - 2s + 4s^2} \, ds$

52. $\int (t^2 + 4t)(t^3 + 6t^2)^6 \, dt$

53. $\int x(2x^2 + 1)^{-1} \, dx$

54. $\int (w^3 - 8w^7 + 1)(w^4 - 4w^8 + 4w)^{-6} \, dw$

55. $\int -(x^2 - 2x^5)(x^3 - x^6)^{-10} \, dx$

56. $\int \frac{3}{7} (v - 2) \, e^{2-4v+v^2} \, dv$

57. $\int (2x^3 + x)(x^4 + x^2) \, dx$

58. $\int (e^{3.1})^2 \, dx$

59. $\int \frac{18 + 12x}{(4 - 9x - 3x^2)^5} \, dx$

60. $\int (e^x - e^{-x})^2 \, dx$

61. $\int x(2x + 1) \, e^{4x^3+3x^2-4} \, dx$

62. $\int (u^2 + 3 - ue^{7-u^2}) \, du$

63. $\int x \sqrt{(7 - 5x^2)^3} \, dx$

64. $\int e^{-x/4} \, dx$

65. $\int \frac{dx}{\sqrt{2x}}$

66. $\int \frac{x^3}{e^{x^4}} \, dx$

67. $\int (x^2 + 1)^2 \, dx$

68. $\int \left[x(x^2 - 16)^2 - \frac{1}{2x + 5} \right] dx$

69. $\int \left[\frac{x}{x^2 + 1} + \frac{x^5}{(x^6 + 1)^2} \right] dx$

70. $\int \left[\frac{1}{x - 1} + \frac{1}{(x - 1)^2} \right] dx$

71. $\int \left[\frac{1}{3x - 5} - (x^2 - 2x^5)(x^3 - x^6)^{-10} \right] dx$

72. $\int (r^3 + 5)^2 \, dr$

73. $\int \left[\sqrt{2x + 3} - \frac{x}{x^2 + 3} \right] dx$

74. $\int \left[\frac{2x}{x^2 + 3} - \frac{x^3}{(x^4 + 2)^2} \right] dx$

75. $\int \frac{e^{\sqrt{x}}}{\sqrt{x}} \, dx$

76. $\int (e^4 - 2^e) \, dx$

In problems 77-80, find y subject to the given conditions.

77. $D_x y = (3 - 2x)^2; \, y(0) = 1$

78. $D_x y = x/(x^2 + 4); \, y(1) = 0$

79. $y'' = 1/x^2; \, y'(-1) = 1, \, y(1) = 0$

80. $y'' = \sqrt{x + 2}; \, y'(2) = \frac{1}{3}, \, y(2) = -\frac{7}{15}$

9-3 MORE TECHNIQUES OF INTEGRATION

Now that you have had some practice in determining indefinite integrals, suppose we consider some problems of a greater degree of difficulty.

EXAMPLE 9

a. $\int \dfrac{x^3 + x - 1}{x^2}\, dx.$

A familiar integration form is not apparent. However, we can write the integrand as the sum of three fractions by dividing each term in the numerator by the denominator.

$$\int \frac{x^3 + x - 1}{x^2}\, dx = \int \left[x + \frac{1}{x} - \frac{1}{x^2} \right] dx$$

$$= \frac{x^2}{2} + \ln|x| - \int x^{-2}\, dx$$

$$= \frac{x^2}{2} + \ln |x| + \frac{1}{x} + C.$$

b. $\int \dfrac{2x^3 + 3x^2 + x + 1}{2x + 1}\, dx.$

Using long division, we first divide the numerator by the denominator.

$$\int \frac{2x^3 + 3x^2 + x + 1}{2x + 1}\, dx = \int \left(x^2 + x + \frac{1}{2x + 1} \right) dx$$

$$= \frac{x^3}{3} + \frac{x^2}{2} + \int \frac{1}{2x + 1}\, dx$$

$$= \frac{x^3}{3} + \frac{x^2}{2} + \frac{1}{2} \int \frac{1}{2x + 1}\, (2\, dx)$$

$$= \frac{x^3}{3} + \frac{x^2}{2} + \frac{1}{2} \ln |2x + 1| + C.$$

EXAMPLE 10

Find the following indefinite integrals.

a. $\int \dfrac{1}{\sqrt{x}\, (\sqrt{x} - 2)^3}\, dx.$

We can write this integral as

$$\int \frac{(\sqrt{x} - 2)^{-3}}{\sqrt{x}} \, dx.$$

Let $u = \sqrt{x} - 2$. Then $du = \dfrac{1}{2\sqrt{x}} \, dx$ and

$$\int \frac{(\sqrt{x} - 2)^{-3}}{\sqrt{x}} \, dx = 2 \int (\sqrt{x} - 2)^{-3} \left(\frac{1}{2\sqrt{x}} \, dx \right)$$

$$= 2 \int u^{-3} \, du$$

$$= 2 \left(\frac{u^{-2}}{-2} \right) + C$$

$$= -u^{-2} + C$$

$$= -(\sqrt{x} - 2)^{-2} + C.$$

b. $\displaystyle \int \frac{1}{x \ln x} \, dx.$

Rewriting the integral, we have

$$\int \frac{1}{\ln x} \left(\frac{1}{x} \, dx \right)$$

If $u = \ln x$, then $du = \dfrac{1}{x} \, dx$ and

$$\int \frac{1}{x \ln x} \, dx = \int \frac{1}{\ln x} \left(\frac{1}{x} \, dx \right)$$

$$= \int \frac{1}{u} \, du$$

$$= \ln |u| + C$$

$$= \ln |\ln x| + C.$$

c. $\displaystyle \int \frac{5}{w(\ln w)^{3/2}} \, dw.$

If $u = \ln w$, then $du = \dfrac{1}{w} \, dw$ and

$$\int \frac{5}{w(\ln w)^{3/2}} \, dw = 5 \int (\ln w)^{-3/2} \left(\frac{1}{w} \, dw \right)$$

$$= 5 \int u^{-3/2} \, du$$

$$= 5 \cdot \frac{u^{-1/2}}{-\frac{1}{2}} + C$$

$$= \frac{-10}{u^{1/2}} + C$$

$$= \frac{-10}{(\ln w)^{1/2}} + C.$$

EXAMPLE 11

Determine $\int 2^{3-x} \, dx$.

Since $2 = e^{\ln 2}$,

$$\int 2^{3-x} \, dx = \int (e^{\ln 2})^{3-x} \, dx = \int e^{(\ln 2)(3-x)} \, dx.$$

If we let $u = (\ln 2)(3 - x)$, then $du = -(\ln 2) \, dx$.

$$\int e^{(\ln 2)(3-x)} \, dx = -\frac{1}{\ln 2} \int e^{(\ln 2)(3-x)} \left[-(\ln 2) \, dx \right]$$

$$= -\frac{1}{\ln 2} \int e^u \, du$$

$$= -\frac{1}{\ln 2} e^u + C$$

$$= -\frac{1}{\ln 2} e^{(\ln 2)(3-x)} + C.$$

Simplifying, we have

$$\int 2^{3-x} \, dx = -\frac{2^{3-x}}{\ln 2} + C.$$

EXAMPLE 12

Mr. John Dirtyneck, Minister of Economic Affairs of the country of Nowashie, determined that for his country the marginal propensity to consume is given by

$$\frac{dC}{dI} = \frac{3}{4} - \frac{1}{2\sqrt{3I}}.$$

Here I represents the Nowashie national income and is expressed in billions of slugs (50 slugs = $.01). Determine the consumption function for Nowashie if it is known that consumption is 10 billion slugs ($C = 10$) when $I = 12$.

Since the marginal propensity to consume is the derivative of the consumption function C,

$$C = \int \left(\frac{3}{4} - \frac{1}{2\sqrt{3I}} \right) dI = \int \frac{3}{4} \, dI - \frac{1}{2} \int (3I)^{-1/2} \, dI$$

$$= \frac{3}{4} I - \frac{1}{2} \int (3I)^{-1/2} \, dI.$$

If we let $u = 3I$, then $du = 3 \, dI$ and

$$C = \frac{3}{4} I - \left(\frac{1}{2} \right) \frac{1}{3} \int (3I)^{-1/2} \, (3 \, dI)$$

$$= \frac{3}{4} I - \frac{1}{6} \frac{(3I)^{1/2}}{\frac{1}{2}} + C_1$$

$$C = \frac{3}{4} I - \frac{\sqrt{3I}}{3} + C_1.$$

When $I = 12$, then $C = 10$ and thus

$$10 = \frac{3}{4} (12) - \frac{\sqrt{3(12)}}{3} + C_1$$

$$= 9 - 2 + C_1.$$

$$C_1 = 3.$$

The Nowashie consumption function is

$$C = \frac{3}{4} I - \frac{\sqrt{3I}}{3} + 3.$$

EXERCISE 9-3

In problems 1–42, determine the indefinite integrals.

1. $\displaystyle\int \frac{3x^3 + x^2 - x}{x^2} \, dx$ **2.** $\displaystyle\int \frac{3x^2 - 7x}{4x} \, dx$

3. $\displaystyle\int (3x^2 + 2) \sqrt{2x^3 + 4x + 1} \, dx$ **4.** $\displaystyle\int \frac{x}{\sqrt[3]{x^2 + 5}} \, dx$

5. $\displaystyle\int \frac{4}{\sqrt{2-3x}}\,dx$

6. $\displaystyle\int \frac{xe^{x^2}\,dx}{e^{x^2}-2}$

7. $\displaystyle\int 4^{7x}\,dx$

8. $\displaystyle\int 3^x\,dx$

9. $\displaystyle\int 2x(7-e^{x^2/4})\,dx$

10. $\displaystyle\int \left(e^x + x^e + ex + \frac{e}{x}\right)dx$

11. $\displaystyle\int \frac{3e^{2x}}{e^{2x}+1}\,dx$

12. $\displaystyle\int (e^{4-3x})^2\,dx$

13. $\displaystyle\int \frac{e^{7/x}}{x^2}\,dx$

14. $\displaystyle\int \frac{2x^4 - 6x^3 + x - 2}{x-2}\,dx$

15. $\displaystyle\int \frac{(\sqrt{x}+2)^2}{3\sqrt{x}}\,dx$

16. $\displaystyle\int \frac{3e^s}{6+5e^s}\,ds$

17. $\displaystyle\int \frac{\ln x}{x}\,dx$

18. $\displaystyle\int \sqrt{t}\,(5 - t\sqrt{t})^{.4}\,dt$

19. $\displaystyle\int \frac{\ln^2(r+1)}{r+1}\,dr$

20. $\displaystyle\int \frac{8x^3 - 6x^2 - ex^4}{3x^3}\,dx$

21. $\displaystyle\int x\sqrt{e^{x^2+3}}\,dx$

22. $\displaystyle\int \frac{x+3}{x+6}\,dx$

23. $\displaystyle\int \frac{1}{(x+3)\ln(x+3)}\,dx$

24. $\displaystyle\int (x e^2 + 2x)\,dx$

25. $\displaystyle\int \left(\frac{x^3}{\sqrt{x^4-1}} - \ln 4\right)dx$

26. $\displaystyle\int \frac{x - x^{-2}}{x^2 + 2x^{-1}}\,dx$

27. $\displaystyle\int \frac{2x^4 - 8x^3 - 6x^2 + 4}{x^3}\,dx$

28. $\displaystyle\int \frac{e^x + e^{-x}}{e^x - e^{-x}}\,dx$

29. $\displaystyle\int \frac{6x^2 - 11x + 5}{3x-1}\,dx$

30. $\displaystyle\int \frac{(2x-1)(x+3)}{x-5}\,dx$

31. $\displaystyle\int \frac{x}{x-1}\,dx$

32. $\displaystyle\int \frac{x}{(x^2+1)\ln(x^2+1)}\,dx$

33. $\displaystyle\int \frac{xe^{x^2}}{\sqrt{e^{x^2}+2}}\,dx$

34. $\displaystyle\int \frac{7}{(2x+1)[1+\ln(2x+1)]^2}\,dx$

35. $\displaystyle\int \frac{(e^{-x}+6)^2}{e^x}\,dx$

36. $\displaystyle\int \left[\frac{1}{8x+1} - \frac{1}{e^x(8+e^{-x})^2}\right]dx$

37. $\int \sqrt{x} \sqrt{(8x)^{3/2} + 3} \, dx$

38. $\int \dfrac{3}{x(\ln x)^{1/2}} \, dx$

39. $\int \dfrac{\sqrt{s}}{e^{\sqrt{s^3}}} \, ds$

40. $\int \dfrac{\ln^3 x}{3x} \, dx$

41. $\int e^{\ln(x+2)} \, dx$

42. $\int dx$

In problems 43–44, dr/dx is a marginal revenue function. Find the demand function.

43. $\dfrac{dr}{dx} = \dfrac{200}{(x + 2)^2}$

44. $\dfrac{dr}{dx} = \dfrac{900}{(2x + 3)^3}$

In problems 45–46, $\dfrac{dc}{dx}$ is a marginal cost function. Find the total cost function if fixed costs in each case are 2000.

45. $\dfrac{dc}{dx} = \dfrac{20}{x + 5}$

46. $\dfrac{dc}{dx} = 2e^{.001x}$

In problems 47–49, dC/dI represents marginal propensity to consume. Find the consumption function subject to the given condition.

47. $\dfrac{dC}{dI} = \dfrac{1}{\sqrt{I}}; \quad C(9) = 8$

48. $\dfrac{dC}{dI} = \dfrac{3}{4} - \dfrac{1}{2\sqrt{3I}}; \quad C(3) = \dfrac{11}{4}$

49. $\dfrac{dC}{dI} = \dfrac{3}{4} - \dfrac{1}{6\sqrt{I}}; \quad C(25) = 23$

9-4   SUMMATION

To prepare you for further applications of integration, let us discuss certain sums.

Consider finding the sum S of the first n positive integers:

$$S = 1 + 2 + \ldots + (n - 1) + n. \tag{1}$$

Writing the right side of Eq. (1) in reverse order, we have

$$S = n + (n - 1) + \ldots + 2 + 1. \tag{2}$$

Adding the corresponding sides of Eqs. (1) and (2) gives

$$
\begin{array}{lllllll}
S = 1 & + & 2 & + \ldots + & (n - 1) & + & n \\
S = n & + & (n - 1) & + \ldots + & 2 & + & 1 \\
\hline
2S = (n + 1) & + & (n + 1) & + \ldots + & (n + 1) & + & (n + 1).
\end{array}
$$

On the right side of the last equation the term $(n + 1)$ occurs n times. Thus $2S = n(n + 1)$ and so

$$S = \frac{n(n + 1)}{2}. \quad [\text{Sum of first } n \text{ positive integers}] \quad (3)$$

For example, the sum of the first 100 positive integers corresponds to $n = 100$ and is $100(100 + 1)/2$ or 5050.

For convenience, to indicate a sum we shall introduce *sigma notation*, so named because the Greek letter Σ (sigma) is used. For example,

$$\sum_{k=1}^{3} (2k + 5)$$

denotes the sum of those numbers obtained from the expression $(2k + 5)$ by first replacing k by 1, then by 2, and finally by 3. Thus

$$\sum_{k=1}^{3} (2k + 5) = [2(1) + 5] + [2(2) + 5] + [2(3) + 5]$$

$$= 7 + 9 + 11 = 27.$$

The letter k is called the *index of summation*; the numbers 1 and 3 are the *limits of summation* (1 is the *lower limit* and 3 is the *upper limit*). The symbol used for the index is a "dummy" symbol in the sense that it does not affect the sum of the terms. Any other letter can be used. For example,

$$\sum_{j=1}^{3} (2j + 5) = 7 + 9 + 11 = \sum_{k=1}^{3} (2k + 5).$$

EXAMPLE 13

Evaluate each of the following.

a. $\displaystyle\sum_{k=4}^{7} \frac{k^2 + 3}{2}$.

$$\sum_{k=4}^{7} \frac{k^2 + 3}{2} = \frac{4^2 + 3}{2} + \frac{5^2 + 3}{2} + \frac{6^2 + 3}{2} + \frac{7^2 + 3}{2}$$

$$= \frac{19}{2} + \frac{28}{2} + \frac{39}{2} + \frac{52}{2} = 69.$$

b. $\displaystyle\sum_{j=0}^{2} (-1)^{j+1} (j - 1)^2$.

$$\sum_{j=0}^{2} (-1)^{j+1} (j - 1)^2 = (-1)^{0+1} (0 - 1)^2 + (-1)^{1+1} (1 - 1)^2 + (-1)^{2+1} (2 - 1)^2$$

$$= (-1) + 0 + (-1) = -2.$$

To express the sum of the first n positive integers in sigma notation we can write

$$\sum_{k=1}^{n} k = 1 + 2 + \ldots + n.$$

By Eq. (3),

$$\boxed{\sum_{k=1}^{n} k = \frac{n(n+1)}{2}.}$$ (4)

Note in (4) that $\displaystyle\sum_{k=1}^{n} k$ is a function of n alone, not of k.

EXAMPLE 14

Evaluate each of the following.

a. $\displaystyle\sum_{k=1}^{60} k.$

Here we must find the sum of the first sixty positive integers. By Eq. (4) with $n = 60$,

$$\sum_{k=1}^{60} k = \frac{60(60+1)}{2} = 1830.$$

b. $\displaystyle\sum_{k=1}^{n-1} k.$

Here we must add the first $n-1$ positive integers. Replacing n by $n-1$ in Eq. (4), we obtain

$$\sum_{k=1}^{n-1} k = \frac{(n-1)[(n-1)+1]}{2} = \frac{(n-1)n}{2}.$$

Another useful formula is that for the sum of the squares of the first n positive integers. We shall use it in the next section.

$$\boxed{\sum_{k=1}^{n} k^2 = \frac{n(n+1)(2n+1)}{6}.}$$ (5)

EXAMPLE 15

Evaluate the following.

a. $1 + 4 + 9 + 16 + 25 + 36$.

This sum can be written as $\sum\limits_{k=1}^{6} k^2$. By Eq. (5) with $n = 6$,

$$\sum_{k=1}^{6} k^2 = \frac{6(6+1)[2(6)+1]}{6} = 91.$$

b. $\sum\limits_{k=1}^{n-1} k^2$.

Replacing n by $n - 1$ in Eq. (5), we have

$$\sum_{k=1}^{n-1} k^2 = \frac{(n-1)[(n-1)+1][2(n-1)+1]}{6}$$

$$= \frac{(n-1)\,n\,(2n-1)}{6}.$$

We conclude with a property of sigma. If $x_1, x_2, ..., x_n$ are real numbers and c is a constant, then

$$\sum_{i=1}^{n} cx_i = cx_1 + cx_2 + ... + cx_n$$

$$= c(x_1 + x_2 + ... + x_n) = c\sum_{i=1}^{n} x_i.$$

Thus,

$$\boxed{\sum_{i=1}^{n} cx_i = c\sum_{i=1}^{n} x_i.}$$

This means that a constant factor can "jump" before sigma. For example,

$$\sum_{i=1}^{5} 3i^2 = 3\sum_{i=1}^{5} i^2.$$

By Eq. (5) we have

$$\sum_{i=1}^{5} 3i^2 = 3\sum_{i=1}^{5} i^2 = 3\left[\frac{5(6)(11)}{6}\right] = 165.$$

PITFALL.   *Although constant factors can "jump" before sigma, nothing else can.*

EXERCISE 9-4

In problems 1–10, evaluate the given sum.

1. $\displaystyle\sum_{k=1}^{5} (k + 4)$

2. $\displaystyle\sum_{k=12}^{15} (5 - 2k)$

3. $\displaystyle\sum_{j=1}^{10} (-1)^j$

4. $\displaystyle\sum_{j=0}^{5} 2^j$

5. $\displaystyle\sum_{n=2}^{3} (3n^2 - 7)$

6. $\displaystyle\sum_{n=2}^{4} \frac{n + 1}{n - 1}$

7. $\displaystyle\sum_{k=3}^{4} \frac{(-1)^k (k + 1)}{2^k}$

8. $\displaystyle\sum_{n=1}^{5} 1$

9. $\displaystyle\sum_{k=1}^{3} \frac{(-1)^{k-1} (1 - k^2)}{k}$

10. $\displaystyle\sum_{n=1}^{4} (n^2 + n)$

In problems 11–16, express the given sums in sigma notation.

11. $1 + 2 + 3 + \ldots + 15$

12. $7 + 8 + 9 + 10$

13. $1 + 3 + 5 + 7$

14. $2 + 4 + 6 + 8$

15. $1^2 + 2^2 + 3^2 + \ldots + 12^2$

16. $3 + 6 + 9 + 12$

By using Eqs. (4) and (5), evaluate the following sums.

17. $\displaystyle\sum_{k=1}^{450} k$

18. $\displaystyle\sum_{k=1}^{10} k^2$

19. $\displaystyle\sum_{j=1}^{6} 4j$

20. $\displaystyle\sum_{i=1}^{40} \frac{i}{2}$

21. $\displaystyle\sum_{i=1}^{6} 3i^2$

22. $\displaystyle\sum_{j=1}^{8} \left(\frac{j}{2}\right)^2$

9-5 THE DEFINITE INTEGRAL

Figure 9-1 shows a right triangle formed by the lines $y = f(x) = 2x$, $y = 0$ (the x-axis), and $x = 1$. If b and h are the length of the base and the height, respectively, then from geometry the area A of the triangle is $A = \frac{1}{2} bh = \frac{1}{2} (1)(2) = 1$ square unit. We shall now determine the area of this region by another method which,

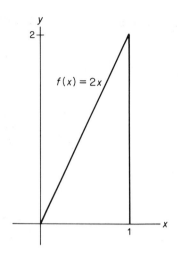

Fig. 9-1

as you will see, applies to more complex regions. This method involves summation of areas of rectangles.

Let us divide the interval $[0, 1]$ on the x-axis into four subintervals of equal length Δx. This is done by the equally spaced points $x_0 = 0$, $x_1 = \frac{1}{4}$, $x_2 = \frac{2}{4}$, $x_3 = \frac{3}{4}$, and $x_4 = \frac{4}{4} = 1$ (see Fig. 9-2). Each subinterval has length $\Delta x = \frac{1}{4}$. These subintervals determine four subregions: R_1, R_2, R_3, and R_4. With each subregion we can associate a *circumscribed* rectangle (Fig. 9-3); that is, a rectangle whose base is the corresponding subinterval and whose height is the *maximum* value of $f(x)$ on that subinterval. Since f is an increasing function,

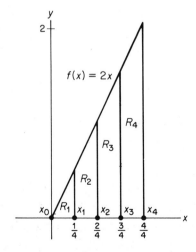

Fig. 9-2

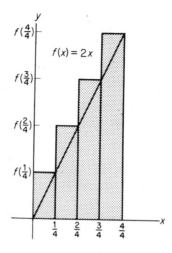

Fig. 9-3

the maximum value of $f(x)$ on each subinterval will occur when x is the right-hand endpoint. Thus the areas of the circumscribed rectangles associated with regions R_1, R_2, R_3, and R_4 are $\frac{1}{4} f(\frac{1}{4})$, $\frac{1}{4} f(\frac{2}{4})$, $\frac{1}{4} f(\frac{3}{4})$, and $\frac{1}{4} f(\frac{4}{4})$, respectively. The area of each rectangle is an approximation to the area of its corresponding subregion. Thus the sum of the areas of these rectangles, denoted by $\bar{S}_4$, (read "S sub 4 upper bar"), is an approximation to the area A of the triangle.

$$\bar{S}_4 = \tfrac{1}{4} f(\tfrac{1}{4}) + \tfrac{1}{4} f(\tfrac{2}{4}) + \tfrac{1}{4} f(\tfrac{3}{4}) + \tfrac{1}{4} f(\tfrac{4}{4})$$

$$= \tfrac{1}{4} [2 (\tfrac{1}{4}) + 2 (\tfrac{2}{4}) + 2 (\tfrac{3}{4}) + 2(1)] = \tfrac{5}{4}.$$

You may verify that we can write $\bar{S}_4$ as $\bar{S}_4 = \sum\limits_{i=1}^{4} f(x_i)\, \Delta x$. The fact that $\bar{S}_4$ is greater than the actual area of the triangle might have been expected, since $\bar{S}_4$ includes areas of shaded regions that are not in the triangle (see Fig. 9-3).

On the other hand, with each subregion we can also associate an *inscribed* rectangle (see Fig. 9-4); that is, a rectangle whose base is the corresponding subinterval and whose height is the *minimum* value of $f(x)$ on that subinterval. Since f is an increasing function, the minimum value of $f(x)$ on each subinterval will occur when x is the left-hand endpoint. Thus the areas of the four inscribed rectangles associated with R_1, R_2, R_3, and R_4 are $\frac{1}{4} f(0)$, $\frac{1}{4} f(\frac{1}{4})$, $\frac{1}{4} f(\frac{2}{4})$, and $\frac{1}{4} f(\frac{3}{4})$ respectively. Their sum, denoted $\underline{S}_4$ (read "S sub 4 lower bar"), is also an approximation to the area A of the triangle.

$$\underline{S}_4 = \tfrac{1}{4} f(0) + \tfrac{1}{4} f(\tfrac{1}{4}) + \tfrac{1}{4} f(\tfrac{2}{4}) + \tfrac{1}{4} f(\tfrac{3}{4})$$

$$= \tfrac{1}{4} [2(0) + 2(\tfrac{1}{4}) + 2(\tfrac{2}{4}) + 2(\tfrac{3}{4})] = \tfrac{3}{4}.$$

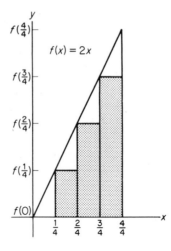

Fig. 9-4

Using sigma notation, we can write $\underline{S}_4$ as $\underline{S}_4 = \sum_{i=1}^{4} f(x_{i-1}) \Delta x$. Clearly $\underline{S}_4$ is less than the area of the triangle because the rectangles do not account for that portion of the triangle which is not shaded (see Fig. 9-4).

Note that $\frac{3}{4} = \underline{S}_4 \le A \le \bar{S}_4 = \frac{5}{4}$. We say that $\underline{S}_4$ is an approximation to A from *below* and $\bar{S}_4$ is an approximation to A from *above*.

If $[0, 1]$ is divided into more subintervals, better approximations to A will occur. For example, let us use six subintervals of equal length $\Delta x = \frac{1}{6}$.

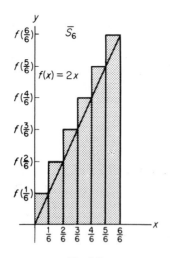

Fig. 9-5

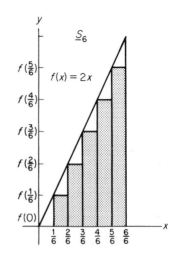

Fig. 9-6

Then $\bar{S}_6$, the total area of six circumscribed rectangles (see Fig. 9-5), and $\underline{S}_6$, the total area of six inscribed rectangles (see Fig. 9-6) are

$$\bar{S}_6 = \tfrac{1}{6}f(\tfrac{1}{6}) + \tfrac{1}{6}f(\tfrac{2}{6}) + \tfrac{1}{6}f(\tfrac{3}{6}) + \tfrac{1}{6}f(\tfrac{4}{6}) + \tfrac{1}{6}f(\tfrac{5}{6}) + \tfrac{1}{6}f(\tfrac{6}{6})$$

$$= \tfrac{1}{6}[2(\tfrac{1}{6}) + 2(\tfrac{2}{6}) + 2(\tfrac{3}{6}) + 2(\tfrac{4}{6}) + 2(\tfrac{5}{6}) + 2(\tfrac{6}{6})] = \tfrac{7}{6}$$

and

$$\underline{S}_6 = \tfrac{1}{6}f(0) + \tfrac{1}{6}f(\tfrac{1}{6}) + \tfrac{1}{6}f(\tfrac{2}{6}) + \tfrac{1}{6}f(\tfrac{3}{6}) + \tfrac{1}{6}f(\tfrac{4}{6}) + \tfrac{1}{6}f(\tfrac{5}{6})$$

$$= \tfrac{1}{6}[2(0) + 2(\tfrac{1}{6}) + 2(\tfrac{2}{6}) + 2(\tfrac{3}{6}) + 2(\tfrac{4}{6}) + 2(\tfrac{5}{6})] = \tfrac{5}{6}.$$

Note that $\underline{S}_6 \leq A \leq \bar{S}_6$ and, with appropriate labelling, both $\bar{S}_6$ and $\underline{S}_6$ will be of the *form* $\Sigma f(x)\Delta x$. Note that using six subintervals gives better approximations to the area than did four subintervals.

More generally, if we divide $[0, 1]$ into n subintervals of equal length Δx, then $\Delta x = 1/n$ and the endpoints of the subintervals are $x = 0, 1/n, 2/n,$ ..., $(n - 1)/n$, and $n/n = 1$. See Fig. 9-7. The total area of n *circumscribed* rectangles is

$$\bar{S}_n = \frac{1}{n}f\left(\frac{1}{n}\right) + \frac{1}{n}f\left(\frac{2}{n}\right) + \dots + \frac{1}{n}f\left(\frac{n}{n}\right) \qquad (1)$$

$$= \frac{1}{n}\left[2\left(\frac{1}{n}\right) + 2\left(\frac{2}{n}\right) + \dots + 2\left(\frac{n}{n}\right)\right]$$

$$= \frac{2}{n^2}[1 + 2 + \dots + n] \qquad \text{(by factoring } \frac{2}{n} \text{ from each term).}$$

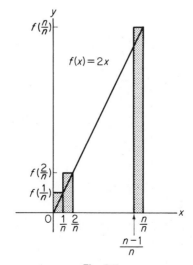

Fig. 9-7

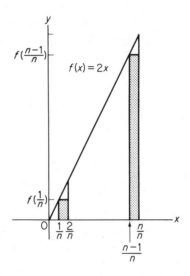

Fig. 9-8

From Sec. 9-4, the sum of the first n positive integers is $\dfrac{n(n+1)}{2}$. Thus

$$\bar{S}_n = \left(\frac{2}{n^2}\right)\frac{n(n+1)}{2} = \frac{n+1}{n}.$$

For n *inscribed* rectangles, the total area determined by the subintervals (see Fig. 9-8) is

$$\underline{S}_n = \frac{1}{n}f(0) + \frac{1}{n}f\left(\frac{1}{n}\right) + \ldots + \frac{1}{n}f\left(\frac{n-1}{n}\right) \qquad (2)$$

$$= \frac{1}{n}\left[2(0) + 2\left(\frac{1}{n}\right) + \ldots + 2\left(\frac{n-1}{n}\right)\right]$$

$$= \frac{2}{n^2}\left[1 + \ldots + (n-1)\right].$$

Summing the first $n-1$ positive integers as we did in Example 14(b), we obtain

$$\underline{S}_n = \left(\frac{2}{n^2}\right)\frac{(n-1)n}{2} = \frac{n-1}{n}.$$

From Equations (1) and (2) we see that both $\bar{S}_n$ and $\underline{S}_n$ are sums of the *form* $\Sigma f(x)\Delta x$.

From the nature of $\bar{S}_n$ and $\underline{S}_n$, it seems reasonable and it is indeed true that

$$\underline{S}_n \le A \le \bar{S}_n.$$

As n becomes larger, $\underline{S}_n$ and $\bar{S}_n$ become better approximations to A from below and above, respectively. In fact, let us take the limit of $\underline{S}_n$ and $\bar{S}_n$ as n approaches ∞ through positive integral values.

$$\lim_{n \to \infty} \underline{S}_n = \lim_{n \to \infty} \frac{n-1}{n} = \lim_{n \to \infty} \left(1 - \frac{1}{n}\right) = 1.$$

$$\lim_{n \to \infty} \bar{S}_n = \lim_{n \to \infty} \frac{n+1}{n} = \lim_{n \to \infty} \left(1 + \frac{1}{n}\right) = 1.$$

Since $\bar{S}_n$ and $\underline{S}_n$ have the same common limit,

$$\lim_{n \to \infty} \bar{S}_n = \lim_{n \to \infty} \underline{S}_n = 1, \tag{3}$$

and since

$$\underline{S}_n \leq A \leq \bar{S}_n,$$

we shall take this limit to be the area of the triangle. Thus $A = 1$ square unit which agrees with our prior finding.

Mathematically, the sums $\bar{S}_n$ and $\underline{S}_n$, as well as their common limit, have a meaning which is independent of area. For the function $f(x) = 2x$ over the interval $[0, 1]$, we define the common limit of $\bar{S}_n$ and $\underline{S}_n$, namely 1, to be the **definite integral** of $f(x) = 2x$ from $x = 0$ to $x = 1$ and we abbreviate this symbolically by writing

$$\int_0^1 2x \, dx = 1. \tag{4}$$

The reason for using the term "definite integral" and the symbolism in Eq. (4) will become apparent in the next section. The numbers 0 and 1 appearing with the integral sign $\int$ in Eq. (4) are called the *limits of integration;* 0 is the *lower limit* and 1 is the *upper limit.*

Two points must be made about the definite integral: first, aside from any geometrical interpretation, it is nothing more than a real number; second, the definite integral is a limit of a sum of the form $\Sigma \, f(x) \, \Delta x$. In fact, one can think of the integral sign as an elongated "S", the first letter of "Summation."

In general, the definite integral of a function $f(x)$ over the interval from $x = a$ to $x = b$, where $a \leq b$, is the common limit of $\bar{S}_n$ and $\underline{S}_n$, if it exists, and is written

$$\int_a^b f(x) \, dx.$$

The symbol x is the *variable of integration* and $f(x)$ is the *integrand.* In terms of a limiting process we have

$$\Sigma \, f(x) \, \Delta x \to \int_a^b f(x) \, dx.$$

As you saw in (3), $\lim\limits_{n\to\infty} S_n$ is equal to $\lim\limits_{n\to\infty} \bar{S}_n$. For an arbitrary function this is not always true. However, for the functions that we shall consider, these limits will be equal and the definite integral will always exist. Hence, to save time we shall just use the right-hand endpoint of each subinterval in computing a sum. We shall denote this sum by S_n.

EXAMPLE 16

a. *Find the area of the region in the first quadrant bounded by* $y = f(x) = 4 - x^2$ *and the lines* $x = 0$ *and* $y = 0$ *(Fig. 9-9).*

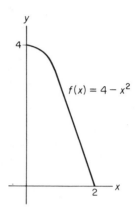

Fig. 9-9

First, the interval over which x varies in this region must be determined. From Fig. 9-9 it is from $x = 0$ to $x = 2$. Second, we divide the interval $[0, 2]$ into n subintervals of equal length Δx. Since the length of $[0, 2]$ is 2, we take $\Delta x = 2/n$. The endpoints of the subintervals are $x = 0,\ 2/n,\ 2(2/n),\ \ldots,\ (n-1)(2/n)$, and $n(2/n) = 2$ (see Fig. 9-10).

Using right-hand endpoints, we get

$$S_n = \frac{2}{n} f\left(\frac{2}{n}\right) + \frac{2}{n} f\left[2\left(\frac{2}{n}\right)\right] + \ldots + \frac{2}{n} f\left[n\left(\frac{2}{n}\right)\right]$$

$$= \frac{2}{n}\left[f\left(\frac{2}{n}\right) + f\left[2\left(\frac{2}{n}\right)\right] + \ldots + f\left[n\left(\frac{2}{n}\right)\right]\right]$$

$$= \frac{2}{n}\left[\left\{4 - \left[\frac{2}{n}\right]^2\right\} + \left\{4 - \left[2\left(\frac{2}{n}\right)\right]^2\right\} + \ldots + \left\{4 - \left[n\left(\frac{2}{n}\right)\right]^2\right\}\right].$$

Since the number 4 occurs n times in the sum, we can simplify S_n.

$$S_n = \frac{2}{n}\left[4n - \left(\frac{2}{n}\right)^2 - 2^2\left(\frac{2}{n}\right)^2 - \ldots - n^2\left(\frac{2}{n}\right)^2\right]$$

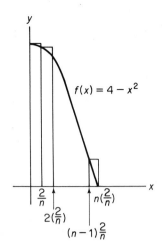

$f(x) = 4 - x^2$

$\frac{2}{n}$ $n(\frac{2}{n})$

$2(\frac{2}{n})$

$(n-1)\frac{2}{n}$

Fig. 9-10

$$= \frac{2}{n}\left[4n - \left(\frac{2}{n}\right)^2 \{1^2 + 2^2 + \ldots + n^2\}\right]$$

From Sec. 9-4, $\displaystyle\sum_{k=1}^{n} k^2 = \frac{n(n+1)(2n+1)}{6}$ and thus

$$S_n = \frac{2}{n}\left[4n - \left(\frac{2}{n}\right)^2 \frac{n(n+1)(2n+1)}{6}\right]$$

$$= 8 - \frac{4(n+1)(2n+1)}{3n^2}$$

$$= 8 - \frac{4}{3}\left(\frac{2n^2 + 3n + 1}{n^2}\right).$$

Next we take the limit of S_n as $n \to \infty$.

$$\lim_{n\to\infty} S_n = \lim_{n\to\infty}\left[8 - \frac{4}{3}\left(\frac{2n^2 + 3n + 1}{n^2}\right)\right]$$

$$= \lim_{n\to\infty}\left[8 - \frac{4}{3}\left(2 + \frac{3}{n} + \frac{1}{n^2}\right)\right]$$

$$= 8 - \frac{8}{3} = \frac{16}{3}.$$

Hence the area of the region is $\frac{16}{3}$ square units.

b. *Evaluate* $\displaystyle\int_0^2 (4 - x^2)\, dx$.

Since $\displaystyle\int_0^2 (4 - x^2)\, dx = \lim_{n \to \infty} S_n$, from part (a) we conclude that

$$\int_0^2 (4 - x^2)\, dx = \frac{16}{3}.$$

EXAMPLE 17

Integrate $f(x) = x - 5$ from $x = 0$ to $x = 3$; that is, evaluate $\displaystyle\int_0^3 (x - 5)\, dx$.

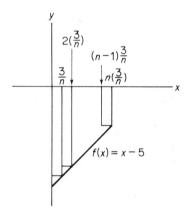

Fig. 9-11

A sketch of $f(x) = x - 5$ over $[0, 3]$ appears in Fig. 9-11. We divide $[0, 3]$ into n subintervals of equal length $\Delta x = 3/n$. The endpoints are $x = 0,\ 3/n,\ 2(3/n),\ \ldots,$ $(n - 1)(3/n)$, and $n(3/n) = 3$. Note that $f(x)$ is negative at each endpoint. We form the sum

$$S_n = \frac{3}{n} f\left(\frac{3}{n}\right) + \frac{3}{n} f\left[2\left(\frac{3}{n}\right)\right] + \ldots + \frac{3}{n} f\left[n\left(\frac{3}{n}\right)\right].$$

Since all terms are negative, they do *not* represent areas of rectangles; in fact, they are the negatives of areas of rectangles. Simplifying, we have

$$S_n = \frac{3}{n}\left[\left\{\frac{3}{n} - 5\right\} + \left\{2\left(\frac{3}{n}\right) - 5\right\} + \ldots + \left\{n\left(\frac{3}{n}\right) - 5\right\}\right]$$

$$= \frac{3}{n}\left[-5n + \frac{3}{n}\{1 + 2 + \ldots + n\}\right]$$

$$= \frac{3}{n}\left[-5n + \left(\frac{3}{n}\right)\frac{n(n + 1)}{2}\right]$$

$$= -15 + \frac{9}{2} \cdot \frac{n+1}{n}$$

$$= -15 + \frac{9}{2}\left(1 + \frac{1}{n}\right).$$

Taking the limit, we obtain

$$\lim_{n \to \infty} S_n = \lim_{n \to \infty}\left[-15 + \frac{9}{2}\left(1 + \frac{1}{n}\right)\right] = -\frac{21}{2}.$$

Thus

$$\int_0^3 (x - 5) \, dx = -\frac{21}{2}.$$

This definite integral is **not** the area of the region bounded by $f(x) = x - 5$, $y = 0$, $x = 0$, and $x = 3$. It represents the negative of that area.

In Example 17 it was shown that the definite integral does not have to represent area. In fact, there the definite integral was negative. However, if f is continuous and $f(x) \geq 0$ on $[a, b]$, then $\int_a^b f(x) \, dx \geq 0$. Furthermore, this definite integral gives the area of the region bounded by $y = f(x)$, $y = 0$, $x = a$ and $x = b$ (see Fig. 9-12).

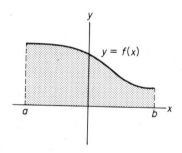

Fig. 9-12

Although the approach which we took to discuss the definite integral is sufficient for our purposes, it is by no means rigorous. **The important thing to remember about the definite integral is that it is the limit of a sum.**

EXERCISE 9-5

In problems 1–4, sketch the region in the first quadrant which is bounded by the given curves. Approximate the area of the region by the indicated sum. Use the right-hand endpoint of each subinterval.

1. $f(x) = x$, $y = 0$, $x = 1$; S_3

2. $f(x) = 3x$, $y = 0$, $x = 1$; S_5

3. $f(x) = x^2$, $y = 0$, $x = 1$; S_3

4. $f(x) = x^2 + 1$, $y = 0$, $x = 0$, $x = 1$; S_2

In problems 5–10, sketch the region in the first quadrant which is bounded by the given curves. Determine the exact area of the region by considering the limit of S_n as $n \to \infty$. Use the right-hand endpoint of each subinterval.

5. Region as described in Problem 1

6. Region as described in Problem 2

7. Region as described in Problem 3

8. Region as described in Problem 4

9. $f(x) = 2x^2$, $y = 0$, $x = 2$

10. $f(x) = 9 - x^2$, $y = 0$, $x = 0$

For each of the following problems, evaluate the given definite integral by taking the limit of S_n. Use the right-hand endpoint of each subinterval. Sketch the graph, over the given interval, of the function to be integrated.

11. $\displaystyle\int_0^4 9\,dx$ **12.** $\displaystyle\int_0^2 3x\,dx$ **13.** $\displaystyle\int_0^3 -4x\,dx$

14. $\displaystyle\int_0^3 (2x - 9)\,dx$ **15.** $\displaystyle\int_0^1 (x^2 + x)\,dx$

16. A company has an asset whose original value is \$3200 and which has no salvage value. The maintenance cost each year is \$100 and increases by \$100 each year. Show that the average annual total cost C over a period of n years is

$$C = \frac{3200}{n} + 50(n + 1).$$

Find the value of n that minimizes C. What is the average annual cost at this value of n?

9-6 THE FUNDAMENTAL THEOREM OF INTEGRAL CALCULUS

Until now the limiting processes of the derivative and definite integral have been considered as distinct concepts. We shall now bring these fundamental ideas together and establish the relationship that exists between them. As a result, definite integrals may be evaluated more efficiently.

In Fig. 9-13 the graph of a function f is given. Note that f is continuous on the interval $[a, b]$ and its graph does not fall below the x-axis. That is,

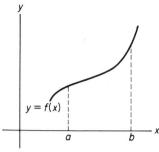

Fig. 9-13

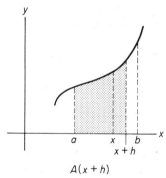

$f(x) \geq 0$. Suppose there is another function $A(x)$, which we shall refer to as an "area" function, that gives the area of the region below the graph and above the x-axis from a to x, where $a \leq x \leq b$. This region is shaded in Fig. 9-14.

From its definition we state two properties of $A(x)$ immediately:

(1) $A(a) = 0$ since there is no area from a to a;
(2) $A(b)$ is the area from a to b.

A(x + h)

Fig. 9-15

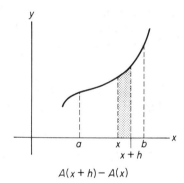

$A(x + h) - A(x)$

Fig. 9-16

If x is increased by h units, then $A(x + h)$ is the area of the shaded region in Fig. 9-15. Hence $A(x + h) - A(x)$ will be the difference of the areas in Figs. 9-15 and 9-14; namely, the area of the shaded region in Fig. 9-16. The area of this region is the same as the area of a rectangle (Fig. 9-17) whose base is h and whose height is some value $\bar{y}$ between $f(x)$ and $f(x + h)$. Thus the area of the rectangle is, on the one hand, $A(x + h) - A(x)$, and on the other hand it is $h\bar{y}$:

$$A(x + h) - A(x) = h\bar{y}$$

or

$$\frac{A(x + h) - A(x)}{h} = \bar{y}.$$

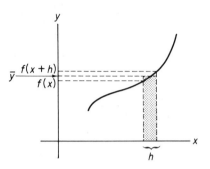

Fig. 9-17

As $h \to 0$, then $\bar{y}$ approaches the number $f(x)$ and so

$$\lim_{h \to 0} \frac{A(x + h) - A(x)}{h} = f(x). \tag{1}$$

But the left side is merely the derivative of $A(x)$. Thus Eq. (1) becomes

$$A'(x) = f(x).$$

We conclude that the area function $A(x)$ has the additional property of having its derivative $A'(x)$ as $f(x)$. That is, $A(x)$ is an antiderivative of $f(x)$. But if $F(x)$ is *any* antiderivative of $f(x)$, then

$$F'(x) = f(x).$$

Since both $A(x)$ and $F(x)$ are antiderivatives of the same function, we conclude that they must differ by a constant C:

$$A(x) = F(x) + C. \tag{2}$$

Since $A(a) = 0$, evaluating both sides of Eq. (2) when $x = a$ gives

$$0 = F(a) + C$$

or

$$C = -F(a).$$

Thus Eq. (2) becomes

$$A(x) = F(x) - F(a). \tag{3}$$

If $x = b$, then from Eq. (3)

$$A(b) = F(b) - F(a). \tag{4}$$

But recall that $A(b)$ is the area from a to b (Fig. 9-18). Since the area of this region can also be obtained by the limit of a sum, we can also refer to it by $\displaystyle\int_a^b f(x)\, dx$. Hence,

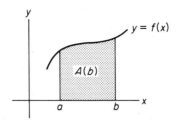

Fig. 9-18

$$A(b) = \int_a^b f(x) \, dx. \qquad (5)$$

From Eqs. (4) and (5) we get

$$\int_a^b f(x) \, dx = F(b) - F(a).$$

Thus a relationship between a definite integral and antidifferentiation has become clear. To find $\int_a^b f(x) \, dx$ it is sufficient to find an antiderivative of $f(x)$, say $F(x)$, and subtract its value at the lower limit a from its value at the upper limit b. Our result can be stated more generally as follows:

Fundamental Theorem of Integral Calculus.
     If f is continuous† on the interval $[a, b]$ and $F(x)$ is any antiderivative of $f(x)$ there, then

$$\int_a^b f(x) \, dx = F(b) - F(a).$$

It is crucial that you understand the distinction between a definite integral and an indefinite integral. The **definite integral** $\int_a^b f(x) \, dx$ **is a number** defined to be the limit of a sum. The Fundamental Theorem says that the **indefinite integral** $\int f(x) \, dx$ (an antiderivative of f), which **is a function** of x and is related to the differentiation process, can be used to determine this limit.

Suppose we apply the Fundamental Theorem to evaluate $\int_0^2 (4 - x^2) \, dx$. Here $f(x) = 4 - x^2$, $a = 0$, $b = 2$, and $F(x) = 4x - (x^3/3)$ is an antiderivative of $4 - x^2$. Thus

---

† If f is continuous on $[a, b]$, it can be shown that $\int_a^b f(x) \, dx$ does indeed exist.

$$\int_0^2 (4 - x^2) \, dx = F(2) - F(0) = \left(8 - \frac{8}{3}\right) - (0) = \frac{16}{3}.$$

This confirms the result in Example 16(b) of Sec. 9-5. If we had chosen $F(x)$ to be $4x - (x^3/3) + C$, then $F(2) - F(0) = [(8 - \frac{8}{3}) + C] - [0 + C] = \frac{16}{3}$ as before. Since the choice of the value of C is immaterial, for convenience we shall always choose it to be 0, as originally done. Usually, $F(b) - F(a)$ is abbreviated by writing

$$F(x) \Big|_a^b.$$

Hence we have

$$\int_0^2 (4 - x^2) \, dx = \left(4x - \frac{x^3}{3}\right)\Big|_0^2 = \left(8 - \frac{8}{3}\right) - 0 = \frac{16}{3}.$$

By convention,

$$\int_b^a f(x) \, dx = -\int_a^b f(x) \, dx.$$

That is, interchanging the limits of integration in a definite integral changes the integral's sign. For example,

$$\int_2^0 (4 - x^2) \, dx = -\int_0^2 (4 - x^2) \, dx.$$

Two properties of the definite integral deserve mention:

(1) $\int_a^b f(x) \, dx = \int_a^b f(t) \, dt$. The variable of integration x used in $\int_a^b f(x) \, dx$ is a "dummy variable" in the sense that any other variable would produce the same result, that is, the same number. You may verify, for example, that $\int_0^2 x^2 \, dx = \int_0^2 t^2 \, dt$.

(2) If f is continuous on an interval I and a, b, and c are in I, then

$$\int_a^c f(x) \, dx = \int_a^b f(x) \, dx + \int_b^c f(x) \, dx.$$

This means that you may subdivide the interval over which a definite integral is to be evaluated. Thus,

$$\int_0^2 (4 - x^2) \, dx = \int_0^{.5} (4 - x^2) \, dx + \int_{.5}^2 (4 - x^2) \, dx.$$

We shall look at some examples of definite integration now and compute some areas in the next section.

EXAMPLE 18

Evaluate each of the following definite integrals.

a. $\displaystyle\int_{-1}^{3} (3x^2 - x + 6)\, dx.$

$$\int_{-1}^{3} (3x^2 - x + 6)\, dx = \left(x^3 - \frac{x^2}{2} + 6x \right)\bigg|_{-1}^{3}$$

$$= \left[3^3 - \frac{3^2}{2} + 6(3) \right] - \left[(-1)^3 - \frac{(-1)^2}{2} + 6(-1) \right]$$

$$= \left(\frac{81}{2} \right) - \left(-\frac{15}{2} \right) = 48.$$

b. $\displaystyle\int_{0}^{1} \frac{x^3}{\sqrt{1 + x^4}}\, dx.$

$$\int_{0}^{1} \frac{x^3}{\sqrt{1 + x^4}}\, dx = \int_{0}^{1} x^3 (1 + x^4)^{-1/2}\, dx$$

$$= \frac{1}{4} \int_{0}^{1} (1 + x^4)^{-1/2} (4x^3\, dx) = \left(\frac{1}{4} \right) \frac{(1 + x^4)^{1/2}}{\frac{1}{2}}\bigg|_{0}^{1}$$

$$= \frac{1}{2} (1 + x^4)^{1/2}\bigg|_{0}^{1}$$

$$= \frac{1}{2} (\sqrt{2} - 1).$$

c. $\displaystyle\int_{1}^{2} [2x^{1/3} + x(x^2 + 1)^6]\, dx.$

$$\int_{1}^{2} [2x^{1/3} + x(x^2 + 1)^6]\, dx = 2 \int_{1}^{2} x^{1/3}\, dx + \frac{1}{2} \int_{1}^{2} (x^2 + 1)^6 (2x\, dx)$$

$$= (2) \frac{x^{4/3}}{\frac{4}{3}}\bigg|_{1}^{2} + \left(\frac{1}{2} \right) \frac{(x^2 + 1)^7}{7}\bigg|_{1}^{2}$$

$$= \frac{3}{2} (2^{4/3} - 1) + \frac{1}{14} (5^7 - 2^7)$$

$$= 3\sqrt[3]{2} - \frac{3}{2} + \frac{5^7}{14} - \frac{2^7}{14}$$

$$= 3\sqrt[3]{2} + \frac{5^7 - 149}{14}.$$

d. $\displaystyle\int_0^1 e^{3t}\,dt$.

$$\int_0^1 e^{3t}\,dt = \tfrac{1}{3}\int_0^1 e^{3t}(3\,dt)$$

$$= (\tfrac{1}{3})\,e^{3t}\,\Big|_0^1 = \tfrac{1}{3}(e^3 - e^0) = \tfrac{1}{3}(e^3 - 1).$$

EXAMPLE 19

Evaluate $\displaystyle\int_{-2}^1 x^3\,dx$.

$$\int_{-2}^1 x^3\,dx = \frac{x^4}{4}\,\Big|_{-2}^1 = \frac{1^4}{4} - \frac{(-2)^4}{4} = \frac{1}{4} - \frac{16}{4} = -\frac{15}{4}.$$

The reason the result is negative is clear from the graph of $y = x^3$ on the interval $[-2, 1]$ (see Fig. 9-19). For $-2 \le x < 0$, $f(x)$ is negative. Since a definite integral is a limit of a sum of the form

$$\Sigma\, f(x)\,\Delta x,$$

then $\displaystyle\int_{-2}^0 x^3\,dx$ is not only a negative number, but it is also the negative of the area

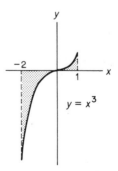

Fig. 9-19

of the shaded region in the third quadrant. On the other hand, $\int_0^1 x^3\,dx$ is the area of the shaded region in the first quadrant. However, the definite integral over the entire interval $[-2, 1]$ is the *algebraic* sum of these numbers since

$$\int_{-2}^1 x^3\,dx = \int_{-2}^0 x^3\,dx + \int_0^1 x^3\,dx.$$

Thus $\int_{-2}^1 x^3\,dx$ does not represent the area between the curve and the x-axis. However, the area can be given in the form

$$\left| \int_{-2}^0 x^3\,dx \right| + \int_0^1 x^3\,dx.$$

PITFALL.   *Remember that $\int_a^b f(x)\,dx$ is a limit of a sum. In certain instances this limit represents area. In others it does not. Do not attach units of area to every definite integral.*

EXERCISE 9-6

In problems 1–38, evaluate the definite integral.

1. $\displaystyle\int_0^3 4\,dx$

2. $\displaystyle\int_1^3 (2 + e)\,dx$

3. $\displaystyle\int_1^2 3x\,dx$

4. $\displaystyle\int_0^2 -5x\,dx$

5. $\displaystyle\int_{-2}^1 (4x - 6)\,dx$

6. $\displaystyle\int_{-1}^1 (5y + 2)\,dy$

7. $\displaystyle\int_0^2 (t^2 + t)\,dt$

8. $\displaystyle\int_1^3 (2w^2 + 1)\,dw$

9. $\displaystyle\int_2^3 (y^2 - 2y + 1)\,dy$

10. $\displaystyle\int_3^2 (2t - t^2)\,dt$

11. $\displaystyle\int_{-2}^{-1} (3w^2 - w - 1)\,dw$

12. $\displaystyle\int_8^9 dt$

13. $\displaystyle\int_{-1}^1 \sqrt[3]{x^5}\,dx$

14. $\displaystyle\int_{1/2}^{3/2} (x^2 + x + 1)\,dx$

15. $\displaystyle\int_2^3 \frac{1}{x^2}\,dx$

16. $\displaystyle\int_4^9 \left(\frac{1}{\sqrt{x}} - 2 \right)\,dx$

17. $\displaystyle\int_{-1}^{1} (z + 1)^5 \, dz$

18. $\displaystyle\int_{1}^{8} (x^{1/3} - x^{-1/3}) \, dx$

19. $\displaystyle\int_{0}^{1} 2x^2(x^3 - 1)^3 \, dx$

20. $\displaystyle\int_{1}^{3} (x + 3)^3 \, dx$

21. $\displaystyle\int_{1}^{8} \frac{4}{y} \, dy$

22. $\displaystyle\int_{0}^{e-1} \frac{1}{x + 1} \, dx$

23. $\displaystyle\int_{0}^{2} x^2 e^{x^3} \, dx$

24. $\displaystyle\int_{0}^{1} (3x^2 + 4x)(x^3 + 2x^2)^4 \, dx$

25. $\displaystyle\int_{4}^{5} \frac{2}{(x - 3)^3} \, dx$

26. $\displaystyle\int_{0}^{6} \sqrt{2x + 4} \, dx$

27. $\displaystyle\int_{1/3}^{2} \sqrt{10 - 3p} \, dp$

28. $\displaystyle\int_{-1}^{1} x\sqrt{x^2 + 3} \, dx$

29. $\displaystyle\int_{0}^{1} x^2 \sqrt[3]{7x^3 + 1} \, dx$

30. $\displaystyle\int_{0}^{\sqrt{7}} \left[2x - \frac{x}{(x^2 + 1)^{5/3}} \right] dx$

31. $\displaystyle\int_{0}^{1} \frac{2x^3 + x}{x^2 + x^4 + 1} \, dx$

32. $\displaystyle\int_{a}^{b} (m + ny) \, dy$

33. $\displaystyle\int_{0}^{1} (e^x - e^{-2x}) \, dx$

34. $\displaystyle\int_{-2}^{1} |x| \, dx$

35. $\displaystyle\int_{1}^{e} (x^{-1} + x^{-2} - x^{-3}) \, dx$

36. $\displaystyle\int_{1}^{2} \left(6\sqrt{x} - \frac{1}{\sqrt{2x}} \right) dx$

37. $\displaystyle\int_{1}^{3} (x + 1)e^{x^2 + 2x} \, dx$

38. $\displaystyle\int_{3}^{4} \frac{e^{\ln x}}{x} \, dx$

39. In statistics, the mean μ (= mu) of the continuous probability density function $f(x)$ defined on the interval (a, b) is

$$\mu = \int_{a}^{b} [x \cdot f(x)] \, dx,$$

and the variance σ^2 (σ = sigma) is

$$\sigma^2 = \int_{a}^{b} (x - \mu)^2 f(x) \, dx.$$

Compute μ and then σ^2 if $a = 0$, $b = 1$, and $f(x) = 1$.

40. In statistics, the cumulative probability function $F(x)$ is obtained from the continuous probability density function $f(x)$ by the formula

$$F(x) = \int_0^x f(t)\, dt$$

If $f(x) = 6x - 6x^2$ on the interval $(0, 1)$, find $F(x)$.

41. The economist Pareto[†] has stated an empirical law of distribution of higher incomes, namely $N = Ax^{-B}$, where N is the number of persons receiving x or more dollars, A and B are constants, and B is approximately 1.5. The total number of persons having incomes between a and b is

$$\int_a^b Ax^{-B}\, dx.$$

Evaluate this integral.

42. If c_0 is the yearly consumption of a mineral at time $t = 0$, then the total amount of the mineral used in the interval $[0, t_1]$ is

$$\int_0^{t_1} c_0 e^{kt}\, dt$$

where k is the rate of increase of consumption. For the rare-earth mineral *junko* it has been determined that $c_0 = 3000$ units and $k = .05$. Evaluate the above integral for these data.

9-7 AREA

In Sec. 9-5 we found the area of a region by evaluating the limit of a sum of the form $\Sigma f(x)\, dx$. Since this limit also is a definite integral, we can use the Fundamental Theorem to evaluate the limit.

    When using the definite integral to determine the area of a region, you should make a rough sketch of this region. Since you are evaluating the limit of the sum of areas of rectangles, a sample rectangle should be included in the sketch in order to gain a clear understanding of the integration process. Such a rectangle (see Fig. 9-20) is called a **vertical element of area** (or a **vertical strip**). In the diagram the width of the vertical element is Δx. The length is the ordinate y_1 of the upper curve minus the ordinate y_2 of the lower curve, henceforth referred to as $y_{upper} - y_{lower}$. In our case, $y_1 = f(x)$ and $y_2 = 0$. Hence, the rectangle has area $(y_1 - y_2)\Delta x = f(x)\Delta x$, and we want to add the areas of all such elements between $x = a$ and $x = b$ by means of definite integration.

$$\Sigma f(x)\, \Delta x \to \int_a^b f(x)\, dx.$$

[†] G. Tintner, *Methodology of Mathematical Economics and Econometrics*, University of Chicago Press, Chicago, 1967, p. 16.

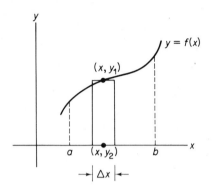

Fig. 9-20

For example, let us find the area of the region bounded by the curve $y = x^2 - 1$, the x-axis, and the line $x = 2$ (see Fig. 9-21). The width of the sample element is Δx and its length is

$$y_{\text{upper}} - y_{\text{lower}} = y_1 - y_2.$$

Thus the area of the element is $(y_1 - y_2)\,\Delta x$. All such areas of elements between $x = 1$ and $x = 2$ are to be summed. Hence the limits of integration are $x = 1$ and $x = 2$.

$$\Sigma\,(y_1 - y_2)\,\Delta x \rightarrow \int_1^2 (y_1 - y_2)\,dx.$$

To evaluate this integral we must express the integrand in terms of the variable of integration x. Since $y_1 = x^2 - 1$ and $y_2 = 0$,

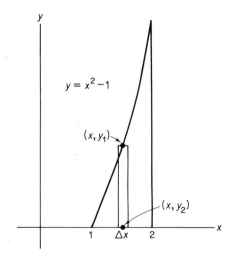

Fig. 9-21

$$\text{area} = \int_1^2 (x^2 - 1)\, dx = \left(\frac{x^3}{3} - x\right)\Bigg|_1^2$$

$$= \left(\frac{8}{3} - 2\right) - \left(\frac{1}{3} - 1\right)$$

$$= \frac{4}{3} \text{ sq units.}$$

EXAMPLE 20

Find the area of the region bounded by the curve $y = 6 - x - x^2$ and the x-axis (Fig. 9-22).

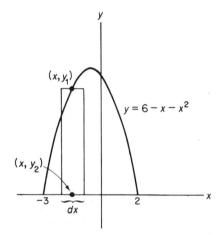

Fig. 9-22

Since $y = -(x^2 + x - 6) = -(x - 2)(x + 3)$, the x-intercepts are $(2, 0)$ and $(-3, 0)$. For the vertical element shown, the width is $dx(= \Delta x)$ and the length is

$$y_{\text{upper}} - y_{\text{lower}} = y_1 - y_2 = (6 - x - x^2) - 0.$$

Hence the area of the element is $(6 - x - x^2)\, dx$. Summing these from $x = -3$ to $x = 2$ gives

$$\text{area} = \int_{-3}^2 (6 - x - x^2)\, dx = \left(6x - \frac{x^2}{2.} - \frac{x^3}{3}\right)\Bigg|_{-3}^2$$

$$= \left(12 - \frac{4}{2} - \frac{8}{3}\right) - \left(-18 - \frac{9}{2} + \frac{27}{3}\right)$$

$$= \frac{125}{6} \text{ sq units.}$$

EXAMPLE 21

Find the area between $y = e^x$ and the x-axis from $x = 1$ to $x = 2$ (see Fig. 9-23).

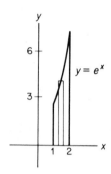

Fig. 9-23

Since the upper part of the element lies on $y = e^x$ and the lower part on $y = 0$,

$$y_{\text{upper}} - y_{\text{lower}} = e^x - 0 = e^x.$$

Hence

$$\text{area} = \int_1^2 e^x \, dx = e^x \Big|_1^2 = e^2 - e$$

$$= e(e - 1) \text{ sq units.}$$

EXAMPLE 22

Find the area of the region bounded by $y = x^2 + 2x + 2$, the x-axis, and the lines $x = -2$ and $x = 1$ (see Fig. 9-24).

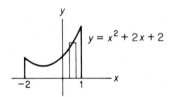

Fig. 9-24

$$\text{area} = \int_{-2}^1 (y_{\text{upper}} - y_{\text{lower}}) \, dx = \int_{-2}^1 [(x^2 + 2x + 2) - (0)] \, dx$$

$$= \left(\frac{x^3}{3} + x^2 + 2x \right) \Big|_{-2}^1 = \left(\frac{1}{3} + 1 + 2 \right) - \left(-\frac{8}{3} + 4 - 4 \right)$$

$$= 6 \text{ sq units.}$$

EXAMPLE 23

Find the area of the region bounded by the curves $y = x^2 - x - 2$ *and* $y = 0$ *(the x-axis)*
from $x = -2$ *to* $x = 2$ *(Fig. 9-25).*

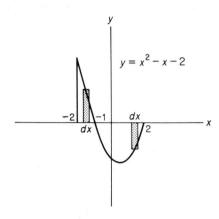

Fig. 9-25

PITFALL.   *It would be wrong to write hastily that the area is* $\displaystyle\int_{-2}^{2} (x^2 - x - 2)\, dx$
since the upper curve is not the same throughout the interval. This points out the importance
of sketching the region.

On $[-2, -1]$, the area of the element is

$$(y_{\text{upper}} - y_{\text{lower}})\, dx = [(x^2 - x - 2) - 0]\, dx.$$

On $[-1, 2]$ it is

$$(y_{\text{upper}} - y_{\text{lower}})\, dx = [0 - (x^2 - x - 2)]\, dx = -(x^2 - x - 2)\, dx.$$

Thus

$$\text{area} = \int_{-2}^{-1} (x^2 - x - 2)\, dx + \int_{-1}^{2} -(x^2 - x - 2)\, dx$$

$$= \left(\frac{x^3}{3} - \frac{x^2}{2} - 2x\right)\Bigg|_{-2}^{-1} - \left(\frac{x^3}{3} - \frac{x^2}{2} - 2x\right)\Bigg|_{-1}^{2}$$

$$= \left[\left(-\frac{1}{3} - \frac{1}{2} + 2\right) - \left(-\frac{8}{3} - \frac{4}{2} + 4\right)\right] -$$

$$\left[\left(\frac{8}{3} - \frac{4}{2} - 4\right) - \left(-\frac{1}{3} - \frac{1}{2} + 2\right)\right] = \frac{19}{3} \text{ sq units.}$$

EXAMPLE 24

It can be shown that the total revenue (similarly, total variable cost) for an output of x units is numerically equal to the area of the region between the marginal revenue (similarly, marginal cost) curve and the x-axis between 0 and x. If the marginal revenue is given by $dr/dx = 15 - (x/15)$, find the revenue obtained from an output of 30 units (Fig. 9-26).

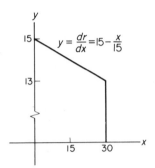

Fig. 9-26

$$\text{total revenue} = \int_0^{30} \frac{dr}{dx}\,dx = \int_0^{30} \left(15 - \frac{x}{15}\right)dx$$

$$= \left(15x - \frac{x^2}{30}\right)\Bigg|_0^{30} = 420.$$

EXERCISE 9-7

In problems 1–34, find the area of the region bounded by the given curves, the x-axis, and the given lines. In each case, sketch the region.

1. $y = 4x$, $x = 2$

2. $y = 3x + 1$, $x = 0$, $x = 4$

3. $y = 3x + 2$, $x = 2$, $x = 3$

4. $y = x + 5$, $x = 2$, $x = 4$

5. $y = x - 1$, $x = 5$

6. $y = 2x^2$, $x = 1$, $x = 2$

7. $y = x^2$, $x = 2$, $x = 3$

8. $y = 2x^2 - x$, $x = -2$, $x = -1$

9. $y = x^2 + 2$, $x = -1$, $x = 2$

10. $y = 2x + x^3$, $x = 1$

11. $y = x^2 - 2x$, $x = -3$, $x = -1$

12. $y = 3x^2 - 4x$, $x = -2$, $x = -1$

13. $y = 9 - x^2$

14. $y = \dfrac{4}{x}$, $x = 1$, $x = 2$

15. $y = 1 - x - x^3$, $x = -2$, $x = 0$

16. $y = e^x$, $x = 1$, $x = 3$

17. $y = 3$, $x = -1$, $x = 1$

18. $y = \dfrac{1}{x^2}$, $x = 2$, $x = 3$

19. $y = \dfrac{1}{x}$, $x = 1$, $x = e$ 20. $y = \dfrac{1}{x}$, $x = 1$, $x = e^2$

21. $y = \sqrt{x + 9}$, $x = -9$, $x = 0$ 22. $y = x^2 - 2x$, $x = 1$, $x = 3$

23. $y = \sqrt{2x - 1}$, $x = 1$, $x = 5$ 24. $y = x^3 + 3x^2$, $x = -2$, $x = 2$

25. $y = \sqrt[3]{x}$, $x = 2$ 26. $y = x^2 - 4$, $x = -2$, $x = 2$

27. $y = e^x$, $x = 0$, $x = 2$ 28. $y = |x|$, $x = -2$, $x = 2$

29. $y = x + \dfrac{2}{x}$, $x = 1$, $x = 2$ 30. $y = 6 - x - x^2$

31. $y = x^3$, $x = -2$, $x = 4$ 32. $y = \sqrt{x - 2}$, $x = 2$, $x = 6$

33. $y = 2x - x^2$, $x = 1$, $x = 3$ 34. $y = x^2 - x + 1$, $x = 0$, $x = 1$

35. Using the definite integral, find the revenue obtained from an output of 10 units given each of the following marginal revenue functions.

     a. $dr/dx = .7$

     b. $dr/dx = 275 - x - .3x^2$

36. Using the definite integral, find the total variable cost of producing 10 units given each of the following marginal cost functions.

     a. $dc/dx = 1.35$

     b. $dc/dx = 2x + 50$

     c. $dc/dx = .09x^2 - 1.2x + 4.5$

37. Under conditions of a continuous uniform distribution, a topic in statistics, the percentage (expressed as a decimal) of persons with incomes between a and t, where $a \le t \le b$, is the area of the region between the curve $y = 1/(b - a)$ and the x-axis from $x = a$ to $x = t$. Sketch the graph of the curve and determine the area of the given region.

38. If

$$f(x) = \begin{cases} 3x^2, & \text{for } 0 \le x \le 2 \\ 16 - 2x, & \text{for } x \ge 2, \end{cases}$$

find the area of the region bounded by the graph of $y = f(x)$, the x-axis, and the line $x = 3$. Sketch the region.

9-8 AREA BETWEEN CURVES

In this section we consider the area of a region enclosed by several curves. As before, our procedure will be to draw a sample element of area and use the definite integral to "add together" the areas of all such elements.

EXAMPLE 25

Find the area of the region bounded by the curves $y = \sqrt{x}$ *and* $y = x$.

A sketch of the region appears in Fig. 9-27. To determine where the curves intersect, we solve the system formed by the equations $y = \sqrt{x}$ and $y = x$. Eliminating y in these equations, we obtain

$$\sqrt{x} = x$$

$$x = x^2$$

$$0 = x^2 - x = x(x - 1)$$

$$x = 0 \quad \text{or} \quad x = 1.$$

If $x = 0$, then $y = 0$; if $x = 1$, then $y = 1$. Thus the curves intersect at $(0, 0)$ and $(1, 1)$. The width of the indicated element of area is dx. If we distinguish between the curves by writing $y_1 = x$ and $y_2 = \sqrt{x}$, then the length of the element is

$$y_{\text{upper}} - y_{\text{lower}} = y_2 - y_1 = \sqrt{x} - x.$$

That is, the upper end of the element lies on $y_2 = \sqrt{x}$ and the lower end lies on $y_1 = x$, the difference between the two being the length. Thus the area of the element is $(\sqrt{x} - x)\, dx$. Summing all such areas from $x = 0$ to $x = 1$ by means of the definite integral, we get the area of the entire region.

$$\sum (\sqrt{x} - x)\, dx \to \int_0^1 (\sqrt{x} - x)\, dx.$$

$$\text{area} = \int_0^1 (x^{1/2} - x)\, dx = \left(\frac{x^{3/2}}{\frac{3}{2}} - \frac{x^2}{2} \right) \Big|_0^1$$

$$= (\tfrac{2}{3} - \tfrac{1}{2}) - (0 - 0) = \tfrac{1}{6} \text{ sq unit.}$$

It should be apparent that the points of intersection are important in determining the limits of integration.

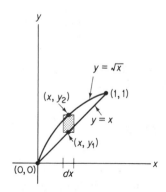

Fig. 9-27

Sometimes area can more easily be determined by integrating with respect to y, rather than x. In the following example this will be shown after area is determined in the usual way.

EXAMPLE 26

Find the area of the region bounded by the curve $y^2 = 4x$ and the lines $y = 3$ and $x = 0$ (the y-axis) (see Fig. 9-28).

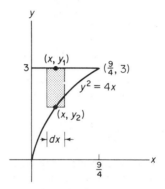

Fig. 9-28

When the curves $y = 3$ and $y^2 = 4x$ intersect, then $9 = 4x$ and so $x = \frac{9}{4}$. Thus the point of intersection is $(\frac{9}{4}, 3)$. Since the width of the vertical strip is dx, we shall integrate with respect to the variable x. Thus y_{upper} and y_{lower} must be expressed as functions of x. For the curve $y^2 = 4x$, we have $y = \pm 2\sqrt{x}$. But for the portion of this curve which bounds the region we must have $y \geq 0$, so we use $y = 2\sqrt{x}$. Thus the length of the strip is $y_{upper} - y_{lower} = 3 - 2\sqrt{x}$. Hence the strip has an area of $(3 - 2\sqrt{x})\,dx$ and we wish to sum up all such areas from $x = 0$ to $x = \dfrac{9}{4}$.

$$\text{area} = \int_0^{9/4} (3 - 2\sqrt{x})\,dx = \left(3x - \frac{4x^{3/2}}{3}\right)\Bigg|_0^{9/4}$$

$$= \left[3\left(\frac{9}{4}\right) - \frac{4}{3}\left(\frac{9}{4}\right)^{3/2}\right] - [(0 - 0)]$$

$$= \frac{27}{4} - \frac{4}{3}\left[\left(\frac{9}{4}\right)^{1/2}\right]^3 = \frac{27}{4} - \frac{4}{3}\left(\frac{3}{2}\right)^3 = \frac{9}{4}\ \text{sq units.}$$

Let us now approach this problem from the point of view of a **horizontal element of area** (or **horizontal strip**) as shown in Fig. 9-29. Since the width of the strip is dy, we must express the strip's length in terms of functions of y. The rightmost end of the element lies on $y^2 = 4x$ (or equivalently, $x = y^2/4$). The leftmost end lies on $x = 0$. Letting $x_1 = y^2/4$ and $x_2 = 0$, we find that the length of the element is $x_1 - x_2$, *the*

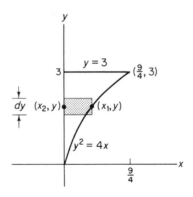

Fig. 9-29

rightmost abscissa minus the leftmost abscissa. The area of the element is $(x_1 - x_2)\, dy$.
We replace x_1 by $y^2/4$ and x_2 by 0 and sum all such areas from $y = 0$ to $y = 3$:

$$\text{area} = \int_0^3 \left(\frac{y^2}{4} - 0 \right) dy = \left. \frac{y^3}{12} \right|_0^3 = \frac{9}{4}\ \text{sq units}.$$

Note that for this region, horizontal strips make the definite integral easier to evaluate
(and set up) than vertical strips. In any case, remember that **the limits of integration
are those limits for the variable of integration.**

EXAMPLE 27

*Find the area of the region bounded by the curves $y = 4x - x^2 + 8$ and $y = x^2 - 2x$
(see Fig. 9-30).*

The curves intersect when

$$4x - x^2 + 8 = x^2 - 2x$$

$$-2x^2 + 6x + 8 = 0$$

$$x^2 - 3x - 4 = 0$$

$$(x + 1)(x - 4) = 0$$

$$x = -1 \quad \text{or} \quad x = 4.$$

When $x = -1$, then $y = 3$; when $x = 4$, then $y = 8$. Thus the curves intersect at $(-1, 3)$
and $(4, 8)$. We shall use vertical strips since they appear to present no difficulty. The
area of the element is

$$(y_{\text{upper}} - y_{\text{lower}})\, dx = [(4x - x^2 + 8) - (x^2 - 2x)]\, dx$$

$$= (-2x^2 + 6x + 8)\, dx.$$

Summing all such elements from $x = -1$ to $x = 4$, we have

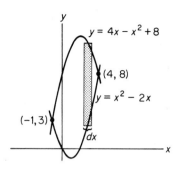

Fig. 9-30

$$\text{area} = \int_{-1}^{4} (-2x^2 + 6x + 8)\,dx = 41\tfrac{2}{3} \text{ sq units.}$$

EXAMPLE 28

Find the area of the region bounded by $y^2 = x$ and $x - y = 2$ (see Fig. 9-31).

The curves intersect when $y^2 = y + 2$. Thus $y^2 - y - 2 = 0$ from which $y = -1$ or $y = 2$; the points of intersection are $(1, -1)$ and $(4, 2)$. Solving $y^2 = x$ for y gives $y = \pm\sqrt{x}$. As seen in Fig. 9-31(a), to the *left* of $x = 1$ the upper end of the element lies on $y = \sqrt{x}$ and the lower end lies on $y = -\sqrt{x}$. To the *right* of $x = 1$, the upper curve is $y = \sqrt{x}$ and the lower curve is $x - y = 2$ (or $y = x - 2$). Thus with vertical strips *two* integrals are needed to evaluate the area.

$$\text{area} = \int_{0}^{1} [\sqrt{x} - (-\sqrt{x})]\,dx + \int_{1}^{4} [\sqrt{x} - (x - 2)]\,dx.$$

Let us consider horizontal strips to see if we can simplify our work. In Fig. 9-31(b), the width of the strip is dy. The rightmost curve is *always* $x - y = 2$ (or $x = y + 2$) and the leftmost curve is *always* $y^2 = x$ (or $x = y^2$). Thus the area of the horizontal strip is $[(y + 2) - y^2]\,dy$ and the total area is

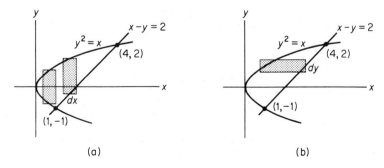

(a)   (b)

Fig. 9-31

$$\text{area} = \int_{-1}^{2} (y + 2 - y^2) \, dy = \frac{9}{2} \text{ sq units.}$$

Clearly the use of horizontal strips is the more desirable approach for the problem.

EXERCISE 9-8

In each of the problems 1–22, find the area of the region bounded by the graphs of the given equations.

1. $y = x^2$, $y = 2x$

2. $y = x$, $y = -x + 3$, $y = 0$

3. $y = x^2$, $x = 0$, $y = 4$ $(x \geq 0)$

4. $y = x^2$, $y = x$

5. $y = x^2 + 3$, $y = 9$

6. $y^2 = x$, $x = 2$

7. $x = 8 + 2y$, $x = 0$, $y = -1$, $y = 3$

8. $y = x - 4$, $y^2 = 2x$

9. $y = 4 - x^2$, $y = -3x$

10. $x = y^2 + 2$, $x = 6$

11. $y^2 = x$, $3x - 2y = 1$

12. $y = x^2$, $y = x + 2$

13. $2y = 4x - x^2$, $2y = x - 4$

14. $y = \sqrt{x}$, $y = x^2$

15. $y^2 = x$, $y = x - 2$

16. $y = 2 - x^2$, $y = x$

17. $y = 8 - x^2$, $y = x^2$, $x = -1$, $x = 1$

18. $y^2 = 4 - x$, $y = x + 2$

19. $y = x^2$, $y = 2$, $y = 5$

20. $y = x^3 - x$, x-axis

21. $y = x^3$, $y = x$

22. $y = x^3$, $y = \sqrt{x}$

23. A *Lorentz curve* is used in studying income distributions. If x is the cumulative percentage of income recipients, ranked from poorest to richest, and y is the cumulative percentage of income, then equality of income distribution is given by the line $y = x$ in Fig. 9-32 where x and y are expressed as decimals. For example, 10 percent of the people receive 10 percent of total income, 20 percent of the people receive 20 percent of the income, etc. Suppose the actual distribution is given by the Lorentz curve defined by $y = \frac{20}{21} x^2 + \frac{1}{21} x$. Note, for example, that 30 percent of the people receive only 10 percent of total income. The degree of deviation from equality is measured by the *coefficient of inequality*† for a Lorentz curve. This coefficient is defined to be the area between the curve and the diagonal, divided by the area under the diagonal:

$$\frac{\text{area between curve and diagonal}}{\text{area under diagonal}}.$$

For example, when all incomes are equal, the coeffient of inequality is zero. Find the coefficient of inequality for the Lorentz curve defined above.

----

†G. Stigler, *The Theory of Price*, 3rd ed., The Macmillan Co., New York, 1966, p. 293–294.

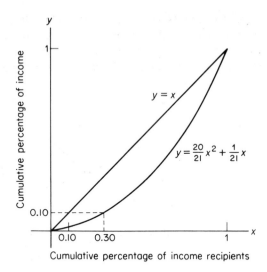

Fig. 9-32

24. Find the coefficient of inequality as in the above problem for the Lorentz curve defined by $y = \frac{11}{12}x^2 + \frac{1}{12}x$.

9-9 CONSUMERS' AND PRODUCERS' SURPLUS

Determining the area of a region in the plane has applications in economics. Figure 9-33 shows the supply and demand curves for a product. Recall from Chapter 4 that the point (x_0, p_0) where these curves intersect is called the *point of equilibrium*. Let us assume that the market is indeed at equilibrium and, consequently, the price per unit of the product is p_0. According to the demand

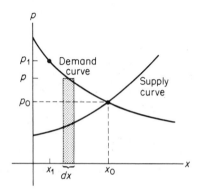

Fig. 9-33

curve there are consumers who would be willing to pay *more* than p_0 for the product. For example, at the price per unit of p_1 there are consumers who would be willing to buy a total of x_1 units. Thus all consumers who are willing to pay more than p_0 are benefiting from the lower equilibrium price.

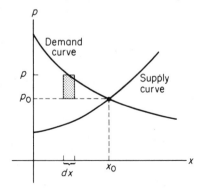

Fig. 9-34

The vertical strip in Fig. 9-33 has area $p\,dx$. This quantity can also be thought of as the total amount of money that consumers would spend by buying dx units of the product if the price per unit were p. Since the price is actually p_0, these consumers spend only $p_0\,dx$ for these dx units and thus benefit by the amount $p\,dx - p_0\,dx$. But $p\,dx - p_0\,dx = (p - p_0)\,dx$ is the area of a rectangle of width dx and length $p - p_0$ (see Fig. 9-34). Summing the areas of all such rectangles from $x = 0$ to $x = x_0$ by using definite integration,

we have $\displaystyle\int_0^{x_0} (p - p_0)\,dx$. This integral, under certain conditions, represents

the total gain to consumers who are willing to pay more than the equilibrium price. This total gain is called **consumers' surplus**, abbreviated *CS*. If the demand function is given by $p = f(x)$, then

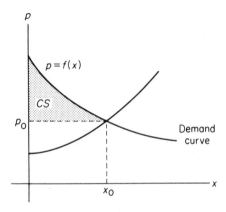

Fig. 9-35

$$CS = \int_0^{x_0} [f(x) - p_0]\ dx.$$

Geometrically (see Fig. 9-35), consumers' surplus is represented by the area between the line $p = p_0$ and the demand curve $p = f(x)$ from $x = 0$ to $x = x_0$.

The producers also benefit from the equilibrium price since they would be willing to supply the product at prices *lower* than p_0. Under certain conditions the total gain to the producers is represented geometrically in Fig. 9-36 by

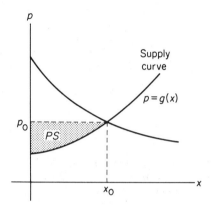

Fig. 9-36

the area between the line $p = p_0$ and the supply curve $p = g(x)$ from $x = 0$ to $x = x_0$. This gain, called **producers' surplus** and abbreviated *PS*, is given by

$$PS = \int_0^{x_0} [p_0 - g(x)]\ dx.$$

EXAMPLE 29

The demand function for a product is $p = f(x) = 100 - .05x$ where p is the price per unit (in dollars) for x units. The supply function is $p = g(x) = 10 + .1x$. Determine consumers' surplus and producers' surplus when market equilibrium has been established.

First we must find the equilibrium point by solving the system formed by $p = 100 - .05x$ and $p = 10 + .1x$. Eliminating p, we have

$$10 + .1x = 100 - .05x$$

$$.15x = 90$$

$$x = 600.$$

When $x = 600$, then $p = 10 + .1(600) = 70$. Thus, $x_0 = 600$ and $p_0 = 70$. Consumers' surplus is

$$CS = \int_0^{x_0} [f(x) - p_0] \, dx = \int_0^{600} (100 - .05x - 70) \, dx$$

$$= \left(30x - .05\frac{x^2}{2}\right)\Bigg|_0^{600} = 18,000 - 9000 = 9000.$$

Producers' surplus is

$$PS = \int_0^{x_0} [p_0 - g(x)] \, dx = \int_0^{600} [70 - (10 + .1x)] \, dx$$

$$\doteq \left(60x - .1\frac{x^2}{2}\right)\Bigg|_0^{600} = 36,000 - 18,000 = 18,000.$$

Therefore, consumers' surplus is $9000 and producers' surplus is $18,000.

EXAMPLE 30

The demand equation for a product is $x = f(p) = (90/p) - 2$ and the supply equation is $x = g(p) = p - 1$. Determine the consumers' surplus and producers' surplus when market equilibrium has been established.

Determining the equilibrium point, we have

$$p - 1 = \frac{90}{p} - 2$$

$$p^2 + p - 90 = 0$$

$$(p + 10)(p - 9) = 0.$$

Thus $p_0 = 9$ and $x_0 = 9 - 1 = 8$ (see Fig. 9-37). Note that the demand equation expresses x as a function of p. Since consumers' surplus can be considered as an area, this area can be determined by means of horizontal strips of width dp and length $x = f(p)$. These strips are summed from $p = 9$ to $p = 45$.

$$CS = \int_9^{45} \left(\frac{90}{p} - 2\right) dp = (90 \ln|p| - 2p)\Bigg|_9^{45}$$

$$= 90 \ln 5 - 72 \approx 72.85.$$

Using horizontal strips for producers' surplus, we have

$$PS = \int_1^9 (p - 1) \, dp = \frac{(p - 1)^2}{2}\Bigg|_1^9 = 32.$$

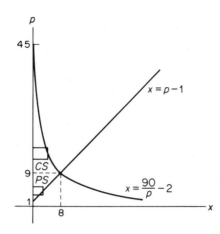

Fig. 9-37

EXERCISE 9-9

In problems 1–6, the first equation is a demand equation and the second is a supply equation of a product. In each case determine the consumers' surplus and producers' surplus when market equilibrium has been established.

1. $p = 20 - .8x$

   $p = 4 + 1.2x$

2. $p = 900 - x^2$

   $p = 100 + x^2$

3. $p = \dfrac{50}{x + 5}$

   $p = \dfrac{x}{10} + 4.5$

4. $p = 400 - x^2$

   $p = 20x + 100$

5. $x = 100(10 - p)$

   $x = 80(p - 1)$

6. $x = \sqrt{100 - p}$

   $x = \dfrac{p}{2} - 10$

9-10   REVIEW

Important Terms and Symbols in Chapter 9

antiderivative *(p. 319)*

indefinite integral *(p. 320)*

definite integral *(p. 355)*

integrand *(p. 320)*

Σ *(p. 346)*

sigma notation *(p. 346)*

index of summation *(p. 346)*

limits of summation *(p. 346)*

limits of integration (p. 355)   element of area (p. 369)

$$\int f(x)\, dx, \int_a^b f(x)\, dx \text{ (p. 363)}$$ consumers' surplus (p. 382)

constant of integration (p. 320)   producers' surplus (p. 383)

Review Section

1. If $F(x)$ is an antiderivative of $f(x)$, then $dF/dx = $ _____ .

> Ans. $f(x)$

2. $\int 5x^4\, dx = $ _____ .

> Ans. $x^5 + C$

3. In $\int f(x)\, dx$, $f(x)$ is called the _____ .

> Ans. integrand

4. $\int_{10}^{20} 2\, dx = $ _____ .

> Ans. 20

5. True or false: $\int x^{-1}\, dx = \dfrac{x^{-1+1}}{-1+1} + C$, __(a)__ ; $\int e^x\, dx = \dfrac{e^{x+1}}{x+1} + C$, __(b)__ .

> Ans. (a) false;   (b) false

6. $\int (2x - 5)^9\, dx = $ _____ .

> Ans. $\dfrac{1}{20}(2x - 5)^{10} + C$

7. $\int e^{2x+1}\, dx = $ _____ .

> Ans. $\frac{1}{2} e^{2x+1} + C$

8. If $\int f(x)\, dx = F(x) + C$, then C is called the _____ .

> Ans. constant of integration

9. $\displaystyle\int \frac{2}{x+5}\, dx =$ _____.

> *Ans.* $2 \ln |x + 5| + C$

10. A definite integral of a function is a (function) (number).

> *Ans.* number

11. $\displaystyle\sum_{k=0}^{2} (k + 1) =$ _____.

> *Ans.* 6

12. True or false: $\displaystyle\sum_{k=1}^{15} (k^2 + 3k + 5) = \sum_{j=1}^{15} (j^2 + 3j + 5).$ _____

> *Ans.* true

13. If $D_x y = 1$ and $y(0) = 1$, then $y =$ _____.

> *Ans.* $x + 1$

14. All antiderivatives of a given function differ at most by a _____.

> *Ans.* constant

15. If $F'(x) = f(x)$, then $\displaystyle\int_{2}^{3} f(x)\, dx =$ _____.

> *Ans.* $F(3) - F(2)$

16. If $f(x) = 0$, then $\displaystyle\int f(x)\, dx =$ _____.

> *Ans.* C, a constant

Review Problems

Determine the integrals in problems 1–26.

1. $\displaystyle\int (x^3 + 2x - 7)\, dx$

2. $\displaystyle\int dx$

3. $\displaystyle\int_{0}^{9} (\sqrt{x} + x)\, dx$

4. $\displaystyle\int \frac{2}{5 - 3x}\, dx$

5. $\displaystyle\int \frac{2}{(x + 5)^3}\, dx$

6. $\displaystyle\int_{4}^{12} (y - 8)^{501}\, dy$

7. $\displaystyle\int \frac{6x^2 - 12}{x^3 - 6x + 1}\, dx$

8. $\displaystyle\int_{0}^{2} x e^{4 - x^2}\, dx$

9. $\displaystyle\int_{1}^{2} \frac{t^2}{2 + t^3}\, dt$

10. $\displaystyle\int \frac{4x^2 - x}{x}\, dx$

11. $\displaystyle\int x^2 \sqrt{3x^3 + 2}\, dx$

12. $\displaystyle\int (2x^3 + x)(x^4 + x^2)^{3/4}\, dx$

13. $\displaystyle\int (e^{2y} - e^{-2y})\, dy$

14. $\displaystyle\int \frac{8x}{3\sqrt[3]{7 - 2x^2}}\, dx$

15. $\displaystyle\int \left(\frac{1}{x} + \frac{2}{x^2}\right) dx$

16. $\displaystyle\int_{0}^{1} \frac{e^{2x}}{1 + e^{2x}}\, dx$

17. $\displaystyle\int_{-2}^{1} (y^4 - y + 1)\, dy$

18. $\displaystyle\int_{7}^{70} dx$

19. $\displaystyle\int_{\sqrt{3}}^{2} 7x\sqrt{4 - x^2}\, dx$

20. $\displaystyle\int_{0}^{1} (2x + 1)(x^2 + x)^4\, dx$

21. $\displaystyle\int_{0}^{1} \left[2x - \frac{1}{(x + 1)^{2/3}}\right] dx$

22. $\displaystyle\int_{2}^{8} (\sqrt{2x} - x + 4)\, dx$

23. $\displaystyle\int \frac{\sqrt{t} - 3}{t^2}\, dt$

24. $\displaystyle\int \frac{z^2}{z - 1}\, dz$

25. $\displaystyle\int_{-1}^{0} \frac{x^2 + 4x - 1}{x + 2}\, dx$

26. $\displaystyle\int \frac{(x^2 + 4)^2}{x^2}\, dx$

In problems 27-34, determine the area of the region bounded by the given curves, the x-axis, and the given lines.

27. $y = x^2 - 1,\ x = 2$

28. $y = 4e^{2x},\ x = 0,\ x = 3$

29. $y = \sqrt{x + 4},\ x = 0$

30. $y = x^2 - x - 2,\ x = -2,\ x = 2$

31. $y = 5x - x^2$

32. $y = \sqrt[4]{x},\ x = 1,\ x = 16$

33. $y = \dfrac{1}{x} + 3,\ x = 1,\ x = 3$

34. $y = x^3 - 1,\ x = -1$

In problems 35-40, find the area of the region bounded by the given curves.

35. $y^2 = 4x,\ x = 0,\ y = 2$

36. $y = 2x^2,\ x = 0,\ y = 2\ (x \geq 0)$

37. $y = x^2 + 4x - 5,\ y = 0$

38. $y = 2x^2,\ y = x^2 + 9$

39. $y = x^2 - 2x,\ y = 12 - x^2$

40. $y = \sqrt{|x|},\ y = 3$

41. If marginal revenue is given by $dr/dx = 100 - (3/2)\sqrt{2x}$, determine the corresponding demand equation.

42. If marginal cost is given by $dc/dx = x^2 + 7x + 6$, and fixed costs are 2500, determine the total cost for producing 6 units.

43. For a product the demand equation is $p = .01x^2 - 1.1x + 30$ and its supply equation is $p = .01x^2 + 8$. Determine consumers' surplus and producers' surplus when market equilibrium has been established.

Chapter **10**

Methods and Applications of Integration

10-1 INTEGRATION BY PARTS†

Many integrals cannot be found by our previous methods. However, there are ways of changing certain integrals to forms that are easier to integrate. Of these methods, we shall discuss two: *integration by parts*, and (in the next section) *integration using partial fractions*.

If u and v are differentiable functions of x, the product rule asserts

$$D_x(uv) = u\frac{dv}{dx} + v\frac{du}{dx}.$$

By rearranging, we obtain

$$u\frac{dv}{dx} = D_x(uv) - v\frac{du}{dx}.$$

_____

† May be omitted without loss of continuity.

Integrating both sides with respect to x, we get

$$\int u \frac{dv}{dx} dx = \int \left[D_x(uv) - v \frac{du}{dx} \right] dx$$

$$= \int D_x(uv) dx - \int v \frac{du}{dx} dx.$$

Since dv/dx and du/dx can be considered quotients of differentials, we have $\int u \frac{dv}{dx} dx = \int u\, dv$ and $\int v \frac{du}{dx} dx = \int v\, du$. Hence from above,

$$\int u\, dv = \int D_x(uv)\, dx - \int v\, du. \tag{1}$$

For $\int D_x(uv)\, dx$, we must find a function whose derivative with respect to x is $D_x(uv)$. Clearly uv is such a function. Hence $\int D_x(uv)\, dx = uv + C_1$ and Eq. (1) becomes

$$\int u\, dv = uv + C_1 - \int v\, du.$$

Incorporating C_1 into the constant of integration for $\int v\, du$, we have the **integration by parts formula:**

$$\boxed{\int u\, dv = uv - \int v\, du.} \tag{2}$$

This formula expresses a given integral $\int u\, dv$ in terms of another integral, $\int v\, du$, which may be easier to find.

To apply the formula to $\int f(x)\, dx$ we must write $f(x)\, dx$ as the product of two factors (or *parts*) by choosing a function u and a differential dv such that $f(x)\, dx = u\, dv$. For the formula to be useful, we must be able to integrate the part chosen for dv. To illustrate, consider

$$\int xe^x\, dx.$$

This integral cannot be determined by previous integration formulas. We now write $xe^x \, dx$ in the form $u \, dv$. Let

$$u = x \quad \text{and} \quad dv = e^x \, dx.$$

Then

$$du = dx$$

and since v is an antiderivative of dv, then

$$v = \int e^x \, dx = e^x + C_1 .$$

Thus

$$\int \underbrace{x}_{u} \underbrace{e^x \, dx}_{dv} = uv - \int v \, du$$

$$= x(e^x + C_1) - \int (e^x + C_1) \, dx$$

$$= xe^x + C_1 x - e^x - C_1 x + C$$

$$= xe^x - e^x + C = e^x(x - 1) + C.$$

The constant C_1 that resulted when we found v from dv does not appear in the final answer. This is a characteristic of integration by parts and from now on this constant will not be included (that is, we choose $C_1 = 0$).

When you are using the integration by parts formula, sometimes the "best choice" for u and dv may not be apparent. In some cases one choice may be as good as another; in other cases only one choice may be suitable. Insight into making a good choice (if any exists) will come only with practice and, of course, trial and error.

EXAMPLE 1

Find $\displaystyle \int \frac{\ln x}{\sqrt{x}} \, dx$ *by integration by parts.*

We try

$$u = \ln x \quad \text{and} \quad dv = \frac{1}{\sqrt{x}} \, dx.$$

Then

$$du = \frac{1}{x} \, dx \quad \text{and} \quad v = \int x^{-1/2} \, dx = 2x^{1/2}.$$

Thus,

$$\int \underbrace{\ln x}_{u} \underbrace{\left(\frac{1}{\sqrt{x}} \, dx \right)}_{dv} = uv - \int v \, du$$

$$= (\ln x)(2\sqrt{x}) - \int (2x^{1/2}) \left(\frac{1}{x} \, dx \right)$$

$$= 2\sqrt{x} \ln x - 2 \int x^{-1/2} \, dx$$

$$= 2\sqrt{x} \ln x - 2(2\sqrt{x}) + C$$

$$= 2\sqrt{x} \, (\ln x - 2) + C.$$

For a definite integral, Eq. (2) becomes

$$\int_a^b u \, dv = uv \Big|_a^b - \int_a^b v \, du.$$

EXAMPLE 2

Evaluate $\displaystyle\int_1^2 x \ln x \, dx.$

If $u = x$ and $dv = \ln x \, dx$, then $du = dx$ but $v = \displaystyle\int \ln x \, dx$ is not apparent by inspection.
Let us try

$$u = \ln x \quad \text{and} \quad dv = x \, dx.$$

Then

$$du = \frac{1}{x} \, dx \quad \text{and} \quad v = \int x \, dx = \frac{x^2}{2}$$

and

$$\int_1^2 x \ln x \, dx = (\ln x) \left(\frac{x^2}{2} \right) \Big|_1^2 - \int_1^2 \left(\frac{x^2}{2} \right) \frac{1}{x} \, dx$$

$$= \frac{x^2 \ln x}{2} \Big|_1^2 - \frac{1}{2} \left(\frac{x^2}{2} \right) \Big|_1^2$$

$$= (2 \ln 2 - 0) - (1 - \tfrac{1}{4}) = 2 \ln 2 - \tfrac{3}{4}.$$

Sometimes integration by parts must be used more than once, as shown in the following example.

EXAMPLE 3

Determine $\int x^2 e^{2x+1} \, dx$.

Let $u = x^2$ and $dv = e^{2x+1} \, dx$. Then $du = 2x \, dx$ and $v = e^{2x+1}/2$.

$$\int x^2 e^{2x+1} \, dx = \frac{x^2 e^{2x+1}}{2} - \int \frac{e^{2x+1}}{2}(2x) \, dx$$

$$= \frac{x^2 e^{2x+1}}{2} - \int xe^{2x+1} \, dx.$$

For $\int xe^{2x+1} \, dx$, let $u = x$ and $dv = e^{2x+1} \, dx$. Then $du = dx$ and $v = e^{2x+1}/2$.

$$\int xe^{2x+1} \, dx = \frac{xe^{2x+1}}{2} - \int \frac{e^{2x+1}}{2} \, dx$$

$$= \frac{xe^{2x+1}}{2} - \frac{e^{2x+1}}{4} + C_1.$$

Thus

$$\int x^2 e^{2x+1} \, dx = \frac{x^2 e^{2x+1}}{2} - \frac{xe^{2x+1}}{2} + \frac{e^{2x+1}}{4} + C$$

$$= \frac{e^{2x+1}}{2}\left(x^2 - x + \frac{1}{2}\right) + C \qquad \text{(where } C = -C_1\text{)}.$$

EXAMPLE 4

Determine $\int \ln y \, dy$.

Let $u = \ln y$ and $dv = dy$. Then $du = (1/y) \, dy$ and $v = y$.

$$\int \ln y \, dy = (\ln y)(y) - \int y\left(\frac{1}{y} \, dy\right)$$

$$= y \ln y - \int dy = y \ln y - y + C$$

$$= y(\ln y - 1) + C.$$

EXAMPLE 5

Determine $\int xe^{x^2}\, dx$.

PITFALL.   *Do not forget about basic integration forms. Integration by parts is not needed here!*

$$\int xe^{x^2}\, dx = \tfrac{1}{2} \int e^{x^2}\,(2x\, dx)$$

$$= \tfrac{1}{2} \int e^u\, du \quad \text{where } u = x^2$$

$$= \tfrac{1}{2} e^u + C$$

$$= \tfrac{1}{2} e^{x^2} + C.$$

EXERCISE 10-1

In problems 1–20, find the integrals.

1. $\displaystyle\int xe^{-x}\, dx$

2. $\displaystyle\int xe^{2x}\, dx$

3. $\displaystyle\int y^3 \ln y\, dy$

4. $\displaystyle\int x^2 \ln x\, dx$

5. $\displaystyle\int \ln (4x)\, dx$

6. $\displaystyle\int \frac{t}{e^t}\, dt$

7. $\displaystyle\int x\sqrt{x + 1}\, dx$

8. $\displaystyle\int \frac{x}{\sqrt{1 + 4x}}\, dx$

9. $\displaystyle\int \sqrt{x}\, \ln x\, dx$

10. $\displaystyle\int \frac{\ln (x + 1)}{2(x + 1)}\, dx$

11. $\displaystyle\int_0^1 xe^{-x^2}\, dx$

12. $\displaystyle\int_0^1 xe^{-x}\, dx$

13. $\displaystyle\int_1^2 xe^{2x}\, dx$

14. $\displaystyle\int \frac{x^3}{\sqrt{4 - x^2}}\, dx$

15. $\displaystyle\int_1^2 \frac{x}{\sqrt{4 - x}}\, dx$

16. $\displaystyle\int (\ln x)^2\, dx$

17. $\displaystyle\int x^2 e^x\, dx$

18. $\displaystyle\int x^2 e^{-2x}\, dx$

19. $\int (x - e^{-x})^2 \, dx$ **20.** $\int x^3 e^{x^2} \, dx$

21. Find the area of the region bounded by the x-axis, the curve $y = \ln x$ and the line $x = e^3$.

22. Find the area of the region bounded by the x-axis and the curve $y = xe^{-x}$ between $x = 0$ and $x = 4$.

23. If $dc/dx = 2 + 2 \ln (x + 2)$ is a marginal cost function, find the total variable cost of producing 100 units of a product. *Hint:* See Example 24 of Chapter 9.

10-2 INTEGRATION BY PARTIAL FRACTIONS†

We now consider the integral of a quotient of two polynomials—that is, the integral of a *rational function*. Without loss of generality, we may assume that the numerator $N(x)$ and denominator $D(x)$ have no common polynomial factor and that the degree of $N(x)$ is less than the degree of $D(x)$ [that is, $N(x)/D(x)$ is a *proper rational function*]. For if the numerator were not of lower degree, we could use long division to divide $N(x)$ by $D(x)$:

$$\begin{array}{r} P(x) \\ D(x) \overline{)N(x)} \\ \vdots \\ \hline R(x) \end{array}; \quad \text{thus} \quad \frac{N(x)}{D(x)} = P(x) + \frac{R(x)}{D(x)}.$$

$P(x)$ would be a polynomial (easily integrable) and $R(x)$ would be a polynomial of lower degree than $D(x)$. Thus $R(x)/D(x)$ would be a proper rational function. For example,

$$\int \frac{2x^4 - 3x^3 - 4x^2 - 17x - 6}{x^3 - 2x^2 - 3x} \, dx = \int \left(2x + 1 + \frac{4x^2 - 14x - 6}{x^3 - 2x^2 - 3x} \right) dx$$

$$= x^2 + x + \int \frac{4x^2 - 14x - 6}{x^3 - 2x^2 - 3x} \, dx.$$

Therefore, we shall consider

$$\int \frac{4x^2 - 14x - 6}{x^3 - 2x^2 - 3x} \, dx = \int \frac{4x^2 - 14x - 6}{x(x + 1)(x - 3)} \, dx.$$

Observe that the denominator of the integrand consists only of **distinct linear factors,** each factor occurring exactly once. It can be shown that to each such factor $(x - a)$ there corresponds a *partial fraction* of the form

$$\frac{A}{x - a} \qquad\qquad (A \text{ a constant})$$

---
† May be omitted without loss of continuity.

such that the integrand is the sum of the partial fractions. If there are n such *distinct* linear factors, there will be n such partial fractions, each of which is easily integrated. Applying these facts, we can write

$$\frac{4x^2 - 14x - 6}{x(x + 1)(x - 3)} = \frac{A}{x} + \frac{B}{x + 1} + \frac{C}{x - 3}. \qquad (1)$$

To determine the constants A, B, and C, we first combine the terms on the right side:

$$\frac{4x^2 - 14x - 6}{x(x + 1)(x - 3)} = \frac{A(x + 1)(x - 3) + Bx(x - 3) + Cx(x + 1)}{x(x + 1)(x - 3)}.$$

Since the denominators of both sides are equal, we may equate their numerators:

$$4x^2 - 14x - 6 = A(x + 1)(x - 3) + Bx(x - 3) + Cx(x + 1). \qquad (2)$$

Although Eq. (1) is not defined for $x = 0$, $x = -1$, and $x = 3$, we want to find values for A, B, and C that will make Eq. (2) true for all values of x. That is, it will be an identity. By successively setting x in Eq. (2) equal to any three different numbers, we can obtain a system of equations which can be solved for A, B, and C. In particular, the work can be simplified by letting x be the roots of $D(x) = 0$, in our case $x = 0$, $x = -1$, and $x = 3$. Using Eq. (2), if $x = 0$, we have

$$-6 = A(1)(-3) + B(0) + C(0) = -3A \quad \text{and} \quad A = 2;$$

if $x = -1$,

$$12 = A(0) + B(-1)(-4) + C(0) = 4B \quad \text{and} \quad B = 3;$$

if $x = 3$,

$$-12 = A(0) + B(0) + C(3)(4) = 12C \quad \text{and} \quad C = -1.$$

Thus Eq. (1) becomes

$$\frac{4x^2 - 14x - 6}{x(x + 1)(x - 3)} = \frac{2}{x} + \frac{3}{x + 1} - \frac{1}{x - 3}.$$

Hence

$$\int \frac{4x^2 - 14x - 6}{x(x + 1)(x - 3)} \, dx = \int \left(\frac{2}{x} + \frac{3}{x + 1} - \frac{1}{x - 3} \right) dx$$

$$= 2 \int \frac{dx}{x} + 3 \int \frac{dx}{x + 1} - \int \frac{dx}{x - 3}$$

$$= 2 \ln |x| + 3 \ln |x + 1| - \ln |x - 3| + C$$

$$= \ln \left| \frac{x^2(x + 1)^3}{x - 3} \right| + C \quad \text{(using properties of logarithms).}$$

For the *original* integral we can now state

$$\int \frac{2x^4 - 3x^3 - 4x^2 - 17x - 6}{x^3 - 2x^2 - 3x} \, dx = x^2 + x + \ln \left| \frac{x^2(x+1)^3}{x-3} \right| + C.$$

There is an alternative method of determining A, B, and C. It involves expanding the right side of Eq. (2) and combining similar terms:

$$4x^2 - 14x - 6 = A(x^2 - 2x - 3) + B(x^2 - 3x) + C(x^2 + x)$$

$$= Ax^2 - 2Ax - 3A + Bx^2 - 3Bx + Cx^2 + Cx$$

$$4x^2 - 14x - 6 = (A + B + C)x^2 + (-2A - 3B + C)x + (-3A).$$

For this identity, coefficients of corresponding powers of x on the left and right sides of the equation must be equal:

$$\begin{cases} 4 = A + B + C \\ -14 = -2A - 3B + C \\ -6 = -3A. \end{cases}$$

Solving gives $A = 2$, $B = 3$, and $C = -1$ as before.

EXAMPLE 6

Determine $\displaystyle\int \frac{2x+1}{3x^2 - 27} \, dx.$

Since the degree of $N(x)$ is less than the degree of $D(x)$, no long division is necessary. The integral can be written as

$$\frac{1}{3} \int \frac{2x+1}{x^2 - 9} \, dx.$$

Expressing $(2x+1)/(x^2 - 9)$ as a sum of partial fractions, we have

$$\frac{2x+1}{x^2 - 9} = \frac{2x+1}{(x+3)(x-3)} = \frac{A}{x+3} + \frac{B}{x-3}.$$

Combining terms and equating numerators, we obtain

$$2x + 1 = A(x - 3) + B(x + 3).$$

If $x = 3$,

$$7 = 6B \quad \text{and} \quad B = \frac{7}{6};$$

if $x = -3$,

$$-5 = -6A \quad \text{and} \quad A = \frac{5}{6}.$$

Thus

$$\int \frac{2x + 1}{3x^2 - 27}\, dx = \frac{1}{3}\left[\int \frac{\frac{5}{6}\, dx}{x + 3} + \int \frac{\frac{7}{6}\, dx}{x - 3}\right]$$

$$= \frac{1}{3}\left[\frac{5}{6}\ln|x + 3| + \frac{7}{6}\ln|x - 3|\right] + C$$

$$= \tfrac{1}{18}\ln|(x + 3)^5(x - 3)^7| + C.$$

If the denominator of $N(x)/D(x)$ contains only linear factors, some of which are repeated, then for each factor $(x - a)^k$, where k is the maximum number of times $(x - a)$ occurs as a factor, there will correspond the sum of k partial fractions:

$$\frac{A}{x - a} + \frac{B}{(x - a)^2} + \ldots + \frac{K}{(x - a)^k}.$$

EXAMPLE 7

Determine $\displaystyle\int \frac{6x^2 + 13x + 6}{(x + 2)(x + 1)^2}\, dx.$

Since the degree of $N(x)$ is less than that of $D(x)$, no long division is necessary. In $D(x)$ the factor $(x + 2)$ occurs once and the factor $(x + 1)$ occurs twice. There will be three partial fractions and three constants to determine.

$$\frac{6x^2 + 13x + 6}{(x + 2)(x + 1)^2} = \frac{A}{x + 2} + \frac{B}{x + 1} + \frac{C}{(x + 1)^2}$$

$$6x^2 + 13x + 6 = A(x + 1)^2 + B(x + 2)(x + 1) + C(x + 2).$$

Let us choose $x = -2$, $x = -1$, and for convenience $x = 0$. Then if $x = -2$,

$$4 = A;$$

if $x = -1$,

$$-1 = C;$$

if $x = 0$,

$$6 = A + 2B + 2C = 4 + 2B - 2 = 2 + 2B$$

$$2 = B.$$

Thus,

$$\int \frac{6x^2 + 13x + 6}{(x + 2)(x + 1)^2}\, dx = 4\int \frac{dx}{x + 2} + 2\int \frac{dx}{x + 1} - \int \frac{dx}{(x + 1)^2}$$

$$= 4 \ln |x + 2| + 2 \ln |x + 1| + \frac{1}{x + 1} + C$$

$$= \ln [(x + 2)^4 (x + 1)^2] + \frac{1}{x + 1} + C.$$

Suppose a quadratic factor $(x^2 + bx + c)$ occurs in $D(x)$ such that $x^2 + bx + c$ cannot be expressed as a product of two linear factors with real coefficients. Such a factor is called *irreducible over the real numbers*. To each irreducible quadratic factor that occurs exactly once in $D(x)$ there will correspond a partial fraction of the form

$$\frac{Ax + B}{x^2 + bx + c}.$$

EXAMPLE 8

Determine $\displaystyle\int \frac{-2x - 4}{x^3 + x^2 + x} dx.$

Since $x^3 + x^2 + x = x(x^2 + x + 1)$, we have the linear factor x and the quadratic factor $x^2 + x + 1$ which does not seem factorable on inspection. If it were factorable into $(x - r_1)(x - r_2)$, where r_1 and r_2 are real, then r_1 and r_2 would be roots of $x^2 + x + 1 = 0$. By the quadratic formula, the roots are

$$x = \frac{-1 \pm \sqrt{1 - 4}}{2}.$$

Since there are no real roots, we conclude that $x^2 + x + 1$ is irreducible. Thus there will be two partial fractions and *three* constants to determine:

$$\frac{-2x - 4}{x(x^2 + x + 1)} = \frac{A}{x} + \frac{Bx + C}{x^2 + x + 1}.$$

$$-2x - 4 = A(x^2 + x + 1) + (Bx + C)x$$

$$= Ax^2 + Ax + A + Bx^2 + Cx$$

$$0x^2 - 2x - 4 = (A + B)x^2 + (A + C)x + A.$$

Equating coefficients of like powers of x, we obtain

$$\begin{cases} 0 = A + B \\ -2 = A + C \\ -4 = A. \end{cases}$$

Solving gives $A = -4$, $B = 4$, and $C = 2$. Thus

$$\int \frac{-2x - 4}{x(x^2 + x + 1)}\, dx = \int \left(\frac{-4}{x} + \frac{4x + 2}{x^2 + x + 1} \right) dx$$

$$= -4 \int \frac{dx}{x} + 2 \int \frac{2x + 1}{x^2 + x + 1}\, dx.$$

Both integrals have the form $\displaystyle\int \frac{du}{u}$.

$$\int \frac{-2x - 4}{x(x^2 + x + 1)}\, dx = -4 \ln |x| + 2 \ln |x^2 + x + 1| + C$$

$$= \ln \left[\frac{(x^2 + x + 1)^2}{x^4} \right] + C.$$

Suppose $D(x)$ contains factors of the form $(x^2 + bx + c)^k$, where k is the maximum number of times the irreducible factor $x^2 + bx + c$ occurs. Then to each such factor there will correspond a sum of k partial fractions of the form

$$\frac{A + Bx}{x^2 + bx + c} + \frac{C + Dx}{(x^2 + bx + c)^2} + \cdots + \frac{M + Nx}{(x^2 + bx + c)^k}.$$

EXAMPLE 9

Determine $\displaystyle\int \frac{x^5}{(x^2 + 4)^2}\, dx$.

Since $N(x)$ has degree 5 and $D(x)$ has degree 4, we first divide $N(x)$ by $D(x)$.

$$\frac{x^5}{x^4 + 8x^2 + 16} = x - \frac{8x^3 + 16x}{(x^2 + 4)^2}.$$

The quadratic factor $(x^2 + 4)$ in the denominator of $(8x^3 + 16x)/(x^2 + 4)^2$ is irreducible and occurs as a factor twice. Thus to $(x^2 + 4)^2$ there correspond two partial fractions and *four* coefficients to be determined.

$$\frac{8x^3 + 16x}{(x^2 + 4)^2} = \frac{Ax + B}{x^2 + 4} + \frac{Cx + D}{(x^2 + 4)^2}$$

$$8x^3 + 16x = (Ax + B)(x^2 + 4) + Cx + D$$

$$8x^3 + 0x^2 + 16x + 0 = Ax^3 + Bx^2 + (4A + C)x + 4B + D.$$

Equating like powers of x, we obtain

$$\begin{cases} 8 = A \\ 0 = B \\ 16 = 4A + C \\ 0 = 4B + D. \end{cases}$$

Solving gives $A = 8$, $B = 0$, $C = -16$, and $D = 0$.

$$\int \frac{x^5}{(x^2 + 4)^2}\, dx = \int \left(x - \left[\frac{8x}{x^2 + 4} - \frac{16x}{(x^2 + 4)^2} \right] \right) dx$$

$$= \int x\, dx - 4 \int \frac{2x}{x^2 + 4}\, dx + 8 \int \frac{2x}{(x^2 + 4)^2}\, dx.$$

The second integral has the form $\int \dfrac{du}{u}$ and the third integral has the form $\int \dfrac{du}{u^2}$.

$$\int \frac{x^5}{(x^2 + 4)^2}\, dx = \frac{x^2}{2} - 4 \ln (x^2 + 4) - \frac{8}{x^2 + 4} + C.$$

From our examples you may have deduced that the number of constants needed to express $N(x)/D(x)$ by partial fractions is equal to the degree of $D(x)$, if it is assumed that $N(x)/D(x)$ is a proper rational function. This is indeed the case. It should be added that the representation of a proper rational function by partial fractions is unique; that is, there is only one choice of constants that can be made. Furthermore, regardless of the complexity of the polynomial $D(x)$, it can always (theoretically) be expressed as a product of linear and irreducible quadratic factors with real coefficients.

EXAMPLE 10

Find $\displaystyle\int \frac{2x + 3}{x^2 + 3x + 1}\, dx.$

PITFALL.   *Do not forget about basic integration forms.*

$$\int \frac{2x + 3}{x^2 + 3x + 1}\, dx = \ln |x^2 + 3x + 1| + C.$$

EXERCISE 10-2

In problems 1–22, determine the integrals.

1. $\displaystyle\int \frac{5x - 2}{x^2 - x}\, dx$

2. $\displaystyle\int \frac{3x + 8}{x^2 + 2x}\, dx$

3. $\displaystyle\int \frac{x + 10}{x^2 - x - 2} \, dx$

4. $\displaystyle\int \frac{dx}{x^2 - 5x + 6}$

5. $\displaystyle\int \frac{3x^3 - 3x + 4}{4x^2 - 4} \, dx$

6. $\displaystyle\int \frac{4 - x^2}{(x - 4)(x - 2)(x + 3)} \, dx$

7. $\displaystyle\int \frac{17x - 12}{x^3 - x^2 - 12x} \, dx$

8. $\displaystyle\int \frac{4 - x}{x^4 - x^2} \, dx$

9. $\displaystyle\int \frac{3x^5 + 4x^3 - x}{x^6 + 2x^4 - x^2 - 2} \, dx$

10. $\displaystyle\int \frac{x^4 - 3x^3 - 5x^2 + 8x - 1}{x^3 - 2x^2 - 8x} \, dx$

11. $\displaystyle\int \frac{2x^2 - 5x - 2}{(x - 2)^2(x - 1)} \, dx$

12. $\displaystyle\int \frac{-3x^3 + 2x - 3}{x^2(x^2 - 1)} \, dx$

13. $\displaystyle\int \frac{x^2 + 8}{x^3 + 4x} \, dx$

14. $\displaystyle\int \frac{2x^3 - 6x^2 - 10x - 6}{x^4 - 1} \, dx$

15. $\displaystyle\int \frac{-x^3 + 8x^2 - 9x + 2}{(x^2 + 1)(x - 3)^2} \, dx$

16. $\displaystyle\int \frac{2x^4 + 9x^2 + 8}{x(x^2 + 2)^2} \, dx$

17. $\displaystyle\int \frac{14x^3 + 24x}{(x^2 + 1)(x^2 + 2)} \, dx$

18. $\displaystyle\int \frac{12x^3 + 20x^2 + 28x + 4}{(x^2 + 2x + 3)(x^2 + 1)} \, dx$

19. $\displaystyle\int \frac{3x^3 + x}{(x^2 + 1)^2} \, dx$

20. $\displaystyle\int \frac{3x^2 - 8x + 4}{x^3 - 4x^2 + 4x - 6} \, dx$

21. $\displaystyle\int_0^1 \frac{2 - 2x}{x^2 + 7x + 12} \, dx$

22. $\displaystyle\int_1^2 \frac{2x^2 + 1}{(x + 3)(x + 2)} \, dx$

23. Find the area bounded by $y = (x^2 + 1)/(x + 2)^2$ and the x-axis from $x = 0$ to $x = 1$.

10-3 INTEGRATION USING TABLES

The fact that certain forms of integrals occur frequently has led to the preparation of extensive tables of integration formulas. Indeed, such tables can be found in book form. Perhaps one can be found in your library. In Appendix C a short table has been provided. In this section its use will be illustrated.

No table of integrals is exhaustive. We may still have to appeal to prior techniques of integration when a suitable form is not listed in the tables. Moreover, a given integral may have to be replaced by an equivalent form before it will fit a formula in the table. The equivalent form must match the formula *exactly.* Consequently, the steps that you perform should *not* be done mentally. *Write them down!* Failure to do this can easily lead to incorrect results. Before proceeding with the exercises, be sure you understand the illustrative examples *thoroughly.*

In the following examples the formula numbers refer to the Table of Selected Integrals given in Appendix C.

EXAMPLE 11

Find $\displaystyle\int \frac{x\,dx}{(2 + 3x)^2}$.

Scanning the tables, we identify the integrand with formula 7:

$$\int \frac{u\,du}{(a + bu)^2} = \frac{1}{b^2}\left(\ln|a + bu| + \frac{a}{a + bu}\right) + C.$$

For the given integrand, let $u = x$, $a = 2$, and $b = 3$. Then $du = dx$ and we have

$$\int \frac{x\,dx}{(2 + 3x)^2} = \int \frac{u\,du}{(a + bu)^2}.$$

By the formula,

$$\int \frac{x\,dx}{(2 + 3x)^2} = \int \frac{u\,du}{(a + bu)^2} = \frac{1}{b^2}\left(\ln|a + bu| + \frac{a}{a + bu}\right) + C.$$

Returning to the variable x and replacing a by 2 and b by 3, we obtain

$$\int \frac{x\,dx}{(2 + 3x)^2} = \frac{1}{9}\left(\ln|2 + 3x| + \frac{2}{2 + 3x}\right) + C.$$

EXAMPLE 12

Find $\displaystyle\int x^2\sqrt{x^2 - 1}\,dx$.

This integral is identified with formula 24:

$$\int u^2\sqrt{u^2 \pm a^2}\,du = \frac{u}{8}(2u^2 \pm a^2)\sqrt{u^2 \pm a^2} - \frac{a^4}{8}\ln|u + \sqrt{u^2 \pm a^2}| + C.$$

Letting $u = x$ and $a = 1$, then we have $du = dx$. Thus

$$\int x^2\sqrt{x^2 - 1}\,dx = \int u^2\sqrt{u^2 - a^2}\,du$$

$$= \frac{u}{8}(2u^2 - a^2)\sqrt{u^2 - a^2} - \frac{a^4}{8}\ln|u + \sqrt{u^2 - a^2}| + C.$$

Since $u = x$ and $a = 1$,

$$\int x^2\sqrt{x^2 - 1}\,dx = \frac{x}{8}(2x^2 - 1)\sqrt{x^2 - 1} - \frac{1}{8}\ln|x + \sqrt{x^2 - 1}| + C.$$

EXAMPLE 13

Find $\displaystyle\int \frac{dx}{x\sqrt{16x^2 + 3}}$.

The integrand can be identified with formula 28:

$$\int \frac{du}{u\sqrt{u^2 + a^2}} = \frac{1}{a}\ln\left|\frac{\sqrt{u^2 + a^2} - a}{u}\right| + C.$$

If we let $u = 4x$ and $a = \sqrt{3}$, then $du = 4\,dx$. Thus (watch closely)

$$\int \frac{dx}{x\sqrt{16x^2 + 3}} = \int \frac{(4\,dx)}{(4x)\sqrt{(4x)^2 + (\sqrt{3})^2}} = \int \frac{du}{u\sqrt{u^2 + a^2}}.$$

By formula 28, the latter integral is

$$\frac{1}{a}\ln\left|\frac{\sqrt{u^2 + a^2} - a}{u}\right| + C.$$

Hence, replacing u by $4x$ and a by $\sqrt{3}$, we have

$$\int \frac{dx}{x\sqrt{16x^2 + 3}} = \frac{1}{\sqrt{3}}\ln\left|\frac{\sqrt{16x^2 + 3} - \sqrt{3}}{4x}\right| + C.$$

Our result may be written in another form. Since $\sqrt{16x^2 + 3} - \sqrt{3} > 0$,

$$\int \frac{dx}{x\sqrt{16x^2 + 3}} = \frac{1}{\sqrt{3}}\ln\left[\frac{\sqrt{16x^2 + 3} - \sqrt{3}}{4|x|}\right] + C$$

$$= \frac{1}{\sqrt{3}}\left(\ln\left[\frac{\sqrt{16x^2 + 3} - \sqrt{3}}{|x|}\right] - \ln 4\right) + C$$

$$= \frac{1}{\sqrt{3}}\ln\left[\frac{\sqrt{16x^2 + 3} - \sqrt{3}}{|x|}\right] - \frac{1}{\sqrt{3}}\ln 4 + C.$$

Letting $C_1 = -\dfrac{1}{\sqrt{3}}\ln 4 + C$, we have

$$\int \frac{dx}{x\sqrt{16x^2 + 3}} = \frac{1}{\sqrt{3}}\ln\left[\frac{\sqrt{16x^2 + 3} - \sqrt{3}}{|x|}\right] + C_1.$$

EXAMPLE 14

Find $\displaystyle\int \frac{dx}{x^2(2 - 3x^2)^{1/2}}$.

The integrand is identified with formula 21:

$$\int \frac{du}{u^2 \sqrt{a^2 - u^2}} = -\frac{\sqrt{a^2 - u^2}}{a^2 u} + C.$$

Letting $u = \sqrt{3}\, x$ and $a^2 = 2$, then we have $du = \sqrt{3}\, dx$. Hence

$$\int \frac{dx}{x^2 (2 - 3x^2)^{1/2}} = \sqrt{3} \int \frac{(\sqrt{3}\, dx)}{(\sqrt{3}\, x)^2 (2 - 3x^2)^{1/2}}$$

$$= \sqrt{3} \int \frac{du}{u^2 (a^2 - u^2)^{1/2}}$$

$$= \sqrt{3} \left[-\frac{\sqrt{a^2 - u^2}}{a^2 u} \right] + C$$

$$= \sqrt{3} \left[-\frac{\sqrt{2 - 3x^2}}{2(\sqrt{3}\, x)} \right] + C$$

$$= -\frac{\sqrt{2 - 3x^2}}{2x} + C.$$

EXAMPLE 15

Find $\int 7x^2 \ln (4x)\, dx.$

This is similar to formula 42 where $n = 2$;

$$\int u^n \ln u\, du = \frac{u^{n+1} \ln u}{n + 1} - \frac{u^{n+1}}{(n + 1)^2} + C.$$

If we let $u = 4x$, then $du = 4\, dx$. Hence

$$\int 7x^2 \ln (4x)\, dx = \frac{7}{64} \int (4x)^2 \ln (4x)\, (4\, dx)$$

$$= \frac{7}{64} \int u^2 \ln u\, du$$

$$= \frac{7}{64} \left(\frac{u^3 \ln u}{3} - \frac{u^3}{9} \right) + C$$

$$= \frac{7}{64} \left[\frac{(4x)^3 \ln (4x)}{3} - \frac{(4x)^3}{9} \right] + C$$

$$= 7x^3 \left[\frac{\ln (4x)}{3} - \frac{1}{9} \right] + C.$$

EXAMPLE 16

Find $\int x^3 e^{3x} dx$.

We shall use formula 39,

$$\int u^n e^{au} du = \frac{u^n e^{au}}{a} - \frac{n}{a} \int u^{n-1} e^{au} du,$$

called a *reduction formula* since it reduces an integral into an expression that involves an integral which is easier to determine. If $u = x$, then $du = dx$ and

$$\int x^3 e^{3x} dx = \int u^3 e^{3u} du$$

$$= \frac{u^3 e^{3u}}{3} - \frac{3}{3} \int u^2 e^{3u} du \qquad (n = 3, a = 3).$$

In the new integral, the exponent of u has been reduced to 2. We apply formula 39 again with $n = 2$ and $a = 3$:

$$\int x^3 e^{3x} dx = \frac{u^3 e^{3u}}{3} - \left(\frac{u^2 e^{3u}}{3} - \frac{2}{3} \int u e^{3u} du \right)$$

$$= \frac{u^3 e^{3u}}{3} - \frac{u^2 e^{3u}}{3} + \frac{2}{3} \int u e^{3u} du.$$

We now apply formula 38,

$$\int u e^{au} du = \frac{e^{au}}{a^2} (au - 1) + C$$

where $a = 3$:

$$\int x^3 e^{3x} dx = \frac{u^3 e^{3u}}{3} - \frac{u^2 e^{3u}}{3} + \frac{2}{3} \left[\frac{e^{3u}}{9} (3u - 1) \right] + C$$

$$= \frac{e^{3u}}{27} (9u^3 - 9u^2 + 6u - 2) + C$$

$$= \frac{e^{3x}}{27} (9x^3 - 9x^2 + 6x - 2) + C.$$

EXAMPLE 17

Find $\int \frac{e^{2x} dx}{7 + e^{2x}}$.

At first glance we do not identify the integrand with any form in the table. Perhaps rewriting the integral will help. Let $u = 7 + e^{2x}$; then $du = 2e^{2x} dx$.

$$\int \frac{e^{2x} dx}{7 + e^{2x}} = \frac{1}{2} \int \frac{(2e^{2x} dx)}{7 + e^{2x}} = \frac{1}{2} \int \frac{du}{u} = \frac{1}{2} \ln |u| + C$$

$$= \tfrac{1}{2} \ln |7 + e^{2x}| + C = \tfrac{1}{2} \ln (7 + e^{2x}) + C.$$

Thus we had only to use our knowledge of basic integration forms. Actually, this form appears as formula 2 in the tables.

EXAMPLE 18

Evaluate $\displaystyle\int_1^4 \frac{dx}{(4x^2 + 2)^{3/2}}.$

We shall use formula 32 to get the indefinite integral first:

$$\int \frac{du}{(u^2 \pm a^2)^{3/2}} = \frac{\pm u}{a^2 \sqrt{u^2 \pm a^2}} + C.$$

Letting $u = 2x$ and $a^2 = 2$, then we have $du = 2\ dx$. Thus

$$\int \frac{dx}{(4x^2 + 2)^{3/2}} = \frac{1}{2} \int \frac{(2\ dx)}{[(2x)^2 + 2]^{3/2}} = \frac{1}{2} \int \frac{du}{(u^2 + 2)^{3/2}}$$

$$= \frac{1}{2} \left[\frac{u}{2\sqrt{u^2 + 2}} \right] + C.$$

Instead of substituting back to x and evaluating from $x = 1$ to $x = 4$, we can determine the corresponding limits of integration with respect to u. Since $u = 2x$, then when $x = 1$ we have $u = 2$; when $x = 4$ we have $u = 8$. Thus

$$\int_1^4 \frac{dx}{(4x^2 + 2)^{3/2}} = \frac{1}{2} \int_2^8 \frac{du}{(u^2 + 2)^{3/2}}$$

$$= \frac{1}{2} \left(\frac{u}{2\sqrt{u^2 + 2}} \right) \Big|_2^8 = \frac{2}{\sqrt{66}} - \frac{1}{2\sqrt{6}}.$$

PITFALL.   *When changing the variable of integration x to the variable of integration u, be certain to change the limits of integration so that they agree with u. **Do not write***

$$\int_1^4 \frac{dx}{(4x^2 + 2)^{3/2}} = \frac{1}{2} \int_1^4 \frac{du}{(u^2 + 2)^{3/2}}.$$

EXERCISE 10-3

In problems 1–34, find the integrals by using the tables in Appendix C.

1. $\int \dfrac{dx}{x(6 + 7x)}$

2. $\int \dfrac{x^2\, dx}{(1 + 2x)^2}$

3. $\int \dfrac{dx}{x\sqrt{x^2 + 9}}$

4. $\int \dfrac{dx}{(x^2 + 7)^{3/2}}$

5. $\int \dfrac{x\, dx}{(2 + 3x)(4 + 5x)}$

6. $\int 2^{5x}\, dx$

7. $\int \dfrac{dx}{4 + 3e^{2x}}$

8. $\int x^2\sqrt{1 + x}\, dx$

9. $\int \dfrac{2\, dx}{x(1 + x)^2}$

10. $\int \dfrac{dx}{x\sqrt{5 - 11x^2}}$

11. $\int \dfrac{x\, dx}{2 + x}$

12. $\int \dfrac{x^2\, dx}{2 + 5x}$

13. $\int \sqrt{x^2 - 3}\, dx$

14. $\int \dfrac{dx}{(4 + 3x)(4x + 3)}$

15. $\int xe^{12x}\, dx$

16. $\int \sqrt{\dfrac{2 + 3x}{5 + 3x}}\, dx$

17. $\int x^2 e^x\, dx$

18. $\int \dfrac{dx}{x^2(1 + x)}$

19. $\int \dfrac{\sqrt{4x^2 + 1}}{x^2}\, dx$

20. $\int \dfrac{dx}{x\sqrt{2 - x}}$

21. $\int \dfrac{x\, dx}{(1 + 3x)^2}$

22. $\int \dfrac{dx}{\sqrt{(1 + 2x)(3 + 2x)}}$

23. $\int \dfrac{dx}{7 - 5x^2}$

24. $\int x^2\sqrt{2x^2 - 9}\, dx$

25. $\int x^5 \ln(3x)\, dx$

26. $\int \dfrac{dx}{x^2(1 + x)^2}$

27. $\int 2x\sqrt{1 + 3x}\, dx$

28. $\int x^2 \ln x\, dx$

29. $\int \dfrac{dx}{\sqrt{4x^2 - 13}}$

30. $\int \dfrac{dx}{x \ln(2x)}$

31. $\displaystyle\int x \ln (2x)\, dx$

32. $\displaystyle\int \frac{\sqrt{2 - 3x^2}}{x}\, dx$

33. $\displaystyle\int \frac{dx}{x^2\sqrt{9 - 4x^2}}$

34. $\displaystyle\int \frac{x^3\, dx}{1 + x^4}$

In problems 35–52, find the integrals by any means.

35. $\displaystyle\int \frac{x\, dx}{x^2 + 1}$

36. $\displaystyle\int \sqrt{x}\; e^{x^{3/2}}\, dx$

37. $\displaystyle\int x\sqrt{2x^2 + 1}\, dx$

38. $\displaystyle\int \frac{4x^2 - \sqrt{x}}{x}\, dx$

39. $\displaystyle\int \frac{dx}{x^2 - 5x + 6}$

40. $\displaystyle\int \frac{e^{2x}}{\sqrt{e^{2x} + 3}}\, dx$

41. $\displaystyle\int x^3 \ln x\, dx$

42. $\displaystyle\int_0^3 xe^{-x}\, dx$

43. $\displaystyle\int xe^{2x}\, dx$

44. $\displaystyle\int_1^2 x^2\sqrt{3 + 2x}\, dx$

45. $\displaystyle\int \ln^2 x\, dx$

46. $\displaystyle\int_1^e \ln x\, dx$

47. $\displaystyle\int_1^2 \frac{x\, dx}{\sqrt{4 - x}}$

48. $\displaystyle\int_1^2 x\sqrt{1 + 2x}\, dx$

49. $\displaystyle\int_0^1 \frac{2x\, dx}{\sqrt{8 - x^2}}$

50. $\displaystyle\int_0^{\ln 2} x^3 e^{2x}\, dx$

51. $\displaystyle\int_1^2 x \ln (2x)\, dx$

52. $\displaystyle\int_1^2 dx$

10-4   IMPROPER INTEGRALS†

A. Infinite Limits

Any integral of the form

$$\int_a^\infty f(x)\, dx, \quad f \text{ continuous on } [a, \infty), \tag{1}$$

---

† May be omitted without loss of continuity.

$$\int_{-\infty}^{b} f(x)\, dx, \quad f \text{ continuous on } (-\infty, b], \tag{2}$$

or

$$\int_{-\infty}^{\infty} f(x)\, dx, \quad f \text{ continuous on } (-\infty, \infty) \tag{3}$$

is called an *improper integral*.† In each case the interval over which the integral is evaluated has infinite length.

We define (1) as follows:

$$\int_{a}^{\infty} f(x)\, dx = \lim_{r \to \infty} \int_{a}^{r} f(x)\, dx.$$

When this limit exists, $\int_{a}^{\infty} f(x)\, dx$ is said to be *convergent* or to *converge to that limit*. When the limit does not exist, the integral is said to be *divergent*.

We can give a geometric interpretation of this improper integral for the case where f is nonnegative for $a < x < \infty$. See Fig. 10-1. The integral $\int_{a}^{r} f(x)\, dx$ is the area under the curve and above the x-axis from $x = a$ to $x = r$. As $r \to \infty$, we may think of $\int_{a}^{r} f(x)\, dx$ as the area of the unbounded region which is shaded in Fig. 10-1. If $\int_{a}^{\infty} f(x)\, dx$ converges, then the unbounded region is considered to have a finite area, and this area is represented by $\int_{a}^{\infty} f(x)\, dx$. If the improper integral is divergent, then the region does not have a finite area.

The improper integral in (2) is defined as

$$\int_{-\infty}^{b} f(x)\, dx = \lim_{r \to -\infty} \int_{r}^{b} f(x)\, dx.$$

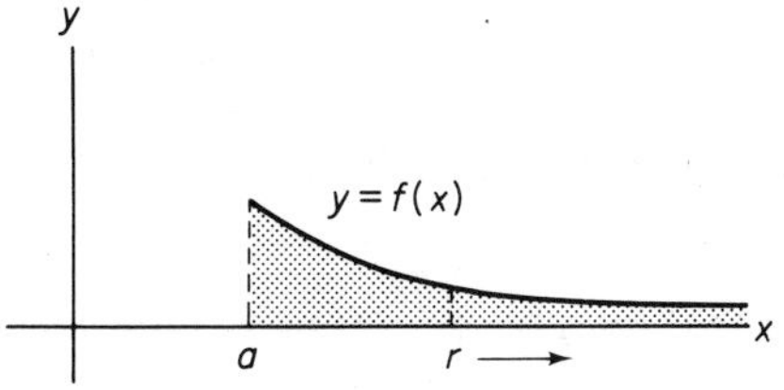

Fig. 10-1

---

†There are also other types of improper integrals.

If this limit exists, $\displaystyle\int_{-\infty}^{b} f(x)\, dx$ is said to be convergent. Otherwise it is divergent.

EXAMPLE 19

Determine whether the following improper integrals are convergent or divergent. If convergent, determine the value of the integral.

a. $\displaystyle\int_{1}^{\infty} \frac{1}{x^3}\, dx.$

$$\int_{1}^{\infty} \frac{1}{x^3}\, dx = \lim_{r\to\infty} \int_{1}^{r} x^{-3}\, dx = \lim_{r\to\infty} -\left.\frac{x^{-2}}{2}\right|_{1}^{r}$$

$$= \lim_{r\to\infty} \left[-\frac{1}{2r^2} + \frac{1}{2} \right] = -0 + \frac{1}{2} = \frac{1}{2}.$$

Therefore $\displaystyle\int_{1}^{\infty} \frac{1}{x^3}\, dx$ converges to $\dfrac{1}{2}$.

b. $\displaystyle\int_{-\infty}^{0} e^x\, dx.$

$$\int_{-\infty}^{0} e^x\, dx = \lim_{r\to-\infty} \int_{r}^{0} e^x\, dx = \lim_{r\to-\infty} e^x \Big|_{r}^{0}$$

$$= \lim_{r\to-\infty} (1 - e^r) = 1 - 0 = 1.$$

Therefore $\displaystyle\int_{-\infty}^{0} e^x\, dx$ converges to 1.

c. $\displaystyle\int_{1}^{\infty} \frac{1}{\sqrt{x}}\, dx.$

$$\int_{1}^{\infty} \frac{1}{\sqrt{x}}\, dx = \lim_{r\to\infty} \int_{1}^{r} x^{-1/2}\, dx = \lim_{r\to\infty} 2x^{1/2} \Big|_{1}^{r}$$

$$= \lim_{r\to\infty} 2(\sqrt{r} - 1) = \infty.$$

Therefore the improper integral diverges.

The improper integral $\displaystyle\int_{-\infty}^{\infty} f(x)\, dx$ is defined in terms of improper integrals of the forms (1) and (2). For any real number a,

$$\int_{-\infty}^{\infty} f(x)\, dx = \int_{-\infty}^{a} f(x)\, dx + \int_{a}^{\infty} f(x)\, dx. \tag{4}$$

If *both* integrals on the right side of (4) are convergent, then $\int_{-\infty}^{\infty} f(x)\, dx$ is said to be convergent; otherwise, it is divergent.

EXAMPLE 20

Determine whether $\int_{-\infty}^{\infty} e^x\, dx$ is convergent or divergent.

$$\int_{-\infty}^{\infty} e^x\, dx = \int_{-\infty}^{a} e^x\, dx + \int_{a}^{\infty} e^x\, dx.$$

Since a can be any real number, we shall choose $a = 0$ for convenience.

$$\int_{-\infty}^{\infty} e^x\, dx = \int_{-\infty}^{0} e^x\, dx + \int_{0}^{\infty} e^x\, dx.$$

By Example 19(b), $\int_{-\infty}^{0} e^x\, dx = 1$. On the other hand,

$$\int_{0}^{\infty} e^x\, dx = \lim_{r \to \infty} \left[\int_{0}^{r} e^x\, dx \right] = \lim_{r \to \infty} e^x \Big|_{0}^{r}$$

$$= \lim_{r \to \infty} (e^r - 1) = \infty.$$

Since $\int_{0}^{\infty} e^x\, dx$ is divergent, $\int_{-\infty}^{\infty} e^x\, dx$ is also divergent.

B. Discontinuous Integrand

Another type of improper integral has the form $\int_{a}^{b} f(x)\, dx$ where f is either

　　i. continuous on $(a, b]$ with an infinite discontinuity as $x \to a^+$,

or

　　ii. continuous on $[a, b)$ with an infinite discontinuity as $x \to b^-$.

When f meets the conditions of i, we define

$$\int_{a}^{b} f(x)\, dx = \lim_{r \to a^+} \int_{r}^{b} f(x)\, dx.$$

When f meets the conditions of ii, we define

$$\int_a^b f(x)\, dx = \lim_{r \to b^-} \int_a^r f(x)\, dx.$$

As usual, these integrals are said to be convergent when the limits exist and divergent otherwise.

EXAMPLE 21

Evaluate each of the following integrals if possible.

a. $\displaystyle\int_0^1 \frac{1}{x}\, dx.$

The function $f(x) = 1/x$ has an infinite discontinuity as $x \to 0^+$ and the integral is improper (see Fig. 10-2).

$$\int_0^1 \frac{1}{x}\, dx = \lim_{r \to 0^+} \int_r^1 \frac{1}{x}\, dx = \lim_{r \to 0^+} [\ln |x|] \Big|_r^1$$

$$= \lim_{r \to 0^+} (\ln 1 - \ln r) = \infty.$$

Therefore, $\displaystyle\int_0^1 \frac{1}{x}\, dx$ does not exist and is divergent.

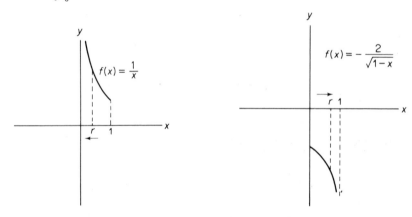

Fig. 10-2	Fig. 10-3

b. $\displaystyle\int_0^1 \frac{-2}{\sqrt{1 - x}}\, dx.$

The integrand has an infinite discontinuity as $x \to 1^-$, and so the integral is improper. See Fig. 10-3.

$$\int_0^1 \frac{-2}{\sqrt{1 - x}}\, dx = \lim_{r \to 1^-} \int_0^r -2(1 - x)^{-1/2}\, dx = \lim_{r \to 1^-} 4(1 - x)^{1/2} \Big|_0^r$$

$$= \lim_{r \to 1^-} 4(\sqrt{1 - r} - 1) = -4;$$

therefore the improper integral converges to -4.

Another type of improper integral has the form $\int_a^b f(x)\,dx$ where f is continuous on $[a, b]$ *except* at c, where $a < c < b$, and such that f has an infinite discontinuity at $x = c$. We define

$$\int_a^b f(x)\,dx = \int_a^c f(x)\,dx + \int_c^b f(x)\,dx.$$

If *both* of the improper integrals on the right are convergent, then $\int_a^b f(x)\,dx$ is convergent; otherwise it is divergent.

EXAMPLE 22

Determine whether $\int_1^5 \dfrac{1}{(x-3)^2}\,dx$ *is convergent or divergent.*

The function $f(x) = 1/(x-3)^2$ has an infinite discontinuity when $x = 3$ and so the integral is improper (see Fig. 10-4).

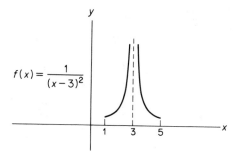

$$f(x) = \frac{1}{(x-3)^2}$$

Fig. 10-4

$$\int_1^5 \frac{1}{(x-3)^2}\,dx = \int_1^3 \frac{1}{(x-3)^2}\,dx + \int_3^5 \frac{1}{(x-3)^2}\,dx.$$

However,

$$\int_1^3 \frac{1}{(x-3)^2}\,dx = \lim_{r \to 3^-} \int_1^r \frac{1}{(x-3)^2}\,dx$$

$$= \lim_{r \to 3^-} -\frac{1}{x-3}\bigg|_1^r$$

$$= \lim_{r \to 3^-} \left[-\frac{1}{r-3} - \frac{1}{2} \right] = \infty.$$

Since $\displaystyle\int_1^3 (x-3)^{-2}\,dx$ is divergent, $\displaystyle\int_1^5 (x-3)^{-2}\,dx$ must also be divergent. In this case

it is immaterial whether $\displaystyle\int_3^5 (x-3)^{-2}\,dx$ is convergent or divergent (although it actually

is divergent).

EXERCISE 10-4

In problems 1–12, determine the integrals, if they exist. Indicate those which are divergent.

1. $\displaystyle\int_3^\infty \frac{1}{x^2}\,dx$

2. $\displaystyle\int_2^\infty \frac{1}{(2x-1)^3}\,dx$

3. $\displaystyle\int_1^\infty \frac{1}{x}\,dx$

4. $\displaystyle\int_1^\infty \frac{1}{\sqrt[3]{x+1}}\,dx$

5. $\displaystyle\int_1^\infty e^{-x}\,dx$

6. $\displaystyle\int_0^\infty (5+e^{-x})\,dx$

7. $\displaystyle\int_1^\infty \frac{1}{\sqrt{x}}\,dx$

8. $\displaystyle\int_4^\infty \frac{x\,dx}{\sqrt{(x^2+9)^3}}$

9. $\displaystyle\int_{-\infty}^{-2} \frac{1}{(x+1)^3}\,dx$

10. $\displaystyle\int_{-\infty}^3 \frac{1}{\sqrt{7-x}}\,dx$

11. $\displaystyle\int_{-\infty}^\infty xe^{-x^2}\,dx$

12. $\displaystyle\int_{-\infty}^\infty (5-3x)\,dx$

In problems 13–24, determine the integrals, if they exist. Indicate those which are divergent.

13. $\displaystyle\int_0^9 \frac{1}{\sqrt{x}}\,dx$

14. $\displaystyle\int_1^2 \frac{1}{x-1}\,dx$

15. $\displaystyle\int_0^3 \frac{x}{\sqrt{9-x^2}}\,dx$

16. $\displaystyle\int_0^1 \frac{1}{\sqrt{1-x}}\,dx$

17. $\displaystyle\int_0^3 \frac{x}{9-x^2}\,dx$

18. $\displaystyle\int_0^1 \frac{1}{x^3}\,dx$

19. $\displaystyle\int_0^1 \frac{1}{x+7}\,dx$

20. $\displaystyle\int_{-1}^1 \frac{dx}{\sqrt[3]{x}}$

21. $\displaystyle\int_{-1}^1 \frac{1}{x^2}\,dx$

22. $\displaystyle\int_{-2}^2 \frac{1}{x-1}\,dx$

23. $\displaystyle\int_{-1}^1 \frac{1}{x^{2/3}}\,dx$

24. $\displaystyle\int_{-100}^0 \frac{1}{\sqrt{-x}}\,dx$

In problems 25–26, determine the integrals, if they exist. Indicate those which are divergent.

25. $\displaystyle\int_1^\infty xe^x\,dx$

26. $\displaystyle\int_1^\infty x\ln x\,dx$

27. In statistics, a function $f(x)$ where $f(x)\ge 0$ is called a density function if

$$\int_{-\infty}^\infty f(x)\,dx = 1.$$

To show that

$$f(x) = \begin{cases} 2e^{-2x}, & \text{if } x \geq 0 \\ 0, & \text{if } x < 0 \end{cases}$$

is a density function, it suffices to show that $\int_0^\infty 2e^{-2x}\,dx = 1$. Evaluate this integral.

28. If $100 is deposited today at 6 percent compounded annually, then in one year its value is $106. We say that $106 one year from now has a *present value* of $100 at 6 percent. For the Steady-State Company, the present value of all total future profits is (in dollars)

$$\int_0^\infty 240{,}000e^{-.06t}\,dt.$$

Evaluate this integral.

29. In discussing entrance of a firm into an industry, Stigler † uses the equation

$$V = \pi_0 \int_0^\infty e^{\theta t}e^{-\rho t}\,dt$$

where π_0, θ, and ρ are constants. Show that $V = \pi_0/(\rho - \theta)$ if $\theta < \rho$.

30. Find the area of the region in the first quadrant bounded by the curve $y = e^{-2x}$ and the x-axis.

10-5　DIFFERENTIAL EQUATIONS

Occasionally you may run into an equation that involves the derivative (or differential) of an unknown function. For example,

$$\frac{dy}{dx} = xy^2 \tag{1}$$

is such an equation. It is called a *differential equation*. More precisely, it is a *first order differential equation* since it involves a derivative of the first order and none of higher order. A solution of Eq. (1) is any function $y = f(x)$ defined on an interval which satisfies Eq. (1) for all x in the interval.

To solve

$$\frac{dy}{dx} = xy^2, \tag{2}$$

we consider dy/dx a quotient of differentials and proceed to "separate variables" by getting x's on one side and y's on the other:

---

† G. Stigler, *The Theory of Price*, 3rd ed., The Macmillan Co., New York, 1966, p. 344.

$$\frac{dy}{y^2} = x\,dx.$$

Integrating both sides, we obtain

$$\int \frac{1}{y^2}\,dy = \int x\,dx$$

$$-\frac{1}{y} = \frac{x^2}{2} + C_1$$

$$-\frac{1}{y} = \frac{x^2 + 2C_1}{2}. \qquad (3)$$

Letting $2C_1 = C$ and solving Eq. (3) for y, we have

$$y = \frac{-2}{x^2 + C}. \qquad (4)$$

On any interval on which y is defined, we can verify that y is a solution to differential equation (2):

$$\frac{dy}{dx} \overset{?}{=} xy^2$$

$$\frac{4x}{(x^2 + C)^2} \overset{?}{=} x\left[\frac{-2}{x^2 + C}\right]^2$$

$$\frac{4x}{(x^2 + C)^2} = \frac{4x}{(x^2 + C)^2}.$$

Note in Eq. (4) that for *each* value of C, a different solution is obtained. We speak of Eq. (4) as the *general solution* of the differential equation. The method that we used to get it is called *separation of variables*.

In the example above, suppose we are given the further condition that $y = -\frac{2}{3}$ when $x = 1$; that is, $y(1) = -\frac{2}{3}$. Then the *particular* function that satisfies Eq. (2) can be found by substituting the values $x = 1$ and $y = -\frac{2}{3}$ into Eq. (4) and solving for C:

$$-\frac{2}{3} = -\frac{2}{1^2 + C}$$

$$C = 2.$$

Therefore, the solution of $dy/dx = xy^2$ such that $y(1) = -\frac{2}{3}$ is

$$y = -\frac{2}{x^2 + 2}. \tag{5}$$

We speak of Eq. (5) as a *particular solution* to the differential equation.

EXAMPLE 23

Find the demand function $p = f(x)$ if the point elasticity of demand is -1 for $x > 0$.

From Sec. 8-7 the point elasticity of demand, η, is given by

$$\eta = \frac{\dfrac{p}{x}}{\dfrac{dp}{dx}}.$$

Since $\eta = -1$ for $x > 0$,

$$-1 = \frac{\dfrac{p}{x}}{\dfrac{dp}{dx}}, \qquad x > 0. \tag{6}$$

Separating variables and integrating, we have

$$\frac{dp}{dx} = -\frac{p}{x}$$

$$\frac{dp}{p} = -\frac{dx}{x}$$

$$\int \frac{1}{p}\, dp = -\int \frac{1}{x}\, dx$$

$$\ln |p| = C_1 - \ln x. \tag{7}$$

Since p represents price and [from Eq. (6)] $p \neq 0$, then $p > 0$. Thus $\ln |p| = \ln p$. The constant of integration, C_1, can be any real number. Since the range of the logarithmic function is all real numbers, C_1 can be replaced by $\ln C$ where $C > 0$. Therefore Eq. (7) becomes

$$\ln p = \ln C - \ln x.$$

Using properties of logarithms, we have

$$\ln p = \ln \left(\frac{C}{x}\right).$$

This can only happen if

$$p = \frac{C}{x}, \qquad C, x > 0.$$

Thus *any demand function with unit elasticity must have the form* $p = C/x$, *where* $C > 0$ *and* $x > 0$.

Let us now focus our attention on compound interest. Suppose P_0 dollars are invested at an annual rate r compounded n times a year. Let the function $P = P(t)$ give the total amount P present after t years from the date of the initial investment. Then the initial principal is $P(0) = P_0$. Furthermore, since there are n interest periods per year, each period has length $1/n$ years, which we shall denote by Δt. At the end of the first period, the accrued interest for that period is added to the principal, and the sum acts as the principal for the second period, etc. Hence, if the beginning of an interest period occurs at time t, then the increase in the amount present (that is, the interest earned) at the end of a period of Δt is $P(t + \Delta t) - P(t) = \Delta P$. Equivalently, the interest earned is principal times rate times time:

$$\Delta P = P \cdot r \cdot \Delta t.$$

Dividing both members by Δt, we obtain

$$\frac{\Delta P}{\Delta t} = rP. \tag{8}$$

As $\Delta t \to 0$, then $n = \dfrac{1}{\Delta t} \to \infty$ and consequently interest is being *compounded continuously*; that is, the principal is subject to continuous growth at every instant. However as $\Delta t \to 0$, then $\Delta P/\Delta t \to dP/dt$ and Eq. (8) takes the form

$$\frac{dP}{dt} = rP. \tag{9}$$

This differential equation means that *when interest is compounded continuously, the rate of change of the amount of money present at time t is proportional to the amount present at time t.*

To determine the actual function P, we solve differential equation (9) by the method of separation of variables.

$$\frac{dP}{dt} = rP$$

$$\frac{dP}{P} = r \, dt$$

$$\int \frac{1}{P} \, dP = \int r \, dt$$

$$\ln |P| = rt + C_1.$$

Since it can be assumed that $P > 0$, then $\ln |P| = \ln P$.

$$\ln P = rt + C_1.$$

Solving for P, we have

$$P = e^{rt + C_1} = e^{C_1} e^{rt}.$$

Replacing e^{C_1} by C, we obtain

$$P = Ce^{rt}.$$

Since $P(0) = P_0$,

$$P_0 = Ce^{r(0)}.$$

Hence $C = P_0$ and

$$P = P_0 e^{rt}. \tag{10}$$

Equation (10) gives the total value after t years of an initial investment of P_0 dollars, compounded continuously at an annual rate r. For example, if \$100 is invested at an annual rate of 5 percent compounded continuously, then the total value of the investment at the end of one year is

$$P = 100e^{.05(1)} = \$105.13.$$

We can compare this value with the value after one year of an initial \$100 investment at an annual rate of 5 percent compounded semiannually—namely, \$105.06. The difference is not significant.

In our compound interest discussion we saw from Eq. (9) that the rate of change in the amount present was proportional to the amount present. There are many natural quantities, such as population, whose rate of growth or decay at any time is considered proportional to the amount of that quantity present.

If N denotes the amount of such a quantity at time t, then the above rate of growth means

$$\frac{dN}{dt} = kN.$$

If we separate variables and solve for N as we did for Eq. (9), we get

$$N = N_0 e^{kt}, \tag{11}$$

where N_0 and k are constants. Due to the form of Eq. (11), we say that the quantity follows an **exponential law of growth.**

EXAMPLE 24

In a certain Australian town, the rate at which the population grows at any time is proportional to the size of the population. If the population was 125,000 in 1940 and 140,000 in 1960, what is the expected population in 1980?

Let N be the size of the population at time t. Since the exponential law of growth applies,

$$N = N_0 e^{kt}.$$

We must first find the constants N_0 and k. The year 1940 will correspond to $t = 0$. Thus $t = 20$ is 1960 and $t = 40$ is 1980. Now, if $t = 0$, then $N = 125{,}000$. Thus

$$N = N_0 e^{kt}$$

$$125{,}000 = N_0 e^0 = N_0.$$

Hence

$$N = 125{,}000 e^{kt}.$$

But if $t = 20$, then $N = 140{,}000$. This means

$$140{,}000 = 125{,}000 e^{20k}.$$

Thus

$$e^{20k} = \frac{140{,}000}{125{,}000} = 1.12$$

$$20k = \ln(1.12)$$

$$k = \tfrac{1}{20} \ln(1.12).$$

Therefore,

$$N = 125{,}000 e^{(t/20)\,\ln\,1.12} \tag{12}$$

$$= 125{,}000 \big[e^{\ln\,1.12} \big]^{t/20}$$

$$N = 125{,}000(1.12)^{t/20}. \tag{13}$$

If $t = 40$,

$$N = 125{,}000(1.12)^2$$

$$= 156{,}800.$$

Note that we can write Eq. (12) in a form different from Eq. (13). Since $\ln 1.12 \approx .11333$, then $k = .11333/20 \approx .0057$. Thus

$$N \approx 125{,}000 e^{.0057t}.$$

EXERCISE 10-5

In problems 1–8, solve the differential equations.

1. $\dfrac{dy}{dx} = 2xy^2$

2. $\dfrac{dy}{dx} = x^3 y^3$

3. $\dfrac{dy}{dx} = y, \quad y > 0$ 4. $\dfrac{dy}{dx} = \dfrac{x}{y}$

5. $\dfrac{dy}{dx} = \dfrac{y}{x}, \quad x, y > 0$ 6. $\dfrac{dy}{dx} = e^x y^2$

7. $\dfrac{dy}{dx} - x\sqrt{x^2 + 1} = 0$ 8. $\dfrac{dy}{dx} + xe^x = 0$

In problems 9–14, solve each of the differential equations subject to the given conditions.

9. $\dfrac{dy}{dx} = \dfrac{1}{y}; \quad y > 0, \ y(2) = 2$

10. $\dfrac{dy}{dx} = e^{x-y}; \quad y(0) = 0.$ *Hint:* $e^{x-y} = e^x/e^y.$

11. $e^y \dfrac{dy}{dx} - x^2 = 0; \quad y = 0$ when $x = 0$

12. $x^2 \dfrac{dy}{dx} + \dfrac{1}{y^2} = 0; \quad y(1) = 2$

13. $(4x^2 + 3)^2 \dfrac{dy}{dx} - 4xy^2 = 0; \quad y(0) = \dfrac{3}{2}$

14. $\dfrac{dy}{dx} + x^2 y = 0; \quad y > 0, \ y = 1$ when $x = 0$

15. Find the demand function $p = f(x)$ for $x > 0$ if the point elasticity of demand is k where k is constant.

16. Find the demand function $p = f(x)$ for $x > 0$ if the point elasticity of demand is $\eta = p/(p - 20)$ and $p = 10$ when $x = 20$. Assume $0 < p < 20$.

17. Find the value of an initial investment of \$200 after 20 years if interest is compounded continuously at an annual rate of 4 percent.

18. Repeat Problem 17 if the initial investment is \$5000 and the period is t years.

19. In a certain town the population at any time changes at a rate proportional to the population. If the population in 1965 was 20,000 and in 1975 it was 24,000, find an equation for the population at time t, where t is the number of years past 1965. Write your answer in two forms, one involving e. You may assume $\ln 1.2 = .18$. What is the expected population in 1985?

20. The population of a town increases by natural growth at a rate which is proportional to the number N of persons present. If the population at time $t = 0$ is 10,000, find two expressions for the population N, t years later, if the population doubles in 50 years. Assume $\ln 2 = .69$. Also, find N for $t = 100$.

21. Suppose the population of the world in 1930 was 2 billion and in 1960 it was 3 billion. If the exponential law of growth is assumed, what is the expected population in 2000? Assume $\ln \frac{3}{2} = .405$.

22. The population of Sigmatown doubles every 10 years due to exponential growth. At a certain time the population is 10,000. Find an expression for the number of people N at time t years later. Assume $\ln 2 = .69$.

23. If exponential growth is assumed, in approximately how many years will a population triple if it doubles in 50 years? *Hint:* Let the population at $t = 0$ be N_0. Assume $\ln 3 = 1.09$ and $\ln 2 = .69$.

10-6 REVIEW

Important Terms and Symbols in Chapter 10

integration by parts *(p. 391)*

partial fractions *(p. 396)*

improper integral *(p. 410)*

separation of variables *(p. 418)*

first-order differential equation *(p. 417)*

interest compounded continuously *(p. 420)*

exponential growth *(p. 421)*

$$\int_a^\infty f(x)\,dx, \int_{-\infty}^b f(x)\,dx,$$

$$\int_{-\infty}^\infty f(x)\,dx \ (p.\ 410)$$

Review Section

†**1.** $\int u\,dv = uv - \int v\,du$ is called the _____ formula.

Ans. integration by parts

†**2.** To express $5/[x^3(x^2 + 9)]$ as a sum of partial fractions, the number of constants that you must determine is _____.

Ans. 5

†**3.** If $\lim\limits_{r \to \infty} \int_a^r f(x)\,dx$ exists, then $\int_a^\infty f(x)\,dx$ is said to be (convergent)(divergent).

Ans. convergent

---

† Refers to Sections 10-1, 10-2, or 10-4.

†4. $\displaystyle\int_0^\infty e^x\, dx$ is (convergent) (divergent).

> *Ans.* divergent

5. The equation $x^3\dfrac{dy}{dx} + y^2 = 0$ is called a _____ equation.

> *Ans.* first-order differential

6. Exponential growth of a quantity means the quantity at any time changes at a rate proportional to _____.

> *Ans.* the amount of the quantity

Review Problems

In problems 1–18, determine the integrals.

1. $\displaystyle\int x \ln x\, dx$

2. $\displaystyle\int \frac{1}{\sqrt{4x^2 + 1}}\, dx$

3. $\displaystyle\int_0^2 \sqrt{4x^2 + 9}\, dx$

4. $\displaystyle\int \frac{2x}{3 - 4x}\, dx$

5. $\displaystyle\int \frac{x\, dx}{(2 + 3x)(3 + x)}$

6. $\displaystyle\int_e^{e^2} \frac{1}{x \ln x}\, dx$

7. $\displaystyle\int \frac{dx}{x(x + 2)^2}$

8. $\displaystyle\int \frac{dx}{x^2 - 1}$

9. $\displaystyle\int \frac{dx}{x^2\sqrt{9 - 16x^2}}$

10. $\displaystyle\int x^2 \ln 4x\, dx$

11. $\displaystyle\int \frac{9\, dx}{x^2 - 9}$

12. $\displaystyle\int \frac{3x}{\sqrt{1 + 3x}}\, dx$

13. $\displaystyle\int xe^{7x}\, dx$

14. $\displaystyle\int \frac{dx}{2 + 3e^{4x}}$

15. $\displaystyle\int \frac{dx}{2x \ln 2x}$

16. $\displaystyle\int \frac{dx}{x(2 + x)}$

17. $\displaystyle\int \frac{2x}{3 + 2x}\, dx$

18. $\displaystyle\int \frac{dx}{\sqrt{4x^2 - 9}}$

---

†Refers to Sections 10-1, 10-2, or 10-4.

In problems 19–24, determine the improper integrals, if they exist.† Indicate those which are divergent.

19. $\displaystyle\int_{3}^{\infty} \frac{1}{x^3}\, dx$

20. $\displaystyle\int_{-\infty}^{0} e^{3x}\, dx$

21. $\displaystyle\int_{0}^{2} \frac{1}{x - 2}\, dx$

22. $\displaystyle\int_{0}^{1} \frac{x}{\sqrt{1 - x^2}}\, dx$

23. $\displaystyle\int_{1}^{\infty} \frac{1}{2x}\, dx$

24. $\displaystyle\int_{-\infty}^{\infty} xe^{1-x^2}\, dx$

In problems 25–26, solve the differential equations.

25. $\displaystyle\frac{dy}{dx} = 3x^2 y + 2xy, \quad y > 0$

26. $\displaystyle\frac{dy}{dx} - 2xe^{x^2 - y + 3} = 0, \quad y(0) = 3$

27. Find the amount after 14 years of an investment of $100 compounded continuously at 5 percent.

28. The population of a city in 1960 was 100,000 and in 1975 it was 120,000. Assuming exponential growth, project the population in 1990.

---

† Refers to Sec. 10-4.

Chapter 11

Multivariable Calculus

11-1 FUNCTIONS OF SEVERAL VARIABLES

Suppose a manufacturer produces two products, X and Y. His total cost is dependent on the levels of production of *both* X and Y. Table 11-1 shows a total cost schedule which indicates his total cost at various levels of production. For example, when 5 units of X and 6 units of Y are produced, the total cost is 17. Corresponding to this particular production situation, it seems natural to associate the number 17 with the ordered pair (5, 6):

$$(5, 6) \to 17.$$

The first element of the ordered pair represents the number of units of X produced while the second element represents the number of units of Y produced. Corresponding to the other production situations, we have

$$(5, 7) \to 19,$$

$$(6, 6) \to 18,$$

and

$$(6, 7) \to 20.$$

TABLE 11-1

NO. OF UNITS OF X PRODUCED (x)	NO. OF UNITS OF Y PRODUCED (y)	TOTAL COST OF PRODUCTION (c)
5	6	17
5	7	19
6	6	18
6	7	20

This correspondence can be considered an input-output relation where the inputs are ordered pairs. Note that with each input we associate exactly one output. Thus the correspondence defines a function f such that

$$\text{domain of } f = \{(5, 6), (5, 7), (6, 6), (6, 7)\}$$

and

$$\text{range of } f = \{17, 19, 18, 20\}.$$

In function notation,

$$f(5, 6) = 17 \qquad f(6, 6) = 18$$
$$f(5, 7) = 19 \qquad f(6, 7) = 20.$$

We say that the total cost schedule of this manufacturer can be described by $c = f(x, y)$, a function of the two independent variables x and y. The letter c is the dependent variable.

Turning to another function of two variables, we see that the equation

$$z = \frac{2}{x^2 + y^2}$$

defines z as a function of x and y:

$$z = f(x, y) = \frac{2}{x^2 + y^2}.$$

The domain of f is all ordered pairs of real numbers (x, y) for which the equation has meaning when the first and second elements of (x, y) are substituted for x and y, respectively, in the equation. Thus the domain of f is all ordered pairs except $(0, 0)$. To find $f(2, 3)$, for example, we substitute $x = 2$ and $y = 3$ into $2/(x^2 + y^2)$. Hence $f(2, 3) = 2/(2^2 + 3^2) = \frac{2}{13}$.

For most functions of two variables that describe business and economic situations, the values of the variables are usually nonnegative.

EXAMPLE 1

a. $f(x, y) = \dfrac{x + 3}{y - 2}$ defines f as a function of two variables. Since $(x + 3)/(y - 2)$ is not defined when $y = 2$, the domain of f is all (x, y) such that $y \neq 2$.

Some functional values of f are

$$f(0, 3) = \frac{0 + 3}{3 - 2} = 3,$$

and

$$f(3, 0) = \frac{3 + 3}{0 - 2} = -3.$$

Note that $f(0, 3) \neq f(3, 0)$.

b. $g(r, s) = 2r - 3s + 5$ defines g as a function of two variables, r and s. The domain of g is all ordered pairs (r, s).

$$g(4, 7) = 2(4) - 3(7) + 5 = -8.$$

$$g(r + h, s) = 2(r + h) - 3s + 5.$$

c. $h(x, y) = 4x$ defines h as a function of x and y. The domain is all ordered pairs of real numbers.

$$h(2, 5) = 4(2) = 8$$

$$h(2, 6) = 4(2) = 8.$$

d. If $z^2 = x^2 + y^2$ and $x = 3$ and $y = 4$, then $z^2 = 3^2 + 4^2 = 25$. Consequently $z = \pm 5$. Thus, with the ordered pair $(3, 4)$ we *cannot* associate exactly one output number. Hence z is not a function of x and y.

     In Chapter 3 we saw that if $y = f(x)$ is a function of one variable, the domain of f can be geometrically represented by points on the real number line. The function itself can be represented by its graph in a rectangular coordinate plane, sometimes called a two-dimensional rectangular coordinate system. However, for a function of two variables, $z = f(x, y)$, its domain (consisting of ordered pairs of real numbers) can be geometrically represented by a *region* in the plane. The function itself can be geometrically represented in a *three-dimensional* rectangular coordinate system. Such a system is formed when three mutually perpendicular real number lines in space intersect at the origin of each line (Fig. 11-1). The three number lines are commonly called the x-, y-, and z-axes and their point of intersection is called the origin of the system.

     With each point P in space we can associate a unique ordered triple of numbers. To do this [see Fig. 11-2(a)], a perpendicular line is constructed from P to the x,y-plane (that is, the *coordinate plane* formed by the x- and

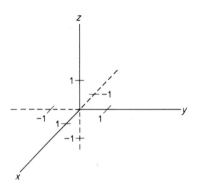

Fig. 11-1

y-axes). Letting *Q* be the point where the line intersects this plane, we construct perpendiculars to the *x*- and *y*-axes from *Q*. These lines intersect the *x*-axis and the *y*-axis at points corresponding to the numbers x_0 and y_0, respectively. From *P* a perpendicular to the *z*-axis is constructed which intersects the *z*-axis at a point corresponding to the number z_0. Thus with the point *P* we associate the ordered triple (x_0, y_0, z_0). The converse should be evident, namely, that with each ordered triple of numbers, we can associate a unique point in space. Due to this one-to-one correspondence between points in space and ordered triples, an ordered triple may be called a point. In Fig. 11-2(b) the points (2, 0, 0), (2, 3, 0), and (2, 3, 4) are illustrated. Note that the origin corresponds to (0, 0, 0).

Suppose we wish to represent geometrically a function of two variables, $z = f(x, y)$. Then to each ordered pair (x, y) in the domain of *f* we assign the point $(x, y, f(x, y))$. The set of all such points is called the *graph* of *f*. Such a graph appears in Fig. 11-3. You can consider $z = f(x, y)$ as representing a surface in space.†

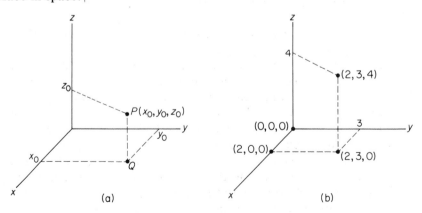

Fig. 11-2

---

†We shall freely use the term "surface" in the intuitive sense.

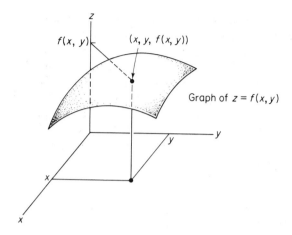

Fig. 11-3

In Chapter 6, continuity of a function of one variable was discussed. We saw there that if $y = f(x)$ defines a function which is continuous at $x = x_0$, then points near x_0 will have their functional values near $f(x_0)$. Extending this concept to a function of two variables, we say that the function $z = f(x, y)$ is continuous at (x_0, y_0) when points near (x_0, y_0) have their functional values near $f(x_0, y_0)$. Loosely interpreting this and without delving into the concept in great depth, we can say that a function will be continuous on its domain (that is, continuous at each point in its domain) if its graph is a "connected surface." In the following sections of this chapter we shall see that when a function is continuous, we can make important mathematical generalizations.

Until now, we have considered only functions of either one or two variables. In general, a function of n variables is one whose domain consists of ordered n-tuples $(x_1, x_2, ..., x_n)$. For example, $f(x, y, z) = 2x + 3y + 4z$ defines a function of three variables with a domain consisting of all ordered triples. The function $g(x_1, x_2, x_3, x_4) = x_1 x_2 x_3 x_4$ is a function of four variables with a domain consisting of all ordered 4-tuples. Although functions of several variables are extremely important and useful, we cannot represent functions of more than two variables geometrically.

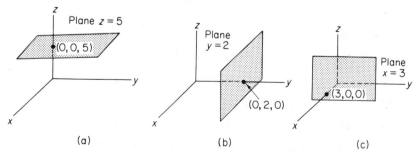

Fig. 11-4

We conclude this section with a discussion of planes that are parallel to a coordinate plane. By "coordinate planes" we mean the x,y-plane, the x,z-plane, and the y,z-plane. Suppose S is a plane which is parallel to the x,y-plane and which also passes through the point $(0, 0, 5)$ [see Fig. 11-4(a)]. Then the point (x, y, z) will lie on S if and only if $z = 5$; that is, x and y can be any real numbers, but z must equal 5. For this reason we say $z = 5$ is an equation of S. Similarly, an equation of the plane parallel to the x,z-plane and passing through the point $(0, 2, 0)$ is $y = 2$ [Fig. 11-4(b)]. The equation $x = 3$ is an equation of the plane passing through $(3, 0, 0)$ and parallel to the y,z-plane [Fig. 11-4(c)].

EXERCISE 11-1

In problems 1–12, determine the given functional values for the indicated functions.

1. $f(x, y) = 3x + y - 1; f(0, 4)$

2. $f(x, y) = xy^2 + 2; f(1, -4)$

3. $g(x, y, z) = ze^{x+y}; g(-2, 2, 6)$

4. $g(x, y, z) = xy + xz + yz; g(1, 2, -3)$

5. $h(r, s, t, u) = \dfrac{r + s^2}{t - u}; h(-3, 3, 5, 4)$

6. $h(r, s, t, u) = \ln(ru); h(1, 5, 3, 1)$

7. $g(p_A, p_B) = 2p_A(p_A^2 - 5); g(4, 8)$

8. $g(p_A, p_B) = p_A\sqrt{p_B} + 10; g(8, 4)$

9. $F(x, y, z) = 3; F(2, 0, -1)$

10. $F(x, y, z) = \dfrac{x}{yz}; F(0, 0, 3)$

11. $f(x, y) = 2x - 5y + 4; f(x_0 + h, y_0)$

12. $f(x, y) = x^2y - 3y^3; f(r + t, r)$

In problems 13–17, find equations of the planes that satisfy the given conditions.

13. Parallel to the x, z-plane and passes through the point $(0, -4, 0)$.

14. Parallel to the y, z-plane and passes through the point $(8, 0, 0)$.

15. Parallel to the x, y-plane and passes through the point $(2, 7, 6)$.

16. Parallel to the y, z-plane and passes through the point $(-4, -2, 7)$.

17. Parallel to the x, z-plane and passes through the point (x_0, y_0, z_0).

11-2   PARTIAL DERIVATIVES

Figure 11-5 shows the graph of a function $z = f(x, y)$ and a plane which is parallel to the x, z-plane and passes through the point $(x_0, y_0, f(x_0, y_0))$ on the graph. An equation of this plane is $y = y_0$. Hence any point on the curve cut from the surface by the plane must have the form $(x, y_0, f(x, y_0))$. Thus

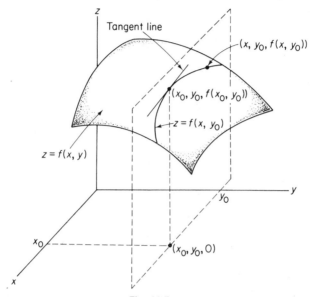

Fig. 11-5

the curve can be described by $z = f(x, y_0)$. Since y_0 is constant, $z = f(x, y_0)$ can be considered a function of one variable, x. When the derivative of this function of x is evaluated at x_0, it gives the slope of the tangent line to this curve at $(x_0, y_0, f(x_0, y_0))$. See Fig. 11-5. This slope is called the partial derivative of f with respect to x at (x_0, y_0) and is denoted $f_x(x_0, y_0)$. In terms of limits,

$$f_x(x_0, y_0) = \lim_{h \to 0} \frac{f(x_0 + h, y_0) - f(x_0, y_0)}{h}. \qquad (1)$$

On the other hand, in Fig. 11-6 the plane $x = x_0$ is parallel to the y, z-plane and cuts the surface $z = f(x, y)$ in a curve given by $z = f(x_0, y)$, a function of y. When the derivative of this function of y is evaluated at y_0, it gives the slope of the tangent line to this curve at the point $(x_0, y_0, f(x_0, y_0))$. This slope is called the partial derivative of f with respect to y at (x_0, y_0) and is denoted $f_y(x_0, y_0)$. In terms of limits,

$$f_y(x_0, y_0) = \lim_{h \to 0} \frac{f(x_0, y_0 + h) - f(x_0, y_0)}{h}. \qquad (2)$$

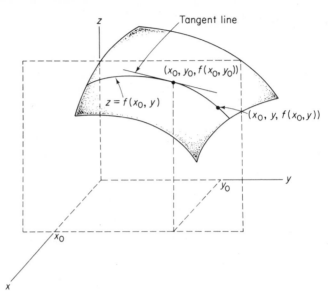

Fig. 11-6

Sometimes $f_x(x_0, y_0)$ is said to be the slope at $(x_0, y_0, f(x_0, y_0))$ of the tangent line to the graph of f *in the x-direction*; similarly $f_y(x_0, y_0)$ is the slope of the tangent line *in the y-direction*.

For generality, by replacing x_0 and y_0 in Eqs. (1) and (2) by x and y, respectively, we get the following definition.

DEFINITION.   *If $z = f(x, y)$, the **partial derivative of f with respect to x**, denoted $f_x(x, y)$, is*

$$f_x(x, y) = \lim_{h \to 0} \frac{f(x + h, y) - f(x, y)}{h}$$

provided this limit exists.
*The **partial derivative of f with respect to y**, denoted $f_y(x, y)$, is*

$$f_y(x, y) = \lim_{h \to 0} \frac{f(x, y + h) - f(x, y)}{h}$$

provided this limit exists.

EXAMPLE 2

If $f(x, y) = xy^2 + x^2 y$, find $f_x(x, y)$ and $f_y(x, y)$. Also find $f_x(3, 4)$ and $f_y(3, 4)$.
By the definition of $f_x(x, y)$,

$$f_x(x, y) = \lim_{h \to 0} \frac{f(x + h, y) - f(x, y)}{h}$$

$$= \lim_{h \to 0} \frac{[(x + h)y^2 + (x + h)^2 y] - [xy^2 + x^2 y]}{h}$$

$$= \lim_{h \to 0} \frac{xy^2 + hy^2 + x^2 y + 2xhy + h^2 y - xy^2 - x^2 y}{h}$$

$$= \lim_{h \to 0} (y^2 + 2xy + hy) = y^2 + 2xy.$$

Therefore,

$$f_x(x, y) = y^2 + 2xy.$$

To find $f_x(3, 4)$ we evaluate $f_x(x, y)$ when $x = 3$ and $y = 4$.

$$f_x(3, 4) = 4^2 + 2(3)(4) = 40.$$

By the definition of $f_y(x, y)$,

$$f_y(x, y) = \lim_{h \to 0} \frac{f(x, y + h) - f(x, y)}{h}$$

$$= \lim_{h \to 0} \frac{[x(y + h)^2 + x^2(y + h)] - [xy^2 + x^2 y]}{h}$$

$$= \lim_{h \to 0} \frac{xy^2 + 2xyh + xh^2 + x^2 y + x^2 h - xy^2 - x^2 y}{h}$$

$$= \lim_{h \to 0} (2xy + xh + x^2) = 2xy + x^2.$$

Therefore,

$$f_y(x, y) = 2xy + x^2.$$

Evaluating when $x = 3$ and $y = 4$, we have

$$f_y(3, 4) = 2(3)(4) + 3^2 = 33.$$

Note that $f_x(x, y)$ and $f_y(x, y)$ are each functions of the two variables x and y.

From its definition we see that to find $f_x(x, y)$ we treat y as a constant and differentiate $f(x, y)$ with respect to x in the usual way. For example, if $f(x, y) = xy^2 + x^2 y$, then by treating y as a constant and differentiating with respect to x we have

$$f_x(x, y) = (1)y^2 + (2x)y = y^2 + 2xy$$

as was shown in Example 2.

Similarly, to find $f_y(x, y)$ we treat x as a constant and differentiate f with respect to y in the usual way. Thus for $f(x, y) = xy^2 + x^2 y$,

$$f_y(x, y) = x(2y) + x^2(1) = 2xy + x^2,$$

as was shown in Example 2.

Other notations for partial derivatives of $z = f(x, y)$ are in Table 11-2.

TABLE 11-2

PARTIAL DERIVATIVE OF f (OR z) WITH RESPECT TO x	PARTIAL DERIVATIVE OF f (OR z) WITH RESPECT TO y
$f_x(x, y)$	$f_y(x, y)$
f_x	f_y
$\dfrac{\partial f}{\partial x}$	$\dfrac{\partial f}{\partial y}$
$\dfrac{\partial}{\partial x}[f(x, y)]$	$\dfrac{\partial}{\partial y}[f(x, y)]$
$\dfrac{\partial z}{\partial x}$	$\dfrac{\partial z}{\partial y}$

Table 11-3 gives notations for partial derivatives evaluated at (x_0, y_0).

TABLE 11-3

PARTIAL DERIVATIVE OF f (OR z) WITH RESPECT TO x EVALUATED AT (x_0, y_0)	PARTIAL DERIVATIVE OF f (OR z) WITH RESPECT TO y EVALUATED AT (x_0, y_0)
$f_x(x_0, y_0)$	$f_y(x_0, y_0)$
$\left.\dfrac{\partial f}{\partial x}\right|_{(x_0, y_0)}$	$\left.\dfrac{\partial f}{\partial y}\right|_{(x_0, y_0)}$
$\left.\dfrac{\partial z}{\partial x}\right|_{(x_0, y_0)}$	$\left.\dfrac{\partial z}{\partial y}\right|_{(x_0, y_0)}$

EXAMPLE 3

a. If $z = 3x^3 y^3 - 9x^2 y + xy^2 + 4y$, find $\dfrac{\partial z}{\partial x}, \dfrac{\partial z}{\partial y}, \left.\dfrac{\partial z}{\partial x}\right|_{(1,0)}$ and $\left.\dfrac{\partial z}{\partial y}\right|_{(1,0)}$.

To find $\partial z/\partial x$ we differentiate z with respect to x, treating y as a constant:

$$\frac{\partial z}{\partial x} = 3(3x^2)y^3 - 9(2x)y + (1)y^2 + 0$$

$$= 9x^2 y^3 - 18xy + y^2.$$

Evaluating at (1, 0), we obtain

$$\frac{\partial z}{\partial x}\bigg|_{(1,0)} = 9(1)^2(0)^3 - 18(1)(0) + 0^2 = 0.$$

To find $\partial z / \partial y$ we differentiate z with respect to y, treating x as a constant.

$$\frac{\partial z}{\partial y} = 3x^3(3y^2) - 9x^2(1) + x(2y) + 4(1)$$

$$= 9x^3 y^2 - 9x^2 + 2xy + 4.$$

Thus,

$$\frac{\partial z}{\partial y}\bigg|_{(1,0)} = -5.$$

b. *If* $g(x, y) = x^2 e^{2x+3y}$, *find* $\partial g / \partial x$ *and* $\partial g / \partial y$.

To find $\partial g / \partial x$, we treat y as a constant and differentiate with respect to x. Since $x^2 e^{2x+3y}$ is a product of two functions, each involving x, we use the product rule.

$$\frac{\partial g}{\partial x} = x^2 \frac{\partial}{\partial x}(e^{2x+3y}) + e^{2x+3y} \frac{\partial}{\partial x}(x^2)$$

$$= x^2(2e^{2x+3y}) + e^{2x+3y}(2x)$$

$$= 2x(x + 1) e^{2x+3y}.$$

To find $\partial g / \partial y$, we treat x as a constant and differentiate with respect to y.

$$\frac{\partial g}{\partial y} = x^2 \frac{\partial}{\partial y}(e^{2x+3y}) = 3x^2 e^{2x+3y}.$$

We have seen that for a function of two variables, two partial derivatives can be considered. Actually the concept of partial derivatives can be extended to functions of more than two variables. For example, with $f(x, y, z)$ we have three partial derivatives:

the partial with respect to x, denoted $f_x(x, y, z)$, $\partial f / \partial x$, etc.;

the partial with respect to y, denoted $f_y(x, y, z)$, $\partial f / \partial y$, etc.;

and the partial with respect to z, denoted $f_z(x, y, z)$, $\partial f / \partial z$, etc.

To determine $\partial f / \partial x$, treat y and z as constants and differentiate with respect to x. For $\partial f / \partial y$, treat x and z as constants and differentiate with respect to y. For $\partial f / \partial z$, treat x and y as constants and differentiate with respect to z. With a function of n variables we have n partial derivatives which are determined in the obvious way.

EXAMPLE 4

a. *If $f(x, y, z) = x^2 + y^2 z + z^3$, find $f_x(x, y, z)$, $f_y(x, y, z)$, and $f_z(x, y, z)$.*

Treating y and z as constants and differentiating with respect to x, we have

$$f_x(x, y, z) = 2x.$$

Treating x and z as constants and differentiating with respect to y, we have

$$f_y(x, y, z) = 2yz.$$

Treating x and y as constants and differentiating with respect to z, we have

$$f_z(x, y, z) = y^2 + 3z^2.$$

b. *If $g(r, s, t, u) = \dfrac{rsu}{rt^2 + s^2 t}$, determine $\dfrac{\partial g}{\partial s}$, $\dfrac{\partial g}{\partial t}$, and $\dfrac{\partial g}{\partial t}\Big|_{(0,1,1,1)}$.*

To find $\partial g/\partial s$, first note that g is a quotient of two functions, each involving the variable s. Thus we use the quotient rule, treating r, t, and u as constants.

$$\frac{\partial g}{\partial s} = \frac{(rt^2 + s^2 t)\dfrac{\partial}{\partial s}(rsu) - rsu\dfrac{\partial}{\partial s}(rt^2 + s^2 t)}{(rt^2 + s^2 t)^2}$$

$$= \frac{(rt^2 + s^2 t)(ru) - (rsu)(2st)}{(rt^2 + s^2 t)^2}.$$

Simplifying, we obtain

$$\frac{\partial g}{\partial s} = \frac{ru(rt - s^2)}{t(rt + s^2)^2}.$$

To find $\partial g/\partial t$ we can write g as

$$g(r, s, t, u) = rsu(rt^2 + s^2 t)^{-1}.$$

Next we use the power rule, treating r, s, and u as constants.

$$\frac{\partial g}{\partial t} = rsu(-1)(rt^2 + s^2 t)^{-2}\frac{\partial}{\partial t}(rt^2 + s^2 t)$$

$$= -rsu(rt^2 + s^2 t)^{-2}(2rt + s^2).$$

Simplifying, we have

$$\frac{\partial g}{\partial t} = -\frac{rsu(2rt + s^2)}{(rt^2 + s^2 t)^2}.$$

Letting $r = 0$, $s = 1$, $t = 1$ and $u = 1$, we have

$$\frac{\partial g}{\partial t}\bigg|_{(0,1,1,1)} = -\frac{0(1)(1)[2(0)(1) + (1)^2]}{[0(1)^2 + (1)^2(1)]^2} = 0.$$

EXERCISE 11-2

In each of problems 1-26, find all partial derivatives.

1. $f(x, y) = x - 5y + 3$ **2.** $f(x, y) = 4 - 5x^2 + 6y^3$

3. $f(x, y) = 3x - 4$ **4.** $f(x, y) = \sqrt{7}$

5. $g(x, y) = x^5 y^4 - 3x^4 y^3 + 7x^3 + 2y^2 - 3xy + 4$

6. $g(x, y) = x^8 - 2x^6 y^5 + 3x^5 y^3 + x^3 y^3 + 3x - 4$

7. $g(p, q) = \sqrt{pq}$ **8.** $g(w, z) = \sqrt[3]{w^2 + z^2}$

9. $h(s, t) = \dfrac{s^2 + 4}{t - 3}$ **10.** $h(u, v) = \dfrac{4uv^2}{u^2 + v^2}$

11. $u(q_1, q_2) = \frac{3}{4}\ln q_1 + \frac{1}{4}\ln q_2$ **12.** $Q(l, k) = 3l^{.41} k^{.59}$

13. $h(x, y) = \dfrac{x^2 + 3xy + y^2}{\sqrt{x^2 + y^2}}$ **14.** $h(x, y) = \dfrac{\sqrt{x + 4}}{x^2 y + y^2 x}$

15. $z = e^{5xy}$ **16.** $z = (x^2 + y) e^{3x+4y}$

17. $z = 5x \ln(x^2 + y)$ **18.** $z = \ln(3x^2 + 4y^4)$

19. $f(r, s) = \sqrt{r + 2s}\,(r^3 - 2rs + s^2)$ **20.** $f(r, s) = \sqrt{rs}\, e^{2+r}$

21. $f(r, s) = e^{3-r} \ln(7 - s)$ **22.** $f(r, s) = (5r^2 + 3s^3)(2r - 5s)$

23. $g(x, y, z) = 3x^2 y + 2xy^2 z + 3z^3$

24. $g(x, y, z) = x^2 y^3 z^5 - 3x^2 y^4 z^3 + 5xz$

25. $g(r, s, t) = e^{s+t}(r^2 + 7s^3)$ **26.** $g(r, s, t, u) = rs \ln(2t + 5u)$

In problems 27-32, evaluate the given partial derivatives.

27. $f(x, y) = x^3 y + 7x^2 y^2$; $f_x(1, -2)$

28. $z = \sqrt{5x^2 + 3xy + 2y}$; $\dfrac{\partial z}{\partial x}\bigg|_{\substack{x=0 \\ y=2}}$

29. $g(x, y, z) = e^x \sqrt{y + 2z}$; $\dfrac{\partial g}{\partial z}\bigg|_{(0,1,4)}$

30. $g(x, y, z) = \dfrac{3x^2 + 2y}{xy + xz}$; $g_y(1, 1, 1)$

31. $h(r, s, t, u) = (s^2 + tu) \ln(2r + 7st)$; $h_s(1, 0, 0, 1)$

32. $h(r, s, t, u) = \dfrac{7r + 3s^2 u^2}{s}; \dfrac{\partial h}{\partial t}\bigg|_{(4,3,2,1)}$

11-3 APPLICATIONS OF PARTIAL DERIVATIVES

Suppose a manufacturer produces x units of product X and y units of product Y. Then the total cost c of these units is a function of x and y and is called a *joint-cost function*. If such a function is $c = f(x, y)$, then $\partial c/\partial x$ is called the *(partial) marginal cost with respect to x*. It is the instantaneous rate of change of c with respect to x when y is held fixed. On the other hand, $\partial c/\partial y$ is the *(partial) marginal cost with respect to y*. It is the instantaneous rate of change of c with respect to y when x is held fixed.

For example, if c is expressed in dollars and $\partial c/\partial y = 2$, then the cost of producing an extra unit of Y when the level of production of X is fixed is approximately two dollars.

If a manufacturer produces n products, his joint-cost function is a function of n variables and there are n (partial) marginal cost functions.

EXAMPLE 5

The Shishka Bobsled Co. manufactures two types of sleds, the Lightning and the Alaskan models. Suppose the joint-cost function for producing x sleds of the Lightning model and y sleds of the Alaskan model is $c = f(x, y) = .06x^2 + 7x + 15y + 1000$ where c is expressed in dollars. Determine $\partial c/\partial x$ and $\partial c/\partial y$ when $x = 100$ and $y = 50$.

Treating y as a constant and differentiating c with respect to x, we obtain

$$\frac{\partial c}{\partial x} = .12x + 7.$$

Treating x as a constant and differentiating c with respect to y, we have

$$\frac{\partial c}{\partial y} = 15.$$

Thus,

$$\frac{\partial c}{\partial x}\bigg|_{(100,50)} = .12(100) + 7 = 19$$

and

$$\frac{\partial c}{\partial y}\bigg|_{(100,50)} = 15.$$

This means that increasing the output of the Lightning model from 100 to 101, while maintaining production of the Alaskan model at 50, increases costs by approximately $19. On the other hand, increasing output of the Alaskan model from 50 to 51 and holding production of the Lightning model at 100 will increase costs by approximately $15.

A manufacturer's total output of a commodity is dependent upon many factors of production. Among these factors may be labor, capital, land, machinery, etc. If the function $Q = f(l, k)$ gives the total output Q produced when a manufacturer uses l units of labor and k units of capital, then this function is called a *production function*. We define the *marginal productivity with respect to l* to be $\partial Q/\partial l$. This is the instantaneous rate of change of Q with respect to l when k is held fixed. Likewise, the *marginal productivity with respect to k* is $\partial Q/\partial k$. It is the instantaneous rate of change of Q with respect to k when l is held fixed.

EXAMPLE 6

National Flim Flam Co. is the manufacturer of the popular Flimsee toy. The company has determined that its production function is $Q = \sqrt{lk}$, where l is the number of man-hours per week and k is the capital (expressed in hundreds of dollars per week) required for a weekly production of Q gross of the Flimsee toy. Determine the marginal productivity functions and evaluate them when l = 400 and k = 16.

Since $Q = (lk)^{1/2}$,

$$\frac{\partial Q}{\partial l} = \frac{1}{2}(lk)^{-1/2}k = \frac{k}{2\sqrt{lk}}$$

and

$$\frac{\partial Q}{\partial k} = \frac{1}{2}(lk)^{-1/2}l = \frac{l}{2\sqrt{lk}}.$$

Evaluating when $l = 400$ and $k = 16$, we obtain

$$\left.\frac{\partial Q}{\partial l}\right|_{\substack{l=400 \\ k=16}} = \frac{16}{2\sqrt{400(16)}} = \frac{1}{10},$$

$$\left.\frac{\partial Q}{\partial k}\right|_{\substack{l=400 \\ k=16}} = \frac{400}{2\sqrt{400(16)}} = \frac{5}{2}.$$

Thus if $l = 400$ and $k = 16$, increasing l to 401 and holding k at 16 will increase output by approximately $\frac{1}{10}$ gross. But if k is increased to 17 while l is held at 400, the output increases by approximately $\frac{5}{2}$ gross.

Sometimes two products may be related so that changes in the price of one of them can affect the demand for the other. A typical example is that of butter and margarine. If such a relationship exists between products A and B, then the demand for each product is dependent on the prices of both. Suppose q_A and q_B are the quantities demanded for A and B respectively, and p_A and p_B are their respective prices. Then both q_A and q_B are functions of p_A and p_B:

$$q_A = f(p_A, p_B), \text{ demand function for } A$$

$$q_B = g(p_A, p_B), \text{ demand function for } B.$$

We can find four partial derivatives:

$\dfrac{\partial q_A}{\partial p_A}$, *the marginal demand for A with respect to* p_A

$\dfrac{\partial q_A}{\partial p_B}$, *the marginal demand for A with respect to* p_B

$\dfrac{\partial q_B}{\partial p_A}$, *the marginal demand for B with respect to* p_A

$\dfrac{\partial q_B}{\partial p_B}$, *the marginal demand for B with respect to* p_B.

Under typical conditions, if the price of B is fixed and the price of A increases, then the quantity of A demanded will decrease. Thus $\partial q_A / \partial p_A < 0$. Similarly, $\partial q_B / \partial p_B < 0$. However, $\partial q_A / \partial p_B$ and $\partial q_B / \partial p_A$ may be either positive or negative. If

$$\frac{\partial q_A}{\partial p_B} > 0 \quad \text{and} \quad \frac{\partial q_B}{\partial p_A} > 0,$$

then A and B are said to be **competitive products.** In this situation an increase in the price of B causes an increase in the demand for A, if it is assumed that the price of A does not change. Likewise, an increase in the price of A causes an increase in the demand for B when the price of B is held fixed. Butter and margarine are examples of such competitive commodities.

Proceeding to a different situation, we say that if

$$\frac{\partial q_A}{\partial p_B} < 0 \quad \text{and} \quad \frac{\partial q_B}{\partial p_A} < 0,$$

then A and B are **complementary products.** In this case an increase in the price of B causes a decrease in the demand for A if the price of A does not change. Similarly, an increase in the price of A causes a decrease in the demand for B when the price of B is held fixed. For example, cameras and film are complementary products. An increase in the price of film will make picture-taking more expensive. Hence the demand for cameras will decrease.

EXAMPLE 7

The demand for widgets and the demand for wadgets are each functions of the prices of both widgets and wadgets. If the demand functions for widgets and wadgets are

$$q_A = \frac{50 \sqrt[3]{p_B}}{\sqrt{p_A}}$$

and

$$q_B = \frac{75 p_A}{\sqrt[3]{p_B^2}}$$

respectively, find the four marginal demand functions and also determine whether widgets and wadgets are competitive or complementary products.

Writing $q_A = 50 p_A^{-1/2} p_B^{1/3}$ and $q_B = 75 p_A p_B^{-2/3}$, we have

$$\frac{\partial q_A}{\partial p_A} = 50 \left(-\frac{1}{2} \right) p_A^{-3/2} p_B^{1/3} = -25 p_A^{-3/2} p_B^{1/3},$$

$$\frac{\partial q_A}{\partial p_B} = 50 p_A^{-1/2} \left(\frac{1}{3} \right) p_B^{-2/3} = \frac{50}{3} p_A^{-1/2} p_B^{-2/3},$$

$$\frac{\partial q_B}{\partial p_A} = 75(1) p_B^{-2/3} = 75 p_B^{-2/3},$$

$$\frac{\partial q_B}{\partial p_B} = 75 p_A \left(-\frac{2}{3} \right) p_B^{-5/3} = -50 p_A p_B^{-5/3}.$$

Since p_A and p_B represent prices, they are both positive. Hence $\partial q_A / \partial p_B > 0$ and $\partial q_B / \partial p_A > 0$. We conclude that widgets and wadgets are competitive products.

EXERCISE 11-3

For the joint-cost functions in problems 1–3, find the indicated marginal cost at the given production level.

1. $c = 4x + .3y^2 + 2y + 500; \dfrac{\partial c}{\partial y}, \; x = 20, \; y = 30$

2. $c = x\sqrt{x + y} + 1000; \dfrac{\partial c}{\partial x}, \; x = 40, \; y = 60$

3. $c = .03(x + y)^3 - .6(x + y)^2 + 4.5(x + y) + 7700; \dfrac{\partial c}{\partial x}, \; x = 50, \; y = 50$

For the production functions in problems 4 and 5, find the marginal production functions $\partial Q/\partial k$ and $\partial Q/\partial l$.

4. $Q = 20lk - 2l^2 - 4k^2 + 800$

5. $Q = 1.582l^{\cdot 192} k^{\cdot 764}$

6. A Cobb-Douglas production function is a production function of the form $Q = Al^{\alpha} k^{\beta}$ where A, α, and β are constants and $\alpha + \beta = 1$. For such a function, show that

    a. $\partial Q/\partial l = \alpha Q/l$ b. $\partial Q/\partial k = \beta Q/k$

In problems 7-9, q_A and q_B are demand functions for products A and B, respectively. In each case, find $\partial q_A/\partial p_A$, $\partial q_A/\partial p_B$, $\partial q_B/\partial p_A$, $\partial q_B/\partial p_B$ and determine whether A and B are competitive, complementary, or neither.

7. $q_A = 1000 - 50p_A + 2p_B; q_B = 500 + 4p_A - 20p_B$

8. $q_A = 20 - p_A - 2p_B'; q_B = 50 - 2p_A - 3p_B$

9. $q_A = \dfrac{100}{p_A \sqrt{p_B}}; q_B = \dfrac{500}{p_B \sqrt[3]{p_A}}$

Suppose f defines a demand function for product A and $q_A = f(p_A, p_B)$ where q_A is the quantity of A demanded when the price per unit of A is p_A and the price per unit of product B is p_B. The partial elasticity of demand for A with respect to p_A, denoted η_{p_A}, is defined as $\eta_{p_A} = (p_A/q_A)(\partial q_A/\partial p_A)$. The partial elasticity of demand for A with respect to p_B, denoted η_{p_B}, is defined as $(p_B/q_A)(\partial q_A/\partial p_B)$. Loosely speaking, η_{p_A} is the ratio of a percentage change in the quantity of A demanded to a percentage change in the price of A when the price of B is fixed. Similarly, η_{p_B} can be loosely interpreted as the ratio of a percentage change in the quantity of A demanded to a percentage change in the price of B when the price of A is fixed.

In problems 10-12, find η_{p_A} and η_{p_B} for the given values of p_A and p_B.

10. $q_A = 1000 - 50p_A + 2p_B; p_A = 2, p_B = 10$

11. $q_A = 100/(p_A \sqrt{p_B}); p_A = 1, p_B = 4$

12. $q_A = 20 - p_A - 2p_B; p_A = 2, p_B = 2$

13. If $f(l, k) = 2l^{\cdot 4} k^{\cdot 6}$, show that

$$l\frac{\partial f}{\partial l} + k\frac{\partial f}{\partial k} = f(l, k).$$

11-4 IMPLICIT PARTIAL DIFFERENTIATION †

In the equation

$$z^2 - x^2 - y^2 = 0, \tag{1}$$

---

† May be omitted without loss of continuity.

if $x = 1$ and $y = 1$, then $z^2 - 1 - 1 = 0$ and so $z = \pm\sqrt{2}$. Thus Eq. (1) does not define z as a function of x and y. However, solving Eq. (1) for z gives

$$z = \sqrt{x^2 + y^2} \quad \text{or} \quad z = -\sqrt{x^2 + y^2},$$

each of which defines z as a function of x and y. Although Eq. (1) does not *explicitly* express z as a function of x and y, it can be thought of as expressing z *implicitly* as two different functions of x and y. Note that $z^2 - x^2 - y^2 = 0$ has the form $F(x, y, z) = 0$. Any equation of the form $F(x, y, z) = 0$ can be thought of as expressing z implicitly as one or more functions of x and y.

To find $\partial z / \partial x$ where

$$z^2 - x^2 - y^2 = 0, \tag{2}$$

we first differentiate both sides of Eq. (2) with respect to x, treating z as a function of x and y, and treating y as a constant.

$$\frac{\partial}{\partial x}(z^2 - x^2 - y^2) = \frac{\partial}{\partial x}(0)$$

$$\frac{\partial}{\partial x}(z^2) - \frac{\partial}{\partial x}(x^2) - \frac{\partial}{\partial x}(y^2) = 0$$

$$2z\frac{\partial z}{\partial x} - 2x - 0 = 0.$$

Solving for $\partial z / \partial x$, we obtain

$$2z\frac{\partial z}{\partial x} = 2x$$

$$\frac{\partial z}{\partial x} = \frac{x}{z}.$$

To find $\partial z / \partial y$ we differentiate both sides of Eq. (2) with respect to y, treating z as a function of x and y, and treating x as a constant.

$$\frac{\partial}{\partial y}(z^2 - x^2 - y^2) = \frac{\partial}{\partial y}(0)$$

$$2z\frac{\partial z}{\partial y} - 0 - 2y = 0$$

$$2z\frac{\partial z}{\partial y} = 2y.$$

Hence,

$$\frac{\partial z}{\partial y} = \frac{y}{z}.$$

The method we used to find $\partial z / \partial x$ and $\partial z / \partial y$ is called *implicit (partial) differentiation.*

EXAMPLE 8

a. If $\dfrac{xz^2}{x + y} + y^2 = 0$, *evaluate* $\partial z / \partial x$ *when* $x = -1$, $y = 2$, *and* $z = 2$.

We treat z as a function of x and y and differentiate both sides of the equation with respect to x,

$$\frac{\partial}{\partial x}\left(\frac{xz^2}{x + y}\right) + \frac{\partial}{\partial x}(y^2) = \frac{\partial}{\partial x}(0).$$

Using the quotient rule for the first term on the left side, we have

$$\frac{(x + y)\dfrac{\partial}{\partial x}(xz^2) - xz^2\dfrac{\partial}{\partial x}(x + y)}{(x + y)^2} + 0 = 0.$$

Using the product rule for $\dfrac{\partial}{\partial x}(xz^2)$, we obtain

$$\frac{(x + y)\left[x\left(2z\dfrac{\partial z}{\partial x}\right) + z^2\,(1)\right] - xz^2\,(1)}{(x + y)^2} = 0.$$

Solving for $\partial z / \partial x$, we obtain

$$2xz(x + y)\frac{\partial z}{\partial x} + z^2(x + y) - xz^2 = 0$$

$$\frac{\partial z}{\partial x} = -\frac{xz^2 - z^2(x + y)}{2xz(x + y)} = -\frac{yz}{2x(x + y)}, \qquad z \neq 0.$$

When $x = -1$, $y = 2$, and $z = 2$, then $\partial z / \partial x = 2$.

b. *If* $se^{r^2 + u^2} = u \ln (t^2 + 1)$, *determine* $\partial t / \partial u$.

We consider t as a function of r, s, and u. By differentiating both sides with respect to u while treating r and s as constants, we get

$$\frac{\partial}{\partial u}(se^{r^2 + u^2}) = \frac{\partial}{\partial u}[u \ln (t^2 + 1)]$$

$$2sue^{r^2 + u^2} = u\frac{\partial}{\partial u}[\ln (t^2 + 1)] + \ln (t^2 + 1)\frac{\partial}{\partial u}(u)$$

$$2sue^{r^2 + u^2} = u\frac{2t}{t^2 + 1}\frac{\partial t}{\partial u} + \ln (t^2 + 1).$$

Thus,

$$\frac{\partial t}{\partial u} = \frac{(t^2 + 1)[2sue^{r^2+u^2} - \ln (t^2 + 1)]}{2ut}.$$

EXERCISE 11-4

In problems 1-11, by the method of implicit partial differentiation find the indicated partial derivatives.

1. $x^2 + y^2 + z^2 = 9$; $\partial z/\partial x$

2. $z^2 - 3x^2 + y^2 = 0$; $\partial z/\partial x$

3. $2z^3 - x^2 - 4y^2 = 0$; $\partial z/\partial y$

4. $3x^2 + y^2 + 2z^3 = 9$; $\partial z/\partial y$

5. $x^2 - 2y - z^2 + x^2 yz^2 = 20$; $\partial z/\partial x$

6. $z^3 - xz - y = 0$; $\partial z/\partial x$

7. $e^x + e^y + e^z = 10$; $\partial z/\partial y$

8. $xyz + 2y^2 x - z^3 = 0$; $\partial z/\partial x$

9. $\ln (z) + z - xy = 1$; $\partial z/\partial x$

10. $\ln x + \ln y - \ln z = e^y$; $\partial z/\partial x$

11. $(z^2 + 6xy) \sqrt{x^3 + 5} = 2$; $\partial z/\partial y$

In problems 12-18, evaluate the indicated partial derivatives for the given values of the variables.

12. $xz + xyz - 5 = 0$; $\partial z/\partial x$, $x = 1$, $y = 4$, $z = 1$

13. $xz^2 + yz - 12 = 0$; $\partial z/\partial x$, $x = 2$, $y = -2$, $z = 3$

14. $e^{zx} = xyz$; $\partial z/\partial y$, $x = 1$, $y = -e^{-1}$, $z = -1$

15. $\ln z = x + y$; $\partial z/\partial x$, $x = 5$, $y = -5$, $z = 1$

16. $\sqrt{xz + y^2} - xy = 0$; $\partial z/\partial y$, $x = 2$, $y = 2$, $z = 6$

17. $\dfrac{s^2 + t^2}{rs} = 10$; $\partial t/\partial r$, $r = 1$, $s = 2$, $t = 4$

18. $\dfrac{rs}{s^2 + t^2} = t$; $\partial r/\partial t$, $r = 0$, $s = 1$, $t = 0$

11-5 HIGHER-ORDER PARTIAL DERIVATIVES

If f is a function of x and y, then both f_x and f_y are also functions of x and y. Hence we may differentiate them (or at least try to) and obtain so-called second-order partial derivatives of f. Symbolically,

$$f_{xx} \quad \text{means} \quad (f_x)_x,$$

$$f_{xy} \quad \text{means} \quad (f_x)_y,$$

$$f_{yx} \quad \text{means} \quad (f_y)_x,$$

and

$$f_{yy} \quad \text{means} \quad (f_y)_y.$$

In terms of ∂-notation,

$$\frac{\partial^2 f}{\partial x^2} \quad \text{means} \quad \frac{\partial}{\partial x}\left[\frac{\partial f}{\partial x}\right],$$

$$\frac{\partial^2 f}{\partial y\,\partial x} \quad \text{means} \quad \frac{\partial}{\partial y}\left[\frac{\partial f}{\partial x}\right],$$

$$\frac{\partial^2 f}{\partial x\,\partial y} \quad \text{means} \quad \frac{\partial}{\partial x}\left[\frac{\partial f}{\partial y}\right],$$

and

$$\frac{\partial^2 f}{\partial y^2} \quad \text{means} \quad \frac{\partial}{\partial y}\left[\frac{\partial f}{\partial y}\right].$$

Note that to find f_{xy}, first differentiate f with respect to x. For $\partial^2 f/\partial x\,\partial y$, first differentiate with respect to y.

We can extend our notation beyond second-order partial derivatives. For example, f_{xyx} (or $\partial^3 f/\partial x\,\partial y\,\partial x$) is a third-order partial derivative of f. It is the partial derivative of f_{xy} (or $\partial^2 f/\partial y\,\partial x$) with respect to x. A generalization regarding higher-order partial derivatives to functions of more than two variables should be obvious.

EXAMPLE 9

Find the four second-order partial derivatives of $f(x, y) = x^2 y + x^2 y^2$.

Since

$$f_x(x, y) = 2xy + 2xy^2,$$

then

$$f_{xx}(x, y) = \frac{\partial}{\partial x}(2xy + 2xy^2) = 2y + 2y^2$$

and

$$f_{xy}(x, y) = \frac{\partial}{\partial y}(2xy + 2xy^2) = 2x + 4xy.$$

Since

$$f_y(x, y) = x^2 + 2x^2 y,$$

then

$$f_{yy}(x, y) = \frac{\partial}{\partial y}(x^2 + 2x^2 y) = 2x^2$$

and

$$f_{yx}(x, y) = \frac{\partial}{\partial x}(x^2 + 2x^2 y) = 2x + 4xy.$$

Observe in Example 9 that $f_{xy}(x, y) = f_{yx}(x, y)$. This equality did not occur by chance. It can be shown that for any function f, if f_{xy} and f_{yx} are both continuous, then $f_{xy} = f_{yx}$; that is, the order of differentiation is of no concern.

EXAMPLE 10

Determine the value of $\dfrac{\partial^3 f}{\partial z\, \partial y\, \partial x}\bigg|_{(1,2,3)}$ *if* $f(x, y, z) = (2x + 3y + 4z)^3$.

$$\frac{\partial f}{\partial x} = 3(2x + 3y + 4z)^2 \frac{\partial}{\partial x}(2x + 3y + 4z)$$

$$= 6(2x + 3y + 4z)^2.$$

$$\frac{\partial^2 f}{\partial y\, \partial x} = 6 \cdot 2(2x + 3y + 4z)\frac{\partial}{\partial y}(2x + 3y + 4z)$$

$$= 36(2x + 3y + 4z).$$

$$\frac{\partial^3 f}{\partial z\, \partial y\, \partial x} = 36 \cdot 4 = 144.$$

Thus

$$\frac{\partial^3 f}{\partial z\, \partial y\, \partial x}\bigg|_{(1,2,3)} = 144.$$

EXAMPLE 11†

Determine $\partial^2 z/\partial x^2$ *if* $z^2 = xy$.

By implicit differentiation we first determine $\partial z/\partial x$:

---

† Omit if Sec. 11-4 was not covered.

$$\frac{\partial}{\partial x}(z^2) = \frac{\partial}{\partial x}(xy)$$

$$2z\frac{\partial z}{\partial x} = y$$

$$\frac{\partial z}{\partial x} = \frac{y}{2z}, \qquad z \neq 0.$$

Differentiating both sides with respect to x, we obtain

$$\frac{\partial}{\partial x}\left[\frac{\partial z}{\partial x}\right] = \frac{\partial}{\partial x}\left[\frac{1}{2}yz^{-1}\right]$$

$$\frac{\partial^2 z}{\partial x^2} = -\frac{1}{2}yz^{-2}\frac{\partial z}{\partial x}.$$

Substituting $y/(2z)$ for $\partial z/\partial x$, we have

$$\frac{\partial^2 z}{\partial x^2} = -\frac{1}{2}yz^{-2}\left(\frac{y}{2z}\right) = -\frac{y^2}{4z^3}, \qquad z \neq 0.$$

EXERCISE 11-5

In problems 1-10, find the indicated higher-order partial derivatives.

1. $f(x, y) = 3x^2 y^2; f_{xy}(x, y)$

2. $f(x, y) = 3x^2 y + 2xy^2 - 7y; f_{xx}(x, y)$

3. $f(x, y) = e^{3xy} + 4x^2 y; f_{yxy}(x, y)$

4. $f(x, y) = 7x^2 + 3y; f_{yyx}(x, y)$

5. $f(x, y) = (x^2 + xy + y^2)(x^2 + xy + 1); f_{xy}(x, y)$

6. $f(x, y) = \ln(x^2 + y^2) + 2; f_{xx}(x, y), f_{xy}(x, y)$

7. $f(x, y) = (x + y)^2(xy); f_{xx}(x, y), f_{yy}(x, y)$

8. $f(x, y, z) = xy^2 z^3; f_{xz}(x, y, z), f_{xy}(x, y, z)$

9. $z = \sqrt{x^2 + y^2}; \dfrac{\partial^2 z}{\partial x^2}$

10. $z = \dfrac{\ln(x^2 + 5)}{y}; \dfrac{\partial^2 z}{\partial y \partial x}$

11. If $f(x, y, z) = 7$, find $f_{yxx}(4, 3, -2)$.

12. If $f(x, y, z) = z^2(3x^2 - 4xy^3)$, find $f_{xyz}(1, 2, 3)$.

13. If $f(l, k) = 5l^3 k^6 - lk^7$, find $f_{kkl}(2, 1)$.

14. If $f(x, y) = 2x^2 y + xy^2 - x^2 y^2$, find $f_{xxy}(0, 1)$.

15. If $f(x, y) = y^2 e^x + \ln(xy)$, find $f_{xyy}(1, 1)$.

16. If $f(x, y) = x^3 - 3xy^2 + x^2 - y^3$, find $f_{xy}(1, -1)$.

17. For $f(x, y) = 8x^3 + 2x^2 y^2 + 5y^4$, show $f_{xy}(x, y) = f_{yx}(x, y)$.

18. For $f(x, y) = x^4 y^4 + 3x^3 y^2 - 7x + 4$, show $f_{xyx}(x, y) = f_{xxy}(x, y)$.

19. For $z = \ln(x^2 + y^2)$, show

$$\frac{\partial^2 z}{\partial x^2} + \frac{\partial^2 z}{\partial y^2} = 0.$$

*20. If $2z^2 - x^2 - 4y^2 = 0$, find $\dfrac{\partial^2 z}{\partial x^2}$.

*21. If $z^2 - 3x^2 + y^2 = 0$, find $\dfrac{\partial^2 z}{\partial y^2}$.

11-6   CHAIN RULE †

Suppose a manufacturer of two related products A and B has a joint-cost function given by

$$c = f(q_A, q_B),$$

where c is the total cost of producing quantities q_A and q_B of A and B respectively. Furthermore, suppose the demand functions for his products are

$$q_A = g(p_A, p_B) \quad \text{and} \quad q_B = h(p_A, p_B),$$

where p_A and p_B are the prices per unit of A and B, respectively. Since c is a function of q_A and q_B and both q_A and q_B are themselves functions of p_A and p_B, then c can be viewed as a function of p_A and p_B. (Appropriately, the variables q_A and q_B are called *intermediate variables* of c.) Consequently, we should be able to determine $\partial c / \partial p_A$, the instantaneous rate of change of total cost with respect to the price of A. One way to do this is to substitute the expressions $g(p_A, p_B)$ and $h(p_A, p_B)$ for q_A and q_B, respectively, into $c = f(q_A, q_B)$. Then c is a function of p_A and p_B and we can differentiate c with respect to p_A directly. This approach has some drawbacks—especially when f, g, or h is given by a complicated expression. Another way to approach the problem would be to use the chain rule (actually *a* chain rule) which we now state without proof.

---

*Omit if Sec. 11-4 was not covered.
†May be omitted without loss of continuity.

CHAIN RULE.   *Let $z = f(x, y)$, where both x and y are functions of r and s given by $x = x(r, s)$ and $y = y(r, s)$. If f, x, and y have continuous partial derivatives, then z is a function of r and s and*

$$\frac{\partial z}{\partial r} = \frac{\partial f}{\partial x}\frac{\partial x}{\partial r} + \frac{\partial f}{\partial y}\frac{\partial y}{\partial r}$$

and

$$\frac{\partial z}{\partial s} = \frac{\partial f}{\partial x}\frac{\partial x}{\partial s} + \frac{\partial f}{\partial y}\frac{\partial y}{\partial s}.$$

Note that in the chain rule the number of intermediate variables of z (two) is the same as the number of terms that compose each of $\partial z/\partial r$ and $\partial z/\partial s$.

Returning to the original situation concerning the manufacturer, we see that if f, q_A, and q_B have continuous partial derivatives, then by the chain rule

$$\frac{\partial c}{\partial p_A} = \frac{\partial c}{\partial q_A}\frac{\partial q_A}{\partial p_A} + \frac{\partial c}{\partial q_B}\frac{\partial q_B}{\partial p_A}.$$

EXAMPLE 12

Peek-a-Boo Company is a manufacturer of a unique type of camera and film. The total cost of producing q_C cameras and q_F units of film is given by

$$c = 30q_C + .015q_C q_F + q_F + 900.$$

The demand functions for the cameras and film are given by

$$q_C = \frac{9000}{p_C \sqrt{p_F}} \quad \text{and} \quad q_F = 2000 - p_C - 400p_F$$

where p_C is the price per camera and p_F is the price per unit of film. Find the instantaneous rate of change of total cost with respect to the price of the camera when $p_C = 50$ and $p_F = 2$.

We must first determine $\partial c/\partial p_C$. By the chain rule,

$$\frac{\partial c}{\partial p_C} = \frac{\partial c}{\partial q_C}\frac{\partial q_C}{\partial p_C} + \frac{\partial c}{\partial q_F}\frac{\partial q_F}{\partial p_C}$$

$$= (30 + .015q_F)\left[\frac{-9000}{p_C^2 \sqrt{p_F}}\right] + (.015q_C + 1)(-1).$$

When $p_C = 50$ and $p_F = 2$, then $q_C = 90\sqrt{2}$ and $q_F = 1150$. Substituting these values into $\partial c/\partial p_C$ and simplifying, we have

$$\frac{\partial c}{\partial p_C}\bigg|_{\substack{p_C=50 \\ p_F=2}} = -123.2 \quad \text{(approximately)}.$$

The chain rule can be extended. For example, suppose $z = f(v, w, x, y)$ and v, w, x, and y are all functions of r, s, and t. Then, if certain conditions of continuity are assumed, z is a function of r, s, and t and

$$\frac{\partial z}{\partial r} = \frac{\partial z}{\partial v}\frac{\partial v}{\partial r} + \frac{\partial z}{\partial w}\frac{\partial w}{\partial r} + \frac{\partial z}{\partial x}\frac{\partial x}{\partial r} + \frac{\partial z}{\partial y}\frac{\partial y}{\partial r},$$

$$\frac{\partial z}{\partial s} = \frac{\partial z}{\partial v}\frac{\partial v}{\partial s} + \frac{\partial z}{\partial w}\frac{\partial w}{\partial s} + \frac{\partial z}{\partial x}\frac{\partial x}{\partial s} + \frac{\partial z}{\partial y}\frac{\partial y}{\partial s},$$

and

$$\frac{\partial z}{\partial t} = \frac{\partial z}{\partial v}\frac{\partial v}{\partial t} + \frac{\partial z}{\partial w}\frac{\partial w}{\partial t} + \frac{\partial z}{\partial x}\frac{\partial x}{\partial t} + \frac{\partial z}{\partial y}\frac{\partial y}{\partial t}.$$

Observe that the number of intermediate variables of z (four) is the same as the number of terms that form each of $\partial z/\partial r$, $\partial z/\partial s$, and $\partial z/\partial t$.

Proceeding to another situation, if $z = f(x, y)$ and $x = x(t)$ and $y = y(t)$, then

$$\frac{dz}{dt} = \frac{\partial z}{\partial x}\frac{dx}{dt} + \frac{\partial z}{\partial y}\frac{dy}{dt}.$$

Here we use the symbol dz/dt rather than $\partial z/\partial t$ since z can be considered a function of the *one* variable t. Likewise, the symbols dx/dt and dy/dt are used rather than $\partial x/\partial t$ and $\partial y/\partial t$. As is typical, the number of terms that compose dz/dt equals the number of intermediate variables of z. Other situations would be treated in a similar way.

EXAMPLE 13

a. If $w = f(x, y, z) = 3x^2 y + xyz - 4y^2 z^3$ where $x = 2r - 3s$, $y = 6r + s$, and $z = r - s$, determine $\partial w/\partial r$ and $\partial w/\partial s$.

Since x, y, and z are functions of r and s, then by the chain rule,

$$\frac{\partial w}{\partial r} = \frac{\partial w}{\partial x}\frac{\partial x}{\partial r} + \frac{\partial w}{\partial y}\frac{\partial y}{\partial r} + \frac{\partial w}{\partial z}\frac{\partial z}{\partial r}$$

$$= (6xy + yz)(2) + (3x^2 + xz - 8yz^3)(6) + (xy - 12y^2 z^2)(1)$$

$$= x(18x + 13y + 6z) + 2yz(1 - 24z^2 - 6yz)$$

and

$$\frac{\partial w}{\partial s} = \frac{\partial w}{\partial x}\frac{\partial x}{\partial s} + \frac{\partial w}{\partial y}\frac{\partial y}{\partial s} + \frac{\partial w}{\partial z}\frac{\partial z}{\partial s}$$

$$= (6xy + yz)(-3) + (3x^2 + xz - 8yz^3)(1) + (xy - 12y^2 z^2)(-1)$$

$$= x(3x - 19y + z) - yz(3 + 8z^2 - 12yz).$$

b. If $z = \dfrac{x + e^y}{y}$ where $x = rs + se^{rt}$ and $y = 9 + rt$, *evaluate* $\partial z/\partial s$ *when* $r = -2$, $s = 5$, *and* $t = 4$.

Since x and y are functions of r, s, and t (note that we can write $y = 9 + rt + 0 \cdot s$), by the chain rule,

$$\frac{\partial z}{\partial s} = \frac{\partial z}{\partial x}\frac{\partial x}{\partial s} + \frac{\partial z}{\partial y}\frac{\partial y}{\partial s}$$

$$= \left(\frac{1}{y}\right)(r + e^{rt}) + \frac{\partial z}{\partial y}\cdot(0) = \frac{r + e^{rt}}{y}.$$

If $r = -2$, $s = 5$, and $t = 4$, then $y = 1$. Thus,

$$\left.\frac{\partial z}{\partial s}\right|_{\substack{r=-2 \\ s=5 \\ t=4}} = -2 + e^{-8}.$$

c. *Determine* $\partial y/\partial r$ *if* $y = x^2 \ln(x^4 + 6)$ *and* $x = (r + 3s)^6$.

By the chain rule,

$$\frac{\partial y}{\partial r} = \frac{dy}{dx}\frac{\partial x}{\partial r}$$

$$= \left[x^2 \cdot \frac{4x^3}{x^4 + 6} + 2x \cdot \ln(x^4 + 6)\right][6(r + 3s)^5]$$

$$= 12x(r + 3s)^5 \left[\frac{2x^4}{x^4 + 6} + \ln(x^4 + 6)\right].$$

EXAMPLE 14

Given that $z = e^{xy}$, $x = r - 4s$, *and* $y = r - s$, *find* $\partial z/\partial r$ *in terms of* r *and* s.

$$\frac{\partial z}{\partial r} = \frac{\partial z}{\partial x}\frac{\partial x}{\partial r} + \frac{\partial z}{\partial y}\frac{\partial y}{\partial r}$$

$$= (ye^{xy})(1) + (xe^{xy})(1)$$

$$= (x + y)e^{xy}.$$

Since $x = r - 4s$ and $y = r - s$,

$$\frac{\partial z}{\partial r} = [(r - 4s) + (r - s)] e^{(r-4s)(r-s)}$$

$$= (2r - 5s) e^{r^2 - 5rs + 4s^2}.$$

EXERCISE 11-6

In problems 1–12, find the indicated partial derivatives by using the chain rule.

1. $z = 5x + 3y$, $x = 2r + 3s$, $y = r - 2s$; $\partial z/\partial r$, $\partial z/\partial s$

2. $z = x^2 + 3xy + 7y^3$, $x = r^2 - 2s$, $y = 5s^2$; $\partial z/\partial r$, $\partial z/\partial s$

3. $z = e^{x+y}$, $x = t^2 + 3$, $y = \sqrt{t^3}$; dz/dt

4. $z = \sqrt{8x + y}$, $x = t^2 + 3t + 4$, $y = t^3 + 4$, dz/dt

5. $w = x^2 z^2 + xyz + yz^2$, $x = 5t$, $y = 2t + 3$, $z = 6 - t$; dw/dt

6. $w = \ln(x^2 + y^2 + z^2)$, $x = 2 - 3t$, $y = t^2 + 3$, $z = 4 - t$; dw/dt

7. $z = (x^2 + xy^2)^3$, $x = r + s + t$, $y = 2r - 3s + t$; $\partial z/\partial t$

8. $z = \sqrt{x^2 + y^2}$, $x = r^2 + s - t$, $y = r - s + t$; $\partial z/\partial r$

9. $w = x^2 + xyz + y^3 z^2$, $x = r - s^2$, $y = rs$, $z = 2r - 5s$; $\partial w/\partial s$

10. $w = e^{xyz}$, $x = r^2 s^3$, $y = r - s$, $z = rs^2$; $\partial w/\partial r$

11. $y = x^2 - 7x + 5$, $x = 15rs + 2s^2 t^2$; $\partial y/\partial r$

12. $y = 4 - x^2$, $x = 2r + 3s - 4t$; $\partial y/\partial t$

13. If $z = (4x + 3y)^3$ where $x = r^2 s$ and $y = r - 2s$, evaluate $\partial z/\partial r$ when $r = 0$ and $s = 1$.

14. If $z = \sqrt{5x + 2y}$ where $x = 4t + 7$ and $y = t^2 - 3t + 4$, evaluate dz/dt when $t = 1$.

15. If $w = e^{3x-y}(x^2 + 4z^3)$ where $x = rs$, $y = 2s - r$, and $z = r + s$, evaluate $\partial w/\partial s$ when $r = 1$ and $s = -1$.

16. If $y = x/(x - 5)$ where $x = 2t^2 - 3rs - r^2 t$, evaluate $\partial y/\partial t$ when $r = 0$, $s = 2$, and $t = -1$.

11-7   MAXIMA AND MINIMA FOR FUNCTIONS OF TWO VARIABLES

We now extend to functions of two variables the notion of relative maxima and minima (or more simply, *extrema*) which was introduced in Chapter 8.

DEFINITION. *A function $z = f(x, y)$ is said to have a **relative maximum** at the point (x_0, y_0), that is, when $x = x_0$ and $y = y_0$, if for all points (x, y) in the plane which are sufficiently "close" to (x_0, y_0) we have*

$$f(x_0, y_0) \geq f(x, y). \tag{1}$$

*For a **relative minimum** we replace $\geq$ by $\leq$ in (1).*

To say that $z = f(x, y)$ has a relative maximum at (x_0, y_0) means geometrically that the point (x_0, y_0, z_0) on the graph of f is higher than (or is as high as) all other points on the surface which are "near" (x_0, y_0, z_0). In Fig. 11-7(a), f has a relative maximum at (x_1, y_1). Similarly, the function f in Fig. 11-7(b) has a relative minimum when $x = y = 0$ which corresponds to a *low* point on the surface.

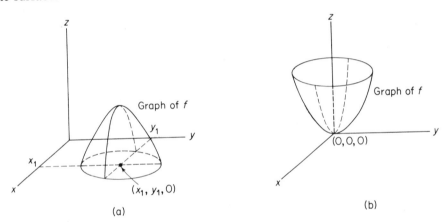

Fig. 11-7

Recall that in locating extrema for a function $y = f(x)$ of one variable, we examined those values of x for which $f'(x) = 0$. For functions of two (or more) variables, a similar procedure is followed.

Suppose $z = f(x, y)$ has a relative maximum at (x_0, y_0) as indicated in Fig. 11-8(a). Then the curve where the plane $y = y_0$ intersects the surface must have a relative maximum when $x = x_0$. Hence the slope of the tangent line to the surface in the x-direction must be 0 at (x_0, y_0). Equivalently, $f_x(x, y) = 0$ at (x_0, y_0). Similarly, on the curve where the plane $x = x_0$ intersects the surface [Fig. 11-8(b)], there must be a relative maximum when $y = y_0$. Thus in the y-direction, the slope of the tangent to the surface must be 0 at (x_0, y_0). Equivalently, $f_y(x, y) = 0$ at (x_0, y_0). Since a similar argument can be given for a relative minimum, we can combine these results as follows.

RULE 1. *If $z = f(x, y)$ has a relative maximum or minimum at (x_0, y_0) and if both f_x and f_y are defined for all points close to (x_0, y_0), it is necessary that (x_0, y_0) be a solution of the system*

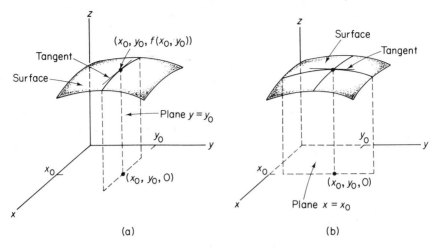

Fig. 11-8

$$\begin{cases} f_x(x,\ y) = 0 \\ f_y(x,\ y) = 0. \end{cases}$$

A point $(x_0,\ y_0)$ for which $f_x(x,\ y) = f_y(x,\ y) = 0$ is called a **critical point** of f. Thus from Rule 1 we infer that to locate extrema for a function we should examine its critical points.

PITFALL. *Rule 1 does not assert that there must be an extremum at a critical point. Just as in the case of functions of one variable, a critical point can give rise to a relative maximum, a relative minimum, or neither.*

Two additional comments: First, Rule 1, as well as the notion of a critical point, can be extended to functions of more than two variables. Thus, to locate possible extrema for $w = f(x,\ y,\ z)$ we would examine those points for which $f_x = f_y = f_z = 0$. Second, for a function whose domain is restricted, a thorough examination for absolute maxima and minima would include consideration of boundary points.

EXAMPLE 15

Examine each of the following for critical points.

a. $f(x,\ y) = 2x^2 + y^2 - 2xy + 5x - 3y + 1$.

Since $f_x(x,\ y) = 4x - 2y + 5$ and $f_y(x,\ y) = 2y - 2x - 3$, we solve the system

$$\begin{cases} 4x - 2y + 5 = 0 \\ -2x + 2y - 3 = 0. \end{cases}$$

This gives $x = -1$ and $y = \frac{1}{2}$. Thus, $(-1, \frac{1}{2})$ is the only critical point.

b. $f(l, k) = l^3 + k^3 - lk$.

$$\begin{cases} f_l(l, k) = 3l^2 - k = 0 & (2) \\ f_k(l, k) = 3k^2 - l = 0. & (3) \end{cases}$$

From Eq. (2), $k = 3l^2$. Substituting for k in Eq. (3) gives $0 = 27l^4 - l = l(27l^3 - 1)$. Hence, $l = 0$ or $l = \frac{1}{3}$. If $l = 0$, then $k = 0$; if $l = \frac{1}{3}$, then $k = \frac{1}{3}$. The critical points are thus $(0, 0)$ and $(\frac{1}{3}, \frac{1}{3})$.

c. $f(x, y, z) = 2x^2 + xy + y^2 + 100 - z(x + y - 100)$.

Solving the system

$$\begin{cases} f_x(x, y, z) = 4x + y - z = 0 \\ f_y(x, y, z) = x + 2y - z = 0 \\ f_z(x, y, z) = -x - y + 100 = 0 \end{cases}$$

gives the critical point $(25, 75, 175)$.

EXAMPLE 16

Find the critical points of $f(x, y) = x^2 - 4x + 2y^2 + 4y + 7$.

We have $\partial f/\partial x = 2x - 4$ and $\partial f/\partial y = 4y + 4$. The system

$$\begin{cases} 2x - 4 = 0 \\ 4y + 4 = 0 \end{cases}$$

gives the critical point $(2, -1)$. Observe that

$$\begin{aligned} f(x, y) &= x^2 - 4x + 4 + 2(y^2 + 2y + 1) + 1 \\ &= (x - 2)^2 + 2(y + 1)^2 + 1 \end{aligned}$$

and $f(2, -1) = 1$. Clearly, if $(x, y) \neq (2, -1)$, then $f(x, y) > 1$. Hence a relative minimum occurs at $(2, -1)$. Moreover, there is an *absolute minimum* at $(2, -1)$ since $f(x, y) > f(2, -1)$ is true for *all* $(x, y) \neq (2, -1)$.

Although in Example 16 we were able to establish that the critical point gave rise to a relative minimum, in many cases this is not so easy. There is, however, a second-derivative test which gives conditions under which a critical point will be a relative maximum or minimum. We state it now, omitting the proof.

RULE 2.   *Second-Derivative Test for Functions of Two Variables. Suppose $z = f(x, y)$ has continuous partial derivatives f_{xx}, f_{yy}, and f_{xy} at all points (x, y) near the critical point (x_0, y_0). Let Δ be defined by*

$$\Delta = f_{xx}(x_0, y_0) f_{yy}(x_0, y_0) - [f_{xy}(x_0, y_0)]^2.$$

Then

a. *if $\Delta > 0$ and $f_{xx}(x_0, y_0) < 0$, f has a relative maximum at (x_0, y_0);*

b. *if $\Delta > 0$ and $f_{xx}(x_0, y_0) > 0$, f has a relative minimum at (x_0, y_0);*

c. *if $\Delta < 0$, f has neither a relative maximum nor a relative minimum at (x_0, y_0);*

d. *if $\Delta = 0$, the test fails, that is, no conclusion can be drawn and further analysis is required.*

EXAMPLE 17

Examine $f(x, y) = x^3 + y^3 - xy$ for relative maxima or minima.

$$f_x(x, y) = 3x^2 - y, \quad f_y(x, y) = 3y^2 - x.$$

In the same manner as in Example 15(b), solving $f_x = f_y = 0$ gives the critical points $(0, 0)$ and $(\frac{1}{3}, \frac{1}{3})$.

At $(0, 0)$,

$$f_{xx} = 6x = 0, \qquad f_{xy} = -1, \qquad f_{yy} = 6y = 0$$

and

$$\Delta = 0(0) - (-1)^2 = -1.$$

Since $\Delta < 0$ there is no extremum at $(0, 0)$.

At $(\frac{1}{3}, \frac{1}{3})$,

$$f_{xx} = 6(\tfrac{1}{3}) = 2, \qquad f_{xy} = -1, \qquad f_{yy} = 6(\tfrac{1}{3}) = 2$$

and

$$\Delta = 2(2) - (-1)^2 = 3.$$

Since $\Delta > 0$ and $f_{xx}(\frac{1}{3}, \frac{1}{3}) > 0$, there is a relative minimum at $(\frac{1}{3}, \frac{1}{3})$. At this point,

$$f(\tfrac{1}{3}, \tfrac{1}{3}) = (\tfrac{1}{3})^3 + (\tfrac{1}{3})^3 - (\tfrac{1}{3})(\tfrac{1}{3}) = -\tfrac{1}{27}.$$

EXAMPLE 18

Examine $f(x, y) = y^2 - x^2$ for extrema.

From

$$\frac{\partial f}{\partial x} = -2x = 0 \quad \text{and} \quad \frac{\partial f}{\partial y} = 2y = 0,$$

we get the critical point $(0, 0)$. Moreover, at $(0, 0)$, and indeed at any point,

$$\frac{\partial^2 f}{\partial x^2} = -2, \qquad \frac{\partial^2 f}{\partial y^2} = 2, \qquad \frac{\partial^2 f}{\partial y \partial x} = 0.$$

Hence $\Delta = (-2)(2) - (0)^2 = -4 < 0$ and no extrema exist. A sketch of $z = f(x, y) = y^2 - x^2$ appears in Fig. 11-9. Note that for the surface curve cut by the plane $y = 0$, there is a maximum at $(0, 0)$; but for the surface curve cut by the plane $x = 0$, there is a minimum at $(0, 0)$. Around the origin the curve is saddle-shaped and $(0, 0)$ is called a *saddle-point* of f.

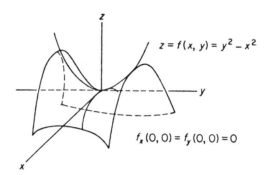

$z = f(x, y) = y^2 - x^2$

$f_x(0, 0) = f_y(0, 0) = 0$

Fig. 11-9

EXAMPLE 19

Examine $f(x, y) = x^4 + (x - y)^4$ for extrema.

If we set

$$f_x(x, y) = 4x^3 + 4(x - y)^3 = 0, \tag{4}$$

$$f_y(x, y) = -4(x - y)^3 = 0, \tag{5}$$

then from Eq. (5) we obtain $x - y = 0$ or $x = y$. Imposing this condition on Eq. (4) implies that $4x^3 = 0$ or $x = 0$. Thus, $x = y = 0$ and $(0, 0)$ is the only critical point. But at $(0, 0)$, $f_{xx} = 12x^2 + 12(x - y)^2 = 0$, $f_{yy} = 12(x - y)^2 = 0$, and $f_{xy} = -12(x - y)^2 = 0$. Hence $\Delta = 0$ and the second-derivative test fails. However, for all nonzero values of x and y we have $f(x, y) > 0$ while $f(0, 0) = 0$. Hence at $(0, 0)$ the graph of f has a low point and we conclude that f has a relative (and absolute) minimum at $(0, 0)$.

In many situations involving functions of two variables, and especially in their applications, the nature of the given problem is an indicator of whether a critical point is in fact a relative (or absolute) maximum or a relative (or absolute) minimum. In such cases the second-derivative test is not needed. Often, in mathematical studies of economic phenomena the appropriate second-order conditions are assumed to hold.

EXAMPLE 20

Let Q be a production function given by

$$Q = f(l, k) = .54l^2 - .02l^3 + 1.89k^2 - .09k^3$$

where l and k are the amounts of labor and capital, respectively, and Q is the quantity of output produced. Find the amounts of l and k so as to maximize Q.

$$f_l(l, k) = 1.08l - .06l^2 \qquad\qquad f_k(l, k) = 3.78k - .27k^2$$

$$= .06l(18 - l) = 0 \qquad\qquad\qquad = .27k(14 - k) = 0$$

$$l = 0, l = 18. \qquad\qquad\qquad\qquad k = 0, k = 14.$$

The critical points are $(0, 0)$, $(0, 14)$, $(18, 0)$, and $(18, 14)$.
At $(0, 0)$,

$$f_{ll} = 1.08 - .12l = 1.08, \qquad f_{lk} = 0, \qquad f_{kk} = 3.78 - .54k = 3.78$$

$$\Delta = 1.08(3.78) - 0 > 0.$$

Since $\Delta > 0$ and $f_{ll} > 0$, there is a relative minimum at $(0, 0)$.
At $(0, 14)$,

$$f_{ll} = 1.08, \qquad f_{lk} = 0, \qquad f_{kk} = -3.78$$

$$\Delta = 1.08(-3.78) - 0 < 0.$$

Since $\Delta < 0$, there is no extremum at $(0, 14)$.
At $(18, 0)$,

$$f_{ll} = -1.08, \qquad f_{lk} = 0, \qquad f_{kk} = 3.78$$

$$\Delta = (-1.08)(3.78) - 0 < 0.$$

Since $\Delta < 0$, there is no extremum at $(18, 0)$.
At $(18, 14)$,

$$f_{ll} = -1.08, \qquad f_{lk} = 0, \qquad f_{kk} = -3.78$$

$$\Delta = (-1.08)(-3.78) - 0 > 0.$$

Since $\Delta > 0$ and $f_{ll} < 0$, there is a relative maximum at $(18, 14)$. The maximum output is obtained when $l = 18$ and $k = 14$.

EXAMPLE 21

A food manufacturer produces two types of candy, A and B, for which the average costs of production are constant at 70 and 80 cents per lb, respectively. The quantities q_A, q_B (in lb) of A and B which can be sold each week are given by the joint-demand functions

$$q_A = 240(p_B - p_A)$$

and

$$q_B = 240(150 + p_A - 2p_B)$$

where p_A and p_B *are the selling prices (in cents per lb) of A and B, respectively. Determine the selling prices that will maximize the manufacturer's profit P.*

For A and B the profits per lb are $(p_A - 70)$ and $(p_B - 80)$, respectively. Hence, total profit P is

$$P = (p_A - 70)q_A + (p_B - 80)q_B$$

$$= (p_A - 70)[240(p_B - p_A)] + (p_B - 80)[240(150 + p_A - 2p_B)].$$

To maximize P, we set its partial derivatives equal to 0:

$$\frac{\partial P}{\partial p_A} = (p_A - 70)[240(-1)] + 240(p_B - p_A)(1) + (p_B - 80)(240)(1) = 0 \qquad (6)$$

$$\frac{\partial P}{\partial p_B} = (p_A - 70)[240(1)] + (p_B - 80)[240(-2)] +$$

$$[240(150 + p_A - 2p_B)](1) = 0. \qquad (7)$$

Simplifying Eqs. (6) and (7) gives

$$\begin{cases} p_B - p_A - 5 = 0 \\ -2p_B + p_A + 120 = 0, \end{cases}$$

whose solution is $p_A = 110$ and $p_B = 115$ (both in cents). Moreover,

$$\frac{\partial^2 P}{\partial p_A^2} = -480 < 0, \qquad \frac{\partial^2 P}{\partial p_B^2} = -960, \qquad \frac{\partial^2 P}{\partial p_B \partial p_A} = 480.$$

Thus $\Delta = (-480)(-960) - (480)^2 > 0$ and we indeed have a maximum. The manufacturer should sell candy A at \$1.10 per lb and B at \$1.15 per lb.

EXAMPLE 22 †

Suppose a monopolist is practicing price discrimination by selling the same product in two separate markets at different prices. Let q_A be the units sold in Market A where the demand function is $p_A = f(q_A)$ and let q_B be the units sold in Market B where the demand function is $p_B = g(q_B)$. Then the revenue functions for the two markets are

$$r_A = q_A f(q_A) \quad \text{and} \quad r_B = q_B g(q_B).$$

---

† Omit if Sec. 11-6 was not covered.

Assuming that all units are produced at one plant, let the cost function for producing $q = q_A + q_B$ units be $c = c(q)$. Keep in mind that r_A is a function of q_A, and r_B is a function of q_B. The monopolist's profit P is

$$P = r_A + r_B - c.$$

To maximize P with respect to outputs q_A and q_B, we set its partial derivatives equal to 0:

$$\frac{\partial P}{\partial q_A} = \frac{dr_A}{dq_A} + 0 - \frac{\partial c}{\partial q_A}$$

$$= \frac{dr_A}{dq_A} - \frac{dc}{dq}\frac{\partial q}{\partial q_A} = 0. \qquad \text{(chain rule)}$$

But

$$\frac{\partial q}{\partial q_A} = \frac{\partial}{\partial q_A}(q_A + q_B) = 1.$$

Thus,

$$\frac{\partial P}{\partial q_A} = \frac{dr_A}{dq_A} - \frac{dc}{dq} = 0. \qquad (8)$$

Similarly,

$$\frac{\partial P}{\partial q_B} = \frac{dr_B}{dq_B} - \frac{dc}{dq} = 0. \qquad (9)$$

From Eqs. (8) and (9) we get

$$\frac{dr_A}{dq_A} = \frac{dc}{dq} = \frac{dr_B}{dq_B}.$$

But dr_A/dq_A and dr_B/dq_B are marginal revenues and dc/dx is marginal cost. Hence, to maximize profit it is necessary to charge prices (and distribute output) so that the marginal revenues in both markets will be the same and, loosely speaking, will also be equal to the cost of the last unit produced in the plant.

EXERCISE 11-7

In problems 1–6, find the critical points of the functions.

1. $f(x, y) = x^2 + y^2 - 5x + 4y + xy$

2. $f(x, y) = x^2 + 4y^2 - 6x + 16y$

3. $f(x, y) = 2x^3 + y^3 - 3x^2 + 1.5y^2 - 12x - 90y$

4. $f(x, y) = xy - \dfrac{1}{x} - \dfrac{1}{y}$

5. $f(x, y, z) = 2x^2 + xy + y^2 + 100 - z(x + y - 200)$

6. $f(x, y, z, w) = x^2 + y^2 + z^2 - w(x - y + 2z - 6)$

In problems 7-18, find the critical points of the functions. Determine, by the second-derivative test, whether these points correspond to a relative maximum, a relative minimum, neither, or whether the test fails.

7. $f(x, y) = x^2 + 3y^2 + 4x - 9y + 3$

8. $f(x, y) = -2x^2 + 8x - 3y^2 + 24y + 7$

9. $f(x, y) = 6x^2 + 3x + y^2 - y$

10. $f(x, y) = x^2 + y^2 + xy - 9x + 1$

11. $f(x, y) = x^3 - 3xy + y^2 + y - 5$

12. $f(x, y) = \dfrac{x^3}{3} + y^2 - 2x + 2y - 2xy$

13. $f(x, y) = \frac{1}{3}(x^3 + 8y^3) - 2(x^2 + y^2) + 1$

14. $f(x, y) = x^2 + y^2 - xy + x^3$

15. $f(l, k) = 2lk - l^2 + 264k - 10l - 2k^2$

16. $f(l, k) = l^3 + k^3 - 3lk$

17. $f(p, q) = pq - \dfrac{1}{p} - \dfrac{1}{q}$

18. $f(x, y) = (x - 3)(y - 3)(x + y - 3)$

In problems 19-26, unless otherwise indicated the variables p_A and p_B denote selling prices of commodities A and B, respectively. Similarly, q_A and q_B denote quantities of A and B which are produced and sold during some time period. In all cases, the variables employed will be assumed to be units of output, input, money, etc.

19. Suppose $Q = f(l, k) = 1.08l^2 - .03l^3 + 1.68k^2 - .08k^3$ is a production function for a firm. Find the quantities of input, l and k, so as to maximize output Q.

20. In a certain automated manufacturing process, machines M and N are utilized for m and n hours, respectively. If daily output Q is a function of m and n, namely $Q = 4.5m + 5n - .5m^2 - n^2 - .25mn$, find the values of m and n which will maximize Q.

21. The Sweet-Tooth Candy Company produces two delectable varieties of candy, A and B, for which the constant average costs of production are 60 and 70 (cents per lb), respectively. The demand functions for A and B are respectively given by $q_A = 230(p_B - p_A)$ and $q_B = 29,440 + 230(p_A - 2p_B)$. Find the selling prices, p_A and p_B, which would maximize the company's profit.

22. Repeat Problem 21 if the constant costs of production of A and B are a and b (cents per lb), respectively.

23. Suppose a monopolist is practicing price discrimination in the sale of his product by charging different prices in two separate markets. In market A the demand function is $p_A = 100 - q_A$ and in B it is $p_B = 84 - q_B$, where q_A and q_B are the quantities sold per week in A and B, and p_A and p_B are the respective prices per unit. If the monopolist's cost function is $c = 600 + 4(q_A + q_B)$, how much should be sold in each market to maximize profit? What selling prices would give this maximum profit? Find the maximum profit.

24. A monopolist sells two competitive products, A and B, for which the demand functions are $q_A = 1 - 2p_A + 4p_B$ and $q_B = 11 + 2p_A - 6p_B$. If the constant average cost of producing a unit of A is 4 and for B it is 1, how many units of A and B should be sold to maximize the monopolist's profit?

25. For products A and B, the joint-cost function for a manufacturer is $c = 1.5q_A^2 + 4.5q_B^2$ and the demand functions are $p_A = 36 - q_A^2$ and $p_B = 30 - q_B^2$. Find the level of production which will maximize profit.

26. For a monopolist's products A and B the joint-cost function is $c = (q_A + q_B)^2$ and the demand functions are $q_A = 26 - p_A$ and $q_B = 10 - .25p_B$. Find the values of p_A and p_B which will maximize profit. What are the quantities of A and B which correspond to these prices? What is the total profit?

27. Suppose A and B are the only two firms in the market selling the same product (we say they are *duopolists*). The industry demand function for the product is $p = 92 - q_A - q_B$ where q_A and q_B denote the output produced and sold by A and B, respectively. For A the cost function is $c_A = 10q_A$ and for B it is $c_B = .5q_B^2$. Suppose the firms decide to enter into an agreement on output and price control by jointly acting as a monopoly. In this case we say they enter into *collusion*. Show that the profit function for the monopoly is given by

$$P = pq_A - c_A + pq_B - c_B.$$

Express P as a function of q_A and q_B and determine how output should be allocated so as to maximize the profit of the monopoly.

11-8 LAGRANGE MULTIPLIERS

We shall now find relative maxima and minima for a function on which certain *constraints* are imposed. Such a situation could arise if a manufacturer wished to minimize the total cost of factors of input and yet obtain a particular level of output.

Suppose we find the extrema of

$$w = x^2 + y^2 + z^2 \tag{1}$$

subject to the constraint that x, y, and z must satisfy

$$x - y + 2z = 6. \tag{2}$$

Solving Eq. (2) for x, we get

$$x = y - 2z + 6, \tag{3}$$

which when substituted for x in Eq. (1) gives

$$w = (y - 2z + 6)^2 + y^2 + z^2. \tag{4}$$

Since w in Eq. (4) has been expressed as a function of two variables, to find extrema we follow the usual procedure of setting its partial derivatives equal to 0.

$$\frac{\partial w}{\partial y} = 2(y - 2z + 6) + 2y = 4y - 4z + 12 = 0 \tag{5}$$

$$\frac{\partial w}{\partial z} = -4(y - 2z + 6) + 2z = -4y + 10z - 24 = 0. \tag{6}$$

Solving Eqs. (5) and (6) simultaneously gives $y = -1$ and $z = 2$. From Eq. (3), $x = 1$. Hence, the only critical point of (1) subject to constraint (2) is $(1, -1, 2)$. Evaluating the second-order derivatives of (4) when $y = -1$ and $z = 2$ gives

$$\frac{\partial^2 w}{\partial y^2} = 4, \qquad \frac{\partial^2 w}{\partial z^2} = 10, \qquad \frac{\partial^2 w}{\partial z \partial y} = -4$$

$$\Delta = 4(10) - (-4)^2 = 24 > 0.$$

Thus w, subject to the constraint, has a relative minimum at $(1, -1, 2)$.

This solution was found by using the constraint to express one of the variables in the original function in terms of the other variables. Often this is not practical, but there is another technique, called the method of **Lagrange multipliers**†, which avoids this step and yet allows us to obtain critical points.

The method is as follows. Suppose we have a function $f(x, y, z)$ subject to the constraint $g(x, y, z) = 0$. We construct a new function F of four variables defined by the following (where λ is the Greek letter lambda):

$$F(x, y, z, \lambda) = f(x, y, z) - \lambda g(x, y, z).$$

It can be shown that if (x_0, y_0, z_0) is a critical point of f subject to the constraint $g(x, y, z) = 0$, then there exists a value of λ, say λ_0, such that $(x_0, y_0, z_0, \lambda_0)$ is a critical point of F. Also, if $(x_0, y_0, z_0, \lambda_0)$ is a critical point of F, then (x_0, y_0, z_0) is a critical point of f subject to the constraint. Thus to find critical points of f subject to $g(x, y, z) = 0$, we instead find critical points of F. These are obtained by solving the simultaneous equations

$$F_x = 0, \qquad F_y = 0, \qquad F_z = 0, \quad \text{and} \quad F_\lambda = 0.$$

At times, ingenuity must be used to do this. Once a critical point $(x_0, y_0,$

---

† After the French mathematician, Joseph-Louis Lagrange (1736–1813).

z_0, λ_0) of F is obtained, we can conclude that (x_0, y_0, z_0) is a critical point of f subject to the constraint.

Let us illustrate for the original situation:

$$f(x, y, z) = x^2 + y^2 + z^2 \quad \text{subject to} \quad x - y + 2z = 6.$$

First, we write the constraint as $g(x, y, z) = x - y + 2z - 6 = 0$. Second, we form the function

$$F(x, y, z, \lambda) = f(x, y, z) - \lambda\, g(x, y, z)$$
$$= x^2 + y^2 + z^2 - \lambda(x - y + 2z - 6).$$

Next we set each partial derivative of F equal to 0.

$$\begin{cases} F_x = 2x - \lambda = 0 & \text{(7)} \\[4pt] F_y = 2y + \lambda = 0 & \text{(8)} \\[4pt] F_z = 2z - 2\lambda = 0 & \text{(9)} \\[4pt] F_\lambda = -x + y - 2z + 6 = 0. & \text{(10)} \end{cases}$$

From Eqs. (7)–(9) we see immediately that

$$x = \frac{\lambda}{2}, \qquad y = -\frac{\lambda}{2}, \quad \text{and} \quad z = \lambda. \tag{11}$$

Substituting these values in Eq. (10), we obtain

$$-\frac{\lambda}{2} - \frac{\lambda}{2} - 2\lambda + 6 = 0$$

$$\lambda = 2.$$

Thus from Eq. (11), $x = 1$, $y = -1$, and $z = 2$. Hence the only critical point of f subject to the constraint is $(1, -1, 2)$ at which there may exist a relative maximum, a relative minimum, or neither of these. The method of Lagrange multipliers does not directly indicate which of these possibilities occur, although from our previous work we saw that it is indeed a relative minimum. In applied problems, the nature of the problem itself may give a clue as to how a critical point is to be regarded. Often the existence of either a relative minimum or a relative maximum is assumed and a critical point is treated accordingly. Actually, sufficient second-order conditions for extrema are available, but we shall not consider them.

The method of Lagrange multipliers is by no means restricted to problems of the type illustrated. For example, suppose $f(x, y, z, w)$ were subject to constraints $g_1(x, y, z, w) = 0$ and $g_2(x, y, z, w) = 0$. Then there would be two Lagrange multipliers, λ_1 and λ_2 (one for each constraint), and we would construct the function $F = f - \lambda_1 g_1 - \lambda_2 g_2$. We would then solve the system $F_x = F_y = F_z = F_w = F_{\lambda_1} = F_{\lambda_2} = 0$.

EXAMPLE 23

Find the critical points for z = f(x, y) = 3x − y + 6 subject to the constraint x² + y² = 4.

We write the constraint as $g(x, y) = x^2 + y^2 - 4 = 0$ and construct the function

$$F(x, y, \lambda) = 3x - y + 6 - \lambda(x^2 + y^2 - 4).$$

Setting $F_x = F_y = F_\lambda = 0$:

$$\left\{ \begin{array}{rll} 3 - 2x\lambda & = 0 & (12) \\ -1 - 2y\lambda & = 0 & (13) \\ -x^2 - y^2 + 4 & = 0. & (14) \end{array} \right.$$

From Eqs. (12) and (13),

$$x = \frac{3}{2\lambda} \quad \text{and} \quad y = -\frac{1}{2\lambda}.$$

Substituting in Eq. (14), we obtain

$$-\frac{9}{4\lambda^2} - \frac{1}{4\lambda^2} + 4 = 0$$

$$\lambda = \pm\frac{\sqrt{10}}{4}.$$

If $\lambda = \sqrt{10}/4$,

$$x = \frac{3}{2\left(\dfrac{\sqrt{10}}{4}\right)} = \frac{3\sqrt{10}}{5}, \qquad y = -\frac{1}{2\left(\dfrac{\sqrt{10}}{4}\right)} = -\frac{\sqrt{10}}{5}.$$

Similarly, if $\lambda = -\sqrt{10}/4$,

$$x = -\frac{3\sqrt{10}}{5}, \qquad y = \frac{\sqrt{10}}{5}.$$

Thus, the critical points are $(3\sqrt{10}/5, -\sqrt{10}/5)$ and $(-3\sqrt{10}/5, \sqrt{10}/5)$.

EXAMPLE 24

Find critical points for f(x, y, z) = xyz, where xyz ≠ 0, subject to the constraint x + 2y + 3z = 36.

$$F(x, y, z, \lambda) = xyz - \lambda(x + 2y + 3z - 36)$$

$$\begin{cases} F_x = yz - \lambda = 0 \\ F_y = xz - 2\lambda = 0 \\ F_z = xy - 3\lambda = 0 \\ F_\lambda = -x - 2y - 3z + 36 = 0. \end{cases}$$

We can write the system as

$$\begin{cases} yz = \lambda & (15) \\ xz = 2\lambda & (16) \\ xy = 3\lambda & (17) \\ x + 2y + 3z - 36 = 0. & (18) \end{cases}$$

Dividing each side of Eq. (15) by the corresponding side of Eq. (16), we get

$$\frac{yz}{xz} = \frac{\lambda}{2\lambda} \quad \text{or} \quad y = \frac{x}{2}.$$

This division is valid since $xyz \neq 0$. Similarly, from Eqs. (15) and (17) we get

$$z = \frac{x}{3}.$$

Substituting into Eq. (18), gives

$$x + 2\left(\frac{x}{2}\right) + 3\left(\frac{x}{3}\right) - 36 = 0$$

$$x = 12.$$

Thus $y = 6$ and $z = 4$. Hence (12, 6, 4) is the only critical point satisfying the given conditions.

EXAMPLE 25

Suppose a firm has an order for 200 units of its product and wishes to distribute their manufacture between two of its plants, Plant 1 and Plant 2. Let q_1 and q_2 denote the outputs of Plants 1 and 2, respectively, and suppose the total cost function is given by $c = f(q_1, q_2) = 2q_1^2 + q_1 q_2 + q_2^2 + 200$. How should the output be distributed in order to minimize costs?

We must minimize $c = f(q_1, q_2)$ subject to the constraint $q_1 + q_2 = 200$.

$$F(q_1, q_2, \lambda) = 2q_1^2 + q_1 q_2 + q_2^2 + 200 - \lambda(q_1 + q_2 - 200)$$

$$\begin{cases} \dfrac{\partial F}{\partial q_1} = 4q_1 + q_2 - \lambda = 0 & (19) \\[2em] \dfrac{\partial F}{\partial q_2} = q_1 + 2q_2 - \lambda = 0 & (20) \\[2em] \dfrac{\partial F}{\partial \lambda} = -q_1 - q_2 + 200 = 0. & (21) \end{cases}$$

Using the method of elimination by addition on Eqs. (19) and (20) gives

$$q_1 = \frac{\lambda}{7}, \qquad q_2 = \frac{3\lambda}{7}.$$

Substituting these values in Eq. (21) gives $\lambda = 350$. Thus $q_1 = 50$ and $q_2 = 150$. Plant 1 should produce 50 units and Plant 2, 150 units, in order to minimize costs.

An interesting observation can be made concerning Example 25. From Eq. (19), $\lambda = 4q_1 + q_2 = \partial c/\partial q_1$, the marginal cost of Plant 1. From Eq. (20), $\lambda = q_1 + 2q_2 = \partial c/\partial q_2$, the marginal cost of Plant 2. Hence, $\partial c/\partial q_1 = \partial c/\partial q_2$ and we conclude that to minimize cost it is necessary that the marginal costs of each plant be equal to each other.

EXAMPLE 26

Suppose a firm must produce a given quantity Q_o of output in the cheapest possible manner. If there are two input factors l and k, and their prices per unit are fixed at p_l and p_k respectively, discuss the economic significance of combining input to achieve least cost. That is, describe the least-cost input combination.

Let $Q = f(l, k)$ be the production function. Then we must minimize the cost function

$$c = lp_l + kp_k$$

subject to

$$Q_0 = f(l, k).$$

We construct

$$F(l, k, \lambda) = lp_l + kp_k - \lambda \left[f(l, k) - Q_0 \right].$$

We have

$$\frac{\partial F}{\partial l} = p_l - \lambda \frac{\partial f}{\partial l} = 0 \tag{22}$$

$$\frac{\partial F}{\partial k} = p_k - \lambda \frac{\partial f}{\partial k} = 0 \tag{23}$$

$$\frac{\partial F}{\partial \lambda} = -f(l, k) + Q_0 = 0.$$

From Eqs. (22) and (23),

$$\lambda = \frac{p_l}{\partial f/\partial l} = \frac{p_k}{\partial f/\partial k}. \tag{24}$$

Hence,

$$\frac{p_l}{p_k} = \frac{\partial f/\partial l}{\partial f/\partial k}.$$

We conclude that when the least-cost combination of factors is used, the ratio of the marginal products of the input factors must be equal to the ratio of their corresponding prices.

EXERCISE 11-8

In problems 1-10 find, by the method of Lagrange multipliers, the critical points of the functions subject to the given constraints.

1. $f(x, y) = x^2 + 4y^2 + 6$; $2x - 8y = 20$

2. $f(x, y) = -2x^2 + 5y^2 + 7$; $3x - 2y = 7$

3. $f(x, y, z) = x^2 + y^2 + z^2$; $2x + y - z = 9$

4. $f(x, y, z) = x + y + z$; $xyz = 27$

5. $f(x, y, z) = x^2 + xy + 2y^2 + z^2$; $x - 3y - 4z = 16$

6. $f(x, y, z) = xyz^2$; $x - y + z = 20$ $(xyz^2 \neq 0)$

7. $f(x, y, z) = xyz$; $x + 2y + 3z = 18$ $(xyz \neq 0)$

8. $f(x, y, z) = x^2 + y^2 + z^2$; $x + y + z = 1$

9. $f(x, y, z) = x^2 + 2y - z^2$; $2x - y = 0$, $y + z = 0$

10. $f(x, y, z, w) = 2x^2 + 2y^2 + 3z^2 - 4w^2$; $4x - 8y + 6z + 16w = 6$

11. To fill an order for 100 units of its product, a firm wishes to distribute the production between its two plants, Plant 1 and Plant 2. The total cost function is $c = f(q_1, q_2) = .1q_1^2 + 7q_1 + 15q_2 + 1000$ where q_1 and q_2 are the units produced at Plants 1 and 2, respectively. How should the output be distributed in order to minimize costs?

12. Repeat Problem 11 if the cost function is $c = 3q_1^2 + q_1q_2 + 2q_2^2$ and a total of 200 units are to be produced.

13. The production function for a firm is $f(l, k) = 12l + 20k - l^2 - 2k^2$. The cost to the firm of l and k is 4 and 8 per unit, respectively. If the firm wants the total cost of input to be 88, find the greatest output possible subject to this budget constraint.

14. Repeat Problem 13 given that $f(l, k) = 60l + 30k - 2l^2 - 3k^2$ and the budget constraint is $2l + 3k = 30$.

Problems 15–18 refer to the following definition. A *utility function* is a function which attaches a measure to the satisfaction or utility a consumer gets from the consumption of products per unit of time. Suppose $U = f(x, y)$ is such a function where x and y are the amounts of two products, X and Y. The *marginal utility* of X is $\partial U/\partial x$ and approximately represents the change in total utility resulting from a one unit change in consumption of product X per unit of time. We define the marginal utility of Y in similar fashion. If the prices of X and Y are p_x and p_y, respectively, and the consumer has an income or budget of I to spend, then his budget constraint is $xp_x + yp_y = I$. In the following problems you are asked to find the quantities of each product which the consumer should buy, subject to his budget, which will allow him to maximize his satisfaction. That is, you are to maximize $U = f(x, y)$ subject to $xp_x + yp_y = I$. Assume such a maximum exists.

15. $U = x^3 y^3$; $p_x = 2$, $p_y = 3$, $I = 48$ $(x^3 y^3 \neq 0)$

16. $U = 46x - (5x^2/2) + 34y - 2y^2$; $p_x = 5$, $p_y = 2$, $I = 30$

17. $U = f(x, y, z) = xyz$; $p_x = 2$, $p_y = 1$, $p_z = 4$, $I = 60$ $(xyz \neq 0)$

18. Let $U = f(x, y)$ be a utility function subject to the budget constraint $xp_x + yp_y = I$ where p_x, p_y, and I are constant. Show that to maximize satisfaction it is necessary that

$$\lambda = \frac{f_x}{p_x} = \frac{f_y}{p_y},$$

where f_x and f_y are the marginal utilities of X and Y, respectively. Deduce that f_x/p_x is the marginal utility of one dollar's worth of X. Hence, maximum satisfaction is obtained when the consumer allocates his budget so that the marginal utility of a dollar's worth of X is equal to the marginal utility per dollar's worth of Y. Performing the same procedure as above, verify that this is true for $U = f(x, y, z, w)$ subject to the corresponding budget equation. In each case, λ is called the *marginal utility of income*.

11-9 LINES OF REGRESSION †

To study the influence of advertising on sales, a firm compiled the data in Table 11-4. The variable x denotes advertising expenditures in hundreds of dollars and the variable y denotes the corresponding yield in sales revenue in thousands of dollars. If each pair (x, y) of data is plotted, the result is called a *scatter diagram* [Fig. 11-10(a)].

From an observation of the distribution of the points, it is reasonable to assume that a relationship exists between x and y and that it is approximately

---

†May be omitted without loss of continuity.

TABLE 11-4

expenditures (x)	2	3	4.5	5.5	7
revenue (y)	3	6	8	10	11

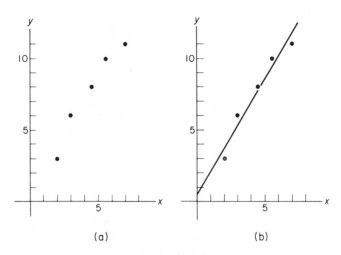

(a)   (b)

Fig. 11-10

linear. On this basis we may fit a straight line "by eye" to the data [Fig. 11-10(b)], and from this line predict a value of *y* for a given value of *x*. This line seems consistent with the trend of the data, although other lines could be drawn as well. Unfortunately, determining a line "by eye" is not very objective. We need a more reliable procedure for judging consistency with data. That is, we want to apply criteria in specifying what we shall call a line of "best fit." A frequently used technique is called the **method of least squares.**

To apply the method of least squares to the data in Table 11-4, we first assume that *x* and *y* are approximately linearly related and that we can fit a straight line

$$\hat{y} = \hat{a} + \hat{b}x \qquad (1)$$

to the given points by a suitable objective choice of the constants $\hat{a}$ and $\hat{b}$ (read "*a* hat" and "*b* hat," respectively). For a given value of *x* in Eq. (1), $\hat{y}$ is the corresponding predicted value of *y* and $(x, \hat{y})$ will be on the line. Our aim is that $\hat{y}$ be near *y*.

When $x = 2$, the observed value of *y* is 3. Our predicted value of *y* is obtained by substituting $x = 2$ in Eq. (1), obtaining $\hat{y} = \hat{a} + 2\hat{b}$. The error of estimation, or vertical deviation of the point (2, 3) from the line, is $\hat{y} - y$ or

$$\hat{a} + 2\hat{b} - 3.$$

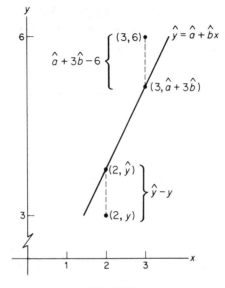

Fig. 11-11

This vertical deviation is indicated (although exaggerated for clarity) in Fig. 11-11. Similarly, the vertical deviation of (3, 6) from the line is $\hat{a} + 3\hat{b} - 6$ as is also illustrated. To avoid possible difficulties associated with positive and negative deviations, we shall consider the squares of the deviations and shall form the sum S of all such squares.

$$S = (\hat{a} + 2\hat{b} - 3)^2 + (\hat{a} + 3\hat{b} - 6)^2 + (\hat{a} + 4.5\hat{b} - 8)^2 + (\hat{a} + 5.5\hat{b} - 10)^2 + $$
$$(\hat{a} + 7\hat{b} - 11)^2.$$

The method of least squares requires that we choose as the line of "best fit" the one obtained by selecting $\hat{a}$ and $\hat{b}$ so as to minimize S. But to minimize S with respect to $\hat{a}$ and $\hat{b}$, it is necessary that we solve the system

$$\begin{cases} \dfrac{\partial S}{\partial \hat{a}} = 0 \\[2mm] \dfrac{\partial S}{\partial \hat{b}} = 0. \end{cases}$$

We have

$$\frac{\partial S}{\partial \hat{a}} = 2(\hat{a} + 2\hat{b} - 3) + 2(\hat{a} + 3\hat{b} - 6) + 2(\hat{a} + 4.5\hat{b} - 8) + 2(\hat{a} + 5.5\hat{b} - 10) + $$
$$2(\hat{a} + 7\hat{b} - 11) = 0$$

$$\frac{\partial S}{\partial \hat{b}} = 4(\hat{a} + 2\hat{b} - 3) + 6(\hat{a} + 3\hat{b} - 6) + 9(\hat{a} + 4.5\hat{b} - 8) + 11(\hat{a} + 5.5\hat{b} - 10) +$$

$$14(\hat{a} + 7\hat{b} - 11) = 0$$

which when simplified gives

$$\begin{cases} 5\hat{a} + 22\hat{b} = 38 \\ 44\hat{a} + 225\hat{b} = 384. \end{cases}$$

Solving for $\hat{a}$ and $\hat{b}$, we obtain

$$\hat{a} = \tfrac{102}{157} \approx .65, \qquad \hat{b} = \tfrac{248}{157} \approx 1.58.$$

It can be shown that the values of $\hat{a}$ and $\hat{b}$ obtained this way always lead to a minimum value of S. Hence, in the sense of least squares the line of best fit is

$$\hat{y} = .65 + 1.58x. \tag{2}$$

This is, in fact, the line indicated in Fig. 11-10(b). It is called the *least squares line of y on x* or the *linear regression line of y on x*. The constants $\hat{a}$ and $\hat{b}$ are called *linear regression coefficients*. To use Eq. (2), we would predict that when $x = 5$ the corresponding value of y is $\hat{y} = .65 + 1.58(5) = 8.55$.

More generally, suppose we are given the following set of n pairs of observations:

$$\{(x_1, y_1), (x_2, y_2), \dots, (x_n, y_n)\}.$$

If we assume that x and y are approximately linearly related and that we can fit a straight line $\hat{y} = \hat{a} + \hat{b}x$ to the data, the sum of the squares of the errors $\hat{y} - y$ is

$$S = (\hat{a} + \hat{b}x_1 - y_1)^2 + (\hat{a} + \hat{b}x_2 - y_2)^2 + \dots + (\hat{a} + \hat{b}x_n - y_n)^2.$$

Since S must be minimized with respect to $\hat{a}$ and $\hat{b}$,

$$\begin{cases} \dfrac{\partial S}{\partial \hat{a}} = 2(\hat{a} + \hat{b}x_1 - y_1) + 2(\hat{a} + \hat{b}x_2 - y_2) + \dots + 2(\hat{a} + \hat{b}x_n - y_n) = 0 \\[2mm] \dfrac{\partial S}{\partial \hat{b}} = 2x_1(\hat{a} + \hat{b}x_1 - y_1) + 2x_2(\hat{a} + \hat{b}x_2 - y_2) + \dots + 2x_n(\hat{a} + \hat{b}x_n - y_n) \\[2mm] \hspace{9cm} = 0. \end{cases}$$

Dividing both equations by 2 and using sigma notation, we have

$$\begin{cases} \hat{a}n + \hat{b} \displaystyle\sum_{i=1}^{n} x_i - \sum_{i=1}^{n} y_i = 0 \\[4mm] \hat{a} \displaystyle\sum_{i=1}^{n} x_i + \hat{b} \sum_{i=1}^{n} x_i^2 - \sum_{i=1}^{n} x_i y_i = 0. \end{cases}$$

Equivalently we have the system of so-called *normal equations:*

$$\begin{cases} \sum_{i=1}^{n} y_i = \hat{a}n + \hat{b}\sum_{i=1}^{n} x_i & (3) \\[4mm] \sum_{i=1}^{n} x_i y_i = \hat{a}\sum_{i=1}^{n} x_i + \hat{b}\sum_{i=1}^{n} x_i^2. & (4) \end{cases}$$

To solve for $\hat{a}$ and $\hat{b}$ we first multiply Eq. (3) by $\sum_{i=1}^{n} x_i$ and Eq. (4) by n:

$$\begin{cases} \left(\sum_{i=1}^{n} x_i\right)\left(\sum_{i=1}^{n} y_i\right) = \hat{a}n\sum_{i=1}^{n} x_i + \hat{b}\left(\sum_{i=1}^{n} x_i\right)^2 & (5) \\[4mm] n\sum_{i=1}^{n} x_i y_i = \hat{a}n\sum_{i=1}^{n} x_i + \hat{b}n\sum_{i=1}^{n} x_i^2. & (6) \end{cases}$$

Subtracting Eq. (5) from Eq. (6), we obtain

$$n\sum_{i=1}^{n} x_i y_i - \left(\sum_{i=1}^{n} x_i\right)\left(\sum_{i=1}^{n} y_i\right) = \hat{b}n\sum_{i=1}^{n} x_i^2 - \hat{b}\left(\sum_{i=1}^{n} x_i\right)^2$$

$$= \hat{b}\left[n\sum_{i=1}^{n} x_i^2 - \left(\sum_{i=1}^{n} x_i\right)^2\right].$$

Thus,

$$\boxed{\hat{b} = \frac{n\sum_{i=1}^{n} x_i y_i - \left(\sum_{i=1}^{n} x_i\right)\left(\sum_{i=1}^{n} y_i\right)}{n\sum_{i=1}^{n} x_i^2 - \left(\sum_{i=1}^{n} x_i\right)^2}.} \qquad (7)$$

It can also be shown that

$$\boxed{\hat{a} = \frac{\left(\sum_{i=1}^{n} x_i^2\right)\left(\sum_{i=1}^{n} y_i\right) - \left(\sum_{i=1}^{n} x_i\right)\left(\sum_{i=1}^{n} x_i y_i\right)}{n\sum_{i=1}^{n} x_i^2 - \left(\sum_{i=1}^{n} x_i\right)^2}.} \qquad (8)$$

Computing the linear regression coefficients $\hat{a}$ and $\hat{b}$ by the formulas of Eqs. (7) and (8) gives the linear regression line of y on x, $\hat{y} = \hat{a} + \hat{b}x$, which can be used to estimate y for a given value of x.

In the next example, as well as in the exercises, you will encounter *index numbers*. They are used to relate a variable in one period of time to the same variable in another period, this latter period called the *base period*. Thus an index number is a *relative* number which describes data that are changing over time. Such data are referred to as *time series*.

For example, consider the time series data of total production of widgets in the United States for 1971–1975 indicated in Table 11-5. If we choose 1972 as the base year and assign to it the index number 100, then the other index

TABLE 11-5

YEAR	PRODUCTION IN THOUSANDS	INDEX [1972 = 100]
1971	828	92
1972	900	100
1973	936	104
1974	891	99
1975	954	106

numbers are obtained by dividing each year's production by the 1972 production of 900 and multiplying the result by 100. We can, for example, interpret the index 106 for 1975 as meaning that production for that year was 106 percent of production in 1972.

In time series analysis, index numbers are obviously of great advantage if the data involve numbers of great magnitude. But regardless of the magnitude of the data, index numbers simplify the task of comparing changes in data over periods of time.

EXAMPLE 27

By means of the least squares linear regression line, represent the trend for the Index of Industrial Production from 1963 to 1968 (Table 11-6 [1967 = 100]).

TABLE 11-6

Year	1963	1964	1965	1966	1967	1968
Index	79	84	91	99	100	105

Source: Economic Report of the President, 1971, U.S. Government Printing Office, Washington, D.C., 1971.

We shall let x denote time and treat the index y as a linear function of x. Also, we shall designate 1963 by $x = 1$, 1964 by $x = 2$, etc. There are $n = 6$ pairs of measurements. To use the formulas of Eqs. (7) and (8) we first find:

$$\sum_{i=1}^{6} x_i = 1 + 2 + 3 + 4 + 5 + 6 = 21,$$

$$\sum_{i=1}^{6} y_i = 79 + 84 + 91 + 99 + 100 + 105 = 558,$$

$$\sum_{i=1}^{6} x_i y_i = 1(79) + 2(84) + 3(91) + 4(99) + 5(100) + 6(105) = 2046,$$

$$\sum_{i=1}^{6} x_i^2 = 1^2 + 2^2 + 3^2 + 4^2 + 5^2 + 6^2 = 91.$$

Hence by Eq. (8),

$$\hat{a} = \frac{91(558) - 21(2046)}{6(91) - (21)^2} = \frac{7812}{105} = 74.4,$$

and by Eq. (7),

$$\hat{b} = \frac{6(2046) - 21(558)}{6(91) - (21)^2} = \frac{558}{105} = 5.31 \text{ (approximately)}.$$

Thus the line of best fit is the regression line of y on x given by the equation

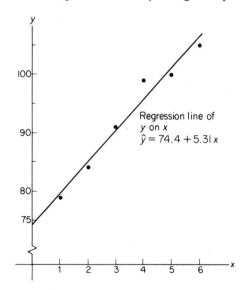

Fig. 11-12

$$\hat{y} = 74.4 + 5.31x,$$

whose graph, as well as a scatter diagram, appears in Fig. 11-12.

EXERCISE 11-9

In problems 1-4, find an equation of the least squares linear regression line of y on x for the given data and sketch both the line and the data. Predict the value of y corresponding to $x = 3.5$.

1.

x	1	2	3	4	5	6
y	1.5	2.3	2.6	3.7	4.0	4.5

2.

x	1	2	3	4	5	6	7
y	1	1.8	2	4	4.5	7	9

3.

x	2	3	4.5	5.5	7
y	3	5	8	10	11

4.

x	2	3	4	5	6	7
y	2.4	2.9	3.3	3.8	4.3	4.9

5. A firm finds that when the price of its product is p dollars per unit, the number of units sold is x as indicated below. Find an equation of the regression line of x on p.

price (p)	10	30	40	50	60	70
demand (x)	70	68	63	50	46	32

6. Old Mac Donald finds that on his farm the amount of water applied (in inches) and the corresponding yield of a certain crop (in tons per acre) are as given below. Find an equation of the regression line of y on x. Predict y when $x = 12$.

water (x)	8	16	24	32
yield (y)	4.1	4.5	5.1	6.1

7. The average cost $\bar{c}$, in dollars per unit, of producing x hundred units of a product is given in the table below. Find an equation of the regression line of $\bar{c}$ on x and predict $\bar{c}$ when $x = 5$.

output (x)	2	4	6	8	10
average cost $(\bar{c})$	7.9	7	6.2	5.5	5

For the time series in problems 8–10 fit a linear regression line by least squares; that is, find an equation of the linear regression line. In each case call the first year in the table, year 1.

8.

WIDGET PRODUCTION IN WESTERN EUPHORIA, 1971–1975
(in thousands of units)

YEAR	PRODUCTION
1971	10
1972	15
1973	16
1974	18
1975	21

9. In the following, let 1961 correspond to $x = 1$, 1963 correspond to $x = 3$, etc.

WHOLESALE PRICE INDEX—LUMBER AND WOOD PRODUCTS
$\left[\textbf{1967} = \textbf{100}\right]$

YEAR	INDEX
1961	91
1963	94
1965	96
1967	100

Source: *Economic Report of the President,* 1971, U.S. Government Printing Office, Washington, D.C., 1971.

10.

EQUIPMENT EXPENDITURES OF ROBBY ROBOT COMPANY, 1970–1975
(in millions of dollars)

YEAR	EXPENDITURES
1970	15
1971	22
1972	21
1973	27
1974	26
1975	34

11. a. By the method of least squares find an equation of the linear regression line that best fits the following data. Refer to 1971 as year 1, etc.

OVERSEAS SHIPMENTS OF BUTTONS BY BELLI BUTTON CO., INC.
(in millions)

YEAR	QUANTITY
1971	35
1972	31
1973	26
1974	24
1975	26

b. For the data in part (a), refer to 1971 as year -2, 1972 as year -1, 1973 as year 0, etc. Then $\sum_{i=1}^{5} x_i = 0$. Fit a least squares line and observe how the calculation is simplified.

12. For the following time series, find an equation of the linear regression line that best fits the data. Refer to 1965 as year -2, 1966 as year -1, etc.

CONSUMER PRICE INDEX—MEDICAL CARE
1965–1969, [1967 = 100]

YEAR	INDEX
1965	90
1966	93
1967	100
1968	106
1969	113

Source: *Economic Report of the President,* 1971, U.S. Government Printing Office, Washington, D.C., 1971.

11-10   A COMMENT ON HOMOGENEOUS FUNCTIONS†

Many of the functions which are useful in economic analysis share the property of being homogeneous.

DEFINITION.   *A function $z = f(x, y)$ is said to be* **homogeneous of degree n** *(n being a constant) if, for* **all** *positive real values of* λ,

$$f(\lambda x, \lambda y) = \lambda^n f(x, y).$$

---

† This section contains material from Sec. 11-6 and may be omitted without loss of continuity.

Verbally, if both x and y are multiplied by the same positive real number, then the resulting functional value is a power of the number times the functional value $f(x, y)$. For example, if

$$f(x, y) = x^3 - 2xy^2,$$

then

$$f(\lambda x, \lambda y) = (\lambda x)^3 - 2(\lambda x)(\lambda y)^2 = \lambda^3 x^3 - 2\lambda^3 xy^2$$
$$= \lambda^3(x^3 - 2xy^2) = \lambda^3 f(x, y).$$

Thus f is homogeneous of degree three.

An important homogeneous function in economics is the Cobb-Douglas production function:

$$Q = f(l, k) = Al^\alpha k^{1-\alpha} \quad (\alpha \text{ and } A \text{ are constants}).$$

We have

$$f(\lambda l, \lambda k) = A(\lambda l)^\alpha (\lambda k)^{1-\alpha} = A\lambda^\alpha l^\alpha \lambda^{1-\alpha} k^{1-\alpha}$$
$$= \lambda Al^\alpha k^{1-\alpha} = \lambda f(l, k).$$

Thus f is homogeneous of degree one. For example, $f(x, y) = 2l^{.3}k^{.7}$ is a homogeneous function of degree one.

Homogeneous production functions of degree one have an interesting property. If f is such a function, then

$$f(\lambda l, \lambda k) = \lambda f(l, k).$$

Thus if all inputs are doubled,

$$f(2l, 2k) = 2f(l, k),$$

then output is doubled. Similarly, if all inputs are tripled, output is tripled, etc. In short, the same proportional change in each input factor of production results in the same proportional change in output.

By considering the partial derivatives of a homogenous function, an important result can be obtained. Let $f(l, k)$ be a homogeneous production function of degree n. Then we have the identity

$$f(\lambda l, \lambda k) = \lambda^n f(l, k). \tag{1}$$

Consider the left side of Eq. (1). If we set $r = \lambda l$ and $s = \lambda k$, then Eq. (1) becomes

$$f(r, s) = \lambda^n f(l, k).$$

Now for each side we take the partial with respect to λ. For the left side, $f(r, s)$:

$$\frac{\partial f}{\partial \lambda} = \frac{\partial f}{\partial r}\frac{\partial r}{\partial \lambda} + \frac{\partial f}{\partial s}\frac{\partial s}{\partial \lambda} \qquad \text{(chain rule)}$$

$$= \frac{\partial f}{\partial r}l + \frac{\partial f}{\partial s}k. \qquad (2)$$

For the right side,

$$\frac{\partial}{\partial \lambda}[\lambda^n f(l, k)] = n\lambda^{n-1}f(l, k). \qquad (3)$$

Setting (2) and (3) equal to each other, we have

$$l\frac{\partial f}{\partial r} + k\frac{\partial f}{\partial s} = n\lambda^{n-1}f(l, k).$$

In particular, if $\lambda = 1$, then $r = l$ and $s = k$. Hence we have what is called *Euler's Theorem* for homogeneous functions:

$$l\frac{\partial f}{\partial l} + k\frac{\partial f}{\partial k} = nf(l, k). \qquad (4)$$

Now, if f is homogenous of degree one, such as the Cobb-Douglas function, then $n = 1$ and Eq. (4) becomes

$$l\frac{\partial f}{\partial l} + k\frac{\partial f}{\partial k} = f(l, k).$$

Thus if we multiply the marginal product of each input by the quantity of the input, the sum is equal to the total product.

11-11   MULTIPLE INTEGRALS

Just as we were able to differentiate functions of two variables, we are also able to integrate them. The symbol

$$\int_0^1 \int_{x^3}^{x^2} (x^3 - xy)\, dy\, dx \quad \text{or} \quad \int_0^1 \left[\int_{x^3}^{x^2} (x^3 - xy)\, dy\right] dx$$

is called a (definite) *double integral*. To evaluate it we use successive integrations starting with the innermost integral.

First, we evaluate

$$\int_{x^3}^{x^2} (x^3 - xy)\, dy$$

by treating x as a constant and integrating with respect to y between the limits x^3 and x^2.

$$\int_{x^3}^{x^2} (x^3 - xy) \, dy = \left(x^3 y - \frac{xy^2}{2} \right) \Big|_{x^3}^{x^2}.$$

Substituting the limits for the variable y, we have

$$= \left[x^3(x^2) - \frac{x(x^2)^2}{2} \right] - \left[x^3(x^3) - \frac{x(x^3)^2}{2} \right]$$

$$= x^5 - \frac{x^5}{2} - x^6 + \frac{x^7}{2} = \frac{x^5}{2} - x^6 + \frac{x^7}{2}.$$

Now we integrate this result with respect to x between the limits 0 and 1.

$$\int_0^1 \left(\frac{x^5}{2} - x^6 + \frac{x^7}{2} \right) dx = \left(\frac{x^6}{12} - \frac{x^7}{7} + \frac{x^8}{16} \right) \Big|_0^1 = \left(\frac{1}{12} - \frac{1}{7} + \frac{1}{16} \right) - 0 = \frac{1}{336}.$$

Thus

$$\int_0^1 \int_{x^3}^{x^2} (x^3 - xy) \, dy \, dx = \frac{1}{336}.$$

Similarly, the integral

$$\int_0^2 \int_3^4 xy \, dx \, dy \quad \text{or} \quad \int_0^2 \left[\int_3^4 xy \, dx \right] dy$$

is evaluated by first treating y as a constant and then integrating xy with respect to x between 3 and 4. Then we integrate the result with respect to y between 0 and 2. Take note of how we shall arrange our work.

$$\int_0^2 \int_3^4 xy \, dx \, dy = \int_0^2 \left[\int_3^4 xy \, dx \right] dy$$

$$= \int_0^2 \left(\frac{x^2 y}{2} \right) \Big|_3^4 dy$$

$$= \int_0^2 \left(8y - \frac{9}{2} y \right) dy$$

$$= \int_0^2 \left(\frac{7}{2} y \right) dy = \frac{7y^2}{4} \Big|_0^2$$

$$= 7 - 0 = 7.$$

EXAMPLE 28

Evaluate $\displaystyle\int_{-1}^1 \int_0^{1-x} (2x + 1) \, dy \, dx.$

$$\int_{-1}^{1}\int_{0}^{1-x}(2x+1)\,dy\,dx = \int_{-1}^{1}\left[\int_{0}^{1-x}(2x+1)\,dy\right]dx$$

$$= \int_{-1}^{1}(2xy+y)\Big|_{0}^{1-x}dx$$

$$= \int_{-1}^{1}\{[2x(1-x)+(1-x)]-0\}\,dx$$

$$= \int_{-1}^{1}(-2x^2+x+1)\,dx$$

$$= \left(-\frac{2x^3}{3}+\frac{x^2}{2}+x\right)\Big|_{-1}^{1}$$

$$= (-\tfrac{2}{3}+\tfrac{1}{2}+1)-(\tfrac{2}{3}+\tfrac{1}{2}-1)$$

$$= \tfrac{2}{3}.$$

EXAMPLE 29

$$Evaluate \int_{1}^{\ln 2}\int_{e^y}^{2}dx\,dy.$$

$$\int_{1}^{\ln 2}\int_{e^y}^{2}dx\,dy = \int_{1}^{\ln 2}\left[\int_{e^y}^{2}dx\right]dy$$

$$= \int_{1}^{\ln 2}x\Big|_{e^y}^{2}dy$$

$$= \int_{1}^{\ln 2}(2-e^y)\,dy$$

$$= (2y-e^y)\Big|_{1}^{\ln 2}$$

$$= (2\ln 2-2)-(2-e)$$

$$= 2\ln 2-4+e$$

$$= \ln 4-4+e.$$

A double integral can be interpreted in terms of volume of the region between the x,y-plane and a surface $z = f(x,\ y)$ if $z \geq 0$. In Fig. 11-13 is a region whose volume we shall consider. The element of volume for this region is a vertical column. It has height $z = f(x,\ y)$ and a base area of $dy\ dx$. Thus

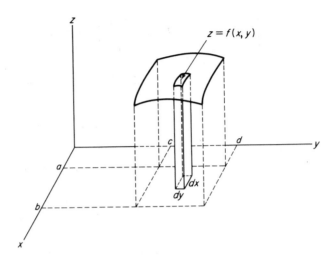

Fig. 11-13

its volume is $f(x, y)\,dy\,dx$. The double integral sums up all such volumes for $a \le x \le b$ and $c \le y \le d$. Thus

$$\text{Volume} = \int_a^b \int_c^d f(x, y)\,dy\,dx.$$

Triple integrals are handled by successively evaluating three integrals.

EXAMPLE 30

$$\text{Evaluate } \int_0^1 \int_0^x \int_0^{x-y} x\,dz\,dy\,dx.$$

$$
\begin{aligned}
\int_0^1 \int_0^x \int_0^{x-y} x\,dz\,dy\,dx &= \int_0^1 \int_0^x \left[\int_0^{x-y} x\,dz \right] dy\,dx \\
&= \int_0^1 \int_0^x (xz) \Big|_0^{x-y} dy\,dx \\
&= \int_0^1 \int_0^x [x(x - y) - 0]\,dy\,dx \\
&= \int_0^1 \int_0^x (x^2 - xy)\,dy\,dx \\
&= \int_0^1 \left[\int_0^x (x^2 - xy)\,dy \right] dx
\end{aligned}
$$

$$= \int_0^1 \left(x^2 y - \frac{xy^2}{2} \right) \Big|_0^x dx$$

$$= \int_0^1 \left[\left(x^3 - \frac{x^3}{2} \right) - 0 \right] dx$$

$$= \int_0^1 \frac{x^3}{2} dx = \frac{x^4}{8} \Big|_0^1$$

$$= \frac{1}{8}.$$

EXERCISE 11-11

In problems 1–20, evaluate the given multiple integrals.

1. $\displaystyle\int_0^3 \int_0^4 x \, dy \, dx$

2. $\displaystyle\int_0^2 \int_1^2 y \, dy \, dx$

3. $\displaystyle\int_0^1 \int_0^1 xy \, dx \, dy$

4. $\displaystyle\int_0^2 \int_0^3 x^2 \, dy \, dx$

5. $\displaystyle\int_1^3 \int_1^2 (x^2 - y) \, dx \, dy$

6. $\displaystyle\int_{-1}^2 \int_1^4 (x^2 - 2xy) \, dy \, dx$

7. $\displaystyle\int_0^1 \int_0^2 (x + y) \, dy \, dx$

8. $\displaystyle\int_0^3 \int_0^x (x^2 + y^2) \, dy \, dx$

9. $\displaystyle\int_0^6 \int_0^{3x} y \, dy \, dx$

10. $\displaystyle\int_1^2 \int_0^{x-1} y \, dy \, dx$

11. $\displaystyle\int_0^1 \int_{3x}^{x^2} 2x^2 y \, dy \, dx$

12. $\displaystyle\int_0^2 \int_0^{x^2} xy \, dy \, dx$

13. $\displaystyle\int_0^2 \int_0^{\sqrt{4-y^2}} x \, dx \, dy$

14. $\displaystyle\int_0^1 \int_y^{\sqrt{y}} y \, dx \, dy$

15. $\displaystyle\int_{-1}^1 \int_x^{1-x} (x + y) \, dy \, dx$

16. $\displaystyle\int_0^3 \int_{y^2}^{3y} x \, dx \, dy$

17. $\displaystyle\int_{-1}^0 \int_{-1}^2 \int_1^2 6xy^2 z^3 \, dx \, dy \, dz$

18. $\displaystyle\int_0^1 \int_0^x \int_0^{x-y} x \, dz \, dy \, dx$

19. $\displaystyle\int_0^1 \int_{x^2}^x \int_0^{xy} dz \, dy \, dx$

20. $\displaystyle\int_0^2 \int_{y^2}^{3y} \int_0^x dz \, dx \, dy$

21. A topic in probability theory is the uniform distribution over the unit square $0 \le x \le 1$,

$0 \le y \le 1$. On the basis of this distribution a student determined that the probability that $\frac{1}{3} < x < \frac{2}{3}$ and $0 < y < \frac{1}{4}$ is

$$\int_{1/3}^{2/3} \int_{0}^{1/4} 1 \cdot dy \, dx.$$

Compute this.

11-12   REVIEW

Important Terms and Symbols in Chapter 11

function of n variables *(p. 431)* x, y-plane; x, z-plane; y, z-plane
                                          (p. 429)

partial derivative *(p. 434)*   production function *(p. 441)*

$\partial f/\partial x$, f_x *(p. 436)*   marginal products *(p. 441)*

$\dfrac{\partial f}{\partial x}\bigg|_{(x_0, y_0)}$, $f_x(x_0, y_0)$ *(p. 436)*   competitive products *(p. 442)*

                                          complementary products *(p. 442)*

                                          relative maxima and minima
                                          (p. 456)

$\dfrac{\partial^2 f}{\partial x \partial y}$, $\dfrac{\partial^2 f}{\partial x^2}$, $\dfrac{\partial^2 f}{\partial y^2}$ *(p. 448)*   critical point *(p. 457)*

f_{xy}, f_{xx}, f_{yy} *(p. 448)*   second-derivative test *(p. 458)*

intermediate variables *(p. 451)*   method of Lagrange multipliers
                                          (p. 466)

chain rule *(p. 452)*   method of least squares *(p. 473)*

joint-cost function *(p. 440)*   index numbers *(p. 477)*

implicit partial differentiation   linear regression line of y on x
(p. 446)   *(p. 475)*

double integral *(p. 483)*   triple integral *(p. 486)*

3-dimensional rectangular coordinate system *(p. 429)*

Review Section

1. If $f(x, y) = 3x^2 y^3$, then to find $\partial f/\partial x$ which do we think of as a constant, x or y? _____

Ans. y

2. If $f(x, y) = x^2 y + 3y$, then $f_x(x, y) = $ __(a)__ and $f_y(x, y) = $ __(b)__ .

Ans. (a) $2xy$;   (b) $x^2 + 3$

3. If $f(x, y) = 2$, then $f_{xy}(x, y) = $ _____ .

Ans. 0

†4. If $w = f(x, y, z)$, $x = g(r, s)$, and $y = h(r, s)$, and $z = k(r, s)$, then the number of terms in $\partial w / \partial s$ is _____ .

Ans. 3

5. If $(1, 2)$ is a critical point of $z = f(x, y)$ and $f_{xx}(1, 2) = f_{yy}(1, 2) = 2$ and $f_{xy}(1, 2) = 1$, then f has a relative (maximum) (minimum) at $(1, 2)$.

Ans. minimum

6. If $f(x, y, z) = x^2 + y^2 + z^2 + 6z$, then f has a critical point at _____ .

Ans. $(0, 0, -3)$

†7. If $yz - x + y = 0$, then $\partial z / \partial x = $ _____ .

Ans. $\dfrac{1}{y}$

†8. Let $z = x^2 + y^2$, $x = r^2 + rs$, $y = s^2 + s$. Then $\partial z / \partial r = $ _____ .

Ans. $2x(2r + s)$

9. If $z = xyw^2$, then $\dfrac{\partial^2 z}{\partial x\, \partial w} = $ _____ .

Ans. $2yw$

10. True or false: If $f(x, y) = 2x^2 + xy + y^2$, then $f_{xy}(1, 2) = f_{yx}(1, 2)$. _____

Ans. true

11. In finding critical points of $f(x, y, z) = x^2 - xy + 2z^2$ subject to $x - y + z = 6$ by the method of Lagrange multipliers, we examine the function $F(x, y, z, \lambda) = $ _____ .

Ans. $x^2 - xy + 2z^2 - \lambda(x - y + z - 6)$ or
$\quad\quad x^2 - xy + 2z^2 - \lambda(6 - x + y - z)$

†12. If $z = f(x, y)$, $x = g(s, t)$, and $y = h(s, t)$, then by the chain rule, $\partial z / \partial s = $ _____ .

Ans. $(\partial z / \partial x)(\partial x / \partial s) + (\partial z / \partial y)(\partial y / \partial s)$

---

†Refers to Secs. 11-4, 11-6, 11-9, or 11-10.

13. A critical point of $z = f(x, y, z)$ is a point where $f_x = f_y = f_z = $ _____.

Ans. 0

14. In a three-dimensional coordinate system, the graph of $y = 2$ is a (a) (line) (plane) parallel to the (b) (x, y) (x, z)-plane.

Ans. (a) plane;   (b) x, z

15. There is a natural one-to-one correspondence between all points in space and all ordered (pairs) (triples) of real numbers.

Ans. triples

16. If $Q = f(l, k)$ is a production function, then in terms of partial derivatives the marginal product of l is _____.

Ans. $\partial Q / \partial l$

†**17.** True or false: If $z = f(x)$ and $x = g(y, w)$, then $\partial z / \partial y = (dz/dx)(\partial x/\partial y)$. _____

Ans. true

†**18.** A function $z = f(x, y)$ is a homogeneous function of degree one if $f(\lambda x, \lambda y) = $ _____.

Ans. $\lambda f(x, y)$

19. In evaluating $\displaystyle\int_0^3 \int_0^2 xy \, dx \, dy$, we integrate first with respect to _____.

Ans. x

Review Problems

In problems 1–12, find the indicated partial derivatives.

1. $f(x, y) = 2x^2 + 3xy + y^2 - 1; f_x, f_y$

2. $Q = l^3 + k^3 - lk; \partial Q/\partial l, \partial Q/\partial k$

3. $z = x/(x + y); \partial z/\partial x, \partial z/\partial y$

4. $w = \dfrac{\sqrt{x^2 + y^2}}{y}; \partial w/\partial x$

5. $w = e^{x^2yz}; w_{xy}(x, y)$

6. $f(x, y) = xy \ln (xy); f_{xy}(x, y)$

---

†Refers to Secs. 11-4, 11-6, 11-9, or 11-10.

7. $f(x, y) = \ln \sqrt{x^2 + y^2}$; $\partial f/\partial y$

8. $f(p_A, p_B) = (p_A - 20)q_A + (p_B - 30)q_B$; $f_{p_A}(p_A, p_B)$

9. $f(x, y, z) = (x + y)(y + z^2)$; $\partial^2 f/\partial z^2$

10. $z = (x^2 - y)(y^2 - 2xy)$; $\partial^2 z/\partial y^2$

11. $w = xe^{yz} \ln z$; $\partial w/\partial y$, $\partial^2 w/\partial x \partial z$

12. $Q = 2.4l^{.11} k^{.89}$; $\partial Q/\partial k$

†13. If $w = x^2 + 2xy + 3y^2$ and $x = e^r$, $y = \ln(r + s)$, find $\partial w/\partial r$ and $\partial w/\partial s$.

†14. If $z = \ln(x/y) + e^y - xy$ and $x = r^2 s^2$, $y = r + s$, find $\partial z/\partial s$.

†15. If $x^2 + 2xy - 2z^2 + xz + 2 = 0$, find $\partial z/\partial x$.

†16. If $z^2 - e^{yz} + \ln z + e^{xz} = 0$, find $\partial z/\partial y$.

17. Examine $f(x, y) = x^2 + 2y^2 - 2xy - 4y + 3$ for extrema.

18. Examine $f(w, z) = 2w^3 + 2z^3 - 6wz + 7$ for extrema.

19. Find all critical points of $f(x, y, z) = x^2 + y^2 + z^2$ subject to the constraint $3x + 2y + z = 14$.

20. Find all critical points of $f(x, y, z) = xyz$ subject to $3x + 2y + 4z - 120 = 0$ $(xyz \neq 0)$.

†21. Find an equation of the linear regression line of y on x given the following data:

x	1	2	3	4	5
y	2.8	5.1	7.1	8.7	10

22. A manufacturer's cost for producing x units of product X and y units of product Y is given by $c = 5x + .03xy + 7y + 200$. Determine the (partial) marginal cost with respect to x when $x = 100$ and $y = 200$.

23. If a manufacturer's production function is defined by $Q = 20l^{.7}k^{.3}$, determine his marginal productivity functions.

24. If $q_A = 200 - 3p_A + p_B$ and $q_B = 50 - 5p_B + p_A$ where q_A and q_B are the number of units demanded of products A and B, respectively, and p_A and p_B are their respective prices per unit, determine whether A and B are competitive or complementary products.

In problems 25–28, evaluate the double integrals.

25. $\displaystyle\int_1^2 \int_0^y x^2 y^2 \, dx \, dy$

26. $\displaystyle\int_0^4 \int_{y/2}^2 xy \, dx \, dy$

27. $\displaystyle\int_0^3 \int_{y^2}^{3y} x \, dx \, dy$

28. $\displaystyle\int_0^1 \int_{\sqrt{x}}^{x^2} (x^2 + 2xy - 3y^2) \, dy \, dx$

---

†Refers to Secs. 11-4, 11-6, 11-9, or 11-10.

Chapter 12

Indeterminate Forms

12-1 L'HOSPITAL'S RULE

In this chapter we shall discuss *indeterminate forms*. The idea of a so-called indeterminate form is not really new to us at all. This form occurs when we find derivatives by the definition. For example, if $f(x) = 2x + 1$, then

$$f'(x) = \lim_{h \to 0} \frac{f(x + h) - f(x)}{h} = \lim_{h \to 0} \frac{(2x + 2h + 1) - (2x + 1)}{h}$$

$$= \lim_{h \to 0} \frac{2h}{h}.$$

As $h \to 0$, both $2h \to 0$ and $h \to 0$ and so we say that the quotient $2h/h$ has the form $0/0$ as $h \to 0$. Since the denominator approaches 0, we cannot use the rule that the limit of a quotient is the quotient of the limits. At this point, knowing only that both the numerator and denominator approach 0 gives no information as to the actual limit. Due to this uncertainty, we call $0/0$ an **indeterminate form.** However, because $h \neq 0$ we can find the limit by dividing both the numerator and denominator by h.

$$f'(x) = \lim_{h \to 0} \frac{2h}{h} = \lim_{h \to 0} 2 = 2.$$

In this chapter we shall consider limits of the form $0/0$ as well as other indeterminate forms.

As another example, consider

$$\lim_{x\to 2}\frac{x^2 + 3x - 10}{x^2 - 4}.$$

Since $\lim_{x\to 2} (x^2 + 3x - 10) = 0$ and $\lim_{x\to 2} (x^2 - 4) = 0$, the quotient has the form $0/0$ as $x\to 2$. But for $x \neq 2$,

$$\lim_{x\to 2}\frac{x^2 + 3x - 10}{x^2 - 4} = \lim_{x\to 2}\frac{(x - 2)(x + 5)}{(x - 2)(x + 2)} = \lim_{x\to 2}\frac{x + 5}{x + 2} = \frac{7}{4}.$$

You may recall this technique. It was used in Chapter 6. However, in many cases algebraic simplification like this is impractical (if not impossible) in finding limits. Another technique, and a powerful one at that, is L'Hospital's rule (pronounced Low-pee-tal´) which is as follows.†

L'HOSPITAL'S RULE.   *If $\lim_{x\to a} f(x) = 0$ and $\lim_{x\to a} g(x) = 0$ and both $f'(x)$ and $g'(x)$ exist, then*

$$\lim_{x\to a}\frac{f(x)}{g(x)} = \lim_{x\to a}\frac{f'(x)}{g'(x)}$$

provided the limit on the right exists or is ∞ or $-\infty$.

This rule says that if $f(x)/g(x)$ has the form $0/0$ as $x \to a$, then to find the limit of $f(x)/g(x)$ just differentiate the numerator and denominator separately and then find the limit of the ratio of the two derivatives.

PITFALL.   *In applying L'Hospital's rule to $f(x)/g(x)$, do not differentiate the quotient $f(x)/g(x)$. Rather, differentiate the numerator and denominator independently, obtaining $f'(x)/g'(x)$. Also, do not apply L'Hospital's rule to forms which are not considered indeterminate.*

Let us apply L'Hospital's rule to the quotient above. Letting $f(x)/g(x) = (x^2 + 3x - 10)/(x^2 - 4)$, we get $f'(x) = 2x + 3$ and $g'(x) = 2x$. Thus

$$\lim_{x\to 2}\frac{x^2 + 3x - 10}{x^2 - 4} = \lim_{x\to 2}\frac{f'(x)}{g'(x)} = \lim_{x\to 2}\frac{2x + 3}{2x} = \frac{7}{4}.$$

EXAMPLE 1

Evaluate the given limit.

a. $\displaystyle\lim_{x\to -1}\frac{x^3 - 3x^2 + 4x + 8}{x^3 + 1}$.

---

† A rigorous statement of L'Hospital's rule requires that other conditions be imposed. For our purposes, the given statement suffices.

As $x \to -1$, both the numerator and denominator approach 0. Thus the quotient has the form $0/0$ and L'Hospital's rule applies. Differentiating the numerator and denominator and taking the limit gives

$$\lim_{x \to -1} \frac{x^3 - 3x^2 + 4x + 8}{x^3 + 1} = \lim_{x \to -1} \frac{3x^2 - 6x + 4}{3x^2} = \frac{13}{3}.$$

b. $\displaystyle \lim_{x \to 4} \frac{\ln (x - 3)}{x - 4}$.

If $x \to 4$, then $[\ln (x - 3)] \to 0$ and $(x - 4) \to 0$. Thus the quotient has the form $0/0$ and L'Hospital's rule applies. Since $D_x[\ln (x - 3)] = 1/(x - 3)$ and $D_x(x - 4) = 1$,

$$\lim_{x \to 4} \frac{\ln (x - 3)}{x - 4} = \lim_{x \to 4} \frac{\dfrac{1}{x - 3}}{1} = \frac{1}{1} = 1.$$

c. $\displaystyle \lim_{x \to 0} \frac{x}{e^x}$.

Since $\lim_{x \to 0} x = 0$ and $\lim_{x \to 0} e^x = 1$, this quotient is *not* an indeterminate form. L'Hospital's rule does *not* apply.

$$\lim_{x \to 0} \frac{x}{e^x} = \frac{0}{1} = 0.$$

The error of using L'Hospital's rule gives

$$\lim_{x \to 0} \frac{x}{e^x} = \lim_{x \to 0} \frac{1}{e^x} = \frac{1}{1} = 1$$

which is *false*.

d. $\displaystyle \lim_{x \to 2} \frac{\sqrt{5} - \sqrt{x + 3}}{x - 2}$.

As $x \to 2$, both the numerator and the denominator approach 0 and so L'Hospital's rule applies.

$$\lim_{x \to 2} \frac{\sqrt{5} - \sqrt{x + 3}}{x - 2} = \lim_{x \to 2} \frac{-\dfrac{1}{2\sqrt{x + 3}}}{1} = -\frac{1}{2\sqrt{5}}.$$

If an indeterminate form occurs after applying L'Hospital's rule, you may apply the rule again as we now show.

EXAMPLE 2

Evaluate $\lim\limits_{x \to 2} \dfrac{2x^3 - 3x^2 - 12x + 20}{2x^3 - 9x^2 + 12x - 4}$.

As $x \to 2$, both the numerator and denominator approach 0 and so L'Hospital's rule applies.

$$\lim_{x \to 2} \frac{2x^3 - 3x^2 - 12x + 20}{2x^3 - 9x^2 + 12x - 4} = \lim_{x \to 2} \frac{6x^2 - 6x - 12}{6x^2 - 18x + 12}.$$

The last quotient also has the form $0/0$ as $x \to 2$. Thus we apply L'Hospital's rule to that quotient.

$$\lim_{x \to 2} \frac{6x^2 - 6x - 12}{6x^2 - 18x + 12} = \lim_{x \to 2} \frac{12x - 6}{12x - 18} = \frac{18}{6} = 3.$$

If both $f(x)$ and $g(x)$ become infinite as $x \to a$ (that is, $f(x) \to \pm\infty$ and $g(x) \to \pm\infty$), then $f(x)/g(x)$ is said to be of the indeterminate form ∞/∞ as $x \to a$. L'Hospital's rule also applies in this case.

EXAMPLE 3

Evaluate $\lim\limits_{x \to 0^+} \dfrac{\ln x}{\dfrac{1}{x^2}}$.

Since $\lim\limits_{x \to 0^+} \ln x = -\infty$ and $\lim\limits_{x \to 0^+} (1/x^2) = \infty$, then the quotient has the form ∞/∞ as $x \to 0^+$. Applying L'Hospital's rule, we obtain

$$\lim_{x \to 0^+} \frac{\ln x}{\dfrac{1}{x^2}} = \lim_{x \to 0^+} \frac{\dfrac{1}{x}}{-\dfrac{2}{x^3}}.$$

The last quotient also has the form ∞/∞ and repeated application of L'Hospital's rule gives the same form. Algebraic manipulation will get us out of trouble, since

$$\frac{\dfrac{1}{x}}{-\dfrac{2}{x^3}} = -\frac{x^2}{2}.$$

Hence,

$$\lim_{x\to0^+} \frac{\ln x}{\dfrac{1}{x^2}} = \lim_{x\to0^+} \frac{\dfrac{1}{x}}{-\dfrac{2}{x^3}} = \lim_{x\to0^+} -\frac{x^2}{2} = 0.$$

L'Hospital's rule also applies if $f(x)/g(x)$ is of the indeterminate form $0/0$ or ∞/∞ as $x \to \infty$ or $x \to -\infty$.

EXAMPLE 4

Evaluate the following limits.

a. $\displaystyle\lim_{x\to\infty} \frac{2x - 6}{3x + 4}$.

Since $\displaystyle\lim_{x\to\infty} (2x - 6) = \infty$ and $\displaystyle\lim_{x\to\infty} (3x + 4) = \infty$, then the quotient has the form ∞/∞ as $x \to \infty$. Applying L'Hospital's rule, we have

$$\lim_{x\to\infty} \frac{2x - 6}{3x + 4} = \lim_{x\to\infty} \frac{2}{3} = \frac{2}{3}.$$

b. $\displaystyle\lim_{x\to\infty} \frac{x^2}{e^x}$.

As $x \to \infty$ both $x^2 \to \infty$ and $e^x \to \infty$. Hence x^2/e^x has the form ∞/∞.

$$\lim_{x\to\infty} \frac{x^2}{e^x} = \lim_{x\to\infty} \frac{2x}{e^x} \qquad\qquad \text{(of form } \infty/\infty)$$

$$= \lim_{x\to\infty} \frac{2}{e^x} = 0.$$

The last equality follows from the fact that as $x \to \infty$, the denominator e^x becomes positively infinite while the numerator remains constant. Hence, the quotient approaches 0.

c. $\displaystyle\lim_{x\to\infty} \frac{\ln x}{x}$.

This has the form ∞/∞.

$$\lim_{x\to\infty} \frac{\ln x}{x} = \lim_{x\to\infty} \frac{\dfrac{1}{x}}{1} = \frac{0}{1} = 0.$$

d. $\displaystyle\lim_{x\to\infty} \frac{e^x}{x}$.

This has the form ∞/∞.

$$\lim_{x \to \infty} \frac{e^x}{x} = \lim_{x \to \infty} \frac{e^x}{1} = \infty.$$

e. $\lim\limits_{x \to \infty} \dfrac{3x^{12} - 8x^8 + 4x^2 - 8}{9x^{15} - 2x^{10} + 3x^5}$.

When $x \to \infty$, both the numerator and the denominator become infinite, so the quotient has the form ∞/∞. Instead of applying L'Hospital's rule, which would involve numerous differentiations, let us divide numerator and denominator by the highest power of x which appears (namely, x^{15}) as was done in Chapter 6.

$$\lim_{x \to \infty} \frac{3x^{12} - 8x^8 + 4x^2 - 8}{9x^{15} - 2x^{10} + 3x^5} = \lim_{x \to \infty} \frac{\dfrac{3}{x^3} - \dfrac{8}{x^7} + \dfrac{4}{x^{13}} - \dfrac{8}{x^{15}}}{9 - \dfrac{2}{x^5} + \dfrac{3}{x^{10}}} = \frac{0}{9} = 0.$$

f. $\lim\limits_{x \to \infty} \dfrac{e^x}{\ln x}$.

This has the form ∞/∞.

$$\lim_{x \to \infty} \frac{e^x}{\ln x} = \lim_{x \to \infty} \frac{e^x}{\dfrac{1}{x}}.$$

The right side has the form $\infty/0$, which is *not* indeterminate. Think of dividing a large positive quantity by a small positive quantity. The result is a large positive quantity. Hence

$$\lim_{x \to \infty} \frac{e^x}{\ln x} = \infty.$$

EXERCISE 12-1

Evaluate the following limits.

1. $\lim\limits_{x \to -6} \dfrac{x^2 - 36}{x + 6}$

2. $\lim\limits_{x \to 1} \dfrac{x^3 - 3x^2 + 3x - 1}{x - 1}$

3. $\lim\limits_{x \to 1} \dfrac{x^3 - 5x^2 + 8x - 4}{x^2 + 5x - 6}$

4. $\lim\limits_{x \to -1} \dfrac{2x^3 + 5x^2 + 4x + 1}{x^3 - x^2 - 5x - 3}$

5. $\lim\limits_{x \to 4} \dfrac{x - 4}{x^2 - 16}$

6. $\lim\limits_{x \to \infty} \dfrac{x^{10} - 1}{x}$

7. $\lim_{x \to -2} \dfrac{2 - x}{(x + 2)^2}$

8. $\lim_{x \to 9} \dfrac{x^2 - 81}{9x}$

9. $\lim_{x \to -2} \dfrac{x^3 - 3x + 4}{x^2 + 4x + 4}$

10. $\lim_{x \to \infty} \dfrac{2x^4 - 12x^2 + x + 6}{5x^4 + 16x^3 - 6x + 4}$

11. $\lim_{x \to \infty} \dfrac{4x^4 - 6x^2 + 2x + 1}{2x^4 - 6x^3 + 7}$

12. $\lim_{x \to \infty} -\dfrac{x}{x^2 + 1}$

13. $\lim_{x \to \infty} \dfrac{x^5 + x^2 - 2x + 2}{2x^6 - 3x^2 + 5x - 2}$

14. $\lim_{x \to \infty} \dfrac{e^x}{x^2}$

15. $\lim_{x \to 3} \dfrac{e^x - e^3}{x - 3}$

16. $\lim_{x \to \infty} \dfrac{2 + 7x + 3x^2}{6 - 7x^2}$

17. $\lim_{x \to \infty} \dfrac{x^4}{e^x}$

18. $\lim_{x \to \infty} \dfrac{x^3}{e^{3x}}$

19. $\lim_{x \to \infty} \dfrac{\ln x}{\sqrt{x}}$

20. $\lim_{x \to \infty} \dfrac{\ln x}{x^2}$

21. $\lim_{x \to \infty} \dfrac{3e^{3x}}{4x^2}$

22. $\lim_{x \to 3} \dfrac{x^4 - 81}{x^2 - 9}$

23. $\lim_{x \to 4^-} \dfrac{x^2 + 3}{x - 4}$

24. $\lim_{x \to \infty} \dfrac{x \ln x}{x + 1}$

25. $\lim_{x \to \infty} \dfrac{3(\ln x) + 4x}{7x + \ln x}$

26. $\lim_{x \to 0} \dfrac{\ln (1 + x)}{x}$

27. $\lim_{x \to e} \dfrac{\ln (x) - 1}{e - x}$

28. $\lim_{x \to \infty} \dfrac{\sqrt{x}}{\ln x}$

29. $\lim_{x \to 0} \dfrac{e^x - 1}{x}$

30. $\lim_{x \to 0^+} \dfrac{e^x}{x}$

31. $\lim_{x \to 0} \dfrac{1 - x}{x^2}$

32. $\lim_{x \to 5} \dfrac{\ln (x - 4)}{x - 5}$

33. $\lim_{x \to 0} \dfrac{\sqrt{1 + x} - 1}{x}$

34. $\lim_{x \to 0} \dfrac{\sqrt[3]{8 + x} - 2}{x}$

35. $\lim_{x \to \infty} \dfrac{\ln (x + 1)^2}{4x}$

36. $\lim_{x \to 1} \dfrac{x - 1}{\ln x}$

37. $\lim_{x \to \infty} \dfrac{e^x + x^2}{2e^x + 3x^2}$

38. $\lim_{x \to 0} \dfrac{e^{2x} - 1}{1 - e^{3x}}$

39. $\lim\limits_{x\to 0} \dfrac{\sqrt{2+x} - \sqrt{2-x}}{x}$

40. $\lim\limits_{x\to 0} \dfrac{xe^x}{1 - e^x}$

41. $\lim\limits_{x\to 1} \dfrac{x + x\ln(x+1)}{\sqrt{x+1} - 1}$

42. $\lim\limits_{x\to\infty} \dfrac{x\ln x}{\ln(x) + x}$

12-2   ADDITIONAL INDETERMINATE FORMS †

If $\lim\limits_{x\to a} f(x) = 0$ and $\lim\limits_{x\to a} g(x) = \pm\infty$, then the product $f(x)g(x)$ is said to have the indeterminate form $0 \cdot \infty$ as $x \to a$. By writing the product as a quotient, such as

$$\frac{f(x)}{\dfrac{1}{g(x)}} \quad \text{or} \quad \frac{g(x)}{\dfrac{1}{f(x)}},$$

we get the indeterminate form $0/0$ or ∞/∞ and L'Hospital's rule applies.

EXAMPLE 5

a. *Evaluate* $\lim\limits_{x\to 0^+} (x\ln x)$.

Since $\lim\limits_{x\to 0^+} x = 0$ and $\lim\limits_{x\to 0^+} \ln x = -\infty$, the product $x \ln x$ has the form $0 \cdot \infty$. Writing it as $(\ln x)/(1/x)$, we get the form ∞/∞, and L'Hospital's rule applies.

$$
\begin{aligned}
\lim_{x\to 0^+} (x\ln x) &= \lim_{x\to 0^+} \frac{\ln x}{\dfrac{1}{x}} \\[2mm]
&= \lim_{x\to 0^+} \frac{\dfrac{1}{x}}{-\dfrac{1}{x^2}} \qquad &\text{(L'Hospital's rule)} \\[2mm]
&= \lim_{x\to 0^+} (-x) \qquad &\text{(simplifying)} \\[2mm]
&= 0.
\end{aligned}
$$

b. *Evaluate* $\lim\limits_{x\to\infty} (x\ln x)$.

As $x \to \infty$, the product has the form $\infty \cdot \infty$ which is *not* indeterminate. Thinking

---

† This section may be omitted without loss of continuity.

of this situation as a product of two positive large "quantities," we conclude that the result is a positive large "quantity."

$$\lim_{x \to \infty} x \ln x = \infty.$$

If $\lim_{x \to a} f(x) = \infty$ and $\lim_{x \to a} g(x) = \infty$, then $f(x) - g(x)$ has the indeterminate form $\infty - \infty$ as $x \to a$. Rewriting $f(x) - g(x)$ as, for example, a quotient (which at times requires ingenuity) *may* lead to a suitable form (0/0 or ∞/∞) to which L'Hospital's rule applies. Also, the indeterminate forms $(\infty) + (-\infty), (-\infty) + (\infty)$, and $(-\infty) - (-\infty)$ are classified under the label $\infty - \infty$.

EXAMPLE 6

a. *Evaluate* $\lim\limits_{x \to 0^+} \left(\dfrac{1}{e^x - 1} - \dfrac{1}{x} \right)$.

This has the form $\infty - \infty$. Adding the fractions, we obtain

$$\frac{1}{e^x - 1} - \frac{1}{x} = \frac{x - e^x + 1}{x(e^x - 1)}$$

which has the form 0/0 as $x \to 0^+$. Applying L'Hospital's rule, we have

$$\lim_{x \to 0^+} \frac{x - e^x + 1}{x(e^x - 1)} = \lim_{x \to 0^+} \frac{1 - e^x}{xe^x + e^x - 1} \qquad \left(\text{form } \frac{0}{0} \right)$$

$$= \lim_{x \to 0^+} \frac{-e^x}{xe^x + e^x + e^x} \qquad \text{(L'Hospital's rule)}$$

$$= -\frac{1}{2}.$$

b. *Evaluate* $\lim\limits_{x \to \infty} (7x^2 - 6x^3)$.

This has the form $\infty - \infty$. But $7x^2 - 6x^3 = x^2(7 - 6x)$. As $x \to \infty$, then $x^2 \to \infty$ and $(7 - 6x) \to -\infty$. The product has the form $(\infty)(-\infty)$, which is *not* indeterminate. Think of this as the product of a positive quantity and a negative quantity, both arbitrarily large in absolute value. The result has the form $-\infty$. Hence

$$\lim_{x \to \infty} (7x^2 - 6x^3) = \lim_{x \to \infty} [x^2(7 - 6x)] = -\infty.$$

We conclude by considering the case when the expression $[f(x)]^{g(x)}$ has the indeterminate form 0^0, 1^∞, or ∞^0 as x approaches some limit. In each case the technique is to first write the expression in exponential form. To do this, recall from Sec. 5-2 that we can write u as $e^{\ln u}$. Hence

$$[f(x)]^{g(x)} = [e^{\ln f(x)}]^{g(x)}.$$

Thus,

$$\lim [f(x)]^{g(x)} = \lim [e^{\ln f(x)}]^{g(x)}$$

$$= \lim e^{g(x)\ln f(x)} \qquad \text{(properties of exponents).}$$

In advanced texts it is shown that the limit can be introduced into the exponent. Thus we have

$$\lim [f(x)]^{g(x)} = e^{\lim [g(x)\ln f(x)]}.$$

In the limit, $g(x) \ln f(x)$ will be of the form $0 \cdot \infty$ and by applying prior techniques we can use L'Hospital's rule. Examples of the forms 0^0, 1^∞, and ∞^0 will now be given.

EXAMPLE 7

Determine $\lim_{x \to 0^+} x^x$.

This has the indeterminate form 0^0. Writing x^x as $(e^{\ln x})^x$, we have

$$\lim_{x \to 0^+} x^x = \lim_{x \to 0^+} (e^{\ln x})^x$$

$$= \lim_{x \to 0^+} e^{x\ln x}$$

$$= e^{\lim_{x \to 0^+} x\ln x}.$$

But from Example 5(a), $\lim_{x \to 0^+} x \ln x = 0$. Thus

$$e^{\lim_{x \to 0^+} x\ln x} = e^0 = 1$$

and so

$$\lim_{x \to 0^+} x^x = 1.$$

EXAMPLE 8

Determine $\lim_{x \to 0^+} (1 + x)^{1/x}$.

This has the indeterminate form 1^∞.

$$\lim_{x \to 0^+} (1 + x)^{1/x} = \lim_{x \to 0^+} [e^{\ln(1+x)}]^{1/x}$$

$$= \lim_{x \to 0^+} e^{(1/x)\ln(1+x)}$$

$$= e^{\lim_{x \to 0^+} [\ln(1 + x)]/x}.$$

In the exponent, $[\ln (1 + x)]/x$ has the form $0/0$ as $x \to 0^+$. Applying L'Hospital's rule to it, we have

$$\lim_{x \to 0^+} \frac{\ln(1+x)}{x} = \lim_{x \to 0^+} \frac{\dfrac{1}{1+x}}{1} = 1.$$

Thus

$$\lim_{x \to 0^+} (1+x)^{1/x} = e^1 = e.$$

EXAMPLE 9

Determine $\lim\limits_{x \to \infty} x^{1/x}$.

As $x \to \infty$, $x^{1/x}$ has the indeterminate form ∞^0.

$$\begin{aligned}
\lim_{x \to \infty} x^{1/x} &= \lim_{x \to \infty} (e^{\ln x})^{1/x} \\
&= \lim_{x \to \infty} e^{(1/x)\ln x} = e^{\lim\limits_{x \to \infty} (\ln x)/x} \\
&= e^0 \qquad\qquad\qquad\qquad\qquad \text{[Example 4(c)]} \\
&= 1.
\end{aligned}$$

EXERCISE 12-2

Evaluate the following limits.

1. $\lim\limits_{x \to 0^+} x^2 \ln x$

2. $\lim\limits_{x \to \infty} x^2 e^x$

3. $\lim\limits_{x \to 1^+} \left(\dfrac{1}{\ln x} - \dfrac{x}{\ln x} \right)$

4. $\lim\limits_{x \to 0^+} x^4 \ln x$

5. $\lim\limits_{x \to 0^+} x^{x^2}$

6. $\lim\limits_{x \to 0^+} x^{\sqrt{x}}$

7. $\lim\limits_{x \to \infty} \left(1 + \dfrac{3}{x} \right)^x$

8. $\lim\limits_{x \to 0^+} \left(\dfrac{1}{x} - \dfrac{1}{x^2} \right)$

9. $\lim\limits_{x \to 0^+} \left(1 + \dfrac{1}{x} \right)^x$

10. $\lim\limits_{x \to 1} x^{1/(1-x)}$

11. $\lim\limits_{x \to 0^+} x e^{1/x}$

12. $\lim\limits_{x \to 0^+} x \ln^2 x$

13. $\lim\limits_{x \to \infty} (x^2 - x)$

14. $\lim\limits_{x \to 0^+} \left(\dfrac{1}{x} + \ln x \right)$

15. $\lim\limits_{x \to 0^+} (x^{e^x} - 1)$

16. $\lim\limits_{x \to 0} x^{5x}$

17. $\lim\limits_{x \to 0} (e^x + x)^{1/x}$

18. $\lim\limits_{x \to 0^+} (1 + 3x)^{1/x}$

19. $\lim\limits_{x \to 0^+} (\sqrt{x} \ln x)$

20. $\lim\limits_{x \to 1^+} [(x-1) \ln(x-1)]$

21. $\lim\limits_{x\to 0^+} \left(\dfrac{1}{x} - \dfrac{1}{xe^x}\right)$

22. $\lim\limits_{x\to 0^+} \left(\dfrac{1}{x} - \ln x\right)$

23. $\lim\limits_{x\to\infty} x^4 e^{-x}$

24. $\lim\limits_{x\to 0^+} \dfrac{1}{x} e^{-1/x}$

25. $\lim\limits_{x\to 0^+} \dfrac{\ln x}{x}$

26. $\lim\limits_{x\to\infty} (1 + 2x)^{1/x}$

27. $\lim\limits_{x\to 5^+} (x^2 - 25)^{x-5}$

28. $\lim\limits_{x\to 1} \left(\dfrac{x}{x-1} - \dfrac{1}{\ln x}\right)$

29. $\lim\limits_{x\to 0} \dfrac{\ln (e^{2x} - 3x)}{x}$

30. $\lim\limits_{x\to 0^+} x^{2/\ln x}$

12-3   REVIEW

Important Terms and Symbols in Chapter 12

L'Hospital's rule *(p. 493)* $0 \cdot \infty$ *(p. 499)*

$\dfrac{0}{0}$ *(p. 492)* $\dfrac{\infty}{\infty}$ *(p. 495)*

$\infty - \infty$ *(p. 500)* 0^0 *(p. 501)*

1^∞ *(p. 501)* ∞^0 *(p. 501)*

Review Section

1. True or false: $\lim\limits_{x\to\infty} x^x$ is an indeterminate form. _____

> *Ans.*   false

2. True or false: $\lim\limits_{x\to -3} \dfrac{x^2 - 9}{x - 3}$ is not an indeterminate form but $\lim\limits_{x\to 3} \dfrac{x^2 - 9}{x - 3}$ is an indeterminate form. _____

> *Ans.*   true

3. It is (always) (not always) necessary to employ L'Hospital's rule to evaluate indeterminate forms.

> *Ans.*   not always

4. $\lim\limits_{x\to\infty} (e^x/x) = $ _____ , $\lim\limits_{x\to 0^+} (e^x/x) = $ _____ , and $\lim\limits_{x\to\infty} 1^x = $ _____ .

> *Ans.*   (a) ∞;   (b) ∞;   (c) 1

5. True or false:

$$\lim_{x \to \infty} \frac{x^2 + 1}{x^2} = \lim_{x \to \infty} D_x \left[\frac{x^2 + 1}{x^2} \right] = \lim_{x \to \infty} \frac{x^2(2x) - (x^2 + 1)(2x)}{x^4}$$

$$= \lim_{x \to \infty} \frac{-2x}{x^4} = -2 \lim_{x \to \infty} \frac{1}{x^3} = 0. \underline{\quad\quad}$$

Ans. false

Review Problems

Evaluate the following limits.

1. $\displaystyle\lim_{x \to 1} \frac{x^3 + x^2 - 5x + 3}{x^3 - 2x^2 + x}$

2. $\displaystyle\lim_{x \to -4} \frac{x^2 + 5x + 4}{x^2 + 2x - 8}$

3. $\displaystyle\lim_{x \to \infty} \frac{3x^2 + 3}{2 - 5x^2}$

4. $\displaystyle\lim_{x \to \infty} \frac{x - 1}{x^2 + 1}$

5. $\displaystyle\lim_{x \to 0^+} \frac{\ln x}{3e^x - 3}$

6. $\displaystyle\lim_{x \to 1^+} \left[\frac{3}{x - 1} - \frac{1}{x^2 - 1} \right]$

7. $\displaystyle\lim_{x \to 0^+} x^2 \ln (1/x)$

8. $\displaystyle\lim_{x \to 1^+} (\ln x)^{x-1}$

9. $\displaystyle\lim_{x \to 5^-} (5 - x)^{1/(5-x)}$

10. $\displaystyle\lim_{x \to 0^+} \left(\frac{5}{x} \right)^x$

11. $\displaystyle\lim_{x \to 1^+} \frac{\sqrt{x + 1}}{\ln x}$

12. $\displaystyle\lim_{x \to \infty} (e^x - e^{-x})$

Chapter 13

Sequences and Series

13-1 SEQUENCES

Suppose f is the function defined by $f(x) = x^2$ and we take the domain of f to be the positive integers. Then we have the correspondence

$$
\begin{array}{ccccccc}
\text{Domain} & 1 & 2 & 3 & \ldots & n & \ldots \\
 & \downarrow & \downarrow & \downarrow & & \downarrow & \\
\text{Range} & 1 & 4 & 9 & \ldots & n^2 & \ldots
\end{array}
$$

A function such as this whose domain is the positive integers is called an *infinite sequence*. By considering the natural ordering of the positive integers, we can list the elements in the range of f in an orderly fashion as follows:

$$f(1), f(2), f(3), \ldots, f(n), \ldots. \tag{1}$$

In fact, we can go one step further if we drop the functional notation in (1) and, instead, adopt a subscript notation. Thus for (1) we can write

$$a_1, a_2, a_3, ..., a_n, ... \tag{2}$$

where $a_n = f(n)$. For example, if $f(n) = n^2$, then $a_1 = 1^2$, $a_2 = 2^2$, $a_3 = 3^2$, etc. Thus the elements in the range of f are

$$1, 4, 9, ..., n^2, ... \tag{3}$$

Since (3) essentially defines a particular sequence, it is commonly referred to as an infinite sequence itself. Similarly, by the infinite sequence

$$\frac{1}{3}, \frac{2}{4}, \frac{3}{5}, ..., \frac{n}{n+2}, ...$$

we mean the function, say g, defined by $g(n) = n/(n+2)$ where n is a positive integer. More generally we have the following definition.

DEFINITION.   *An infinite sequence, denoted a_1, a_2, a_3, ..., a_n, ..., is a function f whose domain is the positive integers and such that $a_n = f(n)$.*

Corresponding to 1 in the domain is the *first term a_1*, to 2 corresponds the *second term a_2*, etc. The nth term, or *general term*, a_n usually defines the function (that is, $a_n = f(n)$). The sequence (2) can also be denoted by the symbol $\{a_n\}$.

EXAMPLE 1

Determine the first four terms of the infinite sequence having the general term

$$a_n = \frac{2n}{3n+1}.$$

In the expression $\dfrac{2n}{3n+1}$ we successively replace n by the integers 1, 2, 3, and 4.

$$n = 1, \quad a_1 = \frac{2(1)}{3(1)+1} = \frac{2}{4} = \frac{1}{2}$$

$$n = 2, \quad a_2 = \frac{2(2)}{3(2)+1} = \frac{4}{7}$$

$$n = 3, \quad a_3 = \frac{2(3)}{3(3)+1} = \frac{6}{10} = \frac{3}{5}$$

$$n = 4, \quad a_4 = \frac{2(4)}{3(4)+1} = \frac{8}{13}.$$

Thus,

$$\left\{\frac{2n}{3n+1}\right\} = \frac{2}{4}, \frac{4}{7}, \frac{6}{10}, \frac{8}{13}, ... = \frac{1}{2}, \frac{4}{7}, \frac{3}{5}, \frac{8}{13}, ...$$

EXAMPLE 2

Write the first four terms of $\{(-1)^{n+1}(n^2+1)\}$.

$$n = 1, \quad a_1 = (-1)^{1+1}(1^2+1) = 2$$

$$n = 2, \quad a_2 = (-1)^{2+1}(2^2+1) = -5$$

$$n = 3, \quad a_3 = (-1)^{3+1}(3^2+1) = 10$$

$$n = 4, \quad a_4 = (-1)^{4+1}(4^2+1) = -17.$$

Thus,

$$\{(-1)^{n+1}(n^2+1)\} = 2, -5, 10, -17, \ldots.$$

EXAMPLE 3

Find a general term for an infinite sequence whose first six terms are

$$1, \sqrt{2}, \sqrt{3}, 2, \sqrt{5}, \sqrt{6}, \ldots.$$

By inspection, a general term is $a_n = \sqrt{n}$.

EXAMPLE 4

Write all the terms of the finite sequence

$$\{n(n+1)\}, \text{ where } n = 1, 2, 3, 4.$$

The domain of this sequence has a finite number of elements (four). Successively substituting 1, 2, 3, and 4 for n in the general term gives $\{n(n+1)\} = 2, 6, 12, 20$. Similarly, the finite sequence $a_1, a_2, \ldots, a_{84}$ has 84 terms. A finite sequence, then, has a last term, as well as a first term.

Let us examine the sequence $\{1/n\}$ rather closely.

$$\left\{\frac{1}{n}\right\} = 1, \frac{1}{2}, \frac{1}{3}, \frac{1}{4}, \ldots, \frac{1}{n}, \ldots.$$

In Fig. 13-1 we indicate some terms on the real number line. Observe that as n increases, the terms get closer to 0. Moreover, although $1/n$ will never equal 0, for large n the corresponding terms will come as close to 0 as we wish. For example, suppose we wish to get within $\frac{1}{1,000,000}$ of a unit distance of 0. Then we must have the inequality

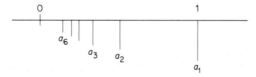

Fig. 13-1

$$\left| \frac{1}{n} - 0 \right| < \frac{1}{1,000,000}.$$

Solving this, we get $n > 1,000,000$. That is, beginning with the 1,000,001st term, each term in the sequence $\{1/n\}$ will satisfy the requirement.

Verbally we say that as n increases indefinitely, the sequence $\{1/n\}$ has 0 for a *limit*, or $\{1/n\}$ *converges* to 0. Symbolically, we write

$$\lim_{n \to \infty} \frac{1}{n} = 0. \tag{4}$$

The notation $n \to \infty$ means that n is increasing indefinitely through positive integral values. Equation (4) can be read: the limit of the sequence $\{1/n\}$ as n-increases without bound is equal to zero. Equivalently, we can state that every interval containing 0, no matter how small, contains all the terms of the sequence $\{1/n\}$ from some term on.

More generally we write

$$\lim_{n \to \infty} a_n = a$$

which means that the limit of the sequence $\{a_n\}$ as $n \to \infty$ is the number a. That is, every interval containing a contains all the terms of the sequence $\{a_n\}$ from some term on. For n sufficiently large, a_n is arbitrarily close to a.

Not every sequence has a limit. For example, the terms of the sequence $\{n^2\} = 1, 4, 9, \ldots$ increase without bound as $n \to \infty$. We denote this situation by writing

$$\lim_{n \to \infty} n^2 = \infty$$

which is read "as n increases without bound, the terms of the sequence $\{n^2\}$ increase without bound." A sequence which has a finite limit is said to *converge* or be *convergent*; otherwise, it *diverges* or is *divergent*. Thus $\{n^2\}$ is a divergent sequence. When a sequence converges, its limit must be unique.

EXAMPLE 5

The sequence 2, -3, -7, -7, $\ldots$, -7, $\ldots$ converges to -7 since *every* interval containing -7 must contain all of the terms of the sequence from the third term on. For most convergent sequences, however, you may have to ignore many, perhaps a million, of the terms in the sequence before all of the remaining terms lie in a given interval.

EXAMPLE 6

a. The terms of the sequence -3, -6, -9, $\ldots$, $-3n$, $\ldots$ decrease without bound and the sequence is said to diverge or have no finite limit. Symbolically,

$$\lim_{n\to\infty} (-3n) = -\infty.$$

b. The sequence $\{(-1)^{n+1}\} = 1, -1, 1, -1, \ldots$ has no limit as $n \to \infty$ and hence is divergent.

EXAMPLE 7

The terms of the sequence

$$\left\{\frac{n+1}{n}\right\} = 2, \frac{3}{2}, \frac{4}{3}, \frac{5}{4}, \frac{6}{5}, \ldots$$

are clearly getting closer to 1 as n increases. In fact, for $n = 1000$,

$$a_{1000} = \frac{1001}{1000} = 1 + \frac{1}{1000}.$$

Later, it will be shown that 1 is indeed the limit.

Without going into their proofs, we shall state some theorems on limits and illustrate their use in determining the behavior of various sequences.

Theorem 1.   If $|r| < 1$, then $\lim_{n\to\infty} r^n = 0$. If $|r| > 1$, then $\lim_{n\to\infty} r_n$ does not exist and $\{r^n\}$ diverges.

Theorem 2. $\lim_{n\to\infty} c = c$ where c is a constant.

Theorem 3. $\lim_{n\to\infty} ca_n = c \lim_{n\to\infty} a_n$ if $\{a_n\}$ is convergent.

Theorem 4.   If each term of a divergent sequence is multiplied by the same non-zero constant, the resulting sequence is also divergent.

EXAMPLE 8

Establish the convergence or divergence of the following sequences.

a. $\{(-\frac{1}{2})^n\} = -\frac{1}{2}, \frac{1}{4}, -\frac{1}{8}, \ldots$.

Since $|-\frac{1}{2}| < 1$, by Theorem 1 we have

$$\lim_{n\to\infty} (-\frac{1}{2})^n = 0.$$

The sequence converges to 0.

b. $\{3\} = 3, 3, 3, \ldots$

From Theorem 2, we have

$$\lim_{n\to\infty} 3 = 3.$$

The sequence converges to 3.

c. $\left\{ \dfrac{3}{4^n} \right\}$.

Since $\dfrac{3}{4^n} = 3\left(\dfrac{1}{4}\right)^n$ and $\left|\dfrac{1}{4}\right| < 1$, by Theorems 3 and 1 we have

$$\lim_{n\to\infty} \frac{3}{4^n} = 3 \lim_{n\to\infty} \left(\frac{1}{4}\right)^n = 3(0) = 0.$$

d. $\{2(\tfrac{4}{3})^n\}$.

Since $|\tfrac{4}{3}| > 1$, Theorem 1 asserts that $\{(\tfrac{4}{3})^n\}$ diverges, and by Theorem 4 so does $\{2(\tfrac{4}{3})^n)\}$.

Theorem 5.   If $\{a_n\}$ and $\{b_n\}$ are convergent sequences, then

a. $\displaystyle\lim_{n\to\infty} (a_n \pm b_n) = \lim_{n\to\infty} a_n \pm \lim_{n\to\infty} b_n$

b. $\displaystyle\lim_{n\to\infty} (a_n b_n) = (\lim_{n\to\infty} a_n)(\lim_{n\to\infty} b_n)$

c. $\displaystyle\lim_{n\to\infty} \frac{a_n}{b_n} = \frac{\lim_{n\to\infty} a_n}{\lim_{n\to\infty} b_n}$ if $b_n \neq 0$ and $\lim_{n\to\infty} b_n \neq 0$.

Theorem 6.   a. For $a_n \neq 0$, $\displaystyle\lim_{n\to\infty} a_n = 0$ if and only if $\displaystyle\lim_{n\to\infty} \frac{1}{|a_n|} = \infty$.

b. For $a_n > 0$, then $\displaystyle\lim_{n\to\infty} a_n = \infty$ if and only if $\displaystyle\lim_{n\to\infty} \frac{1}{a_n} = 0$.

c. For $a_n < 0$, then $\displaystyle\lim_{n\to\infty} a_n = -\infty$ if and only if $\displaystyle\lim_{n\to\infty} \frac{1}{a_n} = 0$.

EXAMPLE 9

a. Since $\displaystyle\lim_{n\to\infty} n^2 = \infty$, then by Theorem 6(b), $\displaystyle\lim_{n\to\infty} \frac{1}{n^2} = 0$.

b. $\displaystyle\lim_{n\to\infty} \left(2 + \frac{1}{n^2}\right) = \lim_{n\to\infty} 2 + \lim_{n\to\infty} \frac{1}{n^2}$ [Theorem 5(a)]

$$= 2 + 0 = 2.$$ [Theorem 2 and Example 9(a)]

EXAMPLE 10

Evaluate $\lim\limits_{n \to \infty} \dfrac{n + 1}{n}$.

As $n \to \infty$, $(n + 1)/n$ has the form ∞/∞. However,

$$\lim_{n \to \infty} \frac{n + 1}{n} = \lim_{n \to \infty} \left(\frac{n}{n} + \frac{1}{n} \right)$$

$$= \lim_{n \to \infty} 1 + \lim_{n \to \infty} \frac{1}{n} \qquad \text{[Theorem 5(a)]}$$

$$= 1 + 0 \qquad \text{[Theorem 2 and previous result]}$$

$$= 1.$$

Alternatively, if n could be *any* real number, then by L'Hospital's rule we differentiate both numerator and denominator with respect to n:

$$\lim_{n \to \infty} \frac{n + 1}{n} = \lim_{n \to \infty} \frac{1}{1} = 1.$$

Since the limit is 1 for arbitrarily large values of n, it must also be 1 for arbitrarily large integral values of n. As in this case, L'Hospital's rule is a great aid in finding limits of sequences.

EXAMPLE 11

a. *Evaluate* $\lim\limits_{n \to \infty} \dfrac{2n^2 + 3n}{3n^2 + 4n}$.

Although L'Hospital's rule applies, we shall try a different technique. Dividing both the numerator and denominator by n^2 (that is, the highest power of n that occurs) and applying Theorem 5, we obtain

$$\lim_{n \to \infty} \frac{2n^2 + 3n}{3n^2 + 4n} = \lim_{n \to \infty} \frac{\dfrac{2n^2}{n^2} + \dfrac{3n}{n^2}}{\dfrac{3n^2}{n^2} + \dfrac{4n}{n^2}}$$

$$= \lim_{n \to \infty} \frac{2 + \dfrac{3}{n}}{3 + \dfrac{4}{n}}$$

$$= \frac{2 + 0}{3 + 0} = \frac{2}{3}.$$

b. *Evaluate* $\lim\limits_{n \to \infty} \dfrac{e^n}{n}$.

By L'Hospital's rule and Theorem 1 (since $|e| > 1$),

$$\lim_{n \to \infty} \frac{e^n}{n} = \lim_{n \to \infty} \frac{e^n}{1} = \infty.$$

EXERCISE 13-1

In problems 1–12, write the first four terms of the given sequence.

1. $\{2n - 1\}$

2. $\{n^2 + 4\}$

3. $\left\{ \dfrac{n}{n + 1} \right\}$

4. $\left\{ \dfrac{n - 1}{n} \right\}$

5. $\{(-1)^{n+1} n^2\}$

6. $\{(-1)^{n+1} (2n)^2\}$

7. $\left\{ \dfrac{e^n}{3} \right\}$

8. $\left\{ \dfrac{n^2 - 1}{n^2 - 2} \right\}$

9. $\left\{ \dfrac{n - 1}{n + 1} \right\}$

10. $\left\{ \dfrac{3^n}{n} \right\}$

11. $\left\{ \dfrac{n}{2^n} \right\}$

12. $\left\{ \dfrac{3}{2n + 5} \right\}$

In problems 13–20, find an expression for the nth term of the indicated sequence.

13. $\frac{1}{2}, -\frac{1}{3}, \frac{1}{4}, -\frac{1}{5}, \ldots$

14. $1, \frac{1}{3}, \frac{1}{9}, \frac{1}{27}, \ldots$

15. $1 \cdot 2, 2 \cdot 3, 3 \cdot 4, 4 \cdot 5, \ldots$

16. $\frac{2}{3^2}, \frac{3}{4^2}, \frac{4}{5^2}, \frac{5}{6^2}, \ldots$

17. $-1, 2, -3, 4, \ldots$

18. $\frac{3}{2}, -\frac{5}{4}, \frac{7}{8}, -\frac{9}{16}, \ldots$

19. $0, -1, 0, -1, \ldots$

20. $1, 0, 1, 0, \ldots$

In problems 21–50, find the limit, if it exists, of the given sequence as $n \to \infty$.

21. $\{2n\}$

22. $\{2n + 5\}$

23. $\left\{ \dfrac{3n - 1}{2n} \right\}$

24. $\left\{ \dfrac{n + 1}{2n} \right\}$

25. $\left\{ 2 + \dfrac{n^3 - 2}{n^2} \right\}$

26. $\left\{ \dfrac{n^2 - n + 4}{2n^2} \right\}$

27. $\left\{ \left(\dfrac{4}{5} \right)^n \right\}$

28. $\left\{ \left(\dfrac{17}{16} \right)^n \right\}$

29. $\left\{\dfrac{(100)^n}{(101)^n}\right\}$

30. $\{7 - \frac{1}{3}\}$

31. $\{3 - \frac{1}{4}\}$

32. $\left\{1 + \dfrac{n-1}{n}\right\}$

33. $\left\{\dfrac{6}{n}\right\}$

34. $\left\{-\dfrac{6}{n}\right\}$

35. $\left\{\dfrac{2n^4 - 6n^2 + 5}{n^5}\right\}$

36. $\left\{\dfrac{3n^2 + 7n - 4}{4n^2}\right\}$

37. $\left\{3\left(\dfrac{1}{2}\right)^n\right\}$

38. $\left\{8\left(\dfrac{1}{3^n}\right)\right\}$

39. $\left\{\dfrac{n+3}{4-n}\right\}$

40. $\left\{\dfrac{n}{\ln(n+1)}\right\}$

41. $\left\{\dfrac{e^n}{n}\right\}$

42. $\left\{\dfrac{n^{12} + 6}{3n^2 + 1}\right\}$

43. $\left\{\dfrac{2\ln n}{n}\right\}$

44. $\left\{\dfrac{1}{n\sqrt{n}}\right\}$

45. $\left\{\dfrac{1}{2^n + 1}\right\}$

46. $\left\{\dfrac{n}{e^{2n}}\right\}$

47. $\left\{\dfrac{n}{n + e^n}\right\}$

48. $\left\{\left(\dfrac{2}{3}\right)^n\right\}$

49. $\left\{\dfrac{1}{5}\left(\dfrac{7}{4}\right)^n\right\}$

50. $\left\{1 - \dfrac{1}{n}\right\}$

13-2 SERIES

DEFINITION. *An infinite series is an expression of the form*

$$a_1 + a_2 + a_3 + \ldots + a_n + \ldots$$

where the terms are those of an infinite sequence.

If a sequence is finite, the series corresponding to it is called a *finite series*. An *infinite series* can be represented by the *sigma* or summation notation

$$\sum_{n=1}^{\infty} a_n = a_1 + a_2 + a_3 + \ldots + a_n + \ldots$$

where the index n is replaced successively by the integers 1, 2, 3, ... For the series $\sum\limits_{n=1}^{\infty} a_n$, a_1 is the first term, a_2 the second term, etc., and a_n is the nth or general term.

EXAMPLE 12

a. $\sum\limits_{n=1}^{\infty} \dfrac{1}{n^3} = \dfrac{1}{1^3} + \dfrac{1}{2^3} + \dfrac{1}{3^3} + \ldots + \dfrac{1}{n^3} + \ldots.$

b. $\sum\limits_{n=1}^{3} (-1)^{n+1}(n^2 + 2) = 3 - 6 + 11 = 8$ is a *finite series*.

c. $\sum\limits_{n=1}^{\infty} 4 = 4 + 4 + 4 + 4 + \ldots + 4 + \ldots.$

d. $\sum\limits_{k=0}^{\infty} \dfrac{k-1}{k+1} = -1 + 0 + \dfrac{1}{3} + \dfrac{2}{4} + \ldots + \dfrac{k-1}{k+1} + \ldots.$

Here the summation begins with $k = 0$. In fact, by a proper choice of indexing the limits of summation may begin with any integer.

If we are given a series $\sum\limits_{n=1}^{\infty} a_n$, then the sequence $\{S_n\}$ where

$$S_1 = a_1$$
$$S_2 = a_1 + a_2 = S_1 + a_2$$
$$S_3 = a_1 + a_2 + a_3 = S_2 + a_3$$
$$\vdots$$
$$S_n = a_1 + a_2 + \ldots + a_n = S_{n-1} + a_n$$

etc.

is called the sequence of *partial sums* of the series. S_1 is the first partial sum, S_2 the second partial sum, etc. Observe that $S_2 = S_1 + a_2$, $S_3 = S_2 + a_3$, ..., $S_n = S_{n-1} + a_n$ and $S_n = \sum\limits_{k=1}^{n} a_k$.

EXAMPLE 13

Write the first four partial sums of $\sum\limits_{n=1}^{\infty} \dfrac{1}{n(n+1)}$.

$$S_1 = \frac{1}{1(1 + 1)} = \frac{1}{2}$$

$$S_2 = S_1 + \frac{1}{2(2 + 1)} = \frac{1}{2} + \frac{1}{6} = \frac{2}{3}$$

$$S_3 = S_2 + \frac{1}{3(4)} = \frac{2}{3} + \frac{1}{12} = \frac{3}{4}$$

$$S_4 = S_3 + \frac{1}{4(5)} = \frac{3}{4} + \frac{1}{20} = \frac{4}{5}.$$

Thus $\{S_n\} = \frac{1}{2}, \frac{2}{3}, \frac{3}{4}, \frac{4}{5}, \ldots$

If the sequence $\{S_n\}$ of partial sums of the series Σa_n† converges to a finite number L, this limit is defined to be the *sum* of the series. That is

$$\sum_{n=1}^{\infty} a_n = \lim_{n \to \infty} S_n = L.$$

In this case Σa_n is said to **converge**, or be **convergent**, to L. This means that by adding up a sufficient number of terms of the series, we can approach L as arbitrarily closely as we wish. If $\lim_{n \to \infty} S_n = \pm \infty$ or does not exist, the series is said to **diverge** or be **divergent**.

For the case of the series $\sum \frac{1}{n(n + 1)}$, we saw in Example 13 that

$$\{S_n\} = \frac{1}{2}, \frac{2}{3}, \frac{3}{4}, \frac{4}{5}, \ldots$$

It is easily established that a general term for this sequence is $S_n = \frac{n}{n + 1}$. Thus

$$\lim_{n \to \infty} S_n = \lim_{n \to \infty} \frac{n}{n + 1}$$

$$= \lim_{n \to \infty} \frac{1}{1} = 1. \qquad \text{(L'Hospital's rule)}$$

Hence

$$\sum_{n=1}^{\infty} \frac{1}{n(n + 1)} = 1.$$

---

†Whenever no confusion arises, we omit the limits of summation for convenience.

It should be pointed out that we have used the notation $\Sigma\, a_n$ in two ways: first, to denote an infinite series and second, to denote its sum, if it exists. The appropriate meaning will be clear from the context in which it appears.

Since $S_n = S_{n-1} + a_n$, for $\{S_n\}$ to converge to a number L it must be the case that a_n is getting closer to zero. Indeed, we have the following.

Theorem 7.   If $\Sigma\, a_n$ converges, then $\lim\limits_{n\to\infty} a_n = 0$. That is, if a series converges, its general term must approach 0 as $n \to \infty$. Equivalently, if the general term of a series does not approach 0, then the series must diverge.

PITFALL.   *Just knowing that the general term of a series approaches 0 signifies the possibility that the series might converge. It does not guarantee that the series converges. In short, the converse of Theorem 7, that is, if $a_n \to 0$ then Σa_n converges, is false. However, knowing that $a_n \nrightarrow 0$ tells us immediately that Σa_n diverges.*

The series $\sum\limits_{n=1}^{\infty} \dfrac{1}{n}$ is called the **harmonic series.** Clearly

$$\lim_{n\to\infty} a_n = \lim_{n\to\infty} \frac{1}{n} = 0.$$

Since $\sum\limits_{n=1}^{\infty} \dfrac{1}{n} = 1 + \dfrac{1}{2} + \dfrac{1}{3} + \dfrac{1}{4} + \dfrac{1}{5} + \dfrac{1}{6} + \dfrac{1}{7} + \dfrac{1}{8} + \dots,$

$$S_2 = 1 + \frac{1}{2} > \frac{1}{2}$$

$$S_4 = \left(1 + \frac{1}{2}\right) + \left(\frac{1}{3} + \frac{1}{4}\right) > \left(\frac{1}{2}\right) + \left(\frac{1}{4} + \frac{1}{4}\right) = 2\left(\frac{1}{2}\right)$$

$$S_8 = \left(1 + \frac{1}{2}\right) + \left(\frac{1}{3} + \frac{1}{4}\right) + \left(\frac{1}{5} + \frac{1}{6} + \frac{1}{7} + \frac{1}{8}\right)$$

$$> \left(\frac{1}{2}\right) + \left(\frac{1}{2}\right) + \left(\frac{1}{8} + \frac{1}{8} + \frac{1}{8} + \frac{1}{8}\right) = 3\left(\frac{1}{2}\right)$$

$$S_{2^n} > n\left(\frac{1}{2}\right).$$

Thus as $n \to \infty$, S_n increases without bound and we conclude that the harmonic series $\sum \dfrac{1}{n}$ diverges. This shows that the converse of Theorem 7 is false.

EXAMPLE 14

Apply Theorem 7 to each of the following.

a. $\displaystyle\sum_{n=1}^{\infty} \frac{e^n}{n}$.

Since

$$\lim_{n\to\infty} a_n = \lim_{n\to\infty} \frac{e^n}{n} = \infty, \qquad\qquad \text{[Example 11(b)]}$$

the general term does not tend to zero and the series diverges.

b. $\displaystyle\sum_{n=1}^{\infty} \frac{1}{n^2 + n} = \sum_{n=1}^{\infty} \frac{1}{n(n+1)}$.

Since $(n^2 + n) \to \infty$ as $n \to \infty$, then

$$\lim_{n\to\infty} \frac{1}{n^2 + n} = 0.$$

Hence the series *may* converge (or diverge). Actually, we saw earlier that it converges.

c. $\displaystyle\sum_{n=1}^{\infty} \frac{(-1)^{n+1}}{2^n + 6}$.

As $n \to \infty$, $(2^n + 6) \to \infty$ and $\dfrac{1}{2^n + 6} \to 0$. Hence

$$\lim_{n\to\infty} |a_n| = \lim_{n\to\infty} \frac{1}{2^n + 6} = 0.$$

Recall that the absolute value of a number is its distance from 0. As $n \to \infty$, the absolute value of a_n goes to 0. Thus $(-1)^{n+1}/(2^n + 6)$ must also be getting close to 0 and hence

$$\lim_{n\to\infty} \frac{(-1)^{n+1}}{2^n + 6} = 0.$$

We conclude that the series might converge.

d. $\displaystyle\sum_{n=1}^{\infty} \frac{(-1)^{n+1}}{\sqrt[3]{n}} = 1 - \frac{1}{\sqrt[3]{2}} + \frac{1}{\sqrt[3]{3}} - \frac{1}{\sqrt[3]{4}} + \dots.$

As $n \to \infty$, $|a_n| = 1/\sqrt[3]{n} \to 0$. By an argument similar to that given in (c), we conclude that

$$\lim_{n\to\infty} a_n = \lim_{n\to\infty} \frac{(-1)^{n+1}}{\sqrt[3]{n}} = 0$$

and the series might converge.

e. $\displaystyle\sum_{k=1}^{\infty} \frac{k}{6k + 4}$.

By L'Hospital's rule,

$$\lim_{k\to\infty} \frac{k}{6k + 4} = \lim_{k\to\infty} \frac{1}{6} = \frac{1}{6} \neq 0.$$

Thus the series diverges.

PITFALL. *Do not confuse convergence or divergence of sequences with convergence or divergence of series. For example,*

$$\lim_{n\to\infty} \frac{3n^2 + 2}{1 + 5n^2} = \lim_{n\to\infty} \frac{6n}{10n} = \lim_{n\to\infty} \frac{6}{10} = \frac{3}{5}.$$

Hence the sequence $\left\{\dfrac{3n^2 + 2}{1 + 5n^2}\right\}$ *converges to* $\dfrac{3}{5}$. *But the series*

$$\sum_{n=1}^{\infty} \frac{3n^2 + 2}{1 + 5n^2}$$

diverges since

$$\lim_{n\to\infty} \frac{3n^2 + 2}{1 + 5n^2} = \frac{3}{5} \neq 0.$$

EXERCISE 13-2

In problems 1–10, write the first four terms of the series.

1. $\displaystyle\sum_{n=1}^{\infty} (n + 1)$

2. $\displaystyle\sum_{k=1}^{\infty} (2k + 1)$

3. $\displaystyle\sum_{k=1}^{\infty} (k^2 - 2k)$

4. $\displaystyle\sum_{n=2}^{10} (-n^2 + 3n)$

5. $\displaystyle\sum_{n=1}^{\infty} [(-1)^n(n^2 + 1)]$

6. $\displaystyle\sum_{n=1}^{\infty} \left[(-1)^{n+1}\left(1 + \frac{1}{n}\right)\right]$

7. $2\displaystyle\sum_{n=1}^{\infty} 2n$

8. $\displaystyle\sum_{n=1}^{\infty} \frac{3}{4^n}$

9. $\displaystyle\sum_{n=1}^{\infty} 2(\tfrac{1}{2})^n$

10. $\displaystyle\sum_{n=0}^{\infty} (-1)^n \frac{1}{n + 1}$

11. Evaluate $\displaystyle\sum_{n=1}^{5} [(\tfrac{1}{2})^n - (\tfrac{1}{3})^n]$.

12. If $f(n + 1) - f(n) = -2$ and $f(2) = 4$, find $\displaystyle\sum_{n=1}^{10} f(n)$.

In problems 13–18, find an expression for the general term of the series.

13. $\frac{1}{4} + \frac{1}{7} + \frac{1}{10} + \dots$

14. $\dfrac{3}{1 \cdot 2} + \dfrac{4}{2 \cdot 3} + \dfrac{5}{3 \cdot 4} + \dots$

15. $1 - \frac{1}{2} + \frac{1}{3} - \frac{1}{4} + \dots$

16. $\dfrac{e}{2} + \dfrac{e^2}{3} + \dfrac{e^3}{4} + \dots$

17. $\frac{3}{2} + \frac{4}{4} + \frac{5}{8} + \frac{6}{16} + \dots$

18. $\frac{1}{5} - \frac{1}{10} + \frac{1}{15} - \frac{1}{20} + \dots$

In problems 19–26, find the first four partial sums of the series.

19. $\displaystyle\sum_{n=1}^{\infty} 3n$

20. $\displaystyle\sum_{n=1}^{\infty} 24(\tfrac{1}{2})^{n-1}$

21. $\displaystyle\sum_{n=1}^{\infty} (.3)^n$

22. $\displaystyle\sum_{n=1}^{\infty} \dfrac{n}{10^n}$

23. $\displaystyle\sum_{n=1}^{\infty} (-1)^n \dfrac{1}{n^2}$

24. $\displaystyle\sum_{n=1}^{\infty} \left(1 - \dfrac{1}{4^n}\right)$

25. $\displaystyle\sum_{n=1}^{\infty} 5$

26. $\displaystyle\sum_{n=1}^{\infty} (\tfrac{3}{2})^{n+1}$

By appealing to Theorem 7, in problems 27–36 determine those series which must diverge.

27. $\displaystyle\sum_{n=1}^{\infty} \dfrac{n + 5}{n}$

28. $\displaystyle\sum_{n=1}^{\infty} \dfrac{2n}{e^n}$

29. $\displaystyle\sum_{n=1}^{\infty} \dfrac{(-1)^{n+1}}{n^2}$

30. $\displaystyle\sum_{n=1}^{\infty} \sqrt{n + 1}$

31. $\displaystyle\sum_{n=1}^{\infty} 3$

32. $\displaystyle\sum_{n=2}^{\infty} \dfrac{n}{\ln n}$

33. $\displaystyle\sum_{k=1}^{\infty} \dfrac{e^{k+5}}{k^3 + 1}$

34. $\displaystyle\sum_{k=1}^{\infty} \dfrac{(-1)^k k}{k^3 + 2k^2 + 1}$

35. $\displaystyle\sum_{n=1}^{\infty} \dfrac{n^2 + 3}{n^5 + 5}$

36. $\displaystyle\sum_{n=1}^{\infty} \dfrac{1}{n^2 \sqrt{n + 2}}$

13-3 THE GEOMETRIC SERIES

If the ratio of every two consecutive terms in a series is a constant r, that is

$$\frac{a_2}{a_1} = \frac{a_3}{a_2} = \dots = \frac{a_{n+1}}{a_n} = r,$$

the series is called a *geometric series*. A more precise definition follows.

DEFINITION.   *The series*

$$\sum_{n=1}^{\infty} ar^{n-1} = a + ar + ar^2 + \dots + ar^{n-1} + \dots, \text{ where } a \neq 0\dagger$$

is called a **geometric series** *with common ratio r.*

For example, the series

$$\sum_{n=1}^{\infty} 2\left(\frac{1}{2}\right)^{n-1} = 2 + 1 + \frac{1}{2} + \dots$$

is a geometric series with common ratio $\frac{1}{2}$. The series

$$\sum_{n=1}^{\infty} \left(\frac{3}{4}\right)^{n} = \frac{3}{4} + \frac{3}{4}\left(\frac{3}{4}\right) + \frac{3}{4}\left(\frac{3}{4}\right)^{2} + \dots$$

is a geometric series with common ratio $\frac{3}{4}$.

Let us consider the nth partial sum, S_n, of the geometric series in the definition above:

$$S_n = a + ar + ar^2 + \dots + ar^{n-1}. \tag{1}$$

Multiplying both sides by r, we obtain

$$rS_n = ar + ar^2 + ar^3 + \dots + ar^n. \tag{2}$$

Substracting corresponding sides of Eq. (2) from Eq. (1), we have

$$S_n - rS_n = a - ar^n$$
$$S_n(1 - r) = a(1 - r^n).$$

Hence the sum of the first n terms of a geometric series is

$$S_n = \frac{a(1 - r^n)}{1 - r}.$$

If $|r| < 1$, then by Theorem 1, $\lim_{n \to \infty} r^n = 0$ and

$$\lim_{n \to \infty} S_n = \lim_{n \to \infty} \frac{a(1 - r^n)}{1 - r} = \frac{a}{1 - r}.$$

$\dagger$If $a = 0$, then $\Sigma ar^{n-1} = 0 + 0 + \dots + 0 + \dots$ and $\lim_{n \to \infty} S_n = 0$. We shall not consider this uninteresting
case.

Thus if $|r| < 1$, the geometric series converges to the sum $a/(1 - r)$. But if $|r| > 1$, then $\lim\limits_{n \to \infty} r^n$ does not exist and so neither does $\lim\limits_{n \to \infty} S_n$. If $r = 1$, then

$$S_n = a + a + \dots + a = na$$

which has no limit as $n \to \infty$. If $r = -1$, then

$$S_n = a - a + a - a + \dots + (\pm a).$$

This is 0 if n is even and is a if n is odd. Hence, the series diverges. In summary we have the following.

Theorem 8.   The geometric series $\sum\limits_{n=1}^{\infty} ar^{n-1}$ converges if $|r| < 1$ and diverges

if $|r| \geq 1$. If the series is convergent, its sum is $\dfrac{a}{1 - r}$.

EXAMPLE 15

Test the following series for convergence or divergence. In the case of convergence, find the sum.

a. $\displaystyle\sum_{n=1}^{\infty} 8(\tfrac{1}{2})^{n-1} = 8 + 4 + 2 + \dots.$

The series is geometric with $a = 8$ and $r = \tfrac{1}{2}$. Since $|r| < 1$, the series converges to

$$\frac{a}{1 - r} = \frac{8}{1 - \tfrac{1}{2}} = 16.$$

b. $6 - 1 + \tfrac{1}{6} - \tfrac{1}{36} + \dots = \displaystyle\sum_{n=1}^{\infty} 6(-\tfrac{1}{6})^{n-1}.$

The series is geometric with $a = 6$ and $r = -\tfrac{1}{6}$. Since $|-\tfrac{1}{6}| < 1$, the series converges to

$$\frac{6}{1 - (-\tfrac{1}{6})} = \frac{36}{7}.$$

c. $\displaystyle\sum_{n=1}^{\infty} \frac{1}{4^n} = \frac{1}{4} + \frac{1}{16} + \frac{1}{64} + \dots = \sum_{n=1}^{\infty} \frac{1}{4}\left(\frac{1}{4}\right)^{n-1}.$

Here $a = \tfrac{1}{4}$, $r = \tfrac{1}{4}$, and the series converges to

$$\frac{\frac{1}{4}}{1 - \frac{1}{4}} = \frac{1}{3}.$$

d. $\sum_{n=1}^{\infty} 4(\frac{5}{3})^n = \sum_{n=1}^{\infty} 4(\frac{5}{3})(\frac{5}{3})^{n-1} = \sum_{n=1}^{\infty} \frac{20}{3}(\frac{5}{3})^{n-1}.$

The series is geometric with $|r| = \frac{5}{3} > 1$ and hence diverges.

e. $\sum_{n=1}^{\infty} [\frac{1}{10} + (\frac{1}{10})^n].$

The series is *not* geometric. Moreover,

$$\lim_{n \to \infty} a_n = \lim_{n \to \infty} [\frac{1}{10} + (\frac{1}{10})^n] = \frac{1}{10} \neq 0.$$

This series must diverge since a_n does not approach 0.

A useful symbol in the study of series is that of *n factorial, n!*

DEFINITION. *If n is a positive integer, then **n factorial**, written "n!," is defined by*

$$n! = 1 \cdot 2 \cdot 3 \cdot \ldots \cdot n.$$

If n = 0, then

$$0! = 1.$$

EXAMPLE 16

a. $3! = 1 \cdot 2 \cdot 3 = 6$

b. $6! = 1 \cdot 2 \cdot 3 \cdot 4 \cdot 5 \cdot 6 = 720$

c. $n! = n(n - 1)(n - 2) \ldots (1) = n(n - 1)!$

d. $2n! = 2(1 \cdot 2 \cdot 3 \cdot \ldots \cdot n)$, but $(2n)! = 1 \cdot 2 \cdot 3 \cdot \ldots \cdot (2n).$

EXAMPLE 17

Show $\sum_{n=1}^{\infty} n! = 1! + 2! + 3! + \ldots$ *diverges.*

Since

$$n! = 1 \cdot 2 \cdot 3 \cdot \ldots \cdot n \geq 1 \cdot 2 \cdot 2 \cdot \ldots \cdot 2 = 2^{n-1}$$

and 2^{n-1} does not tend to zero as $n \to \infty$, neither does the general term $a_n = n!$ Hence the series diverges.

In testing for convergence or divergence of a series, three useful theorems are as follows.

Theorem 9.   If the series obtained from a given series by deleting or inserting a finite number of terms is convergent (divergent), then the given series is convergent (divergent).†

Theorem 10.   Multiplying every term of a series by a nonzero constant does not affect the convergence or divergence of the series.† That is, if Σa_n converges, then $\Sigma c a_n$ converges, and the converse is also true.

Theorem 11.   If Σa_n and Σb_n are both convergent series, then $\Sigma(a_n + b_n)$ and $\Sigma(a_n - b_n)$ are also convergent series.

EXAMPLE 18

Test the following series for convergence or divergence.

a. $\displaystyle\sum_{n=1}^{\infty} \frac{6}{n} = \sum_{n=1}^{\infty} 6\left(\frac{1}{n}\right).$

Each term is a constant multiple of the corresponding term of the divergent harmonic series, $\Sigma\ 1/n$. Thus the given series diverges by Theorem 10.

b. $\displaystyle\sum_{n=1}^{\infty} \frac{1}{4n} = \sum_{n=1}^{\infty} \left(\frac{1}{4}\right)\left(\frac{1}{n}\right).$

As in (a) the series diverges.

c. $\displaystyle\sum_{n=1}^{\infty} \frac{1}{n+6} = \frac{1}{7} + \frac{1}{8} + \frac{1}{9} + \ \dots.$

The series is a harmonic series with the first six terms deleted. Thus it diverges (Theorem 9).

d. $\displaystyle\sum_{k=1}^{\infty} \frac{3}{k+6}.$

From (c), $\displaystyle\sum \frac{1}{k+6}$ diverges. Since each term of the given series is a constant multiple of the corresponding term of this series, the given series must also diverge (Theorem 10).

e. $5 + 4 + 3 + \frac{1}{3} + \frac{1}{9} + \frac{1}{27} + \ \dots.$

---

† Although, of course, the sum could be affected in the event of convergence.

From the fourth term on, the series is a convergent geometric series ($r = \frac{1}{3}$). Thus the given series must converge (Theorem 9).

f. $\displaystyle\sum_{n=1}^{\infty} [(\tfrac{1}{2})^n - (\tfrac{1}{3})^n]$.

Both $\displaystyle\sum_{n=1}^{\infty} (\tfrac{1}{2})^n$ and $\displaystyle\sum_{n=1}^{\infty} (\tfrac{1}{3})^n$ are convergent geometric series. Thus, $\displaystyle\sum_{n=1}^{\infty} [(\tfrac{1}{2})^n - (\tfrac{1}{3})^n]$ is also convergent by Theorem 11.

EXERCISE 13-3

Test each of the following for convergence or divergence. In the case of convergence, find the sum.

1. $\displaystyle\sum_{n=1}^{\infty} (\tfrac{1}{2})^n$

2. $\displaystyle\sum_{n=1}^{\infty} (\tfrac{3}{4})^n$

3. $\displaystyle\sum_{n=1}^{\infty} (-\tfrac{2}{3})^n$

4. $\displaystyle\sum_{n=1}^{\infty} (1.2)^n$

5. $\displaystyle\sum_{n=1}^{\infty} (\tfrac{7}{6})^n$

6. $\displaystyle\sum_{n=1}^{\infty} 4\left(\frac{1}{1.1}\right)^n$

7. $\displaystyle\sum_{k=3}^{\infty} (\tfrac{3}{5})^{k+2}$

8. $\displaystyle\sum_{i=5}^{\infty} (-\tfrac{4}{9})^i$

9. $\displaystyle\sum_{n=1}^{\infty} 3(-.2)^n$

10. $\displaystyle\sum_{n=1}^{\infty} 3(1 - \tfrac{1}{3})^n$

11. $\displaystyle\sum_{n=1}^{\infty} 100\left(\frac{1}{4^n}\right)$

12. $\displaystyle\sum_{n=1}^{\infty} \tfrac{1}{4}(3^n)$

13. $\displaystyle\sum_{n=1}^{\infty} [(\tfrac{1}{3})^n + \tfrac{1}{3}]$

14. $\displaystyle\sum_{n=1}^{\infty} \tfrac{9}{4}(\tfrac{4}{9})^{n+3}$

15. $3 + \tfrac{3}{2} + \tfrac{3}{4} + \ldots$

16. $4 + 1 + \tfrac{1}{4} + \ldots$

17. $12 + 4 + \tfrac{4}{3} + \ldots$

18. $\dfrac{1}{1.2} + \dfrac{1}{(1.2)^2} + \dfrac{1}{(1.2)^3} + \ldots$

19. $-4 + 2 - 1 + \ldots$

20. $100 - 10 + 1 - .1 + \ldots$

21. $\tfrac{5}{3} + \tfrac{1}{6} + \tfrac{1}{60} + \ldots$

22. $\dfrac{3}{4} + \dfrac{3}{4^2} + \dfrac{3}{4^3} + \ldots$

23. $\dfrac{1}{(.1)} + \dfrac{1}{(.1)^2} + \dfrac{1}{(.1)^3} + \ldots$

24. $.02 + .002 + .0002 + \ldots$

25. $\displaystyle\sum_{n=1}^{\infty} (n + 2)!$

26. $\displaystyle\sum_{n=1}^{\infty} (n - 1)!$

27. $\displaystyle\sum_{n=1}^{\infty} 4n!$

28. $\displaystyle\sum_{n=1}^{\infty} \frac{(n - 1)!}{n!}$

29. $\displaystyle\sum_{n=1}^{\infty} \frac{1}{n + 7}$

30. $\displaystyle\sum_{n=1}^{\infty} \frac{4}{5}\left(\frac{1}{n + 2}\right)$

31. $\displaystyle\sum_{n=1}^{\infty} \frac{.1}{n}$

32. $\displaystyle\sum_{n=1}^{\infty} \frac{1/2}{n}$

33. $\displaystyle\sum_{n=1}^{\infty} \frac{3}{5n}$

34. $\displaystyle\sum_{n=1}^{\infty} 5\left(\frac{1}{8n}\right)$

35. In Samuelson's† discussion of the amplified effect of investment on income, he gives the following example. Suppose you invest \$1000 for the construction of a garage. Furthermore, those who receive this sum for building it spend $\frac{2}{3}$ of it on new goods. That is, they have a marginal propensity to consume of $\frac{2}{3}$. Continuing, suppose the producers of these goods in turn spend $\frac{2}{3}$ of this $[\frac{2}{3}$ of $\frac{2}{3}(1000)]$. Continuing in this manner, each new round of spending is $\frac{2}{3}$ the previous round. Find the total sum of this endless chain of money. That is, find $1000 + (\frac{2}{3})(1000) + (\frac{2}{3})(\frac{2}{3})(1000) + \ldots$.

13-4   THE COMPARISON TEST

Usually it is quite difficult to determine the convergence or divergence of a series by considering the limit of its partial sums. In this section and the ones following, we shall consider various tests which often will help us determine the behavior of certain types of series.

One method involves comparing the terms of a given series with those of a series whose convergence or divergence is known. Of course, at this stage the only series at our disposal for comparison purposes are the geometric and harmonic series. Therefore, before stating the so-called comparison test we shall introduce another series whose behavior is known.

The p-series.   The series

$$\sum_{n=1}^{\infty} \frac{1}{n^p} = 1 + \frac{1}{2^p} + \frac{1}{3^p} + \ldots + \frac{1}{n^p} + \ldots,$$

referred to as the p-series, converges if $p > 1$ and diverges if $p \leq 1$.

---

†Paul A. Samuelson, *Economics*, 9th ed. (New York: McGraw-Hill Book Company, 1973), p. 229.

Note that when $p = 1$, the p-series is merely the harmonic series which you should recall is divergent.

EXAMPLE 19

a. The series

$$\sum_{n=1}^{\infty} \frac{1}{n^2} = 1 + \frac{1}{2^2} + \frac{1}{3^2} + \dots + \frac{1}{n^2} + \dots$$

is a p-series with $p = 2 > 1$ and thus converges.

b. The series

$$\sum_{n=1}^{\infty} \frac{1}{\sqrt{n}} = 1 + \frac{1}{\sqrt{2}} + \frac{1}{\sqrt{3}} + \dots + \frac{1}{\sqrt{n}} + \dots$$

has the general term $1/\sqrt{n} = 1/n^{1/2}$ and is a divergent p-series ($p = 1/2 < 1$).

c. Since the series

$$\sum_{n=1}^{\infty} \frac{1}{20\sqrt[3]{n^2}} \quad \text{can be written} \quad \frac{1}{20} \sum_{n=1}^{\infty} \frac{1}{n^{2/3}},$$

it is a multiple of a divergent p-series ($p = \frac{2}{3} < 1$) and is therefore divergent itself.

d. The series

$$\sum_{n=1}^{\infty} \frac{2}{(n+9)^3}$$

is a constant multiple of the series $\sum \dfrac{1}{(n+9)^3}$. But

$$\sum_{n=1}^{\infty} \frac{1}{(n+9)^3} = \frac{1}{10^3} + \frac{1}{11^3} + \frac{1}{12^3} + \dots$$

is the p-series $\sum \dfrac{1}{n^3}$ with the first nine terms deleted and is therefore convergent.

Hence the given series converges.

We are now ready to state the comparison test which applies to a *nonnegative series* (that is, one in which the terms are each greater than or equal to zero).

Comparison Test.   Let $\Sigma\, a_n$ and $\Sigma\, b_n$ be nonnegative series.

1. If $\Sigma\, b_n$ converges and $a_n \le b_n$ for all n, then $\Sigma\, a_n$ converges also.

2. If $\Sigma\, b_n$ diverges and $a_n \ge b_n$ for all n, then $\Sigma\, a_n$ also diverges.

The convergence or divergence of a series is not affected by deleting or inserting a finite number of terms at the beginning of the series. Thus the comparison test essentially states that a nonnegative series is convergent when each term, from some point on, is less than or equal to the corresponding term of a convergent series. A series is divergent when each term, from some point on, is greater than or equal to the corresponding term of a nonnegative divergent series.

EXAMPLE 20

Test each of the following series for convergence or divergence.

a. $\displaystyle\sum_{n=1}^{\infty} \frac{1}{4^n + 5}$.

We first note that the general term approaches 0:

$$\lim_{n \to \infty} \frac{1}{4^n + 5} = 0.$$

At this stage we do not know whether or not the series converges. For large values of n, $4^n + 5$ behaves like 4^n. Thus the general term of the series is similar to $\dfrac{1}{4^n} = \left(\dfrac{1}{4}\right)^n$, which is the general term of a convergent geometric series ($r = \frac{1}{4}$). On this basis we "guess" that the given series is convergent and try to show that it is term by term *less than or equal to* $\displaystyle\sum \frac{1}{4^n}$. The inequality

$$\frac{1}{4^n + 5} \le \frac{1}{4^n}$$

is equivalent to

$$4^n \le 4^n + 5$$

which is true for each n. Since $\displaystyle\sum \frac{1}{4^n}$ converges, by the comparison test so does the given series.

b. $\displaystyle\sum_{n=1}^{\infty} \frac{3}{n^2 + 4}$.

For large values of n, the general term approaches 0 and the series behaves like $\displaystyle\sum \frac{3}{n^2}$. But this series is a multiple of the convergent p-series $\displaystyle\sum \frac{1}{n^2}$ and converges also. Believing that the given series is also convergent, we would like to show the inequality

$$\frac{3}{n^2 + 4} \le \frac{3}{n^2}.$$

This is equivalent to $3n^2 \le 3n^2 + 12$ which is true for each n. Thus, by the comparison test the given series converges.

c. $\displaystyle\sum_{n=1}^{\infty} \frac{n^3}{n^2 + 2}.$

Since

$$\lim_{n\to\infty} \frac{n^3}{n^2 + 2} = \lim_{n\to\infty} \frac{\dfrac{n^3}{n^3}}{\dfrac{n^2}{n^3} + \dfrac{2}{n^3}} = \lim_{n\to\infty} \frac{1}{\dfrac{1}{n} + \dfrac{2}{n^3}} = \infty,$$

the general term does not approach 0. So the series diverges.

d. $\displaystyle\sum_{n=1}^{\infty} \frac{1}{20n + 7}.$

The general term approaches 0. We note that $20n + 7 > 20n$ and hence

$$\frac{1}{20n + 7} < \frac{1}{20n}.$$

Since $\displaystyle\sum \frac{1}{n}$ diverges, so does $\displaystyle\frac{1}{20}\sum \frac{1}{n}$. This means the given series is term by term *less* than a *divergent* series. With only this information we *cannot* apply the comparison test. We can, however, appeal to our ingenuity and write

$$20n + 7 < 20n + 20 = 20(n + 1).$$

Thus

$$\frac{1}{20n + 7} > \frac{1}{20(n + 1)}.$$

Since

$$\sum_{n=1}^{\infty} \frac{1}{n + 1} = \frac{1}{2} + \frac{1}{3} + \cdots$$

is the divergent harmonic series with the first term deleted, $\displaystyle\sum \frac{1}{20(n + 1)}$ diverges also. Thus, the given series is term by term greater than a divergent series, and by the comparison test it too must diverge.

PITFALL.   *Remember that if $a_n \leq b_n$ and Σb_n diverges, we can draw no conclusion about Σa_n. Similarly, if $a_n \geq b_n$ and Σb_n converges, we can draw no conclusion concerning Σa_n.*

e. $\displaystyle\sum_{n=1}^{\infty} \frac{1}{50n + 17}$.

This series can be analyzed as in d, but another approach will be shown instead. Since

$$50n + 17 \leq 51n, \qquad\qquad (n \geq 17)$$

then

$$\frac{1}{50n + 17} \geq \frac{1}{51n}. \qquad\qquad (n \geq 17)$$

Since $\displaystyle\sum \frac{1}{51n} = \frac{1}{51} \sum \frac{1}{n}$ diverges, so does the given series by the comparison test.

EXAMPLE 21

Test each of the following series for convergence or divergence.

a. $\displaystyle\sum_{n=1}^{\infty} \frac{1}{n(n + 1)(n + 2)}$.

Observing that the degree of the denominator is 3 leads us to compare the general term to $1/n^3$. Since

$$n(n + 1)(n + 2) > n \cdot n \cdot n,$$

it follows that

$$\frac{1}{n(n + 1)(n + 2)} < \frac{1}{n^3}.$$

But $\displaystyle\sum \frac{1}{n^3}$ is a convergent *p*-series, and so by the comparison test the given series converges.

b. $\displaystyle\sum_{n=1}^{\infty} \frac{1}{n^n} = 1 + \frac{1}{2^2} + \frac{1}{3^3} + \frac{1}{4^4} + \ldots + \frac{1}{n^n} + \ldots.$

Since

$$1 \geq 1,\ 2^2 \geq 2^1,\ 3^3 \geq 2^2,\ 4^4 \geq 2^3,\ \ldots,\ n^n \geq 2^{n-1},\ \ldots$$

it follows that

$$1 \leq 1,\ \frac{1}{2^2} \leq \frac{1}{2^1},\ \frac{1}{3^3} \leq \frac{1}{2^2},\ \frac{1}{4^4} \leq \frac{1}{2^3},\ \ldots,\ \frac{1}{n^n} \leq \frac{1}{2^{n-1}},\ \ldots.$$

Since

$$\sum_{n=1}^{\infty} \frac{1}{2^{n-1}} = \sum_{n=1}^{\infty} \left(\frac{1}{2}\right)^{n-1}$$

is a convergent geometric series $(r = \frac{1}{2})$, by the comparison test the given series converges.

c. $\sum_{n=1}^{\infty} \frac{1}{n!}$.

Since $n! = 1 \cdot 2 \cdot 3 \cdot \ldots \cdot n \geq 1 \cdot 2 \cdot 2 \cdot 2 \cdot \ldots \cdot 2 = 2^{n-1}$, then

$$\frac{1}{n!} \leq \frac{1}{2^{n-1}}.$$

By an argument similar to that in the preceding problem, the given series converges.

d. $\sum_{n=1}^{\infty} \frac{1}{(2n)!}$.

Since $(2n)! > n!$, then

$$\frac{1}{(2n)!} < \frac{1}{n!}.$$

But from c, $\sum \frac{1}{n!}$ converges, and by the comparison test so does the given series.

e. $\sum_{n=1}^{\infty} \frac{n^2 + n + 1}{n^3}$.

We have

$$n^2 + n + 1 > n^2.$$

Thus

$$\frac{n^2 + n + 1}{n^3} > \frac{n^2}{n^3} = \frac{1}{n}.$$

Since $\sum \frac{1}{n}$ (the harmonic series) diverges, so does the given series.

We conclude this section with a discussion of $\sum \frac{1}{\ln n}$. First we shall show that $\ln n < n$ [or equivalently $(\ln n) - n < 0$] by considering the function $f(x) = (\ln x) - x$. Now $f(1) = -1$ and

$$f'(x) = \frac{1}{x} - 1.$$

If $x > 1$, then $f'(x) < 0$ and f is a decreasing function. Since f is negative when $x = 1$ and decreasing for $x > 1$, it follows that f must always be negative for $x \geq 1$. Hence

$$(\ln x) - x < 0 \quad (x \geq 1)$$

or

$$(\ln n) - n < 0. \quad (n \geq 1)$$

This means

$$\ln n < n.$$

Thus

$$\frac{1}{\ln n} > \frac{1}{n}$$

and since $\sum \dfrac{1}{n}$ diverges, so does the given series.

EXERCISE 13-4

Test each of the following series for convergence or divergence.

1. $\displaystyle\sum_{n=1}^{\infty} \frac{1}{n^3}$

2. $\displaystyle\sum_{n=1}^{\infty} \frac{1}{\sqrt[3]{n}}$

3. $\displaystyle\sum_{n=1}^{\infty} \frac{1}{\sqrt[6]{n}}$

4. $\displaystyle\sum_{n=1}^{\infty} \frac{\sqrt{n}}{n^2}$

5. $\displaystyle\sum_{n=1}^{\infty} \frac{1}{n\sqrt{n}}$

6. $\displaystyle\sum_{n=1}^{\infty} \frac{2}{(n+1)^5}$

7. $\displaystyle\sum_{n=1}^{\infty} \frac{1}{(5n)^5}$

8. $\displaystyle\sum_{n=1}^{\infty} \frac{4}{\sqrt{(n+5)^3}}$

9. $\displaystyle\sum_{n=1}^{\infty} \frac{6}{n+7}$

10. $\displaystyle\sum_{n=1}^{\infty} \frac{2}{3\sqrt[3]{n^2}}$

11. $\displaystyle\sum_{n=5}^{\infty} \frac{1}{n-4}$

12. $\displaystyle\sum_{n=1}^{\infty} \frac{n^2}{n+6}$

13. $\displaystyle\sum_{n=6}^{\infty} \frac{1}{3(n-5)^4}$

14. $\displaystyle\sum_{n=1}^{\infty} \frac{4}{(n+6)!}$

15. $\displaystyle\sum_{n=1}^{\infty} \frac{(n+2)^3}{n}$

16. $\displaystyle\sum_{n=2}^{\infty} \frac{1}{6\ln n}$

17. $\displaystyle\sum_{n=1}^{\infty} \frac{1}{6n + 4}$

18. $\displaystyle\sum_{n=1}^{\infty} \frac{1}{(n + 2)(2n + 2)}$

19. $\displaystyle\sum_{n=1}^{\infty} \frac{1}{2n!}$

20. $\displaystyle\sum_{n=1}^{\infty} \frac{1}{n\sqrt{n} + 7}$

21. $\displaystyle\sum_{n=1}^{\infty} \frac{1}{(10n)!}$

22. $\displaystyle\sum_{n=1}^{\infty} \frac{1}{5^n + 10}$

23. $\displaystyle\sum_{n=1}^{\infty} \frac{3n^2 + 3n + 1}{n^4}$

24. $\displaystyle\sum_{n=1}^{\infty} \frac{n^2 + n}{n}$

25. $\displaystyle\sum_{n=1}^{\infty} \frac{2}{\ln (n + 2)}$

26. $\displaystyle\sum_{n=1}^{\infty} \frac{1}{\sqrt{n(n + 2)}}$

27. $\displaystyle\sum_{n=1}^{\infty} \frac{1}{\sqrt{n^3 + 2}}$

28. $\displaystyle\sum_{n=1}^{\infty} \frac{\ln n}{n^3}$

29. $\displaystyle\sum_{n=1}^{\infty} \frac{5}{n^2 + 1}$

30. $\displaystyle\sum_{n=1}^{\infty} \frac{1}{n4^n}$

31. $\displaystyle\sum_{n=1}^{\infty} \frac{1}{1 + \ln n}$

32. $\displaystyle\sum_{n=1}^{\infty} \frac{n(n - 1)}{n^4}$

33. $\displaystyle\sum_{n=1}^{\infty} \frac{1}{n(n + 1)(n + 2)(n + 3)(n + 4)}$

34. $\displaystyle\sum_{n=1}^{\infty} \frac{1}{2}$

35. $\displaystyle\sum_{n=1}^{\infty} \frac{1}{(1.1)^n + 2.2}$

36. $\displaystyle\sum_{n=1}^{\infty} [(\tfrac{4}{3})^n (\tfrac{3}{5})^n]$

13-5   THE RATIO TEST FOR POSITIVE SERIES

For a *positive series* (a series with each term positive), a test frequently used for convergence or divergence is the *ratio test*.

The Ratio Test.   For the positive series Σa_n, let L be the limit, if it exists (or is ∞), of the ratio of the $(n + 1)$th term to the nth term as $n \to \infty$:

$$L = \lim_{n \to \infty} \frac{a_{n+1}}{a_n}.$$

If

   a. $L < 1$, then Σa_n converges;
   b. $L > 1$ or $L = \infty$, then Σa_n diverges;
   c. $L = 1$, then the test provides no information.

EXAMPLE 22

Determine whether the following series are convergent or divergent.

a. $\displaystyle\sum_{n=1}^{\infty} \frac{n}{5^n} = \frac{1}{5} + \frac{2}{5^2} + \frac{3}{5^3} + \dots + \frac{n}{5^n} + \dots.$

We have

$$a_n = \frac{n}{5^n} \quad \text{and} \quad a_{n+1} = \frac{n+1}{5^{n+1}}.$$

Thus

$$L = \lim_{n\to\infty} \frac{a_{n+1}}{a_n} = \lim_{n\to\infty} \frac{\dfrac{n+1}{5^{n+1}}}{\dfrac{n}{5^n}} = \lim_{n\to\infty} \left[\frac{n+1}{5^{n+1}} \cdot \frac{5^n}{n} \right]$$

$$= \lim_{n\to\infty} \frac{n+1}{5n} \qquad\qquad (\text{form } \infty/\infty)$$

$$L = \lim_{n\to\infty} \frac{1}{5} = \frac{1}{5}. \qquad\qquad (\text{L'Hospital's rule})$$

Since the limit is less than 1, the series converges by the ratio test.

b. $\displaystyle\sum_{n=1}^{\infty} \frac{n!}{2^n}.$

We have

$$a_n = \frac{n!}{2^n} \quad \text{and} \quad a_{n+1} = \frac{(n+1)!}{2^{n+1}}$$

and

$$L = \lim_{n\to\infty} \frac{a_{n+1}}{a_n} = \lim_{n\to\infty} \left[\frac{(n+1)!}{2^{n+1}} \cdot \frac{2^n}{n!} \right] = \lim_{n\to\infty} \left[\frac{(n+1)!}{n!} \cdot \frac{2^n}{2^{n+1}} \right].$$

Since $(n+1)!/n! = n+1$ and $2^n/2^{n+1} = \frac{1}{2}$,

$$\lim_{n\to\infty} \frac{a_{n+1}}{a_n} = \lim_{n\to\infty} \frac{n+1}{2} = \infty.$$

By the ratio test the series diverges since $L = \infty$.

c. $\displaystyle\sum_{n=1}^{\infty} \frac{\sqrt{n}}{n^2+1}.$

$$\lim_{n \to \infty} \frac{a_{n+1}}{a_n} = \lim_{n \to \infty} \left[\frac{\sqrt{n+1}}{(n+1)^2 + 1} \cdot \frac{n^2 + 1}{\sqrt{n}} \right]$$

$$= \lim_{n \to \infty} \left[\frac{\sqrt{n+1}}{\sqrt{n}} \cdot \frac{n^2 + 1}{n^2 + 2n + 2} \right]$$

$$= \lim_{n \to \infty} \left[\sqrt{1 + \frac{1}{n}} \cdot \frac{1 + \dfrac{1}{n^2}}{1 + \dfrac{2}{n} + \dfrac{2}{n^2}} \right]$$

$$= 1 \cdot 1 = 1.$$

Since the limit is 1, the ratio test fails. However, note that the numerator and denominator of a_n are of degrees $\frac{1}{2}$ and 2, respectively. Thus a_n appears to behave like $1/n^{3/2}$ and we shall try the comparison test. The inequality

$$\frac{\sqrt{n}}{n^2 + 1} \le \frac{1}{n^{3/2}}$$

is equivalent to $n^2 \le n^2 + 1$, which is always true. Since $\displaystyle\sum \frac{1}{n^{3/2}}$ is a convergent p-series which is term by term larger than the given series, we conclude that the given series converges.

d. $\displaystyle\sum_{n=1}^{\infty} \frac{n^3}{e^{n^2}}$.

$$\lim_{n \to \infty} \frac{a_{n+1}}{a_n} = \lim_{n \to \infty} \left[\frac{(n+1)^3}{e^{(n+1)^2}} \cdot \frac{e^{n^2}}{n^3} \right]$$

$$= \lim_{n \to \infty} \left[\left(\frac{n+1}{n} \right)^3 \cdot \frac{e^{n^2}}{e^{n^2 + 2n + 1}} \right]$$

$$= \lim_{n \to \infty} \left[\left(1 + \frac{1}{n} \right)^3 \frac{1}{e^{2n+1}} \right] = 1 \cdot 0 = 0.$$

By the ratio test the series converges $(0 < 1)$.

EXAMPLE 23

Determine whether the following series are convergent or divergent.

a. $\displaystyle\sum_{n=1}^{\infty} \frac{(n+1)(n+2)}{n!}$.

$$\lim_{n\to\infty} \frac{a_{n+1}}{a_n} = \lim_{n\to\infty} \left[\frac{(n+2)(n+3)}{(n+1)!} \cdot \frac{n!}{(n+1)(n+2)} \right]$$

$$= \lim_{n\to\infty} \frac{n+3}{(n+1)^2} \qquad\qquad (\text{form } \infty/\infty)$$

$$= \lim_{n\to\infty} \frac{1}{2(n+1)} \qquad\qquad (\text{L'Hospital's rule})$$

$$= 0.$$

By the ratio test the series is convergent $(0 < 1)$.

b. $\displaystyle\sum_{n=1}^{\infty} \frac{e^{2n}}{n^2 + 4}.$

Since

$$\lim_{n\to\infty} a_n = \lim_{n\to\infty} \frac{e^{2n}}{n^2 + 4} = \lim_{n\to\infty} \frac{2e^{2n}}{2n} = \lim_{n\to\infty} \frac{4e^{2n}}{2} = \infty,$$

the series diverges $(a_n \not\to 0)$.

c. $\displaystyle\sum_{n=1}^{\infty} n\left(\frac{1}{4}\right)^n.$

$$\lim_{n\to\infty} \frac{a_{n+1}}{a_n} = \lim_{n\to\infty} \frac{(n+1)(\frac{1}{4})^{n+1}}{n(\frac{1}{4})^n} = \lim_{n\to\infty} \left[\left(\frac{n+1}{n}\right)\left(\frac{1}{4}\right) \right]$$

$$= \lim_{n\to\infty} \left[\left(1 + \frac{1}{n}\right)\left(\frac{1}{4}\right) \right] = 1 \cdot \frac{1}{4} = \frac{1}{4}.$$

By the ratio test the series converges $(\frac{1}{4} < 1)$.

d. $\displaystyle\sum_{n=1}^{\infty} n!$

$$\lim_{n\to\infty} \frac{a_{n+1}}{a_n} = \lim_{n\to\infty} \frac{(n+1)!}{n!} = \lim_{n\to\infty} (n+1) = \infty.$$

Hence $\Sigma\, n!$ diverges, confirming a previously known result.

e. $\displaystyle\sum_{n=1}^{\infty} \frac{2n + 5}{n^4}.$

$$\lim_{n \to \infty} \frac{a_{n+1}}{a_n} = \lim_{n \to \infty} \frac{\dfrac{2(n+1)+5}{(n+1)^4}}{\dfrac{2n+5}{n^4}} = \lim_{n \to \infty} \left[\frac{2n+7}{2n+5} \cdot \frac{n^4}{(n+1)^4} \right]$$

$$= \lim_{n \to \infty} \left[\frac{2n+7}{2n+5} \left(\frac{n}{n+1} \right)^4 \right]$$

$$= \lim_{n \to \infty} \left[\frac{2 + \dfrac{7}{n}}{2 + \dfrac{5}{n}} \left(\frac{1}{1 + \dfrac{1}{n}} \right)^4 \right] = \frac{2}{2} \cdot 1 = 1$$

and the ratio test fails. We try the comparison test. Since

$$2n + 5 \le 3n, \quad (n \ge 5)$$

then

$$\frac{2n+5}{n^4} \le \frac{3n}{n^4} = \frac{3}{n^3}.$$

Since $\displaystyle\sum \frac{3}{n^3} = 3 \sum \frac{1}{n^3}$ converges, so does the given series.

EXERCISE 13-5

In problems 1–24, use the ratio test to determine convergence or divergence of the series.

1. $\displaystyle\sum_{n=1}^{\infty} \frac{1}{6^n}$ **2.** $\displaystyle\sum_{n=1}^{\infty} \left(\tfrac{2}{3}\right)^n$

3. $\displaystyle\sum_{n=1}^{\infty} \left(\tfrac{6}{5}\right)^n$ **4.** $\displaystyle\sum_{n=1}^{\infty} \frac{1}{(.5)^n}$

5. $\displaystyle\sum_{n=1}^{\infty} \frac{n}{3^n}$ **6.** $\displaystyle\sum_{n=1}^{\infty} \frac{n+5}{5^n}$

7. $\displaystyle\sum_{n=1}^{\infty} \frac{n!}{5^n}$ **8.** $\displaystyle\sum_{n=1}^{\infty} \frac{3^n}{n!}$

9. $\displaystyle\sum_{n=1}^{\infty} 5\left(\tfrac{2}{3}\right)^n$ **10.** $\displaystyle\sum_{n=1}^{\infty} 2\left(\tfrac{5}{4}\right)^n$

11. $\displaystyle\sum_{n=1}^{\infty} \frac{n^2}{e^{n^2}}$ **12.** $\displaystyle\sum_{n=1}^{\infty} n\left(\tfrac{2}{3}\right)^n$

13. $\displaystyle\sum_{n=1}^{\infty} n\left(\tfrac{4}{3}\right)^n$

14. $\displaystyle\sum_{n=1}^{\infty} (n+1)!$

15. $\displaystyle\sum_{n=1}^{\infty} \frac{e^{3n}}{n^2+9}$

16. $\displaystyle\sum_{n=1}^{\infty} \frac{n+1}{n!}$

17. $\displaystyle\sum_{n=1}^{\infty} \frac{1}{n2^n}$

18. $\displaystyle\sum_{n=1}^{\infty} \frac{n}{e^n}$

19. $\displaystyle\sum_{n=1}^{\infty} \frac{(1/2)^{2n+1}}{2n+1}$

20. $\displaystyle\sum_{n=1}^{\infty} \frac{n^3}{2^n}$

21. $\displaystyle\sum_{n=1}^{\infty} \frac{(n+2)(n-4)}{n!}$

22. $\displaystyle\sum_{n=1}^{\infty} \frac{n!}{2n}$

23. $\displaystyle\sum_{n=1}^{\infty} \frac{3^n}{n2^n}$

24. $\displaystyle\sum_{n=1}^{\infty} \frac{1+n^2}{2^n}$

In problems 25–44, test the series for convergence or divergence by using the ratio test. If it fails, use prior techniques.

25. $\displaystyle\sum_{n=1}^{\infty} \frac{n^2}{2^n}$

26. $\displaystyle\sum_{n=1}^{\infty} \frac{n+10}{n^3}$

27. $\displaystyle\sum_{n=1}^{\infty} \frac{2}{n^7}$

28. $\displaystyle\sum_{n=1}^{\infty} \frac{3}{n^{3/2}}$

29. $\displaystyle\sum_{n=1}^{\infty} \frac{n+6}{n^3}$

30. $\displaystyle\sum_{n=1}^{\infty} \frac{1}{(5n)n!}$

31. $\displaystyle\sum_{n=1}^{\infty} \frac{1}{(2n+1)!}$

32. $\displaystyle\sum_{n=1}^{\infty} \frac{3^n}{(n+3)!}$

33. $\displaystyle\sum_{n=1}^{\infty} \frac{5^n}{3n-2}$

34. $\displaystyle\sum_{n=1}^{\infty} \frac{2n+1}{3^n}$

35. $\displaystyle\sum_{n=1}^{\infty} \frac{\sqrt[3]{n}}{n^3+2}$

36. $\displaystyle\sum_{n=1}^{\infty} \frac{(2n)!}{(n!)^2}$

37. $\displaystyle\sum_{n=1}^{\infty} \frac{n+.7}{n^2}$

38. $\displaystyle\sum_{n=1}^{\infty} \frac{n^2}{n!}$

39. $\displaystyle\sum_{n=1}^{\infty} \frac{(\ln 100)^n}{n^2}$

40. $\displaystyle\sum_{n=1}^{\infty} \frac{n^2}{(\ln 100)^n}$

41. $\displaystyle\sum_{n=1}^{\infty} \frac{n}{2^{2n}}$

42. $\displaystyle\sum_{n=1}^{\infty} \frac{1}{(2n+1)^2}$

43. $\displaystyle\sum_{n=1}^{\infty} \frac{n}{n+1}$

44. $\displaystyle\sum_{n=1}^{\infty} \frac{n(n+2)(n+4)}{3^n}$

13-6   ALTERNATING SERIES

An **alternating series** is one in which successive terms alternate in sign, that is, a series of the form

$$b_1 - b_2 + b_3 - b_4 + \ldots + (-1)^{n+1} b_n + \ldots$$

or $-b_1 + b_2 - b_3 + b_4 - \ldots + (-1)^n b_n + \ldots$

where all of the b's are positive.

EXAMPLE 24

The following are alternating series:

a. $\displaystyle\sum_{n=1}^{\infty} (-1)^{n+1} \frac{1}{n} = 1 - \frac{1}{2} + \frac{1}{3} - \frac{1}{4} + \ldots + (-1)^{n+1} \frac{1}{n} + \ldots$, which is called the **alternating harmonic series.**

b. $\displaystyle\sum_{n=1}^{\infty} (-1)^{n+1} \frac{1}{2^{n-1}} = 1 - \frac{1}{2} + \frac{1}{4} - \frac{1}{8} + \ldots + (-1)^{n+1} \frac{1}{2^{n-1}} + \ldots$, which is an alternating

geometric series ($a = 1$, $r = -\frac{1}{2}$).

c. $\displaystyle\sum_{n=1}^{\infty} \frac{(-1)^n (n+1)}{n^3} = -2 + \frac{3}{8} - \frac{4}{27} + \ldots + \frac{(-1)^n (n+1)}{n^3} + \ldots$.

There are conditions which guarantee convergence of alternating series:

Alternating Series Test.   If Σa_n is an alternating series, then Σa_n converges when both

    1. $\displaystyle\lim_{n\to\infty} |a_n| = 0$ and

    2. $|a_n| > |a_{n+1}|$.

Condition 1 is similar to the requirement that the general term of a convergent series approach 0. The second condition requires that successive terms of the series decrease in absolute value (except, perhaps, for a finite number of terms).

EXAMPLE 25

Determine the convergence or divergence of each of the following alternating series by using the alternating series test if possible.

a. $\displaystyle\sum_{n=1}^{\infty} (-1)^{n+1} \left(\frac{1}{n}\right)$.

Here $a_n = (-1)^{n+1} \left(\dfrac{1}{n} \right)$ and $|a_n| = \dfrac{1}{n}$. Now,

$$\lim_{n \to \infty} |a_n| = \lim_{n \to \infty} \frac{1}{n} = 0$$

and condition 1 is met. Also, since $n < n + 1$, then

$$|a_n| = \frac{1}{n} > \frac{1}{n+1} = |a_{n+1}|$$

and condition 2 is met. Hence, by the alternating series test **the alternating harmonic series converges.**

b. $\displaystyle\sum_{n=1}^{\infty} (-1)^n \frac{n^2 + 2}{n + 1}$.

Since

$$\lim_{n \to \infty} |a_n| = \lim_{n \to \infty} \frac{n^2 + 2}{n + 1} = \lim_{n \to \infty} \frac{2n}{1} = \infty, \qquad \text{(L'Hospital's rule)}$$

condition 1 is not met. This leads us to consider $\lim_{n \to \infty} a_n$, and clearly $a_n \nrightarrow 0$. Thus the series diverges. Note that the fact $|a_n| \to \infty$ did not allow us to declare divergence immediately, for the alternating series test provides sufficient conditions for convergence, not necessary conditions.

c. $\displaystyle\sum_{n=1}^{\infty} (-1)^{n+1} \frac{2}{n^{3/2}}$.

$$\lim_{n \to \infty} |a_n| = \lim_{n \to \infty} \frac{2}{n^{3/2}} = 0.$$

Also, since $n^{3/2} < (n + 1)^{3/2}$,

$$|a_n| = \frac{2}{n^{3/2}} > \frac{2}{(n + 1)^{3/2}} = |a_{n+1}|.$$

Thus the series converges.

d. $\displaystyle\sum_{n=1}^{\infty} (-1)^n \frac{\ln n}{n}$.

$$\lim_{n \to \infty} |a_n| = \lim_{n \to \infty} \frac{\ln n}{n}$$

$$= \lim_{n \to \infty} \frac{1/n}{1} = 0. \qquad \text{(L'Hospital's rule)}$$

To show $|a_n| > |a_{n+1}|$, it suffices to show that $f(x) = (\ln x)/x$ is a decreasing function, that is, its derivative is negative. (Note that $f(n) = |a_n|$.)

$$f'(x) = \frac{x \dfrac{1}{x} - \ln x}{x^2} = \frac{1 - \ln x}{x^2}.$$

The condition that $f'(x)$ be negative is equivalent to $1 - \ln x < 0$ or $\ln x > 1$. This is true if $x > e$. Hence condition 2 is met for $n > 3 > e$ (that is, $|a_n| > |a_{n+1}|$ for $n > 3$). Thus the series converges.

If $a_n = (-1)^{n+1}/2^n$, then

$$\sum_{n=1}^{\infty} a_n = \frac{1}{2} - \frac{1}{4} + \frac{1}{8} - \frac{1}{16} + \ldots + \frac{(-1)^{n+1}}{2^n} + \ldots$$

is a convergent series (geometric: $r = -\frac{1}{2}$) and so is the series of absolute values $\Sigma |a_n|$:

$$\sum_{n=1}^{\infty} |a_n| = \frac{1}{2} + \frac{1}{4} + \frac{1}{8} + \frac{1}{16} + \ldots + \frac{1}{2^n} + \ldots \qquad \text{(geometric: } r = \tfrac{1}{2}\text{)}.$$

On the other hand, if $a_n = (-1)^{n+1}(1/n)$, then by Example 25,

$$\sum_{n=1}^{\infty} a_n = 1 - \frac{1}{2} + \frac{1}{3} - \frac{1}{4} + \ldots + \frac{(-1)^{n+1}}{n} + \ldots$$

is *convergent*, while the series of absolute values

$$\sum_{n=1}^{\infty} |a_n| = 1 + \frac{1}{2} + \frac{1}{3} + \ldots + \frac{1}{n} + \ldots$$

is the *divergent* harmonic series. Thus, although a series Σa_n may converge, the corresponding series of absolute values $\Sigma |a_n|$ may either converge or diverge. These situations are described by the following terminology.

DEFINITION.   *The series Σa_n is said to be **absolutely convergent** if and only if the series of absolute values $\Sigma |a_n|$ converges. If Σa_n converges but $\Sigma |a_n|$ diverges, then Σa_n is said to be conditionally convergent.*

From the above definition and discussion, we conclude that $\Sigma (-1)^{n+1}/2^n$ is absolutely convergent while the alternating harmonic series $\Sigma (-1)^{n+1}/n$ is conditionally convergent.

In determining convergence of series, the following theorem is most important.

Theorem 12.   If Σa_n is absolutely convergent, then Σa_n is convergent.

In particular, if we can show that the series of absolute values of an alternating series is a convergent series, the theorem asserts that the given alternating series is also convergent.

EXAMPLE 26

Determine whether the following series are absolutely convergent, conditionally convergent, or divergent.

a. $\displaystyle\sum_{n=1}^{\infty} (-1)^n \frac{1}{n^3}$.

The series of absolute values $\displaystyle\sum \frac{1}{n^3}$ is a convergent p-series. Thus the given series is absolutely convergent (and is therefore convergent).

b. $\displaystyle\sum_{n=1}^{\infty} (-1)^{n+1} \frac{1}{\sqrt[3]{n}}$.

The series of absolute values is $\displaystyle\sum \frac{1}{n^{1/3}}$ which is a divergent p-series. Thus the given series is not absolutely convergent. It may still be convergent. Applying the alternating series test to the given series:

1. $\displaystyle\lim_{n\to\infty} |a_n| = \lim_{n\to\infty} \frac{1}{n^{1/3}} = 0$.

2. Since $\sqrt[3]{n} < \sqrt[3]{n+1}$, then

$$|a_n| = \frac{1}{\sqrt[3]{n}} > \frac{1}{\sqrt[3]{n+1}} = |a_{n+1}|.$$

Since the given series converges but the series of absolute values does not converge, the series is conditionally convergent.

c. $\displaystyle\sum_{n=1}^{\infty} \frac{1}{(n+6)^4}$.

The series is a convergent p-series ($p = 4$) with the first six terms deleted and hence is convergent. Since $\Sigma a_n = \Sigma |a_n|$, it is absolutely convergent.

As we saw in Example 26(c), every positive series $\Sigma\, a_n$ which is convergent is automatically absolutely convergent since $a_n = |a_n|$. It is therefore redundant to speak of a positive series as absolutely convergent. Henceforth, we shall confine the term absolutely convergent to those series which consist of terms that are not all positive.

Since testing a series for absolute convergence involves $|a_n|$, not a_n, we can extend the ratio test so that it applies to an arbitrary series.

Generalized Ratio Test.   For the arbitrary series $\Sigma\, a_n$, let L be the limit, if it exists (or is ∞), as follows:

$$L = \lim_{n\to\infty} \left| \frac{a_{n+1}}{a_n} \right|.$$

If

a. $L < 1$, then $\Sigma\, a_n$ is absolutely convergent
b. $L > 1$ (or $L = \infty$), then $\Sigma\, a_n$ is divergent
c. $L = 1$, the test provides no information.

Note that condition (a) implies that Σa_n is convergent, and condition (b) implies that the given series, as well as the series of absolute values, is divergent.

We usually apply the (generalized) ratio test first in determining the nature of a series. Should it fail, we then go to comparison tests or the alternating series test if appropriate. Remember, in all cases of convergence we must have $a_n \to 0$.

EXAMPLE 27

Determine whether the following are absolutely convergent, conditionally convergent, or divergent.

a. $\displaystyle\sum_{n=1}^{\infty} (-1)^{n+1}\, \frac{n^3}{2^n}$.

Here $|a_n| = n^3/2^n$ and $|a_{n+1}| = (n + 1)^3/2^{n+1}$.

$$L = \lim_{n\to\infty} \left| \frac{a_{n+1}}{a_n} \right| = \lim_{n\to\infty} \frac{\dfrac{(n + 1)^3}{2^{n+1}}}{\dfrac{n^3}{2^n}} = \lim_{n\to\infty} \left[\frac{(n + 1)^3}{2^{n+1}} \cdot \frac{2^n}{n^3} \right]$$

$$= \lim_{n\to\infty} \left[\frac{1}{2} \left(\frac{n + 1}{n} \right)^3 \right] = \lim_{n\to\infty} \left[\frac{1}{2} \left(1 + \frac{1}{n} \right)^3 \right]$$

$$= \frac{1}{2}.$$

Since $L = \frac{1}{2} < 1$, the given series is absolutely convergent (and therefore convergent) by the ratio test.

b. $\displaystyle\sum_{n=1}^{\infty} (-1)^{n+1}\, \frac{n!}{3^n}$.

$$L = \lim_{n \to \infty} \left| \frac{a_{n+1}}{a_n} \right| = \lim_{n \to \infty} \frac{\dfrac{(n+1)!}{3^{n+1}}}{\dfrac{n!}{3^n}} = \lim_{n \to \infty} \left[\frac{(n+1)!}{3^{n+1}} \cdot \frac{3^n}{n!} \right]$$

$$= \lim_{n \to \infty} \frac{n+1}{3} = \infty.$$

By the ratio test the given series is divergent.

c. $\displaystyle\sum_{n=1}^{\infty} (-1)^{n+1} \frac{n}{e^n}.$

$$L = \lim_{n \to \infty} \left| \frac{a_{n+1}}{a_n} \right| = \lim_{n \to \infty} \frac{\dfrac{n+1}{e^{n+1}}}{\dfrac{n}{e^n}} = \lim_{n \to \infty} \left[\frac{n+1}{e^{n+1}} \cdot \frac{e^n}{n} \right]$$

$$= \lim_{n \to \infty} \left[\frac{1}{e} \cdot \frac{n+1}{n} \right] = \frac{1}{e} \lim_{n \to \infty} \left(1 + \frac{1}{n} \right)$$

$$= \frac{1}{e}.$$

Since $e > 1$, then $L = 1/e < 1$ and the given series is absolutely convergent.

d. $\displaystyle\sum_{n=1}^{\infty} \frac{(-1)^{n+1}(n+1)}{n\sqrt{n}}.$

$$L = \lim_{n \to \infty} \left| \frac{a_{n+1}}{a_n} \right| = \lim_{n \to \infty} \frac{\dfrac{n+2}{(n+1)\sqrt{n+1}}}{\dfrac{n+1}{n\sqrt{n}}}$$

$$= \lim_{n \to \infty} \left[\frac{n+2}{(n+1)^{3/2}} \cdot \frac{n^{3/2}}{n+1} \right]$$

$$= \lim_{n \to \infty} \left[\left(\frac{n+2}{n+1} \right) \left(\frac{n}{n+1} \right)^{3/2} \right]$$

$$= \lim_{n \to \infty} \left[\left(\frac{1 + \dfrac{2}{n}}{1 + \dfrac{1}{n}} \right) \left(\frac{1}{1 + \dfrac{1}{n}} \right)^{3/2} \right]$$

$$= 1 \cdot 1 = 1.$$

Since $L = 1$, the ratio test fails. But

$$n^{3/2} < (n + 1)^{3/2}$$

and so

$$\frac{1}{n^{3/2}} > \frac{1}{(n + 1)^{3/2}}.$$

Hence

$$\frac{n + 1}{n^{3/2}} > \frac{n + 1}{(n + 1)^{3/2}} = \frac{1}{(n + 1)^{1/2}}.$$

Since $\sum \dfrac{1}{(n + 1)^{1/2}}$ is a divergent p-series $(p = \frac{1}{2})$ with the first term deleted, then by the comparison test the series of absolute values of the given series is divergent. Hence, the given series is not absolutely convergent. We test for conditional convergence by the alternating series test. First,

$$\lim_{n \to \infty} |a_n| = \lim_{n \to \infty} \frac{n + 1}{n^{3/2}} = \lim_{n \to \infty} \frac{1}{\frac{3}{2} n^{1/2}} = 0. \qquad \text{(L'Hospital's rule)}$$

Second, to prove $|a_n| > |a_{n+1}|$ we shall show that

$$f(x) = \frac{x + 1}{x^{3/2}} = \frac{1}{x^{1/2}} + \frac{1}{x^{3/2}}$$

is a decreasing function.

$$f'(x) = -\frac{1}{2x^{3/2}} - \frac{3}{2x^{5/2}} < 0.$$

Thus the given series is conditionally convergent.

e. $\displaystyle\sum_{n=1}^{\infty} (-1)^{n+1} 7\left(\frac{1}{2}\right)^{n-1}.$

$$L = \lim_{n \to \infty} \left|\frac{a_{n+1}}{a_n}\right| = \lim_{n \to \infty} \frac{7\left(\dfrac{1}{2}\right)^n}{7\left(\dfrac{1}{2}\right)^{n-1}} = \lim_{n \to \infty} \frac{1}{2} = \frac{1}{2}.$$

Since $L < 1$, the series is absolutely convergent.

EXERCISE 13-6

In each of the following determine whether the series is absolutely convergent, conditionally convergent, or divergent.

1. $\displaystyle\sum_{n=1}^{\infty} (-1)^{n+1} \frac{1}{\sqrt[3]{n}}$

2. $\displaystyle\sum_{n=1}^{\infty} (-1)^{n+1} \frac{1}{n^2 + 3}$

3. $\displaystyle\sum_{n=1}^{\infty} (-1)^{n+1} \frac{2}{5n}$

4. $\displaystyle\sum_{n=1}^{\infty} (-1)^{n+1} \frac{3}{3n + 13}$

5. $\displaystyle\sum_{n=1}^{\infty} (-1)^{n+1} \left(\tfrac{3}{4}\right)^n$

6. $\displaystyle\sum_{n=1}^{\infty} (-1)^{n+1} \frac{1}{\sqrt[3]{(n + 3)^2}}$

7. $\displaystyle\sum_{n=1}^{\infty} (-1)^{n+1} \frac{1}{n^3}$

8. $\displaystyle\sum_{n=1}^{\infty} (-1)^{n+1} \frac{2n + 3}{3n + 2}$

9. $\displaystyle\sum_{n=4}^{\infty} (-1)^{n+1} \frac{1}{2n - 7}$

10. $\displaystyle\sum_{n=1}^{\infty} (-1)^{n+1} \left(\tfrac{1}{2}\right)^{n-1}$

11. $\displaystyle\sum_{n=1}^{\infty} (-1)^{n+1} \frac{2n + 1}{15n - 6}$

12. $\displaystyle\sum_{n=1}^{\infty} (-1)^{n+1} \frac{\ln n}{n}$

13. $\displaystyle\sum_{n=3}^{\infty} (-1)^{n+1} \frac{1}{\sqrt{n - 2}}$

14. $\displaystyle\sum_{n=1}^{\infty} (-1)^{n+1} \frac{n + 1}{3n^2 - 2}$

15. $\displaystyle\sum_{n=1}^{\infty} (-1)^{n+1} \frac{1}{n\sqrt{n}}$

16. $\displaystyle\sum_{n=1}^{\infty} (-1)^{n+1} \left(\frac{1}{n}\right)^{10}$

17. $\displaystyle\sum_{n=1}^{\infty} (-1)^{n+1} \frac{1}{(n + 5)^7}$

18. $\displaystyle\sum_{n=1}^{\infty} (-1)^{n+1} \frac{n^3}{3^n}$

19. $\displaystyle\sum_{n=1}^{\infty} (-1)^{n+1} \frac{n^4}{4^n}$

20. $\displaystyle\sum_{n=1}^{\infty} (-1)^{n+1} \frac{n}{3^n}$

21. $\displaystyle\sum_{n=1}^{\infty} (-1)^{n+1} \frac{n!}{5^n}$

22. $\displaystyle\sum_{n=1}^{\infty} (-1)^{n+1} \frac{1}{(4n + 1)^2}$

23. $\displaystyle\sum_{n=1}^{\infty} (-1)^{n+1} \frac{n}{n^2 + 2}$

24. $\displaystyle\sum_{n=1}^{\infty} (-1)^{n+1} \frac{6}{7n}$

25. $\displaystyle\sum_{n=1}^{\infty} (-1)^{n+1} \frac{8^n}{n!}$

26. $\displaystyle\sum_{n=1}^{\infty} (-1)^{n+1} \frac{n + 1}{n^3 + 2n^2}$

27. $\displaystyle\sum_{n=1}^{\infty} (-1)^{n+1} \frac{1}{n \cdot 2^n}$

28. $\displaystyle\sum_{n=1}^{\infty} (-1)^{n+1} \frac{1}{1 + n\sqrt{n}}$

29. $\displaystyle\sum_{n=1}^{\infty} (-1)^{n+1} \frac{n^2 + 2}{4^n}$

30. $\displaystyle\sum_{n=1}^{\infty} (-1)^{n+1} \frac{n - 1}{ne^n}$

31. $\displaystyle\sum_{n=1}^{\infty} (-1)^{n+1} \frac{n + 1}{n\sqrt{n}}$

32. $\displaystyle\sum_{n=1}^{\infty} (-1)^{n+1} \frac{2^n}{3^{n+1}}$

33. $\displaystyle\sum_{n=1}^{\infty} (-1)^{n+1} \frac{1}{\sqrt{n^2+1}}$

34. $\displaystyle\sum_{n=1}^{\infty} (-1)^{n+1} \frac{n^2}{2^n}$

35. $\displaystyle\sum_{n=1}^{\infty} (-1)^{n+1} \frac{n!}{2n}$

36. $\displaystyle\sum_{n=1}^{\infty} (-1)^{n+1} \frac{1}{e^n-1}$

13-7   POWER SERIES

So far we have examined series of the form Σa_n where a_n is a constant for each n. Now we shall consider series of the form

$$a_0 + a_1(x-a) + a_2(x-a)^2 + \ldots + a_n(x-a)^n + \ldots \tag{1}$$

consisting of powers of $x - a$, where $a, a_0, a_1, \ldots$ are constants. The series in (1), called a *power series in* $x - a$, is abbreviated by using the notation $\displaystyle\sum_{n=0}^{\infty} a_n(x-a)^n$:

$$\sum_{n=0}^{\infty} a_n(x-a)^n = a_0 + a_1(x-a) + a_2(x-a)^2 + \ldots.$$

Note that the indexing here begins at $n = 0$.

DEFINITION.   *A power series in* $x - a$ *is a series of the form*

$$\sum_{n=0}^{\infty} a_n(x-a)^n$$

where $a, a_0, a_1, \ldots$ *are constants. If* $a = 0$, *then the series has the form*

$$\sum_{n=0}^{\infty} a_n x^n$$

and is called a **power series in** x.

EXAMPLE 28

a. $\displaystyle\sum_{n=0}^{\infty} \frac{n^2}{n+1}(x-4)^n$ is a power series in $x - 4$. Here $a = 4$.

b. $\displaystyle\sum_{n=1}^{\infty} \frac{1}{\sqrt{n}}(x+2)^n$ is a power series in $x + 2$. Here $a = -2$.

c. $\displaystyle\sum_{k=0}^{\infty} \frac{(-1)^k}{k!} x^k$ is a power series in x.

d. $3x^2 + 7x + 2$ is a power series in x since

$$3x^2 + 7x + 2 = \sum_{n=0}^{\infty} a_n x^n$$

where $a_0 = 2$, $a_1 = 7$, $a_2 = 3$, and $a_n = 0$ for $n \geq 3$.

For each fixed real number x, $\Sigma\, a_n(x - a)^n$ is nothing more than a series of constant terms and either converges or diverges. Thus $\Sigma\, a_n(x - a)^n$ defines a function f where

$$f(x) = \sum_{n=0}^{\infty} a_n(x - a)^n$$

and the domain of f consists of all x such that the above series converges.

If $x = a$, then $\Sigma\, a_n(x - a)^n$ will *always* converge because

$$\Sigma\, a_n(x - a)^n = a_0 + 0 + 0 + \ldots = a_0.$$

Thus a is in the domain of f. To completely determine the domain, we use the ratio test as the following examples show.

EXAMPLE 29

Determine the values of x for which $\displaystyle\sum_{n=0}^{\infty} n!(x - 5)^n$ *converges.*

We know the series converges for $x = 5$. For $x \neq 5$ (to avoid division by 0), the limit as $n \to \infty$ of the absolute value of the ratio of successive terms of the series is

$$\lim_{n \to \infty} \left| \frac{(n + 1)!(x - 5)^{n+1}}{n!(x - 5)^n} \right| = \lim_{n \to \infty} |(n + 1)(x - 5)|$$

$$= \lim_{n \to \infty} [|n + 1| \cdot |x - 5|] = |x - 5| \lim_{n \to \infty} (n + 1) = \infty.$$

Therefore, for $x \neq 5$ the series diverges by the ratio test. Hence the series converges only for $x = 5$.

EXAMPLE 30

Determine the values of x for which $\displaystyle\sum_{n=0}^{\infty} \frac{(-1)^n}{2^n(n + 1)}(x + 2)^n$ *converges.*

If $x \neq -2$,

$$\lim_{n \to \infty} \left| \frac{\dfrac{(-1)^{n+1}}{2^{n+1}[(n + 1) + 1]}(x + 2)^{n+1}}{\dfrac{(-1)^n}{2^n(n + 1)}(x + 2)^n} \right| = \lim_{n \to \infty} \left| \frac{n + 1}{2(n + 2)}(x + 2) \right|$$

$$= \frac{|x + 2|}{2} \lim_{n \to \infty} \frac{n + 1}{n + 2} = \frac{|x + 2|}{2}(1) = \frac{|x + 2|}{2}.$$

By the ratio test the series converges if

$$\frac{|x + 2|}{2} < 1, \quad x \neq -2.$$

However, if $x = -2$, then not only does the series converge but the inequality is also satisfied. Thus the restriction that $x \neq -2$ can be lifted. Solving the inequality gives

$$\frac{|x + 2|}{2} < 1$$

$$|x + 2| < 2$$

$$-2 < x + 2 < 2$$

$$-4 < x < 0.$$

Therefore, the series converges for $-4 < x < 0$. If $|x + 2|/2 > 1$, then by the ratio test the series diverges. That is, it diverges for $x < -4$ and for $x > 0$ (see Fig. 13-2). If

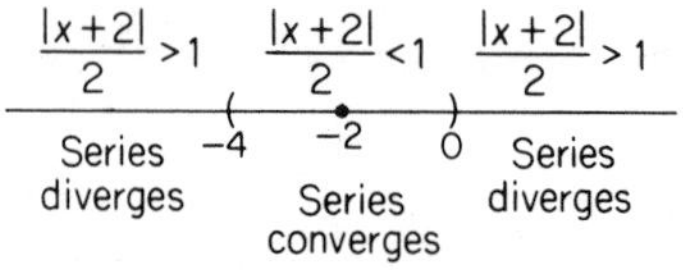

Fig. 13-2

$x = -4$ or $x = 0$, then $|x + 2|/2 = 1$ and the ratio test gives us no information. Consequently we must use other tests for these values.
If $x = -4$, then

$$\sum_{n=0}^{\infty} \frac{(-1)^n}{2^n(n + 1)} (x + 2)^n = \sum_{n=0}^{\infty} \frac{(-1)^n}{2^n(n + 1)} (-2)^n$$

$$= \sum_{n=0}^{\infty} \frac{(-1)^n[(-1)^n 2^n]}{2^n(n + 1)} = \sum_{n=0}^{\infty} \frac{1}{n + 1}.$$

But this is the harmonic series and diverges.
If $x = 0$, then

$$\sum_{n=0}^{\infty} \frac{(-1)^n}{2^n(n + 1)} (x + 2)^n = \sum_{n=0}^{\infty} \frac{(-1)^n}{2^n(n + 1)} (2)^n = \sum_{n=0}^{\infty} \frac{(-1)^n}{n + 1}.$$

This is the alternating harmonic series and is convergent by the alternating series test. We conclude that the given power series converges for $-4 < x \leq 0$.

EXAMPLE 31

Determine the values of x for which $\displaystyle\sum_{n=0}^{\infty} \frac{x^n}{n!}$ *converges.*

If $x \neq 0$,

$$\lim_{n \to \infty} \left| \frac{x^{n+1}/(n+1)!}{x^n/n!} \right| = |x| \lim_{n \to \infty} \frac{1}{n+1} = |x| \cdot 0 = 0 < 1.$$

By the ratio test the series converges for all $x \neq 0$. However, since the series must converge for $x = 0$, it converges for $-\infty < x < \infty$.

Let us now discuss the nature of the set of values of x for which a power series converges.

Each series in the three preceding examples has the form $\Sigma\, a_n(x - a)^n$ (with $a = 5$, $a = -2$, and $a = 0$ in Examples 29, 30, and 31, respectively). In Example 29 the series converges only for $x = a$. In Example 30 the series converges on an interval of finite length and centered about a. And in Example 31 the series converges for all values of x. In general, these situations are the only possibilities as the following theorem states.

Theorem 13.   If $\Sigma\, a_n(x - a)^n$ is a power series in $x - a$, then the series either
    (i) converges only at $x = a$,

or   (ii) converges for all x such that $|x - a| < r$ where r is some real number (that is, it converges for $a - r < x < a + r$) and diverges for $|x - a| > r$,

or   (iii) converges for all x.

In case (ii) of Theorem 13, no information as to convergence or divergence is given for the endpoints of the interval $(a - r, a + r)$. The behavior of the series at these points must be tested separately. Some power series converge at both endpoints, some diverge at both endpoints, and there are yet others, as in Example 30, that converge at one endpoint and diverge at the other.

Figure 13-3 illustrates the three possible cases of convergence for a power series $\Sigma\, a_n(x - a)^n$.

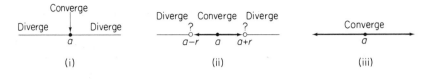

Converge

Diverge   ↓   Diverge
           a
           (i)

Diverge Converge Diverge
   ?   ?
   $a-r$ a $a+r$
           (ii)

Converge
   a
   (iii)

Fig. 13-3

EXAMPLE 32

Determine the values of x for which $\displaystyle\sum_{n=0}^{\infty} \frac{n+5}{n+3}(x-2)^n$ converges.

Using the ratio test, we have

$$\lim_{n \to \infty} \left| \frac{\dfrac{n + 6}{n + 4}(x - 2)^{n+1}}{\dfrac{n + 5}{n + 3}(x - 2)^n} \right| = |x - 2| \lim_{n \to \infty} \frac{(n + 6)(n + 3)}{(n + 4)(n + 5)}$$

$$= |x - 2|(1) = |x - 2|.$$

If $|x - 2| < 1$, the series converges. That is, when

$$|x - 2| < 1$$
$$-1 < x - 2 < 1$$
$$1 < x < 3.$$

For $x < 1$ or $x > 3$ the series diverges.
When $x = 1$,

$$\sum_{n=0}^{\infty} \frac{n + 5}{n + 3}(x - 2)^n = \sum_{n=0}^{\infty} (-1)^n \frac{n + 5}{n + 3}$$

which diverges because

$$\lim_{n \to \infty} \left[(-1)^n \frac{n + 5}{n + 3} \right] \neq 0.$$

When $x = 3$,

$$\sum_{n=0}^{\infty} \frac{n + 5}{n + 3}(x - 2)^n = \sum_{n=0}^{\infty} \frac{n + 5}{n + 3}$$

which also diverges since $\lim_{n \to \infty} [(n + 5)/(n + 3)] \neq 0$. Therefore, the given series converges for $1 < x < 3$ and diverges elsewhere.

EXERCISE 13-7

Determine the values of x for which the following power series converge.

1. $\displaystyle\sum_{n=0}^{\infty} x^n$

2. $\displaystyle\sum_{n=2}^{\infty} \frac{(-1)^n}{\ln n} x^n$

3. $\displaystyle\sum_{n=0}^{\infty} (5x)^n$

4. $\displaystyle\sum_{n=0}^{\infty} \frac{(-1)^n}{n + 1}(x - 3)^n$

5. $\displaystyle\sum_{n=0}^{\infty} (n + 1)!(x - 1)^n$

6. $\displaystyle\sum_{n=1}^{\infty} \frac{(-1)^n \sqrt{n}}{n!}(x + 6)^n$

7. $\displaystyle\sum_{n=1}^{\infty} \left[\frac{1}{\sqrt{n^3}} \left(\frac{x - 7}{2} \right)^n \right]$

8. $\displaystyle\sum_{n=1}^{\infty} \frac{(-1)^{n+1}}{3^{n-1} n^2 \sqrt{n}}(x + 3)^n$

9. $\displaystyle\sum_{n=0}^{\infty} \frac{(-1)^n(n+1)}{6(n+4)} x^n$

10. $\displaystyle\sum_{n=1}^{\infty} (\ln n)\, x^n$

11. $\displaystyle\sum_{n=5}^{\infty} \frac{(-1)^{n-1}}{\sqrt{n-4}} x^n$

12. $\displaystyle\sum_{n=1}^{\infty} \frac{2^n}{n} (x-4)^n$

13. $\displaystyle\sum_{n=0}^{\infty} \frac{(-1)^n(2n+3)}{(n+4)!} (x-9)^n$

14. $\displaystyle\sum_{n=1}^{\infty} \frac{(2n-1)!}{2^n(3n+4)} x^n$

15. $\displaystyle\sum_{n=0}^{\infty} (-1)^n \sqrt{n}\, (x-\tfrac{1}{2})^n$

16. $\displaystyle\sum_{n=0}^{\infty} \frac{n^2+n-2}{n+4} (x+8)^n$

17. $\displaystyle\sum_{n=1}^{\infty} \frac{4^n}{n^2} (x+1)^n$

18. $\displaystyle\sum_{n=1}^{\infty} \frac{(-1)^{n+1}}{n^5} (x-6)^n$

19. $\displaystyle\sum_{n=0}^{\infty} \left(\frac{x+2}{8}\right)^n$

20. $\displaystyle\sum_{n=1}^{\infty} \frac{2n-3}{7n} (x-4)^n$

21. $\displaystyle\sum_{n=0}^{\infty} \frac{1}{4(n!)^2} x^n$

22. $\displaystyle\sum_{n=1}^{\infty} \frac{(-1)^n n!}{\sqrt{n}} (x+6)^n$

23. $\displaystyle\sum_{n=0}^{\infty} n(x-2)^n$

24. $\displaystyle\sum_{n=0}^{\infty} 2(x+5)^n$

25. $\displaystyle\sum_{n=1}^{\infty} \frac{n+1}{n^2} x^n$

26. $\displaystyle\sum_{n=1}^{\infty} \frac{1}{4^n \sqrt{n}} (x+1)^n$

13-8   TAYLOR'S THEOREM AND TAYLOR'S SERIES

Sometimes, instead of working with a function that is complicated, we replace it by one that approximates the function but is less complicated. In fact, as a consequence of Taylor's theorem, which we state below, it is possible under certain conditions to approximate functions by polynomials. Although we shall not give examples here, in economic analyses these approximations prove to be quite advantageous.

Taylor's Theorem.   If f is a function such that the first $n + 1$ derivatives exist on some interval containing a and x, then

$$f(x) = \frac{f(a)}{0!} + \frac{f'(a)}{1!} (x-a) + \frac{f''(a)}{2!} (x-a)^2 + \ldots +$$

$$\frac{f^{(n)}(a)}{n!} (x-a)^n + \frac{f^{(n+1)}(c)}{(n+1)!} (x-a)^{n+1}$$

where c lies between x and a and is also dependent on n.

Some comments on Taylor's theorem are appropriate. In this theorem let us set

$$P_n(x) = \frac{f(a)}{0!} + \frac{f'(a)}{1!}(x - a) + \frac{f''(a)}{2!}(x - a)^2 + \ldots + \frac{f^{(n)}(a)}{n!}(x - a)^n$$

and

$$R_n(x) = \frac{f^{(n+1)}(c)}{(n + 1)!}(x - a)^{n+1}.$$

Then we can write

$$f(x) = P_n(x) + R_n(x).$$

The polynomial $P_n(x)$ is called the *Taylor polynomial* of f in $x - a$ and is of degree n provided $f^{(n)}(a) \neq 0$. $R_n(x)$ is called the *remainder*. The significant aspect of the theorem is that $f(x)$ can be approximated by the polynomial $P_n(x)$ *provided $R_n(x)$ is small in absolute value.* The smaller $R_n(x)$ is, the better the approximation.

To illustrate Taylor's theorem, let $f(x) = e^x$ for $-1 < x < 1$, $a = 0$, and $n = 3$. Then

$$P_3(x) = \frac{f(0)}{0!} + \frac{f'(0)}{1!}x + \frac{f''(0)}{2!}x^2 + \frac{f'''(0)}{3!}x^3$$

and

$$R_3(x) = \frac{f^{(4)}(c)}{4!}x^4$$

where c lies between 0 and x. We have

$$f(x) = e^x, \qquad f(0) = e^0 = 1.$$

Also,

$$f'(x) = e^x, \qquad f'(0) = e^0 = 1;$$
$$f''(x) = e^x, \qquad f''(0) = e^0 = 1;$$
$$f'''(x) = e^x, \qquad f'''(0) = e^0 = 1;$$
$$f^{(4)}(x) = e^x, \qquad f^{(4)}(c) = e^c.$$

Therefore,

$$f(x) = e^x = P_3(x) + R_3(x)$$

$$= 1 + x + \frac{x^2}{2!} + \frac{x^3}{3!} + \frac{e^c x^4}{4!}.$$

We shall now determine bounds on $|R_3(x)|$:

$$|R_3(x)| = \frac{e^c |x|^4}{4!}.$$

Since $-1 < x < 1$ and c lies between 0 and x, then $|x| < 1$ and $e^c < e^1 = e < 3$. Thus,

$$|R_3(x)| < \frac{3 \cdot 1^4}{4!} = \frac{1}{8}.$$

Consequently on the given interval we have

$$e^x \approx P_3(x)$$

where the error involved is less than $\frac{1}{8}$.

If e^x, for $-1 < x < 1$, were approximated by a fourth-degree Taylor polynomial in x (that is, $a = 0$), then

$$P_4(x) = 1 + x + \frac{x^2}{2!} + \frac{x^3}{3!} + \frac{x^4}{4!}$$

and

$$|R_4(x)| = \left| \frac{e^c x^5}{5!} \right| < \frac{3 \cdot 1}{5!} = \frac{1}{40}.$$

Thus the error involved in approximating e^x by $P_4(x)$ is less than $\frac{1}{40}$. For example, to approximate $e^{.5}$ we have

$$e^{.5} \approx P_4(.5) = 1 + \frac{1}{2} + \frac{\left(\frac{1}{2}\right)^2}{2!} + \frac{\left(\frac{1}{2}\right)^3}{3!} + \frac{\left(\frac{1}{2}\right)^4}{4!}$$

$$= 1.6484 \qquad \text{(to four decimal places)}$$

and we are assured that the error in the approximation is no greater than $\frac{1}{40} = .025$. Actually the error is much less than .025. Since

$$R_4(x) = \frac{e^c x^5}{5!}$$

where c lies between 0 and x, then for $x = .5 = \frac{1}{2}$,

$$|R_4(.5)| = \left| \frac{e^c (1/2)^5}{5!} \right| < \frac{3(1/2)^5}{5!} < .0008.$$

EXAMPLE 33

Approximate $f(x) = (x + 2)^{-1}$ for $0 < x < 2$ by its fourth-degree Taylor polynomial in powers of $x - 1$ and estimate the error.

Here $a = 1$ and

$$f(x) = (x + 2)^{-1}, \qquad\qquad f(1) = \frac{1}{3}$$

$$f'(x) = -1(x + 2)^{-2}, \qquad\qquad f'(1) = -\frac{1}{3^2}$$

$$f''(x) = 2!(x + 2)^{-3}, \qquad\qquad f''(1) = \frac{2!}{3^3}$$

$$f^{(3)}(x) = -3!(x + 2)^{-4}, \qquad\qquad f^{(3)}(1) = -\frac{3!}{3^4}$$

$$f^{(4)}(x) = 4!(x + 2)^{-5}, \qquad\qquad f^{(4)}(1) = \frac{4!}{3^5}$$

$$f^{(5)}(x) = -5!(x + 2)^{-6}, \qquad\qquad f^{(5)}(c) = -\frac{5!}{(c + 2)^6}.$$

$$\frac{1}{x + 2} \approx P_4(x)$$

$$= \frac{f(1)}{0!} + \frac{f'(1)}{1!}(x - 1) + \frac{f''(1)}{2!}(x - 1)^2 + \frac{f^{(3)}(1)}{3!}(x - 1)^3 + \frac{f^{(4)}(1)}{4!}(x - 1)^4$$

$$= \frac{1}{3} - \frac{x - 1}{3^2} + \frac{(x - 1)^2}{3^3} - \frac{(x - 1)^3}{3^4} + \frac{(x - 1)^4}{3^5}.$$

To estimate the error in the approximation, consider

$$|R_4(x)| = \left| \frac{f^{(5)}(c)}{5!}(x - 1)^5 \right| = \left| -\frac{(x - 1)^5}{(c + 2)^6} \right| = \frac{|x - 1|^5}{|c + 2|^6}$$

where c lies between 1 and x. Since $0 < x < 2$, then $|x - 1| < 1$ and $|c + 2| > 2$. Thus,

$$|R_4(x)| = \frac{|x - 1|^5}{|c + 2|^6} < \frac{1^5}{2^6} = \frac{1}{64}$$

and the error is no more than $\frac{1}{64}$.

EXAMPLE 34

Use Taylor's theorem to express the polynomial function $f(x) = x^3 - 3x^2 + 4x + 2$ in powers of $x + 4$.

By Taylor's theorem with $a = -4$,

$$f(x) = P_n(x) + R_n(x)$$

where

$$R_n(x) = \frac{f^{(n+1)}(c)}{(n+1)!}(x+4)^{n+1}.$$

Since the fourth derivative of a polynomial of degree three is 0, by choosing $n = 3$ we get $R_3(x) = 0$. Hence we can represent f by a third-degree Taylor polynomial.

$$f(x) = P_3(x)$$

$$= \frac{f(-4)}{0!} + \frac{f'(-4)}{1!}(x+4) + \frac{f''(-4)}{2!}(x+4)^2 + \frac{f'''(-4)}{3!}(x+4)^3.$$

$$f(x) = x^3 - 3x^2 + 4x + 2 \qquad\qquad f(-4) = -126$$

$$f'(x) = 3x^2 - 6x + 4 \qquad\qquad f'(-4) = 76$$

$$f''(x) = 6x - 6 \qquad\qquad\qquad f''(-4) = -30$$

$$f'''(x) = 6 \qquad\qquad\qquad\qquad f'''(-4) = 6$$

Hence, $f(x) = -126 + 76(x+4) - 15(x+4)^2 + (x+4)^3$.

Suppose a function f is such that all of its higher-order derivatives exist on some interval containing a. Then

$$f(x) = \frac{f(a)}{0!} + \frac{f'(a)}{1!}(x-a) + \ldots + \frac{f^{(k)}(a)}{k!}(x-a)^k + R_k(x)$$

$$= P_k(x) + R_k(x).$$

In terms of Σ-notation we write $P_k(x)$ as

$$P_k(x) = \sum_{n=0}^{k} \frac{f^{(n)}(a)}{n!}(x-a)^n$$

where $f^{(0)}(a)$ is defined to be $f(a)$. Hence,

$$f(x) - \sum_{n=0}^{k} \frac{f^{(n)}(a)}{n!}(x-a)^n = R_k(x).$$

If $R_k(x) \to 0$ on the interval as $k \to \infty$, then

$$\lim_{k\to\infty}\left[f(x) - \sum_{n=0}^{k} \frac{f^{(n)}(a)}{n!}(x-a)^n\right] = \lim_{k\to\infty} R_k(x) = 0.$$

Thus,

$$f(x) = \sum_{n=0}^{\infty} \frac{f^{(n)}(a)}{n!}(x-a)^n.$$

That is, if $R_k \to 0$ on the interval as $k \to \infty$, then the power series not only converges but converges to $f(x)$. We say f can be represented as a power series in $x - a$. This power series, $\Sigma \ [f^{(n)}(a)/n!](x - a)^n$, is called the **Taylor series for f about a.** If $a = 0$, the series is usually called a **Maclaurin series.**

EXAMPLE 35

Determine the Maclaurin series for $f(x) = e^x$, and show that it converges to f for all x.

The Maclaurin series is given by

$$\sum_{n=0}^{\infty} \frac{f^{(n)}(0)}{n!}(x - 0)^n \quad \text{or} \quad \sum_{n=0}^{\infty} \frac{f^{(n)}(0)}{n!} x^n.$$

Since the nth derivative of $f(x) = e^x$ is

$$f^{(n)}(x) = e^x,$$

then

$$f^{(n)}(0) = e^0 = 1.$$

Therefore the Maclaurin series for e^x is

$$\sum_{n=0}^{\infty} \frac{1}{n!} x^n.$$

To show that this series converges to e^x for all x, we must show that $R_k \to 0$ as $k \to \infty$. Now

$$R_k(x) = \frac{f^{(k+1)}(c)}{(k + 1)!} x^{k+1}$$

$$= \frac{e^c}{(k + 1)!} x^{k+1} \qquad (c \text{ between } 0 \text{ and } x).$$

If $x \geq 0$, then since f is an increasing function, $e^c \leq e^x$. On the other hand, if $x < 0$, $e^c < e^0 = 1$. In either case e^c is no greater than the maximum of e^x and 1. Denoting this maximum by M, we have

$$|R_k(x)| = \left| \frac{e^c}{(k + 1)!} x^{k+1} \right| \leq \frac{M}{(k + 1)!} |x|^{k+1}.$$

The expression $[M/(k + 1)!] \ |x|^{k+1}$ can be considered as the general term of a series and by the ratio test that series converges. Hence, we have $[M/(k + 1)!] \cdot |x|^{k+1} \to 0$ as $k \to \infty$ and

$$\lim_{k \to \infty} R_k(x) = 0.$$

Therefore, e^x can be represented by its Maclaurin series for all x:

$$e^x = \sum_{n=0}^{\infty} \frac{1}{n!} x^n.$$

EXAMPLE 36

Show that the Taylor series for $f(x) = 2x^3 - 3x^2 + 7x - 1$ about $a = -2$ converges to f for all x.

$$f(x) = 2x^3 - 3x^2 + 7x - 1 \qquad\qquad f(-2) = -43$$
$$f'(x) = 6x^2 - 6x + 7 \qquad\qquad f'(-2) = 43$$
$$f''(x) = 12x - 6 \qquad\qquad f''(-2) = -30$$
$$f^{(3)}(x) = 12 \qquad\qquad f^{(3)}(-2) = 12$$
$$f^{(4)}(x) = 0 \qquad\qquad f^{(4)}(-2) = 0$$

$$f^{(n)}(x) = 0 \qquad\qquad f^{(n)}(-2) = 0 \quad \text{for} \quad n \geq 4.$$

The Taylor series for f is

$$-\frac{43}{0!} + \frac{43}{1!}(x+2) - \frac{30}{2!}(x+2)^2 + \frac{12}{3!}(x+2)^3 + 0 + 0 + \cdots$$

or more simply

$$2(x+2)^3 - 15(x+2)^2 + 43(x+2) - 43.$$

For $-\infty < x < \infty$ and $k \geq 3$, since $f^{(k+1)}(c) = 0$, we have

$$R_k(x) = \frac{f^{(k+1)}(c)}{(k+1)!}(x+2)^{k+1} = 0.$$

Thus as $k \to \infty$, $R_k(x) \to 0$. Therefore f can be represented by its Taylor series about $a = -2$ for all x:

$$2x^3 - 3x^2 + 7x - 1 = 2(x+2)^3 - 15(x+2)^2 + 43(x+2) - 43.$$

From Example 36 it should be clear that any polynomial function can be represented for $-\infty < x < \infty$ by its Taylor series about a for any real number a.

EXAMPLE 37

Find the Taylor series for $f(x) = 1/(x - 5)$ about $a = 7$.

$$f(x) = (x-5)^{-1} \qquad\qquad f(7) = 2^{-1}$$
$$f'(x) = -1(x-5)^{-2} \qquad\qquad f'(7) = -(2)^{-2}$$
$$f''(x) = 2(x-5)^{-3} \qquad\qquad f''(7) = 2(2)^{-3}$$
$$f^{(3)}(x) = -3 \cdot 2(x-5)^{-4} \qquad\qquad f^{(3)}(7) = -3 \cdot 2(2)^{-4}$$
$$f^{(4)}(x) = 4 \cdot 3 \cdot 2(x-5)^{-5} \qquad\qquad f^{(4)}(7) = 4 \cdot 3 \cdot 2(2)^{-5}$$

Notice that a general pattern is forming for higher-order derivatives of f. We conclude that

$$f^{(n)}(x) = (-1)^n [n(n-1) \cdot \ldots \cdot 2](x-5)^{-(n+1)}$$

$$= (-1)^n n!(x-5)^{-(n+1)}$$

for $n = 0, 1, 2, \ldots$. Thus,

$$f^{(n)}(7) = (-1)^n n! \, (2)^{-(n+1)} = \frac{(-1)^n n!}{2^{n+1}}.$$

The Taylor series for f is

$$\sum_{n=0}^{\infty} \frac{f^{(n)}(7)}{n!} (x - 7)^n = \sum_{n=0}^{\infty} \frac{(-1)^n}{2^{n+1}} (x - 7)^n.$$

EXERCISE 13-8

For each function in problems 1–8, determine the Taylor polynomial in $x - a$ of the indicated degree.

1. $f(x) = e^{2x}$; $a = 0$;   degree 4

2. $f(x) = e^{x/2}$; $a = 0$;   degree 3

3. $f(x) = (x + 1)^{-1}$; $a = -\frac{1}{2}$;   degree 4

4. $f(x) = \dfrac{32}{x - 7}$; $a = 5$;   degree 5

5. $f(x) = \dfrac{1}{x^2 + 1}$; $a = 0$;   degree 2

6. $f(x) = xe^x$; $a = 0$;   degree 5

7. $f(x) = \sqrt[3]{9 - x}$; $a = 1$;   degree 2

8. $f(x) = \sqrt{x^2 + 9}$; $a = -4$;   degree 2

In problems 9–12, do the same as in problems 1–8. Also, approximate the value of $f(x_0)$ by evaluating the Taylor polynomial at x_0. Express your answer to three decimal places.

9. $f(x) = e^x$; $a = 0$;   degree 2; $x_0 = .1$

10. $f(x) = \ln x$; $a = 1$;   degree 2; $x_0 = .99$

11. $f(x) = \sqrt{x}$; $a = 49$;   degree 2; $x_0 = 50$

12. $f(x) = \sqrt[3]{x}$; $a = 27$;   degree 2; $x_0 = 26$

In problems 13–16, express the polynomial functions in powers of $x - a$.

13. $f(x) = x^2 - 7x + 10$; $a = 5$

14. $f(x) = 4x^3 - 6x^2 + 5$; $a = -1$

15. $f(x) = 3x^5 - 4x^3 + 7x - 1$; $a = -1$

16. $f(x) = x^4 + x^3 + x^2 + x + 1$; $a = 1$

In problems 17–26, find the Taylor series about a for each of the given functions.

17. $f(x) = e^{5-2x}; \quad a = \dfrac{5}{2}$

18. $f(x) = \dfrac{x+1}{x-1}; \quad a = 2$

19. $f(x) = \dfrac{1}{11-2x}; \quad a = 4$

20. $f(x) = \sqrt{x}; \quad a = 1$

21. $f(x) = xe^x; \quad a = 0$

22. $f(x) = x^5; \quad a = 0$

23. $f(x) = \ln x; \quad a = 1$

24. $f(x) = \ln(x+2); \quad a = -1$

25. $f(x) = \sqrt[3]{6-x}; \quad a = -2$

26. $f(x) = x \ln x; \quad a = 1$

27. In his article on social security taxes, Brittain† states: "The term $\log(1 + st)$ is awkward for estimation purposes, but the parameter s can be extricated by approximating $\log(1 + st)$ . . . by . . . the Taylor expansion . . .." By treating s as a constant, show that a linear approximation to $\log(1 + st)$ is $s(.434t)$. That is, find the sum of the first two terms of the Taylor expansion of $\log(1 + st)$ about $t = 0$.

13-9 REVIEW

Important Terms and Symbols in Chapter 13

sequence *(p. 505)*	ratio test *(p. 532)*
$\{a_n\}$ *(p. 506)*	alternating series *(p. 538)*
series *(p. 513)*	alternating harmonic series *(p. 538)*
$\displaystyle\sum_{n=1}^{\infty} a_n$ *(p. 513)*	alternating series test *(p. 538)*
	generalized ratio test *(p. 542)*
sequence of partial sums *(p. 514)*	absolutely convergent series *(p. 540)*
convergent series *(p. 515)*	conditionally convergent series *(p. 540)*
divergent series *(p. 515)*	n factorial *(p. 522)*
geometric series *(p. 520)*	$n!$ *(p. 522)*
harmonic series *(p. 516)*	power series *(p. 546)*
p-series *(p. 525)*	Taylor's theorem *(p. 551)*

---

†J. A. Brittain, "The Incidence of Social Security Payroll Taxes." *The American Economic Review*, LXI, No. 1, March, 1971, p. 118.

comparison test *(p. 526)*   Taylor polynomial *(p. 552)*
nonnegative series *(p. 526)*   Taylor series *(p. 556)*
positive series *(p. 532)*   Maclaurin series *(p. 556)*

Review Section

1. An infinite sequence is a function whose domain is the set of _____.

Ans. positive integers (or natural numbers)

2. The sixth term of the sequence $\left\{(-1)^{n+1}\dfrac{2n}{n+1}\right\}$ is _____.

Ans. $-\dfrac{12}{7}$

3. The sequence $\frac{1}{2}, \frac{2}{4}, \frac{3}{3}, \ldots$ has a general term given by _____.

Ans. $n/2^n$

4. The sequence $4, -4, 4, -4, \ldots$ (does) (does not) converge.

Ans. does not

5. As $n \to \infty$, the sequence $\left\{\dfrac{1}{n^2+4}\right\}$ converges to _____.

Ans. 0

6. True or false: For a sequence to converge to 3, all the terms from some point on must be equal to 3. _____

Ans. false

7. The fifth term of the series $\displaystyle\sum_{n=1}^{\infty}(-1)^{n+1}2^n$ is _____.

Ans. 32

8. $\displaystyle\sum_{n=1}^{\infty} r^n$ converges if _____.

Ans. $|r| < 1$

9. If $S_n = a_1 + a_2 + \ldots + a_n$, then $\displaystyle\sum_{n=1}^{\infty} a_n$ converges if as $n \to \infty$, the sequence _____ converges.

Ans. $\{S_n\}$

10. True or false: If Σa_n converges, then $\lim_{n\to\infty} a_n = 0$. __(a)__

If $\lim_{n\to\infty} a_n = 0$, then Σa_n converges. __(b)__

> *Ans.* (a) true;   (b) false

11. The sum of the geometric series $2 + 1 + \frac{1}{2} + \dots$ equals _____.

> *Ans.* 4

12. A series in which successive terms are of opposite sign is called a(n) _____ series.

> *Ans.* alternating

13. The series $\sum \dfrac{1}{n^p}$ converges if _____.

> *Ans.* $p > 1$

14. True or false: If $a_n \le b_n$ and Σb_n diverges, then Σa_n must diverge. _____

> *Ans.* false

15. Given the series Σa_n and the fact that $\lim_{n\to\infty} \left| \dfrac{a_{n+1}}{a_n} \right| < 1$, what conclusion, if any, can be reached concerning convergence or divergence of the given series? _____

> *Ans.* series converges

16. If Σa_n converges, then $\Sigma 1{,}000{,}000 a_n$ (converges) (diverges).

> *Ans.* converges

17. The series $\sum \dfrac{(-1)^{n+1}}{n^2}$ converges (absolutely) (conditionally).

> *Ans.* absolutely

18. The series $1 - \dfrac{1}{2} + \dfrac{1}{3} - \dfrac{1}{4} + \dots + (-1)^{n+1}\dfrac{1}{n} + \dots$ (converges) (diverges).

> *Ans.* converges

19. The value of 4! is _____.

> *Ans.* 24

20. The sequence $\{1/n\}$ (converges) (diverges) (a) and the series $\sum \dfrac{1}{n}$ (converges) (diverges) (b).

> *Ans.* (a) converges;   (b) diverges

21. A Taylor series about $a = 0$ is usually called a _____ series.

> *Ans.* Maclaurin

22. A series of the form $\Sigma\, a_n(x - a)^n$ is called a __(a)__ series and will always converge for $x = $ __(b)__ .

> *Ans.* (a) power;   (b) a

23. The coefficient of the x^3 term in the Maclaurin series for a function f is _____ .

> *Ans.* $f^{(3)}(0)/3!$

24. The Maclaurin series for the function $f(x) = x^2 + 3x + 1$ is _____ .

> *Ans.* $x^2 + 3x + 1$

25. True or false: If a power series converges for $a < x < b$ and diverges for $x < a$ and for $x > b$, then it must also converge at a and at b. _____

> *Ans.* false

Review Problems

For each of the sequences in problems 1-6, determine the limit as $n \to \infty$ providing the limit exists.

1. $\left\{ \dfrac{n}{n + 5} \right\}$

2. $\left\{ \dfrac{5}{n^2 + 4} \right\}$

3. $\left\{ \dfrac{e^{2n}}{n + 5} \right\}$

4. $\left\{ \dfrac{3n^2 + 5}{4n^2 + 2n + 1} \right\}$

5. $\left\{ \dfrac{(-1)^n}{2^n} \right\}$

6. $\left\{ \dfrac{n^3}{\ln n} \right\}$

For each of problems 7-26, determine whether the series is absolutely convergent, conditionally convergent, or divergent.

7. $\displaystyle\sum_{n=1}^{\infty} \frac{n + 5}{n}$

8. $\displaystyle\sum_{n=1}^{\infty} \frac{(-1)^{n+1}}{n + 4}$

9. $\displaystyle\sum_{n=1}^{\infty} \frac{(-1)^n n}{\sqrt{3n}}$

10. $\displaystyle\sum_{n=1}^{\infty} \frac{n}{\sqrt{3n}}$

11. $\displaystyle\sum_{k=1}^{\infty} \frac{1}{k^2 + 2k + 1}$

12. $\displaystyle\sum_{k=1}^{\infty} \frac{(-1)^{k+1}}{(k + 7)k!}$

13. $\displaystyle\sum_{k=2}^{\infty} \frac{(-1)^k}{\ln \sqrt{k}}$

14. $\displaystyle\sum_{k=5}^{\infty} \frac{k}{k^2 - 20}$

15. $\displaystyle\sum_{n=1}^{\infty} \frac{(-1)^{n+1}}{n^4}$

16. $\displaystyle\sum_{n=1}^{\infty} (-1)^{n+1} \, n^{-.2}$

17. $\displaystyle\sum_{n=1}^{\infty} \frac{(-1)^{n+1}}{\sqrt[4]{n}}$

18. $\displaystyle\sum_{n=1}^{\infty} \frac{(-1)^{n+1}(n+1)}{n^2 e^n}$

19. $\displaystyle\sum_{n=1}^{\infty} \frac{(-1)^n(n+2)}{(n+4)!}$

20. $\displaystyle\sum_{n=1}^{\infty} \frac{1}{6^n}$

21. $\displaystyle\sum_{n=1}^{\infty} \frac{(-1)^{n+1} \, n}{3^n}$

22. $\displaystyle\sum_{n=1}^{\infty} \frac{(-3)^{n+1}}{n}$

23. $\displaystyle\sum_{n=1}^{\infty} \frac{(-4)^n \, n}{n^3 + 7}$

24. $\displaystyle\sum_{n=1}^{\infty} \frac{(-1)^{n+1}}{\sqrt{2n+3}}$

25. $\displaystyle\sum_{n=1}^{\infty} \frac{(-1)^{n+1}}{\sqrt{n^2+1}}$

26. $\displaystyle\sum_{n=1}^{\infty} \frac{(-1)^{n+1}(2n+1)}{n^3}$

In problems 27–34, determine the values of x for which the power series converge.

27. $\displaystyle\sum_{n=0}^{\infty} \frac{n}{n+6} (x-4)^n$

28. $\displaystyle\sum_{n=0}^{\infty} \frac{1}{4^n(n+2)} (x+6)^n$

29. $\displaystyle\sum_{n=1}^{\infty} \frac{(-1)^n 3^n}{n} x^n$

30. $\displaystyle\sum_{n=0}^{\infty} \frac{2n^2 + 3n - 1}{n^2 + 5} x^n$

31. $\displaystyle\sum_{n=0}^{\infty} \frac{n!}{n+1} (x-1)^n$

32. $\displaystyle\sum_{n=0}^{\infty} \frac{7n+4}{(n+3)!} (x-5)^n$

33. $\displaystyle\sum_{n=0}^{\infty} \frac{1}{\sqrt{n!}} (x-3)^n$

34. $\displaystyle\sum_{n=0}^{\infty} (n+5)!(x+3)^n$

For the functions in problems 35–36, determine the Taylor polynomial in $x - a$ of the indicated degree.

35. $f(x) = e^{x^2}; \quad a = 0; \quad$ degree 2

36. $f(x) = \sqrt{x^3}; \quad a = 1; \quad$ degree 3

In problems 37–40, determine the Taylor series about a for each function.

37. $f(x) = 1/(3x - 4); \quad a = 2$ **38.** $f(x) = \ln \sqrt{x}; \quad a = 1$

39. $f(x) = (x + 4) \ln (x + 4); \quad a = -3$

40. $f(x) = 3x^3 + 2x^2 - 4x + 1; \quad a = -1$

Chapter 14

Matrix Algebra

14-1 MATRICES

Finding ways to describe many situations in mathematics and economics leads to the study of rectangular arrays of numbers. Consider, for example, the system of linear equations

$$\begin{cases} 3x + 4y + 3z = 0 \\ 2x + y - z = 0 \\ 9x - 6y + 2z = 0. \end{cases}$$

The features which characterize this system are the numerical coefficients in the equations, together with their relative positions. For this reason the system can be described by the rectangular array

$$\begin{bmatrix} 3 & 4 & 3 \\ 2 & 1 & -1 \\ 9 & -6 & 2 \end{bmatrix}$$

which is called a *matrix* (plural: *matrices,* pronounced may'tri sees). We shall consider such rectangular arrays to be objects in themselves and our custom, as shown above, will be to enclose them by brackets. Parentheses ( ) are also commonly used.

PITFALL.   *Do not use vertical bars,* | |, *instead of brackets or parentheses, for they have a different meaning.*

In symbolically representing matrices, we shall use bold capital letters such as **A, B, C,** etc.

In economics it is often convenient to use matrices in formulating problems and summarizing data. For example, a manufacturer who produces products *A*, *B*, and *C* could represent the units of labor and material involved in one week's production of these items as in Table 14-1.

TABLE 14-1

		PRODUCT	
	A	*B*	*C*
labor	10	12	16
material	5	9	7

More simply, these data can be represented by the matrix

$$\mathbf{A} = \begin{bmatrix} 10 & 12 & 16 \\ 5 & 9 & 7 \end{bmatrix}.$$

The horizontal rows of a matrix are numbered consecutively from top to bottom, and the vertical columns are numbered from left to right. For matrix **A** above we have

$$\begin{array}{cccc} & \text{column 1} & \text{column 2} & \text{column 3} \\ \text{row 1} & \begin{bmatrix} 10 & 12 & 16 \\ \text{row 2} & 5 & 9 & 7 \end{bmatrix} = \mathbf{A}. \end{array}$$

Since **A** has two rows and three columns, we say **A** has *order* (or *dimension*) 2 × 3 (read "2 by 3"), the number of rows being specified first. Similarly, the matrices

$$\mathbf{B} = \begin{bmatrix} 1 & 6 & -2 \\ 5 & 1 & -4 \\ -3 & 5 & 0 \end{bmatrix} \text{ and } \mathbf{C} = \begin{bmatrix} 1 & 2 \\ -3 & 4 \\ 5 & 6 \\ 7 & -8 \end{bmatrix}$$

have orders 3×3 and 4×2, respectively.

The numbers in a matrix are called its **entries** or **elements.** To denote arbitrary entries in a matrix, say one of order 2×3, there are two common methods. First, we may use different letters:

$$A = \begin{bmatrix} a & b & c \\ d & e & f \end{bmatrix}.$$

Second, a single letter may be used, say a, along with appropriate *double* subscripts to indicate position:

$$\begin{bmatrix} a_{11} & a_{12} & a_{13} \\ a_{21} & a_{22} & a_{23} \end{bmatrix}.$$

For the entry a_{12} (read "a sub one-two"), the first subscript 1 specifies the row and the second subscript 2, the column in which the entry appears. Similarly, the entry a_{23} (read "a sub two-three") is the entry in the second row and the third column. Generalizing, we say that the symbol a_{ij} denotes the entry in the ith row and jth column.

Our concern in this chapter is the manipulation and application of various types of matrices. For completeness, we now give a formal definition of a matrix.

DEFINITION.   *A rectangular array of numbers consisting of* m *rows and* n *columns,*

$$\begin{bmatrix} a_{11} & a_{12} & \cdots & a_{1n} \\ a_{21} & a_{22} & \cdots & a_{2n} \\ \cdot & \cdot & \cdots & \cdot \\ \cdot & \cdot & \cdots & \cdot \\ \cdot & \cdot & \cdots & \cdot \\ a_{m1} & a_{m2} & \cdots & a_{mn} \end{bmatrix},$$

is called an $m \times n$ *matrix or a* **matrix of order (dimension)** $m \times n$. *For the entry* a_{ij}, *i is the row subscript and j the column subscript.*

For brevity, an $m \times n$ matrix can be denoted by the symbol $[a_{ij}]_{m \times n}$ or more simply $[a_{ij}]$, where the dimension is understood to be that which is appropriate for the given context. Thus if $[a_{ij}]$ is 2×3, then $i = 1, 2$ and $j = 1, 2, 3$ and $[a_{ij}]$ has six entries. More generally, $m \times n$ matrices have mn entries.

PITFALL.   *Do not confuse the general entry* a_{ij} *with the matrix* $[a_{ij}]$.

A matrix which has exactly one row, such as

$$\mathbf{A} = [1 \quad 7 \quad 12 \quad 3],$$

is called a **row matrix.** Here **A** has order 1×4. Similarly, a matrix consisting of a single column, such as the 5×1 matrix

$$\mathbf{B} = \begin{bmatrix} 1 \\ -2 \\ 15 \\ 9 \\ 16 \end{bmatrix},$$

is called a **column matrix.**

EXAMPLE 1

The matrices

$$\mathbf{A} = [1 \quad 2 \quad 0], \quad \mathbf{B} = \begin{bmatrix} 1 & -6 \\ 5 & 1 \\ 9 & 4 \end{bmatrix}, \quad \mathbf{C} = [7], \quad \mathbf{D} = \begin{bmatrix} 1 & 3 & 7 & -2 & 4 \\ 9 & 11 & 5 & 6 & 8 \\ 6 & -2 & -1 & 1 & 1 \end{bmatrix}$$

have orders 1×3, 3×2, 1×1, and 3×5, respectively.

EXAMPLE 2

a. *Construct a 3-entry column matrix such that* $a_{21} = 6$ *and* $a_{ij} = 0$ *otherwise.*

The matrix is given by

$$\begin{bmatrix} 0 \\ 6 \\ 0 \end{bmatrix}.$$

b. *If* $\mathbf{A} = [a_{ij}]$ *has order* 3×4 *and* $a_{ij} = i + j$, *find* $\mathbf{A}$.

Here $i = 1, 2, 3$ and $j = 1, 2, 3, 4$, and $\mathbf{A}$ has $(3)(4) = 12$ entries. Since $a_{ij} = i + j$, the entry in row i and column j is obtained by adding the numbers i and j. Hence, $a_{11} = 1 + 1 = 2$, $a_{12} = 1 + 2 = 3$, $a_{13} = 1 + 3 = 4$, etc., and

$$\mathbf{A} = \begin{bmatrix} 1+1 & 1+2 & 1+3 & 1+4 \\ 2+1 & 2+2 & 2+3 & 2+4 \\ 3+1 & 3+2 & 3+3 & 3+4 \end{bmatrix} = \begin{bmatrix} 2 & 3 & 4 & 5 \\ 3 & 4 & 5 & 6 \\ 4 & 5 & 6 & 7 \end{bmatrix}.$$

c. *Construct the* 3×3 *matrix* **I** *given that* $a_{11} = a_{22} = a_{33} = 1$ *and* $a_{ij} = 0$ *otherwise.*

The matrix is given by

$$\mathbf{I} = \begin{bmatrix} 1 & 0 & 0 \\ 0 & 1 & 0 \\ 0 & 0 & 1 \end{bmatrix}.$$

DEFINITION.   *Two matrices are **equal** if and only if they have the same order and corresponding entries are equal.*

For example,

$$\begin{bmatrix} 1+1 & \frac{2}{2} \\ 2\cdot3 & 0 \end{bmatrix} = \begin{bmatrix} 2 & 1 \\ 6 & 0 \end{bmatrix}$$

but

$$\begin{bmatrix} 1 & 1 \end{bmatrix} \neq \begin{bmatrix} 1 \\ 1 \end{bmatrix}$$

and

$$\begin{bmatrix} 1 & 1 \end{bmatrix} \neq \begin{bmatrix} 1 & 1 & 1 \end{bmatrix}.$$

By the definition of equality, for the matrix equation

$$\begin{bmatrix} x & y+1 \\ 2z & 5w \end{bmatrix} = \begin{bmatrix} 2 & 7 \\ 4 & 2 \end{bmatrix}$$

to be a true statement, it must be equivalent to the system

$$\begin{cases} x = 2 \\ y+1 = 7 \\ 2z = 4 \\ 5w = 2. \end{cases}$$

Solving gives $x = 2$, $y = 6$, $z = 2$, and $w = \frac{2}{5}$. It is a significant fact that a matrix equation can define a system of linear equations as has been shown above.

Certain types of matrices play important roles in matrix theory. We now consider three such types.

An $m \times n$ matrix whose entries are all 0 is called the $m \times n$ **zero matrix,** denoted $\mathbf{O}_{m \times n}$ or, more simply, $\mathbf{O}$. Thus the 2×3 zero matrix is

$$\mathbf{O} = \begin{bmatrix} 0 & 0 & 0 \\ 0 & 0 & 0 \end{bmatrix}$$

and in general

$$\mathbf{O} = \begin{bmatrix} 0 & 0 & \cdots & 0 \\ 0 & 0 & \cdots & 0 \\ \cdot & \cdot & \cdots & \cdot \\ \cdot & \cdot & \cdots & \cdot \\ \cdot & \cdot & \cdots & \cdot \\ 0 & 0 & \cdots & 0 \end{bmatrix}.$$

PITFALL.   *Do not confuse the matrix* **O** *with the real number* 0.

A matrix having the same number of columns as rows, for example n rows and n columns, is called a **square matrix** of order n. That is, an $m \times n$ matrix is square if and only if $m = n$. Thus

$$\begin{bmatrix} -2 & 7 & 4 \\ 6 & 2 & 0 \\ 4 & 6 & 1 \end{bmatrix} \quad \text{and} \quad [3]$$

are square matrices of orders 3 and 1, respectively.

In a square matrix of order n, the entries a_{11}, a_{22}, a_{33}, ..., a_{nn} which lie on the diagonal extending from the upper left corner to the lower right corner are called the **main diagonal** entries, or more simply the **main diagonal.** Thus in the matrix

$$\begin{bmatrix} 1 & 2 & 3 \\ 4 & 5 & 6 \\ 7 & 8 & 9 \end{bmatrix},$$

the main diagonal consists of $a_{11} = 1$, $a_{22} = 5$, and $a_{33} = 9$.

A square matrix is said to be an **upper (lower) triangular matrix** if all entries below (above) the main diagonal are zero. Thus

$$\begin{bmatrix} 5 & 1 & 1 \\ 0 & -3 & 7 \\ 0 & 0 & 4 \end{bmatrix} \quad \text{and} \quad \begin{bmatrix} 7 & 0 & 0 & 0 \\ -3 & 2 & 0 & 0 \\ 6 & 5 & -4 & 0 \\ 1 & 6 & 0 & 1 \end{bmatrix}$$

are upper and lower triangular matrices, respectively.

EXERCISE 14-1

1. Given the matrices

$$A = \begin{bmatrix} 1 & -6 & 2 \\ -4 & 2 & 1 \end{bmatrix} \qquad B = \begin{bmatrix} 1 & 2 & 3 \\ 4 & 5 & 6 \\ 7 & 8 & 9 \end{bmatrix} \qquad C = \begin{bmatrix} 1 & 1 \\ 2 & 2 \\ 3 & 3 \end{bmatrix}$$

$$D = \begin{bmatrix} 1 & 0 \\ 2 & 3 \end{bmatrix} \qquad E = \begin{bmatrix} 1 & 2 & 3 & 4 \\ 0 & 1 & 6 & 0 \\ 0 & 0 & 2 & 0 \\ 0 & 0 & 6 & 1 \end{bmatrix} \qquad F = [6 \quad 2]$$

$$G = \begin{bmatrix} 5 \\ 6 \\ 1 \end{bmatrix} \qquad H = \begin{bmatrix} 1 & 6 & 2 \\ 0 & 0 & 0 \\ 0 & 0 & 0 \end{bmatrix} \qquad J = [4]$$

a. State the order of each matrix.

b. Which matrices are square?

c. Which matrices are upper triangular? lower triangular?

d. Which are row matrices?

e. Which are column matrices?

In problems 2-9 let

$$A = [a_{ij}] = \begin{bmatrix} 7 & -2 & 14 & 6 \\ 6 & 2 & 3 & -2 \\ 5 & 4 & 1 & 0 \\ 8 & 0 & 2 & 0 \end{bmatrix}.$$

2. What is the order of A?

Find

3. a_{43} **4.** a_{12} **5.** a_{32} **6.** a_{34} **7.** a_{14} **8.** a_{55}

9. What are the main diagonal entries?

10. Write the upper triangular matrix of order 5 given that all entries which are not required to be 0 are equal to 1.

11. Write $A = [a_{ij}]$ if A is 3×4 and $a_{ij} = 2i + 3j$.

12. Write $B = [b_{ij}]$ if B is 2×2 and $b_{ij} = (-1)^{i+j}(i^2 + j^2)$.

13. If $A = [a_{ij}]$ is 12×10, how many entries does A have? If $a_{ij} = 1$ for $i = j$, and $a_{ij} = 0$ for $i \neq j$, find a_{33}, a_{52}, $a_{10,10}$, and $a_{12,10}$.

14. List the main diagonal of

a. $\begin{bmatrix} 1 & 4 & -2 & 0 \\ 7 & 0 & 4 & -1 \\ -6 & 6 & -5 & 1 \\ 2 & 1 & 7 & 2 \end{bmatrix}$ b. $\begin{bmatrix} x & 1 & y \\ 9 & y & 7 \\ y & 0 & z \end{bmatrix}$.

15. Write the zero matrix of order (a) 4; (b) 6.

In problems 16-19, solve the matrix equation.

16. $\begin{bmatrix} 2x & y \\ z & 3w \end{bmatrix} = \begin{bmatrix} 4 & 6 \\ 0 & 7 \end{bmatrix}$

17. $\begin{bmatrix} 6 & 2 \\ x & 7 \\ 3y & 2z \end{bmatrix} = \begin{bmatrix} 6 & 2 \\ 6 & 7 \\ 2 & 7 \end{bmatrix}$

18. $\begin{bmatrix} 4 & 2 & 1 \\ 3x & y & 3z \\ 0 & w & 7 \end{bmatrix} = \begin{bmatrix} 4 & 2 & 1 \\ 6 & 7 & 9 \\ 0 & 9 & 8 \end{bmatrix}$

19. $\begin{bmatrix} 2x & 7 \\ 7 & 2y \end{bmatrix} = \begin{bmatrix} y & 7 \\ 7 & y \end{bmatrix}$

20. A stock broker sold a customer 200 shares of Stock A, 300 shares of Stock B, 500 shares of Stock C and 300 shares of Stock D. Write a row matrix which gives the number of shares of each stock sold. If the stocks sell for $20, $30, $45, and $100 per share, respectively, write this information as a column matrix.

21. The Wala-Wala Widget Company has its monthly sales reports given by means of matrices where the rows, in order, represent the number of regular, deluxe, and super-duper models sold, and the columns, in order, give the number of red, white, blue, and purple units sold. The matrices for January (J) and February (F) are

$$J = \begin{bmatrix} 2 & 6 & 1 & 2 \\ 0 & 1 & 3 & 5 \\ 2 & 7 & 6 & 0 \end{bmatrix}; \quad F = \begin{bmatrix} 0 & 2 & 4 & 4 \\ 2 & 3 & 3 & 2 \\ 4 & 0 & 2 & 6 \end{bmatrix}.$$

How many white super-duper models were sold in January? How many blue deluxe models were sold in February? In which month were more purple regular models sold? Which model and color sold the same number of units in both months. In which month were more deluxe models sold? In which month were more red widgets sold? How many widgets were sold in January?

22. Input-output matrices, which were developed by W. W. Leontief, indicate the interrelationships that exist among the various sectors of an economy during some period of time. A hypothetical example for a simplified economy is given by matrix M below. The consuming sectors are the same as the producing sectors and can be thought of as manufacturers, government, steel, agriculture, households, etc. Each row shows how the output of a given sector is consumed by the four sectors. For example, of the total output of Industry A, 50 went to Industry A itself, 70 to B, 200 to C, and 360 to all others. The sum of the entries in row 1, namely 680, gives the total output of A for a given time period. Each column gives the output of each sector that is consumed by a given sector. For example, in producing 680 units, Industry A consumed 50 units of A, 90 of B, 120 of C, and 420 from all other producers. For each column, find the sum of the entries. Do the same for each row. What do you observe in comparing these totals? Suppose sector A increases its output by 20 percent, namely by 136 units. Assuming this results in a uniform 20 percent increase of all its inputs, by how many units will sector B have to increase its output? Answer the same question for C and D.

CONSUMERS

	Industry A	Industry B	Industry C	All Other Consumers
PRODUCERS:				

$$\text{M} = \begin{array}{l} \text{Industry } A \\ \text{Industry } B \\ \text{Industry } C \\ \text{All Other} \\ \text{Producers} \end{array} \begin{bmatrix} 50 & 70 & 200 & 360 \\ 90 & 30 & 270 & 320 \\ 120 & 240 & 100 & 1,050 \\ 420 & 370 & 940 & 4,960 \end{bmatrix}$$

14-2 MATRIX ADDITION AND SCALAR MULTIPLICATION

Consider a snowmobile dealer who sells two models, Deluxe and Super. Each is available in one of two colors, red and blue. Suppose his sales for January and February are represented respectively by the sales matrices

$$\begin{array}{cc} & \text{Deluxe \quad Super} \\ \text{J} = \begin{array}{l} \text{red} \\ \text{blue} \end{array} \begin{bmatrix} 1 & 2 \\ 3 & 5 \end{bmatrix}, & \text{F} = \begin{bmatrix} 3 & 1 \\ 4 & 2 \end{bmatrix}. \end{array}$$

Each row of **J** and **F** gives the number of each model sold for a given color. Each column gives the number of each color sold for a given model. A matrix representing total sales for each model and color for both months can be obtained by adding the corresponding entries in **J** and **F**:

$$\begin{bmatrix} 4 & 3 \\ 7 & 7 \end{bmatrix}.$$

This situation provides some motivation for introducing the operation of matrix addition for two matrices of the same order.

DEFINITION. *If **A** and **B** are $m \times n$ matrices, then **A** + **B** is the $m \times n$ matrix obtained by adding corresponding entries of **A** and **B**.*

Thus if

$$\text{A} = \begin{bmatrix} a_{11} & a_{12} & a_{13} \\ a_{21} & a_{22} & a_{23} \end{bmatrix} \quad \text{and} \quad \text{B} = \begin{bmatrix} b_{11} & b_{12} & b_{13} \\ b_{21} & b_{22} & b_{23} \end{bmatrix},$$

then **A** and **B** have the same order (2×3) and

$$\text{A} + \text{B} = \begin{bmatrix} a_{11} + b_{11} & a_{12} + b_{12} & a_{13} + b_{13} \\ a_{21} + b_{21} & a_{22} + b_{22} & a_{23} + b_{23} \end{bmatrix}.$$

EXAMPLE 3

a. $\begin{bmatrix} 1 & 2 \\ 3 & 4 \\ 5 & 6 \end{bmatrix} + \begin{bmatrix} 7 & -2 \\ -6 & 4 \\ 3 & 0 \end{bmatrix} = \begin{bmatrix} 1+7 & 2-2 \\ 3-6 & 4+4 \\ 5+3 & 6+0 \end{bmatrix} = \begin{bmatrix} 8 & 0 \\ -3 & 8 \\ 8 & 6 \end{bmatrix}.$

b. $\begin{bmatrix} 1 & 2 \\ 3 & 4 \end{bmatrix} + \begin{bmatrix} 2 \\ 1 \end{bmatrix}$

is not defined since the matrices do not have the same order.

If **A, B, C,** and **O** have the same order, then the following properties hold for matrix addition:

    a. $\mathbf{A + B = B + A}$ Commutative Property
    b. $\mathbf{A + (B + C) = (A + B) + C}$ Associative Property
    c. $\mathbf{A + O = O + A = A}$ Identity Property

These properties are illustrated in the following example.

EXAMPLE 4

Let

$$\mathbf{A} = \begin{bmatrix} 1 & 2 & 1 \\ -2 & 0 & 1 \end{bmatrix}, \mathbf{B} = \begin{bmatrix} 0 & 1 & 2 \\ 1 & -3 & 1 \end{bmatrix}, \mathbf{C} = \begin{bmatrix} -2 & 1 & -1 \\ 0 & -2 & 1 \end{bmatrix}, \mathbf{O} = \begin{bmatrix} 0 & 0 & 0 \\ 0 & 0 & 0 \end{bmatrix}.$$

a. $\mathbf{A + B} = \begin{bmatrix} 1 & 3 & 3 \\ -1 & -3 & 2 \end{bmatrix}; \ \mathbf{B + A} = \begin{bmatrix} 1 & 3 & 3 \\ -1 & -3 & 2 \end{bmatrix}.$

b. $\mathbf{A + (B + C)} = \mathbf{A} + \begin{bmatrix} -2 & 2 & 1 \\ 1 & -5 & 2 \end{bmatrix} = \begin{bmatrix} -1 & 4 & 2 \\ -1 & -5 & 3 \end{bmatrix},$

     $\mathbf{(A + B) + C} = \begin{bmatrix} 1 & 3 & 3 \\ -1 & -3 & 2 \end{bmatrix} + \mathbf{C} = \begin{bmatrix} -1 & 4 & 2 \\ -1 & -5 & 3 \end{bmatrix}.$

c. $\mathbf{A + O} = \begin{bmatrix} 1 & 2 & 1 \\ -2 & 0 & 1 \end{bmatrix} + \begin{bmatrix} 0 & 0 & 0 \\ 0 & 0 & 0 \end{bmatrix} = \begin{bmatrix} 1 & 2 & 1 \\ -2 & 0 & 1 \end{bmatrix} = \mathbf{A}.$

Thus the zero matrix plays the same role in matrix addition as the number zero does in addition of real numbers.

Returning to the snowmobile dealer, recall that February sales were given by the matrix

$$\mathbf{F} = \begin{bmatrix} 3 & 1 \\ 4 & 2 \end{bmatrix}.$$

If in March the dealer doubles February's sales of each model and color of snowmobile, the sales matrix **M** for March could be obtained by multiplying each entry in **F** by 2:

$$\mathbf{M} = \begin{bmatrix} 2 \cdot 3 & 2 \cdot 1 \\ 2 \cdot 4 & 2 \cdot 2 \end{bmatrix}.$$

It seems reasonable to write this operation as

$$\mathbf{M} = 2\mathbf{F} = 2\begin{bmatrix} 3 & 1 \\ 4 & 2 \end{bmatrix} = \begin{bmatrix} 2 \cdot 3 & 2 \cdot 1 \\ 2 \cdot 4 & 2 \cdot 2 \end{bmatrix} = \begin{bmatrix} 6 & 2 \\ 8 & 4 \end{bmatrix}$$

which is thought of as multiplying a matrix by a real number. Indeed, we have the following definition.

DEFINITION. *If* **A** *is an* $m \times n$ *matrix and* k *is a real number (also called a* scalar*), then by* $k\mathbf{A}$ *we denote the* $m \times n$ *matrix obtained by multiplying each entry in* **A** *by* k. *This operation is called* **scalar multiplication.**

Thus if

$$\mathbf{A} = \begin{bmatrix} a_{11} & a_{12} \\ a_{21} & a_{22} \end{bmatrix},$$

then

$$k\mathbf{A} = \begin{bmatrix} ka_{11} & ka_{12} \\ ka_{21} & ka_{22} \end{bmatrix}.$$

EXAMPLE 5

Let

$$\mathbf{A} = \begin{bmatrix} 1 & 2 \\ 4 & -2 \end{bmatrix}, \quad \mathbf{B} = \begin{bmatrix} 3 & -4 \\ 7 & 1 \end{bmatrix}, \quad \mathbf{O} = \begin{bmatrix} 0 & 0 \\ 0 & 0 \end{bmatrix}.$$

Find

a. 4**A**.

$$4\mathbf{A} = 4\begin{bmatrix} 1 & 2 \\ 4 & -2 \end{bmatrix} = \begin{bmatrix} 4 \cdot 1 & 4 \cdot 2 \\ 4 \cdot 4 & 4 \cdot (-2) \end{bmatrix} = \begin{bmatrix} 4 & 8 \\ 16 & -8 \end{bmatrix}.$$

b. $-\dfrac{2}{3}\mathbf{B}$.

$$-\frac{2}{3}\mathbf{B} = \begin{bmatrix} -\dfrac{2}{3}(3) & -\dfrac{2}{3}(-4) \\ -\dfrac{2}{3}(7) & -\dfrac{2}{3}(1) \end{bmatrix} = \begin{bmatrix} -2 & \dfrac{8}{3} \\ -\dfrac{14}{3} & -\dfrac{2}{3} \end{bmatrix}.$$

c. $\dfrac{1}{2}A + 3B$.

$$\frac{1}{2}A + 3B = \frac{1}{2}\begin{bmatrix} 1 & 2 \\ 4 & -2 \end{bmatrix} + 3\begin{bmatrix} 3 & -4 \\ 7 & 1 \end{bmatrix}$$

$$= \begin{bmatrix} \frac{1}{2} & 1 \\ 2 & -1 \end{bmatrix} + \begin{bmatrix} 9 & -12 \\ 21 & 3 \end{bmatrix} = \begin{bmatrix} \frac{19}{2} & -11 \\ 23 & 2 \end{bmatrix}.$$

d. $0A$.

$$0A = 0\begin{bmatrix} 1 & 2 \\ 4 & -2 \end{bmatrix} = \begin{bmatrix} 0 & 0 \\ 0 & 0 \end{bmatrix} = O.$$

e. kO.

$$kO = k\begin{bmatrix} 0 & 0 \\ 0 & 0 \end{bmatrix} = \begin{bmatrix} 0 & 0 \\ 0 & 0 \end{bmatrix} = O.$$

If **A**, **B**, and **O** have the same order, then for any scalars k, k_1, and k_2 we have the following properties of scalar multiplication:

a. $k(A + B) = kA + kB$
b. $(k_1 + k_2)A = k_1 A + k_2 A$
c. $k_1(k_2 A) = (k_1 k_2)A$
d. $0A = O$
e. $kO = O$.

Properties (d) and (e) were illustrated in (d) and (e) of Example 5; the others will be illustrated in the exercises. Remember that $O \neq 0$, for 0 is a *scalar* and **O** is a zero *matrix*.

For the case that $k = -1$, then $kA = (-1)A$ which will be denoted by simply writing $-A$, called the *negative* of **A**. Thus if

$$A = \begin{bmatrix} 3 & 1 \\ -4 & 5 \end{bmatrix},$$

then

$$-A = (-1)\begin{bmatrix} 3 & 1 \\ -4 & 5 \end{bmatrix} = \begin{bmatrix} -3 & -1 \\ 4 & -5 \end{bmatrix}.$$

Note that $-A$ is the matrix obtained by multiplying each entry of **A** by -1. Subtraction of matrices can now be defined.

DEFINITION.   *If A and B have the same order, then by A − B we mean the matrix A + (−B).*

EXAMPLE 6

a.
$$\begin{bmatrix} 2 & 6 \\ -4 & 1 \\ 3 & 2 \end{bmatrix} - \begin{bmatrix} 6 & -2 \\ 4 & 1 \\ 0 & 3 \end{bmatrix} = \begin{bmatrix} 2 & 6 \\ -4 & 1 \\ 3 & 2 \end{bmatrix} + (-1) \begin{bmatrix} 6 & -2 \\ 4 & 1 \\ 0 & 3 \end{bmatrix}$$

$$= \begin{bmatrix} 2 & 6 \\ -4 & 1 \\ 3 & 2 \end{bmatrix} + \begin{bmatrix} -6 & 2 \\ -4 & -1 \\ 0 & -3 \end{bmatrix}$$

$$= \begin{bmatrix} 2-6 & 6+2 \\ -4-4 & 1-1 \\ 3+0 & 2-3 \end{bmatrix} = \begin{bmatrix} -4 & 8 \\ -8 & 0 \\ 3 & -1 \end{bmatrix}.$$

More simply, to find $A - B$ we can subtract each entry in B from the corresponding entry in A.

b.
$$\begin{bmatrix} 6 & -4 & 7 & 1 \\ -1 & 6 & 0 & -4 \\ 2 & -1 & 3 & 1 \end{bmatrix} - \begin{bmatrix} 2 & -3 & 3 & 2 \\ 4 & 2 & 1 & 3 \\ 1 & 0 & -1 & -4 \end{bmatrix}$$

$$= \begin{bmatrix} 6-2 & -4+3 & 7-3 & 1-2 \\ -1-4 & 6-2 & 0-1 & -4-3 \\ 2-1 & -1-0 & 3+1 & 1+4 \end{bmatrix} = \begin{bmatrix} 4 & -1 & 4 & -1 \\ -5 & 4 & -1 & -7 \\ 1 & -1 & 4 & 5 \end{bmatrix}.$$

EXAMPLE 7

Solve $2 \begin{bmatrix} x_1 \\ x_2 \end{bmatrix} - \begin{bmatrix} 3 \\ 4 \end{bmatrix} = 5 \begin{bmatrix} 5 \\ -4 \end{bmatrix}.$

$$2 \begin{bmatrix} x_1 \\ x_2 \end{bmatrix} - \begin{bmatrix} 3 \\ 4 \end{bmatrix} = 5 \begin{bmatrix} 5 \\ -4 \end{bmatrix}$$

$$\begin{bmatrix} 2x_1 \\ 2x_2 \end{bmatrix} - \begin{bmatrix} 3 \\ 4 \end{bmatrix} = \begin{bmatrix} 25 \\ -20 \end{bmatrix}$$

$$\begin{bmatrix} 2x_1 - 3 \\ 2x_2 - 4 \end{bmatrix} = \begin{bmatrix} 25 \\ -20 \end{bmatrix}.$$

By equality of matrices we must have $2x_1 - 3 = 25$, which gives $x_1 = 14$; from $2x_2 - 4 = -20$ we get $x_2 = -8$.

EXAMPLE 8

Consider a simplified hypothetical economy having three industries, say coal, electricity, and steel, and three consumers 1, 2, and 3. Moreover, assume each consumer may use some of the output of each industry, and also that each industry uses some of the output of each other industry. The needs of each consumer and industry can be represented by a (row) demand matrix where the entries, in order, give the amount of coal, electricity, and steel needed by the consumer or industry in some convenient units. For example, the demand matrices for the consumers might be

$$\mathbf{D}_1 = [3 \quad 2 \quad 5], \qquad \mathbf{D}_2 = [0 \quad 17 \quad 1], \qquad \mathbf{D}_3 = [4 \quad 6 \quad 12],$$

and for the industries they might be

$$\mathbf{D}_C = [0 \quad 1 \quad 4], \qquad \mathbf{D}_E = [20 \quad 0 \quad 8], \qquad \mathbf{D}_S = [30 \quad 5 \quad 0],$$

where the subscripts C, E, and S stand for coal, electricity, and steel respectively. The total demand for these goods by the consumers is given by the sum

$$\mathbf{D}_1 + \mathbf{D}_2 + \mathbf{D}_3 = [3 \quad 2 \quad 5] + [0 \quad 17 \quad 1] + [4 \quad 6 \quad 12] = [7 \quad 25 \quad 18].$$

The total industrial demand is given by the sum

$$\mathbf{D}_C + \mathbf{D}_E + \mathbf{D}_S = [0 \quad 1 \quad 4] + [20 \quad 0 \quad 8] + [30 \quad 5 \quad 0] = [50 \quad 6 \quad 12].$$

Therefore, the total overall demand is given by

$$[7 \quad 25 \quad 18] + [50 \quad 6 \quad 12] = [57 \quad 31 \quad 30].$$

Thus the coal industry sells a total of 57 units, the total units of electricity sold are 31, and the total units of steel which are sold are 30.†

EXERCISE 14-2

In problems 1-12 perform the indicated operations.

1. $\begin{bmatrix} 2 & 0 & -3 \\ -1 & 4 & 0 \\ 1 & -6 & 5 \end{bmatrix} + \begin{bmatrix} 2 & -3 & 4 \\ -1 & 6 & 5 \\ 9 & 11 & -2 \end{bmatrix}$ 2. $\begin{bmatrix} 2 & -7 \\ -6 & 4 \end{bmatrix} + \begin{bmatrix} 7 & -4 \\ -2 & 1 \end{bmatrix} + \begin{bmatrix} 2 & 7 \\ 7 & 2 \end{bmatrix}$

3. $\begin{bmatrix} 1 & 4 \\ -2 & 7 \\ 6 & 9 \end{bmatrix} - \begin{bmatrix} 6 & -1 \\ 7 & 2 \\ 1 & 0 \end{bmatrix}$ 4. $2\begin{bmatrix} 3 & -1 & 4 \\ 2 & 1 & -1 \\ 0 & 0 & 2 \end{bmatrix}$

5. $3[1 \quad -3 \quad 2 \quad 1] + 2[-6 \quad 1 \quad 0 \quad 4] - 0[-2 \quad 7 \quad 6 \quad 4]$

6. $[7 \quad 7] + 66$

7. $\begin{bmatrix} 1 & 2 \\ 3 & 4 \end{bmatrix} + \begin{bmatrix} 5 \\ 6 \end{bmatrix}$ 8. $\begin{bmatrix} 2 & -1 \\ 7 & 4 \end{bmatrix} + 3\begin{bmatrix} 0 & 0 \\ 0 & 0 \end{bmatrix}$

---

†This example, as well as some others in this chapter, are from John G. Kemeny, J. Laurie Snell and Gerald L. Thompson, INTRODUCTION TO FINITE MATHEMATICS, 3rd ed, © 1974. Reprinted by permission of Prentice-Hall, Inc., Englewood Cliffs, New Jersey.

9. $-6\begin{bmatrix} 2 & -6 & 7 & 1 \\ 7 & 1 & 6 & -2 \end{bmatrix}$

10. $\begin{bmatrix} 1 & -1 \\ 2 & 0 \\ 3 & -6 \\ 4 & 9 \end{bmatrix} - 3\begin{bmatrix} -6 & 9 \\ 2 & 6 \\ 1 & -2 \\ 4 & 5 \end{bmatrix}$

11. $\begin{bmatrix} 2 & -4 & 0 \\ 0 & 6 & -2 \\ -4 & 0 & 10 \end{bmatrix} + \frac{1}{3}\begin{bmatrix} 9 & 0 & 3 \\ 0 & 3 & 0 \\ 3 & 9 & 9 \end{bmatrix}$

12. $2\begin{bmatrix} 1 & 0 & 0 \\ 0 & 1 & 0 \\ 0 & 0 & 1 \end{bmatrix} - 3\left(\begin{bmatrix} 2 & 1 & 0 \\ 1 & -2 & 3 \\ 1 & 0 & 0 \end{bmatrix} - \begin{bmatrix} 6 & -2 & 1 \\ -5 & 1 & -2 \\ 0 & 1 & 3 \end{bmatrix}\right)$

In problems 13–24, compute the required matrices if

$$A = \begin{bmatrix} 2 & 1 \\ 3 & -3 \end{bmatrix}, \quad B = \begin{bmatrix} -6 & -5 \\ 2 & -3 \end{bmatrix}, \quad C = \begin{bmatrix} -2 & -1 \\ -3 & 3 \end{bmatrix}, \quad O = \begin{bmatrix} 0 & 0 \\ 0 & 0 \end{bmatrix}.$$

13. $-B$

14. $-(A - B)$

15. $2O$

16. $A + B - C$

17. $2(A - 2B)$

18. $O(A + B)$

19. $3(A - C) + 6$

20. $A + (C + 2O)$

21. $2B - 3A + 2C$

22. $3C - 2B$

23. $\frac{1}{2}A - 2(B + 2C)$

24. $2A - \frac{1}{2}(B - C)$

For matrices **A, B,** and **C** above, verify that

25. $3(A + B) = 3A + 3B$

26. $(2 + 3)A = 2A + 3A$

27. $k_1(k_2 A) = (k_1 k_2)A$

28. $k(A + B + C) = kA + kB + kC$

29. Express the matrix equation

$$x\begin{bmatrix} 2 \\ 1 \end{bmatrix} - y\begin{bmatrix} -3 \\ 5 \end{bmatrix} = 2\begin{bmatrix} 8 \\ 11 \end{bmatrix}$$

as a system of linear equations and solve.

30. In the reverse of the manner used in problem 29, write the system

$$\begin{cases} 3x + 5y = 16 \\ 2x - 6y = -4 \end{cases}$$

as a matrix equation.

In problems 31–34, solve the matrix equations.

31. $3\begin{bmatrix} x \\ y \end{bmatrix} - 3\begin{bmatrix} -2 \\ 4 \end{bmatrix} = 4\begin{bmatrix} 6 \\ -2 \end{bmatrix}$

32. $3\begin{bmatrix} x \\ 2 \end{bmatrix} - 4\begin{bmatrix} 7 \\ -y \end{bmatrix} = \begin{bmatrix} -x \\ 2y \end{bmatrix}$

33. $\begin{bmatrix} 2 \\ 4 \\ 6 \end{bmatrix} + 2\begin{bmatrix} x \\ y \\ 4z \end{bmatrix} = \begin{bmatrix} -10 \\ -24 \\ 14 \end{bmatrix}$

34. $x\begin{bmatrix} 2 \\ 0 \\ 3 \end{bmatrix} + 2\begin{bmatrix} -1 \\ 0 \\ 6 \end{bmatrix} + y\begin{bmatrix} 0 \\ 2 \\ -3 \end{bmatrix} = \begin{bmatrix} 8 \\ 4 \\ 3x + 12 - 3y \end{bmatrix}$

35. Suppose the sales prices of commodities A, B, and C are given, in that order, by the price matrix

$$\mathbf{P} = [p_1 \quad p_2 \quad p_3].$$

If the sales prices are to be increased by 10 percent, the matrix of the new prices can be obtained by multiplying $\mathbf{P}$ by what scalar?

14-3 MATRIX MULTIPLICATION

Besides the operations of matrix addition and scalar multiplication, the product $\mathbf{AB}$ of matrices $\mathbf{A}$ and $\mathbf{B}$ can be defined under certain conditions, namely that the number of columns of $\mathbf{A}$ is equal to the number of rows of $\mathbf{B}$.

DEFINITION. *Let* $\mathbf{A}$ *be an* $m \times n$ *matrix and* $\mathbf{B}$ *be an* $n \times p$ *matrix. Then the product* $\mathbf{AB}$ *is the* $m \times p$ *matrix* $\mathbf{C}$ *whose entry* c_{ij} *in the i-th row and j-th column is obtained as follows: sum the products formed by multiplying, in order, each entry (that is, first, second, etc.) in the i-th row of* $\mathbf{A}$ *by the "corresponding" entry (that is, first, second, etc.) in the j-th column of* $\mathbf{B}$.

Three points must be completely understood regarding the above definition of $\mathbf{AB}$. First, the condition that $\mathbf{A}$ be $m \times n$ and $\mathbf{B}$ be $n \times p$ is equivalent to saying that the number of columns of $\mathbf{A}$ must be equal to the number of rows of $\mathbf{B}$. Second, the product will be a matrix of order $m \times p$; it will have as many rows as $\mathbf{A}$ and as many columns as $\mathbf{B}$. Third, the definition refers to the product $\mathbf{AB}$, *in that order;* $\mathbf{A}$ is the left factor and $\mathbf{B}$ is the right factor. For $\mathbf{AB}$ we say $\mathbf{B}$ is *premultiplied* by $\mathbf{A}$ or $\mathbf{A}$ is *postmultiplied* by $\mathbf{B}$.

To apply the definition, let us find the product

$$\mathbf{AB} = \begin{bmatrix} 2 & 1 & -6 \\ 1 & -3 & 2 \end{bmatrix}\begin{bmatrix} 1 & 0 & -3 \\ 0 & 4 & 2 \\ -2 & 1 & 1 \end{bmatrix}.$$

The number of columns of **A** is equal to the number of rows of **B** and so the product is defined. Since **A** is $2 \times 3 \ (m \times n)$ and **B** is $3 \times 3 \ (n \times p)$, the product **C** will have order $2 \times 3 \ (m \times p)$:

$$\mathbf{C} = \begin{bmatrix} c_{11} & c_{12} & c_{13} \\ c_{21} & c_{22} & c_{23} \end{bmatrix}.$$

The entry c_{11} is obtained by summing the products of each entry in row 1 of **A** by the "corresponding" entry in column 1 of **B**. That is,

row 1 entries of **A**

$$c_{11} = (2)(1) + (1)(0) + (-6)(-2) = 14.$$

column 1 entries of **B**

Similarly, for c_{21} we use the entries in row 2 of **A** and those in column 1 of **B**:

row 2 entries of **A**

$$c_{21} = (1)(1) + (-3)(0) + (2)(-2) = -3.$$

column 1 entries of **B**

Also,

$$c_{12} = (2)(0) + (1)(4) + (-6)(1) = -2$$

$$c_{22} = (1)(0) + (-3)(4) + (2)(1) = -10$$

$$c_{13} = (2)(-3) + (1)(2) + (-6)(1) = -10$$

$$c_{23} = (1)(-3) + (-3)(2) + (2)(1) = -7.$$

Thus

$$\mathbf{AB} = \begin{bmatrix} 2 & 1 & -6 \\ 1 & -3 & 2 \end{bmatrix} \begin{bmatrix} 1 & 0 & -3 \\ 0 & 4 & 2 \\ -2 & 1 & 1 \end{bmatrix} = \begin{bmatrix} 14 & -2 & -10 \\ -3 & -10 & -7 \end{bmatrix}.$$

If we reverse the order of the factors, then

$$\mathbf{BA} = \begin{bmatrix} 1 & 0 & -3 \\ 0 & 4 & 2 \\ -2 & 1 & 1 \end{bmatrix} \begin{bmatrix} 2 & 1 & -6 \\ 1 & -3 & 2 \end{bmatrix}.$$

This product is *not* defined since the number of columns of **B** does *not* equal the number of rows of **A**. This shows that matrix multiplication is not commutative. That is, for any matrices **A** and **B** it is usually the case that $\mathbf{AB} \neq \mathbf{BA}$ (even if both products are defined).

EXAMPLE 9

Determine

$$\mathbf{AB} = \begin{bmatrix} 2 & -4 & 2 \\ 0 & 1 & -3 \end{bmatrix} \begin{bmatrix} 2 & 1 \\ 0 & 4 \\ 2 & 2 \end{bmatrix}.$$

Since **A** is 2×3 and **B** is 3×2, the product **AB** is defined and will have order 2×2. By simultaneously moving the index finger of your left hand along the rows of **A** and the index finger of your right hand along the columns of **B**, you can find mentally the entries of the product.

$$\begin{bmatrix} 2 & -4 & 2 \\ 0 & 1 & -3 \end{bmatrix} \begin{bmatrix} 2 & 1 \\ 0 & 4 \\ 2 & 2 \end{bmatrix} = \begin{bmatrix} 8 & -10 \\ -6 & -2 \end{bmatrix}.$$

EXAMPLE 10

Evaluate each of the following.

a. $[1 \quad 2 \quad 3] \begin{bmatrix} 4 \\ 5 \\ 6 \end{bmatrix}.$

The product has order 1×1:

$$[1 \quad 2 \quad 3] \begin{bmatrix} 4 \\ 5 \\ 6 \end{bmatrix} = [32].$$

b. $\begin{bmatrix} 1 \\ 2 \\ 3 \end{bmatrix} [1 \quad 6].$

The product has order 3×2:

$$\begin{bmatrix} 1 \\ 2 \\ 3 \end{bmatrix} [1 \quad 6] = \begin{bmatrix} 1 & 6 \\ 2 & 12 \\ 3 & 18 \end{bmatrix}.$$

c. $\begin{bmatrix} 1 & 3 & 0 \\ -2 & 2 & 1 \\ 1 & 0 & -4 \end{bmatrix} \begin{bmatrix} 1 & 0 & 2 \\ 5 & -1 & 3 \\ 2 & 1 & -2 \end{bmatrix} = \begin{bmatrix} 16 & -3 & 11 \\ 10 & -1 & 0 \\ -7 & -4 & 10 \end{bmatrix}.$

d. $\begin{bmatrix} a_{11} & a_{12} \\ a_{21} & a_{22} \end{bmatrix} \begin{bmatrix} b_{11} & b_{12} \\ b_{21} & b_{22} \end{bmatrix} = \begin{bmatrix} a_{11}b_{11} + a_{12}b_{21} & a_{11}b_{12} + a_{12}b_{22} \\ a_{21}b_{11} + a_{22}b_{21} & a_{21}b_{12} + a_{22}b_{22} \end{bmatrix}.$

EXAMPLE 11

Find **AB** *and* **BA** *if*

$$\mathbf{A} = \begin{bmatrix} 2 & -1 \\ 3 & 1 \end{bmatrix} \quad and \quad \mathbf{B} = \begin{bmatrix} -2 & 1 \\ 1 & 4 \end{bmatrix}.$$

We have

$$\mathbf{AB} = \begin{bmatrix} 2 & -1 \\ 3 & 1 \end{bmatrix}\begin{bmatrix} -2 & 1 \\ 1 & 4 \end{bmatrix} = \begin{bmatrix} -5 & -2 \\ -5 & 7 \end{bmatrix},$$

$$\mathbf{BA} = \begin{bmatrix} -2 & 1 \\ 1 & 4 \end{bmatrix}\begin{bmatrix} 2 & -1 \\ 3 & 1 \end{bmatrix} = \begin{bmatrix} -1 & 3 \\ 14 & 3 \end{bmatrix}.$$

Although both **AB** and **BA** are defined, **AB** ≠ **BA**.

Matrix multiplication satisfies the following properties if it is assumed that all sums and products are defined:

(1) **A(BC) = (AB)C**   Associative Property

(2) $\left.\begin{array}{l} \mathbf{A(B + C) = AB + AC} \\ \mathbf{(A + B)C = AC + BC} \end{array}\right\}$ Distributive Properties

EXAMPLE 12

If

$$\mathbf{A} = \begin{bmatrix} 1 & -2 \\ -3 & 4 \end{bmatrix}, \quad \mathbf{B} = \begin{bmatrix} 3 & 0 & -1 \\ 1 & 1 & 2 \end{bmatrix}, \quad and \quad \mathbf{C} = \begin{bmatrix} 1 & 0 \\ 0 & 2 \\ 1 & 1 \end{bmatrix},$$

find **ABC** *in two ways.*

$$\mathbf{A(BC)} = \begin{bmatrix} 1 & -2 \\ -3 & 4 \end{bmatrix}\left(\begin{bmatrix} 3 & 0 & -1 \\ 1 & 1 & 2 \end{bmatrix}\begin{bmatrix} 1 & 0 \\ 0 & 2 \\ 1 & 1 \end{bmatrix}\right)$$

$$= \begin{bmatrix} 1 & -2 \\ -3 & 4 \end{bmatrix}\begin{bmatrix} 2 & -1 \\ 3 & 4 \end{bmatrix} = \begin{bmatrix} -4 & -9 \\ 6 & 19 \end{bmatrix}.$$

$$\mathbf{(AB)C} = \left(\begin{bmatrix} 1 & -2 \\ -3 & 4 \end{bmatrix}\begin{bmatrix} 3 & 0 & -1 \\ 1 & 1 & 2 \end{bmatrix}\right)\begin{bmatrix} 1 & 0 \\ 0 & 2 \\ 1 & 1 \end{bmatrix}$$

$$= \begin{bmatrix} 1 & -2 & -5 \\ -5 & 4 & 11 \end{bmatrix} \begin{bmatrix} 1 & 0 \\ 0 & 2 \\ 1 & 1 \end{bmatrix} .$$

$$= \begin{bmatrix} -4 & -9 \\ 6 & 19 \end{bmatrix} .$$

EXAMPLE 13

Verify that $A(B + C) = AB + AC$ *if*

$$A = \begin{bmatrix} 1 & 0 \\ 2 & 3 \end{bmatrix}, \quad B = \begin{bmatrix} -2 & 0 \\ 1 & 3 \end{bmatrix}, \quad and \quad C = \begin{bmatrix} -2 & 1 \\ 0 & 2 \end{bmatrix}.$$

$$A(B + C) = \begin{bmatrix} 1 & 0 \\ 2 & 3 \end{bmatrix} \left(\begin{bmatrix} -2 & 0 \\ 1 & 3 \end{bmatrix} + \begin{bmatrix} -2 & 1 \\ 0 & 2 \end{bmatrix} \right)$$

$$= \begin{bmatrix} 1 & 0 \\ 2 & 3 \end{bmatrix} \begin{bmatrix} -4 & 1 \\ 1 & 5 \end{bmatrix} = \begin{bmatrix} -4 & 1 \\ -5 & 17 \end{bmatrix}.$$

$$AB + AC = \begin{bmatrix} 1 & 0 \\ 2 & 3 \end{bmatrix} \begin{bmatrix} -2 & 0 \\ 1 & 3 \end{bmatrix} + \begin{bmatrix} 1 & 0 \\ 2 & 3 \end{bmatrix} \begin{bmatrix} -2 & 1 \\ 0 & 2 \end{bmatrix}$$

$$= \begin{bmatrix} -2 & 0 \\ -1 & 9 \end{bmatrix} + \begin{bmatrix} -2 & 1 \\ -4 & 8 \end{bmatrix} = \begin{bmatrix} -4 & 1 \\ -5 & 17 \end{bmatrix}.$$

Thus $A(B + C) = AB + AC$.

A square matrix of order n whose main diagonal entries are all 1 and all of whose other entries are 0 is called the **identity matrix** of order n. It is denoted by **I**. For example, the identity matrices of orders 3 and 4, respectively, are

$$I = \begin{bmatrix} 1 & 0 & 0 \\ 0 & 1 & 0 \\ 0 & 0 & 1 \end{bmatrix} \quad and \quad I = \begin{bmatrix} 1 & 0 & 0 & 0 \\ 0 & 1 & 0 & 0 \\ 0 & 0 & 1 & 0 \\ 0 & 0 & 0 & 1 \end{bmatrix}.$$

If **A** is a square matrix and both **A** and **I** have the same order, then

$$AI = IA = A.$$

Thus the identity matrix plays the same role in matrix multiplication as does the number 1 in the multiplication of real numbers. For example,

$$\begin{bmatrix} 2 & 4 \\ 1 & 5 \end{bmatrix}\begin{bmatrix} 1 & 0 \\ 0 & 1 \end{bmatrix} = \begin{bmatrix} 2 & 4 \\ 1 & 5 \end{bmatrix}$$

and

$$\begin{bmatrix} 1 & 0 \\ 0 & 1 \end{bmatrix}\begin{bmatrix} 2 & 4 \\ 1 & 5 \end{bmatrix} = \begin{bmatrix} 2 & 4 \\ 1 & 5 \end{bmatrix}.$$

EXAMPLE 14

If

$$\mathbf{A} = \begin{bmatrix} 3 & 2 \\ 1 & 4 \end{bmatrix}, \quad \mathbf{B} = \begin{bmatrix} \frac{2}{5} & -\frac{1}{5} \\ -\frac{1}{10} & \frac{3}{10} \end{bmatrix}, \quad \mathbf{I} = \begin{bmatrix} 1 & 0 \\ 0 & 1 \end{bmatrix}, \quad and \quad \mathbf{O} = \begin{bmatrix} 0 & 0 \\ 0 & 0 \end{bmatrix},$$

determine
a. $\mathbf{I} - \mathbf{A}$.

$$\mathbf{I} - \mathbf{A} = \begin{bmatrix} 1 & 0 \\ 0 & 1 \end{bmatrix} - \begin{bmatrix} 3 & 2 \\ 1 & 4 \end{bmatrix} = \begin{bmatrix} -2 & -2 \\ -1 & -3 \end{bmatrix}.$$

b. $3(\mathbf{A} - 2\mathbf{I})$.

$$3(\mathbf{A} - 2\mathbf{I}) = 3\left(\begin{bmatrix} 3 & 2 \\ 1 & 4 \end{bmatrix} - 2\begin{bmatrix} 1 & 0 \\ 0 & 1 \end{bmatrix}\right)$$

$$= 3\left(\begin{bmatrix} 3 & 2 \\ 1 & 4 \end{bmatrix} - \begin{bmatrix} 2 & 0 \\ 0 & 2 \end{bmatrix}\right)$$

$$= 3\begin{bmatrix} 1 & 2 \\ 1 & 2 \end{bmatrix} = \begin{bmatrix} 3 & 6 \\ 3 & 6 \end{bmatrix}.$$

c. $\mathbf{AO}$.

$$\mathbf{AO} = \begin{bmatrix} 3 & 2 \\ 1 & 4 \end{bmatrix}\begin{bmatrix} 0 & 0 \\ 0 & 0 \end{bmatrix} = \begin{bmatrix} 0 & 0 \\ 0 & 0 \end{bmatrix} = \mathbf{O}.$$

d. $\mathbf{AB}$.

$$\mathbf{AB} = \begin{bmatrix} 3 & 2 \\ 1 & 4 \end{bmatrix}\begin{bmatrix} \frac{2}{5} & -\frac{1}{5} \\ -\frac{1}{10} & \frac{3}{10} \end{bmatrix} = \begin{bmatrix} 1 & 0 \\ 0 & 1 \end{bmatrix} = \mathbf{I}.$$

Systems of linear equations can be represented by using matrix multiplication. Consider the left side of the matrix equation

$$\begin{bmatrix} a_{11} & a_{12} \\ a_{21} & a_{22} \end{bmatrix} \begin{bmatrix} x_1 \\ x_2 \end{bmatrix} = \begin{bmatrix} c_1 \\ c_2 \end{bmatrix}. \qquad (1)$$

The product on the left side has order 2×1 and hence is a column matrix:

$$\begin{bmatrix} a_{11} x_1 + a_{12} x_2 \\ a_{21} x_1 + a_{22} x_2 \end{bmatrix} = \begin{bmatrix} c_1 \\ c_2 \end{bmatrix}.$$

By equality of matrices we must have

$$\begin{cases} a_{11} x_1 + a_{12} x_2 = c_1 \\ a_{21} x_1 + a_{22} x_2 = c_2. \end{cases}$$

Hence, a system of linear equations can be defined by a matrix equation. We usually describe Eq. (1) by saying it has the form

$$\mathbf{AX = C.}$$

EXAMPLE 15

Represent the system

$$\begin{cases} 2x_1 + 5x_2 = 4 \\ 8x_1 + 3x_2 = 7 \end{cases}$$

in terms of matrices.

If

$$\mathbf{A} = \begin{bmatrix} 2 & 5 \\ 8 & 3 \end{bmatrix}, \quad \mathbf{X} = \begin{bmatrix} x_1 \\ x_2 \end{bmatrix}, \quad \text{and} \quad \mathbf{C} = \begin{bmatrix} 4 \\ 7 \end{bmatrix},$$

then the given system is equivalent to

$$\mathbf{AX = C}$$

or

$$\begin{bmatrix} 2 & 5 \\ 8 & 3 \end{bmatrix} \begin{bmatrix} x_1 \\ x_2 \end{bmatrix} = \begin{bmatrix} 4 \\ 7 \end{bmatrix}.$$

EXAMPLE 16

Suppose the prices (in dollars per unit) for products A, B, and C are represented by the price matrix

Price of
A B C

$$\mathbf{P} = \begin{bmatrix} 2 & 3 & 4 \end{bmatrix}.$$

If the quantities (in units) of A, B, and C which are purchased are given by the column matrix

$$\mathbf{Q} = \begin{bmatrix} 7 \\ 5 \\ 11 \end{bmatrix} \begin{array}{l} \text{units of } A \\ \text{units of } B \\ \text{units of } C, \end{array}$$

then the total cost (in dollars) of the purchases is given by the entry in **PQ**:

$$\mathbf{PQ} = [2 \quad 3 \quad 4] \begin{bmatrix} 7 \\ 5 \\ 11 \end{bmatrix} = [(2 \cdot 7) + (3 \cdot 5) + (4 \cdot 11)] = [73].$$

EXAMPLE 17

Suppose a building contractor has accepted orders for five ranch-style houses, seven Cape Cod-style houses, and twelve Colonial-style houses. Then his orders can be represented by the row matrix

$$\mathbf{Q} = [5 \quad 7 \quad 12].$$

Furthermore, suppose the "raw materials" that go into each type of house are steel, wood, glass, paint, and labor. The entries in the matrix **R** below give the number of units of each raw material going into each type of house.

STEEL WOOD GLASS PAINT LABOR

$$\begin{array}{l} \textit{Ranch} \\ \textit{Cape Cod} \\ \textit{Colonial} \end{array} \begin{bmatrix} 5 & 20 & 16 & 7 & 17 \\ 7 & 18 & 12 & 9 & 21 \\ 6 & 25 & 8 & 5 & 13 \end{bmatrix} = \mathbf{R}.$$

Each row indicates the amount of each raw material needed for a given kind of house; each column indicates the amount of a given raw material needed for each type of house. Suppose now that the contractor wishes to compute the amount of each raw material needed to fulfill his contracts. Then such information is given by **QR**:

$$\mathbf{QR} = [5 \quad 7 \quad 12] \begin{bmatrix} 5 & 20 & 16 & 7 & 17 \\ 7 & 18 & 12 & 9 & 21 \\ 6 & 25 & 8 & 5 & 13 \end{bmatrix}$$

$$= [146 \quad 526 \quad 260 \quad 158 \quad 388].$$

Thus, the contractor should order 146 units of steel, 526 units of wood, 260 units of glass, etc.

The contractor is also interested in the costs he will have to pay for these materials. Suppose steel costs $15 per unit, wood costs $8 per unit, and glass, paint, and labor cost $5, $1, and $10 per unit, respectively. These data can be written as the column cost matrix

$$C = \begin{bmatrix} 15 \\ 8 \\ 5 \\ 1 \\ 10 \end{bmatrix}.$$

Then **RC** gives the cost of each type of house:

$$RC = \begin{bmatrix} 5 & 20 & 16 & 7 & 17 \\ 7 & 18 & 12 & 9 & 21 \\ 6 & 25 & 8 & 5 & 13 \end{bmatrix} \begin{bmatrix} 15 \\ 8 \\ 5 \\ 1 \\ 10 \end{bmatrix} = \begin{bmatrix} 492 \\ 528 \\ 465 \end{bmatrix}.$$

Thus, the cost of materials for the ranch-style house is $492, for the Cape Cod house, $528, and for the Colonial house, $465.

The total cost of raw materials for all the houses is given by

$$QRC = Q(RC) = \begin{bmatrix} 5 & 7 & 12 \end{bmatrix} \begin{bmatrix} 492 \\ 528 \\ 465 \end{bmatrix} = [11,736].$$

The total cost is $11,736.

EXAMPLE 18

In Example 8 of Sec. 14-2, suppose the price of coal is $1 per unit, the price of electricity is $2 per unit, and the price of steel is $4 per unit. These prices can be represented by the (column) price matrix

$$P = \begin{bmatrix} 1 \\ 2 \\ 4 \end{bmatrix}.$$

Consider the steel industry. It sells a total of 30 units of steel at $4 per unit and its total income is therefore $120. Its costs for the various goods are given by the matrix product

$$D_S P = \begin{bmatrix} 30 & 5 & 0 \end{bmatrix} \begin{bmatrix} 1 \\ 2 \\ 4 \end{bmatrix} = [40].$$

Hence the profit for the steel industry is $120 − $40 = $80.

EXERCISE 14-3

If

$$A = \begin{bmatrix} 1 & 3 & -2 \\ -2 & 1 & -1 \\ 0 & 4 & 3 \end{bmatrix}, \quad B = \begin{bmatrix} 0 & -2 & 3 \\ -2 & 4 & -2 \\ 3 & 1 & -1 \end{bmatrix},$$

and $AB = C$, find

1. c_{11}
2. c_{23}

3. c_{32}
4. c_{33}

5. c_{22}
6. c_{13}

If A is 2×3, B is 3×1, C is 2×5, D is 4×3, E is 3×2, and F is 2×3, find the order and number of entries of

7. AE
8. DE

9. EC
10. DB

11. FB
12. BA

13. EA
14. E(AE)

15. E(FB)
16. (F + A)B

Write the identity matrix of order

17. 4
18. 6

In problems 19–34 perform the indicated operations.

19. $\begin{bmatrix} 2 & -4 \\ 3 & 2 \end{bmatrix} \begin{bmatrix} 3 & 0 \\ -1 & 4 \end{bmatrix}$

20. $\begin{bmatrix} -1 & 1 \\ 0 & 4 \\ 2 & 1 \end{bmatrix} \begin{bmatrix} 1 & -2 \\ 3 & 4 \end{bmatrix}$

21. $\begin{bmatrix} 2 & 0 & 3 \\ -1 & 4 & 5 \end{bmatrix} \begin{bmatrix} 1 \\ 4 \\ 7 \end{bmatrix}$

22. $\begin{bmatrix} 1 & 0 & 6 & 2 \end{bmatrix} \begin{bmatrix} 0 \\ 1 \\ 2 \\ 3 \end{bmatrix}$

23. $\begin{bmatrix} 1 & 4 & -1 \\ 0 & 0 & 2 \\ -2 & 1 & 1 \end{bmatrix} \begin{bmatrix} -2 & 1 & 0 \\ 0 & 1 & 1 \\ 1 & 1 & 2 \end{bmatrix}$

24. $\begin{bmatrix} 3 & 2 & -1 \\ 4 & 10 & 0 \\ 0 & 1 & 2 \end{bmatrix} \begin{bmatrix} 2 & 0 & 1 & 0 \\ 0 & 1 & 0 & 0 \\ 0 & 1 & 0 & 1 \end{bmatrix}$

25. $\begin{bmatrix} -1 & 2 & 3 \end{bmatrix} \begin{bmatrix} 3 & 1 & -1 & 2 \\ 0 & 4 & 3 & 1 \\ -1 & 3 & 1 & -2 \end{bmatrix}$

26. $\begin{bmatrix} 1 & -4 \end{bmatrix} \begin{bmatrix} -2 & 1 \\ 0 & 5 \\ 1 & 0 \end{bmatrix}$

27. $\begin{bmatrix} 2 \\ 3 \\ -4 \\ 1 \end{bmatrix}$ [2 3 -2 3]

28. $\begin{bmatrix} 0 & 1 \\ 2 & 3 \end{bmatrix} \left(\begin{bmatrix} 1 & 0 & 1 \\ 0 & 1 & 0 \end{bmatrix} + \begin{bmatrix} 0 & 1 & 0 \\ 0 & 0 & 1 \end{bmatrix} \right)$

29. $3 \left(\begin{bmatrix} -2 & 0 & 2 \\ 3 & -1 & 1 \end{bmatrix} + 2 \begin{bmatrix} -1 & 0 & 2 \\ 1 & 1 & -2 \end{bmatrix} \right) \begin{bmatrix} 1 & 2 \\ 3 & 4 \\ 5 & 6 \end{bmatrix}$

30. $\begin{bmatrix} -1 & 3 \\ -1 & 0 \end{bmatrix} \begin{bmatrix} -1 & 0 & 2 & -1 \\ 2 & 1 & -3 & -2 \end{bmatrix}$

31. $\begin{bmatrix} 1 & 2 \\ 3 & 4 \end{bmatrix} \left(\begin{bmatrix} 2 & 0 & 1 \\ 1 & 0 & -2 \end{bmatrix} \begin{bmatrix} 1 & -2 \\ 2 & 1 \\ 3 & 0 \end{bmatrix} \right)$

32. $3 \begin{bmatrix} 1 & 2 \\ -1 & 4 \end{bmatrix} - 4 \left(\begin{bmatrix} 1 & 0 \\ 0 & 1 \end{bmatrix} \begin{bmatrix} -2 & 4 \\ 6 & 1 \end{bmatrix} \right)$

33. $\begin{bmatrix} 1 & 0 & 0 \\ 0 & 1 & 0 \\ 0 & 0 & 1 \end{bmatrix} \begin{bmatrix} x \\ y \\ z \end{bmatrix}$

34. $\begin{bmatrix} a_{11} & a_{12} \\ a_{21} & a_{22} \end{bmatrix} \begin{bmatrix} x_1 \\ x_2 \end{bmatrix}$

In problems 35–49 compute the required matrices if

$$A = \begin{bmatrix} 1 & -2 \\ 0 & 3 \end{bmatrix} \qquad B = \begin{bmatrix} -2 & 3 & 0 \\ 1 & -4 & 1 \end{bmatrix} \qquad C = \begin{bmatrix} -1 & 1 \\ 0 & 3 \\ 2 & 4 \end{bmatrix}$$

$$D = \begin{bmatrix} 1 & 0 & 0 \\ 0 & 1 & 1 \\ 1 & 2 & 1 \end{bmatrix} \qquad E = [1 \quad 2 \quad 4] \qquad F = \begin{bmatrix} 2 \\ 1 \end{bmatrix}$$

$$G = \begin{bmatrix} 3 & 0 & 0 \\ 0 & 6 & 0 \\ 0 & 0 & 3 \end{bmatrix} \qquad H = \begin{bmatrix} \frac{1}{3} & 0 & 0 \\ 0 & \frac{1}{6} & 0 \\ 0 & 0 & \frac{1}{3} \end{bmatrix} \qquad I = \begin{bmatrix} 1 & 0 & 0 \\ 0 & 1 & 0 \\ 0 & 0 & 1 \end{bmatrix}.$$

35. AB

36. BD

37. CF

38. FE − 3B

39. DG

40. $D^2 (= DD)$

41. EC

42. GC

43. $DI - \frac{1}{3} G$

44. B(D + G)

45. 3A − 2BC

46. G(2D − 3I)

47. $2I - \frac{1}{2} GH$

48. A(BC)

49. (DC)A

In problems 50–53 represent the given system using matrix multiplication.

$$\begin{vmatrix} 1 & 1 & 1 \\ 1 & -1 & 1 \\ 2 & -1 & 3 \end{vmatrix} \times \begin{vmatrix} x \\ y \\ z \end{vmatrix} = \begin{vmatrix} 6 \\ 2 \\ 6 \end{vmatrix}$$

50. $\begin{cases} 2x - y = 4 \\ 3x + y = 5 \end{cases}$

51. $\begin{cases} 3x + y = 6 \\ 7x - 2y = 5 \end{cases}$

52. $\begin{cases} x + y + z = 6 \\ x - y + z = 2 \\ 2x - y + 3z = 6 \end{cases}$

53. $\begin{cases} 4r - s + 3t = 9 \\ 3r \quad - t = 7 \\ 3s + 2t = 15 \end{cases}$

54. A stock broker sold a customer 200 shares of Stock A, 300 shares of Stock B, 500 shares of Stock C, and 250 shares of Stock D. The prices per share of A, B, C, and D are \$100, \$150, \$200, and \$300, respectively. Write a row matrix representing the number of shares of each stock bought. Write a column matrix representing the price per share of each stock. Using matrix multiplication, find the total cost of the stocks.

55. In Example 17 assume that the contractor is to build seven ranch-style, three Cape Cod, and five Colonial-type houses. Compute, using matrix multiplication, the total cost of raw materials.

56. In Example 17 assume that the contractor wishes to take into account the cost of transporting raw materials to the building site as well as the purchasing cost. Suppose the costs are given in the matrix below.

	Purchase	Transport	
	15	4.5	Steel
	8	2	Wood
$\mathbf{C} =$	5	3	Glass
	1	0.5	Paint
	10	0	Labor

a. By computing $\mathbf{RC}$, find a matrix whose entries give the purchase and transportation costs of the materials for each kind of house.

b. Find the matrix $\mathbf{QRC}$ whose first entry gives the total purchase price and whose second entry gives the total transportation cost.

c. Let $\mathbf{Z} = \begin{bmatrix} 1 \\ 1 \end{bmatrix}$ and then compute $\mathbf{QRCZ}$, which gives the total cost of materials and transportation for all houses being built.

57. Perform the following calculations for Example 18:

a. Compute the amount that each industry and each consumer have to pay for the goods they receive.

b. Compute the profit earned by each industry.

c. Find the total amount of money that is paid out by all the industries and consumers.

d. Find the proportion of the total amount of money found in (c) paid out by the industries. Find the proportion of the total amount of money found in (c) that is paid out by the consumers.

14-4 METHOD OF REDUCTION

In this section we shall illustrate a method by which matrices can be used to solve a system of linear equations, *the method of reduction*. In introducing the method we shall first solve a system in the usual way. Then we shall obtain the same solution by using matrices.

Let us consider the system

$$\begin{cases} 3x - y = 1 & \text{(1)} \\ x + 2y = 5 & \text{(2)} \end{cases}$$

consisting of two linear equations in two unknowns, x and y. Although this system can be solved by various algebraic methods, we shall solve it by a method which is readily adapted to matrices.

For reasons that will be obvious later, we begin by replacing Eq. (1) by Eq. (2), and Eq. (2) by Eq. (1), thus obtaining the equivalent system

$$\begin{cases} x + 2y = 5 & \text{(3)} \\ 3x - y = 1. & \text{(4)} \end{cases}$$

In $x + 2y = 5$, multiplying both sides by -3 gives $-3x - 6y = -15$. Adding the left and right sides of this equation to the corresponding sides of Eq. (4) gives the equivalent system

$$\begin{cases} x + 2y = 5 & \text{(5)} \\ 0x - 7y = -14. & \text{(6)} \end{cases}$$

Multiplying both sides of Eq. (6) by $-\frac{1}{7}$ gives the equivalent system

$$\begin{cases} x + 2y = 5 & \text{(7)} \\ 0x + y = 2. & \text{(8)} \end{cases}$$

By Eq. (8), $y = 2$ and hence $-2y = -4$. Adding the sides of $-2y = -4$ to the corresponding sides of Eq. (7), we get the equivalent system

$$\begin{cases} x + 0y = 1 \\ 0x + y = 2. \end{cases}$$

Therefore, $x = 1$ and $y = 2$, and the original system is solved.

Before showing a method of solving

$$\begin{cases} 3x - y = 1 \\ x + 2y = 5 \end{cases}$$

by matrices, we first define some terms. We say that the matrix

$$\begin{bmatrix} 3 & -1 \\ 1 & 2 \end{bmatrix}$$

is the **coefficient matrix** of this system. The entries in the first column correspond to the coefficients of the x's in the equations. For example, the entry in the first row and first column corresponds to the coefficient of x in the first equation; the entry in the second row and first column corresponds to the coefficient of x in the second equation. Similarly, the entries in the second column correspond to the coefficients of the y's.

Another matrix associated with this system is called the **augmented coefficient matrix** and is given by

$$\begin{bmatrix} 3 & -1 & \vdots & 1 \\ 1 & 2 & \vdots & 5 \end{bmatrix}.$$

The first and second columns are the first and second columns, respectively, of the coefficient matrix. The entries in the third column correspond to the constant terms in the system: the entry in the first row of this column is the constant term of the first equation, while the entry in the second row is the constant term of the second equation. Although it is not necessary to include the broken line in the augmented coefficient matrix, it serves to remind us that the 1 and the 5 are the constant terms that appear on the right sides of the equations. The augmented coefficient matrix itself completely describes the system of equations.

The procedure which was used to solve the original system involved a number of equivalent systems. With each of these systems we can associate its augmented coefficient matrix. Listed below are the systems that were involved, together with their corresponding augmented coefficient matrices which we have labeled **A, B, C, D,** and **E.**

$$\begin{cases} 3x - y = 1 \\ x + 2y = 5 \end{cases} \qquad \begin{bmatrix} 3 & -1 & \vdots & 1 \\ 1 & 2 & \vdots & 5 \end{bmatrix} = \mathbf{A}$$

$$\begin{cases} x + 2y = 5 \\ 3x - y = 1 \end{cases} \qquad \begin{bmatrix} 1 & 2 & \vdots & 5 \\ 3 & -1 & \vdots & 1 \end{bmatrix} = \mathbf{B}$$

$$\begin{cases} x + 2y = 5 \\ 0x - 7y = -14 \end{cases} \qquad \begin{bmatrix} 1 & 2 & \vdots & 5 \\ 0 & -7 & \vdots & -14 \end{bmatrix} = \mathbf{C}$$

$$\begin{cases} x + 2y = 5 \\ 0x + y = 2 \end{cases} \qquad \begin{bmatrix} 1 & 2 & \vdots & 5 \\ 0 & 1 & \vdots & 2 \end{bmatrix} = \mathbf{D}$$

$$\begin{cases} x + 0y = 1 \\ 0x + y = 2 \end{cases} \qquad \begin{bmatrix} 1 & 0 & \vdots & 1 \\ 0 & 1 & \vdots & 2 \end{bmatrix} = \mathbf{E}.$$

Let us see how these matrices are related.

B can be obtained from **A** by interchanging the first and second rows of **A**. This operation corresponds to the interchanging of the two equations in the original system.

C can be obtained from **B** by adding to each entry in the second row of **B**, -3 times the corresponding entry in the first row of **B**.

$$\mathbf{C} = \begin{bmatrix} 1 & 2 & \vdots & 5 \\ 3 + (-3)(1) & -1 + (-3)(2) & \vdots & 1 + (-3)(5) \end{bmatrix}$$

$$= \begin{bmatrix} 1 & 2 & \vdots & 5 \\ 0 & -7 & \vdots & -14 \end{bmatrix}.$$

This operation is described as the addition of -3 times the first row of **B** to the second row of **B**.

D can be obtained from **C** by multiplying each entry in the second row of **C** by $-\frac{1}{7}$. This operation is referred to as multiplying the second row of **C** by $-\frac{1}{7}$.

E can be obtained from **D** by adding -2 times the second row of **D** to the first row of **D**.

Observe that **E**, which essentially gives the solution, can be obtained from **A** by a series of operations which include:

(1) **interchanging two rows of a matrix;**
(2) **adding a multiple of one row of a matrix to another row of that matrix;**
(3) **multiplying a row of a matrix by a nonzero scalar.**

We refer to these operations as **elementary row operations.** Whenever a matrix can be obtained from another by one or more elementary row operations, we say that the matrices are **equivalent.** Thus **A** is equivalent to **E**, and we write $\mathbf{A} \sim \mathbf{E}$.

We are now ready to describe a matrix procedure for solving a system of linear equations. First, form the augmented coefficient matrix of the system; then, by means of elementary row operations, determine an equivalent matrix which clearly indicates the solution. Let us be quite specific as to what we mean by a matrix which clearly indicates the solution. It is a matrix, called a **reduced matrix,** such that

(1) **the first nonzero entry in each row is 1 while all other entries in the column in which the 1 appears are zeros,**

(2) **the first nonzero entry in each row is to the right of the first nonzero entry of each preceding row,**

(3) **each row that consists entirely of zeros is below each row which contains a nonzero entry.**†

In other words, to solve the system we must find a reduced matrix such that the augmented coefficient matrix is equivalent to it. Note that **E** above,

$$\mathbf{E} = \begin{bmatrix} 1 & 0 & \vdots & 1 \\ 0 & 1 & \vdots & 2 \end{bmatrix},$$

is a reduced matrix.

EXAMPLE 19

For each matrix below, determine whether it is reduced or not reduced.

a. $\begin{bmatrix} 1 & 0 \\ 0 & 3 \end{bmatrix}$
    b. $\begin{bmatrix} 1 & 0 & 0 \\ 0 & 1 & 0 \end{bmatrix}$

c. $\begin{bmatrix} 0 & 1 \\ 1 & 0 \end{bmatrix}$
    d. $\begin{bmatrix} 0 & 0 & 0 \\ 0 & 0 & 0 \end{bmatrix}$

e. $\begin{bmatrix} 1 & 0 & 0 \\ 0 & 0 & 0 \\ 0 & 1 & 0 \end{bmatrix}$
    f. $\begin{bmatrix} 0 & 1 & 0 & 3 \\ 0 & 0 & 1 & 2 \\ 0 & 0 & 0 & 0 \end{bmatrix}$

a. Not a reduced matrix since the first nonzero entry in the second row is not 1.

b. Reduced matrix.

c. Not a reduced matrix since the first nonzero entry in the second row is not to the right of the first nonzero entry in the first row.

d. Reduced matrix.

e. Not a reduced matrix since the second row, consisting entirely of zeros, is not below each row which contains nonzero entries.

f. Reduced matrix.

The method of reduction we have described for solving our original system can be generalized to systems consisting of m linear equations in n unknowns. To solve such a system as

---

†From Paul C. Shields, *Elementary Linear Algebra* (New York: Worth Publishers, Inc., 2nd ed., 1973), p. 7.

$$\begin{cases} a_{11}x_1 + a_{12}x_2 + \cdots + a_{1n}x_n = c_1 \\ a_{21}x_1 + a_{22}x_2 + \cdots + a_{2n}x_n = c_2 \\ \quad\vdots \qquad\quad \vdots \qquad\qquad\quad \vdots \qquad \vdots \\ a_{m1}x_1 + a_{m2}x_2 + \cdots + a_{mn}x_n = c_m \end{cases}$$

involves

i. determining the augmented coefficient matrix of the system:

$$\begin{bmatrix} a_{11} & a_{12} & \cdots & a_{1n} & \vdots & c_1 \\ a_{21} & a_{22} & \cdots & a_{2n} & \vdots & c_2 \\ \vdots & \vdots & & \vdots & \vdots & \vdots \\ a_{m1} & a_{m2} & \cdots & a_{mn} & \vdots & c_m \end{bmatrix}$$

and

ii. determining a reduced matrix such that the augmented coefficient matrix is equivalent to it.

Frequently, step ii is called *reducing the augmented coefficient matrix.*

EXAMPLE 20

By using matrix reduction, solve the system

$$\begin{cases} 2x + 3y = -1 \\ 2x + \;\; y = \;\;\; 5 \\ \;\; x + \;\; y = \;\;\; 1. \end{cases}$$

The augmented coefficient matrix of the system is

$$\begin{bmatrix} 2 & 3 & \vdots & -1 \\ 2 & 1 & \vdots & 5 \\ 1 & 1 & \vdots & 1 \end{bmatrix}.$$

Reducing this matrix, we have

$$\begin{bmatrix} 2 & 3 & \vdots & -1 \\ 2 & 1 & \vdots & 5 \\ 1 & 1 & \vdots & 1 \end{bmatrix}$$

$$\sim \begin{bmatrix} 1 & 1 & \vdots & 1 \\ 2 & 1 & \vdots & 5 \\ 2 & 3 & \vdots & -1 \end{bmatrix}$$
(by interchanging the first and third rows)

$$\sim \begin{bmatrix} 1 & 1 & \vdots & 1 \\ 0 & -1 & \vdots & 3 \\ 2 & 3 & \vdots & -1 \end{bmatrix}$$
(by adding -2 times the first row to the second)

$$\sim \begin{bmatrix} 1 & 1 & \vdots & 1 \\ 0 & -1 & \vdots & 3 \\ 0 & 1 & \vdots & -3 \end{bmatrix}$$
(by adding -2 times the first row to the third)

$$\sim \begin{bmatrix} 1 & 1 & \vdots & 1 \\ 0 & 1 & \vdots & -3 \\ 0 & 1 & \vdots & -3 \end{bmatrix}$$
(by multiplying the second row by -1)

$$\sim \begin{bmatrix} 1 & 0 & \vdots & 4 \\ 0 & 1 & \vdots & -3 \\ 0 & 1 & \vdots & -3 \end{bmatrix}$$
(by adding -1 times the second row to the first)

$$\sim \begin{bmatrix} 1 & 0 & \vdots & 4 \\ 0 & 1 & \vdots & -3 \\ 0 & 0 & \vdots & 0 \end{bmatrix}$$
(by adding -1 times the second row to the third).

The last matrix is reduced and corresponds to the system

$$\begin{cases} x + 0y = & 4 \\ 0x + y = & -3 \\ 0x + 0y = & 0. \end{cases}$$

Since the original system is equivalent to this system, it has a unique solution, namely

$$x = \quad 4$$
$$y = -3.$$

EXAMPLE 21

Using matrix reduction, solve

$$\begin{cases} x + 2y + 4z - 6 = 0 \\ 2z + y - 3 = 0 \\ x + y + 2z - 1 = 0. \end{cases}$$

Rewriting the system so that the variables are aligned and the constant terms appear on the right sides of the equations, we have

$$\begin{cases} x + 2y + 4z = 6 \\ y + 2z = 3 \\ x + y + 2z = 1. \end{cases}$$

Reducing the augmented coefficient matrix, we have

$$\begin{bmatrix} 1 & 2 & 4 & \vdots & 6 \\ 0 & 1 & 2 & \vdots & 3 \\ 1 & 1 & 2 & \vdots & 1 \end{bmatrix}$$

$$\sim \begin{bmatrix} 1 & 2 & 4 & \vdots & 6 \\ 0 & 1 & 2 & \vdots & 3 \\ 0 & -1 & -2 & \vdots & -5 \end{bmatrix} \qquad \text{(by adding } -1 \text{ times the first row to the third)}$$

$$\sim \begin{bmatrix} 1 & 0 & 0 & \vdots & 0 \\ 0 & 1 & 2 & \vdots & 3 \\ 0 & 0 & 0 & \vdots & -2 \end{bmatrix} \qquad \begin{array}{l} \text{(by adding } -2 \text{ times the second row to the first, and} \\ \text{adding the second row to the third)} \end{array}$$

$$\sim \begin{bmatrix} 1 & 0 & 0 & \vdots & 0 \\ 0 & 1 & 2 & \vdots & 3 \\ 0 & 0 & 0 & \vdots & 1 \end{bmatrix} \qquad \text{(by multiplying the third row by } -\tfrac{1}{2}).$$

The last matrix is reduced and corresponds to

$$\begin{cases} x = 0 \\ y + 2z = 3 \\ 0 = 1. \end{cases}$$

Since $0 \neq 1$, there are no values of x, y, and z for which all equations are satisfied simultaneously. Thus, the original system has no solution.

EXAMPLE 22

Using matrix reduction, solve

$$\begin{cases} 2x_1 + 3x_2 + 2x_3 + 6x_4 = 10 \\ x_2 + 2x_3 + x_4 = 2 \\ 3x_1 - 3x_3 + 6x_4 = 9. \end{cases}$$

Reducing the augmented coefficient matrix, we have

$$\begin{bmatrix} 2 & 3 & 2 & 6 & \vdots & 10 \\ 0 & 1 & 2 & 1 & \vdots & 2 \\ 3 & 0 & -3 & 6 & \vdots & 9 \end{bmatrix}$$

$$\sim \begin{bmatrix} 1 & \frac{3}{2} & 1 & 3 & \vdots & 5 \\ 0 & 1 & 2 & 1 & \vdots & 2 \\ 3 & 0 & -3 & 6 & \vdots & 9 \end{bmatrix} \quad \text{(by multiplying the first row by } \tfrac{1}{2}\text{)}$$

$$\sim \begin{bmatrix} 1 & \frac{3}{2} & 1 & 3 & \vdots & 5 \\ 0 & 1 & 2 & 1 & \vdots & 2 \\ 0 & -\frac{9}{2} & -6 & -3 & \vdots & -6 \end{bmatrix} \quad \text{(by adding } -3 \text{ times the first row to the third)}$$

$$\sim \begin{bmatrix} 1 & 0 & -2 & \frac{3}{2} & \vdots & 2 \\ 0 & 1 & 2 & 1 & \vdots & 2 \\ 0 & 0 & 3 & \frac{3}{2} & \vdots & 3 \end{bmatrix} \quad \begin{matrix}\text{(by adding } -\tfrac{3}{2} \text{ times the second row to the}\\ \text{first, and adding } \tfrac{9}{2} \text{ times the second row to the}\\ \text{third)}\end{matrix}$$

$$\sim \begin{bmatrix} 1 & 0 & -2 & \frac{3}{2} & \vdots & 2 \\ 0 & 1 & 2 & 1 & \vdots & 2 \\ 0 & 0 & 1 & \frac{1}{2} & \vdots & 1 \end{bmatrix} \quad \text{(by multiplying the third row by } \tfrac{1}{3}\text{)}$$

$$\sim \begin{bmatrix} 1 & 0 & 0 & \frac{5}{2} & \vdots & 4 \\ 0 & 1 & 0 & 0 & \vdots & 0 \\ 0 & 0 & 1 & \frac{1}{2} & \vdots & 1 \end{bmatrix} \quad \begin{matrix}\text{(by adding 2 times the third row to the first,}\\ \text{and adding } -2 \text{ times the third row to the}\\ \text{second).}\end{matrix}$$

The last matrix is reduced and corresponds to the system

$$\begin{cases} x_1 + \dfrac{5}{2} x_4 = 4 \\ \qquad\quad x_2 = 0 \\ x_3 + \dfrac{1}{2} x_4 = 1. \end{cases}$$

Thus,

$$x_1 = -\frac{5}{2} x_4 + 4 \qquad\qquad (9)$$

$$x_2 = 0 \qquad\qquad (10)$$

$$x_3 = -\frac{1}{2}x_4 + 1 \qquad (11)$$

$$x_4 = x_4. \qquad (12)$$

If x_4 is any real number, then Eqs. (9)-(12) determine a particular solution to the original system. For example if $x_4 = 0$, then a *particular* solution is $x_1 = 4$, $x_2 = 0$, $x_3 = 1$, and $x_4 = 0$. If $x_4 = 2$, then $x_1 = -1$, $x_2 = 0$, $x_3 = 0$, and $x_4 = 2$ is a particular solution. The variable x_4, on which x_1 and x_3 depend, is called a *parameter*. Clearly, there are an infinite number of solutions to the system—one corresponding to each value of the parameter. We say that the *general* solution of the original system is given by Eqs. (9)-(12).

EXERCISE 14-4

In each of problems 1-6, determine whether the matrix is reduced or not reduced.

1. $\begin{bmatrix} 1 & 2 \\ 3 & 0 \end{bmatrix}$
   2. $\begin{bmatrix} 1 & 0 & 0 & 3 \\ 0 & 0 & 1 & 2 \end{bmatrix}$
   3. $\begin{bmatrix} 1 & 0 & 0 \\ 0 & 1 & 0 \\ 0 & 0 & 1 \end{bmatrix}$

4. $\begin{bmatrix} 1 & 1 \\ 0 & 1 \\ 0 & 0 \\ 0 & 0 \end{bmatrix}$
   5. $\begin{bmatrix} 0 & 0 & 0 & 0 \\ 0 & 1 & 0 & 0 \\ 0 & 0 & 1 & 0 \\ 0 & 0 & 0 & 0 \end{bmatrix}$
   6. $\begin{bmatrix} 0 & 0 & 5 \\ 1 & 0 & 4 \\ 0 & 1 & 2 \\ 0 & 0 & 0 \end{bmatrix}$

In each of problems 7-12, reduce the given matrix.

7. $\begin{bmatrix} 1 & 3 \\ 4 & 0 \end{bmatrix}$
   8. $\begin{bmatrix} 0 & -2 & 0 & 1 \\ 1 & 2 & 0 & 4 \end{bmatrix}$
   9. $\begin{bmatrix} 2 & 4 & 6 \\ 1 & 2 & 3 \\ 1 & 2 & 3 \end{bmatrix}$

10. $\begin{bmatrix} 2 & 3 \\ 1 & -6 \\ 4 & 8 \\ 1 & 7 \end{bmatrix}$
   11. $\begin{bmatrix} 2 & 0 & 3 & 1 \\ 1 & 4 & 2 & 2 \\ -1 & 3 & 1 & 4 \\ 0 & 2 & 1 & 0 \end{bmatrix}$
   12. $\begin{bmatrix} 0 & 0 & 2 \\ 2 & 0 & 3 \\ 0 & -1 & 0 \\ 0 & 4 & 1 \end{bmatrix}$

Solve problems 13-26 by the method of reduction.

13. $\begin{cases} 2x + 3y = 5 \\ x - 2y = -1 \end{cases}$
   14. $\begin{cases} x - 3y = -11 \\ 4x + 3y = 9 \end{cases}$

15. $\begin{cases} 3x + y = 4 \\ 12x + 4y = 2 \end{cases}$
   16. $\begin{cases} x + 2y - 3z = 0 \\ -2x - 4y + 6z = 1 \end{cases}$

17. $\begin{cases} x + 2y + z - 4 = 0 \\ 3x \quad\quad + 2z - 5 = 0 \end{cases}$

18. $\begin{cases} x + 2y + 5z - 1 = 0 \\ x + y + 3z - 2 = 0 \end{cases}$

19. $\begin{cases} x_1 - 3x_2 = 0 \\ 2x_1 + 2x_2 = 3 \\ 5x_1 - x_2 = 1 \end{cases}$

20. $\begin{cases} x_1 + 3x_2 = 5 \\ 2x_1 + x_2 = 5 \\ x_1 + x_2 = 3 \end{cases}$

21. $\begin{cases} x - y - 3z = -4 \\ 2x - y - 4z = -7 \\ x + y - z = -2 \end{cases}$

22. $\begin{cases} x + y - z = 6 \\ 2x - 3y - 2z = 2 \\ x - y - 5z = 18 \end{cases}$

23. $\begin{cases} 2x \quad\quad - 4z = 8 \\ x - 2y - 2z = 14 \\ x + y - 2z = -1 \\ 3x + y + z = 0 \end{cases}$

24. $\begin{cases} x \quad\quad + 3z = -1 \\ 3x + 2y + 11z = 1 \\ x + y + 4z = 1 \\ 2x - 3y + 3z = -8 \end{cases}$

25. $\begin{cases} x_1 + x_2 - x_3 + x_4 + x_5 = 0 \\ x_1 + x_2 + x_3 - x_4 + x_5 = 0 \\ x_1 - x_2 - x_3 + x_4 - x_5 = 0 \\ x_1 + x_2 - x_3 - x_4 - x_5 = 0 \end{cases}$

26. $\begin{cases} x_1 + x_2 - x_3 + x_4 = 0 \\ x_1 + x_2 + x_3 - x_4 = 0 \\ x_1 - x_2 - x_3 + x_4 = 0 \\ x_1 + x_2 - x_3 - x_4 = 0 \end{cases}$

Solve problems 27–31 by using matrix reduction.

27. A company has taxable income of $312,000. The federal tax is 25 percent of that portion which is left after the state tax has been paid. The state tax is 10 percent of that portion which is left after the federal tax has been paid. Find the federal and state taxes.

28. A manufacturer produces two products, A and B. For each unit of A sold the profit is $8, and for each unit of B sold the profit is $11. From past experience it has been found that 25 percent more of A can be sold than of B. Next year the manufacturer desires a total profit of $42,000. How many units of each product must be sold?

29. A manufacturer produces three products, A, B, and C. The profits for each unit sold of A, B, and C are $1, 2, and $3, respectively. Fixed costs are $17,000 per year and the costs of producing each unit of A, B, and C are $4, $5, and $7, respectively. Next year, a total of 11,000 units of all three products is to be produced and sold, and a total profit of $25,000 is to be realized. If total cost is to be $80,000, how many units of each of the products should be produced next year?

30. National Totem Pole Co. has plants for producing totem poles on both the east and west coasts. At the east coast plant, fixed costs are $16,000 per year and the cost of producing each totem pole is $90. At the west coast plant, fixed costs are $20,000 per year and the cost of producing each totem pole is $80. Next year the company wants to produce a total of 800 totem poles. Determine the production order for each plant for the forthcoming year if the total cost for each plant is to be the same.

31. A man is ordered by his doctor to take 10 units of vitamin A, 9 units of vitamin D, and 19 units of vitamin E each day. The man can choose from three brands of vitamin pills. Brand X contains two units of vitamin A, three units of vitamin D, and five units of vitamin E; brand Y has 1, 3, and 4 units, respectively; and brand Z has 1 unit of vitamin A, none of vitamin D, and 1 of vitamin E.
   a. Find all possible combinations of pills that will provide exactly the required amounts of vitamins.
   b. If brand X costs 1¢ a pill, brand Y 6¢, and brand Z 3¢, is there a solution costing exactly 15¢ a day?
   c. What is the least expensive solution? The most expensive?

14-5 METHOD OF REDUCTION (CONTINUED)

As we saw in Sec. 14-4, a system of linear equations may have a unique solution, no solution, or an infinite number of solutions. When there are infinitely many, the general solution is expressed in terms of at least one parameter. For example, the general solution in Example 22 was given in terms of the parameter x_4:

$$x_1 = -\tfrac{5}{2}x_4 + 4$$

$$x_2 = 0$$

$$x_3 = -\tfrac{1}{2}x_4 + 1$$

$$x_4 = x_4.$$

At times, more than one parameter is necessary, as the following example shows.

EXAMPLE 23

Using matrix reduction, solve

$$\begin{cases} x_1 + 2x_2 + 5x_3 + 5x_4 = -3 \\ x_1 + x_2 + 3x_3 + 4x_4 = -1 \\ x_1 - x_2 - x_3 + 2x_4 = 3. \end{cases}$$

The augmented coefficient matrix is

$$\begin{bmatrix} 1 & 2 & 5 & 5 & \vdots & -3 \\ 1 & 1 & 3 & 4 & \vdots & -1 \\ 1 & -1 & -1 & 2 & \vdots & 3 \end{bmatrix},$$

which is equivalent to the reduced matrix

$$\begin{bmatrix} 1 & 0 & 1 & 3 & \vdots & 1 \\ 0 & 1 & 2 & 1 & \vdots & -2 \\ 0 & 0 & 0 & 0 & \vdots & 0 \end{bmatrix}.$$

Hence,

$$\begin{cases} x_1 + x_3 + 3x_4 = 1 \\ x_2 + 2x_3 + x_4 = -2. \end{cases}$$

Thus the general solution can be given by

$$x_1 = 1 - x_3 - 3x_4$$

$$x_2 = -2 - 2x_3 - x_4$$

$$x_3 = x_3$$

$$x_4 = x_4,$$

where parameters x_3 and x_4 are involved. By assigning specific values to x_3 and x_4, we get particular solutions. For example, if $x_3 = 1$ and $x_4 = 2$, then the corresponding particular solution is $x_1 = -6$, $x_2 = -6$, $x_3 = 1$, and $x_4 = 2$.

It is customary to classify a system of linear equations as being either *homogeneous* or *nonhomogeneous*. The appropriate classification depends on the constant terms; as the following definition indicates.

DEFINITION.   *The system*

$$\begin{cases} a_{11}x_1 + a_{12}x_2 + \cdots + a_{1n}x_n = c_1 \\ a_{21}x_1 + a_{22}x_2 + \cdots + a_{2n}x_n = c_2 \\ \vdots \qquad\quad \vdots \qquad\qquad\quad \vdots \qquad\quad \vdots \\ a_{m1}x_1 + a_{m2}x_2 + \cdots + a_{mn}x_n = c_n \end{cases}$$

*is a **homogeneous** system if $c_1 = c_2 = \cdots = c_n = 0$. The system is a **nonhomogeneous** system if at least one of the c's is not equal to 0.*

EXAMPLE 24

The system

$$\begin{cases} 2x + 3y = 4 \\ 3x - 4y = 0 \end{cases}$$

is nonhomogeneous due to the 4 in the top equation. The system

$$\begin{cases} 2x + 3y = 0 \\ 3x - 4y = 0 \end{cases}$$

is homogeneous.

If the homogeneous system

$$\begin{cases} 2x + 3y = 0 \\ 3x - 4y = 0 \end{cases}$$

were solved by the method of reduction, first the augmented coefficient matrix would be written:

$$\begin{bmatrix} 2 & 3 & | & 0 \\ 3 & -4 & | & 0 \end{bmatrix}.$$

Observe that the last column consists entirely of zeros. This is typical of the augmented coefficient matrix of any homogeneous system. We would then reduce this matrix by using elementary row operations:

$$\begin{bmatrix} 2 & 3 & | & 0 \\ 3 & -4 & | & 0 \end{bmatrix} \sim \cdots \sim \begin{bmatrix} 1 & 0 & | & 0 \\ 0 & 1 & | & 0 \end{bmatrix}.$$

The last column of the reduced matrix also consists only of zeros. This does not occur by chance. When any elementary row operation is performed on a matrix which has a column consisting entirely of zeros, the corresponding column of the resulting matrix will also be all zeros. For convenience it will be our custom when solving a homogeneous system by matrix reduction to delete the last column of the matrices involved. That is, we shall only reduce the *coefficient matrix* of the system. For the above system we would have

$$\begin{bmatrix} 2 & 3 \\ 3 & -4 \end{bmatrix} \sim \cdots \sim \begin{bmatrix} 1 & 0 \\ 0 & 1 \end{bmatrix}.$$

Here the reduced matrix, called the *reduced coefficient matrix*, corresponds to

$$\begin{cases} x + 0y = 0 \\ 0x + y = 0 \end{cases}$$

and so the solution is $x = 0$ and $y = 0$.

Let us now consider the number of solutions of the homogeneous system

$$\begin{cases} a_{11} x_1 + a_{12} x_2 + \cdots + a_{1n} x_n = 0 \\ a_{21} x_1 + a_{22} x_2 + \cdots + a_{2n} x_n = 0 \\ \quad \vdots \qquad\quad \vdots \qquad\qquad\quad \vdots \\ a_{m1} x_1 + a_{m2} x_2 + \cdots + a_{mn} x_n = 0. \end{cases}$$

One solution always occurs when $x_1 = 0$, $x_2 = 0$, $\cdots$, and $x_n = 0$ since each equation is satisfied for these values. This solution, called the **trivial solution,** is a solution of *every* homogeneous system.

There is a theorem which allows us to determine whether a homogeneous system has a unique solution (the trivial solution only) or an infinite number of solutions. The theorem is based on the number of nonzero rows that appear in the reduced coefficient matrix of the system. A *nonzero row* is a row that does not consist entirely of zeros.

Theorem.   Let **A** be the *reduced* coefficient matrix of a homogeneous system of m linear equations in n unknowns. If **A** has exactly k nonzero rows, then $k \le n$. Moreover,

a. if $k < n$, the system has an infinite number of solutions;

and

b. if $k = n$, the system has a unique solution (the trivial solution).

If a homogeneous system consists of m equations in n unknowns, then the coefficient matrix of the system has dimension $m \times n$. Thus, if $m < n$ and k is the number of nonzero rows in the reduced coefficient matrix, then $k \le m$ and hence $k < n$. By the theorem, the system must have an infinite number of solutions. Consequently we have the following.

Corollary.   A homogeneous system of linear equations with fewer equations than unknowns has an infinite number of solutions.

EXAMPLE 25

Determine whether the system

$$\begin{cases} x + y - 2z = 0 \\ 2x + 2y - 4z = 0 \end{cases}$$

has a unique solution or an infinite number of solutions.

There are two equations in this homogeneous system and this number is less than the number of unknowns (three). Thus by the corollary above, the system has an infinite number of solutions.

PITFALL.   *The theorem and corollary above apply only to **homogeneous systems of** linear equations. For example, consider the system*

$$\begin{cases} x + y - 2z = 3 \\ 2x + 2y - 4z = 4, \end{cases}$$

*which consists of two linear equations in three unknowns. We **cannot** conclude that this system has an infinite number of solutions since it is not homogeneous. Indeed, you should verify that it has no solution.*

EXAMPLE 26

Determine whether the following homogeneous systems have a unique solution or an infinite number of solutions; then solve the system.

a.
$$\begin{cases} x - 2y + z = 0 \\ 2x - y + 5z = 0 \\ x + y + 4z = 0. \end{cases}$$

Reducing the coefficient matrix, we have

$$\begin{bmatrix} 1 & -2 & 1 \\ 2 & -1 & 5 \\ 1 & 1 & 4 \end{bmatrix} \sim \cdots \sim \begin{bmatrix} 1 & 0 & 3 \\ 0 & 1 & 1 \\ 0 & 0 & 0 \end{bmatrix}.$$

The number of nonzero rows (2) in the reduced coefficient matrix is less than the number of variables (3) in the system. By the theorem above, there are an infinite number of solutions.

Since the reduced coefficient matrix corresponds to

$$\begin{cases} x + 3z = 0 \\ y + z = 0, \end{cases}$$

the solution may be given by

$$x = -3z$$
$$y = -z$$
$$z = z$$

where z is any real number.

b.
$$\begin{cases} 3x + 4y = 0 \\ x - 2y = 0 \\ 2x + y = 0 \\ 2x + 3y = 0. \end{cases}$$

Reducing the coefficient matrix, we have

$$\begin{bmatrix} 3 & 4 \\ 1 & -2 \\ 2 & 1 \\ 2 & 3 \end{bmatrix} \sim \cdots \sim \begin{bmatrix} 1 & 0 \\ 0 & 1 \\ 0 & 0 \\ 0 & 0 \end{bmatrix}.$$

The number of nonzero rows (2) in the reduced coefficient matrix equals the number of variables in the system. By the theorem the system must have a unique solution, namely the trivial solution $x = 0$, $y = 0$.

EXERCISE 14-5

In problems 1-8, solve the systems by using matrix reduction.

1. $\begin{cases} w - x - y + 4z = 5 \\ 2w - 3x - 4y + 9z = 13 \\ 2w + x + 4y + 5z = 1 \end{cases}$

2. $\begin{cases} 3w - x + 12y + 18z = -4 \\ w - 2x + 4y + 11z = -13 \\ w + x + 4y + 2z = 8 \end{cases}$

3. $\begin{cases} 3w - x - 3y - z = -2 \\ 2w - 2x - 6y - 6z = -4 \\ 2w - x - 3y - 2z = -2 \\ 3w + x + 3y + 7z = 2 \end{cases}$

4. $\begin{cases} w + x + 5z = 1 \\ w + y + 2z = 1 \\ w - 3x + 4y - 7z = 1 \\ x - y + 3z = 0 \end{cases}$

5. $\begin{cases} w + x + 3y - z = 2 \\ 2w + x + 5y - 2z = 0 \\ 2w - x + 3y - 2z = -8 \\ 3w + 2x + 8y - 3z = 2 \\ w + 2y - z = -2 \end{cases}$

6. $\begin{cases} w + x + y + 2z = 4 \\ 2w + x + 2y + 2z = 7 \\ w + 2x + y + 4z = 5 \\ 3w - 2x + 3y - 4z = 7 \\ 4w - 3x + 4y - 6z = 9 \end{cases}$

7. $\begin{cases} 4x_1 - 3x_2 + 5x_3 - 10x_4 + 11x_5 = -8 \\ 2x_1 + x_2 + 5x_3 + 3x_5 = 6 \end{cases}$

8. $\begin{cases} x_1 + 2x_3 + x_4 + 4x_5 = 1 \\ x_2 + x_3 - 3x_4 = -2 \\ 4x_1 - 3x_2 + 5x_3 + 13x_4 + 16x_5 = 10 \\ x_1 + 2x_2 + 4x_3 - 5x_4 + 4x_5 = -3 \end{cases}$

For each of problems 9-14, determine whether the system has an infinite number of solutions or only the trivial solution. Do not solve the systems.

9. $\begin{cases} .07x + .3y + .02z = 0 \\ .053x - .4y + .08z = 0 \end{cases}$

10. $\begin{cases} 3w + 5x - 4y + 2z = 0 \\ 7w - 2x + 9y + 3z = 0 \end{cases}$

11. $\begin{cases} 3x - 4y = 0 \\ x + 5y = 0 \\ 4x - y = 0 \end{cases}$

12. $\begin{cases} 2x + 3y + 12z = 0 \\ 3x - 2y + 5z = 0 \\ 4x + y + 14z = 0 \end{cases}$

13. $\begin{cases} x + y + z = 0 \\ x - z = 0 \\ x - 2y - 5z = 0 \end{cases}$

14. $\begin{cases} 2x + 5y = 0 \\ x + 4y = 0 \\ 3x - 2y = 0 \end{cases}$

Solve each of the following systems.

15. $\begin{cases} x + y = 0 \\ 3x - 4y = 0 \end{cases}$

16. $\begin{cases} 2x - 5y = 0 \\ 8x - 20y = 0 \end{cases}$

17. $\begin{cases} x + 6y - 2z = 0 \\ 2x - 3y + 4z = 0 \end{cases}$

18. $\begin{cases} 4x + 7y = 0 \\ 2x + 3y = 0 \end{cases}$

19. $\begin{cases} x + y = 0 \\ 3x - 4y = 0 \\ 5x - 8y = 0 \end{cases}$

20. $\begin{cases} 4x - 3y + 2z = 0 \\ x + 2y + 3z = 0 \\ x + y + z = 0 \end{cases}$

21. $\begin{cases} x + y + z = 0 \\ 5x - 2y - 9z = 0 \\ 3x + y - z = 0 \\ 3x - 2y - 7z = 0 \end{cases}$

22. $\begin{cases} x + y + 7z = 0 \\ x - y - z = 0 \\ 2x - 3y - 6z = 0 \\ 3x + y + 13z = 0 \end{cases}$

23. $\begin{cases} w + x + y + 4z = 0 \\ w + x + 5z = 0 \\ 2w + x + 3y + 4z = 0 \\ w - 3x + 2y - 9z = 0 \end{cases}$

24. $\begin{cases} w + x + 2y + 7z = 0 \\ w - 2x - y + z = 0 \\ w + 2x + 3y + 9z = 0 \\ 2w - 3x - y + 4z = 0 \end{cases}$

14-6   INVERSES

We have seen how useful the method of reduction is for solving systems of linear equations. But it is by no means the only method which uses matrices. In this section we shall discuss a different method which applies to many systems of n linear equations in n unknowns.

To introduce the general technique, we consider the system

$$\begin{cases} a_{11} x_1 + a_{12} x_2 = c_1 \\ a_{21} x_1 + a_{22} x_2 = c_2. \end{cases}$$

We know from Sec. 14–3 that this system can be represented by the matrix equation

$$\begin{bmatrix} a_{11} & a_{12} \\ a_{21} & a_{22} \end{bmatrix} \begin{bmatrix} x_1 \\ x_2 \end{bmatrix} = \begin{bmatrix} c_1 \\ c_2 \end{bmatrix}. \tag{1}$$

Note that the 2×2 matrix in Eq. (1), which we shall denote by $\mathbf{A}$, is the coefficient matrix of the system. Let us assume that there exists a 2×2 matrix $\mathbf{B}$,

$$\mathbf{B} = \begin{bmatrix} p & q \\ r & s \end{bmatrix},$$

such that **B** times **A** is the identity matrix:

$$\begin{bmatrix} p & q \\ r & s \end{bmatrix} \begin{bmatrix} a_{11} & a_{12} \\ a_{21} & a_{22} \end{bmatrix} = \begin{bmatrix} 1 & 0 \\ 0 & 1 \end{bmatrix}.$$

If both sides of Eq. (1) are premultiplied by **B**, we have

$$\begin{bmatrix} p & q \\ r & s \end{bmatrix} \begin{bmatrix} a_{11} & a_{12} \\ a_{21} & a_{22} \end{bmatrix} \begin{bmatrix} x_1 \\ x_2 \end{bmatrix} = \begin{bmatrix} p & q \\ r & s \end{bmatrix} \begin{bmatrix} c_1 \\ c_2 \end{bmatrix}$$

$$\begin{bmatrix} 1 & 0 \\ 0 & 1 \end{bmatrix} \begin{bmatrix} x_1 \\ x_2 \end{bmatrix} = \begin{bmatrix} p & q \\ r & s \end{bmatrix} \begin{bmatrix} c_1 \\ c_2 \end{bmatrix}$$

$$\begin{bmatrix} x_1 \\ x_2 \end{bmatrix} = \begin{bmatrix} pc_1 + qc_2 \\ rc_1 + sc_2 \end{bmatrix}.$$

Thus, $x_1 = pc_1 + qc_2$, $x_2 = rc_1 + sc_2$, and the system is solved.

Summarizing our procedure, we first express the system as a matrix equation of the form

$$AX = C. \tag{2}$$

Then, provided there exists a matrix **B** such that **BA** = **I**, we premultiply both sides of Eq. (2) by **B**:

$$BAX = BC.$$

Simplifying, we have

$$IX = BC$$

$$X = BC. \tag{3}$$

Thus the solution is given by **X** = **BC**. This procedure is based on our assuming the existence of a matrix **B** such that **BA** = **I**. When such a matrix does exist, we say that it is an *inverse* matrix of **A**.

DEFINITION.   *If* **A** *and* **B** *are* $n \times n$ *matrices, then* **B** *is an* **inverse matrix** *of* **A** *(or* **B** *is an inverse of* **A***) if and only if* **BA** = **I**.

EXAMPLE 27

Let $\mathbf{A} = \begin{bmatrix} 1 & 2 \\ 3 & 7 \end{bmatrix}$ and $\mathbf{B} = \begin{bmatrix} 7 & -2 \\ -3 & 1 \end{bmatrix}$.   Since

$$\mathbf{BA} = \begin{bmatrix} 7 & -2 \\ -3 & 1 \end{bmatrix} \begin{bmatrix} 1 & 2 \\ 3 & 7 \end{bmatrix} = \begin{bmatrix} 1 & 0 \\ 0 & 1 \end{bmatrix},$$

B is an inverse matrix of **A**.

It can be shown that if **B** is an inverse matrix of **A**, then that inverse is unique. Thus in Example 27, **B** is the *only* matrix that has the property that **BA** = **I.** In keeping with common practice, we denote *the* inverse of a matrix **A** by $\mathbf{A}^{-1}$. Hence, **B** = $\mathbf{A}^{-1}$ and

$$\mathbf{A}^{-1}\mathbf{A} = \mathbf{I}.$$

We may now write Eq. (3) as

$$\mathbf{X} = \mathbf{A}^{-1}\mathbf{C}. \tag{4}$$

It is also true that $\mathbf{A}^{-1}\mathbf{A} = \mathbf{A}\mathbf{A}^{-1}$. When $\mathbf{A}^{-1}$ does exist, we say **A** is **invertible** (or **nonsingular**).

Not all square matrices are invertible. For example, if

$$\mathbf{A} = \begin{bmatrix} 0 & 1 \\ 0 & 1 \end{bmatrix},$$

then

$$\begin{bmatrix} a & b \\ c & d \end{bmatrix}\begin{bmatrix} 0 & 1 \\ 0 & 1 \end{bmatrix} = \begin{bmatrix} 0 & a+b \\ 0 & c+d \end{bmatrix} \neq \begin{bmatrix} 1 & 0 \\ 0 & 1 \end{bmatrix}.$$

Hence there is no matrix which when postmultiplied by **A** yields the identity matrix. Thus **A** is not invertible.

Before discussing a procedure for finding the inverse of an invertible matrix, we introduce the concept of *elementary matrices*. An $n \times n$ **elementary matrix** is a matrix obtained from the $n \times n$ identity matrix **I** by an elementary row operation. Thus there are three basic types of elementary matrices:

(1) one obtained by interchanging two rows of I;
(2) one obtained by multiplying a row of I by a nonzero scalar; and
(3) one obtained by adding a multiple of one row of I to another.

EXAMPLE 28

$$\mathbf{E}_1 = \begin{bmatrix} 1 & 0 & 0 \\ 0 & 0 & 1 \\ 0 & 1 & 0 \end{bmatrix}, \quad \mathbf{E}_2 = \begin{bmatrix} -4 & 0 \\ 0 & 1 \end{bmatrix}, \quad \text{and} \quad \mathbf{E}_3 = \begin{bmatrix} 1 & 0 \\ 3 & 1 \end{bmatrix}$$

are elementary matrices. $\mathbf{E}_1$ is obtained from the 3×3 identity matrix by interchanging the second and third rows. $\mathbf{E}_2$ is obtained from the 2×2 identity matrix by multiplying the first row by -4. $\mathbf{E}_3$ is obtained from the 2×2 identity matrix by adding 3 times the first row to the second.

Suppose **E** is an $n \times n$ elementary matrix obtained from **I** by a certain elementary row operation, and **A** is an $n \times n$ matrix. Then it can be shown that the product **EA** is equal to the matrix which is obtained from **A** by applying the same elementary row operation to **A**. For example, let

$$A = \begin{bmatrix} 1 & 2 \\ 3 & 4 \end{bmatrix}, \quad E_1 = \begin{bmatrix} 0 & 1 \\ 1 & 0 \end{bmatrix}, \quad E_2 = \begin{bmatrix} 1 & 0 \\ 0 & 2 \end{bmatrix}, \quad \text{and} \quad E_3 = \begin{bmatrix} 1 & -2 \\ 0 & 1 \end{bmatrix}.$$

E_1, E_2, and E_3 are elementary matrices. E_1 is obtained by interchanging the first and second rows of **I**. Likewise,

$$E_1 A = \begin{bmatrix} 0 & 1 \\ 1 & 0 \end{bmatrix} \begin{bmatrix} 1 & 2 \\ 3 & 4 \end{bmatrix} = \begin{bmatrix} 3 & 4 \\ 1 & 2 \end{bmatrix}$$

is the matrix obtained from **A** by interchanging the first and second rows of **A**. E_2 is obtained by multiplying the second row of **I** by 2. Accordingly, the product

$$E_2 A = \begin{bmatrix} 1 & 0 \\ 0 & 2 \end{bmatrix} \begin{bmatrix} 1 & 2 \\ 3 & 4 \end{bmatrix} = \begin{bmatrix} 1 & 2 \\ 6 & 8 \end{bmatrix}$$

is the matrix obtained by multiplying the second row of **A** by 2. E_3 is obtained by adding -2 times the second row of **I** to the first row. The product

$$E_3 A = \begin{bmatrix} 1 & -2 \\ 0 & 1 \end{bmatrix} \begin{bmatrix} 1 & 2 \\ 3 & 4 \end{bmatrix} = \begin{bmatrix} -5 & -6 \\ 3 & 4 \end{bmatrix}$$

is the matrix obtained from **A** by the same elementary row operation.

If we wanted to reduce the matrix

$$A = \begin{bmatrix} 1 & 0 \\ 2 & 2 \end{bmatrix},$$

we might proceed through a sequence of steps as follows:

$$A = \begin{bmatrix} 1 & 0 \\ 2 & 2 \end{bmatrix}$$

$$\sim \begin{bmatrix} 1 & 0 \\ 0 & 2 \end{bmatrix} \qquad \text{(by adding } -2 \text{ times the first row to the second)}$$

$$\sim \begin{bmatrix} 1 & 0 \\ 0 & 1 \end{bmatrix} \qquad \text{(by multiplying the second row by } \tfrac{1}{2} \text{).}$$

Since this involves elementary row operations, it seems natural that elementary matrices can be used to reduce **A**. If **A** is premultiplied by the elementary matrix $E_1 = \begin{bmatrix} 1 & 0 \\ -2 & 1 \end{bmatrix}$, then $E_1 A$ is the matrix obtained from **A** by adding -2 times the first row to the second row:

$$E_1 A = \begin{bmatrix} 1 & 0 \\ -2 & 1 \end{bmatrix} \begin{bmatrix} 1 & 0 \\ 2 & 2 \end{bmatrix} = \begin{bmatrix} 1 & 0 \\ 0 & 2 \end{bmatrix}.$$

Premultiplying $\mathbf{E}_1 \mathbf{A}$ by the elementary matrix $\mathbf{E}_2 = \begin{bmatrix} 1 & 0 \\ 0 & \frac{1}{2} \end{bmatrix}$ gives the matrix

obtained by multiplying the second row of $\mathbf{E}_1 \mathbf{A}$ by $\frac{1}{2}$:

$$\mathbf{E}_2(\mathbf{E}_1 \mathbf{A}) = \begin{bmatrix} 1 & 0 \\ 0 & \frac{1}{2} \end{bmatrix} \begin{bmatrix} 1 & 0 \\ 0 & 2 \end{bmatrix} = \begin{bmatrix} 1 & 0 \\ 0 & 1 \end{bmatrix} = \mathbf{I}.$$

Thus we have reduced $\mathbf{A}$ by multiplying $\mathbf{A}$ by a product of elementary matrices.

Since $(\mathbf{E}_2 \mathbf{E}_1)\mathbf{A} = \mathbf{E}_2(\mathbf{E}_1 \mathbf{A}) = \mathbf{I}$, the product $\mathbf{E}_2 \mathbf{E}_1$ is $\mathbf{A}^{-1}$. However, $\mathbf{A}^{-1} = \mathbf{E}_2 \mathbf{E}_1 = (\mathbf{E}_2 \mathbf{E}_1)\mathbf{I} = \mathbf{E}_2(\mathbf{E}_1 \mathbf{I})$. Thus $\mathbf{A}^{-1}$ can be obtained by applying the same elementary row operations, beginning with $\mathbf{I}$, that were used to reduce $\mathbf{A}$ to $\mathbf{I}$.

$$\mathbf{I} = \begin{bmatrix} 1 & 0 \\ 0 & 1 \end{bmatrix}$$

$$\sim \begin{bmatrix} 1 & 0 \\ -2 & 1 \end{bmatrix} \qquad \text{(by adding } -2 \text{ times the first row to the second)}$$

$$\sim \begin{bmatrix} 1 & 0 \\ -1 & \frac{1}{2} \end{bmatrix} \qquad \text{(by multiplying the second row by } \frac{1}{2}\text{)}.$$

Therefore,

$$\mathbf{A}^{-1} = \begin{bmatrix} 1 & 0 \\ -1 & \frac{1}{2} \end{bmatrix}.$$

Our result can be verified by showing $\mathbf{A}^{-1}\mathbf{A} = \mathbf{I}$:

$$\mathbf{A}^{-1}\mathbf{A} = \begin{bmatrix} 1 & 0 \\ -1 & \frac{1}{2} \end{bmatrix} \begin{bmatrix} 1 & 0 \\ 2 & 2 \end{bmatrix} = \begin{bmatrix} 1 & 0 \\ 0 & 1 \end{bmatrix} = \mathbf{I}.$$

In summary, to find $\mathbf{A}^{-1}$ we apply the identical elementary row operations beginning with $\mathbf{I}$ and proceeding in the same order as was followed to reduce $\mathbf{A}$ to $\mathbf{I}$. finding $\mathbf{A}^{-1}$ by this technique can be done conveniently by using the following format. First, write the matrix

$$[\mathbf{A} \vdots \mathbf{I}] = \begin{bmatrix} 1 & 0 & \vdots & 1 & 0 \\ 2 & 2 & \vdots & 0 & 1 \end{bmatrix}.$$

Then apply elementary row operations until $[\mathbf{A} \vdots \mathbf{I}]$ is equivalent to a matrix which has $\mathbf{I}$ as its first two columns. The last two columns of this matrix will be $\mathbf{A}^{-1}$. Thus,

$$[\mathbf{A} \vdots \mathbf{I}] = \begin{bmatrix} 1 & 0 & \vdots & 1 & 0 \\ 2 & 2 & \vdots & 0 & 1 \end{bmatrix} \sim \begin{bmatrix} 1 & 0 & \vdots & 1 & 0 \\ 0 & 2 & \vdots & -2 & 1 \end{bmatrix}$$

$$\sim \begin{bmatrix} 1 & 0 & \vdots & 1 & 0 \\ 0 & 1 & \vdots & -1 & \frac{1}{2} \end{bmatrix} = [\mathbf{I} \vdots \mathbf{A}^{-1}].$$

Note that the first two columns of $[\mathbf{I} \mid \mathbf{A}^{-1}]$ form a reduced matrix.

This procedure can be extended to find the inverse of *any* invertible $n \times n$ matrix. If $\mathbf{M}$ is such a matrix, form the $n \times (2n)$ matrix $[\mathbf{M} \mid \mathbf{I}]$. Then perform elementary row operations until the first n columns form a reduced matrix equal to $\mathbf{I}$. The last n columns will be $\mathbf{M}^{-1}$.

$$[\mathbf{M} \mid \mathbf{I}] \sim \cdot \cdot \cdot \sim [\mathbf{I} \mid \mathbf{M}^{-1}].$$

If $\mathbf{M}$ does not reduce to $\mathbf{I}$, then $\mathbf{M}^{-1}$ does not exist.

EXAMPLE 29

Determine $\mathbf{A}^{-1}$ *if* $\mathbf{A}$ *is invertible.*

a. $\mathbf{A} = \begin{bmatrix} 1 & 0 & -2 \\ 4 & -2 & 1 \\ 1 & 2 & -10 \end{bmatrix}.$

$$[\mathbf{A} \mid \mathbf{I}] = \begin{bmatrix} 1 & 0 & -2 & 1 & 0 & 0 \\ 4 & -2 & 1 & 0 & 1 & 0 \\ 1 & 2 & -10 & 0 & 0 & 1 \end{bmatrix}$$

$$\sim \cdot \cdot \cdot \sim \begin{bmatrix} 1 & 0 & 0 & -9 & 2 & 2 \\ 0 & 1 & 0 & -\frac{41}{2} & 4 & \frac{9}{2} \\ 1 & 0 & 1 & -5 & 1 & 1 \end{bmatrix}.$$

The first three columns of the last matrix form $\mathbf{I}$. Thus $\mathbf{A}$ is invertible and

$$\mathbf{A}^{-1} = \begin{bmatrix} -9 & 2 & 2 \\ -\frac{41}{2} & 4 & \frac{9}{2} \\ -5 & 1 & 1 \end{bmatrix}.$$

b. $\mathbf{A} = \begin{bmatrix} 3 & 2 \\ 6 & 4 \end{bmatrix}.$

$$[\mathbf{A} \mid \mathbf{I}] = \begin{bmatrix} 3 & 2 & 1 & 0 \\ 6 & 4 & 0 & 1 \end{bmatrix} \sim \begin{bmatrix} 3 & 2 & 1 & 0 \\ 0 & 0 & -2 & 1 \end{bmatrix}$$

$$\sim \begin{bmatrix} 1 & \frac{2}{3} & \frac{1}{3} & 0 \\ 0 & 0 & -2 & 1 \end{bmatrix}.$$

The first two columns of the last matrix form a reduced matrix different from $\mathbf{I}$. Thus $\mathbf{A}$ is not invertible.

EXAMPLE 30

Solve each system by finding the inverse of the coefficient matrix.

a. $\begin{cases} x_1 + 2x_2 = 0 \\ 4x_1 + 9x_2 = 1. \end{cases}$

The system can be expressed as the matrix equation $\mathbf{AX} = \mathbf{C}$, where $\mathbf{A}$ is the coefficient matrix of the system.

$$\begin{bmatrix} 1 & 2 \\ 4 & 9 \end{bmatrix} \begin{bmatrix} x_1 \\ x_2 \end{bmatrix} = \begin{bmatrix} 0 \\ 1 \end{bmatrix}.$$

Since $\mathbf{AX} = \mathbf{C}$, then $\mathbf{A}^{-1}\mathbf{AX} = \mathbf{A}^{-1}\mathbf{C}$ and so our solution is given by

$$\mathbf{X} = \mathbf{A}^{-1}\mathbf{C}.$$

Thus we need to find $\mathbf{A}^{-1}$.

$$\begin{bmatrix} 1 & 2 & | & 1 & 0 \\ 4 & 9 & | & 0 & 1 \end{bmatrix} \sim \cdots \sim \begin{bmatrix} 1 & 0 & | & 9 & -2 \\ 0 & 1 & | & -4 & 1 \end{bmatrix}$$

$$\mathbf{A}^{-1} = \begin{bmatrix} 9 & -2 \\ -4 & 1 \end{bmatrix}.$$

Hence

$$\mathbf{X} = \begin{bmatrix} x_1 \\ x_2 \end{bmatrix} = \mathbf{A}^{-1}\mathbf{C} = \begin{bmatrix} 9 & -2 \\ -4 & 1 \end{bmatrix} \begin{bmatrix} 0 \\ 1 \end{bmatrix} = \begin{bmatrix} -2 \\ 1 \end{bmatrix}.$$

Therefore, $x_1 = -2$ and $x_2 = 1$.

b. $\begin{cases} x_1 \quad\quad - 2x_3 = 1 \\ 4x_1 - 2x_2 + \quad x_3 = 2 \\ x_1 + 2x_2 - 10x_3 = -1. \end{cases}$

The coefficient matrix of the system is

$$\mathbf{A} = \begin{bmatrix} 1 & 0 & -2 \\ 4 & -2 & 1 \\ 1 & 2 & -10 \end{bmatrix}.$$

By Example 29(a),

$$\mathbf{A}^{-1} = \begin{bmatrix} -9 & 2 & 2 \\ -\frac{41}{2} & 4 & \frac{9}{2} \\ -5 & 1 & 1 \end{bmatrix}.$$

Thus,

$$\begin{bmatrix} x_1 \\ x_2 \\ x_3 \end{bmatrix} = \begin{bmatrix} -9 & 2 & 2 \\ -\frac{41}{2} & 4 & \frac{9}{2} \\ -5 & 1 & 1 \end{bmatrix} \begin{bmatrix} 1 \\ 2 \\ -1 \end{bmatrix} = \begin{bmatrix} -7 \\ -17 \\ -4 \end{bmatrix}.$$

Consequently, $x_1 = -7$, $x_2 = -17$, and $x_3 = -4$.

It can be shown that a system of n linear equations in n unknowns has a unique solution if and only if the coefficient matrix is invertible. Indeed, in both parts of the last example the coefficient matrices were invertible and unique solutions did in fact exist. When the coefficient matrix is not invertible, the system will have either no solution or an infinite number of solutions.

EXAMPLE 31

Solve the system

$$\begin{cases} x - 2y + z = 0 \\ 2x - y + 5z = 0 \\ x + y + 4z = 0. \end{cases}$$

The coefficient matrix is

$$\begin{bmatrix} 1 & -2 & 1 \\ 2 & -1 & 5 \\ 1 & 1 & 4 \end{bmatrix}.$$

Since

$$\begin{bmatrix} 1 & -2 & 1 & \vdots & 1 & 0 & 0 \\ 2 & -1 & 5 & \vdots & 0 & 1 & 0 \\ 1 & 1 & 4 & \vdots & 0 & 0 & 1 \end{bmatrix} \sim \cdots \cdots \sim \begin{bmatrix} 1 & 0 & 3 & \vdots & -\frac{1}{3} & \frac{2}{3} & 0 \\ 0 & 1 & 1 & \vdots & -\frac{2}{3} & \frac{1}{3} & 0 \\ 0 & 0 & 0 & \vdots & 1 & -1 & 1 \end{bmatrix},$$

the coefficient matrix is not invertible. Hence, the system *cannot* be solved by inverses. Another method must be used. In Example 26(a) of Sec. 14-5, the solution was found to be $x = -3z$, $y = -z$, $z = z$.

EXERCISE 14-6

In each of problems 1-18, if the given matrix is invertible, find its inverse.

1. $\begin{bmatrix} 6 & 1 \\ 5 & 1 \end{bmatrix}$

2. $\begin{bmatrix} 2 & 8 \\ 3 & 12 \end{bmatrix}$

3. $\begin{bmatrix} 1 & 1 \\ 1 & 1 \end{bmatrix}$

4. $\begin{bmatrix} 4 & 9 \\ 0 & -6 \end{bmatrix}$

5. $\begin{bmatrix} 1 & 0 & 0 \\ 0 & -3 & 0 \\ 0 & 0 & 4 \end{bmatrix}$

6. $\begin{bmatrix} 2 & 0 & 8 \\ -1 & 4 & 0 \\ 2 & 1 & 0 \end{bmatrix}$

7. $\begin{bmatrix} 1 & 2 & 3 \\ 0 & 0 & 4 \\ 0 & 0 & 5 \end{bmatrix}$

8. $\begin{bmatrix} 2 & 0 & 0 \\ 0 & 0 & 0 \\ 0 & 0 & -4 \end{bmatrix}$

9. $\begin{bmatrix} 2 & 4 \\ 8 & 1 \\ 6 & 3 \end{bmatrix}$

10. $\begin{bmatrix} 0 & 0 & 0 \\ 0 & 0 & 0 \\ 0 & 0 & 0 \end{bmatrix}$

11. $\begin{bmatrix} 1 & 1 & 1 \\ 0 & 1 & 1 \\ 0 & 0 & 1 \end{bmatrix}$

12. $\begin{bmatrix} 1 & 2 & -1 \\ 0 & 1 & 4 \\ 1 & -1 & 2 \end{bmatrix}$

13. $\begin{bmatrix} 7 & 0 & -2 \\ 0 & 1 & 0 \\ -3 & 0 & 1 \end{bmatrix}$

14. $\begin{bmatrix} 7 & -8 & 5 \\ -4 & 5 & -3 \\ 1 & -1 & 1 \end{bmatrix}$

15. $\begin{bmatrix} 2 & 1 & 0 \\ 4 & -1 & 5 \\ 1 & -1 & 2 \end{bmatrix}$

16. $\begin{bmatrix} -5 & 4 & -3 \\ 10 & -7 & 6 \\ 8 & -6 & 5 \end{bmatrix}$

17. $\begin{bmatrix} 1 & 2 & 3 \\ 1 & 3 & 5 \\ 1 & 5 & 12 \end{bmatrix}$

18. $\begin{bmatrix} 2 & -1 & 3 \\ 0 & 2 & 0 \\ 2 & 1 & 1 \end{bmatrix}$

For each of problems 19–32, if the coefficient matrix of the system is invertible, solve the system by using the inverse. If not, solve the system by the method of reduction.

19. $\begin{cases} 6x + 5y = 2 \\ x + y = -3 \end{cases}$

20. $\begin{cases} 2x + 3y = 4 \\ -x + 5y = -2 \end{cases}$

21. $\begin{cases} 2x + y = 5 \\ 3x - y = 0 \end{cases}$

22. $\begin{cases} 3x + 2y = 26 \\ 4x + 3y = 37 \end{cases}$

23. $\begin{cases} 2x + 6y = 2 \\ 3x + 9y = 3 \end{cases}$

24. $\begin{cases} 2x + 8y = 3 \\ 3x + 12y = 6 \end{cases}$

25. $\begin{cases} x + 2y + z = 4 \\ 3x + z = 2 \\ x - y + z = 1 \end{cases}$

26. $\begin{cases} x + y + z = 2 \\ x - y + z = -2 \\ x - y - z = 0 \end{cases}$

27. $\begin{cases} x + y + z = 2 \\ x - y + z = 1 \\ x - y - z = 0 \end{cases}$

28. $\begin{cases} 2x \quad\quad + 8z = 8 \\ -x + 4y \quad\quad = 36 \\ 2x + \ y \quad\quad = 9 \end{cases}$

29. $\begin{cases} x + 3y + 3z = 7 \\ 2x + \ y + \ z = 4 \\ x + \ y + \ z = 4 \end{cases}$

30. $\begin{cases} x + 3y + 3z = 7 \\ 2x + \ y + \ z = 4 \\ x + \ y + \ z = 3 \end{cases}$

31. $\begin{cases} w \quad\quad + 2y + \ z = 4 \\ w - \ x \quad\quad + 2z = 12 \\ 2w + \ x \quad\quad + \ z = 12 \\ w + 2x + \ y + \ z = 12 \end{cases}$

32. $\begin{cases} w + x \quad\quad + z = 2 \\ w \quad\quad + y \quad\quad = 0 \\ x + y + z = 4 \\ y + z = 1 \end{cases}$

Find $(\mathbf{I} - \mathbf{A})^{-1}$ for each of the following matrices $\mathbf{A}$.

33. $\begin{bmatrix} 2 & -1 \\ 1 & 3 \end{bmatrix}$

34. $\begin{bmatrix} -3 & 2 \\ 4 & 3 \end{bmatrix}$

35. Solve the following problems by using the inverse of the matrix involved.
(a) An automobile factory produces two models. The first requires 1 man-hour to paint and $\frac{1}{2}$ man-hour to polish; the second requires 1 man-hour for each process. During each hour that the assembly line is operating, there are 100 man-hours available for painting and 80 man-hours for polishing. How many of each model can be produced each hour if all the man-hours available are to be utilized?
(b) Suppose each car of the first type requires 10 widgets and 14 shims, and each car of the second type requires 7 widgets and 10 shims. The factory can obtain 800 widgets and 1130 shims each hour. How many cars of each model can it produce while utilizing all the parts available?

14-7 DETERMINANTS

We now introduce a new function, the *determinant function*. Here our inputs will be *square* matrices, but our outputs will be real numbers. If $\mathbf{A}$ is a square matrix, then the determinant function associates with $\mathbf{A}$ exactly one real number called the *determinant* of $\mathbf{A}$. Denoting the determinant of $\mathbf{A}$ by $|\mathbf{A}|$ (that is, using vertical bars), we can think of the determinant function as a correspondence:

$$\mathbf{A} \longrightarrow |\mathbf{A}|$$

$$\begin{matrix} \text{Square} & \text{Real} & \\ \text{Matrix} & \text{Number} & = \end{matrix} \begin{matrix} \text{Determinant} \\ \text{of } \mathbf{A} \end{matrix}$$

The use of determinants in solving systems of linear equations will be discussed later. Turning to how a real number is assigned to a square matrix, we shall first consider the special cases of matrices of orders one and two.

Then we shall extend the definition to matrices of order n.

DEFINITION.   *If* $A = [a_{11}]$ *is a square matrix of order one, then* $|A| = a_{11}$.

   That is, the determinant function assigns to the one entry matrix $[a_{11}]$ the number a_{11}. Hence if $A = [6]$, then $|A| = 6$.

DEFINITION.   *If*

$$A = \begin{bmatrix} a_{11} & a_{12} \\ a_{21} & a_{22} \end{bmatrix}$$

is a square matrix of order two, then

$$|A| = a_{11}\,a_{22} - a_{12}\,a_{21}.$$

   Verbally, the determinant of a 2×2 matrix is obtained by taking the product of the entries in the main diagonal and subtracting from it the product of the entries in the other diagonal. We speak of the determinant of a 2×2 matrix as a *determinant of order* 2.

EXAMPLE 32

Find $|A|$ *if* $A =$

$$a.\ \begin{bmatrix} 2 & 1 \\ 3 & -4 \end{bmatrix} \quad b.\ \begin{bmatrix} -3 & -2 \\ 0 & 1 \end{bmatrix} \quad c.\ \begin{bmatrix} 1 & 0 \\ 0 & 1 \end{bmatrix} \quad d.\ \begin{bmatrix} x & 0 \\ y & 1 \end{bmatrix}$$

We have

a. $|A| = \begin{vmatrix} 2 & 1 \\ 3 & -4 \end{vmatrix} = (2)(-4) - (1)(3) = -8 - 3 = -11.$

b. $|A| = \begin{vmatrix} -3 & -2 \\ 0 & 1 \end{vmatrix} = (-3)(1) - (-2)(0) = -3 - 0 = -3.$

c. $|A| = \begin{vmatrix} 1 & 0 \\ 0 & 1 \end{vmatrix} = (1)(1) - (0)(0) = 1.$

d. $|A| = \begin{vmatrix} x & 0 \\ y & 1 \end{vmatrix} = (x)(1) - (0)(y) = x.$

   The determinant of a square matrix A of order n $(n > 2)$ is defined in the following manner. With a given entry of A we associate the square matrix of order $n - 1$ obtained by deleting the entries in the row and column in which the given entry lies. For example, given the matrix

$$\begin{bmatrix} a_{11} & a_{12} & a_{13} \\ a_{21} & a_{22} & a_{23} \\ a_{31} & a_{32} & a_{33} \end{bmatrix},$$

with entry a_{21} we delete the entries in row 2 and column 1,

$$\begin{bmatrix} a_{11} & a_{12} & a_{13} \\ a_{21} & a_{22} & a_{23} \\ a_{31} & a_{32} & a_{33} \end{bmatrix},$$

leaving the matrix of order 2

$$\begin{bmatrix} a_{12} & a_{13} \\ a_{32} & a_{33} \end{bmatrix}.$$

The *determinant* of this matrix is called the **minor** of a_{21}. Similarly, the minor of a_{22} is

$$\begin{vmatrix} a_{11} & a_{13} \\ a_{31} & a_{33} \end{vmatrix},$$

and for a_{23} it is

$$\begin{vmatrix} a_{11} & a_{12} \\ a_{31} & a_{32} \end{vmatrix}.$$

With each entry a_{ij} we also associate a number determined by the subscript of the entry:

$$(-1)^{i+j}$$

where $i + j$ is the sum of the row number i and column number j in which the entry lies. With a_{21} we associate $(-1)^{2+1} = -1$, with a_{22} the number $(-1)^{2+2} = 1$, and with a_{23} the number $(-1)^{2+3} = -1$. The **cofactor** c_{ij} of the entry a_{ij} is the product of $(-1)^{i+j}$ and the minor of a_{ij}. For example, the cofactor of a_{21} is

$$c_{21} = (-1)^{2+1} \begin{vmatrix} a_{12} & a_{13} \\ a_{32} & a_{33} \end{vmatrix}.$$

The only difference between a cofactor and a minor is the factor $(-1)^{i+j}$.

To find the determinant of any square matrix **A** of order n, select *any* row (or column) of **A** and multiply each entry in the row (column) by its cofactor. The sum of these numbers is defined to be the determinant of **A** and is called a **determinant of order** n.

Let us find the determinant of

$$\begin{bmatrix} 2 & -1 & 3 \\ 3 & 0 & -5 \\ 2 & 1 & 1 \end{bmatrix}$$

by applying the above rule to the first row (sometimes referred to as "expanding along the first row"). For

$$a_{11} \text{ we obtain } (2)(-1)^{1+1} \begin{vmatrix} 0 & -5 \\ 1 & 1 \end{vmatrix} = (2)(1)(5) = 10,$$

$$a_{12} \text{ we obtain } (-1)(-1)^{1+2} \begin{vmatrix} 3 & -5 \\ 2 & 1 \end{vmatrix} = (-1)(-1)(13) = 13,$$

$$a_{13} \text{ we obtain } (3)(-1)^{1+3} \begin{vmatrix} 3 & 0 \\ 2 & 1 \end{vmatrix} = 3(1)(3) = 9.$$

Hence

$$\begin{vmatrix} 2 & -1 & 3 \\ 3 & 0 & -5 \\ 2 & 1 & 1 \end{vmatrix} = 10 + 13 + 9 = 32.$$

If we had expanded along the second column, then

$$\begin{vmatrix} 2 & -1 & 3 \\ 3 & 0 & -5 \\ 2 & 1 & 1 \end{vmatrix} = (-1)(-1)^{1+2} \begin{vmatrix} 3 & -5 \\ 2 & 1 \end{vmatrix} + 0 + (1)(-1)^{3+2} \begin{vmatrix} 2 & 3 \\ 3 & -5 \end{vmatrix}$$

$$= 13 + 0 + 19 = 32 \text{ as before.}$$

It can be shown that the determinant of a matrix is unique and does not depend on the row or column chosen for its evaluation. In the above problem, the second expansion is preferable since the 0 in column 2 contributed nothing to the sum, thus simplifying the calculation.

EXAMPLE 33

Find $|\mathbf{A}|$ *if*

$$\text{a. } \mathbf{A} = \begin{bmatrix} 12 & -1 & 3 \\ -3 & 1 & -1 \\ -10 & 2 & -3 \end{bmatrix}.$$

Expanding along the first row, we have

$$|A| = 12(-1)^{1+1}\begin{vmatrix} 1 & -1 \\ 2 & -3 \end{vmatrix} + (-1)(-1)^{1+2}\begin{vmatrix} -3 & -1 \\ -10 & -3 \end{vmatrix} + 3(-1)^{1+3}\begin{vmatrix} -3 & 1 \\ -10 & 2 \end{vmatrix}$$

$$= 12(1)(-1) + (-1)(-1)(-1) + 3(1)(4) = -1.$$

b. $A = \begin{bmatrix} 0 & 1 & 1 \\ 2 & 3 & 2 \\ 0 & -1 & 3 \end{bmatrix}$.

Expanding along column 1 for convenience, we have

$$|A| = 0 + 2(-1)^{2+1}\begin{vmatrix} 1 & 1 \\ -1 & 3 \end{vmatrix} + 0 = 2(-1)(4) = -8.$$

EXAMPLE 34

Evaluate

$$|A| = \begin{vmatrix} 2 & 0 & 0 & 1 \\ 0 & 1 & 0 & 3 \\ 0 & 0 & 1 & 2 \\ 1 & 2 & 3 & 0 \end{vmatrix}$$

by expanding along the first row,

$$|A| = 2(-1)^{1+1}\begin{vmatrix} 1 & 0 & 3 \\ 0 & 1 & 2 \\ 2 & 3 & 0 \end{vmatrix} + 1(-1)^{1+4}\begin{vmatrix} 0 & 1 & 0 \\ 0 & 0 & 1 \\ 1 & 2 & 3 \end{vmatrix}.$$

We have now expressed $|A|$ in terms of determinants of order three. Expanding each of these along the first row, we have

$$|A| = 2(1)\left[1(-1)^{1+1}\begin{vmatrix} 1 & 2 \\ 3 & 0 \end{vmatrix} + 3(-1)^{1+3}\begin{vmatrix} 0 & 1 \\ 2 & 3 \end{vmatrix}\right] + 1(-1)\left[1(-1)^{1+2}\begin{vmatrix} 0 & 1 \\ 1 & 3 \end{vmatrix}\right]$$

$$= 2[1(1)(-6) + 3(1)(-2)] + (-1)[(1)(-1)(-1)] = -25.$$

The evaluation of determinants is often simplified by the use of various properties, some of which we now list. In each case, A denotes a square matrix.

(1) **If each of the entries in a row (or column) of A is 0, then $|A| = 0$.**
Thus

$$\begin{vmatrix} 6 & 2 & 5 \\ 7 & 1 & 4 \\ 0 & 0 & 0 \end{vmatrix} = 0.$$

(2) If two rows (or columns) of A are identical, $|A| = 0$.

Thus

$$\begin{vmatrix} 2 & 5 & 2 & 1 \\ 2 & 6 & 2 & 3 \\ 2 & 4 & 2 & 1 \\ 6 & 5 & 6 & 1 \end{vmatrix} = 0, \text{ since column } 1 = \text{column } 3.$$

(3) If all the entries below (or above) the main diagonal of A are 0, then $|A|$ is equal to the product of the main diagonal entries.

Thus

$$\begin{vmatrix} 2 & 6 & 1 & 0 \\ 0 & 5 & 7 & 6 \\ 0 & 0 & -2 & 5 \\ 0 & 0 & 0 & 1 \end{vmatrix} = (2)(5)(-2)(1) = -20.$$

From this property we conclude that the determinant of an identity matrix is 1.

(4) If B is the matrix obtained by adding a multiple of one row (or column) of A to another row (column), then $|B| = |A|$.

Thus if

$$A = \begin{bmatrix} 2 & 4 & 2 & 6 \\ 1 & 3 & 5 & 2 \\ 1 & 2 & 1 & 3 \\ 0 & 5 & 6 & 2 \end{bmatrix}$$

and **B** is the matrix obtained from **A** by adding -2 times row 3 to row 1, then

$$|A| = \begin{vmatrix} 2 & 4 & 2 & 6 \\ 1 & 3 & 5 & 2 \\ 1 & 2 & 1 & 3 \\ 0 & 5 & 6 & 2 \end{vmatrix} = \begin{vmatrix} 0 & 0 & 0 & 0 \\ 1 & 3 & 5 & 2 \\ 1 & 2 & 1 & 3 \\ 0 & 5 & 6 & 2 \end{vmatrix} = |B|.$$

By property 1, $|B| = 0$ and hence $|A| = 0$.

(5) If B is the matrix obtained by interchanging two rows (or columns) of A, then $|A| = -|B|$.

Thus if

$$A = \begin{bmatrix} 2 & 2 & 1 & 6 \\ 0 & 0 & 0 & 1 \\ 0 & 0 & 2 & 0 \\ 0 & 1 & -3 & 4 \end{bmatrix}$$

and **B** is obtained from **A** by interchanging rows 2 and 4, then

$$|\mathbf{A}| = \begin{vmatrix} 2 & 2 & 1 & 6 \\ 0 & 0 & 0 & 1 \\ 0 & 0 & 2 & 0 \\ 0 & 1 & -3 & 4 \end{vmatrix} = - \begin{vmatrix} 2 & 2 & 1 & 6 \\ 0 & 1 & -3 & 4 \\ 0 & 0 & 2 & 0 \\ 0 & 0 & 0 & 1 \end{vmatrix} = -|\mathbf{B}|.$$

By property 3, $|\mathbf{B}| = 4$ and hence $|\mathbf{A}| = -4$.

(6) **If B is the matrix obtained by multiplying each entry of a row (or column) of A by the same real number k, then $|\mathbf{B}| = k\,|\mathbf{A}|$.**
Thus,

$$\begin{vmatrix} 2\cdot3 & 2\cdot5 & 2\cdot7 \\ 5 & 2 & 1 \\ 6 & 4 & 3 \end{vmatrix} = 2 \begin{vmatrix} 3 & 5 & 7 \\ 5 & 2 & 1 \\ 6 & 4 & 3 \end{vmatrix}.$$

Essentially, a real number can be "factored out" of one row or column.

(7) **The determinant of the product of two matrices of order n is the product of their determinants. That is, $|\mathbf{AB}| = |\mathbf{A}|\,|\mathbf{B}|$.**
Thus if

$$\mathbf{A} = \begin{bmatrix} 1 & 2 \\ 3 & 4 \end{bmatrix} \quad \text{and} \quad \mathbf{B} = \begin{bmatrix} 1 & 2 \\ 0 & 3 \end{bmatrix},$$

then

$$|\mathbf{AB}| = |\mathbf{A}| \cdot |\mathbf{B}| = \begin{vmatrix} 1 & 2 \\ 3 & 4 \end{vmatrix} \cdot \begin{vmatrix} 1 & 2 \\ 0 & 3 \end{vmatrix} = (-2)(3) = -6.$$

EXAMPLE 35

Evaluate

$$|\mathbf{A}| = \begin{vmatrix} 1 & 1 & 0 & 5 \\ 1 & 2 & 1 & 0 \\ 0 & 2 & 1 & 1 \\ 3 & 0 & 0 & -4 \end{vmatrix}.$$

Our technique will be to express **A** in upper triangular form (we say we "triangulate") and then, by property 3, take the product of the main diagonal.

$$\begin{vmatrix} 1 & 1 & 0 & 5 \\ 1 & 2 & 1 & 0 \\ 0 & 2 & 1 & 1 \\ 3 & 0 & 0 & -4 \end{vmatrix} = \begin{vmatrix} 1 & 1 & 0 & 5 \\ 0 & 1 & 1 & -5 \\ 0 & 2 & 1 & 1 \\ 0 & -3 & 0 & -19 \end{vmatrix}$$

(by adding -1 times row 1 to row 2; adding -3 times row 1 to row 4)

$$= \begin{vmatrix} 1 & 1 & 0 & 5 \\ 0 & 1 & 1 & -5 \\ 0 & 0 & -1 & 11 \\ 0 & 0 & 3 & -34 \end{vmatrix}$$

(by adding -2 times row 2 to row 3; adding 3 times row 2 to row 4)

$$= \begin{vmatrix} 1 & 1 & 0 & 5 \\ 0 & 1 & 1 & -5 \\ 0 & 0 & -1 & 11 \\ 0 & 0 & 0 & -1 \end{vmatrix}$$

(by adding 3 times row 3 to row 4)

$$= (1)(1)(-1)(-1) = 1.$$

A quick way to evaluate a determinant of order 3 is shown in Fig. 14-1.

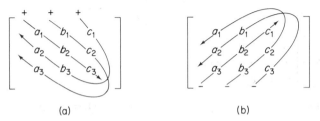

(a)   (b)

Fig. 14-1

Take the sum of the products of the three entries joined by the arrows in the left diagram. In the right diagram, take the sum of the products of the three entries, but precede each product by a minus sign. Then add the two sums. For example,

$$\begin{vmatrix} 12 & -1 & 3 \\ -3 & 1 & -1 \\ -10 & 2 & -3 \end{vmatrix}.$$

$$= (12)(1)(-3) + (-1)(-1)(-10) + (3)(2)(-3) -$$
$$(-10)(1)(3) - (2)(-1)(12) - (-3)(-1)(-3)$$

$$= -36 - 10 - 18 + 30 + 24 + 9$$

$$= -1.$$

This confirms the result of Example 33(a).

PITFALL.   *The above technique works for determinants of order 3 only.*

EXERCISE 14-7

Evaluate the determinants in problems 1-6.

1. $\begin{vmatrix} 2 & 1 \\ 3 & 2 \end{vmatrix}$

2. $\begin{vmatrix} 3 & 2 \\ -5 & -4 \end{vmatrix}$

3. $\begin{vmatrix} -2 & -3 \\ -4 & -6 \end{vmatrix}$

4. $\begin{vmatrix} -3 & 1 \\ -a & b \end{vmatrix}$

5. $\begin{vmatrix} 1 & x \\ 0 & y \end{vmatrix}$

6. $\begin{vmatrix} -2 & -a \\ -a & 2 \end{vmatrix}$

In problems 7 and 8, evaluate the given expressions.

7. $\dfrac{\begin{vmatrix} 1 & 2 \\ 3 & 4 \end{vmatrix}}{\begin{vmatrix} 2 & 1 \\ 5 & 6 \end{vmatrix}}$

8. $\dfrac{\begin{vmatrix} 6 & 2 \\ 1 & 5 \end{vmatrix}}{\begin{vmatrix} 2 & -6 \\ 5 & 3 \end{vmatrix}}$

9. Solve for k if

$$\begin{vmatrix} 2 & 3 \\ 4 & k \end{vmatrix} = 12.$$

If $\mathbf{A} = \begin{bmatrix} 1 & 2 & 3 \\ 4 & 5 & 6 \\ 7 & 8 & 9 \end{bmatrix}$, evaluate

10. the minor of a_{31}

11. the minor of a_{22}

12. the cofactor of a_{23}

13. the cofactor of a_{32}

14. If $\mathbf{A} = [a_{ij}]$ is 50×50 and the minor of $a_{43,47}$ equals 20, what is the value of the cofactor of $a_{43,47}$?

If

$$\mathbf{A} = \begin{bmatrix} a_{11} & a_{12} & a_{13} & a_{14} \\ a_{21} & a_{22} & a_{23} & a_{24} \\ a_{31} & a_{32} & a_{33} & a_{34} \\ a_{41} & a_{42} & a_{43} & a_{44} \end{bmatrix},$$

write

15. the minor of a_{32}

16. the minor of a_{24}

17. the cofactor of a_{13}

18. the cofactor of a_{43}

In problems 19–34, evaluate the determinant. Use properties of determinants if possible.

19. $\begin{vmatrix} 2 & 1 & 3 \\ 2 & 0 & 1 \\ -4 & 0 & 6 \end{vmatrix}$

20. $\begin{vmatrix} 3 & 2 & 1 \\ 1 & -2 & 3 \\ -1 & 3 & 2 \end{vmatrix}$

21. $\begin{vmatrix} 1 & 2 & -3 \\ 4 & 5 & 4 \\ 3 & -2 & 1 \end{vmatrix}$

22. $\begin{vmatrix} 1 & 0 & -1 \\ 0 & 1 & 0 \\ 1 & -1 & 1 \end{vmatrix}$

23. $\begin{vmatrix} 2 & 1 & 5 \\ -3 & 4 & -1 \\ 0 & 6 & -1 \end{vmatrix}$

24. $\begin{vmatrix} 1 & 2 & 3 \\ 4 & 5 & 4 \\ 3 & 2 & 1 \end{vmatrix}$

25. $\begin{vmatrix} 2 & -1 & 3 \\ 1 & 1 & -1 \\ 1 & 2 & -3 \end{vmatrix}$

26. $\begin{vmatrix} 1 & 2 & 3 \\ 4 & 5 & 6 \\ 7 & 8 & 9 \end{vmatrix}$

27. $\begin{vmatrix} \frac{1}{2} & \frac{2}{3} & -\frac{1}{2} \\ -1 & \frac{1}{3} & \frac{2}{3} \\ 3 & -4 & 1 \end{vmatrix}$

28. $\begin{vmatrix} -\frac{1}{3} & \frac{1}{4} & 4 \\ \frac{3}{2} & \frac{3}{8} & -2 \\ -\frac{1}{8} & \frac{9}{2} & 1 \end{vmatrix}$

29. $\begin{vmatrix} 1 & 0 & 3 & 2 \\ 4 & -1 & 0 & 1 \\ 2 & 1 & 0 & 3 \\ -1 & 2 & 3 & -1 \end{vmatrix}$

30. $\begin{vmatrix} 7 & 6 & 0 & 5 \\ -3 & 2 & 0 & 1 \\ 4 & -3 & 0 & 2 \\ 1 & 0 & 0 & 6 \end{vmatrix}$

31. $\begin{vmatrix} 1 & 7 & -3 & 8 \\ 0 & 1 & -5 & 4 \\ 0 & 0 & 1 & 7 \\ 0 & 0 & 0 & 1 \end{vmatrix}$

32. $\begin{vmatrix} 1 & 2 & -3 & 4 \\ 3 & -1 & 2 & 4 \\ -2 & -4 & 6 & -8 \\ 0 & 3 & -1 & 2 \end{vmatrix}$

33. $\begin{vmatrix} 1 & 0 & 0 & 0 \\ 0 & -2 & 0 & 0 \\ 0 & 0 & 4 & 0 \\ 0 & 0 & 0 & -3 \end{vmatrix}$

34. $\begin{vmatrix} 1 & -3 & 2 & 6 & 4 \\ 0 & 13 & 0 & 1 & 5 \\ -2 & 1 & 2 & 3 & 4 \\ 1 & 1 & 4 & 5 & 9 \end{vmatrix}$

Solve for x.

35. $\begin{vmatrix} x & -2 \\ 7 & 7-x \end{vmatrix} = 26$

36. $\begin{vmatrix} 3 & x & 2x \\ 0 & x & 99 \\ 0 & 0 & x-1 \end{vmatrix} = 60$

37. If $\mathbf{A}$ is of order 4×4 and $|\mathbf{A}| = 12$, what is the value of the determinant obtained by multiplying every element in $\mathbf{A}$ by 2?

14-8 CRAMER'S RULE

Determinants can be applied to solving a system of n linear equations in n unknowns. In fact, it is from the analysis of such systems that the study of determinants took its origin. Although the method of reduction is more practical for systems involving a large number of unknowns, the method of solution by determinants is interesting enough to warrant some attention here. We shall first consider a system of two linear equations in two unknowns. Then the results will be extended to include more general situations.

Let us solve

$$\begin{cases} a_{11}x + a_{12}y = c_1 \\ a_{21}x + a_{22}y = c_2. \end{cases} \tag{1}$$

To find an explicit formula for x, we look at $x \begin{vmatrix} a_{11} & a_{12} \\ a_{21} & a_{22} \end{vmatrix}$.

$$x \begin{vmatrix} a_{11} & a_{12} \\ a_{21} & a_{22} \end{vmatrix} = \begin{vmatrix} a_{11}x & a_{12} \\ a_{21}x & a_{22} \end{vmatrix} \qquad \text{(property 6 of Sec. 14-7)}$$

$$= \begin{vmatrix} a_{11}x + a_{12}y & a_{12} \\ a_{21}x + a_{22}y & a_{22} \end{vmatrix} \qquad \text{(adding } y \text{ times column 2 to column 1)}$$

$$= \begin{vmatrix} c_1 & a_{12} \\ c_2 & a_{22} \end{vmatrix}. \qquad \text{[from Eq. (1)]}$$

Thus,

$$x \begin{vmatrix} a_{11} & a_{12} \\ a_{21} & a_{22} \end{vmatrix} = \begin{vmatrix} c_1 & a_{12} \\ c_2 & a_{22} \end{vmatrix}$$

and so

$$x = \frac{\begin{vmatrix} c_1 & a_{12} \\ c_2 & a_{22} \end{vmatrix}}{\begin{vmatrix} a_{11} & a_{12} \\ a_{21} & a_{22} \end{vmatrix}}. \tag{2}$$

To find a formula for y, we look at $y \begin{vmatrix} a_{11} & a_{12} \\ a_{21} & a_{22} \end{vmatrix}$.

$$y \begin{vmatrix} a_{11} & a_{12} \\ a_{21} & a_{22} \end{vmatrix} = \begin{vmatrix} a_{11} & a_{12}y \\ a_{21} & a_{22}y \end{vmatrix} \qquad \text{(property 6 of Sec. 14-7)}$$

$$= \begin{vmatrix} a_{11} & a_{11}x + a_{12}y \\ a_{21} & a_{21}x + a_{22}y \end{vmatrix} \qquad \text{(adding } x \text{ times column 1 to column 2)}$$

$$= \begin{vmatrix} a_{11} & c_1 \\ a_{21} & c_2 \end{vmatrix}. \qquad \text{[from Eq. (1)]}$$

Thus,

$$y \begin{vmatrix} a_{11} & a_{12} \\ a_{21} & a_{22} \end{vmatrix} = \begin{vmatrix} a_{11} & c_1 \\ a_{21} & c_2 \end{vmatrix}$$

and so

$$y = \frac{\begin{vmatrix} a_{11} & c_1 \\ a_{21} & c_2 \end{vmatrix}}{\begin{vmatrix} a_{11} & a_{12} \\ a_{21} & a_{22} \end{vmatrix}}. \qquad (3)$$

Note that in Eqs. (2) and (3) the denominators are the same, namely the determinant of the coefficient matrix of the given system. In finding x, the numerator in Eq. (2) is the determinant of the matrix obtained by replacing the "x-column" (that is, column 1) of the coefficient matrix by the column of constants $\begin{matrix} c_1 \\ c_2 \end{matrix}$. Similarly, the numerator in Eq. (3) is the determinant of the matrix obtained from the coefficient matrix when the "y-column" (that is, column 2) is replaced by $\begin{matrix} c_1 \\ c_2 \end{matrix}$. Provided that the determinant of the coefficient matrix is not zero, the original system will have a unique solution. However, if this determinant is zero, the procedure is not applicable and the system may have either no solution or an infinite number of solutions.

We shall illustrate the above results by solving the system

$$\begin{cases} 2x + y + 5 = 0 \\ \qquad 3y + x = 6. \end{cases}$$

First, the system is written in the appropriate form:

$$\begin{cases} 2x + y = -5 \\ x + 3y = \quad 6. \end{cases}$$

The determinant Δ of the coefficient matrix is

$$\Delta = \begin{vmatrix} 2 & 1 \\ 1 & 3 \end{vmatrix} = 2(3) - 1(1) = 5.$$

Since $\Delta \ne 0$, there is a unique solution. Solving for x, we have

$$x = \frac{\begin{vmatrix} -5 & 1 \\ 6 & 3 \end{vmatrix}}{\Delta} = \frac{-21}{5} = -\frac{21}{5}.$$

Solving for y, we obtain

$$y = \frac{\begin{vmatrix} 2 & -5 \\ 1 & 6 \end{vmatrix}}{\Delta} = \frac{17}{5}.$$

Thus the solution is $x = -\frac{21}{5}$ and $y = \frac{17}{5}$.

The method described above can be extended to systems of n linear equations in n unknowns and is referred to as *Cramer's rule*.

Cramer's Rule.   Let a system of n linear equations in n unknowns be given by

$$\begin{cases} a_{11}x_1 + a_{12}x_2 + \cdots + a_{1n}x_n = c_1 \\ a_{21}x_1 + a_{22}x_2 + \cdots + a_{2n}x_n = c_2 \\ \quad \vdots \qquad \vdots \qquad\qquad \vdots \qquad \vdots \\ a_{n1}x_1 + a_{n2}x_2 + \cdots + a_{nn}x_n = c_n. \end{cases}$$

If the determinant Δ of the coefficient matrix **A** is different from 0, then the system has a unique solution. Moreover, the solution is given by

$$x_1 = \frac{\Delta_1}{\Delta}, \qquad x_2 = \frac{\Delta_2}{\Delta}, \qquad \dots, \qquad x_n = \frac{\Delta_n}{\Delta}$$

where Δ_k, the numerator of x_k, is the determinant of the matrix obtained by replacing the kth column of **A** by the column of constants.

EXAMPLE 36

Solve the following system by Cramer's rule.

$$\begin{cases} 2x + y + z = 0 \\ 4x + 3y + 2z = 2 \\ 2x - y - 3z = 0. \end{cases}$$

The determinant of the coefficient matrix (by using the "quick" way to find a determinant of order 3) is

$$\Delta = \begin{vmatrix} 2 & 1 & 1 \\ 4 & 3 & 2 \\ 2 & -1 & -3 \end{vmatrix} = -18 + 4 - 4 - (6) - (-4) - (-12) = -8.$$

Since $\Delta \neq 0$, there is a unique solution. Solving for x, we obtain

$$x = \frac{\begin{vmatrix} 0 & 1 & 1 \\ 2 & 3 & 2 \\ 0 & -1 & -3 \end{vmatrix}}{\Delta} = \frac{0 + 0 - 2 - (0) - (0) - (-6)}{-8} = \frac{4}{-8} = -\frac{1}{2}.$$

Similarly,

$$y = \frac{\begin{vmatrix} 2 & 0 & 1 \\ 4 & 2 & 2 \\ 2 & 0 & -3 \end{vmatrix}}{\Delta} = \frac{-12 + 0 + 0 - (4) - (0) - (0)}{-8} = \frac{-16}{-8} = 2.$$

$$z = \frac{\begin{vmatrix} 2 & 1 & 0 \\ 4 & 3 & 2 \\ 2 & -1 & 0 \end{vmatrix}}{\Delta} = \frac{0 + 4 + 0 - (0) - (-4) - (0)}{-8} = \frac{8}{-8} = -1.$$

The solution is $x = -\frac{1}{2}$, $y = 2$, and $z = -1$.

EXAMPLE 37

Solve the following system for z, using Cramer's rule.

$$\begin{cases} x + y & + 5w = 6 \\ x + 2y + z & = 4 \\ 2y + z + w = 6 \\ 3x & -4w = 2. \end{cases}$$

$$\Delta = \begin{vmatrix} 1 & 1 & 0 & 5 \\ 1 & 2 & 1 & 0 \\ 0 & 2 & 1 & 1 \\ 3 & 0 & 0 & -4 \end{vmatrix} = \begin{vmatrix} 1 & 1 & 0 & 5 \\ 0 & 1 & 1 & -5 \\ 0 & 0 & -1 & 11 \\ 0 & 0 & 0 & -1 \end{vmatrix} = 1.$$

Here we transformed into upper-triangular form and found the product of the main diagonal entries (Sec. 14-7, Example 35). In a similar fashion we obtain

$$\Delta_z = \begin{vmatrix} 1 & 1 & 6 & 5 \\ 1 & 2 & 4 & 0 \\ 0 & 2 & 6 & 1 \\ 3 & 0 & 2 & -4 \end{vmatrix} = \begin{vmatrix} 1 & 1 & 6 & 5 \\ 0 & 1 & -2 & -5 \\ 0 & 0 & 10 & 11 \\ 0 & 0 & 0 & -\frac{49}{5} \end{vmatrix} = -98.$$

Hence $z = \Delta_z / \Delta = -98/1 = -98$.

EXERCISE 14-8

Solve each of the following by Cramer's rule, if possible.

1. $\begin{cases} 2x - y = 4 \\ 3x + y = 5 \end{cases}$ 2. $\begin{cases} 3x + y = 6 \\ 7x - 2y = 5 \end{cases}$

3. $\begin{cases} -2x = 4 - 3y \\ y = 6x - 1 \end{cases}$ 4. $\begin{cases} x + 2y - 6 = 0 \\ y - 1 = 3x \end{cases}$

5. $\begin{cases} 3(x + 2) = 5 \\ 6(x + y) = -8 \end{cases}$ 6. $\begin{cases} w - 2z = 4 \\ 3w - 4z = 6 \end{cases}$

7. $\begin{cases} \frac{3}{2}x - \frac{1}{4}z = 1 \\ \frac{1}{3}x + \frac{1}{2}z = 2 \end{cases}$ 8. $\begin{cases} .6x - .7y = .33 \\ 2.1x - .9y = .69 \end{cases}$

9. $\begin{cases} x + y + z = 6 \\ x - y + z = 2 \\ 2x - y + 3z = 6 \end{cases}$ 10. $\begin{cases} 2x - y + 3z = 12 \\ x + y - z = -3 \\ x + 2y - 3z = -10 \end{cases}$

11. $\begin{cases} 2x - 3y + 4z = 0 \\ x + y - 3z = 4 \\ 3x + 2y - z = 0 \end{cases}$ 12. $\begin{cases} 3r \qquad - t = 7 \\ 4r - s + 3t = 9 \\ 3s + 2t = 15 \end{cases}$

13. $\begin{cases} 2x - 3y + z = -2 \\ x - 6y + 3z = -2 \\ 3x + 3y - 2z = 2 \end{cases}$ 14. $\begin{cases} x - z = 14 \\ y + z = 21 \\ x - y + z = -10 \end{cases}$

In each of the following solve for the indicated unknowns.

15. $\begin{cases} x - y + 3z + w = -14 \\ x + 2y \qquad - 3w = 12 \\ 2x + 3y + 6z + w = 1 \\ x + y + z + w = 6 \end{cases}$; y, w

16. $\begin{cases} x + y + 5z = 6 \\ x + 2y + w = 4 \\ 2y + z + w = 6 \\ 3x - 4z = 2 \end{cases}$; x, y

17. Show that Cramer's rule does *not* apply to

$$\begin{cases} 2 - y = x \\ 3 + x = -y, \end{cases}$$

but that from geometrical considerations we can assert there is no solution.

14-9   INVERSES USING THE ADJOINT

Determinants and cofactors can be used to find the inverse of a matrix, if it exists. To begin we need the idea of the *transpose* of a matrix.

DEFINITION.   *The **transpose** of an m by n matrix* $\mathbf{A}$, *denoted* $\mathbf{A}^T$, *is the n by m matrix whose i-th row is the i-th column of* $\mathbf{A}$.

EXAMPLE 38

If $\mathbf{A} = \begin{bmatrix} 1 & 2 & 3 \\ 4 & 5 & 6 \\ 7 & 8 & 9 \end{bmatrix}$, *find* $\mathbf{A}^T$.

Column 1 of $\mathbf{A}$ becomes row 1 of $\mathbf{A}^T$, column 2 becomes row 2, and column 3 becomes row 3. Thus

$$\mathbf{A}^T = \begin{bmatrix} 1 & 4 & 7 \\ 2 & 5 & 8 \\ 3 & 6 & 9 \end{bmatrix}.$$

DEFINITION.   *The **adjoint** of a square matrix* $\mathbf{A}$, *denoted adj* $\mathbf{A}$, *is the transpose of the matrix obtained by replacing each entry* a_{ij} *in* $\mathbf{A}$ *by its cofactor* c_{ij}. *That is, it is the transpose of the cofactor matrix* $[c_{ij}]$.

EXAMPLE 39

If $\mathbf{A} = \begin{bmatrix} 2 & -1 & 3 \\ 3 & 0 & -5 \\ 2 & 1 & 1 \end{bmatrix}$, *find adj* $\mathbf{A}$.

We first find the cofactor c_{ij} of each entry a_{ij} in $\mathbf{A}$.

$$c_{11} = (-1)^{1+1} \begin{vmatrix} 0 & -5 \\ 1 & 1 \end{vmatrix} = (1)(5) = 5$$

$$c_{12} = (-1)^{1+2} \begin{vmatrix} 3 & -5 \\ 2 & 1 \end{vmatrix} = (-1)(13) = -13$$

$$c_{13} = (-1)^{1+3} \begin{vmatrix} 3 & 0 \\ 2 & 1 \end{vmatrix} = (1)(3) = 3$$

$$c_{21} = (-1)^{2+1} \begin{vmatrix} -1 & 3 \\ 1 & 1 \end{vmatrix} = (-1)(-4) = 4$$

$$c_{22} = (-1)^{2+2} \begin{vmatrix} 2 & 3 \\ 2 & 1 \end{vmatrix} = (1)(-4) = -4$$

$$c_{23} = (-1)^{2+3} \begin{vmatrix} 2 & -1 \\ 2 & 1 \end{vmatrix} = (-1)(4) = -4$$

$$c_{31} = (-1)^{3+1} \begin{vmatrix} -1 & 3 \\ 0 & -5 \end{vmatrix} = (1)(5) = 5$$

$$c_{32} = (-1)^{3+2} \begin{vmatrix} 2 & 3 \\ 3 & -5 \end{vmatrix} = (-1)(-19) = 19$$

$$c_{33} = (-1)^{3+3} \begin{vmatrix} 2 & -1 \\ 3 & 0 \end{vmatrix} = (1)(3) = 3$$

The cofactor matrix $[c_{ij}]$ is thus

$$[c_{ij}] = \begin{bmatrix} 5 & -13 & 3 \\ 4 & -4 & -4 \\ 5 & 19 & 3 \end{bmatrix}.$$

The adjoint is

$$\text{adj } \mathbf{A} = [c_{ij}]^{\mathsf{T}} = \begin{bmatrix} 5 & 4 & 5 \\ -13 & -4 & 19 \\ 3 & -4 & 3 \end{bmatrix}.$$

It can be shown that if $|\mathbf{A}| \neq 0$, then $\mathbf{A}^{-1}$ exists and

$$\boxed{\mathbf{A}^{-1} = \frac{1}{|\mathbf{A}|} \text{ adj } \mathbf{A}.}$$

EXAMPLE 40

If $\mathbf{A} = \begin{bmatrix} 2 & -1 & 3 \\ 3 & 0 & -5 \\ 2 & 1 & 1 \end{bmatrix}$, *find* $\mathbf{A}^{-1}$.

We find that

$$|\mathbf{A}| = 0 + 10 + 9 - (0) - (-10) - (-3) = 32 \neq 0.$$

Thus $\mathbf{A}^{-1}$ exists. Also, from Example 39,

$$\text{adj } \mathbf{A} = \begin{bmatrix} 5 & 4 & 5 \\ -13 & -4 & 19 \\ 3 & -4 & 3 \end{bmatrix}.$$

Thus

$$\mathbf{A}^{-1} = \frac{1}{|\mathbf{A}|} \text{adj } \mathbf{A}$$

$$= \frac{1}{32} \begin{bmatrix} 5 & 4 & 5 \\ -13 & -4 & 19 \\ 3 & -4 & 3 \end{bmatrix}$$

$$= \begin{bmatrix} \frac{5}{32} & \frac{1}{8} & \frac{5}{32} \\ -\frac{13}{32} & -\frac{1}{8} & \frac{19}{32} \\ \frac{3}{32} & -\frac{1}{8} & \frac{3}{32} \end{bmatrix}$$

You should verify that $\mathbf{A}^{-1}\mathbf{A} = \mathbf{A}\mathbf{A}^{-1} = \mathbf{I}$.

EXAMPLE 41

Find $\mathbf{A}^{-1}$ *if* $\mathbf{A} = \begin{bmatrix} 1 & 0 & -2 \\ 4 & -2 & 1 \\ 1 & 2 & -10 \end{bmatrix}.$

We first find the cofactors of $\mathbf{A}$.

$$c_{11} = (-1)^2 \begin{vmatrix} -2 & 1 \\ 2 & -10 \end{vmatrix} = 18$$

$$c_{12} = (-1)^3 \begin{vmatrix} 4 & 1 \\ 1 & -10 \end{vmatrix} = 41$$

$$c_{13} = (-1)^4 \begin{vmatrix} 4 & -2 \\ 1 & 2 \end{vmatrix} = 10$$

$$c_{21} = (-1)^3 \begin{vmatrix} 0 & -2 \\ 2 & -10 \end{vmatrix} = -4$$

$$c_{22} = (-1)^4 \begin{vmatrix} 1 & -2 \\ 1 & -10 \end{vmatrix} = -8$$

$$c_{23} = (-1)^5 \begin{vmatrix} 1 & 0 \\ 1 & 2 \end{vmatrix} = -2$$

$$c_{31} = (-1)^4 \begin{vmatrix} 0 & -2 \\ -2 & 1 \end{vmatrix} = -4$$

$$c_{32} = (-1)^5 \begin{vmatrix} 1 & -2 \\ 4 & 1 \end{vmatrix} = -9$$

$$c_{33} = (-1)^6 \begin{vmatrix} 1 & 0 \\ 4 & -2 \end{vmatrix} = -2$$

Since the adjoint of **A** involves $|\mathbf{A}|$, we compute $|\mathbf{A}|$ next. We already have the cofactors, so we shall find $|\mathbf{A}|$ by expanding along the first row.

$$|\mathbf{A}| = (1)(18) + 0 + (-2)(10) = -2.$$

The cofactor matrix is

$$[c_{ij}] = \begin{bmatrix} 18 & 41 & 10 \\ -4 & -8 & -2 \\ -4 & -9 & -2 \end{bmatrix}$$

and the adjoint is $[c_{ij}]^{\mathrm{T}}$:

$$\text{adj } \mathbf{A} = \begin{bmatrix} 18 & -4 & -4 \\ 41 & -8 & -9 \\ 10 & -2 & -2 \end{bmatrix}.$$

Thus

$$\mathbf{A}^{-1} = \frac{1}{|\mathbf{A}|} \text{adj } \mathbf{A}$$

$$= \frac{1}{-2} \begin{bmatrix} 18 & -4 & -4 \\ 41 & -8 & -9 \\ 10 & -2 & -2 \end{bmatrix}$$

$$= \begin{bmatrix} -9 & 2 & 2 \\ -\frac{41}{2} & 4 & \frac{9}{2} \\ -5 & 1 & 1 \end{bmatrix}.$$

This result was obtained in Example 29(a) by row reduction.

EXAMPLE 42

Find $\mathbf{A}^{-1}$ *if* $\mathbf{A} = \begin{bmatrix} \frac{4}{5} & -\frac{1}{3} \\ -\frac{3}{10} & \frac{13}{15} \end{bmatrix}$.

Since $|\mathbf{A}| = (\frac{4}{5})(\frac{13}{15}) - (-\frac{1}{3})(-\frac{3}{10}) = \frac{89}{150} \neq 0$, $\mathbf{A}^{-1}$ exists. The cofactors are (the vertical bars here denote determinants, not absolute value)

$$c_{11} = (-1)^2 |\tfrac{13}{15}| = \tfrac{13}{15} \qquad\qquad c_{12} = (-1)^3 |-\tfrac{3}{10}| = \tfrac{3}{10}$$

$$c_{21} = (-1)^3 |-\tfrac{1}{3}| = \tfrac{1}{3} \qquad\qquad c_{22} = (-1)^4 |\tfrac{4}{5}| = \tfrac{4}{5}.$$

The cofactor matrix is

$$[c_{ij}] = \begin{bmatrix} \frac{13}{15} & \frac{3}{10} \\ \frac{1}{3} & \frac{4}{5} \end{bmatrix}$$

and the adjoint is

$$\text{adj } \mathbf{A} = [c_{ij}]^T = \begin{bmatrix} \frac{13}{15} & \frac{1}{3} \\ \frac{3}{10} & \frac{4}{5} \end{bmatrix}.$$

Hence,

$$\mathbf{A}^{-1} = \frac{1}{|\mathbf{A}|} \text{adj } \mathbf{A} = \frac{150}{89} \begin{bmatrix} \frac{13}{15} & \frac{1}{3} \\ \frac{3}{10} & \frac{4}{5} \end{bmatrix}$$

$$= \begin{bmatrix} \frac{130}{89} & \frac{50}{89} \\ \frac{45}{89} & \frac{120}{89} \end{bmatrix}.$$

EXERCISE 14-9

For the following, use adjoints to find the inverses.

1. $\begin{bmatrix} 3 & -2 \\ 1 & 2 \end{bmatrix}$

2. $\begin{bmatrix} 2 & -1 \\ 1 & 3 \end{bmatrix}$

3. $\begin{bmatrix} \frac{1}{4} & \frac{3}{8} \\ 0 & \frac{1}{6} \end{bmatrix}$

4. $\begin{bmatrix} \frac{1}{2} & \frac{1}{4} \\ \frac{1}{3} & \frac{2}{3} \end{bmatrix}$

5. $\begin{bmatrix} 2 & 3 & -1 \\ 1 & 2 & 1 \\ -1 & -1 & 3 \end{bmatrix}$

6. $\begin{bmatrix} -1 & 2 & -3 \\ 2 & 1 & 0 \\ 4 & -2 & 5 \end{bmatrix}$

7. $\begin{bmatrix} 1 & -\frac{2}{3} & \frac{5}{3} \\ -1 & \frac{4}{3} & -\frac{10}{3} \\ -1 & 1 & -2 \end{bmatrix}$

8. $\begin{bmatrix} 1 & 2 & 3 \\ 1 & 3 & 5 \\ 1 & 5 & 12 \end{bmatrix}$

9. $\begin{bmatrix} -\frac{1}{4} & -\frac{1}{2} & \frac{3}{4} \\ 0 & \frac{1}{2} & 0 \\ \frac{1}{2} & \frac{1}{2} & -\frac{1}{2} \end{bmatrix}$

10. $\begin{bmatrix} \frac{11}{2} & -\frac{5}{2} & -\frac{3}{2} \\ -4 & 2 & 1 \\ -\frac{7}{2} & \frac{3}{2} & \frac{1}{2} \end{bmatrix}$

11. $\begin{bmatrix} \frac{2}{5} & -\frac{1}{5} & \frac{9}{15} \\ \frac{4}{15} & \frac{1}{5} & -\frac{4}{15} \\ -\frac{1}{15} & \frac{1}{5} & \frac{1}{15} \end{bmatrix}$

12. $\begin{bmatrix} 0 & -\frac{1}{9} & \frac{4}{9} \\ 0 & \frac{2}{9} & \frac{1}{9} \\ \frac{1}{8} & \frac{1}{36} & -\frac{1}{9} \end{bmatrix}$

14-10 INPUT-OUTPUT ANALYSIS

Input-output matrices, which were developed by Wassily W. Leontief† of Harvard, indicate the supply and demand interrelationships that exist between the various sectors of an economy during some time period. The phrase "input-output" is used because the matrices show how much each sector buys from other sectors as well as how much it sells to them.

A hypothetical example for an oversimplified two-industry economy is given by the matrix below. Before we explain the matrix, let us say that the

	Consumers (input)			
	Industry *A*	Industry *B*	Final Demand	*Totals*
Producers (output):				
Industry *A*	240	500	460	1200
Industry *B*	360	200	940	1500
Labor	600	800	1400	2800

industrial sectors can be thought of as manufacturing, steel, agriculture, coal, etc. The final demand sector could be households, government, etc.

Each row shows how the output of each sector is consumed by the three sectors. The entries represent the value of the products and might be

---

†Leontief won the 1973 Nobel prize in economic science for the development of the "input-output" method and its applications to economic problems.

in units of millions of dollars of product. For example, of the total output of industry A, 240 went to industry A itself (for internal use), 500 to industry B, and 460 went direct to consumers for final use (hence the term *final demand*). The total output of A is the sum of industrial demand and final demand (240 + 500 + 460 = 1200).

Each column gives the value of what each sector consumes from the other sectors. For example, in producing its 1200 units, A consumed 240 units of output from itself, 360 of B's output, and 600 of labor's output.

Note that the sum of the entries in each row is equal to the sum of the entries in each column. That is, A consumed from all sectors the same amount as it produced for them.

Input-output analysis allows us to estimate the total production of each *industrial* sector if there is a change in final demand *as long as the basic structure of the economy remains the same.* This important assumption means that for each industry, the amount spent on each input for each dollar's worth of output must remain fixed.

For example, in producing 1200 units, industry A uses 240 units from industry A, 360 units from B, and 600 units of labor. Thus for each dollar's worth of output, industry A spends $\frac{240}{1200} = \frac{1}{5}$ ($=\$0.20$) on A, $\frac{360}{1200} = \frac{3}{10}$ ($=\$0.30$) on B, and $\frac{600}{1200} = \frac{1}{2}$ ($=\$0.50$) on labor. Combining these fixed ratios of industry A with those of industry B, we can give the requirements per dollar of output for each industry.

$$
\begin{array}{c}
 \\
A \\
B \\
\text{Labor}
\end{array}
\begin{array}{cc}
A & B \\
\left[\begin{array}{cc}
\frac{240}{1200} & \frac{500}{1500} \\
\frac{360}{1200} & \frac{200}{1500} \\
\hline
\frac{600}{1200} & \frac{800}{1500}
\end{array}\right]
\end{array}
=
\begin{array}{cc}
A & B \\
\left[\begin{array}{cc}
\frac{1}{5} & \frac{1}{3} \\
\frac{3}{10} & \frac{2}{15} \\
\hline
\frac{1}{2} & \frac{8}{15}
\end{array}\right]
\end{array}
\begin{array}{c}
 \\
A \\
B \\
\text{Labor}
\end{array}
$$

The entries in the matrix are called *input-output coefficients*. The sum of each column is 1.

Now, suppose final demand changes from 460 to 500 for industry A and from 940 to 1200 for industry B. We would like to estimate the *total* output that A and B must produce for both industry and final demand to meet this goal, assuming the structure in the preceding matrix remains the same.

Let the new values of total outputs for industries A and B be X_A and X_B, respectively. Then

$$
\begin{array}{ccccc}
\text{Total value of} & = & \text{Value consumed} & + & \text{Value consumed} & + & \text{Value consumed} \\
\text{output of } A & & \text{by } A & & \text{by } B & & \text{by final demand}
\end{array}
$$

$$X_A = \tfrac{1}{5}X_A + \tfrac{1}{3}X_B + 500.$$

Similarly,

$$X_B = \tfrac{3}{10}X_A + \tfrac{2}{15}X_B + 1200.$$

In matrix notation,

$$\begin{bmatrix} X_A \\ X_B \end{bmatrix} = \begin{bmatrix} \tfrac{1}{5} & \tfrac{1}{3} \\ \tfrac{3}{10} & \tfrac{2}{15} \end{bmatrix} \begin{bmatrix} X_A \\ X_B \end{bmatrix} + \begin{bmatrix} 500 \\ 1200 \end{bmatrix}. \qquad (1)$$

Let

$$\mathbf{X} = \begin{bmatrix} X_A \\ X_B \end{bmatrix}, \qquad \mathbf{A} = \begin{bmatrix} \tfrac{1}{5} & \tfrac{1}{3} \\ \tfrac{3}{10} & \tfrac{2}{15} \end{bmatrix}, \quad \text{and} \quad \mathbf{C} = \begin{bmatrix} 500 \\ 1200 \end{bmatrix}.$$

We call **X** the **output matrix,** **A** the **coefficient matrix,** and **C** the **final demand matrix.** From Eq. (1)

$$\mathbf{X} = \mathbf{AX} + \mathbf{C}$$

$$\mathbf{X} - \mathbf{AX} = \mathbf{C}.$$

If **I** is the 2×2 identity matrix, then

$$\mathbf{IX} - \mathbf{AX} = \mathbf{C}$$

$$(\mathbf{I} - \mathbf{A})\mathbf{X} = \mathbf{C}.$$

If $(\mathbf{I} - \mathbf{A})^{-1}$ exists, then

$$\boxed{\mathbf{X} = (\mathbf{I} - \mathbf{A})^{-1}\mathbf{C}.}$$

The matrix $\mathbf{I} - \mathbf{A}$ is called the **Leontief matrix.** Now,

$$\mathbf{I} - \mathbf{A} = \begin{bmatrix} 1 & 0 \\ 0 & 1 \end{bmatrix} - \begin{bmatrix} \tfrac{1}{5} & \tfrac{1}{3} \\ \tfrac{3}{10} & \tfrac{2}{15} \end{bmatrix}$$

$$= \begin{bmatrix} \tfrac{4}{5} & -\tfrac{1}{3} \\ -\tfrac{3}{10} & \tfrac{13}{15} \end{bmatrix}.$$

From Example 42,

$$(\mathbf{I} - \mathbf{A})^{-1} = \begin{bmatrix} \tfrac{130}{89} & \tfrac{50}{89} \\ \tfrac{45}{89} & \tfrac{120}{89} \end{bmatrix}.$$

Hence the output matrix is

$$\mathbf{X} = (\mathbf{I} - \mathbf{A})^{-1}\mathbf{C} = \begin{bmatrix} \tfrac{130}{89} & \tfrac{50}{89} \\ \tfrac{45}{89} & \tfrac{120}{89} \end{bmatrix} \begin{bmatrix} 500 \\ 1200 \end{bmatrix}$$

$$= \begin{bmatrix} 1404.49 \\ 1870.79 \end{bmatrix}.$$

Thus to meet the goal, industry A must produce 1404.49 units of value and industry B must produce 1870.79. If we were interested in the labor requirements for A then

$$L_A = \tfrac{1}{2}X_A = 702.25.$$

EXAMPLE 43

Given the input-output matrix below, suppose final demand for industry A changes to 77 for A, 154 for B, and 231 for C. Find the output matrix for the economy. (The entries are in millions of dollars.)

		Consumer		
		Industry		Final
Producer	A	B	C	Demand
Industry: A	240	180	144	36
B	120	36	48	156
C	120	72	48	240
Labor	120	72	240	—

We separately add the entries in the first three rows. The total value of output for industries A, B, and C are 600, 360, and 480 respectively. To get the coefficient matrix, we divide the industry entries in each industry column by the total value of output for that industry.

$$\mathbf{A} = \begin{bmatrix} \frac{240}{600} & \frac{180}{360} & \frac{144}{480} \\ \frac{120}{600} & \frac{36}{360} & \frac{48}{480} \\ \frac{120}{600} & \frac{72}{360} & \frac{48}{480} \end{bmatrix} = \begin{bmatrix} \frac{2}{5} & \frac{1}{2} & \frac{3}{10} \\ \frac{1}{5} & \frac{1}{10} & \frac{1}{10} \\ \frac{1}{5} & \frac{1}{5} & \frac{1}{10} \end{bmatrix}.$$

Thus, if $\mathbf{I}$ is the 3×3 identity matrix,

$$\mathbf{I} - \mathbf{A} = \begin{bmatrix} \frac{3}{5} & -\frac{1}{2} & -\frac{3}{10} \\ -\frac{1}{5} & \frac{9}{10} & -\frac{1}{10} \\ -\frac{1}{5} & -\frac{1}{5} & \frac{9}{10} \end{bmatrix}.$$

We can find $(\mathbf{I} - \mathbf{A})^{-1}$ using the adjoint. Computing the cofactors, we have

$$c_{11} = (-1)^{1+1} \begin{vmatrix} \frac{9}{10} & -\frac{1}{10} \\ -\frac{1}{5} & \frac{9}{10} \end{vmatrix} = \frac{79}{100}$$

$$c_{12} = (-1)^{1+2} \begin{vmatrix} -\frac{1}{5} & -\frac{1}{10} \\ -\frac{1}{5} & \frac{9}{10} \end{vmatrix} = \frac{1}{5}$$

$$c_{13} = (-1)^{1+3} \begin{vmatrix} -\frac{1}{5} & \frac{9}{10} \\ -\frac{1}{5} & -\frac{1}{5} \end{vmatrix} = \frac{11}{50}.$$

At this point we can evaluate $|\mathbf{I} - \mathbf{A}|$ along row 1 by using cofactors.

$$|\mathbf{I} - \mathbf{A}| = \tfrac{3}{5}(\tfrac{79}{100}) - \tfrac{1}{2}(\tfrac{1}{5}) - \tfrac{3}{10}(\tfrac{11}{50}) = \tfrac{77}{250}.$$

Continuing, we obtain

$$c_{21} = (-1)^{2+1} \begin{vmatrix} -\frac{1}{2} & -\frac{3}{10} \\ -\frac{1}{5} & \frac{9}{10} \end{vmatrix} = \frac{51}{100}$$

$$c_{22} = (-1)^{2+2} \begin{vmatrix} \frac{3}{5} & -\frac{3}{10} \\ -\frac{1}{5} & \frac{9}{10} \end{vmatrix} = \frac{12}{25}$$

$$c_{23} = (-1)^{2+3} \begin{vmatrix} \frac{3}{5} & -\frac{1}{2} \\ -\frac{1}{5} & -\frac{1}{5} \end{vmatrix} = \frac{11}{50}$$

$$c_{31} = (-1)^{3+1} \begin{vmatrix} -\frac{1}{2} & -\frac{3}{10} \\ \frac{9}{10} & -\frac{1}{10} \end{vmatrix} = \frac{8}{25}$$

$$c_{32} = (-1)^{3+2} \begin{vmatrix} \frac{3}{5} & -\frac{3}{10} \\ -\frac{1}{5} & -\frac{1}{10} \end{vmatrix} = \frac{3}{25}$$

$$c_{33} = (-1)^{3+3} \begin{vmatrix} \frac{3}{5} & -\frac{1}{2} \\ -\frac{1}{5} & \frac{9}{10} \end{vmatrix} = \frac{11}{25}.$$

Thus,

$$\mathbf{(I} - \mathbf{A})^{-1} = \frac{1}{|\mathbf{I} - \mathbf{A}|} \text{ adj } (\mathbf{I} - \mathbf{A})$$

$$= \frac{250}{77} \begin{bmatrix} \frac{79}{100} & \frac{51}{100} & \frac{8}{25} \\ \frac{1}{5} & \frac{12}{25} & \frac{3}{25} \\ \frac{11}{50} & \frac{11}{50} & \frac{11}{25} \end{bmatrix}$$

$$= \begin{bmatrix} \frac{395}{154} & \frac{255}{154} & \frac{80}{77} \\ \frac{50}{77} & \frac{120}{77} & \frac{30}{77} \\ \frac{5}{7} & \frac{5}{7} & \frac{10}{7} \end{bmatrix}.$$

Hence

$$\mathbf{X} = (\mathbf{I} - \mathbf{A})^{-1}\mathbf{C}$$

$$= \begin{bmatrix} \frac{395}{154} & \frac{255}{154} & \frac{80}{77} \\[2mm] \frac{50}{77} & \frac{120}{77} & \frac{30}{77} \\[2mm] \frac{5}{7} & \frac{5}{7} & \frac{10}{7} \end{bmatrix} \begin{bmatrix} 77 \\[2mm] 154 \\[2mm] 231 \end{bmatrix}$$

$$= \begin{bmatrix} 692.5 \\ 380 \\ 495 \end{bmatrix}.$$

EXERCISE 14-10

1. Given the input-output matrix below, find the output matrix if final demand changes to 600 for A and 805 for B. Find the total labor requirement this involves.

	Industry		Final
	A	B	Demand
Producer: A	200	500	500
B	400	200	900
Labor	600	800	—

2. Given the input-output matrix below, find the output matrix if final demand changes to (a) 200 for A and 300 for B; (b) 64 for A and 64 for B.

	Industry		Final
	A	B	Demand
Producer: A	40	120	40
B	120	90	90
Labor	40	90	—

3. Given the input-output matrix below, find the output matrix if final demand changes to (a) 50 for A, 40 for B, and 30 for C; (b) 10 for A, 10 for B, and 24 for C.

	Industry			Final
	A	B	C	Demand
Producer: A	18	30	45	15
B	27	30	60	3
C	54	40	60	26
Labor	9	20	15	—

4. Given the input-output matrix below, find the output matrix if final demand changes to 300 for A, 200 for B, and 400 for C.

	Industry			Final
	A	B	C	Demand
Producer: A	100	400	240	260
B	100	80	480	140
C	300	160	240	500
Labor	500	160	240	—

14-11   REVIEW

Important Terms and Symbols in Chapter 14

matrix *(p. 566)*

order (dimension) *(p. 566)*

entry *(p. 566)*

a_{ij} *(p. 566)*

determinant *(p. 616)*

square matrix *(p. 569)*

elementary row operation
   (p. 593)

elementary matrices *(p. 609)*

zero matrix, **O** *(p. 568)*

inverse matrix *(p. 608)*

Cramer's rule *(p. 628)*

reduced matrix *(p. 593)*

equivalent matrices *(p. 593)*

homogeneous system *(p. 602)*

trivial solution *(p. 604)*

invertible *(p. 609)*

adjoint *(p. 631)*

row matrix *(p. 567)*

column matrix *(p. 567)*

main diagonal *(p. 569)*

upper triangular matrix *(p. 569)*

equality of matrices *(p. 568)*

matrix multiplication *(p. 579)*

scalar multiplication *(p. 574)*

identity matrix, **I** *(p. 583)*

matrix addition *(p. 572)*

coefficient matrix *(p. 592)*

augmented coefficient matrix
   (p. 592)

minor *(p. 618)*

cofactor *(p. 618)*

nonhomogeneous system
   (p. 602)

parameter *(p. 599)*

$[a_{ij}]$ *(p. 566)*

transpose *(p. 631)*

Review Section

1. The order of the matrix given below is __(a)__ and the entry in the third row and second column is __(b)__ .

$$\begin{bmatrix} 2 & 3 & 0 & 1 \\ 1 & 4 & 6 & 0 \\ 7 & 5 & 2 & 3 \end{bmatrix}$$

Ans. (a) 3×4;   (b) 5

2. A matrix of order 3×1 is a (a) (row) (column) matrix while a matrix of order 1×3 is a (b) (row) (column) matrix.

Ans. (a) column;   (b) row

3. If $[3x \quad 5] = [6 \quad 5]$, then $x = \underline{\quad\quad}$.

Ans. 2

4. If $[4 \quad 1] = k[12 \quad 3]$, then $k = \underline{\quad\quad}$.

Ans. $\frac{1}{3}$

5. The main diagonal entries of $\begin{bmatrix} 1 & 3 \\ 2 & 4 \end{bmatrix}$ are $\underline{\quad\quad}$ and $\underline{\quad\quad}$.

Ans. 1, 4

6. If $2\begin{bmatrix} 3 & -4 \\ 0 & 1 \end{bmatrix} - 3\begin{bmatrix} 0 & 1 \\ -2 & 3 \end{bmatrix} = \begin{bmatrix} p & q \\ r & s \end{bmatrix}$, then $p = \underline{\text{(a)}}$, $q = \underline{\text{(b)}}$, $r = \underline{\text{(c)}}$, and $s = \underline{\text{(d)}}$.

Ans. (a) 6;   (b) -11;   (c) 6;   (d) -7

7. True or false: Both matrix addition and multiplication are commutative. $\underline{\quad\quad}$

Ans. false

8. The entry in the first row and second column of the product

$$\begin{bmatrix} 2 & 1 \\ 3 & 4 \end{bmatrix} \cdot \begin{bmatrix} 0 & 1 \\ 2 & 3 \end{bmatrix} \text{ is } \underline{\quad\quad}.$$

Ans. 5

9. True or false: In order to multiply two matrices, it is necessary that they be of the same order. $\underline{\quad\quad}$

Ans. false

10. True or false: The identity matrix is an upper triangular matrix. $\underline{\quad\quad}$

Ans. true

11. With respect to the system

$$\begin{cases} 2x + y = 4 \\ 3x + 2y = 5, \end{cases}$$

the matrix $\begin{bmatrix} 2 & 1 \\ 3 & 2 \end{bmatrix}$ is called the ___(a)___ matrix, while $\begin{bmatrix} 2 & 1 & \vdots & 4 \\ 3 & 2 & \vdots & 5 \end{bmatrix}$ is called the ___(b)___ matrix.

Ans. (a) coefficient; (b) augmented coefficient

12. If **B** is obtained from **A** by an elementary row operation, then **A** is said to be _____ to **B**.

Ans. equivalent

13. True or false: The 3×3 identity matrix and the 3×3 zero matrix are both reduced matrices. _____

Ans. true

14. A system of m linear equations in n unknowns has either a unique solution, an infinite number of solutions, or _____.

Ans. no solution

15. The system

$$\begin{cases} 2x - 3y + 4z = 0 \\ 3x - 4y + 2z = 0 \end{cases}$$

is (a) (homogeneous) (nonhomogeneous) and it has a(n) (b) (finite) (infinite) number of solutions.

Ans. (a) homogeneous; (b) infinite

16. If a homogeneous system of three linear equations in the variables x, y, and z has only the trivial solution, then
$x =$ ___(a)___ , $y =$ ___(b)___ , and $z =$ ___(c)___ .

Ans. (a) 0; (b) 0; (c) 0

17. The inverse of **I** is _____.

Ans. **I**

18. True or false: Every square matrix is invertible. ___(a)___ . If **A** is invertible, then $\mathbf{A}^{-1}\mathbf{A} = \mathbf{I}$. ___(b)___

Ans. (a) false; (b) true

19. If the inverse of $\begin{bmatrix} 3 & 7 \\ 2 & 5 \end{bmatrix}$ is $\begin{bmatrix} 5 & -7 \\ -2 & 3 \end{bmatrix}$, and

$$\begin{cases} 3x + 7y = 0 \\ 2x + 5y = 1, \end{cases}$$

then $x = $ __(a)__ and $y = $ __(b)__ .

Ans. (a) −7;   (b) 3

20. $[4]^{-1} = $ _____.

Ans. $[\frac{1}{4}]$

21. If $[\mathbf{A} \mid \mathbf{I}] \sim \ldots \sim [\mathbf{I} \mid \mathbf{B}]$, then $\mathbf{A}^{-1} = $ _____.

Ans. **B**

22. The determinant of a 2×2 matrix is a (real number) $(2 \times 2$ matrix).

Ans. real number

23. $|[5]| = $ __(a)__ and $\begin{vmatrix} 1 & 3 \\ 2 & 4 \end{vmatrix} = $ __(b)__ .

Ans. (a) 5;   (b) −2

24. The minor of the element 3 in the matrix $\begin{bmatrix} 0 & 1 & 3 \\ 2 & 4 & 0 \\ 1 & 5 & 2 \end{bmatrix}$ is __(a)__ and its cofactor

is __(b)__ .

Ans. (a) 6;   (b) 6

25. $\begin{vmatrix} 0 & 0 & 0 \\ 4 & 5 & 1 \\ 2 & 3 & 4 \end{vmatrix} = $ __(a)__ and $\begin{vmatrix} 1 & 2 & 3 \\ 0 & 5 & 6 \\ 0 & 0 & 4 \end{vmatrix} = $ __(b)__ .

Ans. (a) 0;   (b) 20

26. Cramer's rule is applicable in solving systems of n linear equations in __(a)__ unknowns providing the determinant of the coefficient matrix is __(b)__ .

Ans. (a) n;   (b) different from 0

27. $\begin{bmatrix} 1 & 1 \\ 2 & 2 \end{bmatrix}^T = $ _____.

Ans. $\begin{bmatrix} 1 & 2 \\ 1 & 2 \end{bmatrix}$

28. If adj $\mathbf{A} = \begin{bmatrix} \frac{1}{2} & 0 \\ 0 & 1 \end{bmatrix}$ and $|\mathbf{A}| = \frac{1}{2}$, then $\mathbf{A}^{-1} =$ _____.

Ans. $\begin{bmatrix} 1 & 0 \\ 0 & 2 \end{bmatrix}$

Review Problems

In problems 1-6, simplify.

1. $3\begin{bmatrix} 3 & 4 \\ -5 & 1 \end{bmatrix} - 2\begin{bmatrix} 1 & 0 \\ 2 & 4 \end{bmatrix}$

2. $5\begin{bmatrix} 1 & 2 \\ 7 & 0 \end{bmatrix} - 6\begin{bmatrix} 1 & 0 \\ 0 & 1 \end{bmatrix}$

3. $\begin{bmatrix} 1 & 7 \\ 2 & -3 \\ 1 & 0 \end{bmatrix}\begin{bmatrix} 1 & 0 & -2 \\ 0 & 5 & 1 \end{bmatrix}$

4. $\begin{bmatrix} 1 & 4 & 5 \end{bmatrix}\begin{bmatrix} 2 & 1 \\ 0 & -1 \\ 8 & 1 \end{bmatrix}$

5. $\begin{bmatrix} 1 & 0 \\ -1 & 4 \end{bmatrix}\left(\begin{bmatrix} 1 & 4 \\ 6 & 5 \end{bmatrix} - \begin{bmatrix} 2 & 6 \\ 5 & 0 \end{bmatrix}\right)$

6. $-\left(\begin{bmatrix} 2 & 0 \\ 7 & 8 \end{bmatrix} + 2\begin{bmatrix} 0 & -5 \\ 6 & -4 \end{bmatrix}\right)$

In problems 7-8, solve for x and y.

7. $\begin{bmatrix} 5 \\ 2 \end{bmatrix}[x] = \begin{bmatrix} 15 \\ y \end{bmatrix}$

8. $\begin{bmatrix} 1 & x \\ 2 & y \end{bmatrix}\begin{bmatrix} 2 & 1 \\ x & 3 \end{bmatrix} = \begin{bmatrix} 3 & 4 \\ 3 & y \end{bmatrix}$

In problems 9-12, reduce the given matrices.

9. $\begin{bmatrix} 1 & 4 \\ 5 & 8 \end{bmatrix}$

10. $\begin{bmatrix} 0 & 0 & 4 \\ 0 & 3 & 5 \end{bmatrix}$

11. $\begin{bmatrix} 2 & 4 & 3 \\ 1 & 2 & 3 \\ 4 & 8 & 6 \end{bmatrix}$

12. $\begin{bmatrix} 0 & 0 & 0 & 1 \\ 0 & 0 & 0 & 0 \\ 1 & 0 & 0 & 0 \end{bmatrix}$

In problems 13-16, solve each of the systems by the method of reduction.

13. $\begin{cases} 2x - 5y = 0 \\ 4x + 3y = 0 \end{cases}$

14. $\begin{cases} x - y + 2z = 3 \\ 3x + y + z = 5 \end{cases}$

15. $\begin{cases} x + y + 2z = 1 \\ 3x - 2y - 4z = -7 \\ 2x - y - 2z = 2 \end{cases}$

16. $\begin{cases} x - y - z - 2 = 0 \\ x + y + 2z + 5 = 0 \\ 2x + z + 3 = 0 \end{cases}$

In problems 17–20, find the inverses of the matrices by using reduction.

17. $\begin{bmatrix} 1 & 5 \\ 3 & 9 \end{bmatrix}$

18. $\begin{bmatrix} 0 & 1 \\ 1 & 0 \end{bmatrix}$

19. $\begin{bmatrix} 1 & 3 & -2 \\ 4 & 1 & 0 \\ 3 & -2 & 2 \end{bmatrix}$

20. $\begin{bmatrix} 1 & 0 & 0 \\ 2 & 3 & -1 \\ 1 & -1 & 2 \end{bmatrix}$

In problems 21 and 22, solve the given system by finding the inverse of the coefficient matrix.

21. $\begin{cases} 3x - y + 4z = 1 \\ x + z = 0 \\ 2y + z = 2 \end{cases}$

22. $\begin{cases} 2x + y - z = 0 \\ 3x + z = 0 \\ x - y + z = 0 \end{cases}$

In problems 23–28, evaluate the determinants.

23. $\begin{vmatrix} 2 & -1 \\ 4 & 7 \end{vmatrix}$

24. $\begin{vmatrix} 5 & 8 \\ 3 & 0 \end{vmatrix}$

25. $\begin{vmatrix} 1 & 2 & -1 \\ 0 & 1 & 4 \\ 1 & 2 & 2 \end{vmatrix}$

26. $\begin{vmatrix} 2 & 0 & 3 \\ 1 & 4 & 6 \\ -1 & 2 & -1 \end{vmatrix}$

27. $\begin{vmatrix} r & p & q & a \\ 0 & i & j & m \\ 0 & 0 & c & n \\ 0 & 0 & 0 & h \end{vmatrix}$

28. $\begin{vmatrix} e & 0 & 0 & 0 \\ a & r & 0 & 0 \\ p & j & n & 0 \\ s & k & t & i \end{vmatrix}$

Solve the systems in problems 29 and 30 by using Cramer's rule.

29. $\begin{cases} 3x - y = 1 \\ 2x + 3y = 8 \end{cases}$

30. $\begin{cases} x + 2y - z = 0 \\ y + 4z = 0 \\ x + 2y + 2z = 0 \end{cases}$

In problems 31–32, use the adjoint to find the inverse of each matrix.

31. $\begin{bmatrix} 1 & 1 & 1 \\ 0 & 2 & 1 \\ 1 & 3 & 1 \end{bmatrix}$

32. $\begin{bmatrix} 2 & 1 & -1 \\ 1 & 1 & 3 \\ -1 & 1 & -1 \end{bmatrix}$

33. Given the input-output matrix below, find the output matrix if final demand changes to 2 for *A* and 2 for *B*. (Data are in tens of billions of dollars.)

$$
\begin{array}{cc}
& \begin{array}{cc} \underline{\text{Industry}} & \text{Final} \\ A \qquad B & \text{Demand} \end{array} \\
\begin{array}{r} \text{Producer: } A \\ B \\ \text{Labor} \end{array} &
\left[\begin{array}{cc|c} 0 & 2 & 1 \\ 1 & 0 & 3 \\ \hline 2 & 2 & - \end{array} \right]
\end{array}
$$

Chapter 15

Linear Programming

15-1 LINEAR INEQUALITIES IN TWO VARIABLES

Suppose a consumer receives a fixed income of $60 per week and uses it all to purchase products A and B. If x kg of A cost $2 per kg and y kg of B cost $3 per kg, then the possible combinations of A and B which can be purchased must satisfy the consumer's *budget equation*

$$2x + 3y = 60 \quad \text{where } x, y \geq 0.$$

The solution is represented by the *budget line* in Fig. 15-1. For example, if 15 kg of A are purchased at a total cost of $30, then 10 kg of B must be bought at a total cost of $30. Thus (15, 10) lies on the line.

On the other hand, suppose the consumer does not necessarily wish to spend his *total* income. In this case the possible combinations are described by the inequality

$$2x + 3y \leq 60 \quad \text{where } x, y \geq 0. \tag{1}$$

649

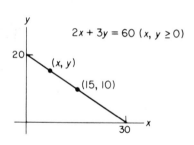

Fig. 15-1

When inequalities in one variable were discussed in Chapter 2, their solutions were represented geometrically by *intervals* on the real number line. However for an inequality in two variables, as in (1), the solution is usually represented by a *region* in the coordinate plane. We shall find the region corresponding to (1) after considering such inequalities in general.

DEFINITION.   *A **linear inequality** in the variables x and y is an inequality which can be written in the form*

$$ax + by + c < 0 \quad (or \leq 0, \geq 0, > 0)$$

where a, b, and c are constants and a and b are not both zero.

Geometrically, the solution of a linear inequality in x and y is all points (x, y) in the plane whose coordinates satisfy the inequality. In particular, the graph of the line $y = mx + b$ separates the plane into three distinct parts (Fig. 15-2):

(a) the line itself, consisting of all points (x, y) whose coordinates satisfy $y = mx + b$;

(b) the region above the line, consisting of all points (x, y) which satisfy $y > mx + b$;

(c) the region below the line, consisting of all points (x, y) satisfying $y < mx + b$.

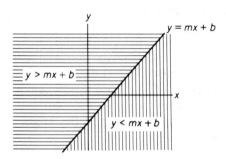

Fig. 15-2

For a vertical line, $x = a$, we speak of regions to the right $(x > a)$ or to the left $(x < a)$ of the line (Fig. 15-3).

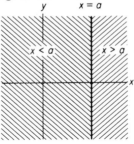

Fig. 15-3

To apply these facts we shall solve $2x + y < 5$. The corresponding *line* $2x + y = 5$ is first sketched by choosing two points on it, for instance the intercepts $(\frac{5}{2}, 0)$ and $(0, 5)$ [Fig. 15-4]. By writing the inequality in the equiva-

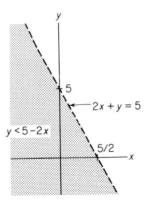

Fig. 15-4

lent form $y < 5 - 2x$, we conclude from (c) above that the solution consists of all points below the line. Part of this region is shaded in the diagram. Thus if (x_0, y_0) is *any* point in this region, then its ordinate y_0 is less than the quantity $5 - 2x_0$ (Fig. 15-5). For example, the point $(-2, -1)$ is in the region and $-1 < 5 - 2(-2)$. If we had required that $y \leq 5 - 2x$, the line $y = 5 - 2x$ would also have been included in the solution as indicated by the solid line in Fig. 15-6. We shall adopt the conventions that a solid line *is* included in the solution, and a broken line *is not*.

EXAMPLE 1

    a. *Find the region described by* $y \leq 5$.

        Since x does not appear, the inequality is assumed to be true for all values of x.

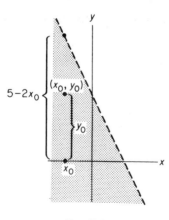

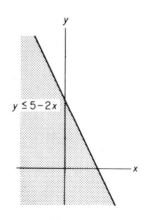

Fig. 15-5   **Fig. 15-6**

Thus the solution consists of the line $y = 5$ *and* the region below it (see Fig. 15-7) since the y-coordinate of each point in that region is less than 5.

b. *Solve* $2(2x - y) < 2(x + y) - 4$.

The inequality is equivalent to

$$4x - 2y < 2x + 2y - 4$$

$$-4y < -2x - 4$$

$$y > \frac{x}{2} + 1.$$

We first sketch the line $y = (x/2) + 1$ by noting that its intercepts are $(0, 1)$ and $(-2, 0)$. Then we shade the region above it (see Fig. 15-8). Every point in this region is a solution.

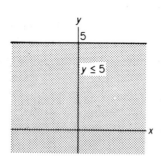

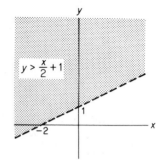

Fig. 15-7   **Fig. 15-8**

The solution of a *system* of inequalities is all points whose coordinates simultaneously satisfy all of the given inequalities. Geometrically, it is the region which is common to all the regions determined by the given inequalities. For example, let us solve

$$\begin{cases} 2x + y > 3 \\ \quad\ x \geq y \\ 2y - 1 > 0. \end{cases}$$

The system is equivalent to

$$\begin{cases} y > -2x + 3 \\ y \leq x \\ y > \dfrac{1}{2}. \end{cases}$$

Note that each inequality has been written so that y is isolated. Thus, the appropriate regions with respect to the corresponding lines will be apparent. We now sketch the lines $y = -2x + 3$, $y = x$, and $y = \frac{1}{2}$ and then shade the region which is simultaneously above the first line, on or below the second line, and above the third line (see Fig. 15-9). This region is the solution. When

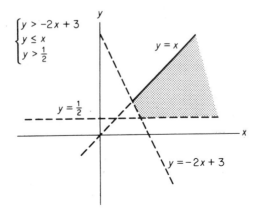

Fig. 15-9

sketching the lines, it is best to draw broken lines everywhere until it is clear which portions of the lines are to be included in the solution.

EXAMPLE 2

Solve

$$\begin{cases} y \geq -2x + 10 \\ y \geq x - 2. \end{cases}$$

The solution is all points which are simultaneously on or above $y = -2x + 10$ and on or above $y = x - 2$. It is the shaded region in Fig. 15-10.

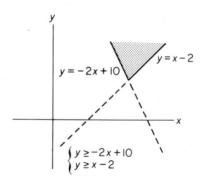

Fig. 15-10

EXAMPLE 3

Find the region described by

$$\begin{cases} 2x + 3y \le 60 \\ \qquad x \ge 0 \\ \qquad y \ge 0. \end{cases}$$

This system relates to the discussion of budget lines earlier in this section. The latter two inequalities restrict the solution to points which are both on or to the right of the *y*-axis *and* also on or above the *x*-axis. The desired region is shaded in Fig. 15-11.

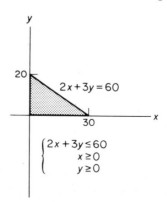

Fig. 15-11

EXERCISE 15-1

Sketch the region described by the following inequalities.

1. $2x + 3y > 6$ 2. $3x - 2y \ge 12$

3. $x + 2y \le 7$ 4. $y > 6 - 2x$

5. $-x \le 2y - 4$

6. $2x + y \ge 10$

7. $3x + y < 0$

8. $x + 5y < -5$

9. $\begin{cases} 3x - 2y < 6 \\ x - 3y > 9 \end{cases}$

10. $\begin{cases} 2x + 3y > -6 \\ 3x - y < 6 \end{cases}$

11. $\begin{cases} 2x + 3y \le 6 \\ x \ge 0 \end{cases}$

12. $\begin{cases} 2y - 3x < 6 \\ x < 0 \end{cases}$

13. $\begin{cases} y - 3x < 6 \\ x - y > -3 \end{cases}$

14. $\begin{cases} x - y < 1 \\ y - x < 1 \end{cases}$

15. $\begin{cases} 2x - 2 \ge y \\ 2x \le 3 - 2y \end{cases}$

16. $\begin{cases} 2y < 4x + 2 \\ y < 2x + 1 \end{cases}$

17. $\begin{cases} x - y > 4 \\ x < 2 \\ y > -5 \end{cases}$

18. $\begin{cases} 2x + y < -1 \\ y > -x \\ 2x + 6 < 0 \end{cases}$

19. $\begin{cases} y < 2x + 4 \\ x \ge -2 \\ y < 1 \end{cases}$

20. $\begin{cases} 4x + 3y \ge 12 \\ y \ge x \\ 2y \le 3x + 6 \end{cases}$

21. $\begin{cases} x + y > 1 \\ 3x - 5 \le y \\ y < 2x \end{cases}$

22. $\begin{cases} 2x - 3y > -12 \\ 3x + y > -6 \\ y > x \end{cases}$

23. $\begin{cases} 3x + y > -6 \\ x - y > -5 \\ x \ge 0 \end{cases}$

24. $\begin{cases} 5y - 2x \le 10 \\ 4x - 6y \le 12 \\ y \ge 0 \end{cases}$

If a consumer wants to spend no more than P dollars to purchase quantities x and y of two products having prices p_1 and p_2 per unit, respectively, then $p_1 x + p_2 y \le P$ where x, $y \ge 0$. Find the possible combinations of purchases by finding the solution of this system if:

25. $p_1 = 5$, $p_2 = 3$, $P = 15$

26. $p_1 = 6$, $p_2 = 4$, $P = 24$

27. If a manufacturer wishes to purchase a *total* of no more than 100 lb of Product Z from suppliers A and B, set up a system of inequalities which describes the possible combinations of quantities which can be purchased from each supplier. Sketch the solution in the plane.

15-2   LINEAR PROGRAMMING

Linear programming is a technique emphasized today in both industrial and economic analysis. Essentially, a problem in linear programming involves two things: first, there is a system of linear inequalities which represents some basic restrictions (or *constraints*) in the problem; and second, there is an objective which is represented by a linear function. Although there are usually infinitely many solutions to the system of inequalities (these are called *feasible points*), the aim is to find one such solution which is also the "best" solution as far as the objective is concerned. Such a solution is called an *optimum solution.* For example, in manufacturing the restrictions might be limitations on the use of machinery or labor in producing a product, and the objective would be maximization of a profit function, subject to these restrictions. We shall now illustrate a geometrical approach to such a problem. In the next section another approach will be discussed.

Suppose a company produces two types of widgets, manual and electric. Each requires in its manufacture the use of three machines: *A*, *B*, and *C*. A manual widget requires the use of machine *A* for 2 hours, machine *B* for 1 hour, and machine *C* for 1 hour. An electric widget requires 1 hour on *A*, 2 hours on *B*, and 1 hour on *C*. Furthermore, suppose the maximum numbers of hours available per month for the use of machines *A*, *B*, and *C* are 180, 160, and 100, respectively. The profit on a manual widget is $4 and on an electric widget it is $6. (See Table 15-1 for a summary of data.) If the company can sell all the widgets it can produce, how many of each type should it make in order to maximize the monthly profit?

TABLE 15-1

	A	*B*	*C*	PROFIT/UNIT
Manual	2 hr	1 hr	1 hr	$4
Electric	1 hr	2 hr	1 hr	$6
Hours Available	180	160	100	

To answer the question we let x and y denote the number of manual and electric widgets, respectively, which are made in a month. Since the number of widgets made is not negative, we have

$$x \geq 0, \, y \geq 0.$$

For machine *A*, the time needed for making x manual widgets is $2x$ hours, and the time needed for making y electric widgets is $1y$ hours. The sum of these times cannot be greater than 180, and so we have

$$2x + y \leq 180.$$

Similarly, the restrictions for machines *B* and *C* give

$$x + 2y \leq 160$$

and

$$x + y \leq 100.$$

The profit P is a function of x and y and is given by the *profit function*

$$P = 4x + 6y.$$

Summarizing, we want to maximize the *objective function*

$$P = 4x + 6y \tag{1}$$

subject to the condition that x and y must be a solution to the system of constraints

$$\begin{cases} x \geq 0 & (2) \\ y \geq 0 & (3) \\ 2x + y \leq 180 & (4) \\ x + 2y \leq 160 & (5) \\ x + y \leq 100. & (6) \end{cases}$$

The region simultaneously satisfying (2)–(6) is shaded in Fig. 15-12. Each point in this region is a feasible point and the region is called the *feasible region*. Thus there are infinitely many feasible points. We must now find one that maximizes the profit function.

Since $P = 4x + 6y$ is equivalent to

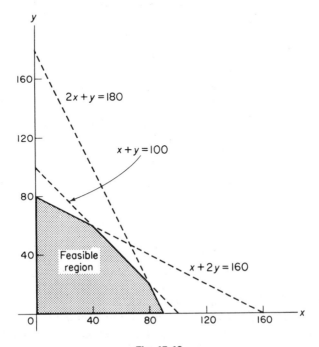

Fig. 15-12

$$y = -\frac{2}{3}x + \frac{P}{6},$$

it defines a so-called "family" of parallel lines, each having a slope of $-\frac{2}{3}$ and y-intercept $(0, P/6)$. For example, if $P = 600$, then we get the line $y = -\frac{2}{3}x + 100$ shown in Fig. 15-13. This line, called an *isoprofit line*, gives all possible combinations of x and y which yield the same profit, \$600. Note

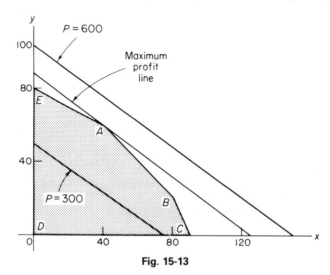

Fig. 15-13

that this isoprofit line has no point in common with the feasible region, whereas the isoprofit line for $P = 300$ has infinitely many such points. Let us look for the member of the family which will maximize profit. *It will be the line whose y-intercept is furthest from the origin (this gives a maximum value of P) and which has at least one point in common with the feasible region.* It is not difficult to observe that such a line will contain the corner point A. Any isoprofit line with a greater profit will contain no points of the feasible region.

From Fig. 15-12, A lies on both the line $x + y = 100$ and the line $x + 2y = 160$. Thus its coordinates may be found by merely solving the system

$$\begin{cases} x + y = 100 \\ x + 2y = 160. \end{cases}$$

This gives $x = 40$ and $y = 60$. Substituting these values in $P = 4x + 6y$, we find the maximum possible profit is \$520 which is obtained by producing 40 manual widgets and 60 electric widgets per month.

It can be shown that *a linear function defined on a feasible region such as we have will take on its maximum (or minimum) value at one of the corner points of the region.* This statement gives us a way of finding an optimum solution without drawing isoprofit lines as we did above. We could just evaluate the objective function at each of the corner points of the feasible region and then choose a corner point at which the function is a maximum.

For example, from Fig. 15-13 the corner points are A, B, C, D, and E. We found A before to be (40, 60). To find B, we see from Fig. 15-12 that we must solve $2x + y = 180$ and $x + y = 100$ simultaneously. This gives $B = (80, 20)$. In this way we obtain all the corner points:

$$A = (40, 60), \qquad B = (80, 20), \qquad C = (90, 0), \qquad D = (0, 0), \qquad E = (0, 80).$$

We now evaluate the objective function $P = 4x + 6y$ at each point:

$$P(A) = 4(40) + 6(60) = 520$$
$$P(B) = 4(80) + 6(20) = 440$$
$$P(C) = 4(90) + 6(0) = 360$$
$$P(D) = 4(0) + 6(0) = 0$$
$$P(E) = 4(0) + 6(80) = 480.$$

Thus P is maximum at A where $x = 40$ and $y = 60$.

EXAMPLE 4

Maximize the objective function

$$Z = 3x + y$$

subject to the constraints

$$2x + y \leq 8$$
$$2x + 3y \leq 12$$
$$x \geq 0$$
$$y \geq 0.$$

From Fig. 15-14 the feasible region has four corner points. The coordinates of A, B, and D are obvious on inspection. To get C we solve $2x + y = 8$ and $2x + 3y = 12$ simultaneously. Thus,

$$A = (0, 0), \qquad B = (4, 0), \qquad C = (3, 2), \qquad D = (0, 4).$$

Evaluating Z at these points, we obtain

$$Z(A) = 3(0) + 0 = 0$$
$$Z(B) = 3(4) + 0 = 12$$
$$Z(C) = 3(3) + 2 = 11$$
$$Z(D) = 3(0) + 4 = 4.$$

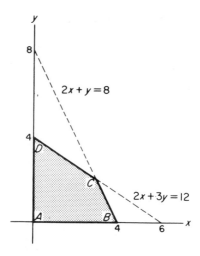

Fig. 15-14

Hence the maximum value of Z, subject to the constraints, is 12 and it occurs when $x = 4$ and $y = 0$.

EXAMPLE 5

A produce grower decides to purchase fertilizer containing three nutrients, A, B, and C, to be spread on his field. The minimum needs are 160 units of A, 200 units of B, and 80 units of C. There are two popular brands of fertilizer on the market. Fast Grow, costing $4 a bag, contains 3 units of A, 5 units of B, and 1 unit of C. Easy Grow, costing $3 a bag, contains 2 units of each nutrient. If the grower wishes to minimize his cost while still maintaining the nutrients required, how many bags of each brand should he buy? The information is summarized in Table 15-2.

TABLE 15-2

	A	B	C	COST/BAG
Fast Grow	3 units	5 units	1 unit	$4
Easy Grow	2 units	2 units	2 units	$3
Units Required	160	200	80	

Let x be the number of bags of Fast Grow that are bought and y the number of bags of Easy Grow that are bought. Then we wish to *minimize* the cost function

$$C = 4x + 3y \qquad (7)$$

subject to the constraints

$$x \geq 0 \qquad (8)$$

$$y \geq 0 \tag{9}$$

$$3x + 2y \geq 160 \tag{10}$$

$$5x + 2y \geq 200 \tag{11}$$

$$x + 2y \geq 80. \tag{12}$$

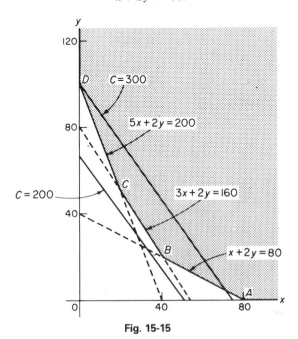

Fig. 15-15

The feasible region satisfying (8)-(12) is shaded in Fig. 15-15, along with *isocost lines* for $C = 200$ and $C = 300$. We observe that the member of the family of lines $C = 4x + 3y$ which will give a minimum cost will intersect the feasible region at the corner point B. Here we chose the isocost line whose y-intercept was *closest* to the origin and which had at least one point in common with the feasible region. Solving

$$\begin{cases} 3x + 2y = 160 \\ x + 2y = 80, \end{cases}$$

we find that $x = 40$ and $y = 20$, which gives a minimum cost of $220. The produce grower should buy 40 bags of Fast Grow and 20 bags of Easy Grow.

To reach the same conclusion another way, we first find the coordinates of all the corner points:

$$A = (80, 0), \quad B = (40, 20), \quad C = (20, 50), \quad D = (0, 100).$$

Next we evaluate the cost function at each point:

$$C(A) = 4(80) + 3(0) = 320$$

$$C(B) = 4(40) + 3(20) = 220$$

$$C(C) = 4(20) + 3(50) = 230$$

$$C(D) = 4(0) + 3(100) = 300.$$

Thus C is a minimum when $x = 40$ and $y = 20$.

PITFALL.   *When using the method of testing corner points in the objective function, you still must draw the graph of the feasible region. This is so that you will know which equations must be solved to get the corner points. Do not pick a pair of equations at random and solve. This may give a point of intersection, but this point may not necessarily be a corner point of the feasible region (see Fig. 15-15).*

EXERCISE 15-2

1. Maximize the function $P = 10x + 12y$ subject to the constraints $x \geq 0$, $y \geq 0$, $x + y \leq 60$, and $x - 2y \geq 0$.

2. Maximize the function $P = 5x + 6y$ subject to the constraints $x \geq 0$, $y \geq 0$, $x + y \leq 80$, $3x + 2y \leq 220$, and $2x + 3y \leq 210$.

3. Minimize the function $C = 2x + y$ subject to the constraints $x \geq 0$, $y \geq 0$, $3x + y \geq 3$, $4x + 3y \geq 6$, and $x + 2y \geq 2$.

4. Minimize the function $C = 2x + 2y$ subject to the constraints $x \geq 0$, $y \geq 0$, $x + 2y \geq 80$, $3x + 2y \geq 160$, and $5x + 2y \geq 200$.

5. A toy manufacturer preparing his production schedule for two new toys, widgets and wadgits, must use the information concerning their construction times given in the table below. The available employee hours per week are as follows: for operating machine *A*, 70 hours; for *B*, 40 hours; for finishing, 90 hours. If the profits on each widget and wadgit are $4 and $6, respectively, how many of each toy should he make per week in order to maximize his profit? What would the maximum profit be?

	MACHINE *A*	MACHINE *B*	FINISHING
Widgets	2 hr	1 hr	1 hr
Wadgits	1 hr	1 hr	3 hr

6. A manufacturer produces two types of barbecue grills, Old Smokey and Blaze Away. During production, the grills require the use of two machines, *A* and *B*. The number of hours needed on both are indicated below. If each machine can be used 24 hours a day, and the profits on the Old Smokey and Blaze Away models are $4 and $6, respectively, how many of each type of grill should be made per day to obtain maximum profit?

	MACHINE *A*	MACHINE *B*
Old Smokey	2 hr	4 hr
Blaze Away	4 hr	2 hr

7. A diet is to contain at least 16 units of carbohydrates and 20 units of protein. Food *A* contains 2 units of carbohydrates and 4 of protein; Food *B* contains 2 units of carbohydrates and 1 of protein. If Food *A* costs $1.20 per unit and Food *B* costs $0.80 per unit, how many units of each food should be purchased in order to minimize cost?

8. A produce grower is purchasing fertilizer containing three nutrients: *A*, *B*, and *C*. The minimum weekly requirements are 80 units of *A*, 120 of *B*, and 240 of *C*. There are two popular blends of fertilizer on the market. Blend I, costing $4 a bag, contains 2 units of *A*, 6 of *B*, and 4 of *C*. Blend II, costing $5 a bag, contains 2 units of *A*, 2 of *B*, and 12 of *C*. How many bags of each blend should the grower buy each week so as to minimize his cost of meeting the nutrient requirements?

15-3 THE SIMPLEX METHOD

In the last section we solved linear programming problems by a geometric method. Now we shall look at a different technique—the *simplex method.*

The simplex method begins with a feasible solution and tests whether or not it is optimum. If not optimum, the method proceeds to a *better* solution. We say "better" in the sense that the new solution brings you closer to optimization of the objective function.† Should this new solution not be optimum, then we repeat the procedure. Eventually the simplex method leads to an optimum solution, if one exists.

Besides being efficient, there are other advantages to the simplex method. It is completely mechanical (we use matrices, elementary row operations, and basic arithmetic). Moreover, no geometry is involved. This allows us to solve linear programming problems having any number of constraints and variables.

We shall now apply the simplex method to the problem in Example 4:

$$\text{Maximize: } Z = 3x + y$$

subject to the constraints

$$2x + y \le 8, \tag{1}$$

and

---

†In most cases this is true. In some situations, however, the new solution may be just as good as the previous one. Example 7 will illustrate this.

$$2x + 3y \le 12, \tag{2}$$

where $x \ge 0$ and $y \ge 0$. We begin by expressing constraints (1) and (2) as equations. In (1), $2x + y$ will *equal* 8 if we add some nonnegative quantity s to $2x + y$:

$$2x + y + s = 8 \quad \text{where } s \ge 0.$$

We call s a **slack variable.** Similarly, inequality (2) can be written as an equation by using the slack variable t:

$$2x + 3y + t = 12 \quad \text{where } t \ge 0.$$

The variables x and y are called **structural variables.**

Now we can restate the problem in terms of equations.

$$\text{Maximize: } Z = 3x + y \tag{3}$$

such that

$$2x + \quad y + s = 8 \tag{4}$$

and

$$2x + 3y + t = 12 \tag{5}$$

where x, y, s, and t are nonnegative.

From Sec. 15-2 we know that the optimum solution occurs at a corner point of the feasible region in Fig. 15-16. At each of these points *at least two* of the variables x, y, s, and t are 0.

(a) At A, we have $x = 0$ and $y = 0$.

(b) At B, $x = 4$ and $y = 0$. But from Eq. (4), $2(4) + 0 + s = 8$. Thus $s = 0$.

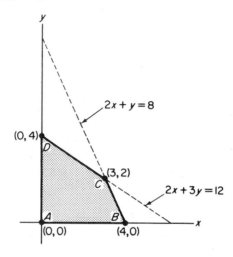

Fig. 15-16

(c) At C, $x = 3$ and $y = 2$. But from Eq. (4), $2(3) + 2 + s = 8$. Thus $s = 0$. From Eq. (5), $2(3) + 3(2) + t = 12$. Thus $t = 0$.

(d) At D, $x = 0$ and $y = 4$. From Eq. (5), $2(0) + 3(4) + t = 12$ and so $t = 0$.

On the other hand, it can be shown that any solution to Eqs. (3)-(5), where x, y, s, $t \geq 0$ and at least two of these variables are 0, corresponds to a corner point. Any solution where at least two (the *number* of structural variables) of these variables are 0 is called a **basic feasible solution** (abbreviated B.F.S.). Thus we eventually want to find a B.F.S. that maximizes Z.

If we write Eq. (3) as $-3x - y + Z = 0$, then Eqs. (4), (5), and (3) form the system

$$\begin{cases} 2x + y + s && = 8 \\ 2x + 3y & + t & = 12 \\ -3x - y & & + Z = 0. \end{cases}$$

In terms of an augmented coefficient matrix (also called a *simplex tableau*), we have

$$\begin{array}{c} & x & y & s & t & Z \\ \begin{array}{c} s \\ t \\ Z \end{array} & \left[\begin{array}{ccccc|c} 2 & 1 & 1 & 0 & 0 & 8 \\ 2 & 3 & 0 & 1 & 0 & 12 \\ \hline -3 & -1 & 0 & 0 & 1. & 0 \end{array} \right]. \end{array}$$

The first two rows correspond to the constraints, and the last row corresponds to the objective equation.

Notice that if $x = 0$ and $y = 0$, then from rows 1, 2, and 3 we can directly read off the values of s, t and Z; $s = 8$, $t = 12$, $Z = 0$, respectively. This is why we placed the letters s, t, and Z to the left of the rows. Thus, the two slack variables provide our initial basic feasible solution:

$$x = 0, \, y = 0, \, s = 8, \, t = 12, \, Z = 0 \text{ is a B.F.S.}$$

Let us see if we can find a B.F.S. that gives a larger value of Z. We shall look for one where not both x and y are 0.

Since $Z = 3x + y$, if x changes by 1 (unit), then Z changes by 3. On the other hand, if y changes by 1, then Z changes by 1. Thus, choosing between x and y, we get a larger value of Z by dropping the condition that $x = 0$. We say that x is an **entering variable**, since it enters the category of those B.F.S.'s where x does not have to equal 0. In terms of the simplex tableau below, this variable can be found by looking at the most negative of the numbers enclosed by the brace in the last row. Since that number is -3 and appears in the x-column, x is the entering variable. The numbers in the brace are called **indicators**.

$$
\begin{array}{c}
\begin{array}{ccccc}
x & y & s & t & Z
\end{array} \\
\begin{array}{c}
s \\
t \\
Z
\end{array}
\left[
\begin{array}{ccccc|c}
2 & 1 & 1 & 0 & 0 & 8 \\
2 & 3 & 0 & 1 & 0 & 12 \\
\hline
-3 & -1 & 0 & 0 & 1 & 0
\end{array}
\right]
\end{array}
$$

↑   indicators
entering
variable

Now, along with $y = 0$ we must decide whether to choose s or t to be 0. There are two cases to consider: $y = 0$, $s = 0$; and $y = 0$, $t = 0$.

Case 1. Suppose $y = 0$ and $s = 0$. From the first row of the tableau above,

$$2x = 8$$

or $x = \frac{8}{2} (=4).$

From the second row, $2x + t = 12$. Thus

$$2(\tfrac{8}{2}) + t = 12$$

or $t = 4.$

Case 2. Suppose $y = 0$ and $t = 0$. From the second row,

$$2x = 12$$

or $x = \frac{12}{2} (=6).$

From the first row, $2x + s = 8$. Thus

$$2(\tfrac{12}{2}) + s = 8$$

or $s = -4.$

But s cannot be negative!

Discussion of Cases. We got into trouble in Case 2 since the quotient $\frac{12}{2}$ was too large when substituted into $2x + s = 8$. In fact, if we use the original inequalities $2x + y \le 8$ and $2x + 3y \le 12$ along with the condition that $y = 0$, we find

$$x \le \tfrac{8}{2} \quad \text{and} \quad x \le \tfrac{12}{2}.$$

Thus x must be less than or equal to the smaller of the quotients $\frac{8}{2} (=4)$ and $\frac{12}{2} (=6)$. Therefore, we must choose the case corresponding to $y = 0$ and $s = 0$. We call s the **departing variable** because s drops out of the category of B.F.S.'s where s does not have to equal 0 (that is, $s = 0$).

To the right of the tableau below, the quotients $\frac{8}{2}$ and $\frac{12}{2}$ are indicated. We get them by dividing each entry in the first two rows of the b-column by the entry in the corresponding row of the entering variable column. Notice

$$
\begin{array}{c}
\quad\quad x \quad y \quad s \quad t \quad Z \quad\quad b \quad\quad \textit{Quotients} \\
\text{departing} \rightarrow s \\
\text{variable} \quad\quad t \\
Z
\end{array}
\begin{bmatrix}
2 & 1 & 1 & 0 & 0 & \vdots & 8 \\
2 & 3 & 0 & 1 & 0 & \vdots & 12 \\
\hline
-3 & -1 & 0 & 0 & 1 & \vdots & 0
\end{bmatrix}
\begin{array}{l}
8 \div 2 = 4 \\
12 \div 2 = 6
\end{array}
$$

$$\uparrow$$
$$\text{entering variable}$$

that the departing variable is in the same row as the smaller quotient 8 ÷ 2.

In Case 1 we saw that when $y = 0$ and $s = 0$, then $x = 4$ and $t = 4$. It certainly would be nice to change our tableau above by elementary row operations into a form where these values of x and t can be read off with ease (just as we were able to do with the solution corresponding to $x = 0$ and $y = 0$). To do this we want to find a matrix which is equivalent to the tableau above but which has the form

$$
\begin{array}{ccccc}
x & y & s & t & Z \\
\end{array}
$$
$$
\begin{bmatrix}
1 & ? & ? & 0 & 0 & \vdots & ? \\
0 & ? & ? & 1 & 0 & \vdots & ? \\
\hline
0 & ? & ? & 0 & 1 & \vdots & ?
\end{bmatrix}
$$

where the question marks represent numbers to be determined. Notice here that if $y = 0$ and $s = 0$, then x equals the number in row 1 of the last column, t equals the number in row 2, and Z is the number in row 3. Thus we must transform the tableau

$$
\begin{array}{c}
\quad\quad\quad x \quad y \quad s \quad t \quad Z \\
\text{departing} \rightarrow s \\
\text{variable} \quad\quad t \\
Z
\end{array}
\begin{bmatrix}
② & 1 & 1 & 0 & 0 & \vdots & 8 \\
2 & 3 & 0 & 1 & 0 & \vdots & 12 \\
\hline
-3 & -1 & 0 & 0 & 1 & \vdots & 0
\end{bmatrix} \quad\quad (6)
$$

$$\uparrow$$
$$\text{entering variable}$$

into an equivalent matrix which has a 1 where the circle appears and 0's elsewhere in the first column. The entry in the circle is called the **pivot entry**—it is in the column of the entering variable and the row of the departing variable.

$$
\begin{array}{ccccc}
x & y & s & t & Z \\
\end{array}
$$
$$
\begin{bmatrix}
② & 1 & 1 & 0 & 0 & \vdots & 8 \\
2 & 3 & 0 & 1 & 0 & \vdots & 12 \\
\hline
-3 & -1 & 0 & 0 & 1 & \vdots & 0
\end{bmatrix}
$$

$$\sim \left[\begin{array}{ccccc|c} 1 & \frac{1}{2} & \frac{1}{2} & 0 & 0 & 4 \\ \hline 2 & 3 & 0 & 1 & 0 & 12 \\ \hline -3 & -1 & 0 & 0 & 1 & 0 \end{array}\right]$$

(by multiplying first row by $\frac{1}{2}$)

$$\sim \left[\begin{array}{ccccc|c} 1 & \frac{1}{2} & \frac{1}{2} & 0 & 0 & 4 \\ \hline 0 & 2 & -1 & 1 & 0 & 4 \\ \hline 0 & \frac{1}{2} & \frac{3}{2} & 0 & 1 & 12 \end{array}\right]$$

(by adding -2 times first row to the second, and adding 3 times first row to the third)

Thus we have

$$\begin{array}{c} \quad\quad x \quad\; y \quad\; s \quad\; t \quad\; Z \\ \begin{array}{c} x \\ t \\ Z \end{array} \left[\begin{array}{ccccc|c} 1 & \frac{1}{2} & \frac{1}{2} & 0 & 0 & 4 \\ 0 & 2 & -1 & 1 & 0 & 4 \\ \hline 0 & \frac{1}{2} & \frac{3}{2} & 0 & 1 & 12 \end{array}\right]. \end{array} \quad (7)$$

$$\underbrace{}_{\text{indicators}}$$

When $y = 0$ and $s = 0$, then from the first row we have $x = 4$; from the second, $t = 4$. These values give us another B.F.S. Note that we replaced the s located to the left of the initial tableau in (6) by x in our new tableau (7)—thus s *departed* and x *entered*. From row 3, when $y = 0$ and $s = 0$ we get $Z = 12$, which is a larger value than we had before (it was $Z = 0$).

Notice in the last row of (7) that all indicators are nonnegative. That row's corresponding equation is $\frac{1}{2}y + \frac{3}{2}s + Z = 12$ or

$$Z = 12 - \tfrac{1}{2}y - \tfrac{3}{2}s. \quad (8)$$

Since we must have $y \geq 0$ and $s \geq 0$, and their coefficients in Eq. (8) are negative, then Z is maximum when $y = 0$ and $s = 0$. That is, *having all nonnegative indicators means that we have an optimum solution*. In this case the maximum occurs when $x = 4$, $y = 0$, $s = 0$, and $t = 4$, and the maximum value of Z is 12.

In terms of our original problem, if

$$Z = 3x + y,$$

such that

$$2x + y \leq 8, \quad\quad 2x + 3y \leq 12, \quad\quad x \geq 0, \quad \text{and} \quad y \geq 0,$$

then Z is maximum when $x = 4$ and $y = 0$, and the maximum value of Z is 12 (confirming our result in Example 4). Note that the values of s and t do not have to appear here.

Let us outline the simplex method for a more general linear programming problem.

Simplex Method

Problem:

$$\text{Maximize: } Z = c_1 x_1 + c_2 x_2 + c_3 x_3$$

such that

$$a_{11} x_1 + a_{12} x_2 + a_{13} x_3 \le b_1,$$

$$a_{21} x_1 + a_{22} x_2 + a_{23} x_3 \le b_2,$$

$$a_{31} x_1 + a_{32} x_2 + a_{33} x_3 \le b_3,$$

and the x's and b's are nonnegative.

Method:

(1) Set up the initial simplex tableau.

	x_1	x_2	x_3	s_1	s_2	s_3	Z	b
s_1	a_{11}	a_{12}	a_{13}	1	0	0	0	b_1
s_2	a_{21}	a_{22}	a_{23}	0	1	0	0	b_2
s_3	a_{31}	a_{32}	a_{33}	0	0	1	0	b_3
Z	$-c_1$	$-c_2$	$-c_3$	0	0	0	1	0

indicators

There are three slack variables, s_1, s_2, and s_3—one for each constraint.

(2) If all the indicators in the last row are nonnegative, then Z has a maximum when $x_1 = 0$, $x_2 = 0$, and $x_3 = 0$ and the maximum value is 0.

If there are any negative indicators, locate the column in which the most negative indicator appears. This column gives the entering variable.

(3) Divide each *positive* entry above the broken line in the entering variable column *into* the corresponding value of b.

(4) Place a circle around the entry in the entering variable column which corresponds to the smallest quotient in step (3). This is the pivot entry. The departing variable is the one to the left of the pivot entry row.

(5) Use elementary row operations to transform the tableau into a new equivalent tableau which has a 1 where the pivot entry was and 0's elsewhere in that column.

(6) On the left side of this tableau the entering variable replaces the departing variable.

(7) If the indicators of the new tableau are all nonnegative, you have an optimum solution. The maximum value of Z is the entry in the last row and last column. It occurs when the variables to the left of the tableau are equal to the corresponding entries in the last column. All other variables are 0.

If at least one of the indicators is negative, repeat the process beginning with step (2) applied to the new tableau.

For the procedure above, we had three structural variables and three constraints. However, the simplex method works with any number of structural variables or constraints.

EXAMPLE 6

$$Maximize: Z = 5x + 4y$$

subject to

$$x + y \leq 20,$$

$$2x + y \leq 35,$$

$$-3x + y \leq 12,$$

and $x \geq 0$, $y \geq 0$.

The initial simplex tableau is

		x	y	s_1	s_2	s_3	Z	b	Quotients
	s_1	1	1	1	0	0	0	20	$20 \div 1 = 20$
departing variable $\rightarrow$	s_2	②	1	0	1	0	0	35	$35 \div 2 = \frac{35}{2}$
	s_3	-3	1	0	0	1	0	12	no quotient since -3 is not positive
	Z	-5	-4	0	0	0	1	0	

$\uparrow$ entering variable — indicators

The most negative indicator, -5, occurs in the x-column. Thus x is the entering variable. The smaller quotient is $\frac{35}{2}$, and so s_2 is the departing variable. The pivot entry is 2. Using elementary row operations to get a 1 in the pivot position and 0's elsewhere in its column, we have

x	y	s_1	s_2	s_3	Z	b
1	1	1	0	0	0	20
②	1	0	1	0	0	35
-3	1	0	0	1	0	12
-5	-4	0	0	0	1	0

$$\sim \begin{bmatrix} 1 & 1 & 1 & 0 & 0 & 0 & \vdots & 20 \\ 1 & \frac{1}{2} & 0 & \frac{1}{2} & 0 & 0 & \vdots & \frac{35}{2} \\ -3 & 1 & 0 & 0 & 1 & 0 & \vdots & 12 \\ -5 & -4 & 0 & 0 & 0 & 1 & \vdots & 0 \end{bmatrix}$$ (by multiplying row two by $\frac{1}{2}$)

$$\sim \begin{bmatrix} 0 & \frac{1}{2} & 1 & -\frac{1}{2} & 0 & 0 & \vdots & \frac{5}{2} \\ 1 & \frac{1}{2} & 0 & \frac{1}{2} & 0 & 0 & \vdots & \frac{35}{2} \\ 0 & \frac{5}{2} & 0 & \frac{3}{2} & 1 & 0 & \vdots & \frac{129}{2} \\ 0 & -\frac{3}{2} & 0 & \frac{5}{2} & 0 & 1 & \vdots & \frac{175}{2} \end{bmatrix}$$ (by adding -1 times row two to row one; adding 3 times row two to row three; adding 5 times row two to row four)

Our new tableau is

	x	y	s_1	s_2	s_3	Z	b	Quotients
departing variable $\rightarrow s_1$	0	$\left(\frac{1}{2}\right)$	1	$-\frac{1}{2}$	0	0	$\frac{5}{2}$	$\frac{5}{2} \div \frac{1}{2} = 5$
x	1	$\frac{1}{2}$	0	$\frac{1}{2}$	0	0	$\frac{35}{2}$	$\frac{35}{2} \div \frac{1}{2} = 35$
s_3	0	$\frac{5}{2}$	0	$\frac{3}{2}$	1	0	$\frac{129}{2}$	$\frac{129}{2} \div \frac{5}{2} = \frac{129}{5} = 25\frac{4}{5}$
Z	0	$-\frac{3}{2}$	0	$\frac{5}{2}$	0	1	$\frac{175}{2}$	

$\uparrow$ indicators
entering variable

Note that on the left side, x replaced s_2. Since $-\frac{3}{2}$ is the most negative indicator, we must continue our process. The entering variable is now y. The smallest quotient is 5. Thus s_1 is the departing variable and $\frac{1}{2}$ is the pivot entry. Using elementary row operations, we have

$$\begin{array}{cccccccc} x & y & s_1 & s_2 & s_3 & Z & b \end{array}$$
$$\begin{bmatrix} 0 & \left(\frac{1}{2}\right) & 1 & -\frac{1}{2} & 0 & 0 & \vdots & \frac{5}{2} \\ 1 & \frac{1}{2} & 0 & \frac{1}{2} & 0 & 0 & \vdots & \frac{35}{2} \\ 0 & \frac{5}{2} & 0 & \frac{3}{2} & 1 & 0 & \vdots & \frac{129}{2} \\ 0 & -\frac{3}{2} & 0 & \frac{5}{2} & 0 & 1 & \vdots & \frac{175}{2} \end{bmatrix}$$

$$\sim \begin{bmatrix} 0 & \frac{1}{2} & 1 & -\frac{1}{2} & 0 & 0 & \vdots & \frac{5}{2} \\ 1 & 0 & -1 & 1 & 0 & 0 & \vdots & 15 \\ 0 & 0 & -5 & 4 & 1 & 0 & \vdots & 52 \\ 0 & 0 & 3 & 1 & 0 & 1 & \vdots & 95 \end{bmatrix}$$ (by adding -1 times row one to row two; adding -5 times row one to row three; adding 3 times row one to row four)

$$\sim \begin{bmatrix} 0 & 1 & 2 & -1 & 0 & 0 & \vdots & 5 \\ 1 & 0 & -1 & 1 & 0 & 0 & \vdots & 15 \\ 0 & 0 & -5 & 4 & 1 & 0 & \vdots & 52 \\ \hdashline 0 & 0 & 3 & 1 & 0 & 1 & \vdots & 95 \end{bmatrix} \quad \text{(by multiplying row one by 2).}$$

Our new tableau is

$$\begin{array}{c} \\ y \\ x \\ s_3 \\ Z \end{array} \begin{array}{cccccccc} x & y & s_1 & s_2 & s_3 & Z & & b \\ \begin{bmatrix} 0 & 1 & 2 & -1 & 0 & 0 & \vdots & 5 \\ 1 & 0 & -1 & 1 & 0 & 0 & \vdots & 15 \\ 0 & 0 & -5 & 4 & 1 & 0 & \vdots & 52 \\ \hdashline 0 & 0 & 3 & 1 & 0 & 1 & \vdots & 95 \end{bmatrix} \end{array}$$

$$\underbrace{\qquad\qquad\qquad\qquad}_{}$$

indicators

where y replaced s_1 on the left side. Since all indicators are nonnegative, the maximum value of Z is 95 and occurs when $y = 5$ and $x = 15$ (and $s_3 = 52$, $s_1 = 0$, and $s_2 = 0$).

It is interesting to see how the values of Z got progressively "better" in successive tableaus in Example 6. These are the entries in the last row and column of each tableau. In the initial tableau we had $Z = 0$. From then on we got $Z = \frac{175}{2} = 87\frac{1}{2}$ and then $Z = 95$, the maximum.

At times several indicators may "tie" for being most negative. In this case, choose any one of the indicators to give the column for the entering variable. Likewise, there may be several quotients which "tie" for being the smallest. You may choose any one of the quotients to give you the departing variable and pivot entry.

EXAMPLE 7

$$\text{Maximize:} \quad Z = 3x_1 + 4x_2 + 2x_3$$

subject to

$$x_1 + 2x_2 \quad\ \leq\ 10,$$

$$2x_1 + 2x_2 + x_3 \leq 10,$$

and $x_1 \geq 0$, $x_2 \geq 0$, $x_3 \geq 0$.

Our initial simplex tableau is Tableau I.

Simplex Tableau I

	x_1	x_2	x_3	s_1	s_2	Z	b	Quotients
departing variable → s_1	1	②	0	1	0	0	10	$10 \div 2 = 5$
s_2	2	2	1	0	1	0	10	$10 \div 2 = 5$
Z	-3	-4	-2	0	0	1	0	

↑ indicators
entering
variable

The entering variable is x_2. Since there is a tie for the smallest quotient, we can choose either s_1 or s_2 as the departing variable. Let us choose s_1. The pivot entry is circled. Using elementary row operations, we get Tableau II.

Simplex Tableau II

	x_1	x_2	x_3	s_1	s_2	Z	b	Quotients
								no quotient since 0 is
departing x_2	$\frac{1}{2}$	1	0	$\frac{1}{2}$	0	0	5	not positive.
variable → s_2	1	0	①	-1	1	0	0	$0 \div 1 = 0$
Z	-1	0	-2	2	0	1	20	

↗ indicators
entering
variable

Since there are negative indicators, we continue. The entering variable is now x_3, the departing variable is s_2, and the pivot is circled. Using elementary row operations, we get Tableau III.

Simplex Tableau III

	x_1	x_2	x_3	s_1	s_2	Z	b
x_2	$\frac{1}{2}$	1	0	$\frac{1}{2}$	0	0	5
x_3	1	0	1	-1	1	0	0
Z	1	0	0	0	2	1	20

indicators

Since all indicators are nonnegative, Z is maximum when $x_2 = 5$ and $x_3 = 0$, and $x_1 = s_1 = s_2 = 0$. The maximum value is $Z = 20$. Note that this value is the same as that value of Z corresponding to Tableau II. This occurred because we had a tie for the smallest quotient. When such a tie exists, we say that we have a *degeneracy*. In degenerate problems it is possible to arrive at the same value of Z at various stages of the simplex process. In Exercise 15-3 you are asked to solve this example problem using s_2 as the departing variable in the initial tableau.

In the next section we shall use the simplex method on minimization problems.

EXERCISE 15–3

Use the simplex method to solve the following problems.

1. Maximize
$$Z = x + 2y$$
subject to
$$2x + y \leq 8$$
$$2x + 3y \leq 12$$
$$x, y \geq 0.$$

2. Maximize
$$Z = 2x + y$$
subject to
$$-x + y \leq 4$$
$$x + y \leq 6$$
$$x, y \geq 0.$$

3. Maximize
$$Z = -x + 3y$$
subject to
$$x + y \leq 6$$
$$-x + y \leq 4$$
$$x, y \geq 0.$$

4. Maximize
$$Z = 3x + 8y$$
subject to
$$x + 2y \leq 8$$
$$x + 6y \leq 12$$
$$x, y \geq 0.$$

5. Maximize
$$Z = 8x + 2y$$
subject to
$$x - y \leq 1$$
$$x + 2y \leq 8$$
$$x + y \leq 5$$
$$x, y \geq 0.$$

6. Maximize
$$Z = 3x - 3y$$
subject to
$$x - y \leq 4$$
$$-x + y \leq 4$$
$$x + y \leq 6$$
$$x, y \geq 0.$$

7. Solve the problem in Example 7 by choosing s_2 as the departing variable in Tableau I.

8. Maximize
$$Z = 2x_1 - x_2 + x_3$$
subject to
$$2x_1 + x_2 - x_3 \leq 4$$
$$x_1 + x_2 + x_3 \leq 2$$
$$x_1, x_2, x_3 \geq 0.$$

9. Maximize
$$Z = 2x_1 + x_2 - x_3$$
subject to
$$x_1 + x_2 \leq 1$$
$$-x_1 + 2x_2 + x_3 \leq 2$$
$$x_1, x_2, x_3 \geq 0.$$

10. Maximize
$$Z = -x + 2y$$
subject to
$$x + y \leq 1$$
$$x - y \leq 1$$
$$-x + y \leq 2$$
$$x \leq 2$$
$$x, y \leq 0.$$

11. Maximize
$$Z = x + y$$
subject to
$$x - y \le 4$$
$$-x + y \le 4$$
$$8x + 5y \le 40$$
$$x + y \le 6$$
$$x, y \ge 0.$$

12. Maximize
$$W = 2x + y - 2z$$
subject to
$$2x - y - z \le 2$$
$$x - y + z \le 4$$
$$x + y + 2z \le 6$$
$$x, y, z \ge 0.$$

13. Maximize
$$W = x - 12y + 4z$$
subject to
$$4x + 3y - z \le 1$$
$$-x - y + z \le 2$$
$$x - y - z \le 1$$
$$x, y, z \ge 0.$$

14. Maximize
$$Z = 4x_1 + 10x_2 - 6x_3 - x_4$$
subject to
$$x_1 \quad + x_3 - x_4 \le 1$$
$$x_1 - x_2 \quad + x_4 \le 2$$
$$x_1 + x_2 - x_3 + x_4 \le 4$$
$$x_1, x_2, x_3, x_4 \ge 0.$$

15. Maximize
$$Z = 50x_1 + 0x_2 + 100x_3 + 0x_4$$
subject to
$$x_1 - 2x_2 \qquad \le 2$$
$$x_1 + x_2 \qquad \le 5$$
$$x_3 + x_4 \le 4$$
$$x_3 - 2x_4 \le 7$$
$$x_1, x_2, x_3, x_4 \ge 0.$$

16. A company manufactures three products: X, Y, and Z. Each product requires machine time and finishing time as given in the table below. The numbers of hours of machine time and finishing time available per month are 900 and 5000, respectively. The unit profit on X, Y, and Z is $3, $4, and $6, respectively. What is the maximum profit per month that can be obtained?

	MACHINE TIME	FINISHING TIME
X	1 hr	4 hr
Y	2 hr	4 hr
Z	3 hr	8 hr

17. The Flip-Flop Company manufactures three types of patio furniture: chairs, rockers, and chaise lounges. Each requires wood, plastic, and aluminum as given in the table below. The company has available 400 units of wood, 600 units of plastic, and 1500 units of aluminum. Each chair, rocker, and chaise lounge sells at $6, $8, and $12, respectively. Assuming that all furniture can be sold, determine a production order so that total revenue will be maximum. What is the maximum revenue?

	WOOD	PLASTIC	ALUMINUM
Chair	1 unit	1 unit	2 units
Rocker	1 unit	1 unit	3 units
Chaise lounge	1 unit	2 units	5 units

15-4   ARTIFICIAL VARIABLES

In this section we shall extend the range of problems that can be solved by the simplex method. One type is as follows.

$$\text{Maximize:}\quad Z = x + 2y$$

subject to

$$x + y \le 9, \tag{1}$$

$$x - y \ge 1, \tag{2}$$

and $x \ge 0$, $y \ge 0$. This problem differs from those in the last section because constraint (2) involves the symbol "$\ge$." To begin, constraints (1) and (2) are written as equations. Constraint (1) becomes

$$x + y + s_1 = 9, \tag{3}$$

where s_1 is a slack variable and $s_1 \ge 0$. For constraint (2), $x - y$ will equal 1 if we *subtract* a nonnegative slack variable from $x - y$. Thus

$$x - y - s_2 = 1, \tag{4}$$

where $s_2 \ge 0$. We can now restate the problem.

$$\text{Maximize:}\ Z = x + 2y \tag{5}$$

subject to

$$x + y + s_1 = 9, \tag{6}$$

$$x - y - s_2 = 1, \tag{7}$$

and $x, y, s_1, s_2 \ge 0$.

With the simplex method we previously got an initial solution by setting the structural variables equal to 0. However, if we do that in this problem, we get into trouble. Namely, when $x = 0$ and $y = 0$ are substituted into Eq. (7), then

$$0 - 0 - s_2 = 1$$

or

$$s_2 = -1.$$

But this contradicts the condition that $s_2 \geq 0$. Thus we must modify our procedure when "$\geq$" is involved.

To do this we work with a maximization problem related to Eqs. (5)–(7) and which, you will see, allows the simplex method to get off the ground.

$$\text{Maximize: } W = Z - nt = x + 2y - nt \qquad (8)$$

subject to

$$x + y + s_1 = 9, \qquad (9)$$

$$x - y - s_2 + t = 1, \qquad (10)$$

where x, y, s_1, s_2, $t \geq 0$ and n is a fixed large positive number. We shall not worry about the particular value of n. The variable t is called an **artificial variable.** It appears in the new objective equation and in the equation in which the coefficient of the slack variable is -1. In Eq. (8), note that W is a maximum when Z is as large as possible (that is, when Z is a maximum as we originally wanted) and nt is as small as possible. The latter occurs when $t = 0$. Thus to maximize Z, it suffices to maximize W.

After expressing Eq. (8) as

$$-x - 2y + nt + W = 0, \qquad (11)$$

we write the augmented coefficient matrix of Eqs. (9)–(11).

$$
\begin{array}{cccccc}
x & y & s_1 & s_2 & t & W \\
\end{array}
$$

$$
\left[
\begin{array}{cccccc|c}
1 & 1 & 1 & 0 & 0 & 0 & 9 \\
1 & -1 & 0 & -1 & 1 & 0 & 1 \\
\hline
-1 & -2 & 0 & 0 & n & 1 & 0
\end{array}
\right] \qquad (12)
$$

To begin the simplex method for maximizing W, we need an initial basic feasible solution. Since the objective function $W = x + 2y - nt$ has three variables (x, y, and t), any B.F.S. must have at least three variables equal to 0. If we let $x = 0$, $y = 0$, and $s_2 = 0$, then from row 1 we get $s_1 = 9$; from row 2, $t = 1$. From row 3, $nt + W = 0$. Since $t = 1$, then $W = -n$. But in a simplex tableau we want the value of W to appear in the last row and last column. This is not so in (12), and thus we must modify that matrix.

To do this, we transform (12) into an equivalent matrix whose last row has the form

$$
\begin{array}{cccccc}
x & y & s_1 & s_2 & t & W \\
? & ? & 0 & ? & 0 & 1 & ?
\end{array}
$$

That is, the n in the t-column is replaced by 0. As a result, if $x = y = s_2 = 0$, then W equals the last entry.

$$
\begin{array}{cccccc}
x & y & s_1 & s_2 & t & W \\
\end{array}
$$

$$
\left[
\begin{array}{cccccc|c}
1 & 1 & 1 & 0 & 0 & 0 & 9 \\
1 & -1 & 0 & -1 & 1 & 0 & 1 \\
\hline
-1 & -2 & 0 & 0 & n & 1 & 0
\end{array}
\right]
$$

$$
\begin{array}{cccccc}
x & y & s_1 & s_2 & t & W \\
\end{array}
$$

$$
\sim
\left[
\begin{array}{cccccc|c}
1 & 1 & 1 & 0 & 0 & 0 & 9 \\
1 & -1 & 0 & -1 & 1 & 0 & 1 \\
\hline
-1-n & -2+n & 0 & n & 0 & 1 & -n
\end{array}
\right].
\qquad
\begin{array}{l}
\text{(by adding } -n \text{ times} \\
\text{row 2 to row 3)}
\end{array}
$$

Let us now check things out. If $x = 0$, $y = 0$, and $s_2 = 0$, then from row 1 we get $s_1 = 9$; from row 2, $t = 1$; and from row 3, $W = -n$. Thus we now have initial simplex Tableau I.

Simplex Tableau I

$$
\begin{array}{ccccccc}
& x & y & s_1 & s_2 & t & W & \textit{Quotients}
\end{array}
$$

$$
\begin{array}{c}
\text{departing} \\
\text{variable}
\end{array}
\!\!\to\!\!
\begin{array}{c}
s_1 \\
t \\
W
\end{array}
\left[
\begin{array}{cccccc|c}
1 & 1 & 1 & 0 & 0 & 0 & 9 \\
① & -1 & 0 & -1 & 1 & 0 & 1 \\
\hline
-1-n & -2+n & 0 & n & 0 & 1 & -n
\end{array}
\right]
\begin{array}{l}
9 \div 1 = 9 \\
1 \div 1 = 1
\end{array}
$$

$$
\uparrow \qquad \text{indicators}
$$
$$
\text{entering variable}
$$

From this point we can use the procedures of the last section. Since n is a large positive number, the most negative indicator is $-1 - n$. Thus the entering variable is x. From the quotients we choose t as the departing variable. The pivot entry is circled. Using elementary row operations to get 1 in the pivot position and 0's elsewhere in that column, we get Tableau II.

Simplex Tableau II

$$
\begin{array}{ccccccc}
& x & y & s_1 & s_2 & t & W & \textit{Quotients}
\end{array}
$$

$$
\begin{array}{c}
\text{departing} \\
\text{variable} \to
\end{array}
\begin{array}{c}
s_1 \\
x \\
W
\end{array}
\left[
\begin{array}{cccccc|c}
0 & ② & 1 & 1 & -1 & 0 & 8 \\
1 & -1 & 0 & -1 & 1 & 0 & 1 \\
\hline
0 & -3 & 0 & -1 & n+1 & 1 & 1
\end{array}
\right]
\begin{array}{l}
8 \div 2 \\
\text{(no quotient,} \\
\text{since } -1 \text{ is not} \\
\text{positive)}
\end{array}
$$

$$
\uparrow \quad \text{indicators}
$$
$$
\text{entering variable}
$$

Here the entering variable is y, the departing variable is s_1, and the pivot entry is circled. Using elementary row operations we get Tableau III.

Simplex Tableau III

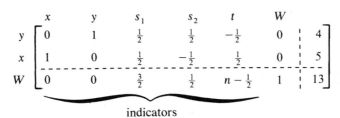

$$
\begin{array}{c}
\begin{array}{cccccc} x & y & s_1 & s_2 & t & W \end{array}\\
\begin{array}{c} y \\ x \\ W \end{array}
\left[
\begin{array}{cccccc|c}
0 & 1 & \frac{1}{2} & \frac{1}{2} & -\frac{1}{2} & 0 & 4 \\
1 & 0 & \frac{1}{2} & -\frac{1}{2} & \frac{1}{2} & 0 & 5 \\
\hline
0 & 0 & \frac{3}{2} & \frac{1}{2} & n-\frac{1}{2} & 1 & 13
\end{array}
\right]
\end{array}
$$

indicators

Since all the indicators are nonnegative, the maximum value of W, as well as Z, is 13. It occurs when $x = 5$ and $y = 4$.

It is worthwhile to review the steps we performed to solve our problem.

$$\text{Maximize: } Z = x + 2y$$

subject to

$$x + y \le 9, \qquad\qquad (13)$$

$$x - y \ge 1, \qquad\qquad (14)$$

and $x \ge 0$, $y \ge 0$. We write (13) as

$$x + y + s_1 = 9. \qquad\qquad (15)$$

Since (14) involves the symbol $\ge$, we write (14) in a form having both a slack variable (with coefficient -1) and an artificial variable.

$$x - y - s_2 + t = 1. \qquad\qquad (16)$$

The objective equation to consider is $W = x + 2y - nt$, or equivalently,

$$-x - 2y + nt + W = 0. \qquad\qquad (17)$$

The augmented coefficient matrix of the system formed by Eqs. (15)–(17) is

$$
\begin{array}{c}
\begin{array}{cccccc} x & y & s_1 & s_2 & t & W \end{array}\\
\left[
\begin{array}{cccccc|c}
1 & 1 & 1 & 0 & 0 & 0 & 9 \\
1 & -1 & 0 & -1 & 1 & 0 & 1 \\
\hline
-1 & -2 & 0 & 0 & n & 1 & 0
\end{array}
\right].
\end{array}
$$

Next we remove the n from the artificial variable column by using elementary row operations. The resulting simplex Tableau I corresponds to the initial solution in which the structural variables, x and y, and the slack variable s_2 (the one associated with the constraint involving the symbol $\ge$) are each 0.

Simplex Tableau I

$$
\begin{array}{c}
 \\
s_1 \\
t \\
W
\end{array}
\begin{array}{cccccc|c}
x & y & s_1 & s_2 & t & W & \\
1 & 1 & 1 & 0 & 0 & 0 & 9 \\
1 & -1 & 0 & -1 & 1 & 0 & 1 \\
\hline
-1-n & -2+n & 0 & n & 0 & 1 & -n
\end{array}
$$

The variables s_1 and t on the left side of the tableau correspond to the nonstructural variables in Eqs. (15) and (16) which have positive coefficients. Using the procedures of the last section on this tableau, we then get the maximum value of W, which is the same as the maximum value of Z.

EXAMPLE 8

Use the simplex method to

$$\textit{Maximize: } Z = 2x + y$$

subject to

$$x + y \le 12, \tag{18}$$

$$x + 2y \le 20, \tag{19}$$

$$-x + y \ge 2, \tag{20}$$

and $x \ge 0$, $y \ge 0$.

The equations for (18)–(20) will involve a total of three slack variables: s_1, s_2, and s_3. Since (20) contains the symbol $\ge$, its equation will also involve an artificial variable t, and the coefficient of its slack variable s_3 will be -1.

$$x + y + s_1 = 12 \tag{21}$$

$$x + 2y + s_2 = 20 \tag{22}$$

$$-x + y - s_3 + t = 2. \tag{23}$$

We consider $W = Z - nt = 2x + y - nt$ as the objective equation, or equivalently,

$$-2x - y + nt + W = 0, \tag{24}$$

where n is a large positive number. Now we construct the augmented coefficient matrix of Eqs. (21)–(24).

$$
\begin{array}{cccccccc}
x & y & s_1 & s_2 & s_3 & t & W & \\
\end{array}
\begin{bmatrix}
1 & 1 & 1 & 0 & 0 & 0 & 0 & 12 \\
1 & 2 & 0 & 1 & 0 & 0 & 0 & 20 \\
-1 & 1 & 0 & 0 & -1 & 1 & 0 & 2 \\
\hline
-2 & -1 & 0 & 0 & 0 & n & 1 & 0
\end{bmatrix}.
$$

To get initial simplex Tableau I, we remove the n from the artificial variable column by adding $-n$ times row 3 to row 4.

Simplex Tableau I

	x	y	s_1	s_2	s_3	t	W			Quotients
s_1	1	1	1	0	0	0	0		12	$12 \div 1 = 12$
s_2	1	2	0	1	0	0	0		20	$20 \div 2 = 10$
departing → t	-1	①	0	0	-1	1	0		2	$2 \div 1 = 2$
variable W	$-2+n$	$-1-n$	0	0	n	0	1		$-2n$	

↑ indicators
entering
variable

The variables s_1, s_2, and t on the left side of Tableau I are the nonstructural variables with positive coefficients in Eqs. (21)–(23). Since n is a large positive number, $-1 - n$ is the most negative indicator. The entering variable is y, the departing variable is t, and the pivot entry is circled. Proceeding, we get Tableau II.

Simplex Tableau II

	x	y	s_1	s_2	s_3	t	W			Quotients
departing → s_1	②	0	1	0	1	-1	0		10	$10 \div 2 = 5$
variable s_2	3	0	0	1	2	-2	0		16	$16 \div 3 = 5\frac{1}{3}$
y	-1	1	0	0	-1	1	0		2	
W	-3	0	0	0	-1	$1+n$	1		2	

↑   indicators
entering
variable

Since -3 is the most negative indicator, we continue the process and get Tableau III.

Simplex Tableau III

	x	y	s_1	s_2	s_3	t	W		
x	1	0	$\frac{1}{2}$	0	$\frac{1}{2}$	$-\frac{1}{2}$	0		5
s_2	0	0	$-\frac{3}{2}$	1	$\frac{1}{2}$	$-\frac{1}{2}$	0		1
y	0	1	$\frac{1}{2}$	0	$-\frac{1}{2}$	$\frac{1}{2}$	0		7
W	0	0	$\frac{3}{2}$	0	$\frac{1}{2}$	$-\frac{1}{2}+n$	1		17

indicators

Since n is a large positive number, all indicators are nonnegative. Thus the maximum value of W, as well as Z, is 17. It occurs when $x = 5$ and $y = 7$.

So far we have used the simplex method to *maximize* objective functions. In general, to *minimize* a function it suffices to maximize the negative of the function. To understand why, consider the function $f(x) = x^2 - 4$. In Fig. 15-17(a), observe that the minimum value of f is -4 and it occurs when $x = 0$. In Fig.

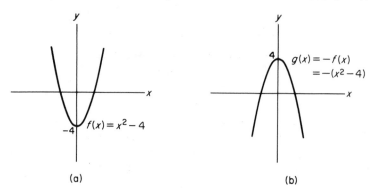

(a)   (b)

Fig. 15-17

15-17(b) is the graph of $g(x) = -f(x) = -(x^2 - 4)$. This graph is the reflection through the x-axis of the graph of f. Notice that the maximum value of g is 4 and occurs also when $x = 0$. Thus the minimum value of $x^2 - 4$ is the negative of the maximum value of $-(x^2 - 4)$. That is,

$$\text{Min } f = -\text{Max } (-f).$$

EXAMPLE 9

Use the simplex method to

$$\text{Minimize: } Z = x + 2y$$

subject to

$$-2x + y \geq 1, \tag{25}$$

$$-x + y \geq 2 \tag{26}$$

and $x \geq 0$, $y \geq 0$.

To minimize Z, we first maximize $-Z = -x - 2y$. Note that (25) and (26) both involve the symbol $\geq$. Thus their equations will involve two slack variables s_1 and s_2, each with coefficient -1, and two artificial variables t_1 and t_2.

$$-2x + y - s_1 + t_1 = 1 \tag{27}$$

$$-x + y - s_2 + t_2 = 2. \tag{28}$$

Since there are *two* artificial variables, we shall maximize the objective function $W = (-Z) - nt_1 - nt_2$, or equivalently,

$$x + 2y + nt_1 + nt_2 + W = 0. \tag{29}$$

The augmented coefficient matrix of Eqs. (27)–(29) is

$$
\begin{array}{ccccccc}
x & y & s_1 & s_2 & t_1 & t_2 & W \\
\end{array}
$$

$$
\left[
\begin{array}{ccccccc|c}
-2 & 1 & -1 & 0 & 1 & 0 & 0 & 1 \\
-1 & 1 & 0 & -1 & 0 & 1 & 0 & 2 \\
\hline
1 & 2 & 0 & 0 & n & n & 1 & 0
\end{array}
\right].
$$

We now remove the n's from *all* of the artificial variable columns. By adding $-n$ times row 1 to row 3, and adding $-n$ times row 2 to row 3, we get initial simplex Tableau I.

Simplex Tableau I

$$
\begin{array}{ccccccc}
x & y & s_1 & s_2 & t_1 & t_2 & W \\
\end{array}
\qquad Quotients
$$

departing variable $\rightarrow$ t_1
t_2
W

$$
\left[
\begin{array}{ccccccc|c}
-2 & ① & -1 & 0 & 1 & 0 & 0 & 1 \\
-1 & 1 & 0 & -1 & 0 & 1 & 0 & 2 \\
\hline
1+3n & 2-2n & n & n & 0 & 0 & 1 & -3n
\end{array}
\right]
$$

$1 \div 1 = 1$
$2 \div 1 = 2$

$\uparrow$ indicators
entering
variable

Since n is a large positive number, the most negative indicator is $2 - 2n$. Proceeding, we get Tableau II.

Simplex Tableau II

$$
\begin{array}{ccccccc}
x & y & s_1 & s_2 & t_1 & t_2 & W \\
\end{array}
\qquad Quotients
$$

y
departing variable $\rightarrow$ t_2
W

$$
\left[
\begin{array}{ccccccc|c}
-2 & 1 & -1 & 0 & 1 & 0 & 0 & 1 \\
1 & 0 & ① & -1 & -1 & 1 & 0 & 1 \\
\hline
5-n & 0 & 2-n & n & -2+2n & 0 & 1 & -2-n
\end{array}
\right]
$$

$1 \div 1 = 1$

$\nearrow$ indicators
entering
variable

The most negative indicator is $2 - n$. Thus we continue and get Tableau III.

Simplex Tableau III

$$
\begin{array}{ccccccc}
x & y & s_1 & s_2 & t_1 & t_2 & W \\
\end{array}
$$

y
s_1
W

$$
\left[
\begin{array}{ccccccc|c}
-1 & 1 & 0 & -1 & 0 & 1 & 0 & 2 \\
1 & 0 & 1 & -1 & -1 & 1 & 0 & 1 \\
\hline
3 & 0 & 0 & 2 & n & -2+n & 1 & -4
\end{array}
\right]
$$

indicators

Since all indicators are nonnegative, W, as well as $-Z$, has a maximum value of -4. Thus the *minimum* of Z is $-(-4)$ or 4. It occurs when $x = 0$ and $y = 2$.

EXERCISE 15-4

Use the simplex method to solve the following problems.

1. Maximize
$$Z = 2x + y$$
subject to
$$x + y \le 6$$
$$-x + y \ge 4$$
$$x, y \ge 0.$$

2. Maximize
$$Z = 2x + 4y$$
subject to
$$x + 2y \le 8$$
$$x + 6y \ge 12$$
$$x, y \ge 0.$$

3. Maximize
$$Z = x - 10y$$
subject to
$$x - y \le 1$$
$$x + 2y \le 8$$
$$x + y \ge 5$$
$$x, y \ge 0.$$

4. Maximize
$$Z = -2x + 2y$$
subject to
$$x - y \le 4$$
$$-x + y \le 4$$
$$x \ge 6$$
$$x, y \ge 0.$$

5. Maximize
$$Z = 2x + y - z$$
subject to
$$x + 2y + z \le 5$$
$$-x + y + z \ge 1$$
$$x, y, z \ge 0.$$

6. Maximize
$$Z = x - y + 4z$$
subject to
$$x + y + z \le 9$$
$$x - 2y + z \ge 6$$
$$x, y, z \ge 0.$$

7. Maximize
$$Z = x - y$$
subject to
$$-x + 2y \le 13$$
$$-x + y \ge 3$$
$$x + y \ge 11$$
$$x, y \ge 0.$$

8. Maximize
$$Z = x + 4y$$
subject to
$$x + 2y \le 8$$
$$x + 6y \ge 12$$
$$y \ge 2$$
$$x, y \ge 0.$$

9. Minimize
$$Z = 3x + 6y$$
subject to
$$-x + y \ge 6$$
$$x + y \ge 10$$
$$x, y \ge 0.$$

10. Minimize
$$Z = 8x + 12y$$
subject to
$$2x + 2y \ge 1$$
$$x + 3y \ge 2$$
$$x, y \ge 0.$$

11. Minimize
$$Z = 4x_1 + 2x_2 + x_3$$
subject to
$$x_1 - x_2 - x_3 \ge 9$$
$$x_1, x_2, x_3 \ge 0.$$

12. Minimize
$$Z = x_1 + x_2 + 2x_3$$
subject to
$$x_1 + 2x_2 - x_3 \ge 4$$
$$x_1, x_2, x_3 \ge 0.$$

13. Minimize

$$Z = x_1 + 8x_2 + 5x_3$$

subject to

$$x_1 + x_2 + x_3 \geq 8$$
$$-x_1 + 2x_2 + x_3 \geq 2$$
$$x_1, x_2, x_3 \geq 0.$$

14. Minimize

$$Z = 4x_1 + 4x_2 + 6x_3$$

subject to

$$x_1 - x_2 - x_3 \leq 3$$
$$x_1 - x_2 + x_3 \geq 3$$
$$x_1, x_2, x_3 \geq 0.$$

15. Because of increased business, a catering service finds that it must rent additional delivery trucks. The minimum needs are 12 units each of refrigerated and nonrefrigerated space. Two standard types of trucks are available in the rental market. Type *A* has 2 units of refrigerated space and 1 unit of nonrefrigerated space. Type *B* has 2 units of refrigerated space and 3 units of nonrefrigerated space. The costs per mile are $0.40 for *A* and $0.60 for *B*. How many of each type of truck should be rented so as to minimize total cost per mile? What is the minimum total cost per mile?

15-5   THE DUAL

With any given linear programming problem, we can associate another linear programming problem called its *dual*. The given problem is called *primal*. If the primal is a maximization problem, then its dual is a minimization. Similarly, if the primal involves minimization, then the dual involves maximization.

For example, suppose the primal problem is

Primal

$$\text{Maximize: } Z = c_1 x_1 + c_2 x_2 + c_3 x_3$$

subject to

$$a_{11} x_1 + a_{12} x_2 + a_{13} x_3 \leq b_1, \tag{1}$$

$$a_{21} x_1 + a_{22} x_2 + a_{23} x_3 \leq b_2, \tag{2}$$

and $x_1, x_2, x_3 \leq 0$.
Then its dual is

Dual

$$\text{Minimize: } W = b_1 y_1 + b_2 y_2$$

subject to

$$a_{11} y_1 + a_{21} y_2 \geq c_1, \tag{3}$$

$$a_{12} y_1 + a_{22} y_2 \geq c_2, \tag{4}$$

$$a_{13} y_1 + a_{23} y_2 \geq c_3, \tag{5}$$

and $y_1, y_2 \geq 0$.

Let us compare the primal and dual. Notice that the primal has three structural variables and will involve two slack variables. In the dual, the reverse is true. It has two structural variables and will involve three slack variables. In (1) and (2) the inequality symbols are all $\leq$. But in (3)–(5) they are all $\geq$. The coefficients of the objective function in the dual are the constant terms in constraints (1) and (2) of the primal. Similarly, the constant terms in constraints (3)–(5) of the dual are the coefficients of the primal objective function. The coefficient matrix of the left sides of (3)–(5) is

$$\begin{bmatrix} a_{11} & a_{21} \\ a_{12} & a_{22} \\ a_{13} & a_{23} \end{bmatrix}$$

This matrix is the *transpose* of the coefficient matrix of the left sides of (1) and (2) in the primal:

$$\begin{bmatrix} a_{11} & a_{12} & a_{13} \\ a_{21} & a_{22} & a_{23} \end{bmatrix}^{T} = \begin{bmatrix} a_{11} & a_{21} \\ a_{12} & a_{22} \\ a_{13} & a_{23} \end{bmatrix}$$

More generally, if the primal problem involves m structural and n slack variables, then its dual involves n structural and m slack variables.

There is an important relationship between the primal and its dual. **The optimum value of the primal's objective function is the *same* as that of the dual's.**

EXAMPLE 10

Find the dual of

$$\text{Maximize: } Z = 3x_1 + 4x_2 + 2x_3$$

subject to

$$x_1 + 2x_2 + 0x_3 \leq 10,$$
$$2x_1 + 2x_2 + x_3 \leq 10,$$

and $x_1, x_2, x_3 \geq 0$.

The dual is

$$\text{Minimize: } W = 10y_1 + 10y_2$$

subject to

$$y_1 + 2y_2 \geq 3,$$
$$2y_1 + 2y_2 \geq 4,$$

$$0y_1 + y_2 \geq 2,$$

and y_1, $y_2 \geq 0$.

In Example 7 we showed that the maximum value of Z is 20. Thus the minimum value of W is also 20.

If the primal problem is a minimization, then its dual is a maximization. For example, suppose the primal is

Primal

$$\text{Minimize: } Z = c_1 x_1 + c_2 x_2 + c_3 x_3$$

subject to

$$a_{11} x_1 + a_{12} x_2 + a_{13} x_3 \geq b_1,$$
$$a_{21} x_1 + a_{22} x_2 + a_{23} x_3 \geq b_2,$$

and x_1, x_2, $x_3 \geq 0$.

Then its dual is

Dual

$$\text{Maximize: } W = b_1 y_1 + b_2 y_2$$

subject to

$$a_{11} y_1 + a_{21} y_2 \leq c_1,$$
$$a_{12} y_1 + a_{22} y_2 \leq c_2,$$
$$a_{13} y_1 + a_{23} y_2 \leq c_3,$$

and y_1, $y_2 \geq 0$.

The optimum values of Z and W are the same.

EXAMPLE 11

Find the dual of

$$\text{Minimize: } Z = 80x_1 + 220x_2 + 210x_3$$

subject to

$$x_1 + 3x_2 + 2x_3 \geq 5,$$
$$x_1 + 2x_2 + 3x_3 \geq 6,$$

and x_1, x_2, $x_3 \geq 0$.

The dual is

$$\text{Maximize: } W = 5y_1 + 6y_2$$

subject to

$$y_1 + y_2 \leq 80,$$
$$3y_1 + 2y_2 \leq 220,$$
$$2y_1 + 3y_2 \leq 210,$$

and $y_1, y_2 \geq 0$.

EXAMPLE 12

Find the dual of

$$\text{Maximize: } Z = 10x + 12y$$

subject to

$$x + y \leq 60, \tag{6}$$
$$x - 2y \geq 0, \tag{7}$$

and $x, y \geq 0$.

First the primal must be put in proper form. Since it is a maximization, we want the inequality symbols in *both* (6) and (7) to be $\leq$. Multiplying (7) by -1 gives

$$-x + 2y \leq 0.$$

Thus the primal problem is

$$\text{Maximize: } Z = 10x + 12y$$

subject to

$$x + y \leq 60,$$
$$-x + 2y \leq 0,$$

and $x, y \geq 0$.
The dual is

$$\text{Minimize: } W = 60u + 0v$$

subject to

$$u - v \geq 10,$$
$$u + 2v \geq 12,$$

and $u, v \geq 0$.

At times it is easier to solve the dual problem rather than the primal. In terms of the number of rows of a simplex tableau, it is usually easier to solve the dual if the primal has fewer structural variables than slack variables. For example, if the primal has 4 structural and 10 slack variables, then its simplex tableau will have $10 + 1 = 11$ rows. On the other hand, the tableau of the dual will have only $4 + 1 = 5$ rows.

In Example 9 we used the simplex method to minimize $Z = x + 2y$ such that

$$-2x + y \geq 1,$$
$$-x + y \geq 2,$$

and x, $y \geq 0$. The simplex tableau had 24 entries and involved two artificial variables. The tableau of the dual has only 18 entries, no artificial variables, and is easier to handle, as Example 13 will show.

EXAMPLE 13

Use the dual and the simplex method to find the minimum value of

$$Z = x + 2y$$

subject to

$$-2x + y \geq 1$$
$$-x + y \geq 2,$$

and x, $y \geq 0$.

The dual is

$$\text{Maximize: } W = u + 2v$$

subject to

$$-2u - v \leq 1,$$
$$u + v \leq 2,$$

and u, $v \geq 0$.
The initial simplex tableau is Tableau I.

Simplex Tableau I

Continuing, we get Tableau II.

Simplex Tableau II

$$
\begin{array}{c@{\quad}c@{\quad}c@{\quad}c@{\quad}c@{\quad}c}
 & u & v & s_1 & s_2 & W & \\
\begin{array}{c} s_1 \\ v \\ W \end{array} &
\left[\begin{array}{ccccc|c}
-1 & 0 & 1 & 1 & 0 & 3 \\
1 & 1 & 0 & 1 & 0 & 2 \\
\hline
1 & 0 & 0 & 2 & 1 & 4
\end{array}\right]
\end{array}
$$

$$\underbrace{\hphantom{-1 \quad 0 \quad 1 \quad 1 \quad 0}}_{\text{indicators}}$$

Since all indicators are nonnegative in Tableau II, the maximum value of W is 4. Hence the minimum value of Z is also 4. This confirms the result in Example 9.

EXERCISE 15-5

In problems 1–8, find the duals. Do not solve.

1. Maximize
$$Z = 2x + 3y$$
subject to
$$x + y \le 6$$
$$-x + y \le 4$$
$$x, y \ge 0.$$

2. Maximize
$$Z = 2x_1 + x_2 - x_3$$
subject to
$$x_1 + x_2 \qquad \le 1$$
$$-x_1 + 2x_2 + x_3 \le 2$$
$$x_1, x_2, x_3 \ge 0.$$

3. Minimize
$$Z = x_1 + 8x_2 + 5x_3$$
subject to
$$x_1 + x_2 + x_3 \ge 8$$
$$-x_1 + 2x_2 + x_3 \ge 2$$
$$x_1, x_2, x_3 \ge 0.$$

4. Minimize
$$Z = 8x + 12y$$
subject to
$$2x + 2y \ge 1$$
$$x + 3y \ge 2$$
$$x, y \ge 0.$$

5. Maximize
$$Z = x - y$$
subject to
$$-x + 2y \le 13$$
$$-x + y \ge 3$$
$$x + y \ge 11$$
$$x, y \ge 0.$$

6. Maximize
$$Z = x - y + 4z$$
subject to
$$x + y + z \le 9$$
$$x - 2y + z \ge 6$$
$$x, y, z \ge 0.$$

7. Minimize
$$Z = 4x_1 + 4x_2 + 6x_3$$
subject to
$$x_1 - x_2 - x_3 \le 3$$
$$x_1 - x_2 + x_3 \ge 3$$
$$x_1, x_2, x_3 \ge 0.$$

8. Minimize
$$Z = 6x + 3y$$
subject to
$$3x - 4y \le 12$$
$$13x - 8y \le 80$$
$$x, y \ge 0.$$

In problems 9–14, solve by using duals and the simplex method.

9. Minimize
$$Z = 4x_1 + 4x_2 + 6x_3$$

10. Minimize
$$Z = x + y$$

subject to

$$x_1 - x_2 + x_3 \geq 1$$
$$-x_1 + x_2 + x_3 \geq 2$$
$$x_1, x_2, x_3 \geq 0.$$

subject to

$$x + 4y \geq 28$$
$$2x - y \geq 2$$
$$-3x + 8y \geq 16$$
$$x, y \geq 0.$$

11. Maximize

$$Z = 3x + 8y$$

subject to

$$x + 2y \leq 8$$
$$x + 6y \leq 12$$
$$x, y \geq 0.$$

12. Maximize

$$Z = 2x + 6y$$

subject to

$$3x + y \leq 12$$
$$x + y \leq 8$$
$$x, y \geq 0.$$

13. Minimize

$$Z = 6x + 4y$$

subject to

$$-x + y \leq 1$$
$$x + y \geq 3$$
$$x, y \geq 0.$$

14. Minimize

$$Z = x_1 + x_2 + 2x_3$$

subject to

$$-x_1 - x_2 + x_3 \leq 1$$
$$x_1 - x_2 + x_3 \geq 2$$
$$x_1, x_2, x_3 \geq 0.$$

15. A firm is comparing the costs of advertising in two media: newspaper and radio. For every dollar's worth of advertising, the accompanying table gives the number of people, by income group, reached by these media. The firm wants to reach

	Under $20,000	Over $20,000
Newspaper	50	100
Radio	50	20

at least 8500 persons earning under $20,000 and at least 5800 earning over $20,000. By using the dual and the simplex method, find the minimum amount of advertising expenditures that must be made so as to reach these numbers of people.

16. Use the dual and the simplex method to find the minimum total cost per mile in Problem 15 of Exercise 15-4.

17. A company pays skilled and semiskilled workers in its assembly department $4 and $7 per hour, respectively. In the shipping department, shipping clerks are paid $5 per hour and shipping clerk apprentices are paid $2 per hour. The company requires at least 100 workers in the assembly department and at least 50 in the shipping department. Because of union agreements, at least twice as many semiskilled workers must be employed as skilled workers. Also, at least twice as many shipping clerks must be employed as shipping clerk apprentices. Use the dual and the simplex method to find the minimum total hourly wages that must be paid to these employees.

15-6 AN ECONOMIC INTERPRETATION OF THE DUAL

To give you an economic interpretation of the dual, consider the following situation. Because of increased business, a catering service finds that it must rent additional delivery trucks. The minimum needs are 12 units each of refrigerated and nonrefrigerated space. Two standard types of truck are available in the rental market. Type A has 2 units of refrigerated space and 1 unit of nonrefrigerated space. Type B has 2 units of refrigerated space and 3 units of nonrefrigerated space. The costs per mile are $0.40 for A and $0.60 for B. How many of each type of truck should be rented so as to minimize total cost per mile?

TABLE 15-3

	Refrigerated	Nonrefrigerated	Cost/mile
Type A	2 units	1 unit	$0.40
Type B	2 units	3 units	$0.60
Requirements	12 units	12 units	

The data are given in Table 15-3. If the catering firm rents x trucks of type A and y trucks of type B, then the problem is to

$$\text{Minimize: } C = .40x + .60y$$

subject to

$$2x + 2y \geq 12$$

$$x + 3y \geq 12$$

$$x \geq 0$$

$$y \geq 0.$$

Solving gives $x = 3$, $y = 3$, and a minimal total cost per mile $C = \$3.00$.

Now, let us look at the situation from another point of view. Suppose the owner of a new rental agency wants to assign a "worth" to each unit of this type of truck space he is renting, subject to the limitations of market prices. That is, he wants to determine a rental price per mile for each unit of refrigerated and nonrefrigerated space that makes up a truck. Let these rental prices be r and n, respectively, where r, $n \geq 0$. Since a truck of type A has 2 units of refrigerated space and 1 unit of nonrefrigerated space, the total worth of the units for such a truck is $2r + 1n$. For competitive reasons, the rental agent wants to be sure that $2r + n$ is no more than the market value

$0.40 (per mile). Otherwise he may not rent the truck. Similarly, for a truck of type B he wants

$$2r + 3n \le .60.$$

Moreover, the agent wants to meet the needs of the catering service and yet maximize his own return. Since these requirements are 12 units of each type of space, the return R is

$$R = 12r + 12n.$$

Thus we have

$$\text{Maximize: } R = 12r + 12n$$

subject to

$$2r + n \le .40$$
$$2r + 3n \le .60$$
$$r \ge 0$$
$$n \ge 0.$$

This problem is the dual to the original (primal) problem. Note that the dual is a maximization problem and the primal involves minimization. Solving the dual gives $r = .15$, $n = .10$, and $R = \$3.00$. In both the primal and dual, the value of the objective function is $\$3.00$. The worth of one unit of refrigerated space is $\$0.15$ per mile and for nonrefrigerated space it is $\$0.10$. In essence, for this problem, the dual involves attaching a "worth" on a particular unit of space.

15-7 REVIEW

Important Terms and Symbols in Chapter 15

linear inequality *(p. 650)*
system of inequalities *(p. 652)*
linear programming problem
    (p. 655)
feasible region *(p. 657)*
feasible point *(p. 656)*
constraints *(p. 656)*
optimum solution *(p. 656)*
objective function *(p. 657)*
isoprofit line *(p. 658)*
isocost line *(p. 661)*

simplex method *(p. 669)*
slack variable *(p. 664)*
structural variable *(p. 664)*
simplex tableau *(p. 665)*
indicators *(p. 665)*
entering variable *(p. 665)*
departing variable *(p. 666)*
pivot entry *(p. 667)*
artificial variable *(p. 677)*
primal, dual *(p. 685)*

Review Section

1. If $y_1 \leq m_1 x + b_1$ and $y_2 \geq m_2 x + b_2$ is a system of inequalities, which of the regions 1, 2, 3, and 4 in Fig. 15-18 would correspond to the solution?_____

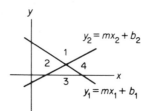

Fig. 15-18

> *Ans.* 2

2. The solution of $x - y > 3$ consists of all points (above)(below) the line $y = x - 3$.

> *Ans.* below

3. True or false: Given a system of linear inequalities in x and y, a solution of any two of the inequalities always gives a feasible point or a corner point._____

> *Ans.* false

4. If a linear programming problem in x and y has three constraints, then there will correspond how many slack variables? _____

> *Ans.* three

5. In the simplex method, an optimum solution is reached when all of the indicators are _____.

> *Ans.* nonnegative

6. Suppose the simplex method is applied to:

$$\text{Maximize: } Z = 3x_1 + 4x_2 + 2x_3$$

subject to

$$2x_1 + 2x_2 + x_3 \leq 10$$
$$x_1 + 2x_2 \qquad \geq 2$$

where $x_1, x_2, x_3 \geq 0$.
Then there will be __(a)__ slack variables and __(b)__ artificial variables. The initial simplex tableau will have __(c)__ rows. The entering variable corresponds to the most __(d)__ indicator.

> *Ans.* (a) 2;   (b) 1;   (c) 3;   (d) negative

7. If the primal problem has 4 structural variables and 2 slack variables, then the dual
has __(a)__ structural variables and __(b)__ slack variables.

> *Ans.* (a) 2;   (b) 4

8. True or false: The optimum value of the primal's objective function is equal to the
optimum value of the dual's objective function. _____

> *Ans.* true

Review Problems

In problems 1–10 solve the given inequality or system of inequalities.

1. $-3x + 2y > -6$

2. $x - 2y + 6 \geq 0$

3. $2y \leq -3$

4. $-x < 2$

5. $\begin{cases} y - 3x < 6 \\ x - y > -3 \end{cases}$

6. $\begin{cases} x - 2y > 4 \\ x + y > 1 \end{cases}$

7. $\begin{cases} x - y < 4 \\ y - x < 4 \end{cases}$

8. $\begin{cases} x > y \\ x + y < 0 \end{cases}$

9. $\begin{cases} 3x + y > -4 \\ x - y > -5 \\ x \geq 0 \end{cases}$

10. $\begin{cases} x - y > 4 \\ x < 2 \\ y < -4 \end{cases}$

11. Maximize the function $Z = x - 2y + 6$ over the region given below by considering
corner points.

$$\begin{cases} y \geq 0 \\ 0 \leq x \leq 3 \\ y - x \leq 2 \\ x + y \leq 4. \end{cases}$$

12. Minimize the function in Problem 11 over the given region by considering corner
points.

Use the simplex method in problems 13–19.

13. Maximize
   $Z = 4x + 5y$
   subject to
   $x + 6y \leq 12$
   $x + 2y \leq 8$
   $x, y \geq 0.$

14. Maximize
   $Z = 18x + 20y$
   subject to
   $2x + 3y \leq 18$
   $4x + 3y \leq 24$
   $y \leq 5$
   $x, y \geq 0.$

15. Minimize

$$Z = 2x + 3y + z$$

subject to

$$x + 2y + 3z \geq 6$$
$$x, y, z \geq 0.$$

16. Minimize

$$Z = x + y$$

subject to

$$3x + 4y \geq 24$$
$$y \geq 3$$
$$x, y \geq 0.$$

17. Maximize

$$Z = x_1 + 2x_2$$

subject to

$$x_1 + x_2 \leq 12$$
$$x_1 + x_2 \geq 5$$
$$x_1 \leq 10$$
$$x_1, x_2 \geq 0.$$

18. Minimize

$$Z = 2x_1 + x_2$$

subject to

$$x_1 + 2x_2 \leq 6$$
$$x_1 + x_2 \geq 1$$
$$x_1, x_2 \geq 0.$$

19. By considering the dual, find the minimum value of

$$Z = 2x + 7y + 8z$$

subject to

$$x + 2y + 3z \geq 35$$

$$x + y + z \geq 25$$

$$x, y, z \geq 0.$$

Appendix A

Tables of Powers—Roots —Reciprocals

n	n^2	$\sqrt{n}$	$\sqrt{10n}$	n^3	$\sqrt[3]{n}$	$\sqrt[3]{10n}$	$\sqrt[3]{100n}$	$1/n$
1.0	1.0000	1.0000	3.1623	1.0000	1.0000	2.1544	4.6416	1.0000
1.1	1.2100	1.0488	3.3166	1.3310	1.0323	2.2240	4.7914	0.9091
1.2	1.4400	1.0954	3.4641	1.7280	1.0627	2.2894	4.9324	0.8333
1.3	1.6900	1.1402	3.6056	2.1970	1.0914	2.3513	5.0658	0.7692
1.4	1.9600	1.1832	3.7417	2.7440	1.1187	2.4101	5.1925	0.7143
1.5	2.2500	1.2247	3.8730	3.3750	1.1447	2.4662	5.3133	0.6667
1.6	2.5600	1.2649	4.0000	4.0960	1.1696	2.5198	5.4288	0.6250
1.7	2.8900	1.3038	4.1231	4.9130	1.1935	2.5713	5.5397	0.5882
1.8	3.2400	1.3416	4.2426	5.8320	1.2164	2.6207	5.6462	0.5556
1.9	3.6100	1.3784	4.3589	6.8590	1.2386	2.6684	5.7489	0.5263
2.0	4.0000	1.4142	4.4721	8.0000	1.2599	2.7144	5.8480	0.5000
2.1	4.4100	1.4491	4.5826	9.2610	1.2806	2.7589	5.9439	0.4762
2.2	4.8400	1.4832	4.6904	10.6480	1.3006	2.8020	6.0368	0.4545
2.3	5.2900	1.5166	4.7958	12.1670	1.3200	2.8439	6.1269	0.4348

n	n^2	$\sqrt{n}$	$\sqrt{10n}$	n^3	$\sqrt[3]{n}$	$\sqrt[3]{10n}$	$\sqrt[3]{100n}$	$1/n$
2.4	5.7600	1.5492	4.8990	13.8240	1.3389	2.8845	6.2145	0.4167
2.5	6.2500	1.5811	5.0000	15.6250	1.3572	2.9240	6.2996	0.4000
2.6	6.7600	1.6125	5.0990	17.5760	1.3751	2.9625	6.3825	0.3846
2.7	7.2900	1.6432	5.1962	19.6830	1.3925	3.0000	6.4633	0.3704
2.8	7.8400	1.6733	5.2915	21.9520	1.4095	3.0366	6.5421	0.3571
2.9	8.4100	1.7029	5.3852	24.3890	1.4260	3.0723	6.6191	0.3448
3.0	9.0000	1.7321	5.4772	27.0000	1.4422	3.1072	6.6943	0.3333
3.1	9.6100	1.7607	5.5678	29.7910	1.4581	3.1414	6.7679	0.3226
3.2	10.2400	1.7889	5.6569	32.7680	1.4736	3.1748	6.8399	0.3125
3.3	10.8900	1.8166	5.7446	35.9370	1.4888	3.2075	6.9104	0.3030
3.4	11.5600	1.8439	5.8310	39.3040	1.5037	3.2396	6.9795	0.2941
3.5	12.2500	1.8708	5.9161	42.8750	1.5183	3.2711	7.0473	0.2857
3.6	12.9600	1.8974	6.0000	46.6560	1.5326	3.3019	7.1138	0.2778
3.7	13.6900	1.9235	6.0828	50.6530	1.5467	3.3322	7.1791	0.2703
3.8	14.4400	1.9494	6.1644	54.8720	1.5605	3.3620	7.2432	0.2632
3.9	15.2100	1.9748	6.2450	59.3190	1.5741	3.3912	7.3061	0.2564
4.0	16.0000	2.0000	6.3246	64.0000	1.5874	3.4200	7.3681	0.2500
4.1	16.8100	2.0248	6.4031	68.9210	1.6005	3.4482	7.4290	0.2439
4.2	17.6400	2.0494	6.4807	74.0880	1.6134	3.4760	7.4889	0.2381
4.3	18.4900	2.0736	6.5574	79.5070	1.6261	3.5034	7.5478	0.2326
4.4	19.3600	2.0976	6.6333	85.1840	1.6386	3.5303	7.6059	0.2273
4.5	20.2500	2.1213	6.7082	91.1250	1.6510	3.5569	7.6631	0.2222
4.6	21.1600	2.1448	6.7823	97.3360	1.6631	3.5830	7.7194	0.2174
4.7	22.0900	2.1679	6.8557	103.823	1.6751	3.6088	7.7750	0.2128
4.8	23.0400	2.1909	6.9282	110.592	1.6869	3.6342	7.8297	0.2083
4.9	24.0100	2.2136	7.0000	117.649	1.6985	3.6593	7.8837	0.2041
5.0	25.0000	2.2361	7.0711	125.000	1.7100	3.6840	7.9370	0.2000
5.1	26.0100	2.2583	7.1414	132.651	1.7213	3.7084	7.9896	0.1961
5.2	27.0400	2.2804	7.2111	140.608	1.7325	3.7325	8.0415	0.1923
5.3	28.0900	2.3022	7.2801	148.877	1.7435	3.7563	8.0927	0.1887
5.4	29.1600	2.3238	7.3485	157.464	1.7544	3.7798	8.1433	0.1852
5.5	30.2500	2.3452	7.4162	166.375	1.7652	3.8030	8.1932	0.1818
5.6	31.3600	2.3664	7.4833	175.616	1.7758	3.8259	8.2426	0.1786
5.7	32.4900	2.3875	7.5498	185.193	1.7863	3.8485	8.2913	0.1754
5.8	33.6400	2.4083	7.6158	195.112	1.7967	3.8709	8.3396	0.1724
5.9	34.8100	2.4290	7.6811	205.379	1.8070	3.8930	8.3872	0.1695
6.0	36.0000	2.4495	7.7460	216.000	1.8171	3.9149	8.4343	0.1667
6.1	37.2100	2.4698	7.8102	226.981	1.8272	3.9365	8.4809	0.1639
6.2	38.4400	2.4900	7.8740	238.328	1.8371	3.9579	8.5270	0.1613
6.3	39.6900	2.5100	7.9372	250.047	1.8469	3.9791	8.5726	0.1587
6.4	40.9600	2.5298	8.0000	262.144	1.8566	4.0000	8.6177	0.1563
6.5	42.2500	2.5495	8.0623	274.625	1.8663	4.0207	8.6624	0.1538
6.6	43.5600	2.5690	8.1240	287.496	1.8758	4.0412	8.7066	0.1515

n	n^2	$\sqrt{n}$	$\sqrt{10n}$	n^3	$\sqrt[3]{n}$	$\sqrt[3]{10n}$	$\sqrt[3]{100n}$	$1/n$
6.7	44.8900	2.5884	8.1854	300.763	1.8852	4.0615	8.7503	0.1493
6.8	46.2400	2.6077	8.2462	314.432	1.8945	4.0817	8.7937	0.1471
6.9	47.6100	2.6268	8.3066	328.509	1.9038	4.1016	8.8366	0.1449
7.0	49.0000	2.6458	8.3666	343.000	1.9129	4.1213	8.8790	0.1429
7.1	50.4100	2.6646	8.4261	357.911	1.9220	4.1408	8.9211	0.1408
7.2	51.8400	2.6833	8.4853	373.248	1.9310	4.1602	8.9628	0.1389
7.3	53.2900	2.7019	8.5440	389.017	1.9399	4.1793	9.0041	0.1370
7.4	54.7600	2.7203	8.6023	405.224	1.9487	4.1983	9.0450	0.1351
7.5	56.2500	2.7386	8.6603	421.875	1.9574	4.2172	9.0856	0.1333
7.6	57.7600	2.7568	8.7178	438.976	1.9661	4.2358	9.1258	0.1316
7.7	59.2900	2.7749	8.7750	456.533	1.9747	4.2543	9.1657	0.1299
7.8	60.8400	2.7928	8.8318	474.552	1.9832	4.2727	9.2052	0.1282
7.9	62.4100	2.8107	8.8882	493.039	1.9916	4.2908	9.2443	0.1266
8.0	64.0000	2.8284	8.9443	512.000	2.0000	4.3089	9.2832	0.1250
8.1	65.6100	2.8460	9.0000	531.441	2.0083	4.3267	9.3217	0.1235
8.2	67.2400	2.8636	9.0554	551.368	2.0165	4.3445	9.3599	0.1220
8.3	68.8900	2.8810	9.1104	571.787	2.0247	4.3621	9.3978	0.1205
8.4	70.5600	2.8983	9.1652	592.704	2.0328	4.3795	9.4354	0.1190
8.5	72.2500	2.9155	9.2195	614.125	2.0408	4.3968	9.4727	0.1176
8.6	73.9600	2.9326	9.2736	636.056	2.0488	4.4140	9.5097	0.1163
8.7	75.6900	2.9496	9.3274	658.503	2.0567	4.4310	9.5464	0.1149
8.8	77.4400	2.9665	9.3808	681.472	2.0646	4.4480	9.5828	0.1136
8.9	79.2100	2.9833	9.4340	704.969	2.0723	4.4647	9.6190	0.1124
9.0	81.000	3.0000	9.4868	729.000	2.0801	4.4814	9.6549	0.1111
9.1	82.8100	3.0166	9.5394	753.571	2.0878	4.4979	9.6905	0.1099
9.2	84.6400	3.0332	9.5917	778.688	2.0954	4.5144	9.7259	0.1087
9.3	86.4900	3.0496	9.6436	804.357	2.1029	4.5307	9.7610	0.1075
9.4	88.3600	3.0659	9.6954	830.584	2.1105	4.5468	9.7959	0.1064
9.5	90.2500	3.0822	9.7468	857.375	2.1179	4.5629	9.8305	0.1053
9.6	92.1600	3.0984	9.7980	884.736	2.1253	4.5789	9.8648	0.1042
9.7	94.0900	3.1145	9.8489	912.673	2.1327	4.5947	9.8990	0.1031
9.8	96.0400	3.1305	9.8995	941.192	2.1400	4.6104	9.9329	0.1020
9.9	98.0100	3.1464	9.9499	970.299	2.1472	4.6261	9.9666	0.1010
10.0	100.000	3.1623	10.000	1000.00	2.1544	4.6416	10.0000	0.1000

Table of e^x and e^{-x}

x	e^x	e^{-x}	x	e^x	e^{-x}
0.00	1.0000	1.0000	2.5	12.182	0.0821
0.05	1.0513	0.9512	2.6	13.464	0.0743
0.10	1.1052	0.9048	2.7	14.880	0.0672
0.15	1.1618	0.8607	2.8	16.445	0.0608
0.20	1.2214	0.8187	2.9	18.174	0.0550
0.25	1.2840	0.7788	3.0	20.086	0.0498
0.30	1.3499	0.7408	3.1	22.198	0.0450
0.35	1.4191	0.7047	3.2	24.533	0.0408
0.40	1.4918	0.6703	3.3	27.113	0.0369
0.45	1.5683	0.6376	3.4	29.964	0.0334
0.50	1.6487	0.6065	3.5	33.115	0.0302
0.55	1.7333	0.5769	3.6	36.598	0.0273
0.60	1.8221	0.5488	3.7	40.447	0.0247
0.65	1.9155	0.5220	3.8	44.701	0.0224
0.70	2.0138	0.4966	3.9	49.402	0.0202
0.75	2.1170	0.4724	4.0	54.598	0.0183

x	e^x	e^{-x}	x	e^x	e^{-x}
0.80	2.2255	0.4493	4.1	60.340	0.0166
0.85	2.3396	0.4274	4.2	66.686	0.0150
0.90	2.4596	0.4066	4.3	73.700	0.0136
0.95	2.5857	0.3867	4.4	81.451	0.0123
1.0	2.7183	0.3679	4.5	90.017	0.0111
1.1	3.0042	0.3329	4.6	99.484	0.0101
1.2	3.3201	0.3012	4.7	109.55	0.0091
1.3	3.6693	0.2725	4.8	121.51	0.0082
1.4	4.0552	0.2466	4.9	134.29	0.0074
1.5	4.4817	0.2231	5	148.41	0.0067
1.6	4.9530	0.2019	6	403.43	0.0025
1.7	5.4739	0.1827	7	1096.6	0.0009
1.8	6.0496	0.1653	8	2981.0	0.0003
1.9	6.6859	0.1496	9	8103.1	0.0001
2.0	7.3891	0.1353	10	22026	0.00005
2.1	8.1662	0.1225			
2.2	9.0250	0.1108			
2.3	9.9742	0.1003			
2.4	11.023	0.0907			

Table of Selected Integrals

Rational Forms Containing ($a + bu$)

1. $\displaystyle \int u^n \, du = \frac{u^{n+1}}{n+1} + C, \quad n \neq -1$

2. $\displaystyle \int \frac{du}{a+bu} = \frac{1}{b} \ln|a+bu| + C$

3. $\displaystyle \int \frac{u \, du}{a+bu} = \frac{u}{b} - \frac{a}{b^2} \ln|a+bu| + C$

4. $\displaystyle \int \frac{u^2 \, du}{a+bu} = \frac{u^2}{2b} - \frac{au}{b^2} + \frac{a^2}{b^3} \ln|a+bu| + C$

5. $\displaystyle \int \frac{du}{u(a+bu)} = \frac{1}{a} \ln\left|\frac{u}{a+bu}\right| + C$

6. $\displaystyle \int \frac{du}{u^2(a+bu)} = -\frac{1}{au} + \frac{b}{a^2} \ln\left|\frac{a+bu}{u}\right| + C$

7. $\displaystyle\int \frac{u\,du}{(a+bu)^2} = \frac{1}{b^2}\left(\ln|a+bu| + \frac{a}{a+bu}\right) + C$

8. $\displaystyle\int \frac{u^2\,du}{(a+bu)^2} = \frac{u}{b^2} - \frac{a^2}{b^3(a+bu)} - \frac{2a}{b^3}\ln|a+bu| + C$

9. $\displaystyle\int \frac{du}{u(a+bu)^2} = \frac{1}{a(a+bu)} + \frac{1}{a^2}\ln\left|\frac{u}{a+bu}\right| + C$

10. $\displaystyle\int \frac{du}{u^2(a+bu)^2} = -\frac{a+2bu}{a^2u(a+bu)} + \frac{2b}{a^3}\ln\left|\frac{a+bu}{u}\right| + C$

11. $\displaystyle\int \frac{du}{(a+bu)(c+eu)} = \frac{1}{bc-ae}\ln\left|\frac{a+bu}{c+eu}\right| + C$

12. $\displaystyle\int \frac{u\,du}{(a+bu)(c+eu)} = \frac{1}{bc-ae}\left[\frac{c}{e}\ln|c+eu| - \frac{a}{b}\ln|a+bu|\right] + C$

Forms Containing $\sqrt{a+bu}$

13. $\displaystyle\int u\sqrt{a+bu}\,du = \frac{2(3bu-2a)(a+bu)^{3/2}}{15b^2} + C$

14. $\displaystyle\int u^2\sqrt{a+bu}\,du = \frac{2(8a^2-12abu+15b^2u^2)(a+bu)^{3/2}}{105b^3} + C$

15. $\displaystyle\int \frac{u\,du}{\sqrt{a+bu}} = \frac{2(bu-2a)\sqrt{a+bu}}{3b^2} + C$

16. $\displaystyle\int \frac{u^2\,du}{\sqrt{a+bu}} = \frac{2(3b^2u^2-4abu+8a^2)\sqrt{a+bu}}{15b^3} + C$

17. $\displaystyle\int \frac{du}{u\sqrt{a+bu}} = \frac{1}{\sqrt{a}}\ln\left|\frac{\sqrt{a+bu}-\sqrt{a}}{\sqrt{a+bu}+\sqrt{a}}\right| + C, \quad a>0$

18. $\displaystyle\int \frac{\sqrt{a+bu}\,du}{u} = 2\sqrt{a+bu} + a\int \frac{du}{u\sqrt{a+bu}}$

Forms Containing $\sqrt{a^2-u^2}$

19. $\displaystyle\int \frac{du}{(a^2-u^2)^{3/2}} = \frac{u}{a^2\sqrt{a^2-u^2}} + C$

20. $\displaystyle\int \frac{du}{u\sqrt{a^2-u^2}} = -\frac{1}{a}\ln\left|\frac{a+\sqrt{a^2-u^2}}{u}\right| + C$

21. $\displaystyle\int \frac{du}{u^2\sqrt{a^2-u^2}} = -\frac{\sqrt{a^2-u^2}}{a^2u} + C$

22. $\displaystyle\int \frac{\sqrt{a^2-u^2}\,du}{u} = \sqrt{a^2-u^2} - a\ln\left|\frac{a+\sqrt{a^2-u^2}}{u}\right| + C, \quad a>0$

Forms Containing $\sqrt{u^2 \pm a^2}$

23. $\displaystyle \int \sqrt{u^2 \pm a^2}\, du = \frac{1}{2}\left(u\sqrt{u^2 \pm a^2} \pm a^2 \ln |u + \sqrt{u^2 \pm a^2}| \right) + C$

24. $\displaystyle \int u^2 \sqrt{u^2 \pm a^2}\, du = \frac{u}{8}(2u^2 \pm a^2)\sqrt{u^2 \pm a^2} - \frac{a^4}{8}\ln |u + \sqrt{u^2 \pm a^2}| + C$

25. $\displaystyle \int \frac{\sqrt{u^2 + a^2}\, du}{u} = \sqrt{u^2 + a^2} - a \ln \left| \frac{a + \sqrt{u^2 + a^2}}{u} \right| + C$

26. $\displaystyle \int \frac{\sqrt{u^2 \pm a^2}\, du}{u^2} = -\frac{\sqrt{u^2 \pm a^2}}{u} + \ln |u + \sqrt{u^2 \pm a^2}| + C$

27. $\displaystyle \int \frac{du}{\sqrt{u^2 \pm a^2}} = \ln |u + \sqrt{u^2 \pm a^2}| + C$

28. $\displaystyle \int \frac{du}{u\sqrt{u^2 + a^2}} = \frac{1}{a}\ln \left| \frac{\sqrt{u^2 + a^2} - a}{u} \right| + C$

29. $\displaystyle \int \frac{u^2\, du}{\sqrt{u^2 \pm a^2}} = \frac{1}{2}\left(u\sqrt{u^2 \pm a^2} \mp a^2 \ln | u + \sqrt{u^2 \pm a^2}| \right) + C$

30. $\displaystyle \int \frac{du}{u^2\sqrt{u^2 \pm a^2}} = -\frac{\pm\sqrt{u^2 \pm a^2}}{a^2 u} + C$

31. $\displaystyle \int (u^2 \pm a^2)^{3/2}\, du = \frac{u}{8}(2u^2 \pm 5a^2)\sqrt{u^2 \pm a^2} + \frac{3a^4}{8}\ln | u + \sqrt{u^2 \pm a^2}| + C$

32. $\displaystyle \int \frac{du}{(u^2 \pm a^2)^{3/2}} = \frac{\pm u}{a^2\sqrt{u^2 \pm a^2}} + C$

33. $\displaystyle \int \frac{u^2\, du}{(u^2 \pm a^2)^{3/2}} = \frac{-u}{\sqrt{u^2 \pm a^2}} + \ln |u + \sqrt{u^2 \pm a^2}| + C$

Rational Forms Containing $a^2 - u^2$ and $u^2 - a^2$

34. $\displaystyle \int \frac{du}{a^2 - u^2} = \frac{1}{2a}\ln \left| \frac{a + u}{a - u} \right| + C$

35. $\displaystyle \int \frac{du}{u^2 - a^2} = \frac{1}{2a}\ln \left| \frac{u - a}{u + a} \right| + C$

Exponential and Logarithmic Forms

36. $\displaystyle \int e^u\, du = e^u + C$

37. $\displaystyle \int a^u\, du = \frac{a^u}{\ln a} + C, \quad a > 0, a \neq 1$

38. $\displaystyle\int ue^{au}\,du = \frac{e^{au}}{a^2}(au-1)+C$

39. $\displaystyle\int u^n e^{au}\,du = \frac{u^n e^{au}}{a} - \frac{n}{a}\int u^{n-1}e^{au}\,du$

40. $\displaystyle\int \frac{e^{au}\,du}{u^n} = -\frac{e^{au}}{(n-1)u^{n-1}} + \frac{a}{n-1}\int \frac{e^{au}\,du}{u^{n-1}}$

41. $\displaystyle\int \ln u\,du = u\ln u - u + C$

42. $\displaystyle\int u^n \ln u\,du = \frac{u^{n+1}\ln u}{n+1} - \frac{u^{n+1}}{(n+1)^2} + C, \quad n \neq -1$

43. $\displaystyle\int u^n \ln^m u\,du = \frac{u^{n+1}}{n+1}\ln^m u - \frac{m}{n+1}\int u^n \ln^{m-1} u\,du, \quad m, n \neq -1$

44. $\displaystyle\int \frac{du}{u\ln u} = \ln|\ln u| + C$

45. $\displaystyle\int \frac{du}{a+be^{cu}} = \frac{1}{ac}(cu - \ln|a+be^{cu}|) + C$

Miscellaneous Forms

46. $\displaystyle\int \sqrt{\frac{a+u}{b+u}}\,du = \sqrt{(a+u)(b+u)} + (a-b)\ln\left(\sqrt{a+u} + \sqrt{b+u}\right) + C$

47. $\displaystyle\int \frac{du}{\sqrt{(a+u)(b+u)}} = \ln\left|\frac{a+b}{2} + u + \sqrt{(a+u)(b+u)}\right| + C$

48. $\displaystyle\int \sqrt{a+bu+cu^2}\,du = \frac{2cu+b}{4c}\sqrt{a+bu+cu^2} -$

$$\frac{b^2-4ac}{8c^{3/2}}\ln|2cu+b+2\sqrt{c}\sqrt{a+bu+cu^2}| + C, \quad c > 0$$

Answers to Odd-Numbered Problems

EXERCISE 0-2

1. true   **3.** false   **5.** true
7. false   **9.** true   **11.** true

EXERCISE 0-3

1. false   **3.** false   **5.** true
7. true   **9.** false   **11.** distributive
13. associative   **15.** commutative
17. definition of subtraction   **19.** distributive   **21.** $5ax + 15a$
23. $2x - 2y$ **25.** $2xy + 4x$ **27.** $ab + ac + ad$

EXERCISE 0-4

1. -6 **3.** 2 **5.** 11 **7.** -2 **9.** -63

11. -6 **13.** $6 - x$ **15.** $-12x + 12y$ (or $12y - 12x$)

17. $-\dfrac{1}{3}$ **19.** -2 **21.** 18 **23.** 25 **25.** $3x - 12$

27. $-x + 2$ **29.** $\dfrac{8}{11}$ **31.** $-\dfrac{5x}{7y}$ **33.** $\dfrac{2}{3x}$ **35.** 3

37. $\dfrac{7}{xy}$ **39.** $\dfrac{5}{6}$ **41.** $-\dfrac{1}{6}$ **43.** $\dfrac{x - y}{9}$ **45.** $\dfrac{1}{24}$

47. $\dfrac{x}{6y}$ **49.** not defined   **51.** not defined

EXERCISE 0-5

1. 5 **3.** -2 **5.** $\dfrac{1}{2}$ **7.** 10 **9.** 8

11. $\dfrac{1}{4}$ **13.** $\dfrac{1}{32}$ **15.** $4\sqrt{2}$ **17.** $x\sqrt[3]{2}$ **19.** $4x^2$

21. $3z^2$ **23.** $\dfrac{9t^2}{4}$

25. $\dfrac{x^3}{y^2 z^2}$ **27.** $\dfrac{2}{x^4}$ **29.** $\dfrac{1}{9t^2}$

31. $7^{1/3} s^{2/3}$ **33.** $x^{1/2} - y^{1/2}$ **35.** $\dfrac{x^{9/4} z^{3/4}}{y^{1/2}}$

37. $\sqrt[5]{(8x - y)^4}$ **39.** $\dfrac{1}{\sqrt[5]{x^4}}$

41. $\dfrac{2}{\sqrt[5]{x^2}} - \dfrac{1}{\sqrt[5]{4x^2}}$ **43.** $\dfrac{2x^6}{y^3}$ **45.** $t^{2/3}$

47. $\dfrac{64y^6 x^{1/2}}{x^2}$ **49.** xyz **51.** $\dfrac{1}{9}$

53. $\dfrac{4y^4}{x^2}$ **55.** $x^2 y^{5/2}$ **57.** $\dfrac{y^{10}}{z^2}$

59. $\dfrac{1}{x^4}$ **61.** $-\dfrac{4}{s^5}$ **63.** $\dfrac{4x^4 z^4}{9y^4}$

65. Rationalization can simplify the approximation of certain irrational numbers.

EXERCISE 0-6

1. $11x - 2y - 3$ **3.** $6t^2 - 2s^2 + 6$ **5.** $2\sqrt{x} + \sqrt{2y} + \sqrt{3z}$

7. $6x^2 - 9xy - 2z + \sqrt{2} - 4$ **9.** $\sqrt{2y} - \sqrt{3z}$

11. $-7x + 14y - 19$ **13.** $x^2 + 9y^2 + xy$ **15.** $6x^2 + 96$

17. $-6x^2 - 18x - 18$ **19.** $x^2 + x - 6$ **21.** $10x^2 + 19x + 6$

23. $x^2 - 10x + 25$ **25.** $2y + 6\sqrt{2y} + 9$ **27.** $4s^2 - 1$

29. $x^3 + 4x^2 - 3x - 12$ **31.** $2x^4 + 2x^3 - 5x^2 - 2x + 3$

33. $5x^3 + 5x^2 + 6x$ **35.** $3x^2 + 2y^2 + 5xy + 2x - 8$

37. $z - 4$ **39.** $3x^3 + 2x - \dfrac{1}{2x^2}$ **41.** $x + \dfrac{-1}{x + 3}$

43. $3x^2 - 8x + 17 + \dfrac{-37}{x + 2}$ **45.** $t + 8 + \dfrac{64}{t - 8}$

47. $x - 2 + \dfrac{7}{3x + 2}$

EXERCISE 0-7

1. $2(3x + 2)$ **3.** $5x(2y + z)$

5. $4bc(2a^3 - 3ab^2 d + b^3 cd^2)$ **7.** $(x - 5)(x + 5)$

9. $(p + 3)(p + 1)$ **11.** $(4x - 3)(4x + 3)$

13. $(z + 4)(z + 2)$ **15.** $(x + 3)^2$

17. $2(x + 4)(x + 2)$ **19.** $3(x - 1)(x + 1)$

21. $(6y + 1)(y + 2)$ **23.** $2s(3s + 4)(2s - 1)$

25. $x^{2/3} y(1 - 2xy)(1 + 2xy)$ **27.** $2x(x + 3)(x - 2)$

29. $4(2x + 1)^2$ **31.** $x(xy - 5)^2$

33. $(x - 2)^2 (x + 2)$ **35.** $(y - 1)(y + 1)(y^4 + 4)^2$

EXERCISE 0-8

1. $x + 2$ **3.** $\dfrac{5}{3t}$ **5.** $-\dfrac{1}{p^2 - 1}$

7. $\dfrac{2x^2 + 3x + 12}{(2x - 1)(x + 3)}$ **9.** $\dfrac{2x - 3}{(x - 2)(x + 1)(x - 1)}$

11. $\dfrac{35 - 8x}{(x - 1)(x + 5)}$ **13.** $-\dfrac{y^2}{(y - 3)(y + 2)}$

15. $\dfrac{3 - 2x}{3 + 2x}$

17. $\dfrac{2(x + 4)}{(x - 4)(x + 2)}$

19. $-\dfrac{(2x + 3)(1 + x)}{x + 4}$

21. $\dfrac{x + 1}{3x}$

23. $\dfrac{(x + 2)(6x - 1)}{2x^2(x + 3)}$

25. $\dfrac{x - \sqrt{5}}{x^2 - 5}$

27. $\dfrac{5\sqrt{3} - 4\sqrt{2} - 13}{2}$

EXERCISE 1-1

1. 0, 2

3. $\dfrac{10}{3}$

5. does not satisfy equation

7. adding 5 to both sides; equivalence guaranteed

9. squaring both sides; equivalence *not* guaranteed

11. dividing both sides by x; equivalence *not* guaranteed

13. multiplying both sides by $x - 1$; equivalence *not* guaranteed

15. multiplying both sides by $(x - 5)/x$; equivalence *not* guaranteed

17. $\dfrac{15}{2}$

19. 0

21. $\dfrac{12}{5}$

23. -1

25. 2

27. $\dfrac{10}{3}$

29. 90

31. 8

33. $-\dfrac{26}{9}$

35. $\dfrac{60}{17}$

37. $-\dfrac{37}{18}$

39. $\dfrac{14}{3}$

41. 3

43. $\dfrac{7}{8}$

45. $P = \dfrac{I}{rt}$

47. $x = \dfrac{p + 1}{6}$

49. $r = \dfrac{S - P}{Pt}$

51. $a_1 = \dfrac{2S - na_n}{n}$

EXERCISE 1-2

1. $\dfrac{1}{4}$

3. $\dfrac{8}{3}$

5. $\dfrac{3}{2}$

7. 0

9. $\dfrac{5}{3}$

11. $\dfrac{1}{8}$

13. 3

15. $\dfrac{5}{13}$

17. $\emptyset$

19. 9

21. $\dfrac{262}{5}$ **23.** $\dfrac{10}{9}$ **25.** 2   **27.** 7   **29.** $\dfrac{49}{36}$

31. $-\dfrac{9}{4}$ **33.** $d = \dfrac{r}{1 + rt}$ **35.** $n = \dfrac{2mI}{rB} - 1$

EXERCISE 1-3

1. $-2, -1$ **3.** 4, 3   **5.** 3, -1

7. 6   **9.** ± 2 **11.** 0, 8

13. $\dfrac{1}{2}$ **15.** 1, $-\dfrac{5}{2}$ **17.** 5, -2

19. 0, $\dfrac{3}{2}$ **21.** 0, $\dfrac{1}{2}$, $-\dfrac{4}{3}$ **23.** 0, ± 8

25. $-3, -1, 2$ **27.** $-5, 3$ **29.** $\dfrac{3}{2}$

31. $\dfrac{5 \pm \sqrt{13}}{2}$ **33.** no real roots   **35.** $\dfrac{1}{2}, -\dfrac{5}{3}$

37. 4, $-\dfrac{5}{2}$ **39.** $\dfrac{-2 \pm \sqrt{14}}{2}$ **41.** 1, $-\dfrac{5}{6}$

43. 6, -2 **45.** $\dfrac{1}{2}$ **47.** 5, -2

49. $\dfrac{3}{2}$ **51.** -2 **53.** 7

55. 4, 8   **57.** 2   **59.** 0, 4

61. 4

REVIEW PROBLEMS—CHAPTER 1

1. $\dfrac{1}{4}$ **3.** $-\dfrac{2}{15}$ **5.** $-\dfrac{1}{2}$

7. $\emptyset$ **9.** $\dfrac{5}{2}$ **11.** $-\dfrac{9}{7}$

13. $-\dfrac{5}{3}, 1$ **15.** 0, $\dfrac{7}{5}$ **17.** 5

19. $\pm\dfrac{\sqrt{15}}{3}$ **21.** $\dfrac{5}{8}, -3$ **23.** $\dfrac{5 \pm \sqrt{13}}{6}$

25. $\dfrac{1}{2}$

27. $\dfrac{4 \pm \sqrt{13}}{3}$

29. 4, 8

EXERCISE 2-1

1. 170,000

3. \$5000 at $5\frac{1}{2}$ percent, \$3000 at 5 percent

5. \$4.25

7. 4 percent

9. 40

11. 46,000 units

13. either \$440 or \$460

15. \$100

17. 77

19. \$112,000

21. 60

23. either 100 winkys and 125 dinkys, or 125 winkys and 150 dinkys.

EXERCISE 2-2

1. $x > 2$

2

3. $x \le 2$

2

5. $y > 0$

0

7. $x \le -\dfrac{1}{2}$

$-\frac{1}{2}$

9. $s < -\dfrac{2}{5}$

$-\frac{2}{5}$

11. $x \ge -\dfrac{7}{5}$

$-\frac{7}{5}$

13. $x > -\dfrac{2}{7}$

$-\frac{2}{7}$

15. $\emptyset$

17. $x < \dfrac{\sqrt{3} - 2}{2}$

$\frac{\sqrt{3} - 2}{2}$

19. $y \le -5$

-5

21. $-\infty < x < \infty$

23. $t > \dfrac{17}{9}$

$\frac{17}{9}$

25. $x \ge -\dfrac{14}{3}$

$-\frac{14}{3}$

27. $r > 0$

0

29. $x \le -2$

-2

31. $y < 0$

0

33. $444{,}000 < S < 636{,}000$

EXERCISE 2-3

1. $-3 < x < 3$

3. $x < -\sqrt{3}, x > \sqrt{3}$

5. $x < -7, x > 1$

7. $-2 < x < 3$

9. $x < -5, x > 4$

11. $0 < s < 5$

13. $-3 \le x \le -2$

15. $-\dfrac{3}{2} < t < \dfrac{1}{2}$

17. $-\infty < x < \infty$

19. $\dfrac{-3 - \sqrt{5}}{2} \le x \le \dfrac{-3 + \sqrt{5}}{2}$

21. $\emptyset$

23. $x > 3$

25. $0 \le x < 4$

27. $t < -3, t > -1$

29. $x < -3, x > \dfrac{1}{2}$

31. $x < -4, 0 < x < 1$

EXERCISE 2-4

1. at least 120,001

3. 11,067

5. $50 \le$ size of group ≤ 100

7. 8000

9. \$150,000; \$112,500

11. 17 in. by 17 in.

13. 1000

15. between 51 and 149

EXERCISE 2-5

1. 13

3. 6

5. 5

7. $-3 < x < 3$

9. $\sqrt{5} - 2$

11. (a) $|x - 7| < 3$

  (b) $|x - 2| < 3$

  (c) $|x - 7| \le 5$

  (d) $|x - 7| = 4$

  (e) $|x + 4| < 2$

  (f) $|x| < 3$

  (g) $|x| > 6$

  (h) $|x - 6| > 4$

  (i) $|x - 105| < 3$

  (j) $|x - 600| < 100$

13. $|p - q| \le 2$

15. ± 7

17. ± 6

19. $-3, 13$

21. $\dfrac{2}{5}$

23. $\dfrac{1}{2}, 3$

25. $-4 < x < 4$

27. $x < -8, x > 8$

29. $-9 < x < -5$

31. $x < 0, x > 1$

33. $2 \le x \le 3$

35. $x \le 0, x \ge \dfrac{16}{3}$

37. $x < \mu - h\sigma, x > \mu + h\sigma.$

REVIEW PROBLEMS—CHAPTER 2

1. $x \leq 0$

3. $\emptyset$

5. $x \leq \dfrac{13}{2}$

7. $-\infty < x < \infty$

9. $-\dfrac{2}{3} \leq x \leq \dfrac{1}{2}$

11. $-2 \leq x < 1$

13. $-2, 5$

15. $0 < t < \dfrac{1}{2}$

17. $x \leq -\dfrac{1}{2}, x \geq \dfrac{7}{2}$

19. 542

21. 6000

EXERCISE 3-1

1. x; all real numbers; $0, 12, -1, 4t$

3. x; all real numbers; $1, 1 + 2u, -13, 1 + 4x, 1 - 2(x + h)$

5. t; all real numbers; $1.02, 1.02, 1.02, 1.02$

7. p; all real numbers; $\dfrac{15}{2}, \dfrac{3(2p + 1)}{2}, \dfrac{3(4 + p)}{2p}$

9. p; all real numbers; $1, 9, x_1^2 + 2x_1 + 1, w^2 + 2w + 1, p^2 + 2ph + h^2 + 2p + 2h + 1$

11. t; all real numbers; $16, 36, h^2 + 12h + 36, h + 12$

13. q; all real numbers; $5, 3, 0, |2x^2 + 3| = 2x^2 + 3$

15. x; all $x \geq -4; 2, 0, 1, \sqrt{5 + x} - \sqrt{4 + x}$

17. s; all $s \neq \pm 3; -\dfrac{1}{2}, -\dfrac{1}{2}, \dfrac{4}{4w^2 - 9}, \dfrac{4}{s^2 - 2s - 8}, \dfrac{13 - s^2}{s^2 - 9}$

19. x; all real numbers; $4, 3, 4, 3$

21. r; all r such that $r < -2$ or $r > 2; 8, 28, 14, 52$

23. z; all $z \neq 3, 4; \dfrac{1}{6}, 1, -\dfrac{1}{15}, \dfrac{z + h}{z^2 + 2zh + h^2 - 7z - 7h + 12}$

25. x; all $x > 0; 1, \dfrac{1}{2}$

27. yes; no, since if $z = 4$, then $x = \pm 1$

29. 3

31. $2x + h + 2$

33. $V = f(t) = 30,000(1 - .02t)$

35. yes; P; x; all integers x such that $0 \leq x \leq 7000$

37. $C = 850 + 3x$

39. (a) $3000, 2900, 2300, 2000; 12, 10;$
(b) $10, 12, 17, 20; 3000, 2300$

EXERCISE 3-2

1. (a) $2x + 9$ (b) 1 (c) $x^2 + 9x + 20$

(d) $\dfrac{x + 5}{x + 4}$ (e) $x + 9$ (f) $x + 9$

3. (a) $x^2 + 3x + 3$ (b) $3x + 5 - x^2$ (c) $3x^3 + 4x^2 - 3x - 4$

(d) $\dfrac{3x + 4}{x^2 - 1}$ (e) $3x^2 + 1$ (f) $9x^2 + 24x + 15$

5. (a) $3x^2 + 3x - 11$ (b) $-x^2 + 3x + 3$ (c) $2x^4 + 6x^3 - 15x^2 - 21x + 28$

(d) $\dfrac{x^2 + 3x - 4}{2x^2 - 7}$ (e) $4x^4 - 22x^2 + 24$ (f) $2x^4 + 12x^3 + 2x^2 - 48x + 25$

7. (a) 26 (b) $20x - 4$ (c) -8 (d) $-2w - 6$ (e) -6

(f) $24x^2 + 34x + 5$ (g) -5 (h) $\dfrac{6t^2 - 5}{4t^2 + 1}$

9. (a) 18 (b) $2x^2 + 4xh + 2h^2 - 3x - 3h + 4$

(c) 4 (d) $2x^2 + 4xh + 2h^2 + 3x + 3h + 2$

(e) 3 (f) $-6x^{3/2} + 2x - 9x^{1/2} + 3$

(g) $-5/2$ (h) $\dfrac{8p^2 + 27}{9(1 - 2p)}$

11. $53;\quad -32$

13. $\dfrac{4}{(t - 1)^2} + \dfrac{6}{t - 1} + 1;\quad \dfrac{2}{t^2 + 3t}$

15. $\dfrac{1}{v + 3};\ \sqrt{\dfrac{2w^2 + 3}{w^2 + 1}}$

17. (a) 14; all real numbers; 14
(b) 2; all real numbers; 2

19. $f(x) = \sqrt{x},\ g(x) = x - 2$

21. $f(x) = x^{2/3},\ g(x) = \dfrac{4x - 5}{x^2 + 1}$

23. $f(x) = x^3 - x^2 + 7,\ g(x) = 3x^3 - 2x$

EXERCISE 3-3

1.

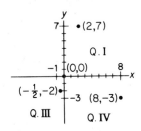

3. Function; all real numbers;
all real numbers

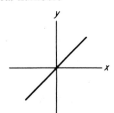

5. Function; all real numbers;
all real numbers

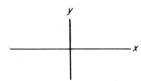

7. Function; all real numbers;
all nonnegative real numbers

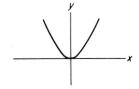

9. Not a function of x

11. Function; all real numbers;
all real numbers

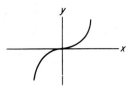

13. Not a function of x

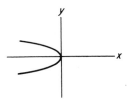

15. Function; all real numbers;
all real numbers

17. All real numbers; 2

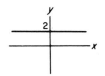

19. All real numbers;
all real numbers

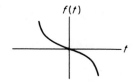

21. All real numbers ≥ 5;
all nonnegative reals

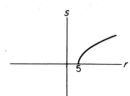

23. All real numbers; all
nonnegative reals

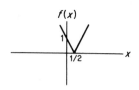

25. All real numbers;
all reals ≥ -3

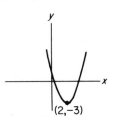

27. All non-zero real numbers;
all positive real numbers

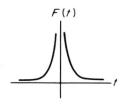

29.

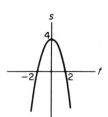

31.

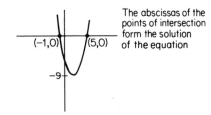

The abscissas of the points of intersection form the solution of the equation

33.

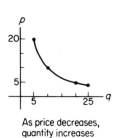

As price decreases, quantity increases

REVIEW PROBLEMS—CHAPTER 3

1. $7, 46, 62, 3x^4 - 4x^2 + 7$; all real numbers

3. $\dfrac{3}{2}, 18, 6\sqrt{u}, 12uh + 6h^2$; all real numbers

5. (a) $-x - 4$ (b) $12 - 5x$ (c) $-6x^2 + 32x - 32$

(d) $\dfrac{4 - 3x}{2x - 8}$ (e) $28 - 6x$ (f) $-6x$

7. $20 + 5\sqrt{23}$; 2

9. All real numbers; all reals ≤ 9

11. All real numbers; all reals ≥ 1

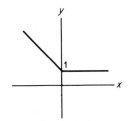

13. All $t \ne 4$; all nonzero real numbers

15. $165,000; yes

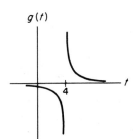

EXERCISE 4-1

1. $\dfrac{3}{2}$ **3.** $-\dfrac{4}{5}$ **5.** not defined

7. 0 **9.** $6x - y - 4 = 0$ **11.** $x + 4y - 18 = 0$

13. $3x - 7y + 25 = 0$ **15.** $8x - 5y - 29 = 0$

17. $y - 5 = 0$ **19.** $x - 2 = 0$ **21.** $4x - y + 7 = 0$

23. 2; $(0, -1)$ **25.** $\dfrac{3}{8}$; $(0, -1)$ **27.** $-\dfrac{1}{2}$; $\left(0, \dfrac{3}{2}\right)$

29. no slope; no y-intercept **31.** 3; $(0, 0)$

33. 0; $(0, 1)$ **35.** $\dfrac{1}{40}$; $\left(0, -\dfrac{1}{2}\right)$

37. $x + 2y - 4 = 0$; $y = -\dfrac{1}{2}x + 2$

39. $4x + 9y - 5 = 0;\ y = -\dfrac{4}{9}x + \dfrac{5}{9}$

41. $9x - 28y - 3 = 0;\ y = \dfrac{9}{28}x - \dfrac{3}{28}$

43. $3x - 2y + 24 = 0;\ y = \dfrac{3}{2}x + 12$

45. $x + y - 1 = 0;\ y = -x + 1$

47. $1;\ (0, 1)$ **49.** $-3;\ (0, 5)$

51. $p = -\dfrac{2}{5}x + 28;\ 16$ **53.** $x + 10y = 100$

EXERCISE 4-2

1. $x = 4,\ y = -5$ **3.** $x = 3,\ y = -1$ **5.** $v = 0,\ w = 18$

7. no solution   **9.** $x = 12,\ y = -12$

11. the coordinates of any point on the line $q = -\dfrac{1}{3}p + \dfrac{1}{2}$

13. $x = \dfrac{1}{2},\ y = \dfrac{1}{2},\ z = \dfrac{1}{4}$ **15.** $x = 1,\ y = 1,\ z = 1$

17. 420 gal of 20 percent solution, 280 gal of 30 percent solution.

19. 240 units (Early American), 200 units (Little Big Horn).

21. 800 forks from Exton plant, 700 from Whyton plant.

23. 4 percent on first \$100,000, 6 percent on remainder.

25. \$10,000 at 4 percent, \$12,000 at 5 percent,

       \$13,000 at 6 percent (later 7 percent).

EXERCISE 4-3

1. $p = \dfrac{1}{3}x + \dfrac{55}{3}$ **3.**

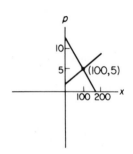

5. (5, 212.50)

7.

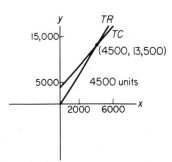

9. Cannot break even at any level of production.

11. (a) $12 (b) $12.18

13. 5840 units; 840 units; 1840 units

15. $4

17. Total cost always exceeds total revenue—no break even point.

19. decreases by $0.70

21. $p_A = 5$, $p_B = 10$

REVIEW PROBLEMS—CHAPTER 4

1. 9

3. $y = -x + 1; x + y - 1 = 0$

5. $y = \dfrac{1}{2}x - 1; x - 2y - 2 = 0$

7. $y = 4; y - 4 = 0$

9. $y = \dfrac{3}{2}x - 2; \dfrac{3}{2}$

11. $y = \dfrac{4}{3}; 0$

13. $x = \dfrac{17}{7}, y = -\dfrac{8}{7}$

15. $x = 2, y = -1$

17. $x = 8, y = 4$

19. $x = 0, y = 1, z = 0$

21. 6

23. (1250, 20,000)

EXERCISE 5-1

1.

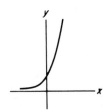

3.

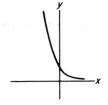

5.

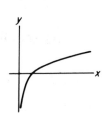

7. $\log_{16} 4 = \dfrac{1}{2}$ **9.** $\log 10{,}000 = 4$ **11.** $2^6 = 64$

13. $2^{14} = x$ **15.** $\ln 1.4 = .33647$ **17.** $e^{1.0986} = 3$

19. 16 **21.** 125 **23.** $\dfrac{1}{10}$ **25.** e^2

27. 2 **29.** 6 **31.** 2 **33.** 4

35. $\dfrac{1}{2}$ **37.** $\dfrac{1}{81}$ **39.** 2 **41.** $\dfrac{5}{3}$

43. $.2241$ **45.** $\$1491.80$ **47.** $\$22{,}465$ **49.** 8 **51.** 6065

EXERCISE 5-2

1. 1.5441 **3.** $.3521$ **5.** 1.3980 **7.** 3.3010

9. $\dfrac{1}{3}$ **11.** 1.9459 **13.** 1.5850 **15.** 48

17. 4 **19.** $\log_2 \dfrac{2x}{x+1}$ **21.** $\log [7^9 (23)^5]$

23. $\log [100(1.05)^{10}]$ **25.** 2 **27.** $\dfrac{1}{12}$ **29.** $\dfrac{5}{2}$

31. ± 2 **33.** 5 **35.** 8

37. $\log x + \log (x + 2) + \log (x - 3)$

39. $\dfrac{3}{2} \log x - \log (x + 2) - 2 \log (x - 3)$

41. $\dfrac{1}{2} [2 \log x + 3 \log (x - 3) - \log (x + 2)]$

43. $p = \dfrac{\log (80 - x)}{\log 2}; \ 4.32$

45. $\dfrac{\log \dfrac{3 - \log x}{\log 2}}{(3 \log 2) - 1}$ **47.** 41.50

REVIEW PROBLEMS—CHAPTER 5

1. $\log_3 81 = 4$ **3.** 3 **5.** $\dfrac{1}{100}$

7. 3 **9.** 3 **11.** 1.2620

13. $2y + \dfrac{1}{2}x$

15. $2x$

17. $y = e^{x^2+2}$

19. 134,060; 109,760

EXERCISE 6-1

1. 14

3. -11

5. 5

7. 2.82

9. 0

11. -1

13. $-\dfrac{5}{2}$

15. 0

17. 5

19. 3

21. $-\dfrac{5\sqrt{3}}{6}$

23. 1

25. 0

27. 4

29. $2e$

31. 4

33. $\dfrac{11}{9}$

35. 0

37. $2x$

EXERCISE 6-2

1. 3

3. 1

5. $-\infty$

7. ∞

9. 0

11. does not exist

13. 0

15. 1

17. 0

19. ∞

21. $-\dfrac{2}{5}$

23. $-\infty$

25. $\dfrac{2}{5}$

27. $\dfrac{11}{5}$

29. $-\dfrac{1}{2}$

31. ∞

33. ∞

35. 0

37. does not exist

39. $-\infty$

41. 0

43. 1

45.

47. 2

49. $2x + 1$

EXERCISE 6-3

11. continuous at -2 and 0

13. discontinuous at ± 3

15. continuous at 2 and 0

21. none

23. $x = 4$

25. none

27. $x = -5, 3$

29. $x = 0, \pm 1$

31. none

33. $x = 2$

35. $x = 4$

37. $x = 0, 2$

39.

41.

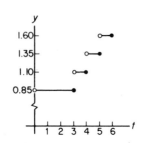

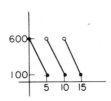

EXERCISE 6-4

1. $x < -1, x > 4$

3. $2 \le x \le 3$

5. $-\dfrac{7}{2} < x < -2$

7. $-1 < x < 0, \quad 0 < x < 1$

9. $x \le -6, -2 \le x \le 3$

11. $x < -4, 0 < x < 5$

13. $x \le -1 - \sqrt{3}, x \ge -1 + \sqrt{3}$

15. $x < -1, 0 < x < 1$

17. $x < -5, -2 \le x < 1, x \ge 3$

19. $-4 < x < -2$

REVIEW PROBLEMS—CHAPTER 6

1. -5

3. 2

5. x

7. 0

9. $\dfrac{3}{5}$

11. does not exist

13. -1

15. 0

17. $\dfrac{1}{9}$

19. 0

23. continuous everywhere

25. $x = -3$

27. $x = -2$

29. $x < -6, x > 2$

31. $x < -4, -3 \le x \le 0, x > 2$

EXERCISE 7-1

1. 0

3. 1

5. 2

7. -2

9. $-\dfrac{1}{x^2}$

11. $2x + 4$

13. $4p + 5$

15. $\dfrac{1}{2\sqrt{x+2}}$

17. -4

19. 0

21. $y = -4x + 2$

23. $x + 3y - 6 = 0$

25. $3x + y + 7 = 0$

EXERCISE 7-2

1. 0

3. 1

5. $2.0721x^{5.907}$

7. $-\dfrac{56}{5}x^{-19/5}$

9. 3

11. $\dfrac{13}{5}$

13. $6x - 5$

15. $-26t + 14 = 2(7 - 13t)$

17. $42x^2 - 12x + 7$

19. $-9q^2 + 9q + 9 = 9(1 + q - q^2)$

21. $8x^7 - 42x^5 + 6x = 2x(4x^6 - 21x^4 + 3)$

23. $1002x^{500} - 12{,}500x^{99} + 108x^{26} + \dfrac{3}{5}x^{-4/5}$

25. $-8x^3$

27. $-\dfrac{4}{3}x^3$

29. $-4x^{-5} - 3x^{-2/3} - 2x^{-7/5}$

31. $-2(27 - 70x^4) = 2(70x^4 - 27)$

33. $-4x + \dfrac{3}{2} + x^3$

35. $-x^{-2}$

37. $-\dfrac{5}{4}s^{-6}$

39. $2u^{-1/2}$

41. $-\dfrac{1}{5}x^{-6/5}$

43. $9x^2 - 14x + 7$

45. $t + 4t^{-3}$

47. $8x - \dfrac{3}{2}\sqrt{x}$

49. $\dfrac{1}{3}x^{-2/3} - \dfrac{10}{3}x^{-5/3} = \dfrac{1}{3}x^{-5/3}(x - 10)$

51. $8q + \dfrac{4}{q^2}$

53. $2(x + 2)$

55. 1

57. $4, 16, -14$

59. $0, 0, 0$

61. $y = 13x - 2$

63. $y = x + 3$

EXERCISE 7-3

1. 1

3. 3

5. $2x$

7. $\dfrac{dc}{dx} = 10; \quad 10$

9. $\dfrac{dc}{dx} = .6x + 2; \quad 3.8$

11. 3.2

13. $\dfrac{dc}{dx} = 2x + 50; \quad 80, \quad 82, \quad 84$

15. $\dfrac{dc}{dx} = .000102x^2 - .034x + 5; \quad 4.6702, \quad 3.555, \quad 2.62$

17. $\dfrac{dc}{dx} = .02x + 5; \quad 6, \quad 7$

19. $\dfrac{dc}{dx} = .00006x^2 - .02x + 6; \quad 4.6, \quad 11$

21. $\dfrac{dr}{dx} = .7; \quad .7, \quad .7, \quad .7$

23. $\dfrac{dr}{dx} = 250 + 90x - 3x^2; \quad 625, \quad 850, \quad 625$

25. $\dfrac{dr}{dx} = 30 - .4x$

27. $-5000; \quad -5000; \quad -5000$

EXERCISE 7-5

1. $(3x - 1)(7) + (7x + 2)(3) = 42x - 1$

3. $(5 - 2x)(2x) + (x^2 + 1)(-2) = -2(3x^2 - 5x + 1)$

5. $(3r^2 - 4)(2r - 5) + (r^2 - 5r + 1)(6r) = 12r^3 - 45r^2 - 2r + 20$

7. $(x^2 + 3x - 2)(4x - 1) + (2x^2 - x - 3)(2x + 3) = 8x^3 + 15x^2 - 20x - 7$

9. $(8w^2 + 2w - 3)(15w^2) + (5w^3 + 2)(16w + 2) = 200w^4 + .40w^3 - 45w^2 + 32w + 4$

11. $3[(x^3 - 2x^2 + 5x - 4)(4x^3 - 6x^2 + 7) + (x^4 - 2x^3 + 7x + 1)(3x^2 - 4x + 5)]$
$= 3(7x^6 - 24x^5 + 45x^4 - 28x^3 - 15x^2 + 66x - 23)$

13. $(x^2 - 1)(9x^2 - 6) + (3x^3 - 6x + 5)(2x) - [(x + 4)(8x + 2) + (4x^2 + 2x + 1)(1)]$
$= 15x^4 - 39x^2 - 26x - 3$

15. $\dfrac{3}{2}\left[(p^{1/2} - 4)(4) + (4p - 5)\left(\dfrac{1}{2}p^{-1/2}\right)\right] = \dfrac{3}{4}(12p^{1/2} - 5p^{-1/2} - 32)$

17. $(2x^{.45} - 3)(1.3x^{.3} - 7) + (x^{1.3} - 7x)(.9x^{-.55}) = 3.5x^{.75} - 20.3x^{.45} - 3.9x^{.3} + 21$

19. $18x^2 + 94x + 31$

21. 0

23. $\dfrac{(x - 1)(1) - (x)(1)}{(x - 1)^2} = -\dfrac{1}{(x - 1)^2}$

25. $\dfrac{(x + 2)(1) - (x - 1)(1)}{(x + 2)^2} = \dfrac{3}{(x + 2)^2}$

27. $\dfrac{(z^2 - 4)(-2) - (5 - 2z)(2z)}{(z^2 - 4)^2} = \dfrac{2(z - 4)(z - 1)}{(z^2 - 4)^2}$

29. $\dfrac{(x^2 - 5x)(16x - 2) - (8x^2 - 2x + 1)(2x - 5)}{(x^2 - 5x)^2} = \dfrac{-38x^2 - 2x + 5}{(x^2 - 5x)^2}$

31. $\dfrac{(2x^2 - 3x + 2)(2x - 4) - (x^2 - 4x + 3)(4x - 3)}{(2x^2 - 3x + 2)^2} = \dfrac{5x^2 - 8x + 1}{(2x^2 - 3x + 2)^2}$

33. $\dfrac{-100x^{99}}{(x^{100} + 1)^2}$ **35.** $\dfrac{4(v^5 + 2)}{v^2}$ **37.** $\dfrac{15x^2 - 2x + 1}{3x^{4/3}}$

39. $\dfrac{4}{(x - 8)^2} + \dfrac{2}{(3x + 1)^2}$

41. $\dfrac{(s - 5)(2s - 2) - [(s + 2)(s - 4)](1)}{(s - 5)^2} = \dfrac{s^2 - 10s + 18}{(s - 5)^2}$

43. $\dfrac{[(x + 2)(x - 4)](1) - (x - 5)(2x - 2)}{[(x + 2)(x - 4)]^2} = \dfrac{-(x^2 - 10x + 18)}{[(x + 2)(x - 4)]^2}$

45. $\dfrac{[(t^2 - 1)(t^3 + 7)](2t + 3) - (t^2 + 3t)(5t^4 - 3t^2 + 14t)}{[(t^2 - 1)(t^3 + 7)]^2}$

$= \dfrac{-3t^6 - 12t^5 + t^4 + 6t^3 - 21t^2 - 14t - 21}{[(t^2 - 1)(t^3 + 7)]^2}$

47. $\dfrac{(x^2 - 7x + 12)(2x - 3) - (x^2 - 3x + 2)(2x - 7)}{[(x - 3)(x - 4)]^2} = \dfrac{-2(2x^2 - 10x + 11)}{[(x - 3)(x - 4)]^2}$

49. $3 - \dfrac{2x^3 + 3x^2 - 12x + 4}{[x(x - 1)(x - 2)]^2}$ **51.** -6

53. $y = 16x + 24$ **55.** $y = \dfrac{1}{16}x - \dfrac{1}{2}$ **57.** $\dfrac{1}{3}; \dfrac{2}{3}$

59. .615; .385   **61.** .536; .464   **63.** $\dfrac{dr}{dx} = 0$

65. $\dfrac{dr}{dx} = \dfrac{x^2 + 100x + 37,500}{(x + 50)^2}$

EXERCISE 7-6

1. $(2u - 2)(2x - 1) = 4x^3 - 6x^2 - 2x + 2$

3. $\left(-\dfrac{2}{w^3}\right)(-1) = \dfrac{2}{(2 - x)^3}$

5. $(2u)\left[\dfrac{-2}{(t-1)^2}\right] = -\dfrac{4(t+1)}{(t-1)^3}$

7. 0

9. $56(7x+4)^7$

11. $-56p(3-2p^2)^{13}$

13. $\dfrac{40(3x^2-2)(4x^3-8x+2)^9}{3}$

15. $-30(4r-5)(4r^2-10r+3)^{-16}$

17. $-49x(3x-2)(x^3-x^2+2)^{-8}$

19. $6z(6z-1)(4z^3-z^2+2)^{-4/5}$

21. $\dfrac{1}{2}(4x-1)(2x^2-x+3)^{-1/2}$

23. $\dfrac{6}{5}x(x^2+1)^{-2/5}$

25. $-6.5(5x^4+21x^2-8)(x^5+7x^3-8x+4)^{-7.5}$

27. $10\left(\dfrac{x-7}{x+4}\right)^9\left[\dfrac{(x+4)(1)-(x-7)(1)}{(x+4)^2}\right] = \dfrac{110(x-7)^9}{(x+4)^{11}}$

29. $10\left(\dfrac{q^3-2q+4}{5q^2+1}\right)^4\left[\dfrac{5q^4+13q^2-40q-2}{(5q^2+1)^2}\right]$

$= \dfrac{10(5q^4+13q^2-40q-2)(q^3-2q+4)^4}{(5q^2+1)^6}$

31. $\dfrac{5}{2(x+3)^2}\left(\dfrac{x-2}{x+3}\right)^{-1/2} = \dfrac{5}{2(x+3)^2}\sqrt{\dfrac{x+3}{x-2}}$

33. $(x^2+2x-1)^3(5) + [3(2x+2)(x^2+2x-1)^2](5x+7)$

$= (x^2+2x-1)^2(35x^2+82x+37)$

35. $8[(4x+3)(6x^2+x+8)]^7[(4x+3)(12x+1) + (6x^2+x+8)(4)]$

$= 8(72x^2+44x+35)[(4x+3)(6x^2+x+8)]^7$

37. $\dfrac{(w^2+4)[6(2w+3)^2] - (2w+3)^3(2w)}{(w^2+4)^2} = \dfrac{2(w^2-3w+12)(2w+3)^2}{(w^2+4)^2}$

39. $6\{(5x^2+2)[2x^3(x^4+5)^{-1/2}] + (x^4+5)^{1/2}(10x)\}$

$= 12x(x^4+5)^{-1/2}(10x^4+2x^2+25)$

41. $8 + \dfrac{5}{(t+4)^2} - (8t-7) = 15 - 8t + \dfrac{5}{(t+4)^2}$

43. $6(2-3x)^5(4-3x^2)^3(21x^2-8x-12)$

45. $\dfrac{(3x-1)^3[40(8x-1)^4] - (8x-1)^5[9(3x-1)^2]}{(3x-1)^6} = \dfrac{(8x-1)^4(48x-31)}{(3x+1)^4}$

47. 0

49. 0

51. $y = 4x - 11$

53. $y = -\dfrac{1}{6}x + \dfrac{5}{3}$

55. 20

57. 13.99

61. -325

63. .456; .544

65. $\dfrac{dc}{dx} = \dfrac{5x(x^2+6)}{(x^2+3)^{3/2}}$

EXERCISE 7-7

1. $\dfrac{3}{3x - 4}$

3. $\dfrac{2}{x}$

5. $-\dfrac{2x}{1 - x^2}$

7. $\dfrac{6p^2 + 3}{2p^3 + 3p} = \dfrac{3(2p^2 + 1)}{p(2p^2 + 3)}$

9. $\dfrac{4 \ln^3(ax)}{x}$

11. $\dfrac{2x + 4}{x^2 + 4x + 5} = \dfrac{2(x + 2)}{x^2 + 4x + 5}$

13. $t\left(\dfrac{1}{t}\right) + (\ln t)(1) = 1 + \ln t$

15. $\dfrac{2 \log_3 e}{2x - 1}$

17. $\dfrac{2(x^2 + 1)}{2x + 1} + 2x \ln (2x + 1)$

19. $\dfrac{4x}{x^2 + 2} + \dfrac{3x^2 + 1}{x^3 + x - 1}$

21. $\dfrac{2}{1 - l^2}$

23. $\dfrac{x}{1 + x^2}$

25. $\dfrac{x}{1 - x^4}$

27. $\dfrac{z\left(\dfrac{1}{z}\right) - (\ln z)(1)}{z^2} = \dfrac{1 - \ln z}{z^2}$

29. $\dfrac{x}{2(x - 1)} + \ln \sqrt{x - 1}$

31. $\dfrac{1}{2x\sqrt{4 + \ln x}}$

33. $2xe^{x^2 + 1}$

35. $-5e^{3 - 5x}$

37. $(6r + 4)e^{3r^2 + 4r + 4} = 2(3r + 2)e^{3r^2 + 4r + 4}$

39. $x(e^x) + e^x(1) = e^x(x + 1)$

41. $2xe^{-x^2}(1 - x^2)$

43. $\dfrac{e^x - e^{-x}}{2}$

45. $(6x)4^{3x^2} \ln 4$

47. $\dfrac{2e^{2w}(w - 1)}{w^3}$

49. $\dfrac{e^{1 + \sqrt{x}}}{2\sqrt{x}}$

51. $\dfrac{2e^x}{(e^x + 1)^2}$

53. $e^{e^x}e^x = e^{e^x + x}$

55. 1

57. $e^{x \ln x}(1 + \ln x)$

59. $(\log 2)^x \ln (\log 2)$

61. $y - e^2 = e^2(x - 2)$ or $y = e^2 x - e^2$

63. $25 \dfrac{(x + 2) \ln (x + 2) - x}{(x + 2) \ln^2 (x + 2)}$

65. $\dfrac{dp}{dx} = -.015e^{-.001x}; -.015e^{-.5}$

69. $\dfrac{dc}{dx} = 10e^{(x + 3)/400}; 10e^{.25}, 10e^{.5}$

71. 0

EXERCISE 7-8

1. $-\dfrac{x}{4y}$

3. $-\dfrac{y}{x}$

5. $\dfrac{4 - y}{x - 1}$

7. $\dfrac{4y - x^2}{y^2 - 4x}$

9. $-\dfrac{y^{1/4}}{x^{1/4}} = -\left(\dfrac{y}{x}\right)^{1/4}$

11. $\dfrac{5}{12y^3}$

13. $-\dfrac{\sqrt{y}}{\sqrt{x}} = -\sqrt{\dfrac{y}{x}}$

15. $\dfrac{6y^{2/3}}{3y^{1/6} + 2}$

17. $\dfrac{xe^y - y}{x(\ln x - xe^y)}$

19. $-\dfrac{e^y}{xe^y + 1}$

21. $-\dfrac{3}{5}$

23. $\dfrac{dx}{dp} = -\dfrac{1}{2x}$

25. $\dfrac{dx}{dp} = -\dfrac{(x + 5)^3}{40}$

EXERCISE 7-9

1. $y\left[\dfrac{2}{x + 1} + \dfrac{1}{x - 1} + \dfrac{2x}{x^2 + 3}\right]$

3. $y\left[\dfrac{18x^2}{3x^3 - 1} + \dfrac{6}{2x + 5}\right]$

5. $\dfrac{y}{2}\left[\dfrac{1}{x + 1} + \dfrac{2x}{x^2 - 2} + \dfrac{1}{x + 4}\right]$

7. $y\left[\dfrac{4x}{x^2 + 1} - \dfrac{2}{x + 1} - \dfrac{3}{3x + 2}\right]$

9. $y\left[\dfrac{4}{8x + 3} + \dfrac{2x}{3(x^2 + 2)} - \dfrac{1}{2(1 + 2x)}\right]$

11. $y\left[\dfrac{x}{x^2 - 1} + \dfrac{2}{1 - 2x}\right]$

13. $\dfrac{y(1 - \ln x)}{x^2}$

15. $y\left[\dfrac{2 \ln x}{x}\right] = (\ln x^2)x^{(\ln x) - 1}$

17. $xy(1 + 2 \ln x)$

19. $y(4 + 3 \ln x)$

21. $\dfrac{y(y - x \ln y)}{x(x - y \ln x)}$

EXERCISE 7-10

1. 24

3. 0

5. e^x

7. $3 + 2 \ln x$

9. $-\dfrac{10}{p^6}$

11. $-\dfrac{1}{4(1 - r)^{3/2}}$

13. $\dfrac{50}{(5x - 6)^3}$

15. $\dfrac{4}{(x - 1)^3}$

17. $-\left[\dfrac{1}{x^2} + \dfrac{1}{(x + 1)^2}\right]$

19. $e^z(z^2 + 4z + 2)$

21. $-\dfrac{1}{y^3}$

23. $-\dfrac{4}{y^3}$

25. $\dfrac{1}{8x^{3/2}}$

27. $\dfrac{2(y - 1)}{(1 + x)^2}$

29. $\dfrac{2y}{(2 - y)^3}$

REVIEW PROBLEMS—CHAPTER 7

1. 0

3. $28x^3 - 18x^2 + 10x = 2x(14x^2 - 9x + 5)$

5. $2e^x + e^{x^2}(2x) = 2(e^x + xe^{x^2})$

7. $\dfrac{1}{r^2 + 5r}(2r + 5) = \dfrac{2r + 5}{r(r + 5)}$

9. $(x^2 + 6x)(3x^2 - 12x) + (x^3 - 6x^2 + 4)(2x + 6)$

   $= 5x^4 - 108x^2 + 8x + 24$

11. $100(2x^2 + 4x)^{99}(4x + 4) = 400(x + 1)[(2x)(x + 2)]^{99}$

13. $(8 + 2x)(4)(x^2 + 1)^3(2x) + (x^2 + 1)^4(2)$

   $= 2(x^2 + 1)^3(9x^2 + 32x + 1)$

15. $e^x(2x) + (x^2 + 2)e^x = e^x(x^2 + 2x + 2)$

17. $\dfrac{(z^2 + 1)(2z) - (z^2 - 1)(2z)}{(z^2 + 1)^2} = \dfrac{4z}{(z^2 + 1)^2}$

19. $\dfrac{e^x\left(\dfrac{1}{x}\right) - (\ln x)(e^x)}{e^{2x}} = \dfrac{1 - x\ln x}{xe^x}$

21. $e^{x^2+4x+5}(2x + 4) = 2(x + 2)e^{x^2+4x+5}$

23. $-\dfrac{y}{x + y}$

25. $\dfrac{y}{2}\left[\dfrac{1}{x - 6} + \dfrac{1}{x + 5} - \dfrac{1}{9 - x}\right] = \dfrac{y}{2}\left[\dfrac{1}{x - 6} + \dfrac{1}{x + 5} + \dfrac{1}{x - 9}\right]$

27. $\dfrac{2}{q + 1} + \dfrac{3}{q + 2}$

29. $-\dfrac{1}{2}(1 - x)^{-3/2}(-1) = \dfrac{1}{2}(1 - x)^{-3/2}$

31. $\dfrac{16\log_2 e}{8x + 5}$

33. $y[1 + \ln(x + 1)]$

35. $\dfrac{\sqrt{x^2 + 5}(2x) - (x^2 + 6)(1/2)(x^2 + 5)^{-1/2}(2x)}{x^2 + 5} = \dfrac{x(x^2 + 4)}{(x^2 + 5)^{3/2}}$

37. $2\left(-\dfrac{3}{8}\right)x^{-11/8} + \left(-\dfrac{3}{8}\right)(2x)^{-11/8}(2) = -\dfrac{3}{4}(1 + 2^{-11/8})x^{-11/8}$

39. $\dfrac{1 + 2l + 3l^2}{1 + l + l^2 + l^3}$

41. $\left(\dfrac{3}{5}\right)(x^3 + 6x^2 + 9)^{-2/5}(3x^2 + 12x) = \dfrac{9}{5}x(x + 4)(x^3 + 6x + 9)^{-2/5}$

43. $2\left(\dfrac{1}{u}\right) + \dfrac{1}{2}\left(\dfrac{1}{1 - u}\right)(-1) = \dfrac{5u - 4}{2u(u - 1)}$

45. $y\left[\dfrac{3}{2}\left(\dfrac{1}{x^2 + 2}\right)(2x) + \dfrac{4}{9}\left(\dfrac{1}{x^2 + 9}\right)(2x) - \dfrac{4}{11}\left(\dfrac{1}{x^3 + 6x}\right)(3x^2 + 6)\right]$

   $= y\left[\dfrac{3x}{x^2 + 2} + \dfrac{8x}{9(x^2 + 9)} - \dfrac{12(x^2 + 2)}{11x(x^2 + 6)}\right]$

47. 12

49. $-\dfrac{1}{128}$

51. $\dfrac{4}{9}$

53. $-\dfrac{1}{4}$ **55.** $y = -4x + 3$ **57.** $y = 2x + 2(1 - \ln 2)$

59. $7x - 2\sqrt{10}\, y - 9 = 0$ **61.** $\dfrac{dr}{dx} = 20 - .2x$

63. .569, .431   **65.** $\dfrac{dr}{dx} = 450 - x$ **67.** 30

EXERCISE 8-1

1. $(0, 0)$; sym. to origin   **3.** $(-2, 0)$; sym. to x-axis

5. $(-21, 0)$, $(0, -7)$, $(0, 3)$

7. $(0, 0)$; sym. to x-axis, y-axis, origin

9. $(-2, 0)$, $(2, 0)$ $(0, 0)$; sym. to origin   **11.** sym. to x-axis

13. $(\pm\sqrt{\ln 5}, 0)$, $(0, \pm\sqrt{\ln 5})$; sym. to x-axis, y-axis, origin

15. $(\pm 3, 0)$; sym. to x-axis, y-axis, origin

17. $(\pm 1, 0)$, $(0, \pm 4)$; sym. to x-axis, y-axis, origin

19. $(0, 0)$; sym. to origin   **21.** $y = 0$, $x = 0$

23. $y = 4$, $x = 6$ **25.** $y = \dfrac{1}{2}$, $x = -\dfrac{3}{2}$ **27.** no asymptotes

29. $y = 4$ **31.** $(0, -3)$; $y = 0$, $x = 1$

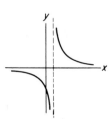

33. sym. to origin; $x = 0$, $y = 0$ **35.** $(0, 0)$; sym. to y-axis; $y = 1$, $x = -2$, $x = 2$

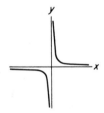

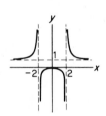

37. $((\ln 3)/2, 0), (0, 2); y = 3$

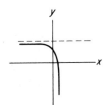

39. $(\pm 3, 0)$; sym. to y-axis

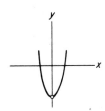

EXERCISE 8-2

1. dec. on $(-\infty, 0)$; inc. on $(0, \infty)$; rel. min. when $x = 0$

3. inc. on $\left(-\infty, \dfrac{1}{2}\right)$; dec. on $\left(\dfrac{1}{2}, \infty\right)$; rel. max. when $x = \dfrac{1}{2}$

5. dec. on $(-\infty, 3)$; inc. on $(3, \infty)$; rel. min. when $x = 3$

7. dec. on $(-\infty, -1)$ and $(1, \infty)$; inc. on $(-1, 1)$; rel. min. when $x = -1$; rel. max. when $x = 1$

9. inc. on $(-\infty, 1)$ and $(2, \infty)$; dec. on $(1, 2)$; rel. max. when $x = 1$; rel. min. when $x = 2$

11. dec. on $(-\infty, -5)$ and $(1, \infty)$; inc. on $(-5, 1)$; rel. min. when $x = -5$; rel. max. when $x = 1$

13. dec. on $(-\infty, -1)$ and $(0, 1)$; inc. on $(-1, 0)$ and $(1, \infty)$; rel. max. when $x = 0$; rel. min. when $x = \pm 1$

15. inc. on $(-\infty, 1)$ and $(3, \infty)$; dec. on $(1, 3)$; rel. max. when $x = 1$; rel. min. when $x = 3$

17. inc. on $(-\infty, -1)$ and $(1, \infty)$; dec. on $(-1, 0)$ and $(0, 1)$; rel. max. when $x = -1$; rel. min. when $x = 1$

19. dec. on $(-\infty, -4)$ and $(0, \infty)$; inc. on $(-4, 0)$; rel. min. when $x = -4$; rel. max. when $x = 0$

21. dec. on $(-\infty, 1)$ and $(1, \infty)$; no rel. max. or min.

23. dec. on $(0, \infty)$; no rel. max. or min.

25. dec. on $(-\infty, 0)$ and $(2, \infty)$; inc. on $(0, 1)$ and $(1, 2)$; rel. min. when $x = 0$; rel. max. when $x = 2$

27. dec. on $(-\infty, \infty)$; no rel. max. or min.

29. dec. on $(0, 1)$; inc. on $(1, \infty)$; rel. min. when $x = 1$

31. dec. on $(-\infty, 0)$; inc. on $(0, \infty)$; rel. min. when $x = 0$

33.   **35.**

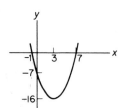   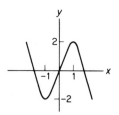

37.

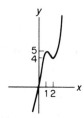

39. ab. max. when $x = -\dfrac{3}{2}$; ab. min. when $x = 3$

41. ab. max. when $x = 0$; ab. min. when $x = 1$

45. never   **47.** 50

EXERCISE 8-3

1. conc. down $(-\infty, \infty)$

3. conc. down $(-\infty, -1)$; conc. up $(-1, \infty)$; inf. pt. when $x = -1$

5. conc. up $(-\infty, -1)$, $(1, \infty)$; conc. down $(-1, 1)$; inf. pt. when $x = \pm 1$

7. conc. up $(-\infty, \infty)$

9. conc. down $(-\infty, -2)$; conc. up $(-2, \infty)$; inf. pt. when $x = -2$

11.

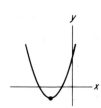

int. $(-3, 0)$, $(-1, 0)$, $(0, 3)$; dec. $(-\infty, -2)$; inc. $(-2, \infty)$; rel. min. when $x = -2$; conc. up $(-\infty, \infty)$

13.

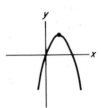

int. (0, 0), (4, 0); inc. $(-\infty, 2)$; dec. $(2, \infty)$; rel. max. when $x = 2$; conc. down $(-\infty, \infty)$

15.

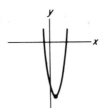

int. $\left(-\dfrac{3}{2}, 0\right)$, (4, 0), (0, −12); dec. $\left(-\infty, \dfrac{5}{4}\right)$; inc. $\left(\dfrac{5}{4}, \infty\right)$; rel. min. when $x = \dfrac{5}{4}$; conc. up $(-\infty, \infty)$

17.

int. (0, −19); inc. $(-\infty, 2)$, $(4, \infty)$; dec. (2, 4); rel. max. when $x = 2$; rel. min. when $x = 4$; conc. down $(-\infty, 3)$; conc. up $(3, \infty)$; inf. pt. when $x = 3$

19.

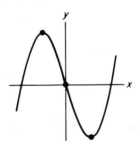

int. $(0, 0)$, $(\pm 3, 0)$; inc. $(-\infty, -\sqrt{3})$, $(\sqrt{3}, \infty)$; dec. $(-\sqrt{3}, \sqrt{3})$; rel. max. when $x = -\sqrt{3}$; rel. min. when $x = \sqrt{3}$; conc. down $(-\infty, 0)$; conc. up $(0, \infty)$; inf. pt. when $x = 0$; sym. to origin

21.

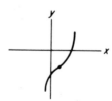

int. $(0, -3)$; inc. $(-\infty, 1)$, $(1, \infty)$; no rel. max. or min.; conc. down $(-\infty, 1)$; conc. up $(1, \infty)$; inf. pt. when $x = 1$

23.

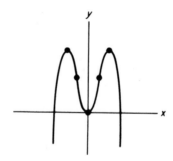

int. $(0, 0)$, $(\pm 2, 0)$; inc. $(-\infty, -\sqrt{2})$, $(0, \sqrt{2})$; dec. $(-\sqrt{2}, 0)$, $(\sqrt{2}, \infty)$; rel. max. when $x = \pm\sqrt{2}$; rel. min. when $x = 0$; conc. down $(-\infty, -\sqrt{2/3})$, $(\sqrt{2/3}, \infty)$; conc. up $(-\sqrt{2/3}, \sqrt{2/3})$; inf. pt. when $x = \pm\sqrt{2/3}$; sym. to y-axis

25.

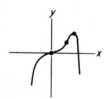

int. $(0, 0)$, $\left(\dfrac{4}{3}, 0\right)$; inc. $(-\infty, 0)$, $(0, 1)$; dec. $(1, \infty)$; rel. max. when $x = 1$; conc.

up $\left(0, \dfrac{2}{3}\right)$; conc. down $(-\infty, 0)$, $\left(\dfrac{2}{3}, \infty\right)$; inf. pt. when $x = 0$, $x = \dfrac{2}{3}$

27.

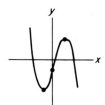

int. (0, −2); dec. (−∞, −2), (2, ∞); inc. (−2, 2); rel. min. when $x = -2$; rel. max. when $x = 2$; conc. up (−∞, 0); conc. down (0, ∞); inf. pt. when $x = 0$

29.

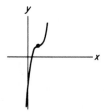

int. (0, −6); inc. (−∞, 2), (2, ∞); conc. down (−∞, 2); conc. up (2, ∞); inf. pt. when $x = 2$

31.

int. (0, 0), $(\pm\sqrt[4]{5}, 0)$; dec. (−∞, −1), (1, ∞); inc. (−1, 1); rel. min. when $x = -1$; rel. max. when $x = 1$; conc. up (−∞, 0); conc. down (0, ∞); inf. pt. when $x = 0$; sym. to origin

33.

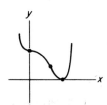

int. (0, 1), (1, 0); dec. (−∞, 0), (0, 1); inc. (1, ∞); rel. min. when $x = 1$; conc.
up (−∞, 0), (2/3, ∞); conc. down (0, 2/3); inf. pt. when $x = 0$, $x = \dfrac{2}{3}$

35.

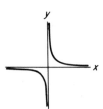

dec. on (−∞, 0), (0, ∞); conc. down (−∞, 0); conc. up (0, ∞); sym. to origin; asymptotes
$x = 0$, $y = 0$

37.

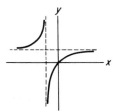

int. (0, 0); inc. (−∞, −1), (−1, ∞); conc. up (−∞, −1); conc. down (−1, ∞); asymptotes
$x = −1$, $y = 1$

39.

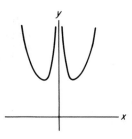

dec. (−∞, −1), (0, 1); inc. (−1, 0), (1, ∞); rel. min. when $x = ±1$; conc. up (−∞,
0), (0, ∞); sym. to y-axis; asymptote $x = 0$

EXERCISE 8-4

1. rel. min. when $x = \dfrac{5}{2}$ **3.** rel. max. when $x = \dfrac{1}{4}$

5. rel. max. when $x = −3$, rel. min. when $x = 3$

7. rel. min. when $x = 0$, rel. max. when $x = 2$

9. test fails, when $x = 0$ there is rel. min. by first deriv. test.

EXERCISE 8-5

1. 100

3. 525, $51, $10,525

5. 625, $4

7. $1.60 \le p \le 2.60$

9. 750

11. 35

13. 130, $p = 340$, $P = 36,980$; 125, $p = 350$, $P = 34,175$

15. 250 per lot (4 lots)

17. 5000

19. 60 mi/hr

21. 30 horsepower

EXERCISE 8-6

1. $3 \, dx$

3. $\dfrac{2x^3}{\sqrt{x^4 + 2}} \, dx$

5. $\dfrac{2(3 - x - x^2)}{(x^2 + 3)^2} \, dx$

7. $\dfrac{2x}{x^2 + 7} \, dx$

9. $4e^{2x^2 + 3}(4x^2 + 3x + 1) \, dx$

11. $-.14$

13. $\dfrac{2}{15}$

15. 44; 41.8

17. 10.05

19. $-.03$

21. $\dfrac{65}{32}$

23. $\dfrac{1}{2}$

25. $\dfrac{1}{6p(p^2 + 5)^2}$

27. $-p^2$

29. $-\dfrac{4}{5}$

31. 2.04

EXERCISE 8-7

1. -3, elastic

3. -1, unit elasticity

5. -1, unit elasticity

7. -1.02, elastic

9. $-\dfrac{9}{32}$, inelastic

11. $-\dfrac{1}{2}$, inelastic

13. $-(150e^{-1} - 1)$, elastic

15. $|\eta| = \dfrac{10}{3}$ when $p = 10$, $|\eta| = \dfrac{3}{10}$ when $p = 3$, $|\eta| = 1$ when $p = 6.50$

17. -1.2, .6 percent decrease   **23.** 5, 30

REVIEW PROBLEMS—CHAPTER 8

1.

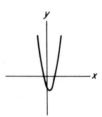

int. $(-4, 0)$, $(6, 0)$, $(0, -24)$; inc. $(1, \infty)$; dec. $(-\infty, 1)$; rel. min. when $x = 1$; conc. up $(-\infty, \infty)$

3.

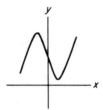

int. $(0, 20)$; inc. $(-\infty, -2)$, $(2, \infty)$; dec. $(-2, 2)$; rel. max. when $x = -2$; rel. min. when $x = 2$; conc. up $(0, \infty)$; conc. down $(-\infty, 0)$; inf. pt. when $x = 0$

5.

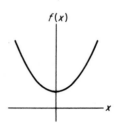

int. $(0, 1)$; inc. $(0, \infty)$; dec. $(-\infty, 0)$; rel. min. when $x = 0$; conc. up $(-\infty, \infty)$; sym. to y-axis

7.

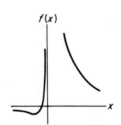

int. $(-5, 0)$; inc. $(-10, 0)$; dec. $(-\infty, -10)$, $(0, \infty)$; rel. min. when $x = -10$; conc. up $(-15, 0)$, $(0, \infty)$; conc. down $(-\infty, -15)$; inf. pt. when $x = -15$; horiz. asym. $y = 0$; vert. asym. $x = 0$

9. $2800

11. 300

13. $\dfrac{x^2 - 14x - 5}{(x - 7)^2}\, dx$

15. .99

17. unit elasticity

EXERCISE 9-1

1. $5x + C$

3. $\dfrac{x^9}{9} + C$

5. $\dfrac{2}{15} t^{15/2} + C$

7. $-\dfrac{1}{6x^6} + C$

9. $-\dfrac{1}{9x^9} + C$

11. $-\dfrac{5}{6y^{6/5}} + C$

13. $\dfrac{5\sqrt[5]{x^{11}}}{11} + C = \dfrac{5x^2\sqrt[5]{x}}{11} + C$

15. $8\sqrt[8]{x} + C$

17. $(7 + e)x + C$

19. $\dfrac{x^{\sqrt{2}+1}}{\sqrt{2} + 1} + C$

21. $\dfrac{3x^8}{8} + C$

23. $8x + \dfrac{x^2}{2} + C$

25. $\dfrac{y^6}{6} + \dfrac{5y^2}{2} + C$

27. $t^3 - 2t^2 - 5t + C$

29. $\dfrac{x^2}{14} - \dfrac{3x^5}{20} + C$

31. $3e^x + C$

33. $6z - \dfrac{5z^3}{12} + 2e^z + C$

35. $\dfrac{e^u}{4} + u + C$

37. $-\dfrac{1}{x} + \dfrac{5}{2x^2} - \dfrac{2}{3x^3} + C$

39. $\dfrac{x^{9.3}}{9.3} - \dfrac{9x^7}{7} - \dfrac{1}{x^3} - \dfrac{1}{2x^2} + C$

41. $\dfrac{x^4}{12} + \dfrac{3}{2x^2} + C$

43. $\dfrac{w^3}{2} + \dfrac{2}{3w} + C$

45. $\dfrac{3x^{4/3}}{4} - \dfrac{4x^{5/4}}{5} + \dfrac{5x^{6/5}}{6} + C$

47. $\dfrac{4x^{3/2}}{3} - \dfrac{12x^{5/4}}{5} + C$

49. $-\dfrac{10}{x^{1/5}} + C$

51. $-\dfrac{3x^{5/3}}{25} - 7x^{1/2} + 3x^2 + C$

53. $\dfrac{x^4}{4} - x^3 + \dfrac{5x^2}{2} - 15x + C$

55. $\dfrac{2x^{5/2}}{5} + 2x^{3/2} + C$

57. $\dfrac{4u^3}{3} + 2u^2 + u + C$

59. $\dfrac{2v^3}{3} + 3v + \dfrac{1}{2v^4} + C$

61. $\dfrac{1}{2}(e^6 x + e^x) + C$

63. $y = 3$

65. $y = \dfrac{x^3}{6} + \dfrac{x^2}{2} + 5$

67. $y = \dfrac{x^4}{12} + x^2 - 5x + 2$

69. $c = 1.35x + 200$

71. 7715

73. \$80 $\left(\dfrac{dc}{dx} = 27.50 \text{ when } x = 50 \text{ is not relevant to problem} \right)$

75. $p = 15 - \dfrac{x}{30}$

77. $-\dfrac{3}{2}$

EXERCISE 9-2

1. $\dfrac{(x + 4)^9}{9} + C$

3. $\dfrac{(x^2 + 16)^4}{4} + C$

5. $\dfrac{3}{5}(y^3 + 3y^2 + 1)^{5/3} + C$

7. $-\dfrac{(3x - 1)^{-2}}{2} + C$

9. $e^{3x} + C$

11. $e^{t^2 + t} + C$

13. $\ln|x + 5| + C$

15. $\ln|x^3 + x^4| + C$

17. $\dfrac{2(x + 10)^{3/2}}{3} + C$

19. $\dfrac{(7x - 6)^5}{35} + C$

21. $\dfrac{(x^2 + 3)^{13}}{26} + C$

23. $\dfrac{3}{20}(27 + x^5)^{4/3} + C$

25. $\dfrac{1}{10}e^{5x^2} + C$

27. $-3e^{-2x} + C$

29. $-\dfrac{3}{4}(z^2 - 6)^{-4} + C$

31. $4\ln|x| + C$

33. $\dfrac{1}{3}\ln|s^3 + 5| + C$

35. $-\dfrac{7}{3}\ln|5 - 3x| + C$

37. $\dfrac{2}{15}(5x)^{3/2} + C = \dfrac{2}{3}x\sqrt{5x} + C$

39. $\sqrt{x^2 - 4} + C$

41. $\dfrac{1}{2}e^{y^4 + 1} + C$

43. $-\dfrac{1}{6}e^{-2v^3 + 1} + C$

45. $-\dfrac{1}{5}e^{-5x} + 2e^x + C$

47. $-\dfrac{1}{24}(3 - 3x^2 - 6x)^4 + C$

49. $\dfrac{1}{3}\ln|x^3 + 6x| + C$

51. $2\ln|3 - 2s + 4s^2| + C$

53. $\dfrac{1}{4}\ln(2x^2 + 1) + C$

55. $\dfrac{1}{27}(x^3 - x^6)^{-9} + C$

57. $\dfrac{1}{4}(x^4 + x^2)^2 + C$

59. $\dfrac{1}{2}(4 - 9x - 3x^2)^{-4} + C$

61. $\dfrac{1}{6}e^{4x^3 + 3x^2 - 4} + C$

63. $-\dfrac{1}{25}(7 - 5x^2)^{5/2} + C$

65. $\sqrt{2x} + C$

67. $\dfrac{x^5}{5} + \dfrac{2x^3}{3} + x + C$

69. $\dfrac{1}{2}\ln(x^2 + 1) - \dfrac{1}{6(x^6 + 1)} + C$

71. $\dfrac{1}{3}\ln|3x - 5| + \dfrac{1}{27}(x^3 - x^6)^{-9} + C$

73. $\dfrac{1}{3}(2x + 3)^{3/2} - \ln\sqrt{x^2 + 3} + C$

75. $2e^{\sqrt{x}} + C$

77. $y = -\dfrac{1}{6}(3 - 2x)^3 + \dfrac{11}{2}$

79. $y = -\ln|x| = \ln|1/x|$

EXERCISE 9-3

1. $\dfrac{3}{2}x^2 + x - \ln|x| + C$

3. $\dfrac{1}{3}(2x^3 + 4x + 1)^{3/2} + C$

5. $-\dfrac{8}{3}\sqrt{2 - 3x} + C$

7. $\dfrac{4^{7x}}{7\ln 4} + C$

9. $7x^2 - 4e^{x^2/4} + C$

11. $\dfrac{3}{2}\ln(e^{2x} + 1) + C$

13. $-\dfrac{1}{7}e^{7/x} + C$

15. $\dfrac{2}{9}(\sqrt{x} + 2)^3 + C$

17. $\dfrac{1}{2}(\ln^2 x) + C$

19. $\dfrac{1}{3}\ln^3(r + 1) + C$

21. $e^{(x^2 + 3)/2} + C$

23. $\ln|\ln(x + 3)| + C$

25. $\dfrac{1}{2}\sqrt{x^4 - 1} - (\ln 4)x + C$

27. $x^2 - 8x - 6\ln|x| - \dfrac{2}{x^2} + C$

29. $x^2 - 3x + \dfrac{2}{3}\ln|3x - 1| + C$

31. $x + \ln|x - 1| + C$

33. $\sqrt{e^{x^2} + 2} + C$

35. $-\dfrac{(e^{-x} + 6)^3}{3} + C$

37. $\dfrac{1}{36\sqrt{2}}[(8x)^{3/2} + 3]^{3/2} + C$

39. $-\dfrac{2}{3}e^{-\sqrt{s^3}} + C$

41. $\dfrac{x^2}{2} + 2x + C$

43. $p = \dfrac{100}{x + 2}$

45. $c = 20 \ln |(x + 5)/5| + 2000$

47. $C = 2(\sqrt{I} + 1)$

49. $C = \dfrac{3}{4} I - \dfrac{1}{3} \sqrt{I} + \dfrac{71}{12}$

EXERCISE 9-4

1. 35

3. 0

5. 25

7. $-\dfrac{3}{16}$

9. $-\dfrac{7}{6}$

11. $\displaystyle\sum_{k=1}^{15} k$

13. $\displaystyle\sum_{k=1}^{4} (2k - 1)$

15. $\displaystyle\sum_{k=1}^{12} k^2$

17. 101,475

19. 84

21. 273

EXERCISE 9-5

1. $\dfrac{2}{3}$ sq unit

3. $\dfrac{14}{27}$ sq unit

5. $\dfrac{1}{2}$ sq unit

7. $\dfrac{1}{3}$ sq unit

9. $\dfrac{16}{3}$ sq unit

11. 36

13. -18

15. $\dfrac{5}{6}$

EXERCISE 9-6

1. 12

3. $\dfrac{9}{2}$

5. -24

7. $\dfrac{14}{3}$

9. $\dfrac{7}{3}$

11. $\dfrac{15}{2}$

13. 0

15. $\dfrac{1}{6}$

17. $\dfrac{32}{3}$

19. $-\dfrac{1}{6}$

21. $4 \ln 8$

23. $\dfrac{1}{3}(e^8 - 1)$

25. $\dfrac{3}{4}$

27. $\dfrac{38}{9}$

29. $\dfrac{15}{28}$

31. $\dfrac{1}{2} \ln 3$

33. $e + \dfrac{1}{2e^2} - \dfrac{3}{2}$

35. $\dfrac{3}{2} - \dfrac{1}{e} + \dfrac{1}{2e^2}$

37. $\dfrac{e^3}{2}(e^{12} - 1)$

39. $\dfrac{1}{2}; \dfrac{1}{12}$

41. $\dfrac{A}{1 - B}(b^{1-B} - a^{1-B})$

EXERCISE 9-7

In problems 1–33, answers are assumed to be expressed in square units.

1. 8   **3.** $\dfrac{19}{2}$ **5.** 8   **7.** $\dfrac{19}{3}$ **9.** 9

11. $\dfrac{50}{3}$ **13.** 36   **15.** 8   **17.** 6   **19.** 1

21. 18   **23.** $\dfrac{26}{3}$ **25.** $\dfrac{3}{2}\sqrt[3]{2}$ **27.** $e^2 - 1$

29. $\dfrac{3}{2} + 2 \ln 2 = \dfrac{3}{2} + \ln 4$ **31.** 68   **33.** 2

35. (a) 7   **37.** $\dfrac{t - a}{b - a}$ sq units

(b) 2600

EXERCISE 9-8

In problems 1–21, the answers are assumed to be expressed in square units.

1. $\dfrac{4}{3}$ **3.** $\dfrac{16}{3}$ **5.** $8\sqrt{6}$

7. 40   **9.** $\dfrac{125}{6}$ **11.** $\dfrac{32}{81}$

13. $\dfrac{125}{12}$ **15.** $\dfrac{9}{2}$ **17.** $\dfrac{44}{3}$

19. $\dfrac{4}{3}(5\sqrt{5} - 2\sqrt{2})$ **21.** $\dfrac{1}{2}$ **23.** $\dfrac{20}{63}$

EXERCISE 9-9

1. $CS = 25.6$, $PS = 38.4$ **3.** $CS = 50 \ln (2) - 25$, $PS = 1.25$

5. $CS = 800$, $PS = 1000$

REVIEW PROBLEMS—CHAPTER 9

1. $\dfrac{x^4}{4} + x^2 - 7x + C$ **3.** $\dfrac{117}{2}$

5. $-(x + 5)^{-2} + C$ **7.** $2 \ln |x^3 - 6x + 1| + C$

9. $\dfrac{1}{3}\ln\dfrac{10}{3}$

11. $\dfrac{2}{27}(3x^3+2)^{3/2}+C$

13. $\dfrac{1}{2}(e^{2y}+e^{-2y})+C$

15. $\ln|x|-\dfrac{2}{x}+C$

17. 11.1

19. $\dfrac{7}{3}$

21. $4-3\sqrt[3]{2}$

23. $\dfrac{3}{t}-\dfrac{2}{\sqrt{t}}+C$

25. $\dfrac{3}{2}-5\ln 2$

In problems 27–39, answers are assumed to be expressed in square units.

27. $\dfrac{4}{3}$ **29.** $\dfrac{16}{3}$ **31.** $\dfrac{125}{6}$ **33.** $6+\ln 3$ **35.** $\dfrac{2}{3}$

37. 36   **39.** $\dfrac{125}{3}$ **41.** $p=100-\sqrt{2x}$ **43.** $CS=166\dfrac{2}{3},\ PS=53\dfrac{1}{3}$

EXERCISE 10-1

1. $-e^{-x}(x+1)+C$

3. $\dfrac{y^4}{4}\left[\ln(y)-\dfrac{1}{4}\right]+C$

5. $x[\ln(4x)-1]+C$

7. $\dfrac{2x}{3}(x+1)^{3/2}-\dfrac{4}{15}(x+1)^{5/2}+C=\dfrac{2}{15}(x+1)^{3/2}(3x-2)+C$

9. $\dfrac{2}{3}x^{3/2}\ln(x)-\dfrac{4}{9}x^{3/2}+C$

11. $\dfrac{1}{2}(1-e^{-1})$, parts not needed

13. $\dfrac{1}{4}e^2(3e^2-1)$

15. $\dfrac{2}{3}(9\sqrt{3}-10\sqrt{2})$

17. $e^x(x^2-2x+2)+C$

19. $\dfrac{x^3}{3}+2e^{-x}(x+1)-\dfrac{e^{-2x}}{2}+C$

21. $2e^3+1$ sq units

23. $204\ln(102)-4\ln(2)=200\ln(2)+204\ln(51)$

EXERCISE 10-2

1. $2\ln|x|+3\ln|x-1|+C=\ln|x^2(x-1)^3|+C$

3. $-3\ln|x+1|+4\ln|x-2|+C=\ln|(x-2)^4/(x+1)^3|+C$

5. $\dfrac{1}{4}\left[\dfrac{3x^2}{2}+2\ln|x-1|-2\ln|x+1|\right]+C=\dfrac{1}{4}\left(\dfrac{3x^2}{2}+\ln\left[\dfrac{x-1}{x+1}\right]^2\right)+C$

7. $\ln |x| + 2 \ln |x - 4| - 3 \ln |x + 3| + C = \ln |x(x - 4)^2/(x + 3)^3| + C$

9. $\dfrac{1}{2} \ln |x^6 + 2x^4 - x^2 - 2| + C$, partial fractions not required

11. $[4/(x - 2)] - 5 \ln |x - 1| + 7 \ln |x - 2| + C$
$= [4/(x - 2)] + \ln |(x - 2)^7/(x - 1)^5| + C$

13. $2 \ln |x| - \dfrac{1}{2} \ln (x^2 + 4) + C = \dfrac{1}{2} \ln \left[\dfrac{x^4}{x^2 + 4} \right] + C$

15. $-\dfrac{1}{2} \ln (x^2 + 1) - \dfrac{2}{x - 3} + C$

17. $5 \ln (x^2 + 1) + 2 \ln (x^2 + 2) + C = \ln [(x^2 + 1)^5 (x^2 + 2)^2] + C$

19. $\dfrac{3}{2} \ln (x^2 + 1) + \dfrac{1}{x^2 + 1} + C$ **21.** $18 \ln (4) - 10 \ln (5) - 8 \ln (3)$

23. $\dfrac{11}{6} + 4 \ln \dfrac{2}{3}$ sq units

EXERCISE 10-3

1. $\dfrac{1}{6} \ln \left| \dfrac{x}{6 + 7x} \right| + C$ **3.** $\dfrac{1}{3} \ln \left| \dfrac{\sqrt{x^2 - 9} - 3}{x} \right| + C$

5. $\dfrac{1}{2} \left[\dfrac{4}{5} \ln |4 + 5x| - \dfrac{2}{3} \ln |2 + 3x| \right] + C$

7. $\dfrac{1}{8} (2x - \ln [4 + 3e^{2x}]) + C$ **9.** $2 \left[\dfrac{1}{1 + x} + \ln \left| \dfrac{x}{1 + x} \right| \right] + C$

11. $x - 2 \ln |2 + x| + C$

13. $\dfrac{1}{2} (x\sqrt{x^2 - 3} - 3 \ln |x + \sqrt{x^2 - 3}|) + C$

15. $\dfrac{e^{12x}}{144} (12x - 1) + C$ **17.** $e^x (x^2 - 2x + 2) + C$

19. $2 \left(-\dfrac{\sqrt{4x^2 + 1}}{2x} + \ln |2x + \sqrt{4x^2 + 1}| \right) + C$

21. $\dfrac{1}{9} \left(\ln |1 + 3x| + \dfrac{1}{1 + 3x} \right) + C$

23. $\dfrac{1}{\sqrt{5}} \left(\dfrac{1}{2\sqrt{7}} \ln \left| \dfrac{\sqrt{7} + \sqrt{5} x}{\sqrt{7} - \sqrt{5} x} \right| \right) + C$

25. $\dfrac{1}{3^6}\left[\dfrac{(3x)^6 \ln{(3x)}}{6} - \dfrac{(3x)^6}{36}\right] + C = \dfrac{x^6}{36}[6 \ln{(3x)} - 1] + C$

27. $\dfrac{4(9x - 2)(1 + 3x)^{3/2}}{135} + C$

29. $\dfrac{1}{2} \ln{|2x + \sqrt{4x^2 - 13}|} + C$

31. $\dfrac{1}{4}[2x^2 \ln{(2x)} - x^2] + C$

33. $-\dfrac{\sqrt{9 - 4x^2}}{9x} + C$

35. $\dfrac{1}{2} \ln{(x^2 + 1)} + C$

37. $\dfrac{1}{6}(2x^2 + 1)^{3/2} + C$

39. $\ln{\left|\dfrac{x - 3}{x - 2}\right|} + C$

41. $\dfrac{x^4}{4}\left[\ln{(x)} - \dfrac{1}{4}\right] + C$

43. $\dfrac{e^{2x}}{4}(2x - 1) + C$

45. $x(\ln x)^2 - 2x \ln{(x)} + 2x + C$

47. $\dfrac{2}{3}(9\sqrt{3} - 10\sqrt{2})$

49. $2(2\sqrt{2} - \sqrt{7})$

51. $\dfrac{7}{2} \ln{(2)} - \dfrac{3}{4}$

EXERCISE 10-4

1. $\dfrac{1}{3}$

3. div.

5. $\dfrac{1}{e}$

7. div.

9. $-\dfrac{1}{2}$

11. 0

13. 6

15. 3

17. div.

19. $\ln{\dfrac{8}{7}}$, integral is not improper

21. div.

23. 6

25. div.

27. 1

EXERCISE 10-5

1. $y = -\dfrac{1}{x^2 + C}$

3. $y = Ce^x,\ C > 0$

5. $y = Cx,\ C > 0$

7. $y = \dfrac{1}{3}(x^2 + 1)^{3/2} + C$

9. $y = \sqrt{2x}$

11. $y = \ln{\dfrac{x^3 + 3}{3}}$

13. $y = \dfrac{4x^2 + 3}{2(x^2 + 1)}$

15. $p = Cx^{1/k},\ C > 0$

17. \$445.10

19. $N = 20,000e^{.018t}$; $N = 20,000(1.2)^{t/10}$; 28,800

21. $2e^{.945}$ billion   **23.** 79

REVIEW PROBLEMS—CHAPTER 10

1. $\dfrac{x^2}{4}[2\ln(x) - 1] + C$ **3.** $5 + \dfrac{9}{4}\ln 3$

5. $\dfrac{1}{21}(9\ln|3 + x| - 2\ln|2 + 3x|) + C$

7. $\dfrac{1}{2(x + 2)} + \dfrac{1}{4}\ln\left|\dfrac{x}{x + 2}\right| + C$

9. $-\dfrac{\sqrt{9 - 16x^2}}{9x} + C$ **11.** $\dfrac{3}{2}\ln\left|\dfrac{x - 3}{x + 3}\right| + C$

13. $\dfrac{e^{7x}}{49}(7x - 1) + C$ **15.** $\dfrac{1}{2}\ln|\ln 2x| + C$

17. $x - \dfrac{3}{2}\ln|3 + 2x| + C$ **19.** $\dfrac{1}{18}$

21. div.   **23.** div.   **25.** $y = Ce^{x^3 + x^2}$

27. \$201.38

EXERCISE 11-1

1. 3   **3.** 6   **5.** 6   **7.** 88   **9.** 3

11. $2x_0 + 2h - 5y_0 + 4$ **13.** $y = -4$ **15.** $z = 6$ **17.** $y = y_0$

EXERCISE 11-2

1. $f_x(x,y) = 1; f_y(x,y) = -5$

3. $f_x(x,y) = 3; f_y(x,y) = 0$

5. $g_x(x,y) = 5x^4 y^4 - 12x^3 y^3 + 21x^2 - 3y$;
$g_y(x,y) = 4x^5 y^3 - 9x^4 y^2 + 4y - 3x$

7. $g_p(p,q) = \dfrac{q}{2\sqrt{pq}}$; $g_q(p,q) = \dfrac{p}{2\sqrt{pq}}$

9. $h_s(s,t) = \dfrac{2s}{t - 3}; h_t(s,t) = -\dfrac{s^2 + 4}{(t - 3)^2}$

11. $u_{q_1}(q_1, q_2) = \dfrac{3}{4q_1}; u_{q_2}(q_1, q_2) = \dfrac{1}{4q_2}$

13. $h_x(x,y) = (x^3 + xy^2 + 3y^3)(x^2 + y^2)^{-3/2};$

$h_y(x,y) = (3x^3 + x^2y + y^3)(x^2 + y^2)^{-3/2}$

15. $\dfrac{\partial z}{\partial x} = 5ye^{5xy}; \dfrac{\partial z}{\partial y} = 5xe^{5xy}$

17. $\dfrac{\partial z}{\partial x} = 5\left[\dfrac{2x^2}{x^2 + y} + \ln(x^2 + y)\right]; \dfrac{\partial z}{\partial y} = \dfrac{5x}{x^2 + y}$

19. $f_r(r,s) = \sqrt{r + 2s}\,(3r^2 - 2s) + \dfrac{r^3 - 2rs + s^2}{2\sqrt{r + 2s}};$

$f_s(r,s) = 2(s - r)\sqrt{r + 2s} + \dfrac{r^3 - 2rs + s^2}{\sqrt{r + 2s}}$

21. $f_r(r,s) = -e^{3-r}\ln(7 - s); \quad f_s(r,s) = \dfrac{-e^{3-r}}{7 - s}$

23. $g_x(x,y,z) = 6xy + 2y^2z; \quad g_y(x,y,z) = 3x^2 + 4xyz;$

$g_z(x,y,z) = 2xy^2 + 9z^2$

25. $g_r(r,s,t) = 2re^{s+t}; \quad g_s(r,s,t) = (7s^3 + 21s^2 + r^2)e^{s+t};$

$g_t(r,s,t) = e^{s+t}(r^2 + 7s^3)$

27. 50   **29.** $\dfrac{1}{3}$ **31.** 0

EXERCISE 11-3

1. 20   **3.** 784.5

5. $\dfrac{\partial Q}{\partial k} = 1.208648 l^{.192} k^{-.236}; \quad \dfrac{\partial Q}{\partial l} = .303744 l^{-.808} k^{.764}$

7. $\dfrac{\partial q_A}{\partial p_A} = -50; \quad \dfrac{\partial q_A}{\partial p_B} = 2; \quad \dfrac{\partial q_B}{\partial p_A} = 4; \quad \dfrac{\partial q_B}{\partial p_B} = -20; \quad$ competitive

9. $\dfrac{\partial q_A}{\partial p_A} = -\dfrac{100}{p_A^2 p_B^{1/2}}; \quad \dfrac{\partial q_A}{\partial p_B} = -\dfrac{50}{p_A p_B^{3/2}}; \quad \dfrac{\partial q_B}{\partial p_A} = -\dfrac{500}{3p_B p_A^{4/3}};$

$\dfrac{\partial q_B}{\partial p_B} = -\dfrac{500}{p_B^2 p_A^{1/3}}; \quad$ complementary

11. $\eta_{p_A} = -1, \eta_{p_B} = -\dfrac{1}{2}$

EXERCISE 11-4

1. $-\dfrac{x}{z}$ **3.** $\dfrac{4y}{3z^2}$ **5.** $\dfrac{x(yz^2 + 1)}{z(1 - x^2y)}$

7. $-e^{y-z}$

9. $\dfrac{yz}{1+z}$

11. $-\dfrac{3x}{z}$

13. $-\dfrac{9}{10}$

15. 1

17. $\dfrac{5}{2}$

EXERCISE 11-5

1. $12xy$

3. $9x(3xy+2)\,e^{3xy}$

5. $6x^2 + 8xy + 3y^2 + 1$

7. $6xy + 4y^2$; $6xy + 4x^2$

9. $y^2(x^2 + y^2)^{-3/2}$

11. 0

13. 1758

15. $2e$

21. $-\dfrac{y^2 + z^2}{z^3} = -\dfrac{3x^2}{z^3}$

EXERCISE 11-6

1. $\dfrac{\partial z}{\partial r} = 13;$ $\dfrac{\partial z}{\partial s} = 9$

3. $\left[2t + \dfrac{3\sqrt{t}}{2}\right] e^{x+y}$

5. $5(2xz^2 + yz) + 2(xz + z^2) - (2x^2 z + xy + 2yz)$

7. $3(x^2 + xy^2)^2 (2x + y^2 + 2xy)$

9. $-2s(2x + yz) + r(xz + 3y^2 z^2) - 5(xy + 2y^3 z)$

11. $15s(2x - 7)$

13. 324

15. -1

EXERCISE 11-7

1. $\left(\dfrac{14}{3}, -\dfrac{13}{3}\right)$

3. $(2,5), (2,-6), (-1,5), (-1,-6)$

5. $(50,150,350)$

7. $\left(-2, \dfrac{3}{2}\right)$, rel. min.

9. $\left(-\dfrac{1}{4}, \dfrac{1}{2}\right)$, rel. min.

11. $(1,1)$, rel. min.; $\left(\dfrac{1}{2}, \dfrac{1}{4}\right)$, neither

13. $(0,0)$, rel. max.; $\left(4, \dfrac{1}{2}\right)$ rel. min.; $\left(0, \dfrac{1}{2}\right)$, $(4,0)$, neither

15. $(122,127)$, rel. max.

17. $(-1,-1)$, rel. min.

19. $l = 24, k = 14$

21. $p_A = 94, p_B = 99$

23. $q_A = 48, q_B = 40, p_A = 52, p_B = 44$, profit $= 3304$

25. $q_A = 3, q_B = 2$

27. $q_A = 31, q_B = 10$

EXERCISE 11-8

1. $(2, -2)$

3. $\left(3, \dfrac{3}{2}, -\dfrac{3}{2}\right)$

5. $\left(\dfrac{4}{3}, -\dfrac{4}{3}, -\dfrac{8}{3}\right)$

7. $(6, 3, 2)$

9. $\left(\dfrac{2}{3}, \dfrac{4}{3}, -\dfrac{4}{3}\right)$

11. Plant 1, 40 units; Plant 2, 60 units

13. 74 units (when $l = 8$, $k = 7$)

15. $x = 12$, $y = 8$

17. $x = 10$, $y = 20$, $z = 5$

EXERCISE 11-9

1. $\hat{y} = .98 + .61x$; 3.12

3. $\hat{y} = .057 + 1.67x$; 5.90

5. $\hat{x} = 82.6 - .641p$

7. $\hat{c} = 8.51 - .365x$; 6.685

9. $\hat{y} = 89.45 + 1.45x$

11. (a) $\hat{y} = 35.9 - 2.5x$

     (b) $\hat{y} = 28.4 - 2.5x$

EXERCISE 11-11

1. 18

3. $\dfrac{1}{4}$

5. $\dfrac{2}{3}$

7. 3

9. 324

11. $-\dfrac{58}{35}$

13. $\dfrac{8}{3}$

15. $-\dfrac{1}{3}$

17. $-\dfrac{27}{4}$

19. $\dfrac{1}{24}$

21. $\dfrac{1}{12}$

REVIEW PROBLEMS—CHAPTER 11

1. $4x + 3y$; $3x + 2y$

3. $\dfrac{y}{(x + y)^2}$; $-\dfrac{x}{(x + y)^2}$

5. $2xze^{x^2 yz}(1 + x^2 yz)$

7. $\dfrac{y}{x^2 + y^2}$

9. $2(x + y)$

11. $xze^{yz}\ln z$; $\dfrac{e^{yz}}{z} + ye^{yz}\ln z = e^{yz}\left(\dfrac{1}{z} + y\ln z\right)$

13. $2(x + y)e^r + 2\left(\dfrac{x + 3y}{r + s}\right)$; $2\left(\dfrac{x + 3y}{r + s}\right)$

15. $\dfrac{2x + 2y + z}{4z - x}$

17. $(2, 2)$, rel. min.

19. $(3, 2, 1)$

21. $\hat{y} = 1.34 + 1.8x$

23. $\dfrac{\partial Q}{\partial l} = 14l^{-.3}\, k^{.3};\quad \dfrac{\partial Q}{\partial k} = 6l^{.7}\, k^{-.7}$

25. $\dfrac{7}{2}$

27. $\dfrac{81}{5}$

EXERCISE 12-1

1. -12

3. $\dfrac{1}{7}$

5. $\dfrac{1}{8}$

7. ∞

9. ∞

11. 2

13. 0

15. e^3

17. 0

19. 0

21. ∞

23. $-\infty$

25. $\dfrac{4}{7}$

27. $-\dfrac{1}{e}$

29. 1

31. ∞

33. $\dfrac{1}{2}$

35. 0

37. $\dfrac{1}{2}$

39. $\dfrac{1}{\sqrt{2}}$

41. $\dfrac{1 + \ln 2}{\sqrt{2} - 1}$

EXERCISE 12-2

1. 0

3. -1

5. 1

7. e^3

9. 1

11. ∞

13. ∞

15. -1

17. e^2

19. 0

21. 1

23. 0

25. $-\infty$

27. 1

29. -1

REVIEW PROBLEMS—CHAPTER 12

1. 4

3. $-\dfrac{3}{5}$

5. $-\infty$

7. 0

9. 0

11. ∞

EXERCISE 13-1

1. $1, 3, 5, 7$

3. $\dfrac{1}{2}, \dfrac{2}{3}, \dfrac{3}{4}, \dfrac{4}{5}$

5. $1, -4, 9, -16$

7. $\dfrac{e}{3}, \dfrac{e^2}{3}, \dfrac{e^3}{3}, \dfrac{e^4}{3}$

9. $0, \dfrac{1}{3}, \dfrac{1}{2}, \dfrac{3}{5}$

11. $\dfrac{1}{2}, \dfrac{1}{2}, \dfrac{3}{8}, \dfrac{1}{4}$

13. $\dfrac{(-1)^{n+1}}{n+1}$

15. $n(n+1)$

17. $(-1)^n n$

19. $\dfrac{(-1)^{n+1} - 1}{2}$

21. ∞

23. $\dfrac{3}{2}$

25. ∞

27. 0

29. 0

31. $\dfrac{11}{4}$

33. 0

35. 0

37. 0

39. -1

41. ∞

43. 0

45. 0

47. 0

49. does not exist (∞)

EXERCISE 13-2

1. $2 + 3 + 4 + 5$

3. $-1 + 0 + 3 + 8$

5. $-2 + 5 - 10 + 17$

7. $4 + 8 + 12 + 16$

9. $1 + \dfrac{1}{2} + \dfrac{1}{4} + \dfrac{1}{8}$

11. $\dfrac{3661}{7776}$

13. $\dfrac{1}{3n + 1}$

15. $(-1)^{n+1}\left(\dfrac{1}{n}\right)$

17. $\dfrac{n+2}{2^n}$

19. $3, 9, 18, 30$

21. $.3, .39, .417, .4251$

23. $-1, -\dfrac{3}{4}, -\dfrac{31}{36}, -\dfrac{115}{144}$

25. $5, 10, 15, 20$

27. yes

29. no

31. yes

33. yes

35. no

EXERCISE 13-3

1. 1

3. $-\dfrac{2}{5}$

5. div.

7. $\dfrac{243}{1250}$

9. $-\dfrac{1}{2}$

11. $\dfrac{100}{3}$

13. div.

15. 6

17. 18

19. $-\dfrac{8}{3}$

21. $\dfrac{50}{27}$

23. div.

25. div.

27. div.

29. div.

31. div.

33. div.

35. $3000

EXERCISE 13-4

1. conv.

3. div.

5. conv.

7. conv.

9. div.

11. div.

13. conv.

15. div.

17. div.

19. conv.

21. conv.

23. conv.

25. div.

27. conv.

29. conv.

31. div.

33. conv.

35. conv.

EXERCISE 13-5

1. conv.

3. div.

5. conv.

7. div.

9. conv.

11. conv.

13. div.

15. div.

17. conv.

19. conv.

21. conv.

23. div.

25. conv.

27. conv.

29. conv.

31. conv.

33. div.

35. conv.

37. div.

39. div.

41. conv.

43. div.

EXERCISE 13-6

1. cond. conv.

3. cond. conv.

5. abs. conv.

7. abs. conv.

9. cond. conv.

11. div.

13. cond. conv.

15. abs. conv.

17. abs. conv.

19. abs. conv.

21. div.

23. cond. conv.

25. abs. conv.

27. abs. conv.

29. abs. conv.

31. cond. conv.

33. cond. conv.

35. div.

EXERCISE 13-7

1. $-1 < x < 1$

3. $-\dfrac{1}{5} < x < \dfrac{1}{5}$

5. $x = 1$

7. $5 \le x \le 9$

9. $-1 < x < 1$

11. $-1 < x \le 1$

13. $-\infty < x < \infty$

15. $-\dfrac{1}{2} < x < \dfrac{3}{2}$

17. $-\dfrac{5}{4} \le x \le -\dfrac{3}{4}$

19. $-10 < x < 6$

21. $-\infty < x < \infty$

23. $1 < x < 3$

25. $-1 \le x < 1$

EXERCISE 13-8

1. $1 + 2x + 2x^2 + \dfrac{4}{3}x^3 + \dfrac{2}{3}x^4$

3. $\dfrac{1}{2} - 4\left(x + \dfrac{1}{2}\right) + 8\left(x + \dfrac{1}{2}\right)^2 - 16\left(x + \dfrac{1}{2}\right)^3 + 32\left(x + \dfrac{1}{2}\right)^4$

5. $1 - x^2$

7. $2 - \dfrac{x - 1}{12} - \dfrac{(x - 1)^2}{288}$

9. $1 + x + \dfrac{x^2}{2}$; 1.105

11. $7 + \dfrac{x - 49}{14} - \dfrac{(x - 49)^2}{2744}$; 7.071

13. $(x - 5)^2 + 3(x - 5)$

15. $3(x + 1)^5 - 15(x + 1)^4 + 26(x + 1)^3 - 18(x + 1)^2 + 10(x + 1) - 7$

17. $\displaystyle\sum_{n=0}^{\infty} \dfrac{(-1)^n 2^n}{n!}\left(x - \dfrac{5}{2}\right)^n$

19. $\displaystyle\sum_{n=0}^{\infty} \dfrac{2^n}{3^{n+1}}(x - 4)^n$

21. $\displaystyle\sum_{n=1}^{\infty} \dfrac{1}{(n - 1)!}x^n$

23. $\displaystyle\sum_{n=1}^{\infty} \dfrac{(-1)^{n+1}}{n}(x - 1)^n$

25. $2 - \dfrac{x + 2}{12} + \displaystyle\sum_{n=2}^{\infty} \dfrac{2 \cdot 5 \cdot \ldots \cdot (3n - 4)}{3^n 2^{3n-1} n!}(x + 2)^n$

REVIEW PROBLEMS—CHAPTER 13

1. 1

3. ∞

5. 0

7. div.

9. div.

11. abs. convergent

13. cond. convergent

15. abs. convergent

17. cond. convergent

19. abs. convergent

21. abs. convergent

23. div.

25. cond. convergent

27. $3 < x < 5$

29. $-\dfrac{1}{3} < x \leq \dfrac{1}{3}$

31. $x = 1$

33. $-\infty < x < \infty$

35. $1 + x^2$

37. $\displaystyle\sum_{n=0}^{\infty} \dfrac{(-1)^n 3^n}{2^{n+1}}(x - 2)^n$

39. $(x + 3) + \displaystyle\sum_{n=2}^{\infty} \dfrac{(-1)^n}{n(n - 1)}(x + 3)^n$

EXERCISE 14-1

1. (a) 2×3, 3×3, 3×2, 2×2, 4×4, 1×2, 3×1, 3×3, 1×1

(b) **B, D, E, H, J**

(c) **H, J** upper triangular;   **D, J** lower triangular   (d) **F, J**   (e) **G, J**

3. 2

5. 4

7. 6

9. 7, 2, 1, 0

11. $\begin{bmatrix} 5 & 8 & 11 & 14 \\ 7 & 10 & 13 & 16 \\ 9 & 12 & 15 & 18 \end{bmatrix}$

13. 120 entries, 1, 0, 1, 0

15. a. $\begin{bmatrix} 0 & 0 & 0 & 0 \\ 0 & 0 & 0 & 0 \\ 0 & 0 & 0 & 0 \\ 0 & 0 & 0 & 0 \end{bmatrix}$
   b. $\begin{bmatrix} 0 & 0 & 0 & 0 & 0 & 0 \\ 0 & 0 & 0 & 0 & 0 & 0 \\ 0 & 0 & 0 & 0 & 0 & 0 \\ 0 & 0 & 0 & 0 & 0 & 0 \\ 0 & 0 & 0 & 0 & 0 & 0 \\ 0 & 0 & 0 & 0 & 0 & 0 \end{bmatrix}$

17. $x = 6$, $y = \dfrac{2}{3}$, $z = \dfrac{7}{2}$ **19.** $x = 0$, $y = 0$

21. 7; 3; February; deluxe blue; February; February; 35

EXERCISE 14-2

1. $\begin{bmatrix} 4 & -3 & 1 \\ -2 & 10 & 5 \\ 10 & 5 & 3 \end{bmatrix}$

3. $\begin{bmatrix} -5 & 5 \\ -9 & 5 \\ 5 & 9 \end{bmatrix}$

5. $[-9 \quad -7 \quad 6 \quad 11]$

7. not defined

9. $\begin{bmatrix} -12 & 36 & -42 & -6 \\ -42 & -6 & -36 & 12 \end{bmatrix}$

11. $\begin{bmatrix} 5 & -4 & 1 \\ 0 & 7 & -2 \\ -3 & 3 & 13 \end{bmatrix}$

13. $\begin{bmatrix} 6 & 5 \\ -2 & 3 \end{bmatrix}$

15. O

17. $\begin{bmatrix} 28 & 22 \\ -2 & 6 \end{bmatrix}$

19. not defined

21. $\begin{bmatrix} -22 & -15 \\ -11 & 9 \end{bmatrix}$

23. $\begin{bmatrix} 21 & \dfrac{29}{2} \\ \dfrac{19}{2} & -\dfrac{15}{2} \end{bmatrix}$

29. $x = \dfrac{146}{13}$, $y = -\dfrac{28}{13}$

31. $x = 6$, $y = \dfrac{4}{3}$

33. $x = -6$, $y = -14$, $z = 1$

35. 1.1

EXERCISE 14-3

1. -12 **3.** 19   **5.** 7

7. $2 \times 2, 4$ **9.** $3 \times 5, 15$ **11.** $2 \times 1, 2$

13. $3 \times 3, 9$ **15.** $3 \times 1, 3$

17. $\begin{bmatrix} 1 & 0 & 0 & 0 \\ 0 & 1 & 0 & 0 \\ 0 & 0 & 1 & 0 \\ 0 & 0 & 0 & 1 \end{bmatrix}$ **19.** $\begin{bmatrix} 10 & -16 \\ 7 & 8 \end{bmatrix}$ **21.** $\begin{bmatrix} 23 \\ 50 \end{bmatrix}$

23. $\begin{bmatrix} -3 & 4 & 2 \\ 2 & 2 & 4 \\ 5 & 0 & 3 \end{bmatrix}$ **25.** $\begin{bmatrix} -6 & 16 & 10 & -6 \end{bmatrix}$

27. $\begin{bmatrix} 4 & 6 & -4 & 6 \\ 6 & 9 & -6 & 9 \\ -8 & -12 & 8 & -12 \\ 2 & 3 & -2 & 3 \end{bmatrix}$ **29.** $\begin{bmatrix} 78 & 84 \\ -21 & -12 \end{bmatrix}$

31. $\begin{bmatrix} -5 & -8 \\ -5 & -20 \end{bmatrix}$ **33.** $\begin{bmatrix} x \\ y \\ z \end{bmatrix}$ **35.** $\begin{bmatrix} -4 & 11 & -2 \\ 3 & -12 & 3 \end{bmatrix}$ **37.** $\begin{bmatrix} -1 \\ 3 \\ 8 \end{bmatrix}$

39. $\begin{bmatrix} 3 & 0 & 0 \\ 0 & 6 & 3 \\ 3 & 12 & 3 \end{bmatrix}$ **41.** $\begin{bmatrix} 7 & 23 \end{bmatrix}$ **43.** $\begin{bmatrix} 0 & 0 & 0 \\ 0 & -1 & 1 \\ 1 & 2 & 0 \end{bmatrix}$

45. $\begin{bmatrix} -1 & -20 \\ -2 & 23 \end{bmatrix}$ **47.** $\begin{bmatrix} \frac{3}{2} & 0 & 0 \\ 0 & \frac{3}{2} & 0 \\ 0 & 0 & \frac{3}{2} \end{bmatrix}$ **49.** $\begin{bmatrix} -1 & 5 \\ 2 & 17 \\ 1 & 31 \end{bmatrix}$

51. $\begin{bmatrix} 3 & 1 \\ 7 & -2 \end{bmatrix} \begin{bmatrix} x \\ y \end{bmatrix} = \begin{bmatrix} 6 \\ 5 \end{bmatrix}$ **53.** $\begin{bmatrix} 4 & -1 & 3 \\ 3 & 0 & -1 \\ 0 & 3 & 2 \end{bmatrix} \begin{bmatrix} r \\ s \\ t \end{bmatrix} = \begin{bmatrix} 9 \\ 7 \\ 15 \end{bmatrix}$

55. $7353

57. (a) $18, $52, $40, $27, $38, $64   (b) $39, $10, $80   (c) $239

     (d) $\dfrac{110}{239}$; $\dfrac{129}{239}$

EXERCISE 14-4

1. not reduced

3. reduced

5. not reduced

7. $\begin{bmatrix} 1 & 0 \\ 0 & 1 \end{bmatrix}$

9. $\begin{bmatrix} 1 & 2 & 3 \\ 0 & 0 & 0 \\ 0 & 0 & 0 \end{bmatrix}$

11. $\begin{bmatrix} 1 & 0 & 0 & 0 \\ 0 & 1 & 0 & 0 \\ 0 & 0 & 1 & 0 \\ 0 & 0 & 0 & 1 \end{bmatrix}$

13. $x = 1, y = 1$

15. no solution

17. $x = -\dfrac{2}{3}z + \dfrac{5}{3}, y = -\dfrac{1}{6}z + \dfrac{7}{6}, z = z$

19. no solution

21. $x = -3, y = 1, z = 0$

23. $x = 2, y = -5, z = -1$

25. $x_1 = 0, x_2 = -x_5, x_3 = -x_5, x_4 = -x_5, x_5 = x_5$

27. federal, \$72,000;   state, \$24,000

29. $A, 2000$; $B, 4000$; $C, 5000$

31. (a) 3 of X, 4 of Z; 2 of X, 1 of Y, 5 of Z; 1 of X, 2 of Y, 6 of Z; 3 of Y, 7 of Z

(b) 3 of X, 4 of Z (c) 3 of X, 4 of Z;   3 of Y, 7 of Z

EXERCISE 14-5

1. $w = -y - 3z + 2, x = -2y + z - 3, y = y, z = z$

3. $w = -z, x = -3y - 4z + 2, y = y, z = z$

5. $w = -2y + z - 2, x = -y + 4, y = y, z = z$

7. $x_1 = -2x_3 + x_4 - 2x_5 + 1, x_2 = -x_3 - 2x_4 + x_5 + 4,$

$x_3 = x_3, x_4 = x_4, x_5 = x_5$

9. infinite

11. trivial

13. infinite

15. $x = 0, y = 0$

17. $x = -\dfrac{6}{5}z, y = \dfrac{8}{15}z, z = z$

19. $x = 0, y = 0$

21. $x = z, y = -2z, z = z$

23. $w = -2z, x = -3z, y = z, z = z$

EXERCISE 14-6

1. $\begin{bmatrix} 1 & -1 \\ -5 & 6 \end{bmatrix}$

3. not invertible

5. $\begin{bmatrix} 1 & 0 & 0 \\ 0 & -\frac{1}{3} & 0 \\ 0 & 0 & \frac{1}{4} \end{bmatrix}$

7. not invertible

9. not invertible (not a square matrix)

11. $\begin{bmatrix} 1 & -1 & 0 \\ 0 & 1 & -1 \\ 0 & 0 & 1 \end{bmatrix}$

13. $\begin{bmatrix} 1 & 0 & 2 \\ 0 & 1 & 0 \\ 3 & 0 & 7 \end{bmatrix}$

15. $\begin{bmatrix} 1 & -\frac{2}{3} & \frac{5}{3} \\ -1 & \frac{4}{3} & -\frac{10}{3} \\ -1 & 1 & -2 \end{bmatrix}$

17. $\begin{bmatrix} \frac{11}{3} & -3 & \frac{1}{3} \\ -\frac{7}{3} & 3 & -\frac{2}{3} \\ \frac{2}{3} & -1 & \frac{1}{3} \end{bmatrix}$

19. $x = 17, y = -20$

21. $x = 1, y = 3$

23. $x = -3y + 1, y = y$

25. $x = 0, y = 1, z = 2$

27. $x = 1, y = \dfrac{1}{2}, z = \dfrac{1}{2}$

29. no solution

31. $w = 1, x = 3, y = -2, z = 7$

33. $\begin{bmatrix} -\frac{2}{3} & -\frac{1}{3} \\ \frac{1}{3} & -\frac{1}{3} \end{bmatrix}$

35. (a) 40 of first model, 60 of second model
(b) 45 of first model, 50 of second model

EXERCISE 14-7

1. 1

3. 0

5. y

7. $-\dfrac{2}{7}$

9. 12

11. -12

13. 6

15. $\begin{vmatrix} a_{11} & a_{13} & a_{14} \\ a_{21} & a_{23} & a_{24} \\ a_{41} & a_{43} & a_{44} \end{vmatrix}$

17. $\begin{vmatrix} a_{21} & a_{22} & a_{24} \\ a_{31} & a_{32} & a_{34} \\ a_{41} & a_{42} & a_{44} \end{vmatrix}$

19. -16

21. 98

23. -89

25. -1

27. 2

29. -90

31. 1

33. 24

35. 3, 4

37. 192

EXERCISE 14-8

1. $x = \dfrac{9}{5},\ y = -\dfrac{2}{5}$ **3.** $x = \dfrac{7}{16},\ y = \dfrac{13}{8}$ **5.** $x = -\dfrac{1}{3},\ y = -1$

7. $x = \dfrac{6}{5},\ z = \dfrac{16}{5}$ **9.** $x = 4,\ y = 2,\ z = 0$

11. $x = \dfrac{2}{3},\ y = -\dfrac{28}{15},\ z = -\dfrac{26}{15}$ **13.** $x = 1,\ y = 3,\ z = 5$

15. $y = 6,\ w = 1$

17. Since $\Delta = \begin{vmatrix} 1 & 1 \\ 1 & 1 \end{vmatrix} = 0$, Cramer's Rule does not apply.

But the equations in

$$\begin{cases} x + y = 2 \\ x + y = -3 \end{cases}$$

represent distinct parallel lines and hence no solution exists.

EXERCISE 14-9

1. $\begin{bmatrix} \dfrac{1}{4} & \dfrac{1}{4} \\[2mm] -\dfrac{1}{8} & \dfrac{3}{8} \end{bmatrix}$ **3.** $\begin{bmatrix} 4 & -9 \\ 0 & 6 \end{bmatrix}$

5. $\begin{bmatrix} 7 & -8 & 5 \\ -4 & 5 & -3 \\ 1 & -1 & 1 \end{bmatrix}$ **7.** $\begin{bmatrix} 2 & 1 & 0 \\ 4 & -1 & 5 \\ 1 & -1 & 2 \end{bmatrix}$

9. $\begin{bmatrix} 2 & -1 & 3 \\ 0 & 2 & 0 \\ 2 & 1 & 1 \end{bmatrix}$ **11.** $\begin{bmatrix} 1 & 2 & -1 \\ 0 & 1 & 4 \\ 1 & -1 & 2 \end{bmatrix}$

EXERCISE 14-10

1. $\begin{bmatrix} 1290 \\ 1425 \end{bmatrix}$;   1405   **3.** (a) $\begin{bmatrix} 297.80 \\ 349.54 \\ 443.12 \end{bmatrix}$ (b) $\begin{bmatrix} 102.17 \\ 125.28 \\ 175.27 \end{bmatrix}$

REVIEW PROBLEMS—CHAPTER 14

1. $\begin{bmatrix} 7 & 12 \\ -19 & -5 \end{bmatrix}$

3. $\begin{bmatrix} 1 & 35 & 5 \\ 2 & -15 & -7 \\ 1 & 0 & -2 \end{bmatrix}$

5. $\begin{bmatrix} -1 & -2 \\ 5 & 22 \end{bmatrix}$

7. $x = 3, y = 6$

9. $\begin{bmatrix} 1 & 0 \\ 0 & 1 \end{bmatrix}$

11. $\begin{bmatrix} 1 & 2 & 0 \\ 0 & 0 & 1 \\ 0 & 0 & 0 \end{bmatrix}$

13. $x = 0, y = 0$

15. no solution

17. $\begin{bmatrix} -\frac{3}{2} & \frac{5}{6} \\ \frac{1}{2} & -\frac{1}{6} \end{bmatrix}$

19. no inverse exists

21. $x = 0, y = 1, z = 0$

23. 18

25. 3

27. rich

29. $x = 1, y = 2$

31. $\begin{bmatrix} \frac{1}{2} & -1 & \frac{1}{2} \\ -\frac{1}{2} & 0 & \frac{1}{2} \\ 1 & 1 & -1 \end{bmatrix}$

33. $\begin{bmatrix} 3.6 \\ 3.2 \end{bmatrix}$

EXERCISE 15-1

1.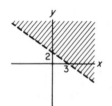

3.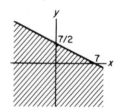

5.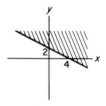

7.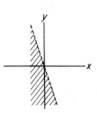

9.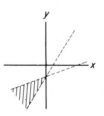

11.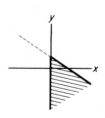

13.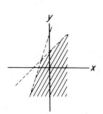

15.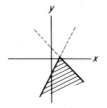

17.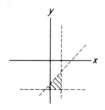

19.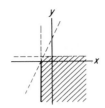

21.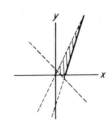

23.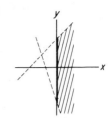

25.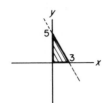

27.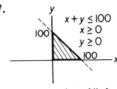

$$x + y \leq 100$$
$$x \geq 0$$
$$y \geq 0$$

x : number of lb. from *A*
y : number of lb. from *B*

EXERCISE 15-2

1. $P = 640$

3. $C = 2.4$

5. 15 widgets, 25 wadgits;   \$210

7. 4 units of Food *A*, 4 units of Food *B*

EXERCISE 15-3

1. 8 (when $x = 0$, $y = 4$)

3. 14 (when $x = 1$, $y = 5$)

5. 28 (when $x = 3$, $y = 2$)

7. 20 (when $x_1 = 0$, $x_2 = 5$, $x_3 = 0$)

9. 2 (when $x_1 = 1$, $x_2 = 0$, $x_3 = 0$)

11. $6\left(\text{when } x = 1, y = 5, \text{ or when } x = \dfrac{10}{3}, y = \dfrac{8}{3}\right)$

13. 13 (when $x = 1$, $y = 0$, $z = 3$)

15. 600 (when $x_1 = 4$, $x_2 = 1$, $x_3 = 4$, $x_4 = 0$)

17. Possible production orders are: 100 chairs, 100 rockers, 200 chaise lounges; or 0 chairs, 250 rockers, 150 chaise lounges. Max. revenue = \$3800

EXERCISE 15-4

1. 7 (when $x = 1$, $y = 5$)

3. -17 (when $x = 3$, $y = 2$)

5. 4 (when $x = 1$, $y = 2$)

7. -3 (when $x = 4$, $y = 7$)

9. 54 (when $x = 2$, $y = 8$)

11. 36 (when $x_1 = 9$, $x_2 = 0$, $x_3 = 0$)

13. 28 (when $x_1 = 3$, $x_2 = 0$, $x_3 = 5$)

15. 3 of type *A*, 3 of type *B*;   \$3.00

EXERCISE 15-5

1. Minimize $W = 6u + 4v$
subject to
$$u - v \geq 2$$
$$u + v \geq 3$$
$$u, v \geq 0$$

3. Maximize $Z = 8x + 2y$
subject to
$$x - y \leq 1$$
$$x + 2y \leq 8$$
$$x + y \leq 5$$
$$x, y \geq 0$$

5. Minimize $W = 13x_1 - 3x_2 - 11x_3$
subject to
$$-x_1 + x_2 - x_3 \geq 1$$
$$2x_1 - x_2 - x_3 \geq -1$$
$$x_1, x_2, x_3 \geq 0$$

7. Maximize $W = -3u + 3v$
subject to
$$-u + v \leq 4$$
$$u - v \leq 4$$
$$u + v \leq 6$$
$$u, v \geq 0$$

9. 11   **11.** 26   **13.** 14   **15.** $170   **17.** $600

REVIEW PROBLEMS—CHAPTER 15

1.

3.

5.

7.

9.

11. $Z = 9$

13. 32 (when $x = 8$, $y = 0$)

15. 2 (when $x = 0$, $y = 0$, $z = 2$)

17. 24 (when $x_1 = 0$, $x_2 = 12$)

19. 70

Index